The
PORTABLE
MBA
in
STRATEGY

The Portable MBA Series

The Portable MBA Series provides managers, executives, professionals, and students with a "hands-on," easy-to-access overview of the ideas and information covered in a typical Masters of Business Administration program. The published and forthcoming books in the program are:

Published

The Portable MBA (0-471-61997-3, cloth; 0-471-54895-2, paper) Eliza G. C. Collins and Mary Anne Devanna

The Portable MBA Desk Reference (0-471-57681-6) Paul A. Argenti

The Portable MBA in Finance and Accounting (0-471-53226-6) John Leslie Livingstone

The Portable MBA in Management (0-471-57379-5) Allan R. Cohen

The Portable MBA in Marketing (0-471-54728-X) Alexander Hiam and Charles Schewe

New Product Development: Managing and Forecasting for Strategic Success (0-471-57226-8) Robert J. Thomas

Real-Time Strategy: Improving Team-Based Planning for a Fast-Changing World (0-471-58564-5) Lee Tom Perry, Randall G. Stott, and W. Norman Smallwood

The Portable MBA in Economics (0-471-59526-8) Philip K. Y. Young and John McCauley

The Portable MBA in Entrepreneurship (0-471-57780-4) William Bygrave

The Portable MBA in Strategy (0-471-58498-3) Liam Fahey and Robert M. Randall

The New Marketing Concept (0-471-59576-4) Frederick E. Webster

Total Quality Management: Strategies and Techniques Proven at Today's Most Successful Companies (0-471-54538-1) Arnold Weimerskirch and Stephen George

Market-Driven Management: Using the New Market Concept to Create a Customer-Oriented Company (0-471-5976-4) Frederick E. Webster

Forthcoming

The Portable MBA in Global Business Leadership (0-471-30410-7) Noel Tichy, Michael Brimm, and Hiro Takeuchi

Analyzing the Balance Sheet (0-471-59191-2) John Leslie Livingstone

Information Technology and Business Strategy (0-471-59659-0) N. Venkatraman and James E. Short

Negotiating Strategically (0-471-1321-8) Roy Lewicki and Alexander Hiam

Psychology for Leaders (0-471-59538-1) Dean Tjosvold and Mary Tjosvold

The

PORTABLE

MBA

in

STRATEGY

Liam Fahey
Robert M. Randall

John Wiley & Sons, Inc.

New York • Chichester • Brisbane • Toronto • Singapore

Library of Congress Cataloging-in Publication Data:

The Portable MBA in strategy / [edited by] Liam Fahey, Robert Randall.
    p.   cm.
    Includes index.
    ISBN 0-471-58498-3 (alk. paper)
    1. Strategic planning. 2. Corporate planning. I. Fahey, Liam,
1951–   . II. Randall, Robert, 1940–
HD30.28.P674 1994
658.4'012—dc20   94-4475

Printed in the United States of America

10 9 8 7 6 5 4 3 2 1

Preface

The design and development of *The Portable MBA in Strategy* was guided by one overarching goal: to bring the best in thought and practice in the field of strategic management (or business strategy) to a number of audiences:

1. Managers and others who possess an MBA degree and are interested in staying abreast of the field of strategic management.
2. Any person working in an organizational setting who is interested in learning about the scope, substance, and processes of strategic management.
3. Students, at both the graduate and undergraduate levels, who need a compendium of material from the leading thinkers in the field. This book could serve as a primary or supplementary text in any mainstream course related to strategic management.

To bring together the best in thought and practice in the strategic management field, we invited a select list of outstanding thought leaders to contribute to the book. Sixteen contributors are leading professors at the most prestigious business schools. Five contributors are innovative consultants. Each contributor is an expert in his or her domain; each has extensive experience in "live" organizations, putting into practice the principles, precepts, and methodologies expounded in each chapter. The work of many of the contributors is internationally known.

The Portable MBA in Strategy addresses the following questions:

1. What is strategic management? What is it that managers do when they engage in strategic management? How and why is strategic management different from other types of management, such as financial management or manufacturing management or human resource management?
2. What is a strategy? How does one identify an organization's strategy? How do strategies differ from one organization to another?

3. What should an organization do when it sets about formulating or changing its strategy? What kinds of analysis should it do? What kinds of analytical methodologies are available?

4. What is involved in implementing strategy? How are strategies translated into action? How can the organization be better managed, with a view to more efficient and effective strategy execution? How can strategy development and execution be more tightly linked?

The book is divided into five parts.

PART ONE: AN INTRODUCTION TO STRATEGIC MANAGEMENT

Chapter 1, *Strategic Management: Today's Most Important Business Challenge,* by Liam Fahey, provides an overview of strategic management. It argues that strategic management's central challenge is the need to lay the foundation for success in tomorrow's marketplace while competing to win in today's marketplace. This challenge lies at the heart of strategic management because the environment confronting every organization is in a constant state of change.

Chapter 1 segments strategic management into three components: (1) managing marketplace strategy, (2) managing the organization, and (3) managing the interface between strategy and the organization. Marketplace strategy incorporates three elements: (1) scope, (2) posture, and (3) goals. Managing the organization incorporates five elements: (1) analytics, (2) mindset, (3) operating processes, (4) infrastructure, and (5) leadership. Managing the linkages between marketplace strategy and organization is the focus of much of the activity that must be accomplished by strategic management.

PART TWO: STRATEGY: WINNING IN THE MARKETPLACE

Strategy, above all else, is about winning in the marketplace—attracting, winning, and retaining customers, and outperforming competitors. To do so requires that the organization create or leverage change in the environment by continually adapting its product offerings and by modifying and enhancing how it competes. It must anticipate changes in competitive conditions—the entry of new types of competitors, the introduction of new products, technology developments, and changes in customers' tastes.

Chapters 2 through 5 address strategy from four distinct vantage points: (1) corporate strategy, (2) business-unit strategy, (3) global strategy, and (4) political strategy. Chapter 2, *Corporate Strategy: Managing a Set of Businesses,* by H. Kurt Christensen, begins by considering the rationale or logic for corporate diversification, a central thrust in many firms' corporate strategy. It then details the principal elements in corporate strategy and examines the most frequently used means by which a corporation can change its scope (internal development, strategic alliances, and divestment).

Chapter 3, *Business-Unit Strategy: Managing the Single Business,* by Anil K. Gupta, examines strategy at the level of a stand-alone organization, that is, a business unit in a multibusiness corporation or single business organization. The author addresses five issues central to strategy development and execution in any single business entity: (1) defining the scope of the business unit, (2) setting business-unit goals, (3) defining the intended bases for competitive advantage, (4) designing the value constellation (what the business unit will do versus what it will rely on its partners to do), and (5) managing the business unit's internal value chain.

Chapter 4, *Global Strategy: Winning in the World-Wide Marketplace,* by Michael E. Porter, considers corporate and business-unit strategy from a global perspective. Porter provides a framework for understanding the nature of competition between rivals in an international arena and the development of a new conception of global strategy.

Chapter 5, *Political Strategy: Managing the Social and Political Environment,* by John F. Mahon, Barbara Bigelow, and Liam Fahey, extends the notion of strategy to incorporate an organization's efforts to deal with the social and political environment. Political strategy is defined as the set of activities undertaken by an organization in the political, regulatory, judicial, or social domain to secure a position of advantage and influence over other actors in the process. Although political strategy is frequently accorded little prominence in strategic management textbooks, this chapter demonstrates how political strategy is sometimes critical to the success of strategy in the marketplace, that is, the corporate, business-unit, and global strategies discussed in the three prior chapters.

PART THREE: STRATEGY INPUTS: ANALYZING THE EXTERNAL AND INTERNAL ENVIRONMENTS

Strategy, as an intentional organizational choice, is always driven by some understanding of the organization's external and internal environment. Unfortunately, in too many organizations, this understanding is, at best, only partially explicated, challenged, and refined. The four chapters in Part Three are intended to show readers what is involved in analyzing organizations' external and internal environments (and many of the connections between these environments).

In Chapter 6, *Industry Analysis: Understanding Industry and Dynamics,* David Collis and Pankaj Ghemawat show how to analyze an industry using two distinct but related frameworks. Industry analysis constitutes the core of the environmental analysis conducted by most firms.

In Chapter 7, *Macroenvironmental Analysis: Understanding the Environment Outside the Industry,* V. K. Narayanan and Liam Fahey show how to analyze the macroenvironment—the political, economic, social, and technological environment external to an industry. In particular, they show how to scan, monitor, and forecast change in each of the four domains within the macroenvironment. Yet, it is not enough to understand what macroenvironmental change is occurring or may occur: the implications of such change for the development and execution of corporate and business-unit strategy are detailed and discussed in the final section of the chapter.

Chapter 8, *Building the Intelligent Enterprise: Leveraging Resources, Services, and Technology,* by James Brian Quinn, focuses on the organization itself as a source of distinctive competitive advantage. In particular, this chapter demonstrates how (and why) intellectual resources rather than physical resources contain the seeds of marketplace success. The core challenge for organizations is to develop knowledge-based service activities—which are, increasingly, the source of value and benefits that are important to customers. Recognition of the need to continually upgrade and enhance intellectual resources is leading many firms to create new organizational configurations involving multiple linkages to suppliers, distributors, end customers, and technology sources.

Chapter 9, *A Strategy for Growth: The Role of Core Competencies in the Corporation,* by C. K. Prahalad, with Liam Fahey and Robert M. Randall also addresses how the organization itself can be a source of marketplace success, with particular reference to multibusiness corporations. The chapter argues that corporations need to develop a strategic intent and strategic architecture as a prelude to the determination of which core competencies need to be developed and refined. Core competencies assume strategic importance because they underlie products provided by a number of business units. As an example, Honda's engine competence is reflected in a range of products.

PART FOUR: STRATEGY MAKING: IDENTIFYING AND EVALUATING STRATEGIC ALTERNATIVES

An understanding of strategy and of an organization's external and internal environment in and of itself does not generate strategy. Managers need to transform knowledge about their industry, about the environment outside the industry, and about their own organization's resources and competencies into opportunities. Thus, they must develop a range of strategy alternatives—some of which may take the organization in a direction that is radically different from its current strategy—and choose their preferred options among those alternatives.

Chapter 10, *Identifying and Developing Strategic Alternatives*, by Marjorie A. Lyles, illustrates why it is so important for any organization to invest considerable time and effort in generating obvious, creative, and unthinkable alternatives. Unless opportunities are detected and developed, they cannot be considered or exploited. This chapter offers various analytical methodologies and organizational processes to capture and develop alternatives in the hope that, by so doing, the organization will never become complacent because of its marketplace success, nor succumb to being a victim of its own historic mindset and way of doing business.

Chapter 11, *Evaluating Strategic Alternatives,* by George S. Day, discusses how to evaluate the strategic alternatives an organization may generate. Poor choices of strategic direction cost organizations dearly. This chapter provides a framework of analysis—a set of tests in the form of questions—that is intended to provide organizations with a comprehensive means of evaluating and testing strategic alternatives before managers commit to a specific strategic direction.

PART FIVE: MANAGING STRATEGIC CHANGE: LINKING STRATEGY AND ACTION

However elegant and grand their design, strategies that do not get executed cannot enhance organizational performance. By the same token, how the organization is managed affects significantly the quality of the strategies developed and the commitment and willingness of the organization's members to execute them. In other words, managing strategy—how the organization seeks to win in the marketplace—and managing the organization are intimately interrelated.

In Chapter 12, *Strategic Change: Realigning the Organization to Implement Strategy,* Russell A. Eisenstat and Michael Beer tackle a challenge that has bedeviled so many organizations' efforts to achieve strategic change—realigning the organization with the intended change in strategic direction. Part of the problem is that it appears so deceptively easy; yet, any manager who has tried to instill new attitudes, new skills, and new behaviors in his or her organization knows how difficult the task is. This chapter lays out a systematic approach to achieving such alignment.

Chapter 13, *Strategic Change: Reconfiguring Operational Processes to Implement Strategy,* by Ellen R. Hart, emphasizes the crucial need to reconfigure organizational processes—to redefine the work organizations do and how they do it. Redesigning core business processes—how products are designed and developed, how products are manufactured, and how products or services are delivered to customers—is central to delivering value to targeted customers. Strategic change increasingly involves reconfiguring multiple core processes. This chapter provides a detailed methodology on how to do so.

In Chapter 14, *Strategic Change: Managing Strategy Making through Planning and Administrative Systems,* John H. Grant argues that strategy making must be coordinated throughout the organization. If left to their own devices, individual units—business units, product groups, and functional departments, among others—will push and pull the organization in conflicting directions. Thus, the role of planning and of related administrative systems is to provide mechanisms for coordinating strategy development and execution. This chapter details a variety of organizational processes to achieve integrated and coordinated strategy making.

Chapter 15, *Strategic Change: Managing Cultural Processes,* by Gerry Johnson, explicates the linkages between organizational culture and strategy. Although these connections often receive minimal attention from managers, strategic change is always either inhibited or fostered by the organization's culture. After delineating the elements that constitute an organization's cultural web, this chapter shows how strategic change can be achieved through managing cultural processes and the closely related political processes.

Chapter 16, *Re-Inventing Strategy and the Organization: Managing the Present from the Future,* by Tracy Goss, Richard Pascale, and Anthony Athos, makes the case that many organizations need to reinvent both their strategy and their entire organization—perhaps many times in the course of a manager's career—if their intent is to get ahead of and stay ahead of competitors. The organization—especially its key executives—must make a complete break with the past and embrace a future that, by definition, will remain murky. Using many different corporate examples, this chapter documents what is involved in reinvention and the steps that an organization must undertake in order to achieve strategic change of this magnitude.

LIAM FAHEY
ROBERT M. RANDALL

Babson Park, Massachusetts
New York, New York
February 1994

Contents

PART ONE

AN INTRODUCTION TO STRATEGIC MANAGEMENT

1 STRATEGIC MANAGEMENT: TODAY'S MOST IMPORTANT BUSINESS CHALLENGE*

Liam Fahey

Babson College and
Cranfield School of Management

Strategic management is the name given to the most important, difficult, and encompassing challenge that confronts any private or public organization: how to lay the foundation for tomorrow's success while competing to win in today's marketplace. Winning today is never enough; unless the seeds of tomorrow's success are planted and cultivated, the organization will not have a future. This challenge is difficult because, as we shall see throughout this book, the choices involved in exploiting the present and building for the future confront managers with complex trade-offs. Managers must resolve conflicting demands from stakeholders; perennial tensions among different groups and levels within the organization must be fairly addressed. It is encompassing because it embraces all the decisions that any organization makes.

The conflict between the demands of the present and the requirements of the future lies at the heart of strategic management for at least three reasons:

1. The environment in which tomorrow's success will be earned is likely to be quite different from the environment that confronts the organization today. Products change as competitors introduce new variations, sometimes radically shifting the nature of the offering made to customers. New models of laptop computers that are smaller, lighter, and more powerful have changed many customers' perceptions of what constitutes a

* The author would like to especially thank Robert M. Randall for his many comments on this chapter, and H. Kurt Christensen, Jeffrey Ellis, Samuel Felton, V. K. Narayanan, G. Richard Patten, and Daniel Simpson for their comments on an earlier draft of this chapter.

3

personal computer. New competitors enter long-established markets with new concepts of how to serve and satisfy customers. For example, Saturn, at the low end of the automobile market, and Lexus, at the high end, have dramatically altered the dynamics of competition within their product categories.[1] Increasingly, the emergence of substitute products causes highly disruptive industry change. Customers' tastes sometimes change in unexpected ways. Technological developments often alter not only the function of products but every facet of how business is conducted: procurement, logistics, manufacturing, marketing, sales, and service. Political, regulatory, social, and economic change often give rise, directly or indirectly, to shifts in industry or competitive conditions.[2]

2. To succeed in the new environment of tomorrow, the organization itself must undergo significant and sometimes radical change. Organizations as large, as diverse, and as historically successful as IBM, General Motors, Sears, Honda, Sony, Philips, and Rolls Royce have learned this painful lesson in the late 1980s and early 1990s. Old ways of thinking have had to be challenged and reconceived: long-held assumptions and beliefs ultimately have become incongruent with the changed environment. New operating processes or ways of doing things must be learned. Organizational structures, systems, and decision processes inherited from outmoded eras need to be redesigned.

3. Adapting to (and, in many cases, driving) change in and around the marketplace during a time of significant *internal* change places an extremely heavy burden on the leaders of any organization. Yet, that is precisely the dual task that confronts strategic managers. They must:

    • Exploit the present while sowing the seeds for a new and very different future and, simultaneously,

    • Build bridges between change in the environment and change within their organizations.[3]

Change is the central concern and focus of strategic management: change in the environment, change inside the organization, and change in how the organization links strategy and the organization. Change means that organizations can never become satisfied with their accomplishments. Unless an organization changes its products over time, it falls behind competitors. Unless the organization changes its own understanding of the environment, it cannot keep abreast of, much less get ahead of, changes in customers, the industry, technology, and governmental policies. The importance and pervasiveness of change is evident in the strategic management principles noted in Table 1–1.

From environmental change springs opportunities. Without change or the potential to affect change, organizations would neither confront nor be able to create opportunities.[4] Without a managed flow of new opportunities, organizations cannot grow and prosper; they are destined to decline and die. Unfortunately, change is also the source of threats to the organization's current and

TABLE 1–1   Some strategic management (SM) principles.

Strategic Management

- Involves the management of marketplace strategy, of the organization, and of the relationship between them.
- Has as a core assignment; management of the interface between the organization and its environment.
- Involves anticipating, adapting to, and creating change both in the environment and within the organization.
- Is driven by the relentless pursuit of opportunities.
- Recognizes that opportunities may arise in the external environment or they may be generated within the organization; in either case, they are realized in the marketplace.
- Necessitates risk taking; the organization commits to pursuing opportunities *before* they have fully materialized (in the environment).
- Is as much about inventing or creating the organization's competitive future as it is about adapting to some understanding of that future.
- Sees the marketplace purpose of an organization as residing outside its (legal) boundaries; it must find, serve, and satisfy customers as a prelude to other returns such as profits.
- Is the task of the *whole* organization; it cannot be delegated to any group within the organization.
- Necessitates the integration of the long-distance and short-distance horizons; the future influences current decisions; current decisions are intended to lead toward some future state or goal.

potential strategies. Thus, organizations must commit themselves to grappling with change—understanding it and transforming it into opportunity. Leveraging and/or shaping change in the environment is, as we shall see in the next section, central to designing and executing strategy.

Although organizations cannot control their environment,[5] they are not helpless in the face of persistent and sometimes unpredictable environmental change. By practicing strategic management, managers can lead more effectively. They can effect change in their strategies: they can introduce new products, enhance their existing products, withdraw from particular markets, compete more smartly against their competitors, and offer better value to customers. Managers can also reconfigure their organization: They can get more output out of existing resources, hone existing capabilities or competencies and develop new ones, and energize the organization through their leadership. As we shall see throughout this chapter, managing more effectively and reconfiguring organizations go hand-in-hand.

To cope with change successfully, strategic management must address three interrelated tasks (see Figure 1–1):

1. Managing strategy in the marketplace: designing, executing, and refining strategies that "win" in a changing marketplace. Strategy is the means by

6

FIGURE 1–1 An integrated model of strategic management.

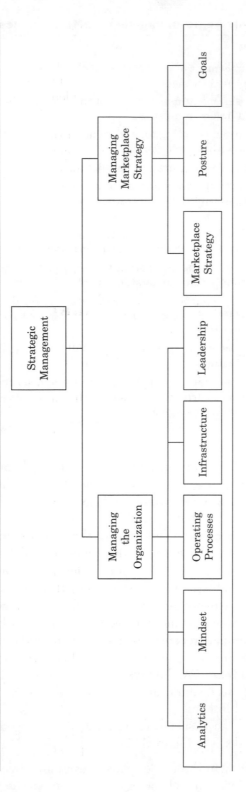

which the organization creates and leverages change in and around the marketplace.

2. Managing the organization: continually reconfiguring the organization—how it thinks, how it operates. Without such internal change, the organization cannot hope to hone its capacity to identify, adapt to, and leverage environmental change.

3. Practicing strategic management: continually enhancing the linkages or "interface" between strategy (what the organization does in the marketplace) and organization (what takes place within the organization). Throughout this book, we shall see that how these linkages are managed determines whether the organization wins today and positions itself for tomorrow.

Each of these three core strategic management tasks will now be discussed in detail.

MANAGING STRATEGY IN THE MARKETPLACE

Few words are as abused in the lexicon of organizations, as ill-defined in the management literature, and as open to multiple meanings as *strategy*.[6] Throughout this book, strategy is a synonym for *choices*. The sum of the choices determines whether the organization has a chance to win in the marketplace—whether it can get and keep customers and outperform competitors. Success in getting and keeping customers allows organizations to achieve their financial, technological, and other stakeholder-related goals. A number of core strategy principles are indicated in Table 1–2.

If a strategy is to successfully create or leverage change, it must manifest an "entrepreneurial content"[7] in the marketplace. Strategies that do not anticipate changes in competitive conditions, such as technological developments, new entrants with distinctly different product offerings, or changes in customers' tastes, will lag behind what is happening in the marketplace and will eventually fail. Strategies that do not create or leverage change to the organization's advantage cannot drive the marketplace; that is, they cannot provide, faster and better than competitors, the offerings that customers want.

How do organizations create or leverage change in the marketplace? What levers can they manipulate to effect changes that are to their advantage? How is change exploited for superior performance? In brief, strategy creates or leverages change in three related ways:

1. Through the choice of products the firm offers and the customers it seeks to serve—commonly referred to as the "scope" issue. For example, should Apple Computer Inc. add more powerful computers to its product line? Should General Motors eliminate its Oldsmobile product line or significantly overhaul it by introducing a new set of models?

TABLE 1–2 Some strategy principles.

Strategy addresses the interface between the organization and its marketplace environment.

Strategy involves three elements: (1) scope, (2) posture, and (3) goals.

Strategy is the means by which the organization creates and/or leverages environmental change.

Strategy is always conditional; the choice of strategy depends on the conditions in the environment and within the organization.

Strategy is in part an intellectual activity; strategies exist in managers' minds.

Strategy is about outwitting and outmaneuvering competitors by anticipating change faster and better and taking actions accordingly.

Strategy's marketplace intent is to be better than competitors at attracting, winning, and retaining customers.

Strategy is not likely to win unless it possesses some degree of entrepreneurial content: its approach is different from competitors'.

Strategy must be continually renovated; scope, posture, and goals are adjusted to enhance the chances of winning in the marketplace.

Strategy often needs to be (re)invented if it is to achieve "breakthrough" success. A strategy that is new to the marketplace *and* significantly outdistances rivals needs to be created.

2. Through how the firm competes in its chosen businesses or product-customer segments to attract, win, and retain customers. We shall refer to this as the "posture" issue. For example, should Apple add functionality—more speed and more features—to its Macintosh line? Should the price on some Cadillac models be lowered to make them more attractive to new customer segments?

3. Through the choice of goals the firm wishes to pursue. Should Apple try to be a major participant in every segment of the personal computer business or aim to be the leader in certain software segments? Should General Motors set out to penetrate the Japanese market?

Scope, posture, and goals will be recurring themes throughout this book. Because of their importance to any understanding of strategy, each will now be briefly discussed.

Business Scope

Central to any consideration of strategy are questions concerning business scope. Scope compels choices because it cannot be unlimited. No organization can market an unlimited array of products, and frequently (even with the assistance of partners) it will not be able to reach all potential customers. Indeed, few firms are able to compete or "be a player" in all product-customer segments of their industry.

Scope determination revolves around three general questions:

1. What products (or product groups) does the organization want to provide to the marketplace?

2. What customers—or, more specifically, what customer needs—does it want to serve?

3. What resources, competencies, and technologies does it possess or can it develop to serve its product-customer segments?

These three questions compel an organization to systematically and carefully assess what business it is in, where opportunities exist in the marketplace, and what capacity it has or can create to avail of these opportunities.[8]

Product-Market Scope

The breadth and complexity of the relevant product-market scope questions are distinctly different at the corporate and business-unit levels, as shown in Table 1–3. At the corporate level, a principal challenge is to identify the businesses in which the corporation can generate value-adding opportunities. What businesses can be developed and enhanced over time? The difficulties inherent in this strategic task are well exemplified in the myriad of household-name corporations in the United States (such as, Westinghouse, Kodak, DuPont), in Europe (such as Mercedes-Benz, Siemens, Philips, Rolls Royce), and in Japan (Matsushita, Mitsubishi, Nissan) that, in the past few years, have reported significantly lower performance results than anticipated. Many of these firms have had to sell off what once were described as promising or "can't miss" businesses.

The case of General Electric (GE), a multibusiness conglomerate, illustrates differences in the context and setting of corporate and business-unit scope issues and questions. Viewed from the perspective of the CEO or the board of directors, GE's *corporate* scope is assessed by continually posing the following types of questions with regard to each of its business areas (see Figure 1–2):

- Which business areas confront the greatest opportunities in the form of potential new businesses (that is, new products that would give rise to a new business for GE)?

- What emerging or potential opportunities might *not* be exploited, given the present configuration of business areas? How might the business areas be realigned to pursue these opportunities?

- Which areas should be encouraged to develop new opportunities through the internal development of new products, based on their current knowledge, capabilities, and competencies?

- Which business areas can take existing products to new types of customers or to customers in new geographic regions?

- Which areas should receive minimal, if any, new funds for business development?

TABLE 1–3   Scope: Some key questions and issues.

Corporate Level

Business Scope	What businesses is the firm in? What business does the firm want to be in?
Stakeholder Scope	What stakeholders can the organization leverage to aid in attaining its goals?
Scope Relatedness	How should the businesses in the corporation be related to each other, if at all?
Means of Changing Scope	Internal development, acquisitions, alliances, divestment; aligning with/opposing stakeholders.
Strategic Issues	In which business sectors should the firm invest? Retain the current level of investment? Reduce investment or divest itself entirely?
Strategic Challenges	How can the corporation add value to its individual businesses? What might be the basis of synergy between two or more businesses within the corporation?

Business-Unit Level

Product Scope	What range of products does the firm want to offer to the marketplace?
Customer Scope	What categories of customers does the organization want to serve? What customer needs does the firm want to satisfy?
Geographic Scope	Within what geographic terrain does the organization want to offer its products to its chosen customers?
Vertical Scope	What linkages does the organization have (and want to have) with suppliers and customers?
Stakeholder Scope	What stakeholders can the organization leverage to aid in attaining its goals?
Means of Changing Scope	Adding/deleting products or customers, moving into/out of geographic regions, aligning with/opposing stakeholders.
Strategic Issues	In what products should the organization invest? Retain at current levels? Divest itself? What relationships does the organization wish to develop with stakeholders?
Strategic Challenges	How can opportunities be identified and exploited? What is the best strategy to do so?

FIGURE 1–2 The GE Corporation's business sectors.

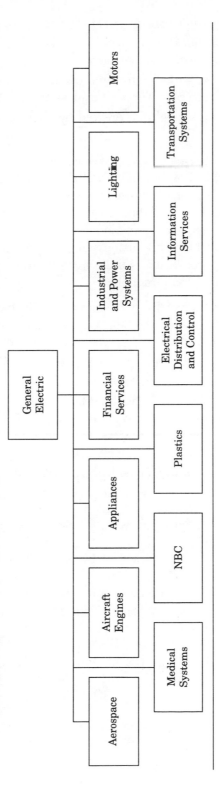

- Which areas should be deemphasized, that is, managed with the intent of generating cash that will be invested elsewhere, perhaps in other areas or in the development of new business areas?
- What new opportunities might be created by linking products, skills, and competencies from two or more business areas?
- What opportunities might be created by aligning with one or more other corporations?

Only a few of the major scope changes noted by GE in its 1992 annual report are indicated in Box 1–1. Yet, even this sampling suggests the extensive changes that most large multibusiness firms make in their corporate scope, sometimes within a single year, but certainly over a five-year period.

Some of the same questions can be directed, with considerably more focus and specificity, to each of GE's business areas. Each area must consider which specialized businesses or business units it wants to grow, hold, or divest. The Financial Services area is an example:

- Which of its 22 specialized businesses or business units should be extended through the introduction of new products or services, the pursuit of international markets, and/or the acquisition of businesses?
- Which business-units ought to be "pruned" or scaled back?
- Are there business-units that should be divested?
- What opportunities can be pursued by combining the products, technologies, and competencies of two or more business units?

Box 1–1

Sample GE Scope Changes*

Aerospace

1. The product-market scope was extended with several major contracts. These included:

   —a Korean Telecom contract for two commercial communications satellites;

   —a U.S. Navy contract for an antisubmarine warfare system;

   —others from the governments of Italy, Canada, and Turkey, for GE-built solid-state radars.

2. To enhance its position in the engine control and flight control markets, it formed a coventure with GE Aircraft Engines to pursue new opportunities.

Aircraft Engines

1. An ambitious development program is under way to certify the GE90 engine in 1994 and introduce it into active service in 1995.

* As noted in GE's 1992 annual report.

2. The aviation service business expanded its worldwide reach and capabilities in 1991 with the purchase of an engine overhaul and maintenance facility in Wales from British Airways.

Appliances

1. Expanded its relationships with MABE (a joint venture in Mexico) and other international partners. MABE's breakthrough product, an oven with 30 percent more usable capacity than any other leading manufacturer's gas range, has received a high degree of market acceptance.

2. Signed an agreement in principle to create a joint venture with Godrej & Boyce Manufacturing Co. Ltd., which would provide an opportunity to compete in India's rapidly growing appliance market.

Financial Services

1. Made a number of acquisitions to extend its product-customer scope in specific business areas. For example, Vendor Financial Services purchased Chase Manhattan's technology equipment leasing business, and Retailer Financial Services added the Harrods/House of Fraser credit card business in Great Britain.

2. Corporate Finance developed a special niche in providing lines of credit to bankrupt companies undergoing reorganization.

Industrial and Power Systems

1. In Asia, the business won $350 million of turbine-generator orders outside of Japan, and a program to intensify sales coverage in this region was announced.

2. A new agreement with ELIN of Austria is intended to enhance GE's presence in Europe.

Lighting

1. The business is emphasizing new product initiatives for global markets; for example, it accelerated its international momentum with the introduction of a complete line of GE brand lamps for the European commercial and industrial market.

2. New products introduced include the energy-efficient Trimline fluorescent lamp.

Medical Systems

1. Introduced a number of products in magnetic resonance—"literally a renewal of the entire product line."

2. Took a series of steps to increase penetration of the Indian, Russian, and Latin American markets.

Geographic Scope

Increasingly, a geographic dimension is unavoidable in scope determination: corporate and business-unit strategy must consider the international or global context of business. Even relatively small firms that sell all of their output in one country (or even within one region of a country) possess a number of options to gain a toehold in foreign markets—among them, exporting directly or partnering with enterprises in other countries. Indeed, it is not uncommon today to find small firms selling a majority of their output in foreign markets.

Without question, one of the most significant forces that has shaped almost every industry in the past 20 or 30 years has been "globalization." Competitors in any geographic market may have their "home" in any number of countries; raw materials and supplies may be obtained from any region of the world; many customers may be purchasing on a global scale. Dramatic improvements in information technology, telecommunications, and transportation allow information, goods, and services to be shipped around the world at a speed that was unimaginable a mere few decades ago.

Global change affects every organization's portfolio of opportunities. Countries and regions experience different rates of economic growth, demographic shifts affect the size of markets, and political change opens up or restricts access to national marketplaces. In short, as business becomes increasingly globalized, organizations will miss out on extensive opportunities unless they try to penetrate nations and regions beyond their "home" or regional market (i.e., their adjacent multicountry market).[9]

Geographic scope thus presents a number of issues and questions:

- What national or regional markets represent opportunities for the firm's current or future products?
- What differences and similarities exist among customers across these national or regional boundaries?
- How can the firm's products be customized or adapted for each customer group?
- How can what is learned about customers, distribution channels, competitors, and the firm's success or failure in one geographic market be leveraged in others?

Stakeholder Scope

Although frequently neglected in the strategic management literature, issues of scope also apply to the "political" arena: the interaction between the organization and its external stakeholders (industry and trade associations, community groups, governmental agencies, the courts, the media, social activist groups, and industry participants such as distributors, end-customers, suppliers, and competitors). Success in dealing with stakeholders is frequently critical to success in the product or economic marketplace. For example, many firms have developed political alliances with some of their product competitors in order to push their preferred technology standard or to obtain favorable treatment from one or more governmental agencies. Scope therefore must include consideration of how the organization wishes to deal with its external stakeholders.[10]

Among the scope issues and questions involving critical stakeholders are the following:

- Which stakeholders can affect attainment of the organization's goals and how can they do so?
- What are the similarities and differences in the "stakes" or interests of these stakeholders?
- Which stakeholders can the organization align itself with to enhance goal attainment and how can it do so?

Scope delineates the businesses or product-customer segments the organization is in or wants to be in. It does not, however, address or provide much guidance as to how to compete in the marketplace in order to attract, win, and retain customers—the substance and focus of competitive posture.

Competitive Posture

Posture embodies how an organization differentiates itself from current and future competitors *as perceived and understood by customers.* Differentiation is the source of the value (as compared to the value provided by competitors) that customers obtain when they buy a firm's product or solution. Without some degree of differentiation, customers have no particular reason to purchase an organization's product offerings rather than those of its competitors. For example, unless customers perceive some unique value associated with buying an automobile produced by General Motors, they will have no specific incentive or reason to buy from General Motors rather than from its competitors. In short, a critical purpose of strategy is to create—and to continue to enhance—some degree of differentiation.

How is differentiation created? What are its principal dimensions? What levers can an organization manipulate to foster and sustain differentiation *as perceived and understood by customers?* Although not intended as an exhaustive listing, Table 1–4 indicates a number of the key dimensions of differentiation that are employed by organizations in almost all industries. Box 1–2 discusses each of these dimensions.

Posture defines the terms of marketplace rivalry—the battle among firms to create new customers, to lure away each other's customers, and to retain customers once they have been won. Almost any industry (or industry segment) could be used to illustrate the efforts of rivals to distinguish themselves in the eyes of customers along the dimensions noted in Table 1–4 and Box 1–2. Rivalry among firms in the personal computer (PC) business is described in Box 1–3.

The intensity of the pressures to attract, win, and retain customers in almost every industry forces organizations into a never-ending race; they struggle

TABLE 1–4   Competitive posture: Sample key dimensions.

Product Line Width	Breadth of the product line
Product Features	Style Design "Bells and whistles" Size and shape
Product Functionality	Performance Reliability Durability Speed Taste
Service	Technical assistance Product repair Hot lines Education about product use
Availability	Access via distribution channels Ability to purchase in bulk How quickly product can be obtained
Image and Reputation	Brand name Image as "high-end" product Reputation for quality of service
Selling and Relationships	Sales force that can detail many products Close ties with distribution channels Historic dealings with large end-users
Price	List price Discounted price Price performance comparisons Price value comparisons

---

Box 1–2

Key Dimensions of Posture

Product Line Width

Providing a full line of products or services is often highly valued by distribution channels and/or end-users. Retailers, distributors, and end-customers often like to be able to do "one-stop" shopping. Other firms focus on a narrow product line (compared to competitors) and promote their specialization and expertise in the narrow product line to customers.

Product Features

Products can vary greatly along physical attributes such as design, style, shape, and color.

Product Functionality

All products provide some type of functional benefit(s) to users: newspapers convey information; personal computers allow individuals to better manage their household finances or write articles and books; bread provides sustenance; CDs facilitate listening pleasure. Functionality thus offers organizations myriad means by which they can differentiate their product offerings.

Service

Increasingly, service is a powerful source of differentiation in all types of products. Indeed, customers—both distribution channels and end-users—now expect high levels of service. Many industrial product firms offer customers varying levels of technical assistance, education about product use, and after-sale support with application or product-use difficulties.

Availability

Wide or highly select distribution can be a significant source of differentiation. Book publishers strive to get their books marketed through as many different types of distribution channels as possible, including specialist book retailers, institutional (i.e., college) book stores, supermarket chains, direct mail catalogs, and industry and trade shows. Other firms choose select distribution channels as a means of augmenting the image and reputation of their products and services.

Image and Reputation

All organizations and their products develop an image and reputation in the eyes of distributors, customers, suppliers, competitors, and governmental agencies. Recognizing the powerful and persuasive image conveyed to customers via brand names, many firms, such as IBM, Pepsi, Honda, and Levi, invest extensive resources to create and foster the "equity" in their brand name. Some discount stores and distribution channels have successfully created a powerful reputation for quality and low price in the form of "generic" products. Many firms have successfully differentiated themselves by crafting a well-earned image and reputation for prompt and supportive service.

Selling and Relationships

Many firms have established such tight relationships with their distribution channels and/or end-users that rivals have extreme difficulty "getting a hearing."

Price

Customers compare the value provided by competitors against the prices asked for their products.

Box 1–3

Rivalry in the Personal Computer Business

Rivalry in the personal computer (PC) business is so intense, business journalists describe it as "the PC wars." A large number of firms—well-known, large computer firms such as IBM, Digital Equipment Corporation, Apple, and Hewlett-Packard; smaller and more recent U.S. entrants such as Tandy, AST, and Compaq; Japanese firms such as Toshiba and NEC; direct mail entrants such as Dell Computer, Gateway 2000, and CompuAdd, as well as many others—are all striving to get and keep customers.

The rivalry has multiple dimensions. All competitors are rapidly extending their product lines. New models and line extensions are announced almost daily. Some firms have announced as many as 40 new products within a year. Firms are fighting furiously to stay ahead of each other with the latest notebook, laptop, and desktop models.

Functionality and features are a fierce battleground. Compaq has historically emphasized the performance capability of its products. The so-called "clone" manufacturers have differentiated themselves on comparatively low levels of functionality (yet sufficient for specific customer needs) but at low prices.

Newly introduced products are often aimed directly at rivals' offerings. IBM's low-end Value-Points were positioned to compete directly against some of Compaq's models.

Dell Computer, Gateway 2000, Zeos International, and CompuAdd have used direct distribution (i.e., selling directly to the end-customer or user) as an initial primary means of attracting and winning customers. The success of this means of reaching customers has caused IBM to create a new organizational unit, Ambra, specifically intended to compete directly against the mail order providers. Compaq and Digital Equipment Corporation have also announced that they plan to develop direct distribution capabilities.

In efforts to create image and reputation, the rivalry is now direct and intense. For example, one of Dell's advertisements asserts: "The gateway to the hottest PC technology isn't Gateway."

Service is now a primary target of differentiation. Almost all firms offer a package of support services that includes an 800 number, installation, assistance, and technical support. The direct distributors—Dell, Gateway, and others—endeavor to use service features such as rapid response to customers' inquiries as a means of distinguishing the value they provide to customers from that of their more "mainline" rivals such as IBM and Compaq. IBM and Compaq have responded by dramatically upgrading the range and quality of the service they offer.

The extent and intensity of the rivalry has been reflected in continually declining prices.

continually to redefine and renew their posture. As detailed in Box 1–3, every firm in the personal computer business continually upgrades its product features; builds greater functionality into the products; adds new service elements; promotes, advertises, and uses every form of customer interaction to advance its image and reputation; broadens the distribution base for its products; works to strengthen its relationships with dealers and users—all with the intent of enhancing the value delivered for the prices charged.

The ultimate power of the modes of differentiation, as illustrated for Dell Computer in Box 1–4, resides in their combination. By providing customers with a continual flow of new models with state-of-the-art functionality, supported by superior service and close working relationships with customers, and prompt delivery at prices that are often below those of many direct competitors, Dell is able to offer customers many reasons for buying its products. Each mode of differentiation contributes to attracting, winning, and retaining customers. Customer-based advantage (why customers buy from one competitor rather than others) always stems from a combination of these modes of differentiation; no one alone is sufficient.

For many products, posture increasingly is tailored to each individual customer—what has become known as mass customization.[11] The modes of differentiation are customized to meet customers' unique needs and wants. Dell Computer is a classic example (see Box 1–4). Dell endeavors to tailor to the needs and demands of each customer the features, power, and capability of each computer as well as the type and level of service offered.

Goals

The choices made in business scope and competitive posture are to achieve some purposes or goals.[12] It is almost impossible to make sense of an organization's changes in its scope and posture without having some knowledge of its goals. For example, unless one understands that GE's overriding marketplace goal is to be first, second, or third in terms of global market share in each of its businesses, it would be difficult to explain why it divested the television receiver business it had acquired in its takeover of Radio Corporation of America (RCA) even though the RCA brand name was one of the market share leaders in the United States. RCA had a very small share of the global market, and it would have been extremely difficult to increase it significantly in the face of intense Japanese competition.

Consideration of goals inevitably leads to two central questions:

1. What does the organization want to achieve in the marketplace?
2. What returns or rewards does it wish to attain for its various stakeholders—its stockholders, employees, customers, suppliers, and the community at large?

(Specific goals typically considered by organizations are noted in Table 1–5.)

Box 1–4

Competitive Posture: Dell Computer, Inc.

Product Line Width

Endeavors to provide a computer configuration to meet the specific needs of each customer.

Features

Varies features to meet customer needs. Uses data about each customer to tailor the feature configuration. Emphasis is on what customers want; technology is not introduced for its own sake.

Functionality

Tries to provide state-of-the-art performance and reliability tailored to how a customer will use the computer.

Service

Has 24-hour customer access via toll-free lines; handles 35,000 service and support calls per day; offers personalized phone numbers for many business customers; provides technical assistance to all customers.

Availability

Distributes directly to customers; uses distribution partners to provide next-day delivery; uses superstore and mass-merchant companies as channels but maintains direct support services to these customers.

Image and Reputation

Working to (1) make a reputation for second-to-none service an integral part of what customers buy when they purchase from Dell and (2) create an image as a firm that will go to any lengths to give customers a computer configuration that meets their needs.

Selling and Relationships

Small field sales force targets business customers; uses direct mail for as many as 15 million catalogs in a quarter. All sales and service calls are aimed at learning about customer needs, wants, and reactions to Dell products.

Price

Historically, has built a reputation for prices lower than those of established computer manufacturers like IBM and Compaq. Now broadly similar to emerging lookalike rivals such as Gateway 2000 and Northgate Computer. Tries to emphasize price–value relationship, with the price including service and customization.

TABLE 1–5   Goals: Key questions.

What does the organization want to achieve in the marketplace?

Vision or Intent	In the broad marketplace, where does the organization want to be 5, 10, or 15 years from today?
Businesses	What primary and secondary businesses does it want to get into, stay in, or get out of?
Position	What ranking does it want to attain in each of its businesses in terms of marketplace leadership?
Products	With regard to each product line: —What market share does it want to strive for, over what time period? —What types of new customers does it want to attract? —Which competitors does it want to take share away from?
Differentiation	What type of differentiation does it want to establish?

What returns or rewards does the organization wish to attain for its various stakeholders?

Shareholders/Owners	What level of shareholder wealth creation does it want to strive for? What returns (e.g., ROI) are sought on specific investments?
Employees	What quality of working experience does it want to provide for employees at all levels? What level of remuneration does it want to provide to all levels in the organization?
Government	How can the organization contribute to attainment of the goals of specific governmental agencies? What other contributions can the organization make to good government?
Customers	What degree of customer satisfaction and value does it want to provide its customers? How can the organization help its customers achieve their goals?
Society	In what ways does the organization want to demonstrate that it is a "good citizen"? Are there specific social projects to which it wants to make a monetary or other contribution?

Every organization has an explicit or implicit *hierarchy* of goals that involve some mixture of the marketplace, finance, technology, and other factors. At least four levels of goals need to be considered: (1) strategic intent/marketplace vision, (2) strategic thrusts/investment programs, (3) objectives, and (4) operating goals (see Figure 1–3). We shall discuss each briefly.

Goals at the level of *strategic intent*[13] or *marketplace vision* refer to the long-run concept of what the organization wants to achieve in the marketplace

FIGURE 1–3   An organization's hierarchy of goals.

in terms of products, customers, and technologies. For example, a number of firms promulgate an intent or vision somewhat akin to the following: To be the leader in the provision of a specific product class to particular types of customers on a global scale.

For some companies, the intent or vision embodies a goal of reshaping and reconfiguring an industry or some industry segment. In any case, intent or vision is broader in scope and more distant in time perspective than the market share goals (that is, the share of customers for existing or planned products) that are the obsessive and dominant focus in some firms.

Strategic thrusts and investment programs refer to the significant product and other investment commitments that the firm is undertaking or plans to undertake to realize its intent or vision over three- to five-year (and sometimes considerably longer) periods. Examples include investments in alliances, research and development (R&D), product line extensions, new manufacturing facilities, and development of marketing capabilities. Representative goals might include: build a leading presence in the European marketplace, reorient R&D toward the development of products that are new to the marketplace, and/or fashion a set of alliance partners that brings together two or three types of related technologies.

Objectives refer to goals that transform strategic thrusts into action programs. Objectives tend to specify results that embrace a time horizon of one to three years and represent the broad targets or milestones that the organization strives to attain. For example, a business unit's strategic thrust to penetrate the European marketplace might be guided by objectives such as: launch each product line in every major European country within three years, attain 15 percent of the European market within three or four years, achieve average gross margins of 22 percent, and be represented in every major distribution channel in each major country.

Operating goals are short-run targets (usually achievable within one year) that are measurable, specific, and detailed. They can be viewed as accomplishments that contribute to the attainment of objectives. Typical operating goals include: attain a particular market share for each product in a specific geographic market or for different specific customer sets, improve margins by a specific amount, and enhance customer satisfaction by some percentage (based on some scale of measurement).

In summary, goals make sense of the organization's actions. The decision by a corporation to divest an entire business often makes sense only when it is known whether its strategic thrust is to refocus on its core business or to raise cash quickly. Goals focus the organization's attention. If the goal is to increase margins, the organization is likely to address those activities that will add to revenues and reduce costs. Goals facilitate coordination of what otherwise might be disparate and conflicting activities. They motivate organizational members and rationalize the organization's actions so that all the stakeholders can contribute to winning.

Linkages among Scope, Posture, and Goals

Strategic management presumes that organizations are goal-directed, although seasoned managers recognize that an organization's goals may not be consistent, integrated, widely disseminated, or understood. This is especially so when goals are related to time. Many firms are too busy pursuing today's opportunities to worry about goal consistency. Others are so committed to outdated goals that they don't react quickly enough to critical changes in the marketplace. Thus, in the challenge of strategic management noted at the beginning of this chapter—laying the foundation for success in tomorrow's environment while competing to win in today's marketplace—a central element is management of the conflict between commitment to goals and the need to adapt scope and posture to changing environmental and organizational conditions.

Managing the conflict is a difficult balancing act. A strategic intent or marketplace vision that is out of touch with the environment and with the organization's resources and capabilities can only lead to shattered dreams, intense frustration, and enormous anxiety.[14] On the other hand, if the goals do not push the organization's scope and posture to create or avail of emerging opportunities, they contribute to inferior performance.[15] For example, William Gates III, CEO of Microsoft, has said that one of his greatest regrets is that he did not commit the firm sooner to a vision of "work-group computing" (i.e., a means of allowing teams to use networks of interconnected personal computers to share data and information and to cooperate on multiple projects). The intent of being the dominant leader in work-group computing is now reflected in a variety of

Microsoft's strategic thrusts and investment programs designed to make a broad-based attack on this marketplace.[16]

In summary, as illustrated for an electronics firm in Box 1–5, scope, posture, and goals are three interrelated elements in marketplace strategy. The electronics firm's long-term goals—its intent and vision—are to establish new technology and customer service standards in a specific domain of industrial applications. These long-term goals create a context for the design and development of scope and posture. The firm's product development thrusts and its search for new customers and new uses or applications refine the firm's marketplace scope over time. Its overall posture of moving toward customizing each "solution" or application for each customer serves as a central plank of its intent to establish a new industry standard for delivering customer-focused value. Its objectives and operating goals furnish milestones and targets to be achieved in the course of executing its strategic thrusts and programs. For example, attainment of the image and reputation objective to become unquestionably the leading brand name is a necessary step on the road to achieving its intent and vision.

A final but critical comment on strategy: Strategy provides a sense of marketplace direction that may remain quite stable over time, but substantial parts of its key elements—scope, posture, and goals—may change. Thus, the electronics firm's intent or vision (noted in Box 1–5) may endure for a number of years as a guide to the direction of many of its principal strategic thrusts and investment programs. However, as the firm strives to reach its overarching vision, the strategy may manifest a number of twists and turns as the firm anticipates, responds to, and leverages environmental change. For example, the firm's own technology development may generate unexpected opportunities for new products, extension of one or more of the existing product lines, or new ways to seek differentiation. As the organization reaches for these opportunities, scope and posture are adapted over time.[17]

MANAGING THE ORGANIZATION

Strategies that continue to win in the marketplace don't just happen. Even if an organization stumbles onto a winning strategy, considerable effort and ingenuity are still needed to continually adapt and amend the strategy in order to leverage internal and environmental change. It is no accident that some organizations successfully adapt to an environment and initiate new ventures in a number of related product areas while others never seem able to repeat a single success. In short, what takes place *within* the organization makes a difference.

Winning in the marketplace is heavily influenced by how well the organization makes and executes its choices of where and how to compete. Figure 1–1 sets out five organizational domains that are critical to crafting and sustaining successful marketplace strategies.

Box 1–5
An Electronics Firm's Marketplace Strategy

Broad Goals

Intent and Vision:

To become the leading supplier of a range of equipment involving specific technologies for a variety of customer uses. (In so doing, to enhance revenues, profits, margins, market share, and image as product/technology leader.)

Marketplace Scope

Products-Customers:

Provides three distinct lines of related products to any type of industrial customer in North America and most European countries. Continues to add variety to its product lines and to search for new applications of its products with both existing and new customers.

Marketplace Posture

Modes of Competing to Achieve Differentiation:

Moving toward customizing its solution for each customer by varying product features and performance to meet each customer's specific needs. Also tailoring service agreements to suit customers' requirements and ability to pay. Using own salesforce and distributors to reach new customers and build customer relationships through provision of technical assistance and attention to evolving customer needs. Building an image of leading technology developer through promotion and marketing programs and salesforce activity. Actual prices tend to be higher than competitors, reflecting superior product functionality, reputation, and added service.

Objectives and Goals

Product development.   To introduce another product line within three years and to add as many variations to the existing lines as customers need.

Market share.   Continue to gain penetration of each major customer class. Attain 25% share of market units within four to five years.

Image and reputation.   To become the recognized leading name for a range of uses of its core product technology (measured by customer surveys).

Distribution channels.   To be the preferred product line of each major channel in every geographic region.

Technology.   To augment technology capabilities in three specific areas in order to enhance product functionality:

1. Increase revenues by 12–14% per year.
2. Increase gross margins 8–10% over three years.
3. Increase net profits 10–12% over three years.

Analytics

The determination of scope, posture, and goals involves a plethora of individual decisions: what products to develop and offer, what customers to seek, how best to compete in the marketplace, and what goals to pursue. These decisions require many types of analytical input; especially important are data and insights about multiple facets of the competitive context as well as the organization itself. These data and insights are the products of analysis. *Analytics* here refers to all of the analysis conducted by an organization in strategy determination and execution.

Analysis is framed and guided by conceptual frameworks and analytical methodologies. As discussed in Chapters 6 through 9, many different types of frameworks and methodologies are available to capture and assess change in any firm's industry and macroenvironment. The outputs of this analysis are threefold:

1. An understanding of the current state of the industry (or industries) and the macroenvironment the firm may enter or in which it currently participates;
2. An identification of likely "alternative futures," that is, potential future states of these industries;
3. An assessment of the implications of the current and potential states of the environment for the organization's existing and potential strategies.

Equally important is analysis of the organization itself. If the organization is unable to take advantage of opportunities or to defend against competitive or environmental threats, there is little benefit in engaging in environmental analysis. The organization's historic practices, policies, and operating processes may facilitate or impede the development and execution of strategy.[18] Moreover, the organization's own resources—its knowledge, skills, and relationships—as well as its capabilities and competencies may be the source of marketplace opportunities.[19] The outputs of organization analysis include:

1. An understanding of the state of the organization's mindset, operating processes, infrastructure, and leadership;
2. An identification of the organization's strengths (such as its capabilities and competencies) and weaknesses (such as its vulnerabilities, constraints, and limitations);
3. An assessment of the implications of the state of the organization for its current and potential strategies.

As emphasized repeatedly in this book, it is never enough merely to analyze. Analyses of the environment and of the organization must be transformed into strategy alternatives that are then assessed before the organization commits to its existing direction or selects new directions. Strategy alternatives need to be articulated in terms of possible alterations to scope, posture, and goals. Analytics therefore needs to be specifically focused on a crucial, complex, and creative task: turning the knowledge and learning acquired as part of ongoing environmental and organizational analysis into the specification of potential opportunities and threats.

Once strategy alternatives are identified and developed and their implications are understood, they can then be evaluated. The analysis of strategy alternatives requires that each alternative be subjected to searching and demanding questions. This level of analysis should be part of a continuous process to enhance an organization's strategy. In our rapidly changing business environment, the product of this analysis is likely to be a set of strategy recommendations for altering the organization's scope, posture, and goals.

Analytics poses a number of managerial challenges. First, analytics must be strategically focused; that is, the analysis must be aimed at detecting opportunities. It is not sufficient merely to capture and promulgate warnings of environmental and organizational change. Second, an emphasis on opportunities compels continuous consideration of the future. Managers conducting analysis often must dare to break free of the intellectual shackles that the past imposes on anyone who tries to anticipate the future.

Mindset

Analysis is conducted by individuals in an organizational setting. It is influenced by the collective state-of-mind or mindset of the organization. Mindset is the sum of vision (what managers see the organization striving to attain), values (what they consider important), beliefs (what they consider to be cause-effect relationships), and assumptions (what they take for granted).

An organization's *vision* offers stakeholders a view of the future it wants to achieve. Apple's vision is to change the world by empowering individuals through personal computing technology. Whether a vision is explicit or implicit, it transmits the organization's overarching strategic goals, as discussed earlier, to its members. Vision thus shapes a common theme in the organization's state-of-mind. For example, in the 1960s, Komatsu established the vision of being the world's leading earth-moving equipment manufacturer. At the time, it seemed an unachievable goal, but this aim served as a rallying cry and unifying force as Komatsu set out to overtake Caterpillar's dominant lead in the global marketplace.[20]

Visions are not likely to move organizations to decisive action unless they are reflected in *values*—what organization members consider important. Values connect a vision to decision making; they link the organization's aspirations and goals to day-to-day actions and decisions. For example, organizations that are product- or technology-driven (versus customer- or marketplace-driven) manifest distinctly different values. In technology-focused firms, driving values might be stated as: "If it is technologically feasible, let's do it" or, "Each product must incorporate the latest technological capability." Customer-focused firms manifest these values: "What the customer wants is more important than what is technologically possible" or, "Each technological development should be tested against customers' needs and perceptions as early as possible."

Most organizations construct value statements that typically address broad items: "a commitment to excellence," "doing what is right," "treating employees with respect and integrity," and "providing value to customers." However, such statements do not provide enough guidance for decision making and action. Excellence at any cost? Doing what is right by what code? Values truly become a core element in an organization's mindset only when they are localized and internalized by organization members. For example, Komatsu could not have sustained its assault on Caterpillar unless the vision of becoming the world's leading earth-moving equipment manufacturer translated into values such as the need to continually upgrade the quality of the product line, the need to provide superior value to customers, the need to manufacture extremely functional and high-performing machines.

Beliefs are the organization's understanding of cause–effect relationships. Beliefs may address matters that are internal (for example, improvements in the manufacturing process will lead to higher product quality and lower costs) or external (for example, competitors' lower prices will not lead to higher market share). In either case, they may be widely shared and embedded in the organization. Beliefs are an important component of mindset because they strongly influence behaviors. If an organization believes that alliances are the only way to quickly penetrate and sustain a dominant position in a particular industry segment, it will likely forgo other options and craft a series of alliances.

Assumptions are distinct from beliefs. They are "givens" such as information or situations that the organization is willing to consider givens. Organizations make assumptions about many internal and external factors, including customers, competitors, industry evolution, regulation, technology, and the organization's resources, competencies, and cash flows. Assumptions such as "Competitors will not be able to introduce a superior product for the next three years" or "Our own organization will be able to generate all the funds it needs for capital investment from cash flow" become central elements in the organization's mindset.

An organization's mindset is the world view that results from its own members' interacting with each other over time. Eventually, organizational members begin to share with each other and reinforce their vision, values, beliefs, and assumptions. The world view defines and shapes opportunity and risk. For example, stories about the difficulties of dealing with a particular distribution channel or an end-customer group may become legend within an organization and implicitly lead it to shy away from doing business with these customer segments.

Mindset is of central importance to strategic management because it can either buttress or inhibit strategy. Its effects on scope, posture, and goals can be dramatic. Visions have frequently transformed the mindset of organizations so that they could then achieve what earlier might have seemed impossible.

False beliefs and assumptions preordain strategy failure. IBM's recent, well-publicized difficulties can in large measure be traced to false beliefs and assumptions about the future of the mainframe segment of the computer industry. The mainframe segment had catapulted IBM to its position of dominance in the computer industry. IBM believed that its technological prowess could add to the mainframe a level of functionality that customers would appreciate and value. It also assumed that the rate of market decline would not increase and that new customers could be attracted to the mainframe. The combination of these beliefs and assumptions allowed IBM to stumble into disaster. The decline of the mainframe sales and profits led to shareholders' losing billions of dollars and employees' losing tens of thousands of jobs.

The managerial challenge therefore is to ensure that mindset recognizes environmental change. This recognition is a prerequisite to developing and executing strategies that can win in the marketplace. Ideally, to achieve strategic leadership, an organization should be able to adopt a new mindset as a way of positioning itself to profit from environmental change. The challenge for managers then becomes one of continually assessing the organization's existing mindset and questioning whether it is reflecting past or emerging potential environmental change.

Operating Processes

Analytics and mindset are necessary, but they are not sufficient for an organization to function—to get things done. Operating processes constitute how work gets done in and around any organization.[21] A large number of operating processes exist in every organization. A listing of critical operating processes for most manufacturing firms is shown in Table 1–6. Each operating process represents a task that must be completed in order for an organization to survive.

TABLE 1–6   Typical operating processes in manufacturing firms.

Scanning the Environment for Marketplace Opportunities.

Designing Products That Meet Customers' Needs.

Acquiring Raw Materials and Components.

Acquiring and Training Personnel.

Building Product Prototypes.

Manufacturing Products.

Marketing.

Selling and Detailing Products to Customers.

Delivering Products to Customers.

Receiving and Fulfilling Customers' Orders.

Providing Pre- and Postsales Service to Customers.

Without operating processes, organizations cannot systematically learn about the marketplace, develop new products, acquire the raw materials and components to assemble and produce products or services, access capital, acquire and develop human resources, market and distribute products, or provide service to intermediate or end-customers. In the execution of these tasks, operating processes are intimately linked to the development and implementation of strategy.

Operating processes have critical import for a strategically managed organization, for many reasons. Among them are:

1. If the organization does not do the right things, then both its thinking and its actions are unlikely to generate competitive success. Each organization must identify its critical or core operating processes—those that are most central to winning in the marketplace.[22]

2. Many core operating processes, such as product development, fulfillment of customers' orders, and learning about marketplace change, transcend organizational boundaries and thus serve to integrate functional groups (such as R&D, manufacturing, and marketing) around common external purposes (such as serving customers better).

3. If operating processes are not well-managed, the organization's overall efficiency will be severely hampered. For example, in the 1990s, managers of operating processes in cutting-edge firms have greatly reduced cycle times (such as speed to market or the time it takes to fulfill a customer's order).

Like analytics and mindset, operating processes can positively or negatively affect each element in strategy: scope, posture, and goals. With regard to scope, many companies, after recognizing the poor returns from their R&D and product commercialization activity, have struggled to redesign and invigorate the new product development process. In particular, in the 1990s, some industrial product companies have established integrated product development teams and radically changed the work flow related to identifying ideas for products, doing basic or applied research, creating product prototypes, and market-testing prototypes in customer facilities. No longer is product development solely the responsibility of the R&D and/or new product development departments. Rather, new product development groups are established with representation from all the affected functional areas or departments—R&D, product design, manufacturing, marketing, sales and service, accounting and finance, and human resources. This integration replaces having one phase of new product development done by one department or group without much consultation with all the others in the development chain, and then "handed-off" to the next department or group.

Operating processes have perhaps a more direct impact on posture than on scope. In company after company, the redesign and enhancement of operating processes are leading to significant improvement in the quality, speed, and responsiveness of these organizations—how they anticipate changing customer needs, acquire and fulfill orders, and ensure that customers are satisfied after they have purchased their products or services.[23]

Managing operating processes presents a number of challenges:

1. Analysis and redesign of operating processes must be guided by their marketplace strategy relevance because their ultimate value resides in how they contribute to getting and keeping customers.[24]

2. Operating processes constitute an integrated organizational system: altering one process often affects many others. Thus, they must be managed at the systemic level, not at the individual level.

3. Because operating processes reside at the heart of an organization's capabilities and competencies, they often are the source of marketplace opportunities.[25]

Infrastructure

Analytics, mindset, and operating processes exist within an organization's infrastructure: its structure, systems and decision-making processes. As with the other organizational elements, infrastructure must be managed with an eye to helping the organization cope with and leverage environmental change.

Structure refers to how the organization is organized internally as well as to its relationships with external entities.[26] Internal structure addresses (1) how the organization divides itself into units (such as business sectors, business units, and departments) and (2) the linkages among these subunits[27] (such as reporting relationships). An increasingly critical element in structure is the linkages that an organization effects with other entities (suppliers, distributors, customers, competitors, technology sources, venture partners, and community and public interest groups) through alliances, partnerships, and networks.[28] External linkages help organizations to gain access to critical resources (such as capital, knowledge, and skills) and facilitate the development of key capabilities and competencies.

An organization's structure, however elegant and innovative its design, is merely a shell. *Systems* are required to move information through the structure, oversee and control the flow of resources, reward and motivate organizational members, and facilitate the making of decisions. Information, control, remuneration, and planning systems play critical roles in ensuring that an organization anticipates, copes with, and leverages change.[29]

Decision processes are the organizational procedures and routines that bring organizational members together in the making of decisions.[30] They may be largely formal, as when planning system procedures, committees, task forces, and regularly scheduled meetings, or informal, as when ad hoc meetings or other get-togethers of individuals are charged with making specific decisions. They may range from consensus-generating routines that involve interaction among many individuals at multiple levels of the organization to top-down, authoritarian routines in which decisions are made and announced by one person or a small number of individuals, with all others then expected to fall in line and execute the decisions.[31]

Infrastructure is not incidental to making and executing strategy. Structure can serve to focus and reinforce an organization's efforts to win in the marketplace or it can hobble managers who might otherwise take initiatives. Many business units have found ways to succeed in reshaping and enhancing their product line and to aggressively pursue customers once they have been freed from the infrastructural shackles of a prior corporate parent. Lexmark, almost as soon as it became independent of IBM, began to change its scope and posture in the printer business and achieved dramatic results; it had struggled to do so for many years as an IBM business unit.

Systems can affect scope, posture, and goals in many ways. For example, managers' incentive systems sometimes have an unintended and unanticipated influence on scope decisions. In one well-known leading U.S. corporation, senior executives did not approve any capital investment in new product development, geographic expansion, or potential alliances if it was likely to have a negative impact on short-run earnings. Why? Because they did not receive *any* bonus if earnings dipped below a prespecified level. On the other hand, if managers' incentives are closely tied to increased sales, a common result is that the organization goes to extraordinary lengths to attract new customers.

Decision processes sometimes directly influence goals. The CEO in a large single-business firm was unable to generate a consensus among his top management team as to which of a number of strategic alternatives or opportunities the firm should pursue. In his estimation, part of the difficulty in reaching a consensus stemmed from the inability of the top management team to devote sufficient time, as a group, to considering the alternatives and choosing among them. His solution was to take the management team for a five-day "retreat" at an executive education facility where the team would have the time and commitment needed to seriously consider the options. The team eliminated some opportunities, identified linkages among others that previously had not been noted, and rank-ordered the opportunities in terms of their potential sales and their fit with the organization's resources, capabilities, and competencies. The short list of opportunities then became the focus of further analysis once the executive team returned home.[32]

Managing infrastructure also presents a number of challenges:

1. Structure, systems, and decision processes tend to ossify: they take on a life of their own. For example, once managers and others get used to a particular information system, they become reluctant to change.

2. Structure, systems, and decision processes that were appropriate for one set of environmental conditions may be ineffectual for identifying and adapting to emerging opportunities spawned by change.

3. Structure, systems, and decision processes are interrelated; thus, like operating processes, they must be managed at the systemic level.

Leadership

A dominant presumption underlying strategic management is that managers can make a difference. The organizational elements discussed above—analytics, mindset, operating processes, and infrastructure—can never be allowed to go on "automatic pilot." Leaders must continually guide the analytics, modify the mindset, orient and integrate the operating processes, and adjust the infrastructure. They should do so in anticipation of change in the environment rather than in reaction to it. Effective managers can create change within the organization *before* performance results suggest that it is necessary.[33] Effective managers continually adapt and sometimes radically alter strategy—scope, posture, and goals. These actions are the substance and focus of *strategic* leadership.

Simply stated, the purpose of leadership is to make a difference by:

- Increasing the chances of winning in the marketplace—the strategy difference;
- Building and sustaining an organization that supports and executes marketplace strategy—the organization difference.

As discussed in the next section, managers must lead if the organization is to outperform its competitors in the marketplace.

The strategy-relevant purpose of leadership *within* the organization is the alignment of the other organizational elements—analytics, mindset, operating processes, and infrastructure—to take maximum advantage of opportunities in the marketplace. In the face of persistent environmental change, organization leaders have little choice but to continually confront and revamp the analytics, mindset, operating processes, and infrastructure. Leadership is thus the distinguishing contribution of managers; it is their "value-add" to the organization. Broadly viewed, leadership is the capacity of individuals *at all levels* of the organization, from team leaders to the CEO, to inspire, motivate, and energize those around them to do what it takes to win in the marketplace and to excel in what the organization does and what they do as individuals.

The challenges inherent in strategic leadership can be best illustrated by considering a specific organization. Consider the leadership challenges confronting Jack Smith, the CEO of General Motors, and his team of senior executives, as noted in a recent *Business Week* article:[34]

- Extend and revamp the product lines of each product group;
- Upgrade the product lines more frequently;
- Lower the cost per vehicle (which exceeds both Ford and Chrysler);
- Mend the tattered relations with suppliers angered by the draconian practices of a former head of purchasing;
- Reduce the bureaucracy and improve upward, downward and lateral communication within the organization;
- Streamline the production and procurement of parts and components.

PRACTICING STRATEGIC MANAGEMENT

As we have defined it, strategic management entails managing strategy, organization, and the linkages between them in order to win both today and tomorrow. Managing strategy or the organization alone is not sufficient. Creating and leveraging change requires a simultaneous focus on both the environment and the organization. Managers must lead by persistently challenging the accepted view of the future and its implications, the basis for success of their strategies, and the ability of their organization to identify and avail itself of opportunities.

This section emphasizes the bridges between strategy and organization by addressing the following key tasks that are central to strategic management:

- Delineating the current state of strategic management;
- Assessing the presence of strategic leadership;
- Identifying and developing strategic alternatives;
- Choosing the preferred strategy;
- Implementing the chosen strategy;
- Outperforming competitors and winning customers;
- Renovating strategy;
- Reinventing strategy.

These tasks serve as the focus of linkages between strategy and organization (see Figure 1–4). Each task will be briefly discussed.

Delineating the Current State of Strategic Management

Delineating the current marketplace strategy (scope, posture, and goals) and the organization's configuration (the state of its analytics, mindset, operating processes, infrastructure, and leadership) is a task that must be undertaken before the development and assessment of a future strategy direction. An understanding of the current marketplace strategy and organization configuration gives essential input to the identification and assessment of the presence and extent of strategic leadership, relevant marketplace opportunities and threats, and the resources and capabilities that can be leveraged for advantage, as well as to recognition of the organization's vulnerabilities, limitations, and constraints.

An understanding of current marketplace strategy develops when the interrelated dimensions of scope, posture, and goals are mapped and detailed as discussed in Chapters 2 through 5 and as summarized for the electronics firm in Box 1–5.

Because analytics, mindset, operating processes, infrastructure, and leadership are so deeply ingrained in the day-to-day activities and functioning of the organization, it may be difficult for managers to delineate their prevailing state. Yet it must be done. Various chapters in this book directly and indirectly address how to detail and document the analytics conducted (such as the tools and techniques used to analyze industries, the broader environment, and the

FIGURE 1–4   Strategic management: Linking marketplace strategy and the organization.

organization's resources), the content of mindset (i.e., vision, values, assumptions, and beliefs), the dominant operating processes, the overarching infrastructure (i.e., structure, systems, and decisions processes), and the extent to which leadership is evident.

As emphasized earlier, it is the interplay between strategy and organization that needs thorough scrutiny, especially if it has previously received minimal attention. Consideration of the linkages between strategy and organization often results in significant surprises. Managers are frequently shocked to discover that their strategy is constrained not by environmental change but by their own values, beliefs, and assumptions.[35] Similarly, a successful strategy may be reinforcing the current operating processes and infrastructure but restricting the organization's ability to win if the marketplace changes.

Assessing the Presence of Strategic Leadership

Merely to understand what the marketplace strategy is or how the organization is configured is not enough. A crucial test of strategic management is whether the organization is attaining and sustaining marketplace leadership: Is it outdistancing its current and future competitors? Is it regarded by customers as the most innovative and premier supplier or merely as one of the pack? Marketplace leadership can be denominated and measured in many ways; the typical indicators are noted in Table 1–7. Without some degree of marketplace leadership, it is difficult to argue that organizations can fend off rivals nipping at their heels or generate long-term superior financial performance.

Marketplace leadership is the ultimate test of any organization's capacity not just to anticipate change but to shape and leverage it in the form of products and services that attract, win, and retain customers. An organization committed to strategic leadership wants:

- To have its product offerings or "solutions" rated as the best in the market;
- To be recognized as the leading innovator in products or solutions in its field;
- To provide customers with not just the best value but with some excitement about their purchase;
- To be the organization with which customers strive to do business;
- To create new ways of obtaining and retaining customers.

Marketplace leadership cannot be achieved and sustained in the absence of organizational leadership. Management must first set strategic intent and direction in terms of scope, posture, and goals; it must decide what product domains it wants to be in, what customers it wants to serve, and how it wants to attract, win, and retain customers. In short, management must provide the over-

TABLE 1–7 Indicators of marketplace leadership.

Is the organization creating new visions of what the industry might look like at some point in the future?

Is the organization the leader in introducing products that are new to the marketplace?

Is the organization the leader in building linkages between products that previously were unrelated?

Is the organization the leader in extending product lines and in modifying existing products?

Is the organization driving change in how customers understand and use products or solutions?

Is the organization serving the most demanding and challenging customers?

Is the organization leading in the creation of new customers?

Is the organization driving technology change that underlies key product changes?

Is the organization seen as the innovator in product functionality?

Is the organization seen as the innovator in new forms of service, distribution, and delivery?

arching intent of what the organization wants to achieve in the marketplace and then lead the organization in the pursuit of its broad goals.

Organization leadership contributes to marketplace leadership not just in terms of focusing and inspiring marketplace goals but in choosing, fostering, and extending the specific capabilities and competencies that can be leveraged for marketplace opportunity. In short, operating processes need to be honed and extended so that they contribute to capabilities and competencies that directly or indirectly result in value and benefits for customers. Increasingly, organizations are building capabilities and competencies around "what we do well" and finding best-in-class outside vendors for products and services that are not central to their skill and knowledge base.[36]

Internal infrastructure, in the form of incentive, control, and planning systems, must be focused on fostering the required capabilities and competencies. External infrastructure must be aimed at cultivating relationships with other organizations that are necessary to augment and extend the organization's capability and competency profile. Organizations as diverse as Honda, IBM, and AT&T have recently acknowledged the need to redirect their internal infrastructure toward developing and refining capabilities and competencies as one of the requirements to gaining and solidifying marketplace leadership.

Organization leadership, as noted earlier, facilitates the entrepreneurship and innovation necessary to attain and sustain marketplace leadership by constantly challenging the organization's analytics and mindset (a challenge to which we return later, in the discussion of strategic renovation and strategic reinvention).

Identifying and Developing Strategic Alternatives

Strategic leadership emanates from the identification, development, and exploitation of marketplace opportunities. Recognized marketplace leaders such as Microsoft, Intel, Merck, Johnson and Johnson, and Procter and Gamble enhance and extend their marketplace leadership by continually shaping new opportunities. New entrants to every industry or market segment are driven by the presumption that they have detected a market opportunity for their products. Each marketplace participant will ultimately falter before the onslaught of existing competitors and new entrants unless it renovates or reinvents its strategy.[37]

Sustained leadership in the marketplace can only result from an obsessive pursuit of opportunities. Opportunities come in many forms. Some are new not just to the organization but to the marketplace; for example, the introduction of Chrysler's minivan created a new product class or category. More typically, opportunities constitute extensions of the present strategy: They broaden the product line, reach more of the existing customers, and offer the current or slightly augmented product line in new geographic markets. Opportunities range from the very promising to the very restricted in terms of sales, customer reach, and profit potential, and firms must estimate the costs and benefits of pursuing each opportunity.

Irrespective of their scope or scale, opportunities do not fall like manna from heaven. Although they are nurtured, exploited, and realized in the market-place, opportunities are first identified, developed, and shaped by individuals *within* the organization. Opportunities therefore must be captured: Individuals must see them in terms of emergent, visible, or potential change. The purpose of the industry, macroenvironmental, and technological assessment discussed in Chapters 6 through 9 is to identify key trends and patterns within the organization's environment, the drivers of these environmental changes, and how they might translate into opportunities.

Opportunity identification and development must be continually managed. Detecting, making sense of, and projecting environmental change must be oriented toward the identification and development of opportunities. Opportunities ranging from the obvious to the "unthinkable" need to be surfaced.[38] Detecting and documenting demographic and life-style changes are comparatively straightforward activities; the difficulties and rewards lie in isolating what opportunities might exist in such change. For example, the rapid explosion of single-person households has created a corresponding upsurge in the demand for convenience foods, yet many food packagers have been slow to detect how such change could be transformed into opportunity. The increasing cost-consciousness in many corporate, governmental, and not-for-profit organizations has given rise to an array of opportunities for "solutions" that help these organizations to become more cost-efficient.

In the absence of leadership that challenges mindsets, opportunities will not be developed and evaluated even though they may be identified. In one consumer goods firm, a group of product managers steadfastly refused to give serious consideration to the option of selling products produced by the firm under a brand name other than its own historic brand name or to provide products to private-label distributors. Only after competitors had successfully done so did the firm belatedly decide to go after these opportunities. It takes effective leadership to promote opportunities that do not fit outdated mindsets.

Infrastructure may help or hinder analytics and mindset in shaping opportunities. Planning systems that do not support interaction among business units do not foster the detection and development of opportunities that lie outside the domain of any one business unit. Conversely, planning and information systems that transmit data about change in customers, technology, and industry growth and evolution across functional boundaries, within a business unit, or across business units may spark an insight that leads to opportunity detection. For example, in one large telecommunications corporation, a report disseminated to all business units by a senior corporate executive detailed some of the current and emerging technological challenges confronting some business units. One unit realized, from reading the report, that a technology it was attempting to develop possessed considerably more market opportunity than had been previously determined.

Choosing the Preferred Strategy Evaluation

Ceaseless opportunity detection, development, and assessment are central to strategic management. A true test of leadership is whether it inspires the organization to surface and develop opportunities that will stretch it beyond its current resources.[39]

The greater the strategic change (i.e., scope, posture, and goals) embedded in an opportunity, the greater both the potential payback (returns) and the risk. The challenge in assessing opportunities resides in the following dilemma: Strategic success requires organizations to create and leverage change in the marketplace. Unfortunately, their efforts to do so may result in strategies (or adjustments to existing strategies) that are inconsistent with current or future environmental change. For example, IBM's efforts to reshape its strategy in the mainframe computer segment may flop in a world where smaller computers can do the work previously performed by mainframes. If strategic change is too far ahead of or behind environmental change, it is not likely to generate superior marketplace or financial performance.

Thus, potential opportunities must be subjected to extensive and intensive scrutiny to ensure, to the extent it is possible to do so, that they are congruent with current and future environmental change.[40] Opportunities must be subjected to the types of questions noted in Table 1–8. Few tasks so test the strategic management prowess of any organization as its capacity to insightfully subject potential opportunities to thorough scrutiny and yet maintain an entrepreneurial orientation.

The analysis challenge (see Chapter 11) is considerable. Opportunities are framed and interpreted through the organization's preferred analytical tools and

---

TABLE 1–8   Assessing opportunities: Key questions.

What is the nature of the opportunity?

What environmental change underlies the opportunity?

—What are the specific industry changes?
    Customer change?
    Supplier change?
    Technology change?
    Substitute product change?

—What is the macroenvironmental change?
    Social change?
    Economic change?
    Technological change?
    Political and regulatory change?

What organizational change supports or is needed to exploit the opportunity?
    Change in mindset?
    Change in operating processes?
    Change in infrastructure?
    Change in leadership?

techniques. For example, in many firms, the early imposition of financial criteria often prematurely leads to the rejection of valuable alternatives.[41] An emphasis on marketplace criteria such as market share and sales growth often propels organizations to favor scope and posture alternatives such as product line development and product proliferation. In some firms, technology reigns supreme, and any opportunity that builds on the organization's technological prowess or takes the organization in new, "exciting" technological directions is accorded favored status. The risk here is that the firm may select alternatives that are inconsistent with emerging or potential industry change or broader environmental change.

Mindset also shapes opportunity selection. A well-disseminated vision, reinforced by widely shared values, can shape the lens through which the organization views specific opportunities. The risk is that an organization's mindset will blind it to opportunities that are radically different from those it is experienced at evaluating. One telecommunications firm that saw itself as a future leader in specific types of equipment missed out on a major new business opportunity: it did not give serious consideration to "wireless" opportunities because they fell outside its designated purview.

Infrastructure must be continually assessed for its opportunity assessment implications. Business-unit or product-group structure can dramatically influence opportunity assessment. If the opportunity is not seen as falling directly within the unit's product-market domain, managers may have little incentive to give it a serious appraisal. Decision-making procedures that emphasize rapid and decisive decision making often eliminate alternatives that have "obvious" potential. Too often, alternatives are rejected before they are fully understood.

Implementing the Chosen Strategy

To realize valuable opportunities, products or services must be created and customers must be won and retained. An action agenda is required to translate the potential of opportunities into the reality of results. Action is required on a myriad of fronts—redesign of the current product or "solution" to meet customers' needs; development of new products; delivery of products and services to customers; execution of marketing, promotion, and sales programs; fulfillment of customer orders; provision of customer service; recruitment and training of personnel; and acquisition of capital. Key milestones for action programs must be developed, the sequence and timing of actions must be determined, and control and monitoring of actions must be given proper attention.

As actions are executed, the organization observes the results and learns from them. Product development may lead to unexpected breakthroughs (or bottlenecks); manufacturing may unearth ways of producing at less cost; sales programs may identify superior ways of reaching customers; order fulfillment may generate more efficient ways of reaching customers. The consequent learning should change the intended actions or plans; some opportunities can be reshaped and refined as the strategy is being executed. For example, as products are introduced to the marketplace, firms frequently find that the intended customers respond less positively than expected but other customers adopt the products with enthusiasm.

As strategy is rolled out, managers must execute it coherently in the marketplace; scope, posture, and goals must be consistent and reinforcing. Scope coherence requires: distinct differences within and across product lines; product lines that are tailored or customized to specific customer segments or niches; products that address distinct customer needs (rather than serving the same customer group or needs). Computer and automobile firms, for example, strive to shape multiple product lines that have distinct features and benefits to satisfy different customer needs.

Coherence is especially critical within posture. For example, an up-market image would be inconsistent with low price; a narrow product line would be inconsistent with an intent to develop a corporate image and reputation as the solution to most customers' needs; availability of a product through all types of distribution channels and retailers, ranging from discount outlets to exclusive, high-end merchandisers, is likely to confuse customers. Yet, posture is not static; for example, Dell Computer (see Box 1–4) is a company with a coherent but constantly changing posture.

Goal coherence is the rock on which strategy execution often founders. Unless the organization's multiple goals support and reinforce each other, the organization is pulled in conflicting directions and sends contradictory messages or signals to its multiple stakeholders: suppliers, distributors, end-customers, competitors, employees, and shareholders. Some classic examples are worth noting. A long-run goal to achieve marketplace leadership in terms of product superiority can be sabotaged by a goal of maximizing short-run financial performance: Investments in research and development and marketing programs intended to build relationships with key customers are postponed. In many firms, manufacturing's pursuit of product standardization and cost minimization conflicts directly with marketing's desire for product and service customization.

Strategy coherence is greatly abetted, of course, by organizational alignment—that is, alignment in the form of linkage and integration among analytics, mindset, operational processes, infrastructure, and leadership, and alignment with the focus, direction, and thrust of the marketplace strategy. Otherwise, the organization is not driving in the direction that is required by marketplace strategy.[42]

To understand the importance of organizational alignment, we need only look at firms striving for rapid sales growth and penetration of many customer segments. In the computer industry, companies such as Microsoft, Compaq, and Dell confront a number of distinct alignment challenges because of the pressures brought about by rapidly expanding sales. In particular:

- Rapid sales growth requires that operational processes and infrastructure be intimately integrated. For example, information and control systems need to be continually adapted to monitor whether such operating processes as order fulfillment and customer service are being over-stretched and thus are detracting from value delivered to customers.

- Leaders need to continually challenge and reinvigorate the analytics and mindset to ensure that they stay congruent with the needs of many distinct types of customers. Many rapidly growing firms, obsessed with meeting current demand, have neglected to think about future product needs.

In particular, strategy execution places heavy demands on the alignment of operational processes (how the work gets done). If the strategy centers on new product introduction, critical operational processes—product design, product testing, product manufacturing, marketing and promotion, sales, and order fulfillment (how orders are taken, filled, and delivered to customers)—must not only be put in place but aligned. Each process contributes to transforming a dream about a new product into an offering that is available to and satisfactory for customers.[43]

The role of infrastructure in strategy execution often receives primary attention in strategy textbooks. However, infrastructural change is not an end in itself; at a minimum, its implications for operational processes need to be carefully considered. Organizational structures, systems, and decision-making procedures often need to be adapted and modified to facilitate the development or refinement of specific operational processes. For example, as illustrated in Chapter 13, departmental structures (and their associated mindsets) often get in the way of developing and shaping the necessary operating processes. In many companies, the so-called functional "silos" that grow up around departmental boundaries prohibit departments such as research and development, marketing, and manufacturing from working together to create better designed products that customers are eager to buy. Needless to say, such organizations experience considerable difficulties in developing a scope and a posture that attract, win, and retain more customers than do their competitors.

Outperforming Competitors and Winning Customers

Opportunities cannot be realized unless competitors are outmaneuvered and outperformed and customers are attracted, won, and retained. These goals take leadership and good management. Customers are the ultimate arbiters of rivalry among competitors. No matter how well strategy is conceived and executed, unless customers want to do business with an organization rather than with its competitors, any success it achieves will be short-lived.

Strategy therefore must generate some measure of distinctive and sustainable advantage in the marketplace. Marketplace advantage is created when both intermediate customers (distribution channels and retailers) and end-customers (those who use the product or service) choose the organization's offerings rather than those of its competitors. Such advantage stems from differentiation.[44]

Unfortunately, marketplace advantage is difficult to sustain. Advantage in product functionality and features is generally easy for competitors to replicate. In automobiles and computers, few product advantages last beyond the next model. The decline in market share of the Honda Accord, for a number of years the number-one-selling model in the U.S. market, attests to the difficulties in sustaining advantage based on functionality and features. American and Japanese manufacturers were able to catch up to the Accord. "Unique" services often can be copied in a matter of months. Advantages in image, reputation, selling, and relationships are typically more enduring. However, the travails of IBM, Digital Equipment Corporation, General Motors, and Ford in the past decade clearly indicate that advantages in these domains can be overcome by aggressive and committed competitors.

Sustaining marketplace advantage thus requires the organization to incessantly enhance its advantage base; it must continue to give customers more reason to do business with it. However, the changes inherent in the dynamics of marketplace rivalry render it difficult to sustain marketplace advantage. Once an advantage (such as superior product functionality, broader distribution, closer relationships with customers or lower price) is attained by one firm, competitors immediately have a long-jump distance not only to be matched but to be surpassed. The competitive rivalry and the consequent need to renovate and reinvent strategy are never-ending.

When marketplace advantage is so difficult to sustain in the face of competitors' moves, can it be created and augmented by anything managers do to (re)configure the organization? The answer is an emphatic *yes!* The key lies in the development and refinement of capabilities and competencies that lead, directly or indirectly, to value or benefits that customers appreciate.[45] Thus, the challenge of strategic management is to develop and refine capabilities and competencies that contribute to products, services, and benefits that result in positive differentiation in the eyes of customers.[46]

Capabilities and competencies drive marketplace advantage in a number of ways. "Invisible" competencies, such as the ability to learn about the marketplace, often give an organization the capacity to detect opportunities before they are manifest to competitors. For example, Dell Computer's intelligence capability enables it to learn very quickly and accurately from customers what they value (and do not value) about new offerings, what they would like Dell to offer, and what they value in competitors' offerings. This capability allows Dell to rapidly and continually refine its product "solutions" to meet specific customers' needs. Technology-based capabilities and competencies, such as the ability to design and develop products or flexible manufacturing systems that allow the rapid production of small lots, promote continuous product development and enhancement. At 3M Company, for example, competencies in substrates, coatings, and adhesives underlie many of its products.[47] The important point here is that capabilities and competencies provide a platform for the development and enhancement of multiple products as well as for how the organization can differentiate these products.

Within the organization, analytics, mindset, infrastructure, and leadership need to be directed toward enhancing capabilities and competencies that increase marketplace advantage. Analytics must be directed toward key questions about existing and desired competencies and how they contribute to marketplace advantage. Mindset suggests that organizations need to think in terms of developing competencies and not in terms of short-run product differentiation. Competency development almost always requires that structural barriers, such as the decision-making and information-retaining prerogatives of individual business units or departments, must be demolished. Leadership necessitates a choice of the competencies that are to be developed and a commitment of the resources to do so.[48]

Renovating Strategy

Winning customers and outperforming competitors can be achieved in two distinct and quite unrelated ways: (1) strategic renovation or renewal and (2) strategic invention or reinvention.

Strategic renovation takes the existing strategy as its point of departure. The search is for opportunities that can be pursued using the organization's current strategy. Product lines are extended, improved, and adapted, and new customers are actively pursued. Posture along many dimensions is enhanced: Product quality and service are upgraded, image and reputation are augmented, distribution is extended, and considerable effort is expended in embellishing selling and relationships. Goal change tends to be incremental and continuous: Gaining more market share, providing greater value at distinct price points, improving margins and profits, and gaining technological advantage over competitors.

The motivation for strategic renovation is clear and specific: If an organization does not continually renew and reinvigorate its strategy—its scope, posture, and goals—it becomes a sitting target for current and potential competitors. Successful computer manufacturers as varied as IBM, Digital, Compaq, and CompuAdd, and automobile firms as diverse as Mercedes-Benz, Honda, and Saab have all learned the hard way that product lines that are not renewed become easy prey for rivals. In short, organizations have little choice but to renovate their marketplace strategy if they want to stay even marginally ahead of their competition.

Strategic renovation is reflected in the dynamics of rivalry in almost all sectors of all industries. Rivals continually extend their product lines; the proliferation of product varieties is most evident in electronics goods such as personal computers, computer accessories, television sets, radios, and stereos. Japanese firms are infamous for continually changing the form, features, and styling of their basic products. Their automobiles undergo hundreds of body modifications from one model year to the next. The features and functionality of many consumer products, such as breakfast cereals, canned food, soft drinks, and frozen meats, often remain significantly unchanged from one year to another, but rivals seek to renew their scope and posture by recrafting their image and reputation through advertising campaigns, augmented relationships within the trade, and experimentation with premiums, minor price changes via discounts and coupons, and other means.

Strategy renewal is mirrored in the need to revitalize the organization: Unless analytics, mindset, operating processes, infrastructure, and leadership are reinvigorated, strategy renewal is less likely to occur or to be sustained.

Strategy renewal is often sparked by change in analytics and mindset. For example, analysis that leads to change in assumptions and beliefs can lead directly to change in product development and customer focus. One industrial products firm concluded from a study of its customers' buying behaviors that service, and not price or loyalty to a long-established vendor, was the primary reason for switching from one competitor to another. It then beefed up its levels of service and matched them to customers' needs. In the process, the firm reconstituted the "product" customers had been purchasing; from a physical product, it became a "solution" for a specific set of needs. The result was a rapid increase in market share and in customer satisfaction and retention.

Infrastructure tends to solidify over time, a process that inhibits strategy renewal. The solution is frequent reviews and critiques. For example, information and control systems designed for one product-customer segment may be inappropriate if an organization renews its strategy (for example, through extending its product line) to win customers in another segment. A leading electronics firm found that its control system, which was designed to have all phone queries answered within five hours, was counterproductive as the firm moved toward higher-end customers. The new customers wanted extensive personal service rather than a quick telephone response.

The linkage between infrastructure and operating processes is evident in this telephone answering example. Strategy renewal often requires extensive change in many operating processes. Indeed, in many cases, as illustrated in Chapters 8, 9, and 13 (and in the discussion above of the linkage between marketplace advantage and organization competency), the revitalization of operating processes (the building blocks of an organization's capabilities and competencies) makes possible extensive strategy renewal.

Reinventing Strategy

Strategic renovation can lead to regaining lost or declining marketplace advantage and rehabilitating or even extending existing competencies and capabilities. Unfortunately, strategic renovation often is not sufficient if the organization wishes to catapult itself "out of the pack" or into the position of a "break-through" leader. Initiatives to create or redefine an industry or market segment require real strategy entrepreneurship. This entails the management of fundamental—and often radical—shifts in scope, posture, and goals.[49] The combination of all three elements of strategy characterizes strategy entrepreneurship. In short, the organization must invent a strategy—new products or solutions that serve distinct customer needs, offer a unique way of competing, and lead to distinctive goals.

Unlike strategy renewal, strategic reinvention necessarily entails radical redirection of scope and posture. The choice is either the creation of products new to the marketplace or the reinvention of existing products and services to set new standards or norms in the marketplace. Such strategy entrepreneurship is likely to be based on the reconceptualization of customer needs. Almost by definition, such strategies lead to the creation of new industries or new industry segments. Apple's creation of the user-friendly computer, Nike's popularization of the running shoe, and Nucor's new specialty steel products are all examples of strategy entrepreneurship.

Indeed, any industry, over time, may witness a series of entrepreneurial strategies. The computer industry has seen IBM's development of the mainframe, Digital Equipment's launch of the minicomputer, Cray's design of the supercomputer, Apple's introduction of the personal computer, and Compaq's pioneering of laptop computers.

Posture reinvention almost always is closely associated with scope reinvention. It entails the creation of new ways of attracting, winning, and retaining customers. Significant deviations from conventional practice in key posture dimensions such as functionality, service, image, reputation, selling, and relationships create new grounds for fostering and sustaining competitive advantage. For example, Apple promulgated "user-friendly" as the means to win customers; it represented a radical departure from how computer firms had previously approached the challenge of making computers attractive to users. Dell's use of direct marketing invented a new way of reaching both commercial and consumer users of personal computers.

Associated with scope and posture reinvention are major shifts in goals. The creation or invention of a new market sector or even a new industry is often the distinguishing feature of organizations' strategic intent and marketplace vision. For example, Apple was driven in its early years by the goal of putting a computer in every home. The Saturn division of General Motors has been driven by the aim of creating an automobile that will be superior in quality to its predominantly Japanese rivals—in short, reinventing the low end of the automobile market.

It is not a coincidence that many of the strategic invention examples noted above cite firms that started from scratch. In going concerns, strategic reinvention necessitates dismembering and reconstructing the organization's historic analytics, mindset, operating processes, and infrastructure. The historic molds of thinking and doing must be broken if reinvention is to occur. Nothing less than *reinventing how the organization does business* is required. Chapter 16 details the magnitude of this challenge and how some organizations have successfully tackled it.

Organizational leadership incurs its most severe challenges in effecting and sustaining strategic entrepreneurship. The weight of the old ways of doing things squashes fragile potential product and operating breakthroughs. The current obsession with business process reengineering[50] reflects a desire to transform how the organization works as a means not just to attain operating efficiencies (such as, lower costs and shorter cycles) but also to facilitate radical product development and posture shifts.[51] For example, radical redesign of how a number of functional departments interrelate in making decisions can lead to dramatic breakthroughs in the design and development of new products as well as in posture dimensions such as product functionality (such as, higher reliability), faster and more effective service levels (such as, providing new types of technical assistance to customers), and closer working relationships with customers (such as, joint development of products or joint debugging of prototype products).

A central challenge in strategic reinvention is the management of analytics and mindset. Strategic entrepreneurship is a product of thinking differently; old ways of thinking cannot suffice. The past offers little guidance to the future. Old paradigms or recipes for industry success or competitive differentiation inhibit the detection, visualization, and development of emerging and potential marketplace opportunities.[52] It is not an overstatement to assert that organizational reinvention presumes that individuals can unlearn their own past as well as that of others.

Leaders committed to strategic reinvention must translate what is to be invented into a vision (including a set of aspirations and motivating targets) and values (a set of principles that guide individuals' behaviors) that are meaningful, tangible, and invigorating for the organization's members. As discussed in Chapter 16, Motorola is an example of a company whose leaders have established visions entailing new product directions (betting the firm on new products long before the opportunity is apparent to others) that inspired the organization to achieve results that few could have expected.

CONCLUSION

Strategic management involves the management of marketplace strategy, the organization, and the linkages between them. It represents the central challenge of management. Given the extensiveness and intensity of change, it is a never-ending challenge. Moreover, there are no simple recipes or algorithms; the fun and the excitement of strategic management lie in the creation of new ways to win in the marketplace and new ways to configure the organization to facilitate doing so.

NOTES

1. Because most people are familiar with the automobile and computer industries, we shall use many examples from these two industries in this chapter.

2. The linkages between political, regulatory, social, and economic change and industry change are addressed in detail in Chapter 7.

3. A number of the principal bridges between strategy and organization are noted and discussed in the last section of this chapter.

4. This argument has been persistently and effectively articulated by Peter Drucker. See, in particular, *Innovation and Entrepreneurship, Practice and Principles* (New York: Harper & Row, 1985).

5. Most organizations can exercise some degree of influence over some sector of their environment, but rarely can an organization impose its will on all institutional sectors of its environment—customers, suppliers, competitors, community groups, and governmental agencies. Demographic, social, and technological changes also lie outside the control of all organizations.

6. Unfortunately, it is commonplace to find the word *strategy* used differently by managers in different subunits or hierarchical levels within the same organization. The absence of a generally accepted meaning of strategy is reflected in and compounded by its association with all spheres of business activity. Thus, one hears frequent reference to human resource strategy, marketing strategy, financial strategy, product strategy, and information strategy.

7. Entrepreneurial content articulates the need for an organization's strategy to be different from that of its competitors; otherwise, it does not possess any degree of differentiation.

8. These and other related questions are explicitly analyzed in Chapters 2 through 4.

9. Chapter 4 deals in detail with the myriad issues involved in global strategy.

10. The issues, questions, and challenges involved in determining stakeholder scope are extensively detailed in Chapter 5.

11. The most extensive development of mass customization can be found in B. Joseph Pine II, *Mass Customization, The New Frontier in Business Competition* (Boston: Harvard Business School Press, 1993).

12. The argument here is that strategy is about both means and ends. Means are meaningless without some understanding of goals, and vice versa. Some authors equate strategy with means and thus keep goals distinct from any consideration of strategy.

13. Strategic intent is a term coined by C. K. Prahalad and Gary Hamel, "Strategic Intent," *Harvard Business Review* (May–June 1989), pp. 63–76. It is discussed in more detail in Chapter 9.

14. Some of the reasons why firms' long-run intent or vision often does not materialize are discussed in Chapters 15 and 16.

15. How an organization's culture affects the choice and pursuit of goals is discussed in Chapter 15. Chapter 16 addresses many of the issues involved in radically shifting an organization's goals.

16. See, for example, *Business Week*, October 12, 1993, pp. 156–158.

17. This discussion reflects the emergent nature of strategy. See Chapter 15 for elaboration of the distinction between emergent and intended strategy.

18. Chapters 12–16 examine how these and other facets of an organization may help or hinder strategy development and execution.

19. Chapters 8 and 9 address this argument in detail.

20. The battle between Komatsu and Caterpillar is delineated in detail in Caterpillar Tractor Co. #9-385-276 and Komatsu Limited #9-385-277, Harvard Business School Cases.

21. Operating processes are the focus of Chapter 13. How knowledge undergirds and creates many key operating processes is the central theme in Chapter 8.

22. A number of authors have recently stressed the importance of identifying and enhancing core operating processes. See, for example, Thomas J. Housel, Chris J. Morris, and Christopher Westland, "Business Process Reengineering at Pacific Bell," *Planning Review* (May–June, 1993), 28–34; Robert B. Kaplan and Laura Murdock, "Core Process Redesign," *The McKinsey Quarterly* (1991), 2: 27–43.

23. This assertion is illustrated in many examples in Chapters 8 and 13.

24. This is the central theme of Chapter 13.

25. This observation is well developed in Chapters 8 and 9.

26. Many issues relevant to structure are discussed in Chapters 12 and 14.

27. Many of the key questions involved in building and fostering linkages among a corporation's business units and among a business unit's product areas have been identified in the GE example earlier in this chapter; they are pursued in greater depth in Chapter 14.

28. Strategic alliances at the corporate level are discussed in Chapter 2. The use of alliances and other relationships with vendors, technology sources, competitors, and distribution channels as sources of knowledge-based competency development is a major focus of Chapters 8 and 9.

29. The role of each of these systems in shaping and executing strategy is covered in detail in Chapters 12 and 14.

30. How planning and other administrative systems affect decision processes is discussed in Chapter 14. Many of the facets of an organization's culture that impact decision-making procedures are discussed in detail in Chapter 15.

31. Organizational decision-making processes affect every phase of decision making: The generation and evaluation of alternatives, and the choice and execution of the preferred course of action. See Chapter 10 for a discussion of how a number of organizational processes affect the identification and development of strategy alternatives. Chapter 16 lays out some of the processes that organizations have found useful in facilitating a radical shift in or a reinvention of strategy.

32. Chapters 10 and 11 address the role of both analytical and organizational processes in identifying and assessing strategic alternatives or opportunities. Neither one alone provides a complete explanation of how and why decisions are made.

33. The discussion of the difficulties in changing "paradigms" (Chapter 15) and effecting the reinvention of strategy (Chapter 16) illustrates why both change within organizations and change in strategy almost always occur *after* the need to change is reflected in such performance criteria as market share, new products developed, margins, and profits.

34. "Can Jack Smith Fix GM?" *Business Week*, November 1, 1993, pp. 126–134.

35. This argument has been extensively documented by Eileen C. Shapiro, *How Organizational Assumptions Become Competitive Traps* (New York: John Wiley & Sons, Inc., 1991).

36. The role and importance of outsourcing as a means of developing capabilities and competencies are discussed in some detail in Chapter 8.

37.   We return to the notions of renovating and reinventing strategy at the end of this chapter. See also Chapter 16.

38.   Chapter 10 distinguishes among obvious, creative, and unthinkable alternatives and discusses the processes involved in identifying and generating each type.

39.   For a forceful and compelling articulation of this argument, see Chapter 9.

40.   This challenge is the focus of Chapter 11.

41.   For further elaboration of this point, see George S. Day and Liam Fahey, "Putting Strategy into Shareholder Value Analysis," *Harvard Business Review* (March–April 1990), 156–162.

42.   This linkage—aligning the organization with marketplace strategy—is the principal focus of Chapter 12.

43.   The alignment of operating processes in executing strategy is the dominant focus of Chapter 13. It is also considered in Chapter 12.

44.   For a considerably more detailed discussion of competitive advantage, see Chapter 3.

45.   The linkage between capabilities and competencies on the one hand and competitive advantage or differentiation on the other is most directly addressed in Chapters 8, 9, and 13.

46.   The point to be emphasized here is that differentiation must be sufficient not just to attract customers but to win and retain them as customers.

47.   The 3M example is discussed in detail in Chapter 8.

48.   Many of the analytics, mindset, infrastructure, and leadership issues and challenges in developing and reinvigorating competencies are discussed in Chapters 8 and 9. See also C. K. Prahalad and Gary Hamel, "The Core Competence of the Corporation," *Harvard Business Review* (May–June 1990), 79–91.

49.   Strategic reinvention is the focus of Chapter 16. A reinvented strategy may also result from the analysis recommended in Chapter 9.

50.   Much of the discussion in Chapter 13 embodies the spirit of process reengineering. For further treatment of the topic, see Thomas H. Davenport, *Process Innovation: Reengineering Work through Information Technology* (Boston: Harvard Business School Press, 1993).

51.   We emphasize here the *desire* to reinvent strategy as well as to transform the organization. Process reengineering in some organizations has led to efficiency improvements but not to strategy reinvention.

52.   The discussion of an organization's "paradigm" or "context" in Chapters 15 and 16 illustrates how the historic mode of thinking or seeing the world within any organization can effectively destroy its ability to anticipate and respond to change in the marketplace.

PART TWO

STRATEGY: WINNING IN THE MARKETPLACE

CORPORATE STRATEGY: MANAGING A SET OF BUSINESSES

2

H. Kurt Christensen

J. L. Kellogg Graduate School of Management,
Northwestern University

- American Express has sold its retail brokerage business to Primerica, in order to focus more attention on its core travel-related services business. Primerica has merged this new acquisition with its Smith-Barney brokerage unit to create the second largest retail brokerage network in the United States.

- Lotus Development Corporation did not develop its Lotus Notes networking product in-house, but rather had it developed by Iris Associates, a very small software boutique. Iris is considered a programmer's utopia, with an "engineering is king" culture and little managerial "hassle."

- Snapple Beverage Corporation's flavored teas and seltzers have been warmly received by affluent, health-conscious consumers in New York, Boston, and Washington. Snapple is now taking its product line nationwide. In so doing, it faces the challenges of building a national distribution network and competing more directly with beverage giants like Coca-Cola and Pepsi.

- Michael Ovitz, chairman of Creative Artists Agency, has long had a reputation as Hollywood's most powerful agent. His agency is leveraging its network of star relationships into several other businesses that utilize star power for commercial ends. For example, it has entered into a joint venture with Nike to produce sporting events for television, it has received the creative portion of Coca-Cola's advertising account, and it has provided investment banking advice to Crédit Lyonnais, Matsushita, and Sony regarding their movie units.

Each of these firms has made a change in corporate strategy. For the most part, such moves are not opportunistic; they are elements of explicitly formulated strategies.

Two factors are motivating corporations to increase the managerial attention given to strategy formulation: (1) rapid environmental change and (2) increasing organizational complexity. In a rapidly changing environment, it is important to take a disciplined look at one's products, markets, customers, and competitors, and to formulate a strategy for marketplace success. A carefully formulated strategy tells how the firm will utilize its resources and capabilities to build and maintain the competitive advantages that will favorably influence its customers' purchase decisions. By focusing on what is critically important, a strategy acts as a compass; it helps management to know when to "stay the course" and when to alter its strategy in the face of changes in its environment.

To manage organizational complexity, strategies need to be stated in the form of strategic plans and circulated within the organization in order to:

- Facilitate communication up and down the organization.
- Focus attention on the intended strategy.
- Enable persons in one part of the organization to see how their work relates to that of others.
- Facilitate monitoring and taking any necessary corrective action.

In large, complex corporations, strategy formulation occurs at the business and corporate levels.[1] To facilitate meaningful strategic planning, corporations with sufficient product-market diversity are subdivided into business units. Business-level planning involves determining the boundaries of the business and deciding how the business should compete in its chosen product-market. At the corporate level, there are similar concerns:

- *The boundaries of the corporation are addressed in the scope decision:* In what businesses should the corporation participate?
- *Scope decisions are guided by the corporation's decisions about relatedness:* On what basis should the businesses in the corporation be related to each other? This is important because, through its relatedness decisions, the corporation determines whether and to what extent *the corporate level* will seek to add value to the businesses within its boundaries. What can the XYZ business do because it is part of ABC Corporation that it could not do if it were outside the corporation?
- *The scope and relatedness decisions jointly determine how diversified a corporation is:* In what array of product-markets does it participate, and how loosely or tightly related to each other are the businesses in the corporation?

Chapter Goals

The focus of this chapter is corporate strategy.[2] The domain and key components of corporate strategy are outlined to provide a context for consideration of the logic of corporate diversification: Why does it have the potential to create economic value? Why does it often not fulfill that potential? Next, each of the dimensions of a corporation's scope is explored: What product markets are served? What geographic areas are served? Is the company vertically integrated? How? Relatedness and the different ways that it can be created are then considered, and the chapter concludes with a discussion of methods that can be used to change a corporation's scope.

THE DOMAIN OF CORPORATE STRATEGY

Corporate strategy concerns itself with three important issues that corporate executives must address:

1. *The corporation's scope:* In what mix of businesses should it participate?
2. *The relatedness of its parts:* On what basis should the business units in the corporation be related to each other?
3. *The methods for managing scope and relatedness:* What particular methods—acquisition, strategic alliances, divestment, or others—should be employed in making specific changes in the corporation's scope and relatedness?

In determining the corporation's scope, central management must consider three dimensions:

1. *Product-market scope:* In what product-markets should the corporation participate?
2. *Geographic scope:* In what countries should the corporation operate?
3. *Vertical scope:* In what stages of the vertical chain (from raw material to consumption) should the company participate?

Each of these dimensions needs to be analyzed separately because, as we shall see later, the underlying rationale for each is different.

In determining relatedness, central management must decide whether it seeks relatedness based on a single, externally perceived, competitive advantage across its businesses. This type of relatedness has provided significant benefit to some companies; for example, Hewlett-Packard has gained a reputation for technically *au courant* products with value-adding features. However, such a strategy is viable only as long as the market rewards the particular competitive advantage that serves as the basis for relatedness. A more common kind of relatedness is based on shared resources and/or on the ability to transfer one or more specific capabilities from one unit to another. A shared resource can relate to everything from a brand name to a machine or a distribution system, and a transferred capability can be in general management or within one of the functional areas, such as marketing.

Scope Expansion

Corporations expanding their scope may decide to use internal development, acquisition, or strategic alliances. Depending on a corporation's current resources and capabilities and how they fit with what is needed to succeed in a particular market, one method may be preferable to the others. Each method poses a significant, but different, organizational challenge:

- *In internal development:* organizing "from nothing."
- *In an acquisition or merger:* successful integration after the deal closes.
- *In a strategic alliance:* managing in a partnership (rather than a hierarchical) mode.

Scope Contraction

Corporations that are reducing their scope may consider five different methods of divesting: sale as a going business, leveraged buyout (LBO), spin-off, harvest, or liquidation. The selection of method is more straightforward because maximizing the return from divestment is the major consideration.

Scope changes are the subject of headlines in the business press each day. The scope changes of major corporations are important news items, as are comments by external parties about a company's current or intended scope. For example, AT&T's recent agreement to purchase McCaw Cellular Communications received much media attention because of AT&T's ability to help McCaw expand its cellular network nationwide. Scope decisions (and their attendant explicit or implicit decisions about relatedness) tend to be the most expensive, most visible, and potentially farthest-reaching decisions central management can make. They represent one major way—and perhaps *the* major way—in which central management can create economic value.

Relatedness and Scope

In combination with the relatedness decision, scope decisions can profoundly affect the economics of the businesses in the corporation. For example, a firm that acquires or internally develops only businesses that leverage its marketing channel will enjoy significant economies of scale. With more products available for amortization of fixed costs, the firm will have a more efficient channel than will competitors who have narrower product lines. And, other things equal, each business in the firm will have lower marketing and distribution costs than it would have as a stand-alone company. Most of Procter & Gamble's and Lever Brothers' businesses are related in this way.

This efficiency generates discretionary funds that can be allocated to some combination of product development, enhanced promotion, lower prices, or higher returns for shareholders. Thus, related diversification, based on product development, manufacturing, or marketing can profoundly affect the economics of the corporation's businesses.

On the other hand, a firm that follows a conglomerate strategy does not strive for such operating synergies across businesses. Rather, it seeks to create only financial and managerial synergies across its businesses. If central management is lean and manages wisely, the businesses in a conglomerate can have the flexibility of a stand-alone business while enjoying some financial resources and general management support often not available to their stand-alone competitors. With the exception of previously undermanaged units, however, the value added at the corporate level by a conglomerate is more modest than is possible with related diversification.

Scope decisions are also important because of their impact on central management's responsibilities. They define the domain of central management's accountability. For example, when a merger or acquisition poses cultural risks in integration, it is central management's role to manage these risks acceptably. Where potential synergies exist, central management is ultimately accountable for seeing that they are created. The odds of successfully creating value at the corporate level depend to a large degree on the quality of the strategic thinking that leads to the decision to make particular scope changes.

Corporate management's collective track record in making scope changes has been far from stellar. Even though diversification has been occurring on a large scale since the 1950s, far too little has been learned from the many mistakes that have been made. Researchers have studied corporate diversification extensively, and most have concluded that diversification has produced far less value than its proponents have predicted. (There are a few big success stories, such as Berkshire Hathaway.) Most firms that diversify do not create economic value; rather, they often destroy it. Typically, value is destroyed because most of the reasons given to justify diversifying moves are flawed.

THE LOGIC OF CORPORATE DIVERSIFICATION

Despite the wide variety of diversifying actions corporations have taken in recent years, most of the reasons stated by their executives and reported in the business press can be clustered into the following list of five. The logic for the first four reasons is flawed. For each, both the rationale and the flaw are considered.

Reason 1: To take advantage of what the buyer perceives to be an exceptional market opportunity. Typically, this opportunity is characterized in terms of an extremely high market-growth rate. As the argument goes, rapidly growing markets provide an exceptional opportunity because new entrants are less likely to evoke retaliation by existing competitors. Consequently, a determined player has a greater chance of becoming the dominant—and most profitable—player.[3]

The flaw. A successful acquisition can be expected only when there will be a fit between the market opportunity and the firm's resources and capabilities. Unfortunately, when pursuing an acquisition, most corporations focus only on the market opportunity part of the equation. The opportunity may be great for some firms, but the opportunity is often not accessible *to the buying firm.* Given its configuration of resources and capabilities, it is frequently not well-positioned to take advantage of that opportunity. To avoid this mistake, it is critically important to ask: "What does our company bring to the venture? Can we do anything in that marketplace that others can't do as well or can't do better?" Both IBM and Kodak entered the copier industry. IBM eventually withdrew, but Kodak has remained a player. Kodak could leverage its in-depth knowledge of imaging technology, a critical area in which IBM was at a relative disadvantage.

Reason 2: To remedy low growth potential in current product-markets. Firms in mature markets often can't achieve their growth goals without diversifying into one or more new businesses.

The flaw. An early diagnosis of the limits of opportunity in an existing business may be a shrewd management judgment,[4] but recognizing the absence of opportunity in an existing business does not confer the capability to succeed in a new one. In fact, the mindset necessary to run a mature business successfully is profoundly different from the mindset necessary for success in a rapidly growing business. R. J. Reynolds diversified because of diminished opportunity. Especially keeping in mind the corporation's problematic acquisitions in the 1970s, shareholders would have been better off if the money spent on diversification had been distributed to them instead.

Reason 3: To create a more stable earnings stream. Companies with more stable earnings over time have slightly lower costs of capital, and, other things being equal, they generate a slightly higher risk-adjusted rate of return. Despite the theoretical correctness of the argument, such efforts typically fail.

The flaw. Diversification undertaken for this reason has very modest upside potential, and the downside risk can be considerable. Businesses whose earnings streams are inversely correlated—one is cascading at the precise time the other is trickling—tend to be fundamentally different and require very different capabilities and management practices. The likelihood of serious management mistakes is therefore quite high. The costs of acquiring such a business can also be high, relative to the increased shareholder value possible from reduced earnings variability. For these reasons, institutional investors (and some individual investors) strongly prefer to manage the earnings variability *of their own portfolio* by changing their mix of holdings, not by having management seek to do this by diversifying.[5] EMI diversified out of the music business and into the electronics and medical equipment businesses in part to smooth its very volatile earnings stream from the music business. It experienced some success in these industries, but it eventually returned to its roots as an entertainment company and gave up its attempt to be strong in technology-based product businesses.

Reason 4: To save the individual investors among shareholders a "double taxation" of their dividends by reinvesting excess cash in new businesses. Given the reality of "double taxation," it is possible for a corporation to diversify and give its individual shareholders an advantage. However, that outcome is not very likely.

The flaw. In most instances, the costs of entry and of learning how to run the new business significantly exceed the tax benefit. Institutional investors are even worse off because they aren't subject to any significant amount of double taxation.

As noted earlier, none of the above four frequently stated reasons should be the impetus for diversification.[6] The fifth reason is the only valid reason.

Reason 5: To exploit synergies across businesses or between a business and its corporate parent. Synergies are the additive benefits sought by having two units within the same corporation.[7] Synergies may increase revenues or reduce costs (or both), by sharing resources or transferring capabilities from one unit to another. Diversification that fosters genuine synergies can create economic value.

Nevertheless, synergistic benefits from diversification are invoked far more frequently than synergy is actually achieved.[8] Sometimes, the alleged synergies do not exist because the underlying rationale is flawed. One common error is to overestimate revenue-generating synergies by a substantial margin. For example, during the 1980s, a number of financial services firms expanded their "product" offerings, expecting that "one-stop shopping" would be a competitive advantage because it would dramatically increase the flow of customers. Overall, these hopes were not realized. Led by CEO James Robinson, American Express, for example, learned this lesson the expensive way.

Another common error is to overestimate the extent to which relationships can be leveraged. Advertising firms that have diversified into management consulting have found that cross-selling is much more difficult than anticipated because a relationship in one department of a client company is generally not leverageable into another department or into the executive suite.

More often, however, synergies are present but are overestimated. Three factors have led to systematic overestimation of synergies:

1. Confusing synergy with net positive synergy.
2. Overestimating the extent of management synergy.

3. Underestimating the administrative challenges in achieving potential synergies.

The tendency to confuse *synergy* with *net positive synergy* has been widespread. Many situations capable of generating some positive synergy cannot generate enough to overcome the negative synergies that are incurred at the same time. In an acquisition, these can include:

- The control premium (the amount by which the price the buyer pays exceeds the market value of the firm prior to the offer).
- Traceable cash flows associated with the deal (fees to investment bankers, lawyers, and accountants).
- The allocation of corporate expenses to the acquired unit.
- Negative synergies with other parts of the business.
- The cost of mistakes made in learning how to oversee or manage the new business.

Typically, in spite of the existence of some positive synergies, not enough are generated for the net synergy to be positive.

Many advocates of diversification have seriously overestimated the extent of management synergy. The argument that management is generic and transportable across all markets and industries, and that it can be applied without acquiring industry knowledge and without paying considerable attention to the substance of the business, has been discredited. Nevertheless, there *are* management skills and practices that can be applied in a wide variety of businesses and settings. Few, if any, are applicable in all settings, however, and attention to the industry context and to the substance of the business is necessary in virtually all cases. Consequently, although managerial synergy exists in some situations, it is less pervasive and has a more modest impact on performance than many persons had believed. Further, managerial synergy can be difficult to institutionalize. Its effectiveness is often more dependent on the style and capabilities of the CEO than many had thought. For example, ITT's management system, developed during Harold Geneen's tenure, was believed to provide an effective and enduring way to manage highly diversified firms. However, it did not transfer effectively to his successors.

Many deal makers have seriously underestimated the administrative challenges in achieving potential synergies across businesses or between an acquired business and its new corporate parent. Achieving synergies across businesses can be deterred by strategy, operating policy, and cultural differences. A new corporate parent often finds it difficult to exercise the right mix of flexibility and firmness in creating synergies with a newly acquired unit.

Net positive synergies can provide a valid motivation to diversify, but considerable care must be exercised to determine the extent of the positive synergies, the negative synergies that can't be avoided, and the net effect. Only when the *net* synergy is positive can diversification create economic value.

DIMENSIONS OF CORPORATE SCOPE

Central management most profoundly impacts the corporation through the scope changes it formulates and implements. How it relates the corporation's businesses to each other, how it manages entry into new businesses and divests an existing business, and how it facilitates or hinders the development of cross-business synergies will directly affect corporate performance.[9] Because of the importance of each major kind of scope decision, these corporate decisions need to be considered in detail. They involve the product-markets chosen (product-market scope), the geographic area served (geographic scope), and the stages in each business's vertical chain in which they will participate (vertical scope).

Product-Market Scope

Whether it thinks about it consciously or not, every corporate management chooses to participate in a particular product market or set of product markets. In some instances, a sound logic frames the choices; in others, they appear more haphazard and opportunistic. Companies seeking to make the best choices about which markets to participate in must address two issues:

1. Whether to diversify around only one or more than one resource or capability?
2. What specific resource and capability choices should serve as the basis for diversification?[10]

When firms diversify on the basis of a single resource or capability associated with their core business, their diversification is quite focused or constrained.[11] A number of pharmaceutical firms have diversified around a tightly focused research capability. Firms that diversify on the basis of different commonalities or links between different pairs of units are less focused (for example, General Electric). Least focused of all are conglomerates, which diversify with little or no regard to product-market commonalities (an example is Loews). In conglomerate diversification, only financial and/or managerial synergies are sought. Both the highest potential for value creation and the greatest organizational challenges reside with related diversification.[12, 13]

Firms can potentially diversify on the basis of common product technology, manufacturing technology, marketing channels, customer needs, related needs of a particular customer group, or some combination of these. For example, 3M has built its strategy around its capability in adhesive chemistry. Leveraging that capability has taken the company into a wide array of businesses, including Post-It™ notes, sandpaper, copying machines (toner must adhere to paper in making a copy), floppy and optical storage disks (coating adheres to disks), coated papers, Scotch™ adhesive tape, and video, correction, and box-sealing tapes.[14] In contrast, Procter & Gamble (P&G) has built its strategy around marketing capability through the grocery and over-the-counter drug channels. Leveraging that capability, P&G participates in a wide array of businesses including laundry detergent, disposable diapers, bathroom tissue, cake mixes, toothpaste, cosmetics, cough medicines, and other in-home remedies. P&G's businesses have different product and manufacturing technologies, but share the same marketing channels; 3M's businesses have the same product technology but reach different customers through several marketing channels.

A successful choice of product-market scope will reflect a company's existing capabilities, its ability to maintain and enhance them over time, the value-creating potential that its capabilities have in its chosen markets, and its consistency and effectiveness in implementation.

Geographic Scope

The second dimension of the corporation's scope is its geographic scope—the geographic boundaries of the markets the corporation serves. Businesses can serve regional, national, or international markets.[15] In many product (and service) businesses, the economics of national or international scope are so compelling that local or regional competitors are few or nonexistent. However, local or regional markets can be viable when:

- Products are perishable (such as, hand-dipped chocolates).
- Transportation costs are a substantial portion of total product costs. This situation usually occurs when the product is inexpensive and bulky (such as, unfilled metal cans) or heavy (such as, gravel).
- Customer needs and wants differ significantly across regions or locales (two examples: Floridians don't need heavy winter coats and barbecue sauce taste preferences vary considerably across regions of the United States).
- There are few (or no) economies of scale (two examples: a fine-cuisine restaurant and a hair-styling salon).

For many businesses, serving a market that crosses national borders is viable; for a growing number, it is becoming essential for survival. When they choose to serve foreign markets, business leaders make several important decisions.

Selection of Served Countries

A key decision is what particular countries to serve (and in what order an expansion will serve them). In making this decision, they must consider the attractiveness of each national market. A critical aspect is the level of country-specific risks—expropriation, onerous legislation, or political or economic instability. Regional considerations may also have an important influence on this decision. (Does the company already operate, or plan to establish operations, in nearby countries? Will the newly targeted country be part of a regional or global manufacturing network?)

Strategy Variation

Central management needs to decide how much strategy variation to have across countries or regions. Firms follow a global strategy when they employ essentially the same strategy in each country where they operate; the amount of local adaptation is kept to a minimum. At the other end of the spectrum, firms follow a multidomestic strategy when their subsidiaries in each country formulate and implement their own strategies. Most firms avoid both extremes by seeking to capture as many economies of global strategies as they can without being insensitive to differences in customer needs and preferences across countries. Global competition in many industries has become sufficiently intense that most companies seek as global a strategy as customer needs permit.[16] Coca-Cola has been able to follow a global strategy because the association it seeks to create in consumers' minds, "a good time," has universal appeal. Philips N.V., The Netherlands-based multinational, had for many years successfully operated with a multidomestic strategy but has moved in recent years toward regional and global strategies in some of its businesses. A multidomestic strategy became an unaffordable luxury in industries that are globalizing and becoming increasingly competitive.

Functional Activities

Executives need to consider what functional activities to carry out in foreign markets. Companies can:

- Export on an order-by-order basis (lowest commitment).
- Warehouse and market in the host country.
- Manufacture, warehouse, and market there.
- Do each of these *and* perform research and development there (highest commitment).

The order of activities indicates increasing commitment to the host country. Some companies move through the sequence one step at a time.[17]

Ownership Form

Central management needs to consider what ownership form to employ. This means assessing the relative benefits of a wholly owned subsidiary, an equity joint venture (typically with a local partner), a licensed subsidiary, a local agent or a franchise. A wholly owned subsidiary is easier to manage, but many firms opt for a local partner (even where not legally required) because of the partner's market knowledge and ability to relate to the host country government. In many industries, the perception of "foreignness" in a wholly-owned subsidiary can be a barrier to effective performance.

Licensing, franchising, and utilizing a local agent are relatively low-risk, low-return options. When considering licensing, management must assess the likelihood that a licensee will eventually become a direct competitor. When hiring a local agent, management must consider whether he or she has sufficient incentive to build the business to its potential in the region. When franchising, management must assure itself that the franchisee can manage the business (and make any needed local adaptations) in a manner consistent with the image of the company.

Reporting Relationship

Corporate management must determine the *reporting relationship*—how the foreign units will be managed. Will the head of the business in the host country have a primary reporting relationship to a regional business-unit head, to a worldwide business-unit head, or to a country manager? With a global strategy, the primary reporting relationship will almost always be to a worldwide business head. Regardless of the primary reporting relationship, there is a need to coordinate action across all other dimensions. Central management needs to determine the form that coordination will take.

These issues—selection of served countries, strategy variation, functional activities, ownership form, and reporting relationship—need thoughtful consideration early in the process of determining geographic scope. The decisions arrived at need to be internally logical and consistent with the corporation's product-market scope.

Vertical Scope

For this third dimension of scope, companies make decisions about the stages in the vertical chain (from raw material to consumed product) in which they will participate. Not every chain has the same number of stages, and some stages can have important subdivisions. A typical set of stages includes raw materials extraction, raw materials processing, component manufacture, product assembly (manufacture), distribution, and consumption. (See Figure 2–1.)

A decision to become more highly integrated has important implications.[18] First, it increases the "bet" (capital investment) that a company is placing on that vertical chain's end-use market. Second, when a company integrates backward (moves closer to the raw material source), it is frequently entering a more

FIGURE 2–1   A typical vertical chain.

Raw Materials Extraction	→	Raw Materials Processing	→	Component Manufacture	→	Product Assembly	→	Distribution	→	Consumption

An Example:

Iron ore mined	→	Steel ingots formed; rolled into sheets	→	Automobile fender formed	→	Automobile assembled	→	Automobile dealer sells car	→	Buyer uses car

capital-intensive business that needs to be managed differently from its core business. When a company integrates forward (moves closer to its customers), the nature of the marketing task becomes sufficiently different that companies very capable in their core business can experience difficulty. When Texas Instruments integrated forward into the watch business, it was successful for a while but eventually found itself at a disadvantage because it had an inadequate understanding of the "jewelry" aspects of the product. It eventually withdrew from the watch business.

Motivated in part by Japanese companies' success with low levels of vertical integration, some U.S. companies are rethinking whether all of their present vertical integration is necessary or desirable. Very few businesses have a technological imperative for integration. (An exception is a company that both makes steel ingots and rolls them into sheets. It saves the time and expense of cooling the ingots for shipment and later reheating them for rolling.) In most cases, integration is not needed to ensure a regular supply of materials or to reduce production costs, despite the rhetoric to the contrary. Carefully drawn long-term contracts can, in most instances, provide the control- or supply-assurance benefits of ownership without ownership's costs and administrative complexity.

Vertical integration may be appropriate to prevent market foreclosure (being shut out of a market). For example, if a company's competitors are purchasing supplier or customer organizations, vertical integration may be warranted to avoid the risk of heavy dependency on an organization that is both a supplier and a competitor. There are also circumstances where contracting gets too expensive, as when there are many possible scenarios in a highly uncertain future (making it too time-consuming to draw up the contract), or when a customer requires the development of expensive, specific assets (like a plant at a location that can economically serve only this customer). Where there is a need for systemic innovation and confidentiality concerns inhibit the necessary flow of information to and from a supplier, vertical integration may also be warranted.[19]

Executives considering vertical integration should be attentive to potential negative synergies. One factor contributing to General Motors' malaise in recent years has been its relatively heavy integration into component manufacturing, where its per-hour labor costs are almost twice those of independently owned component manufacturers. An integrated firm may not require enough output to take advantage of economies of scale. For this reason, most airlines that formerly had catering operations have sold them. In any given city, they were not able to generate the economies of scale available to an independent provider.

Combining the Scope Dimensions

We have discussed each of the three dimensions of scope separately because each has a different focus, set of issues, and set of considerations appropriate for resolving the issues. However, there are two important relationships among product-market, geographic, and vertical scope:

1. Product-market scope decisions concurrently place a company in an industry whose geographic boundaries are strongly influenced by that industry's economics. Where industry economics favor globalization, a decision to enter a particular industry (a product-market decision) largely determines the geographic scope decision. For example, one can't be a major player in the copier industry with a national, or even a regional geographic scope.

2. Substantial breadth in any dimension adds to the complexity of the corporation and, consequently, to the management challenge of operating it. Because of the difficulty of managing a very high level of complexity, corporations that have a very broad product-market scope tend not to have a high vertical integration, and highly integrated corporations (like Exxon or Texaco) tend not to have a very broad product-market scope.

Explicitly or implicitly, corporate executives make these decisions when they formulate their strategies. The experience of Nestlé, detailed in Box 2–1, illustrates how these decisions can transform a firm over a relatively short time period. Whether the executives make sound decisions or not depends in part on the logic undergirding their concept of their corporation. This logic may be explicitly stated, or it may be covered intuitively. For those who choose to formulate strategy explicitly, recent developments in the fields of strategic management and economics provide some insightful ways to think about scope issues.

DETERMINING SCOPE AND RELATEDNESS

Arguably, the major influence on a corporation's scope is its concept of relatedness: On what basis does it seek to have its business units related to each other? Implicit in any relatedness decision is one or more resources or capabilities that central management must build and maintain. As noted earlier, 3M's businesses are related by adhesive chemistry technology. Because this technology is critical to corporate success, 3M's executives need to be certain that this activity is state-of-the-art and capable of serving as its growth engine. Much executive time needs to be expended to see that the needed linkages and synergies across units are in fact developed. Where businesses in a corporation are related on the basis of one of several resources or capabilities (linked diversification) rather than on the basis of a single resource or capability, central management's task is made significantly more complex.

Before considering ways to determine relatedness, it is useful to note how challenging it can be to create value at the corporate level. Placing a formerly independent company into a multibusiness corporation (or creating a new business from the bottom up) unleashes some negative synergies. Even where considerable autonomy is granted to an acquired unit, central management still must make final decisions on major investments, ensure legal compliance, and

Box 2–1

Nestlé and the Coming Food Industry Shakeout*

A shakeout is under way in the food industry worldwide. Nestlé, the world's largest food company with $36 billion in sales, is the world leader in candy, instant coffee, frozen food, mineral water, and instant foods. Chairman Helmut Maucher is determined that Nestlé will retain its number-one position—and double its sales over the next decade—and has initiated several changes in product-market and geographic scope to help accomplish that goal.

To get to its current position, several acquisitions were key. Carnation (a U.S. dairy products company) was acquired in 1985; in 1988, Nestlé acquired Buitoni (Italian pasta maker) and Rowntree Mackintosh (British candy maker). In 1992, it acquired Perrier (mineral water). In addition to its acquisitions, Nestlé has entered joint ventures with General Mills in cereals in Europe, and with Coca-Cola Company in canned coffee and tea drinks. It also has a 25 percent indirect minority interest in French cosmetics maker L'Oréal and has publicly stated its desire eventually to become its majority owner.

In seeking to add value to its acquisitions, it has taken successful products in one country and begun marketing them elsewhere. Rowntree's After Eight dinner mints and Smarties candies are now sold in continental Europe, and Nestlé has plans under way for its Buitoni unit to develop pasta dishes for sale in other European countries. In the United States, it purchased a small New York pasta maker, Pasta and Cheese, Inc., and is marketing its refrigerated pasta products under the Contadina name.

Nestlé has also expanded aggressively into Asia. It has entered into two Chinese joint ventures, one in coffee and dairy products and the second in ice cream. In addition to making Western products for the Chinese market, it is making local products, including soy sauce and frozen *dim sum* (Chinese appetizers).

These scope changes have necessitated far-reaching organizational changes. Operating responsibilities have been shifted from a formerly centralized headquarters staff to seven business-unit general managers. The company is now more nimble, and new products get to market more quickly. In the United States, all operations have been consolidated under a single executive. This has been accomplished by a reduction in distribution centers and sales offices, consolidation in purchasing, and other efficiencies that have reduced operating expenses by $100 million per year.

These changes, combined with Maucher's sense of urgency, have transformed Nestlé from a passive to a very proactive and aggressive competitor.

*Adapted from "Nestlé: A Giant in a Hurry," *Business Week,* March 22, 1993, pp. 50, 51, 54.

see that accounting systems are sufficiently compatible for corporate financial statements to be meaningful. The newly acquired unit will be assigned its portion of corporate overhead. Unless the acquisition has the potential for creating substantial positive synergies, economic value will not be created by the acquisition. The principle is the same for new businesses that are developed internally: On balance, does the company's involvement in this business create *net positive synergy?*

IDENTIFYING OPPORTUNITIES THAT CREATE VALUE

How can executives identify acquisition and self-development opportunities that are likely to create sufficient economic value for their company? These evaluative questions can help:

- How attractive is the industry (or industry segment)?
- Can important resources or capabilities be leveraged?
- Are costs of transactions (with suppliers or customers) high and likely to remain so?
- Can the buyer capture enough of the value it seeks to create?
- Can the initiative be implemented effectively?

Each of these questions is considered here in turn.[20, 21]

How Attractive Is the Industry (or Industry Segment)?

Attractive industries have these characteristics:

- *Their customers have differing needs and wants.* When customers' needs and wants are heterogeneous, companies can often differentiate their products in ways that better meet the needs of one or more market segments. On the other hand, when customers view an industry's products or services as commodities that cannot be meaningfully differentiated, competition centers around price, leading to thin margins and modest earnings at best.
- *They are growing at least moderately.* In growing industries, a new entrant's initiatives (or an acquiree's expansion plans) are less likely to prompt competitors' retaliation—the norm in low- to zero-growth industries.
- *Their members do not perennially generate low average returns on investment.* Perennially low returns are caused by some combination of low entry barriers, high exit barriers, high supplier or customer bargaining power, many substitutes, and aggressive rivalry among direct competitors.[22] Two very unattractive industries are airlines (where ego needs motivate some to enter when "the numbers" don't justify it) and steel (where many competitors are owned by foreign governments more interested in

creating jobs and foreign exchange than profits). On the other hand, at least until recently, the pharmaceutical industry has been very attractive because the large number of therapeutic categories for which drugs can be developed moderates head-to-head competition, and because third-party payers have not been particularly price-sensitive.

Where customer needs are heterogeneous and products can be differentiated, the profitability across different industry segments (or strategic groups) can vary considerably.[23] In one study, the range of earnings *within* an industry was *six times* that across industries.[24] Consequently, a company's acquisition target or new business (internal development) market can be much more attractive than the industry as a whole. When the disparity is large, however, the corporation should satisfy itself that the factors that make the segment so much more attractive are likely to continue. In the minicomputer industry, once-attractive segments that made hardware targeted to specific industries (such as banking) have effectively been replaced by "generic" hardware in combination with industry-specific software. In response to these developments, IBM has reduced its five minicomputer hardware lines to one and now has to compete head-to-head with very aggressive, low-price competitors.

For initiatives that pass this hurdle, attention should turn to the corporation's ability to take advantage of the opportunity: What does it "bring to the table"?

Can Important Resources or Capabilities Be Leveraged?

A corporation can be viewed as a combination of resources and capabilities. Its resources, which enable it to operate and provide value for its customers, are its people, funds, physical assets, external reputation (including corporate and brand names), and intellectual property (such as patents). Company executives adjust the mix of resources (by hiring people, buying machinery, raising capital, and training people) and then apply those resources to create capabilities that support customer-perceived competitive advantages.

The first step in identifying a firm's capabilities is to ask these questions: "What do we do particularly well?" and "Is what we do well important in creating and maintaining the customer-perceived competitive advantages that motivate people to buy our products rather than a competitor's?" It is useful to consider a capability's functional breadth, product-market breadth, imitability, and leverageability.

Functional Breadth

Some capabilities—for example, a product development capability—cross functional lines. Some management capabilities (such as managing decentralized units with the right mix of freedom and control) and financial capabilities (efficient working capital management) also cross functional lines. These capabilities may exist across a wide range of organizations.

Although cross-functional capabilities can be very important, at least some of a company's most important capabilities reside within its "line" functions: R&D, manufacturing, and marketing. Within these functions, the capability often does not encompass the entire functional area. For instance, is a company's capability really R&D, or is it limited to a particular technology or field of science? Is its capability really manufacturing, or is it defined further by material and process technology (small batch, large batch, or mass production)? Is its capability marketing, or is it really advertising or direct sales or market segmentation?

Product-Market Breadth

Marketing capabilities in particular need to be examined to determine their product-market breadth. Marketing to consumers is very different from marketing to business customers, and marketing durable goods is very different from marketing items that are consumed directly. Even within these categories, customers' needs and purchase criteria may vary in ways that require a very different marketing approach.

One can easily overestimate the product-market breadth of a company's capabilities. When Heublein purchased Hamm's Beer, it expected to be able to leverage its capabilities in marketing, only to discover that beer drinkers had different motivations from drinkers of hard liquor. It turned out that Heublein's "alcoholic beverage" capability did not transfer successfully.

Imitability

When other things are equal, capabilities that are hard to imitate create competitive advantages and they, in turn, create economic value. Philip Morris purchased Miller Brewing to leverage its capabilities in marketing "low-cost, mass-produced, disposable consumer goods."[25] It was very successful initially, but became less so when Anheuser-Busch began imitating Miller's marketing capabilities. This step was easy for Anheuser-Busch; it simply hired outstanding marketers with consumer nondurable product experience. On the other hand, Crown Cork & Seal developed a capability for outstanding customer service in the metal container industry, and, after more than 30 years, its capability has not been imitated successfully.

The capabilities that are hardest to imitate are those where competitors lack (and cannot get) critical information, where the time lags in imitation are very long, and where socially complex processes are involved.[26] Product development processes, for example, can be socially complex; several functional areas may be working together under moderate-to-heavy time constraints. In the mid-

1980s, Japanese auto manufacturers were able to develop a new model almost two years faster than their American counterparts. American companies are catching up now, but it has been very difficult, because it has required far-reaching changes in organization processes.[27]

Leverageability

"Leverage" is the advantage gained from using an existing resource or capability in a new market, or improving performance in a market currently served. Leverage can create substantial economic value. In considering the leverageability of resources or capabilities, their operating leverage and capacity are important factors. When fixed costs are a large percentage of total costs, operating leverage is high, and amortizing those costs over a larger output can powerfully reduce average unit cost. Capacity relates to how much output can be expanded without necessitating additional investment. For example, both excess plant capacity and a brand name are leverageable, but plant capacity is more or less fixed. Once the excess capacity is used up, capacity expansion will be necessary, and unit cost will initially increase.[28]

Intangibles, such as a brand name, can be leveraged, too. For example, when using an established brand name in a new, related product area (where the brand name has relevant meaning for customers), the constraint is the need for some additional investment in advertising and promotion. (On the other hand, leveraging it into a new geographic area may necessitate a higher investment to get the name known.)

The same capabilities can be leveraged across a corporation in support of different customer-perceived competitive advantages in different businesses. Some corporations, however, build and maintain *corporate* competitive advantages, which exist across their product lines. For example, customers associate Hewlett-Packard with technically advanced products that have an array of features and cost somewhat more than a low-cost/low-price equivalent.

A major responsibility of corporate executives is to see that cross-business synergies are identified and exploited. Leveraging of resources and capabilities is the major source of these synergies. The next step in identifying value-creating opportunities is to consider transaction costs.

Are Costs of Transactions[29] (with Suppliers or Customers) High and Likely to Remain So?

Much business activity involves a market transaction: hiring employees, purchasing raw materials and components, hiring an advertising agency, and selling products or services through a distributor or franchisee, to name a few. When such transactions can be carried out in a market, there are some powerful incentives for economic efficiency:

- Revenue generation is tightly coupled to meeting customer needs.
- Administrative coordination problems are reduced because organizations are smaller.
- Tendencies toward "political" behavior and "log-rolling" are reduced.

Two organizations in difficulty today, General Motors and IBM, provide negative illustrations of those incentives for economic efficiency. Both of these corporations lost a clear customer focus, had significant administrative coordination problems (in new product development and other areas), and had strong cultures that allowed considerable energy to be devoted to political behavior.

However, in some circumstances, market transactions are far less efficient because transaction costs are high. Whenever transaction costs are high, there is an important information deficiency. In the following three instances, transaction costs are likely to be high:

1. When developing major, systemic innovations, the need for confidentiality may make timely progress difficult or impossible. Because information can flow more freely within an organization, expanding the scope of the corporation to include both units can substantially reduce transaction costs.

2. When one party to a market transaction is much better informed than the other and can't be trusted to be fully honest about sharing that information edge, and when there is only a small number of suppliers (or customers, as the case may be), it makes sense to expand the corporation's scope to include both units in the transaction.

3. When a transaction involves a task of extreme complexity, or when there are so many scenarios about the future that the time and cost to develop a contract for a market transaction would be excessive, placing both units into the same organization and making the decisions sequentially as time passes will be more efficient.[30]

For corporate executives, one major implication of an analysis of transaction costs is that it reveals the situations where vertical integration is typically not needed. This view suggests that vertical integration usually isn't needed to ensure a regular source of supply or to ensure quality: Contracts, if carefully drawn up, usually can provide both.

Can the Buyer Capture Enough of the Acquisition's Value It Seeks to Create?

Many diversification initiatives have not met their proponents' expectations, in spite of a convincing rationale that value could be created. Between persuasive logic and enhanced performance, one important consideration is whether the associated costs cancel out the anticipated benefits. In the case of self-development, how many new business initiatives fail before one succeeds? In the case of an acquisition, can the buyer capture enough of the value it intends to create?

Acquisition costs tend to be quite high. First, there is a *control premium,* the amount by which the price the buyer pays exceeds the market value before acquisition. Historically, in acquisitions of public companies, this has been approximately 40 percent. In the heat of the mid-1980s, it exceeded 60 percent! In another view, the control premium is the present value of the amount of performance improvements which the buyer gives to the seller in return for the privilege of control. Second, boards of directors of selling companies are legally required to act as *fiduciaries* for the shareholders, usually selling to the party that makes the highest offer. In many instances where there are competing bids, an auction is held. Often, an over eager buyer suffers the "winner's curse," or the penalty for overpaying. (In acquiring privately held companies, much less information is publicly available, and competing bids—and, consequently, the winners's curse—are less likely.)

To create net positive synergy, there must be sufficient economic value to cover the net present value of the control premium: deal-related fees to investment bankers, lawyers, and accountants; any additional costs associated with the new corporate parent; any negative synergies. If the value created does not exceed this minimum level, then, on balance, value has been destroyed.

Can the Initiative Be Implemented Effectively?

The greater the intended synergies among new and existing units, the more interaction there needs to be across these units. Units have structures, processes, and cultures, and they may or may not be compatible.[31] Implementation can be difficult when a company positioned in a mature business purchases a company in a rapidly growing segment of the same industry, with the expectation of swift knowledge transfer.

The logic of effectively managing mature units is very different from the logic that is most effective for rapidly expanding units. For mature units, revenues and costs can be predicted more accurately, financial performance is one effective measure of unit performance, a larger portion of communication between units can be in written form (memos and plans), and effective controls can substantially improve performance. In a rapidly growing unit, on the other hand, an effective, expeditious product development process is more important than adherence to budget, organization structure and processes are less developed, and some controls (for example, time clocks) can have negative effects. A new acquirer must ensure that the financial statements of the acquired unit can meaningfully be combined with those of the parent, but most other types of corporate "support" should be withheld. Many of the other elements of the mature parent company's "system" may destroy value in the growing, acquired unit. Before making any other organizational changes, management must consider why the unit was purchased and whether the unit's present arrangements provide a better fit with a rapid growth environment. This approach requires a different mindset on the part of those corporate staff members who see uniformity as an end in itself.

Frequently not asked is the opposite question: "Are there features of *the organization of the acquired unit* that we should emulate if we are trying to reposition ourselves into the growing segments of the market?" Acquirers seem to be much more effective at imposing their processes and culture on the acquiree than the reverse, regardless of the initial motivation for the acquisition.

To summarize, in determining whether particular scope changes are likely to create economic value, careful consideration needs to be given to:

- The attractiveness of the industry (or industry segment).
- Whether important capabilities or competitive advantages can be leveraged from existing to newly acquired businesses (or the reverse).
- Whether, in the case of vertical integration, factors are at work that make an arm's-length market transaction a less attractive alternative.
- Whether the buyer can retain enough of the value created so that the upside potential is sufficient to make the downside risk a prudent one to bear.
- Whether the intended scope change can be implemented effectively.

Most diversifying moves have failed because of deficiencies in one or more of these areas. Creating economic value through diversification is challenging because the corporation has to do many things well in order to succeed. Table 2–1 provides a summary of the questions to consider in identifying value-creating opportunities.

METHODS OF CHANGING SCOPE: EXPANSION AND CONTRACTION

There are many reasons why a company might wish to change its scope:

- Changes in its customer and competitive environments may make its present strategy less attractive;
- Output from its R&D lab may have promising applications outside its present businesses;
- Customers may want a wider range of product offerings;
- The company may have "missed" a major technical development;
- Shareholders may have grown impatient with efforts to create shareholder value in noncore businesses and may want divestment.

Each of these situations, as well as many others, calls for a change in a corporation's scope.

TABLE 2–1   Identifying value-creating opportunities.

1. What are our unique *resources?*

   —Consider brand names, corporate name, proprietary manufacturing technology, patents, and other intellectual property.

2. What are our distinctive *capabilities?* What do we do particularly well?

   —For capabilities *within a single function,* like R&D or marketing, consider the functional and product-market breadth. For example, "Marketing inexpensive products to consumers through the drug and discount channels" is much more useful and accurate than "Marketing."

   —Identify capabilities that *cross functional lines* and specify what makes each distinctive. For example, a product development process might be distinctive because, relative to competitors, it is speedier, involves less redesign, or is better targeted to customer needs.

3. What other companies (if they were fully informed) would want to merge with us, acquire us, or enter into a strategic alliance with us in order to get this benefit?

4. Into what product markets can these resources or capabilities be leveraged?

   —In each market, can our firm create competitive advantages?

   —Are these advantages easily imitated by others?

   —Have unattractive industry segments been avoided?

5. What *complementary* resources or capabilities are needed?

   —To take advantage of this opportunity, what resources do we need that we don't have now?

   —What things do we need to be able to do that we don't do now?

6. Is this initiative likely to generate a satisfactory *return?*

7. Can the organization *implement* this initiative effectively?

Despite the variety of circumstances motivating a change in corporate scope, only a limited range of methods is available for expanding or contracting scope. If scope expansion is desired, it can be done by internal development, acquisition, or some sort of strategic alliance (for example, licensing, franchising, or equity joint venture). Each of these options is considered here.

Internal Development

When a company develops a new business internally, it essentially builds it "from nothing": it develops the product or service, establishes the facilities, runs the operations, and does the marketing. In many instances, this sequence is an alternative to acquisition of an ongoing business.

Several factors affect the ease and desirability of internal new business development. First, how closely related is the new business to one or more of the company's existing businesses? The more closely related it is in product technology, process (manufacturing) technology, and product-market and customer target, the easier it is to develop the new business internally. The less closely related it is, the greater the number of complementary resources and capabilities necessary to bring the new business into operation. Such resources and capabilities are cost-effective to develop only if scale economies and shared resources are not working against them. In other words, are there scale economies that cannot be captured or taken advantage of? Do competitors share significant resources with businesses that are in their portfolio and not in ours? To the degree either situation is true, internal development becomes less cost-effective.

If the primary relationship with the current business is in product technology, the corporation can be propelled into very different product markets. Building on its capability in glass technology, Corning Glass Works has at various times been in the businesses of housewares, electronic components, television tubes, fiber optic cables, medical instruments, laboratory glassware, industrial materials, and ophthalmic products (eyeglass blanks). Despite the company's core capability in glass technology, Corning has entered an array of businesses employing different manufacturing technologies, customer types (business versus consumer), marketing channels, competitive advantages, and customer purchase criteria. Companies defining themselves in terms of a core technological capability need to consider carefully whether they can develop the complementary capabilities (in manufacturing and marketing) necessary for success in each of the product markets to which their technology takes them.

The reverse can occur where an organization's core capability is in marketing. Baxter's hospital supply unit, for example, provides "one-stop shopping" for a wide array of products, including latex gloves, bandages, hospital beds, medical instrumentation, medical devices, and the like. The products Baxter offers have many different technologies and are manufactured by quite different processes.

Internal development has some disadvantages. First, it tends to be very slow. In each area where new capabilities are needed, people need to be identified, hired, and given time to become productive in their new organizational setting. Second, although research is not conclusive, internal development seems to be not particularly profitable. In a careful study, Biggadike found that internally developed new businesses generated returns that were moderate at best.[32] Because of these limitations, acquisition is a frequently used method for diversifying into new businesses.

Acquisition

Acquisitions have several advantages:

1. They are faster to accomplish than internal development, because the company acquired is typically "up and running."
2. Compared to internal development, more information is available to the prospective buyer to evaluate the move. In addition to the information the

candidate provides to the prospective buyer, audited financial statements and filings to government agencies are available for publicly traded corporations; suppliers, customers, and even competitors can also be contacted for information (often through a third party).

3. A certain percentage of internally developed new businesses fail. By acquiring a going concern, the buyer does not need to pay for any of the failures along the way.

Acquisitions are not without their disadvantages:

1. An acquirer never has as much information about the target as it would like (especially in an unfriendly transaction), and it frequently gets some unexpected bad news after the deal closes.

2. Acquisitions can be quite expensive: As noted previously, a control premium of 40 percent is not uncommon for a publicly traded company. In practical terms, that means that the first 40 percent increase in shareholder value created by the new owners goes to the sellers. (The control premium is usually paid at closing, so the sellers receive it whether or not the new owners are actually able to add value.)[33]

3. Integration into the new parent can be very difficult, sometimes destroying more value than the acquisition was expected to create.

An acquisition alternative worthy of consideration is the strategic alliance.

Strategic Alliances

A strategic alliance is any formal, interorganizational, collaborative relationship. In such an alliance, a firm seeks to receive the benefit of another company or business without owning it. A strategic alliance can take many forms, including: a long-term supply or marketing agreement, joint R&D, joint manufacturing, or, in an equity joint venture, the creation of a new legal entity for specified purposes.

One or more of the following motives drives most joint ventures:

- Minimizing costs.
- Improving a firm's competitive position.
- Transferring organizational knowledge.

Merck and Johnson & Johnson, for example, created an equity joint venture to market pharmaceutical products that have moved from prescription to over-the-counter status. Merck gets its over-the-counter products marketed for a lower cost, and Johnson & Johnson is able to leverage its consumer products marketing capability over a wider range of products. An equity joint venture between Toyota and General Motors (GM) to build cars in the United States has provided GM with knowledge of more cost-effective and higher-quality manufacturing processes, as well as with the opportunity to sell a car produced by the joint venture for a lower price. For its part, Toyota has received some U.S. manufacturing plant capacity more quickly than it could have built facilities.

Of all the anticipated knowledge-related benefits from strategic alliances, the hardest to transfer are an organization's complex routines, such as those used in an effective product development process.[34] Frequently, replicating the organization through the creation of a new entity—typically, an equity joint venture—is the only effective way to transfer those routines.

Parties considering strategic alliances need to ask: "What am I giving up, and what am I receiving in return? Is this in my short-run best interest? Is this in my long-run interest? Am I tutoring a new competitor (especially one that could unfavorably alter industry structure)?" The potential benefits of strategic alliances are often readily apparent, while the potential downside is less so. Because the potential downside is so great, partners in strategic alliances should be chosen with great care. For each potential partner, these characteristics should be determined:

- Motivation to participate.
- Potential conflicts of interest.
- Preferred duration for the alliance.
- Level of integrity.

In microcomputer software, Microsoft had a joint venture with IBM to develop OS/2 at the same time it was devoting considerable energy and attention to developing its Windows™ product, a direct competitor. Microsoft's success with Windows™ has negatively impacted sales of OS/2.

In many strategic alliances, the major item of value that changes hands is information. In such arrangements, it is important to make certain that the information that motivated entry into the venture is being received. The requisite number of people in the organization must either have it relayed to them or must be, for a time, assigned to the venture. Many American companies in joint ventures with Japanese companies complain that they spend too much time training the Japanese managers transferred in and out so frequently by their Japanese partners. What the Japanese partners are doing in these instances is ensuring that the information desired from the venture is acquired by many persons in their organization. American venture partners have not always been so effective in gathering information.

When thoughtfully designed and implemented and when partner motives are compatible, strategic alliances can be a great mutual boon to companies. But when these qualities are not present, such alliances can fail—or fail to accomplish one party's objectives and leave that party worse off than if it had not entered into the alliance. It may have tutored or strengthened a competitor, and, if the alliance was intended to create a critically important capability or competitive advantage, the company has lost valuable time in attempting to make the alliance work.

When potential strategic alliances are analyzed with insufficient care and are implemented ineffectively, companies find that they often yield more heartbreak than help. Yet, with thoughtful analysis and implementation, strategic alliances have great potential to build capabilities or competitive advantages that can genuinely "make a difference" in the increasingly competitive business environment.

Thus, in expanding corporate scope, internal development, acquisition, and strategic alliances possess different strengths and challenges. The remaining task is to consider reductions in the corporation's scope.

Divestment

There are several reasons why a corporation might wish to remove one or more units from its portfolio:

1. It may be correcting a past error in which a debatable acquisition was made. Xerox's purchase of Crum & Forster (a financial services firm) in the mid-1980s was greeted skeptically in the financial markets, so it was no surprise to many when Xerox announced its intention to divest it several years later.

2. Changes in the competitive environment may no longer justify retaining a particular unit in the corporation. As the ready-to-eat cereal market has gotten more competitive, both Nabisco and Ralston Purina have considered divesting their cereal businesses because neither has a large enough market share to be a strong player.

3. A corporation may divest a unit that it acquired reluctantly. For example, some businesses in the rapid-growth stage may integrate backward because suppliers do not exist or will not (or cannot) expand capacity rapidly enough to meet the businesses' needs. Later, when a market exists and has become more competitive, divestment may make sense.

4. A corporation in financial difficulty (or seeking to work down a high level of debt) may divest a unit because of its marketability. Such a unit is typically a proven strong performer. TWA's sale of its routes to London is an example.

Companies can utilize different methods to accomplish a divestment. Because a company's goal is to exit from the business in as timely a fashion as is feasible, the objective is quite simply stated: Use the method that realizes the highest return.

In many instances, the most profitable method to the selling company is a *sale of the business* to another company. Where there are operating synergies with other businesses of the buyer, the seller may be able to capture (through a high price) the economic value of a significant portion of the synergies the buyer can create. Unless the sale is explicitly structured otherwise, the seller receives the total proceeds at closing, and these funds can immediately be used for other corporate purposes or for distribution to shareholders. General Dynamics has sold several large businesses due to the decline in defense-related industries and has passed a significant portion of the proceeds to its shareholders in special distributions.

In a *leveraged buyout* (LBO), the unit is sold to a group of managers in partnership with an investment firm in a highly leveraged transaction.[35] Sales to an LBO group can be very attractive to the sellers. However, the buyers may be more astute negotiators, and it is not atypical for the selling company to hold some debt or equity in connection with the transaction. LBOs are not appropriate for rapid-growth businesses because they require too much investment to build the business. LBOs work best in mature markets, which can generate the cash flow needed to service the high level of debt. Because LBOs tend to be rather fully priced, a substantial portion of the debt service comes from funds generated by improved efficiency and the subsequent increases in cash flow. As a result, an undermanaged unit in a mature industry can make a particularly attractive LBO candidate.

When a unit is capable of functioning on a stand-alone basis, a *spin-off* may make sense. A spin-off does not generate revenue for the divesting corporation. Rather, the capital stock of a division or subsidiary of a corporation is transferred to the stockholders of the parent corporation. A major consideration in designing a spin-off is to ensure that the unit is a viable entity on a stand-alone basis. Where the resources (for example, plant, warehouse, or sales force) shared with another unit of the parent are significant, contractual arrangements for continued sharing or for the transfer of sufficient resources to the spin-off are critical. Further, the parent may need to make a cash infusion so that the spin-off's balance sheet is healthy enough for the unit to exist viably on its own. Esmark did this a decade ago when it successfully spun off its Swift meat unit.

A fourth divestment method is a *harvest* of the business. As with other divestment methods, the parent makes a final decision to exit from the business. Unlike the other alternatives, it continues to operate the business because in its judgment the net present value of continuing to operate the business for a specified time significantly exceeds the value available through sale or liquidation. Almost all investments are curtailed, R&D spending is drastically reduced and eventually eliminated, and all expenditures are scrutinized carefully. As sales volume declines, capacity is reduced until all assets are eventually liquidated. Harvesting is most likely when the parent company, with its "inside" knowledge of the business, has a more optimistic view of a declining business's prospects over the next few years than outsiders do.

A *liquidation of assets* is the least profitable avenue of all, because assets are worth much less than a going business. Liquidation is considered seriously only when no buyer is forthcoming, when the business lacks stand-alone capability, and when harvesting is not justified. When Control Data exited from the supercomputer business, it had to liquidate because, despite the investment made in the business over the years, the unit did not have a competitive product and had no value as a going concern.

CONCLUSION

Where an increase in scope is desired, central management can choose among internal development, acquisition, or a strategic alliance. In selecting a method, there are important tradeoffs among speed, cost, and control, and each poses a significant organizational challenge. In reducing scope, the analytical problem is simpler: Which method is likely to generate the highest net present value?

SUMMARY

Corporate strategy addresses three questions:

1. What should the product-market, vertical, and geographic scope of a corporation be?
2. How should the units in the corporation be related to each other?
3. Where scope changes are needed, what method(s) should be used to bring current scope into alignment with desired scope?

Many corporations have been criticized by the capital markets for making what outsiders felt were inappropriate scope decisions. In the increasingly competitive markets of the 1990s, more attention needs to be paid to relatedness, or how the businesses in the corporate fold are linked to each other. When other things are equal, businesses that leverage important capabilities or competitive advantages will perform more strongly than their peers. The alternative methods of changing scope have profound implications for a company's present and future performance. They are equally deserving of corporate management's attention because, through these decisions, a company seeks to accomplish the strategic intentions embodied in its desired relatedness and scope.

NOTES

1. Some companies carry out these activities at intermediate levels as well: at the division, product group, and/or sector level.

2. For a discussion of business unit strategy, see Chapter 3.

3. Boston Consulting Group, *Perspectives on Experience,* 1968.

4. When the judgment is flawed or unduly pessimistic, it can be a substantial management *mis*judgment. Sometimes, it diverts management's attention from alternative ways in which the same needs of existing customers could be met. The problems in the core business may continue to deepen at the same time the company is

adding little to the business it diversifies into. Sears, Roebuck & Co., for example, diversified into financial services, to which it added little, at a time when its retail business problems were not addressed and discount and specialty retailing continued to eat away at its market share.

5.   However, the owner of a single-business firm—with most or all of his or her assets tied up in the firm—might wish to diversify to reduce exposure to a single business. Even in this case, purchasing debt or equity securities in other firms or mutual funds should be considered.

6.   In addition to these stated reasons, three unstated reasons have motivated diversification. Some CEOs have diversified to satisfy ego needs, such as the desire to face a new challenge, to leave a large "imprint" on corporate history, or to have acquisition-related stories to share when in the presence of other CEOs. Second, many executives find it more fun to manage a growing organization than a flat or shrinking one. A third unstated reason has been the increase of the CEO's personal wealth, where a still-too-widespread practice links top executives' compensation to corporate size rather than to corporate performance. See Alfred Rappaport, *Creating Shareholder Value: The New Standard for Corporate Performance* (New York: Free Press, 1986).

7.   Charles W. Hofer and Dan Schendel, *Strategy Formulation: Analytical Concepts* (St. Paul, MN: West, 1978).

8.   This is discussed in H. Kurt Christensen, *Note on Synergy* (unpublished paper).

9.   These are examples at the corporate level of strategic leadership that was discussed in Chapter 1.

10.   This question is the central theme of Chapters 8 and 9.

11.   Richard P. Rumelt, *Strategy, Structure and Economic Performance* (Cambridge, MA: Harvard University Press, 1974).

12.   H. K. Christensen and C. A. Montgomery, "Corporate Economic Performance: Diversification Strategy Versus Market Structure," *Strategic Management Journal* (1981), 2:327–343.

13.   R. Grant, "On 'Dominant Logic,' Relatedness and the Link between Diversity and Performance," *Strategic Management Journal* (1988), 9:639–642.

14.   Readers are referred to Chapter 8 for a more detailed discussion of technology as a source of 3M's competencies.

15   Global strategy is the focus of Chapter 4.

16.   The movement toward creation of trading blocs in Europe, North America, and elsewhere argues for more coordination across national boundaries than the multidomestic strategy implies.

17.   For a discussion of the step-by-step approach of Japanese firms to the European marketplace, see Achim A. Stoehr, "Japanese Positioning for Post-1992 Europe," in Liam Fahey, *Winning in the New Europe: Taking Advantage of the Single Market* (Englewood Cliffs, NJ: Prentice-Hall, 1992).

18.   For a related discussion of the analysis of vertical integration, see Chapter 8.

19.   In some adversarial situations, partial integration may make sense to gain cost (and other) information that will provide leverage in bargaining and will create an implied threat that a company will integrate fully if price or performance becomes unsatisfactory.

20. This discussion utilizes the terminology of product-market scope. However, the same questions can be made appropriate for assessing geographic scope decisions simply by substituting "national market" or "regional market" for "industry," "industry segment," or "product-market."

21. Michael E. Porter, "From Competitive Advantage to Corporate Strategy," *Harvard Business Review* (1987), 65:3, 43–59.

22. See Michael E. Porter, *Competitive Strategy: Techniques for Analyzing Industries and Competitors* (New York: Free Press, 1980), Ch. 1.

23. For explanations of variation in profitability across and within industries, see Chapter 6.

24. Richard P. Rumelt, "How Much Does Industry Matter?," *Strategic Management Journal* (1991), 12:3, 167–185.

25. "The Seven-Up Division of Philip Morris," Harvard Business School, (1985), p. 5.

26. Margaret A. Peteraf, "The Cornerstones of Competitive Advantage: A Resource-Based View," *Strategic Management Journal* (1993), 14:179–191.

27. Kim Clark and Takahira Fujimoto, *Product Development Performance* (Boston: Harvard Business School, 1991).

28. Birger Wernerfelt, "From Critical Resources to Corporate Strategy," *Journal of General Management* (1989), 14:3, 4–12.

29. A transaction is an economic exchange in which one party gives up something in return for something else. The items exchanged can be products, services, or funds. Transaction costs are the costs associated with making a particular transaction. They can range from relatively low (as when a company orders standard office supplies from a catalog) to relatively high (as in a merger with a high control premium). Organizations make most of their transactions externally—in markets. But, when organizations make "something they can buy," that transaction occurs internally—within the *organizational hierarchy*. For a given transaction, lower transaction costs will usually occur in a market, but in some instances these costs are lower in a hierarchy.

30. Oliver E. Williamson, *Markets and Hierarchies: Analysis and Antitrust Implications* (New York: Free Press, 1975).

31. The importance of organization infrastructure was addressed in Chapter One. Chapters 12 and 14 cover in detail the role of structure and decision processes in shaping and executing strategy. How organization culture can be managed to effect strategic change is the focus of Chapter 15.

32. E. Ralph Biggadike, "The Risky Business of Diversification," *Harvard Business Review* (1979), 57:3, 103–111.

33. The exception is when there is an earn-out provision and the final price depends in part on earnings in the years after the acquisition closes. This is more common in acquisitions of a privately held firm.

34. The manner in which routines embodying knowledge constitute a central element in an organization's culture is addressed in Chapter 15.

35. An entire company can be involved in an LBO, but, in the context of divestment, LBOs occur at the unit level.

BUSINESS-UNIT STRATEGY: 3 MANAGING THE SINGLE BUSINESS

Anil K. Gupta

University of Maryland

This chapter examines the management of strategy at the business-unit level. We will use the term *business unit* broadly to refer to a division, a subsidiary, or a profit center within a multibusiness corporation as well as to a single-business company operating independently. There is a fundamental difference between strategic concerns at the corporate versus the business-unit level. Corporate strategy deals with broader issues such as what businesses to be in and how to exploit synergies across businesses; business-unit strategy deals with how to compete successfully within a given industry.[1]

There are five key elements to managing strategy at the business-unit level:

1. Defining the scope of the business unit. What is and is not within the charter of the business unit?

2. Setting business-unit goals. What financial and nonfinancial targets will guide the development of the business unit's strategy, the assessment of its performance, and the taking of corrective actions?

3. Defining the intended bases for competitive advantage. What are the customer-relevant dimensions along which the business unit intends to be not merely good but better than competitors?

4. Designing the value constellation. What will the business unit do and what will it rely on its business partners to do? For example, should General Motors' Saturn division make its own axles or source them?

5. Managing the business unit's internal value chain as well as its integration with the value chains of partners and customers. Is the purpose of value

chain management—to create and sustain competitive superiority along the intended bases of competitive advantage—being fulfilled?

Each of the chapter's sections deals with one of these five key elements. Each section highlights the importance of the particular element, provides guidelines as to what a company should or should not do in managing that element, and illustrates these guidelines through several specific case examples. Table 3–1 summarizes the key questions that need to be addressed in managing each of these elements.

A European firm, Sunds Defibrator Group, is used throughout the chapter as an integrating example of strategic management at the business-unit level. The discussion of this firm serves to illustrate how decisions along each of the five elements interact to yield a comprehensive business strategy for a particular company. Box 3–1 provides a brief profile of the Sunds Defibrator Group.

DEFINING BUSINESS-UNIT SCOPE

The first step in the development of business-unit strategy is to define the scope of the business. Interestingly, the question of what constitutes a single business often does not have an easy answer. Should Procter & Gamble (P&G) manage consumer paper goods as a single business or should it go one level deeper and treat diapers, paper towels, and facial tissues as individual businesses? In another example, Asea Brown Boveri (ABB), the Swiss–Swedish electrotechnical giant, can be viewed as operating in six businesses (such as transportation and power plants) or 65 businesses (such as robotics and electric drives) or several hundred businesses (such as AC motor drives and DC motor drives). The scope of the business clearly becomes narrower and more precisely defined as one goes from higher to lower levels of aggregation. However, defining the scope narrowly is not always superior to defining it broadly—or vice versa.

How then should companies go about defining the scope of a business unit? One of the most useful approaches is to begin by addressing three questions:[2]

1. Who are our target customers? Target customers can be defined in any number of ways. For example, individual customers can be defined by age, sex, income levels, psychosocial characteristics, postal code, ethnic background, country of location, and so on. Similarly, industrial customers can be defined by industry classification, company size, country of location, and many other factors.

2. What customer needs are we trying to fulfill? Customer needs should be defined not in terms of the products or services that the business provides but in terms of the generic problem faced by the customer, to which current products or services might be just one solution. In the case of Federal Express, for example, customer needs would be defined not in terms of "courier services" but in terms such as "the urgent transfer of documents

TABLE 3–1 Defining business unit strategy: Key questions.

Defining the Scope of the Business Unit

- Who are our target customers?

- What customer needs are we trying to fulfill?

- What competencies will serve as the core of how we fulfill the targeted customer needs?

Setting Business-Unit Goals

- What financial goals (e.g., return on assets) are we pursuing?

- What market position and customer satisfaction goals (e.g., market share) are we pursuing?

- What internal business goals (e.g., employee retention, cycle time reduction) are we pursuing?

- What innovation and learning goals (e.g., percent of sales from new products) are we pursuing?

Defining the Intended Bases for Competitive Advantage

- Along which dimensions do we intend to become and remain superior to competitors?

- Along which dimensions will we accept the possibility of being at par with competitors? Why?

- Along which dimensions will we accept the possibility of being at a disadvantage with respect to competitors? Why?

Designing the Value Constellation

- Which customer-relevant activities should we perform ourselves?

- Which customer-relevant activities should we source from business partners (including the option of forming alliances or joint ventures with them)?

- How will we reduce/eliminate the risks of "nonperformance," "profit skimming," and "elimination" by our business partners?

Managing the Value Chain

- For each activity in our value chain, what are the drivers of customer value, cost structure, and asset investment?

- How will we manage each value, cost, and asset driver for competitive superiority?

- How will we ensure high integration across the various value-chain activities, including those performed by our business partners?

and goods from one location to another." In serving customer needs in the area of document transfer, Federal Express faces increasingly tough competition from fax machines and electronic mail; in contrast, in the area of goods transfer, Federal Express is relatively well-protected against substitute technologies.

3. What competencies will form the core of how we serve these needs for these customers in a competitively superior manner? Core competencies

Box 3–1

Sunds Defibrator Group: Corporate Profile

Sunds Defibrator Group, with headquarters in Sundsvall, Sweden, is a world leader in the supply of fiber processing technologies, offering the most comprehensive product range in the industry. It comprises engineering, sales, and service companies and has offices in all major forest products countries.

The company is the only supplier in the world able to deliver complete fiber lines, from woodhandling to the end-product.

The company's R&D activities focus on cost-efficient technologies that meet the demand for environmentally friendly, energy-efficient fiber product solutions that optimize raw material yield.

Annual sales amount to $400 million approximately. The firm has 2,650 employees. Its principal markets are Scandinavia, Europe, North America, South America, and Asia.

The company offers the following products and services:

Woodhandling. Full line of woodyard and woodroom processes and equipment, including debarking, chipping, and screening, as well as chip and bark handling systems.

Chemical pulping. Complete fiber lines including SuperBatch™ cooking, deknotting, screening, brown-stock washing, oxygen and ozone delignification, and bleaching. The company is a leading supplier of totally chlorine free (TCF) pulping technologies.

High-yield and mechanical pulping. High-yield processes based on advanced refiner technology for all grades of pulp. Activities also cover peroxide bleaching, screening, mixing, washing, and fiber classification.

Dewatering, drying, and baling. Plants and equipment for dewatering, drying, bale forming and pressing, wrapping, binding, stacking, and bale finishing of sheet and flash-dried pulp.

Stock preparation. Advanced product lines for slushing, deflaking, Conflo™ refining, and broke treatment applications in paper mills.

Recycled fiber. Equipment and systems for processing of recycled fibers. Activities include pulping, flotation de-inking, washing, dispersion, screening, peroxide bleaching, and fiber classification.

Panelboard. Complete plants for production of dry- and wet-process fiberboard, particleboard, and mineral-bonded boards, as well as panelboard laminating, handling, and finishing.

Refiner segments. Offers customers worldwide the most advanced refiner segments and fillings for all types of refiners.

Customer service and support. Worldwide organization focused on providing customer support throughout the life cycle of customer equipment and process systems.

can include one or more of several types of competencies—product technology, process management, customer service, and short delivery times, to name just a few.[3]

It is not always necessary or even wise to define the scope of a business unit precisely by answering all three of these questions in great detail. An example is the Timex watch company, circa 1970. Suppose management had defined the scope of the business as follows: "To serve the low- to middle-income customers' time-keeping needs through the production of mechanically manufactured pin-levered watches." The definition would have been precise, but, given the coming competitive onslaught by electronic watchmakers, it would have limited the company's options and threatened its survival.

The Timex example is a reminder that changes in the external environment (customer preferences, technological options, growth in market demand, number and identity of competitors, to name a few) can happen suddenly and may have momentous effects on a business unit. Thus, the definition of the scope of a business must simultaneously serve two types of conflicting needs:

1. To provide focus to efforts today.
2. To help in adapting, faster than competitors, to changes in the external environment.

Managers skilled at operating in rapidly changing markets have found an effective way to resolve these apparently conflicting goals. They understand the risk of constraining a business unit's options in all three dimensions of scope: target customers, customer needs, and investment in core competencies. They set constraints on only one or two of the three scope dimensions, and they leave wide latitude for exploration along the remaining one or two dimensions. Here are two examples:

1. FMG Timberjack is the world's market-share leader in forestry equipment. In defining the scope of its business, this company has put fairly tight bounds on who the target customer is (forestry companies), moderately tight bounds on customer needs (currently defined as tree harvesting and forest-to-roadside transportation, but could include tree planting in the future), and fairly loose bounds on the set of underlying competencies that the business might develop and dominate (for example, whole-tree technology, cut-to-length technology, integration of data-processing equipment, and robotization).

2. The inventor of microprocessors, Intel, has been successful in maintaining its technological dominance of this market. However, the uses to which microprocessors can be put are constantly evolving. The biggest volume market at present is personal computers, but microprocessors are also used in the design of massively parallel supercomputers and in medical systems such as CAT scanners. It is entirely likely that the list of target customers and customer needs may be quite different five years from now. Thus, it

would seem to be wiser for Intel's microprocessor business to define its scope primarily in terms of technological competencies rather than target customers or even targeted needs.

To sum up, the starting point of setting business-unit strategy is to define the business unit's scope along one or more of the following three dimensions: target customers, customer needs, and core competencies. Ideally, the scope should be defined specifically enough to help the business discriminate among many opportunities that present themselves and to give it a sense of direction. At the same time, the chosen definition of scope should allow the business unit sufficient room for exploration, adaptation to changing market conditions, and identification of new opportunities.

Sunds Defibrator Group's business scope is delineated in Box 3–2. The target is a broad but clearly focused set of customers: fiber-based process manufacturers, that is, manufacturers of pulp and/or panelboards anywhere in the

---

Box 3–2
Sunds Defibrator Group: Definition of Business Unit Scope

Sunds Defibrator Group defines its business scope primarily in terms of targeted customers and targeted needs, and takes a more flexible evolutionary approach with respect to core competencies. The company proactively seeks to develop new technologies and other competencies rather than remain overly constrained by its historical portfolio of competencies.

Targeted customers. Fiber-based process manufacturers, i.e., manufacturers of pulp and/or panelboards anywhere in the world.

Targeted customer needs. Complete fiber-processing lines (i.e., complete plants) as well as associated machines, parts, and services in three broad areas: (1) chemical pulping systems, (2) mechanical pulping systems, and (3) panelboard systems. In each of these areas, the more specific customer needs are: (a) superior productivity, (b) economical production, (c) environmentally harmonized processes, (d) continuous, long-term, round-the-clock service, and (e) low total investment costs.

Core competencies. Chemical cooking, bleaching, and filtration technologies. Mechanical pulping technologies. Fiber preparation technologies. Customer service. Other competencies that may be developed internally or sourced from business partners.

Source: Derived by the author from "Strategy for the Sunds Defibrator Group: 1992," an open document published by the Sunds Defibrator Group, Sundsvall, Sweden. For the purposes of the illustrations in this chapter, we are treating Sunds Defibrator Group as a "business unit" within Rauma Limited, a large, diversified, industrial corporation headquartered in Finland. Because Sunds Defibrator Group itself is composed of a number of product lines and geographical subsidiaries, this analysis could also be carried out at those finer levels of business-unit definition.

world. These customers seem to manifest a set of consistent needs. However, the firm has chosen to remain more flexible with respect to core competencies; it proactively seeks to develop *new* technologies and other competencies that are relevant to satisfying customers' needs rather than remain overly constrained by its historical portfolio of competencies. The remaining sections of the chapter look at how Sunds Defibrator Group has defined its goals and its intended bases of competitive advantage; how it has designed its value-chain constellation, and how it attempts to manage its value chain.

BUSINESS-UNIT GOALS

Experienced managers are well aware of the saying: "If you don't know where to go, any road will take you there." The establishment of goals is a significant step in the development of a coherent business-unit strategy. But what should these goals be?

Because the ultimate goal of any "business" is to maximize return to shareholders, some companies tend to define business-unit goals primarily or even exclusively in terms of return on capital employed such as: "Every business unit must achieve a minimum of 20 percent return on assets annually." This one-goal-fits-all-units approach is likely to be seriously flawed and can lead to strategies that are myopic and ultimately self-defeating.

Management must recognize that return to shareholders is a function of both short- and long-term profitability, not merely short-term profitability. In other words, what really matters to shareholders is maximization of the net present value (NPV) of all future earnings, not maximization of next year's or even the next five years' earnings. This is an important difference because NPV calculations are affected by the size of future earnings as well as by the discount rates. Thus, if a spanking new business (such as personal digital assistants) is expected to grow significantly, short-term earnings may have a minor impact on NPV estimates. On the other hand, if a market is shrinking (such as mainframe computers), then the next five years' earnings may capture the bulk of the NPV. Similarly, discount rates are a function of the riskiness of the business and, generally, the less risky the business, the lower the discount rate would be.[4]

A direct implication of the above arguments is that the maximization of next year's or even the next five years' earnings would rarely be the ideal goal for all businesses in a corporation. At the same time, the needs of ongoing feedback and managerial control require that business-unit performance be assessed at least annually. The obvious and most common solution to this dilemma lies in adopting a balanced multidimensional approach to the setting of business-unit goals and to the measurement and assessment of business-unit performance. The most extensive recent work in this area has been done by Kaplan and Norton,[5] who suggest that businesses should be assigned goals and measured from four perspectives:

1. Financial perspective (such as return on assets, cash flow).
2. Customer perspective (including market share, customer satisfaction index).
3. Internal business perspective (including employee retention, cycle time reduction).
4. Innovation and learning perspective (for instance, X percent of sales from new products).

Measured by these criteria, business-unit goals would almost always differ across business units and would be a function of industry trends, the nature of competition, the business unit's historical performance, and managerial aggressiveness and ambition.

Box 3–3 shows how Sunds Defibrator Group has chosen to define its business goals. Several aspects of this statement of business goals merit attention. The statement defines the company's goals along both of the most important dimensions—market position and profitability. Too often, firms emphasize one of these goals to the detriment of the other; they forget that long-term financial success is a consequence of winning in the marketplace.

Sunds Defibrator Group's vision sets a real challenge for the organization: To be indisputably recognized as the leading global supplier for the fiber-based process industry by the turn of the century. This vision or intent cannot be achieved without evoking a massive effort from the organization.[6] Yet the vision must be attained while achieving significant financial returns—17 percent on employed capital. The goals are realistic but nonetheless challenging: During the period 1988–1992, the company's market share ranged from 15 percent to 60 percent, depending on the product line; the return on capital employed averaged between 15 percent and 20 percent.

The Sunds Defibrator Group's goals also are stated quantitatively and are given specific target dates, making it feasible for the company to determine whether the goals are being met. The company can therefore monitor its progress toward goal attainment.

INTENDED BASES FOR COMPETITIVE ADVANTAGE

Three core ideas have proved useful for defining a business unit's intended basis for competitive advantage:

1. Relative competitive advantage. Competitive advantage can be defined only in relative, not in absolute terms.
2. Multiple bases for competitive advantage. Competitive advantage must be thought of as existing in layers; that is, a company's offerings can be "better" than the competition's along many different dimensions—price, delivery time, quality, technology, and esthetics, to name a few. The more

---

Box 3–3

Sunds Defibrator Group: Defining Business-Unit Goals

We have two specific Group Objectives.

Preferred Supplier

To be the supplier that the fiber-based process industry prefers to purchase from.

> —It is our vision that, by the turn of the century, we will be indisputably recognized as the leading global supplier for the fiber-based process industry—a supplier with the most comprehensive product program and service network in existence. The number of suppliers will, by then, have been cut by a continual process of consolidation. Two of three highly efficient companies in each global business area and process area will account for more than 90 percent of all major transactions.

> —We intend to be a market leader with market shares exceeding 50 percent. Sunds Defibrator process and equipment solutions in selected business areas will make it possible for us to capture a position of 'qualitative leadership.' With a limited number of suppliers in existence, each will develop its own solutions, and orientation towards technology and know-how will be even more decisive.

Good Return on Employed Capital

To achieve an average return of 17 percent on employed capital over a business cycle (five years).

Source: Abstracted by the author from "Strategy for the Sunds Defibrator Group: 1992," an open document published by the Sunds Defibrator Group, Sundsvall, Sweden. See Box 3–2 regarding application of the term "business unit" to this entity.

---

layers contributing to competitive advantage, the more sustainable the business unit's dominance of its market.

3. The bases of competition shift over time. The relevant bases for competitive advantage can and often do shift over time.

There are many practical implications of these core ideas. Each idea is discussed here in detail.

Relative Competitive Advantage

It is tempting for managers to define the basis for their business's competitive advantage in terms such as excellent products, excellent service, great prices, and so forth. However, these definitions obscure an important issue: What matters in the marketplace is not how good a company's products, services, and prices are, but whether any or all of these attributes are perceived as being superior to those of competitors.[7]

To see how relative competitive advantage can work in a market, consider a ten-year survey on new-car reliability, published by *Consumer Reports* magazine in April 1991. According to this survey, in 1980, on average, General Motors' cars had 110 problems per 100 new cars as compared with about 43 problems per 100 cars for the "worst" of the three major Japanese suppliers (Toyota, Nissan, and Honda). By 1990, the figure for General Motors was down to 40 problems per 100 cars. However, the Japanese companies had, by then, about 17 problems per 100 cars. These data clearly suggest that GM made a remarkable improvement in the reliability of its cars during the 1980s. However, the data also suggest that, in relative terms, in 1990, GM was still at a competitive disadvantage. In terms of the customer's decision to choose one supplier over another, what counts is relative superiority and not absolute performance.

In short, after having defined its scope and set its goals, every business unit must define:

- Those areas in which it must remain superior to competitors.
- Those areas where it will accept the possibility of being on a par with competitors.
- Those areas where it will accept the possibility of being at a disadvantage vis-à-vis competitors.

It is not always essential that the business unit be superior to competitors in all key dimensions. However, lack of superiority along any critical dimension implies that the business unit's current market position is unlikely to be sustainable.

Multiple Bases for Competitive Advantage

Every business should strive for multiple bases (rather than just one base) for competitive advantage. For a number of years, business strategy theory postulated that businesses should strive to compete on the basis of either low cost or differentiation. However, as competition in most industries becomes more global and more intense, the notion that every business must choose between "differentiation" and "cost leadership" is becoming less and less viable.[8]

As an example, we would argue that passionate cost control (not cost reduction per se) is just as critical for Toyota's luxury-market Lexus division as it is for its mass-market Tercel unit. Admittedly, target customers of Lexus are much less price-sensitive than those of Tercel. However, it would be a mistake to conclude that customers' lack of price sensitivity should, in any manner, affect this business unit's passion for cost control. Suppose that Lexus engineers were to figure out how to reduce the cost of the car by 4 percent without affecting its performance or customer-perceived features in any way. Because Lexus customers are not very price-sensitive, the next step may be *not* to reduce the price by 4 percent but, instead, to invest part or all of the cost savings in improved features or higher performance. Because Lexus customers are performance- rather than price-sensitive, it is even conceivable that these improvements could lead to an *increase* in the final price. Thus, passionate cost control in the case of Lexus may well be one of the drivers behind improved performance and higher, rather than lower, price.

In contrast, Toyota's Tercel division, given the high price sensitivity of its target customers, is quite likely to respond to a 4 percent manufacturing cost reduction with a decision to reduce the prices by a like amount. However, de- spite this unit's passion for cost control and lower prices, it would be unwise to suggest that lower prices should constitute the only basis for competitive advan- tage. Tercel customers may not care much about leather seats or high accelera- tion, but they may place very high importance on other differentiable attributes such as reliability, leg room, safety, and fuel efficiency.

There is always more than one way to differentiate any product, even if it is apparently a commodity product, such as steel (where the differentiation may be along attributes such as consistency of product quality and short delivery times). Further, not all types of differentiation necessarily increase the cost structure (as illustrated by Swatch watches, with their wide variety of strap and dial designs). Within the bounds of the prices that the target customer would pay, the more numerous the types of differentiation advantage that a business unit can build in, the more sustainable its dominance of the market.

The Bases of Competition Shift over Time

There are at least two reasons for this shift. Each is examined in turn.

Change in Customers' Priorities and Buying Behavior

Customers' priorities change over time for a variety of reasons—recession, availability of substitutes, changes in the customers' product or process tech- nology. For example, prior to the emergence of the quartz watch, time-keeping quality was the primary differentiating factor among competitors in the indus- try. However, once the quartz watch became ubiquitous, the cheapest quartz watch kept better time than the most expensive mechanical watch. Thus, the differentiating factor switched from time-keeping quality to features (sports watches, watches that also were calculators) and styling design (fancy or tradi- tional dial faces). As another example, consider the case of industrial valves sold by companies such as Fisher Controls, Masoneilan, and Neles-Jamesbury. As the customers of these companies have become increasingly global, the ability to offer a globally coordinated supply of valves has become an impor- tant differentiating factor alongside product features, quality, service, and prices.

Achievement of Competitive Parity

Even when customer priorities remain unchanged, competitive dynamics will often change the relevant bases for competitive advantage. For example, the superior reliability of Honda automobiles was one of the major factors (though not the only one) behind the emergence of Honda Accord as the best selling car in the United States during the late 1980s. However, the obviousness of reliability as a key success factor made weaker competitors push hard in terms of improving their own performance. As the reliability gap between Honda and its competitors has diminished to a marginal level, reliability has become more and more like a commodity attribute. Customers can now assume that several, if not all, competitors are highly reliable. This achievement of competitive parity has shifted the battle to other variables such as styling. Because Honda's styling is viewed by its target customers as "dated," it has suffered a loss in market share even though the reliability of its cars has apparently remained superb. In other words, in any industry, the list of key success factors will invariably change over time, if for no other reason than the achievement of competitive parity along the key success factors of yesterday.

Box 3–4 illustrates Sunds Defibrator Group's intended bases of competitive advantage—the dimensions along which it aims to become or remain superior to its competitors. Consistent with the guidelines suggested in this section, the company has stated its intended bases for competitive advantage in relative rather than absolute terms, as is evident in the use of phrases such as "the *best* economic alternative" and "the *most* optimized modern processes and machinery." The company's aim and commitment are to be better than competitors.

The company is also seeking multiple dimensions of advantage. It recognizes that no one base of advantage, by itself, is likely to be sufficient to attract, win, and retain customers.[9] Thus, it is committed to generating multiple reasons for its customers to do business with it rather than with its competitors.

Sunds Defibrator Group is attempting to define its intended bases for competitive advantage from the perspective of the customer because what customers value is what counts. Indeed, the firm appears to be quite specific in delineating its interpretation of customer needs. Such specificity is valuable in at least two respects: (1) it provides clearer guidance to decision making and action and (2) it makes it easier for people in the company to test their interpretation of the customers' needs against how customers are actually behaving in the marketplace.

Once a business unit has defined the type of competitive advantage that it intends to establish, it faces the challenge of actually creating the intended advantage, a process that has two parts:

1. *Designing the value constellation:* What will the business unit do itself and what will it obtain from business partners?[10]

Box 3–4

**Sunds Defibrator Group:
Intended Bases for Competitive Advantage**

Our business concept is to satisfy customer needs by offering the customer (1) the *best* economic alternative in terms of technology, quality, and service, based on (2) the *most* optimized modern processes and machinery.

Our customers need competitive power. An important part of this power is derived from the process technology and the mechanical equipment selected:

Superior productivity. Our customers seek superior productivity and equipment reliability. They will be constantly on the lookout for the means to improve their manufacturing technology in order to achieve the lowest cost per unit produced.

Economical production. Economical production that is achieved through low raw material consumption, low energy and chemical consumption and through high-quality products and long machinery service life is of the greatest importance for the total profitability of our customers.

Environmentally harmonized processes. To an ever increasing extent, the market and society as a whole will demand fiber products that have been produced with technical methods having a minimum or even zero impact on the environment.

Continuous, long-term, round-the-clock service. To achieve the highest possible utilization of the huge investments associated with the process industry, maintenance and service will continue to grow in importance.

Low total investment costs. Low total investment costs, including well-executed projects, are highly important in achieving cost-effectiveness and competitiveness.

Source: Abstracted by the author from "Strategy for the Sunds Defibrator Group: 1992," an open document published by the Sunds Defibrator Group, Sundsvall, Sweden. See Box 3–2 regarding application of the term "business unit" to this entity.

---

2. *Managing the value chain:* What is required for the actual execution of those activities that the business unit has chosen to do itself? How will they be integrated with the activities of business partners and customers?

These are the topics of the chapter's two remaining sections.

DESIGNING THE VALUE CONSTELLATION

Allowing for some exceptions, the guiding principle underlying the design of a value constellation should be that the business unit itself should not do any activity that other firms can do more effectively and efficiently. Suppose a company is competing in the market for personal computer notebooks and, compared to other firms, this company is relatively weak in flat panel display technologies. For this business, designing the value constellation would refer to the company's decision either to design and manufacture the displays itself or to subcontract this activity. The subcontractors selected would, in effect, become this company's "business partners." If the company decides to make its own flat panel displays, then it controls a larger set of activities internally but risks downgrading the quality and performance of its overall product. The alternative, buy from suppliers, adds to the company's competitive advantage in the eyes of the customer but increases the company's dependence on external partners. In other words, designing the value constellation requires the company to make trade-offs between the size of the total payoffs and the company's share of the total payoffs.

There are no universal guidelines regarding how broadly or how narrowly a company should rely on partners. The optimal solution depends primarily on the specifics of the particular situation and the results of a comparison of the capabilities of the business unit and those of potential business partners. As an example, suppose that, for the PC notebook manufacturer discussed above, the core capabilities needed to dominate the flat panel display market are product technology (design) and process technology (manufacture). If the company is weak in both product and process technologies, then the optimum design of the value constellation might be the purchase of such displays from the best external supplier. However, what if the company is a leader in product technology but weak in process technology? The company may then be better off if it keeps the design activity in-house and gives a product design license to an external subcontractor who will produce the displays exclusively for this company. Alternatively, what if the company is weak in product design but a leader in process technology? In such a scenario, the best course of action may be to seek a product design license from an external partner but retain the actual manufacture of the displays inside the business unit.

As this example illustrates, designing the value constellation requires an extremely sophisticated understanding of the company's dominant skills as well as its relative weaknesses. Without such detailed understanding, there is grave risk of unduly "hollowing the corporation" in the process of relying on external business partners. The following examples show how innovative companies have attempted to build a stronger value constellation through judicious reliance on business partners:

- Host, a division of Marriott Corporation, operates cafeterias at airports and highway plazas. Instead of relying solely on its own recipes and brand name, Host has chosen to develop strategic alliances with national brand-name leaders in selected fast-food segments. For example, Host operates Pizza Hut kiosks inside its own restaurants and has found that pizza sales under this partnership arrangement are significantly higher than when it operates with its own recipe and brand name.

- During the late 1970s, Marriott Corporation concluded that, in the lodging business, its dominating competencies were in hospitality management (its ability at managing people and operations) rather than in real estate management. Yet, the bulk of the company's asset investment was in real estate. This discovery led to a fundamental shift in the company's approach to the allocation of its resources. As one element of its strategy, the company began to sell the real estate to investor syndicates while retaining a long-term (typically, 75-year) contract for the management of the hotels. As the other element of its strategy, the company began an aggressive program of reinvesting the capital generated by the real estate sales for the development of new hotel properties. These, in turn, after appropriate development, were also to be sold to external investors, with Marriott retaining long-term management contracts. From 1975 to 1985, the pursuit of this strategy not only boosted Marriott's return on capital dramatically, but catapulted Marriott from a relative newcomer in the lodging business to the market-share leader in full-service lodging in the United States.

As the reader may have guessed, reliance on other companies to perform essential activities at which they are superior may strengthen the overall bundle of products, services, and prices being offered to the customer, but it is not entirely risk-free.

At least three types of risk are associated with relying on external partners: (1) nonperformance, (2) profit skimming, and (3) elimination.

The Risk of Nonperformance

The partner selected may fail to live up to its obligations either because of a competitive decline in its capabilities or because its priorities no longer include serving the focal business unit. A business unit can guard against this risk in a number of ways:

- Develop alternative suppliers so that there are always multiple options and no one supplier becomes too powerful.
- Maintain a credible threat of eliminating dependence on the supplier by performing at least a portion of the activity in-house through "partial integration."
- Become a part-owner in the supplier by buying an equity stake; the business unit will then be able to monitor and shape the supplier's policies regularly and directly.

The Risk of Profit Skimming

The partners selected may skim most of the profits generated by the value constellation and leave the focal business unit only marginally profitable. From all accounts, it seems that IBM's PC business unit eventually fell into this trap when it decided to rely on Microsoft Corporation to provide the operating system and on Intel Corporation to provide the microprocessor. IBM's PC unit left for itself the task of designing, assembling, and marketing the personal computer. To the extent that IBM did not have a superior operating system and a microprocessor of its own, its decision to rely on Microsoft and Intel was brilliant in terms of creating a stronger value constellation. However, unfortunately for IBM, over time, the operating system and the microprocessor have become more complex and higher value-adding activities over which Microsoft and Intel have an almost monopolistic control. In contrast, the emergence of "clone" manufacturers has made the tasks of designing, assembling, and marketing the PCs almost routine. The net result appears to have been that the value constellation is now controlled more and more by Microsoft and Intel rather than by IBM, enabling these two suppliers to skim the bulk of the profits from the PC business.

To guard against the risk of profit skimming by its partners in a value constellation, a business unit can:

- Retain some critical nonsubstitutable activities.
- Keep upgrading its competencies in these critical activities so that its dominant superiority prevents a decline in partners' dependence on the business unit.
- Acquire an equity stake in the business partners early in the game, before they become too powerful.

In the IBM PC example, it seems that the company suffered on all three counts. Its own activities (design, assembly, and marketing) became less critical and more easily substitutable over time. Microsoft and Intel kept upgrading their own dominance of the activities initially "assigned" to them by IBM. Finally, IBM made the judgmental error of forgoing the option of acquiring and retaining an equity stake in both Microsoft and Intel.

The Risk of Elimination

Business partners might take over the value constellation completely and squeeze out the focal business unit altogether. This risk is basically an extreme version of the risk of profit skimming. The basic safeguards against both risks are the same. The business unit should select and manage its own internal value-chain activities in such a manner that these activities remain critical, superior, nonsubstitutable, and inimitable; alternatively, the focal business unit should attempt to acquire an equity stake in its business partners early in the game.

Box 3–5 summarizes some key features of Sunds Defibrator Group's design of its value constellation. It is important to note that the firm has positioned itself first and foremost as a developer and supplier of process technologies rather than as a manufacturer of machines. This decision yields the company at least two benefits: (1) it keeps investment in fixed assets low, a major advantage in

---

Box 3–5

Sunds Defibrator Group: Designing the Value Constellation

As clarified earlier, Sunds Defibrator Group has defined its business as supplying complete fiber-processing lines and associated machines, parts, and services in three broad areas: chemical pulping systems, mechanical pulping systems, and panelboard systems. In terms of its approach to the market, the company sees itself first and foremost as a developer and supplier of process technologies and systems rather than as a manufacturer of machines. Thus, Sunds Defibrator Group has chosen to concentrate most of its own resources on technology development, project selling, project execution, and customer service and to rely heavily on contract manufacturers for the actual production of the machines. Sunds Defibrator Group does have an internal "Process Machinery Manufacturing" unit. However, this unit manufactures certain key machines only and accounts for only about 20–25 percent of the total value-added. Similar to its approach to manufacturing, Sunds Defibrator Group also relies heavily on external contractors to do on-site plant erection work and has stayed away from these largely civil engineering-oriented activities.

Even in the area of technology development, Sunds Defibrator Group relies selectively on external partners where the partners are global leaders in the particular technology and do not pose an overall competitive challenge to Sunds Defibrator Group. Examples of such technology partnerships are: (1) an alliance with the American company, Union Camp, for the commercialization of the latter's chlorine-free bleaching technology, (2) alliances with two German companies, Kusters and Dieffenbacher, for the use of their continuous presses in Sunds Defibrator Group's panelboard lines, and (3) an exclusive relationship with the Swedish company, ABB Flakt, for the incorporation of the latter's drying and forming machines in Sunds Defibrator Group's panelboard production lines.

Notwithstanding these alliances with external business partners, it appears that Sunds Defibrator Group continuously assesses its value constellation to decide whether some previously internalized activities should be externalized or vice versa.

Source: Derived by the author from "Strategy for the Sunds Defibrator Group: 1992," an open document published by the Sunds Defibrator Group, Sundsvall, Sweden. See Box 3–2 regarding application of the term "business unit" to this entity.

---

a highly cyclical business and (2) it allows the company to build a very focused, technology-driven culture.

However, the company's value constellation design also makes it more dependent on external subcontracted manufacturers. Managing these partner relationships is critical to the success of its marketplace strategy. It would seem that as long as Sunds Defibrator Group is successful in maintaining its technological leadership, its strategy should be both viable and defensible.

MANAGING THE VALUE CHAIN

As discussed in the previous section, after having made a judicious decision regarding which activities to "internalize" (to do itself) and which activities to "externalize" (to source from business partners), the business unit must manage the internalized activities in a manner such that:

- The total bundle of products, services, and prices being offered to the customer remains competitively superior relative to other options.
- The business partners are not able to engage in either profit skimming or elimination.

Following the framework of Michael Porter,[11] we refer to the management of the internalized activities as the management of the business unit's value chain. For effective management of the value chain, excellent execution is required in the following three key elements:

1. Managing individual activities.
2. Managing internal integration across activities.
3. Managing external integration of the value chain with the value chains of suppliers, customers, and other business partners.

Managing Individual Activities

Every business is a collection of activities. For example, a partial list of activities that make up IBM's PC business might be:

- Hiring, training, developing, and retaining people.
- Marketing research.
- Product design.
- Sourcing of raw materials and externally produced components.
- Manufacture of internally produced components.
- Assembly of PCs.
- Marketing and sales of PCs.
- Physical distribution of PCs.
- Management of working capital.
- Management of capital structure.

Three types of outcomes are associated with how every one of these activities is managed: the impact on customer value, the impact on cost structure, and the impact on asset investment.

To study how this works, we can consider product design. The quality of product design makes a difference in how well the PC meets the target customers' expectations and consequently increases or decreases the value perceived by the customers. Similarly, product design affects at least two elements of the cost structure of the PC business: (1) direct costs associated with the design activity (such as salaries of designers, costs of the design center) and (2) impact of product design on manufacturing costs. (Note that assembly costs are generally a function of the number of distinct parts.) How product design is managed also would affect the asset investment in the PC business in at least two significant ways: (1) the asset investment in the design activity itself and (2) the impact of product design on the size of required manufacturing assets.

In managing any value-chain activity, the main goals should be:

- Maximization of resulting customer value.
- Minimization of resulting cost structure.
- Minimization of required asset investment.

The achievement of these goals requires, primarily, a good analysis of the "drivers" of customer value, cost structure, and asset investment associated with the particular activity. For example:

- In managing the product design activity for IBM PCs, decisions need to be made along a number of variables. Where should the design center be located? How many designers should the design center have? What should be the qualifications of the designers? Should the design team consist of only designers or include people from marketing, production, and purchasing? Should product and process design take place serially or in parallel? Each of these variables is in essence a "driver" of how the product design activity impacts on customer value, cost structure, and asset investment. It follows also that managing the product design activity for excellence is, in fact, the same as managing these drivers in competitively superior ways.
- Procter & Gamble's (P&G's) disposable diaper business also presents an interesting example. Suppose we want to understand the drivers of the cost structure in this business. The analysis would begin by first identifying the exact breakdown of the cost structure into its principal components (see Table 3–2). The next step would be to take each of these cost components and determine why the cost is what it is: What keeps it from being higher and how could it be lowered? For example, analysis of why fluff pulp costs $.006 per diaper might lead P&G to identify four main cost drivers of fluff pulp:

1. Product design determines the quantity and quality of fluff pulp needed per diaper.
2. Economies of scale exist in the purchasing of fluff pulp.
3. The timing of purchase decisions affects the market price for fluff pulp paid by P&G.
4. The choice of production technology and learning curve effects jointly determine the yield rate, that is, the percentage of diapers that

TABLE 3–2   Estimated diaper unit cost.

	Dollars per Unit	Percent of Total
Manufacturer sale price	$.040	100.0%
Raw materials		
Fluff pulp	$.006	15.0%
Cover sheet	.005	12.5
Backing sheet	.001	2.5
Packaging	.003	7.5
Manufacturing labor	.003	7.5
Depreciation and maintenance	.001	2.5
Utilities	.001	2.5
Freight	.004	10.0
Selling, general, and administrative expense	.006	15.0
Pretax profit	.010	25.0

Source: "The Disposable Diaper Industry in 1974," Harvard Business School, Cambridge, MA, Case 380-175, p. 7.

are defective and have to be destroyed before final packaging and shipment.

- We could similarly identify the drivers of the cost for each of the other items. Only by managing each of these drivers in competitively superior ways can the diaper business hope to achieve a competitively lower cost.

It might be obvious that, in managing the various drivers of customer value, cost structure, and asset investment, numerous trade-off decisions need to be made. For example, although decreasing the amount of fluff pulp per diaper may reduce the cost structure, it may also make the diaper less absorbent, thereby reducing the value delivered to the customer. Fundamental decisions regarding the business unit's intended bases for competitive advantage should generally serve as the guiding principles for how these trade-off decisions are made.

Managing Internal Integration across Activities

By integration across activities, we mean integration across product design, process design, manufacturing operations, marketing and sales, customer service, distribution, and so forth. The following hypothetical example illustrates how internal integration can affect the total strength of a business unit's value chain. Assume that AIRCON and COOLAIR are the two leading manufacturers of air conditioners. Both companies are absolutely and equally dedicated to customer satisfaction and to the notion that "the customer is king." In the first year of introducing a completely new model, one percent of the customers of each company call in to the service center with some complaints regarding the product. Given the companies' commitment to customer satisfaction, the two customer service centers act courteously and promptly to resolve the customers' problems. At AIRCON, data regarding customer complaints are communicated routinely to the product design, manufacturing, and shipping departments. In sharp contrast, at COOLAIR, such internal integration does not exist and nothing is done beyond satisfying the customer and writing off the cost of the service center as a necessary expense. The likely outcome will be that, over time, AIRCON will become more knowledgeable about the factors that cause customer problems and will take actions to prevent these problems at the source. Consequently, over time, AIRCON is likely to gain a competitive edge over COOLAIR on both counts: delivered quality and the cost of delivering quality.

There are at least three important ways in which internal integration can strengthen any company's value chain:

1. Improving the quality of delivered products and services and lowering the costs of this activity, as illustrated in the AIRCON/COOLAIR example.
2. Slashing the delivery cycle time, from customer order to customer delivery or from raw material input to customer delivery.
3. Reducing the development cycle time, from product conceptualization to product commercialization.

All three types of benefits can be very important. The advantages of higher quality and lower costs are obvious. Shorter delivery cycle times have a significant enabling effect on the lowering of inventory costs, on the customization of products, and on responsiveness to shifts in customer preferences. Finally, development cycle times generally lead to an increase in the rate of new product development and, at the same time, a reduction in the risk of market failure because of shorter time lags between the collection of initial market data and the launching of the new product.

Managing External Integration of the Value Chain

External integration refers to the integration of the company's value chain with the value chains of suppliers, other business partners, and customers. As with internal integration, tighter external integration has the potential to increase delivered value while simultaneously reducing costs. For example:

• Companies such as Motorola and National Semiconductor make semiconductor chips and boards for a variety of industrial markets worldwide. Suppose that one of such a company's business units is charged with the mission to develop a market for the company's products in the automotive industry. One such product might be integrated circuit boards for antilock braking systems (ABS). In this case, several important benefits might result from tight communication between the brake system design team of the auto manufacturer and the ABS electronics design team of the semiconductor company: a shorter design cycle, more customization, and lower costs. If the semiconductor manufacturer is located in the United States and the auto manufacturer is in Germany, for the needed external integration of the value chains to occur, it may well be necessary for the semiconductor manufacturer to establish an ABS design center in close physical proximity to the auto manufacturer's design center in Germany.

• Electronic data interchange (EDI) is rapidly becoming an important means of integration between the buying departments of customers and the sales/distribution departments of sellers in a wide spectrum of industries rang-

---

Box 3–6

Sunds Defibrator Group: Managing the Value Chain

The following are illustrative examples of how Sunds Defibrator Group manages some of its critical value chain activities:

Focused product offering. In each key product area, Sunds Defibrator Group has decided to focus on only one product offering for the entire global market. As the company states, "We believe it is crucial that we clearly focus our product, marketing and sales efforts in order to maximize the impact of our message and not confuse our customers with many different options and alternatives."

Technology development. For virtually all of its product lines, technology development is globally centralized in Sweden or Finland. Because technology development is a fixed cost and any relevant technology is applicable throughout the world, global centralization allows Sunds Defibrator Group to capture the economies of critical mass and scale. Further, the Scandinavian location has been historically very useful in that it is physically proximate to some of the company's largest and most demanding customers.

Project selling and project execution. Selling a new fiber line to a pulp and paper company or a panelboard manufacturer requires first convincing the customer that Sunds Defibrator Group's underlying process technology is superior to competitive options. Thus, project selling is managed by coupling mixed teams of technology experts from Sweden or Finland with local nationals from Sunds Defibrator Group's subsidiary in the country where the customer is located. The same basic approach is utilized for the management of project execution activities.

Customer service. Customer service has to be provided locally on-site wherever the customers' plants are located. Thus, unlike technology development, Sunds Defibrator Group's basic approach to customer service has been to create a decentralized network of local customer service units.

Source: Derived by the author from "Strategy for the Sunds Defibrator Group: 1992," an open document published by the Sunds Defibrator Group, Sundsvall, Sweden. See Box 3–2 regarding application of the term "business unit" to this entity.

ing from consumer goods to pharmaceuticals and plumbing supplies. Such tight integration leads simultaneously to faster deliveries and smaller inventories, which increase customer value and reduce costs.

As illustrated in these two examples, more effective communication is a fundamental requirement for tighter integration of a company's value chain with the value chains of its business partners. Tighter communication can be achieved in a variety of ways: electronic links (like EDI), face-to-face interaction, and physical proximity, to name a few.

Box 3–6 illustrates how Sunds Defibrator Group manages some of the critical activities in its value chain. Details such as how geographically concentrated or dispersed the particular activity should be vary from one activity to another. This is what we would expect in a well-managed company because the drivers of value, cost, and asset investment will generally vary across different value-chain activities.

SUMMARY

This chapter has outlined the main tasks involved in the effective strategic management of a business unit—that is, a division or other type of profit center within a multibusiness company as well as a single-business company operating independently. Business-unit strategy deals primarily with the question of how the business unit should compete within its broadly defined industry.

The five key elements to managing strategy at the business-unit level are:

1. Defining the scope of the business unit.
2. Setting business-unit goals.
3. Defining the intended bases for competitive advantage.
4. Designing the value constellation.
5. Managing the business unit's internal value chain as well as its integration with the value chains of partners and customers.

NOTES

1. As discussed in the previous chapter, strategic management at the level of a multibusiness corporation falls within the realm of what is generally termed "corporate strategy."

2. See Derek F. Abell, *Defining the Business: The Starting Point of Strategic Planning* (Englewood Cliffs, NJ: Prentice-Hall, 1980), for an extensive discussion of how business scope should be defined.

3. The notion of core competencies is the focus of Chapter 9. See also C. K. Prahalad and Gary Hamel, "The Core Competence of the Corporation," *Harvard Business Review* (May–June 1990), 79–91.

4.   For further discussion of the role of financial considerations in evaluating strategy alternatives, see Chapter 10.

5.   Robert S. Kaplan and David P. Norton, "The Balanced Scorecard: Measures that Drive Performance," *Harvard Business Review* (January–February 1992), 71–79.

6.   The importance of goals that challenge the organization to aspire to achievements that go beyond its resources is discussed in more detail in Chapter 9.

7.   This statement is consistent with a dominant theme in Chapter 1: The intent of posture is to differentiate the organization and its product offerings from current and potential competitors as perceived and understood by customers.

8.   It is important to note here the distinction between customer-based advantage—that is, differentiation as discussed in this chapter—and the capabilities and competencies that give rise to differentiation or value for customers. The latter are discussed in detail in Chapters 8 and 9.

9.   This point was emphasized at length in Chapter 1.

10.   Many of the reasons for working with partners and the issues involved in coordinating with partners are discussed in Chapter 8.

11.   See the next chapter by Michael E. Porter for further discussion of the value chain. For a more detailed discussion of the value chain, see Michael E. Porter, *Competitive Advantage* (New York: The Free Press, 1985).

GLOBAL STRATEGY: WINNING IN THE WORLD-WIDE MARKETPLACE*

4

Michael E. Porter

Harvard Business School

One of the seminal forces affecting companies since World War II has been the globalization of competition. Transport and communication costs have fallen, national infrastructures have become more similar, and trade barriers have eased. As a result, international trade and investment have grown markedly. The need for global, as opposed to domestic, strategies has become a given in a wide and ever-widening range of industries.

As the globalization of competition has become more apparent, it is no surprise that research on international strategy has taken on greater prominence. This research, by and large, has concentrated on the power of the multinational company to create competitive advantage through its globalness. A global strategy, involving operations spread among many countries, has been seen as a powerful engine for reaping economies of scale, assimilating and responding to international market needs, and efficiently assembling resources such as capital, labor, raw materials, and technology from around the world. Authors as diverse as Ohmae (1990), Reich (1991b), and Bartlett and Ghoshal (1989) see the global firm as transcending national boundaries. The national identity of a corporation must be replaced, in this view, by a strategic paradigm that knows no borders.

* This chapter draws on research by Rebecca Wayland, MBA 1991 and Hernan Cristerna, MBA 1993, and has also benefited from joint work with Michael Enright and with Örjan Sölvell and Ivo Zander (Stockholm School of Economics). I am also grateful for helpful comments by David Collis, Hans Thorelli, participants in the Integral Strategy Collegium at Indiana University, and participants in the International Business Group seminar at Harvard Business School.

When considering the globalization of competition, however, one must confront an important paradox: Although companies are competing globally, and inputs such as raw materials, capital, and scientific knowledge now move freely around the world, there is strong evidence that location continues to play a crucial role in competitive advantage. There are striking and persistent differences in the economic performance of nations and of states and cities within nations.[1] The world's leading competitors in a wide variety of industries are all based in one or two countries, especially if (1) industries are defined narrowly in ways that are meaningful for setting strategy and (2) cases where government heavily distorts competition are eliminated. This geographic concentration is true not only in established industries such as automobiles and machine tools but also in new industries such as software, biotechnology, and advanced materials. Within companies, global firms have indeed dispersed activities to many countries, but they concentrate in one location a critical mass of their most important activities for competing in each business.

This chapter aims to provide a framework for understanding the nature of international competition and for developing a global strategy. Global strategy combines the role of location with the role of the entire global network of activities as a system in creating competitive advantage. The chapter concludes by examining how to translate this general framework into a new conception of global strategy.

A GENERAL FRAMEWORK FOR GLOBAL STRATEGY

Any effort to create a global strategy must originate from an understanding of the nature of international competition. There is not one single pattern of international competition; there are many. The nature of international competition in industries can be arrayed along a spectrum. On one end are *multidomestic industries,* where the industry is present in many countries but competition takes place on a country-by-country basis with little or no linkage among them. Examples include most types of retailing, metal fabrication, construction, and many services. On the other end of the spectrum are *global industries,* in which competition in different countries is connected because a firm's position in one country is affected by its position elsewhere. Prominent examples are commercial aircraft, consumer electronics, and automobiles. In multidomestic industries, the "global" strategy should be a series of distinct domestic strategies. In global industries, however, firms must create integrated strategies involving all countries simultaneously. Most issues in strategy are the same for domestic and global companies; for both types, performance is a function of the attractiveness of the industry in which the firm competes and its relative position in that industry.[2] The firm's competitive position depends on its competitive advantages (or disadvantages) vis-à-vis its rivals. Competitive advantage is manifested either in lower costs than rivals', or in the ability to differentiate and command a premium price that exceeds the extra cost of differentiating.

Competitive advantage cannot be examined independently of competitive scope or the breadth of the firm's market target. Scope encompasses a number of dimensions, including the product and buyer segments served, the degree of vertical integration, and the extent of related businesses in which the firm has a coordinated strategy. The array of geographic locations at which the firm competes is another dimension of scope and is the one I concentrate on here. Because competitive advantage is attained within some scope, the choice of scope is a central one in strategy. Both domestic and global companies must understand the structure of their industry, identify their sources of competitive advantage, and analyze competitors.

To understand the underpinnings of competitive advantage, we must decompose what firms do into the *value chain* (see Figure 4–1).[3] A firm is a collection of discrete but interrelated economic *activities*—products are assembled, salespeople make sales visits, and orders are processed. These activities involve human resources, physical assets, technologies, routines, and information. "Strengths," "competence," "capabilities," and "resources,"—common phrases in discussions of strategy—are best understood in terms of particular activities in which the firm has advantages, be they skills, physical assets or technologies, or the ability to link the activity with others or improve the activity over time.

A firm's strategy defines its configuration of activities and how they interrelate. Activities are the basic foundation of competitive advantage. Competitive advantage results when, compared to its rivals, a firm has the ability (1) to perform the required activities at a collectively lower cost or (2) to perform some activities in unique ways that create non-price buyer value and support a premium price. Creating buyer value depends, in turn, on how a firm influences the activities of its channels and end-users. Buyer value arises when a firm's activities (including the product itself) lower buyers' cost or raise buyers' performance relative to competitors' activities. The required mix and configuration of activities, in turn, is altered by competitive scope. Broadly targeted competitors seek to gain advantages by sharing activities across an array of industry segments. Narrowly targeted competitors (which I term *focusers*) seek advantage through tailoring activities to the needs of one (or a few) particular segment(s).

The value chain groups a firm's activities into categories, distinguishing between those directly involved in producing, marketing, delivering, and supporting the product and those that create or source inputs required to do so. Discrete activities are much narrower; they include such economic processes as field repair, inbound materials receiving and storage, and billing. The identity of individual discrete activities depends on the particular business. The ability to gain advantages in either cost or differentiation in activities depends on underlying activity economics.

The concept of the value chain provides a way to highlight the strategy issues that are unique to global industries. Both domestic and global firms have value chains, but the global firm has special latitude along two dimensions:

FIGURE 4–1 The value chain.

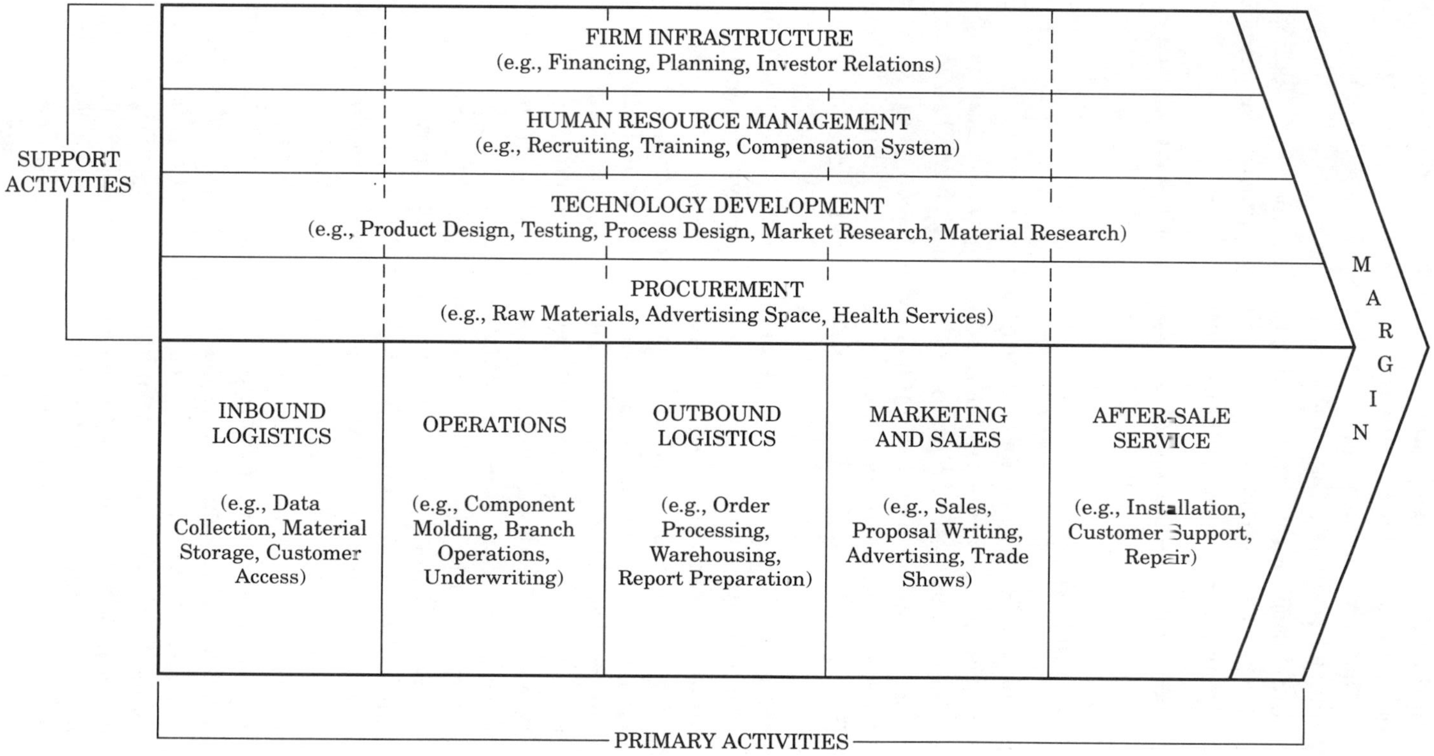

		INBOUND LOGISTICS	OPERATIONS	OUTBOUND LOGISTICS	MARKETING AND SALES	AFTER-SALE SERVICE

FIRM INFRASTRUCTURE
(e.g., Financing, Planning, Investor Relations)

HUMAN RESOURCE MANAGEMENT
(e.g., Recruiting, Training, Compensation System)

TECHNOLOGY DEVELOPMENT
(e.g., Product Design, Testing, Process Design, Market Research, Material Research)

PROCUREMENT
(e.g., Raw Materials, Advertising Space, Health Services)

SUPPORT ACTIVITIES

MARGIN

INBOUND LOGISTICS
(e.g., Data Collection, Material Storage, Customer Access)

OPERATIONS
(e.g., Component Molding, Branch Operations, Underwriting)

OUTBOUND LOGISTICS
(e.g., Order Processing, Warehousing, Report Preparation)

MARKETING AND SALES
(e.g., Sales, Proposal Writing, Advertising, Trade Shows)

AFTER-SALE SERVICE
(e.g., Installation, Customer Support, Repair)

PRIMARY ACTIVITIES

111

1. Configuration, or where the activities in a firm's value chain are located. In a domestic company, all activities are located in a single country. In a global company, however, firms can choose where to locate each activity to enhance competitive advantage. Assembly can be in one country, and product R&D in another.
2. Coordination, or the nature and extent to which the conduct of dispersed activities is coordinated versus allowing activities the autonomy to tailor their approach to local circumstances.

A firm's choice in these two areas gives rise to the unique competitive advantages from competing globally rather than domestically.

Configuration

The international configuration of a firm's activities creates competitive advantage in two ways: (1) choosing where to locate each activity and (2) deciding how many locations should be performing one activity. When choosing where to locate, the firm will know that some activities, such as sales and distribution, are necessarily tied to the customer. A firm seeking to sell in a country must either establish its own activities or rely on others (e.g., distributors, joint venture partners). Other activities, however, can be uncoupled from the customer, giving the global firm greater discretion in the number and location of its activities. For example, the global firm can locate an activity in whatever country has a comparative advantage in that activity, such as low-cost labor or a favorable supply of raw materials. Some multinational software firms have located software debugging and program maintenance activities in India to access low-cost programmers. Because the location that has comparative advantage varies by activity, the global firm has the potential to gain competitive advantage by arbitraging comparative advantages across locations. Other reasons for locating in a particular nation (or state) will be examined later.

In addition to deciding where to locate, a global firm can choose how many locations should be used to perform an activity. The firm might concentrate an activity in one location to serve the world, or disperse the activity to several or many locations. By concentrating an activity, firms may gain economies of scale or may progress rapidly down the learning curve. Concentrating a group of activities in one location may also allow a firm to better coordinate across them.

Dispersing activities, in contrast, may be justified by the need to minimize transportation and storage costs, hedge against the risks of a single activity site, tailor the activity to local market needs, facilitate learning about country and market conditions that can be transmitted to headquarters, and respond to local government pressure or incentives to locate in a country in order to sell or produce there. Sometimes, firms disperse one activity to a country in order to gain the ability (or permission from government) to concentrate others. Establishing local assembly plants in a variety of countries, for example, may allow a company to import scale-sensitive components into each country in which it has an assembly operation and hence concentrate its production of them. The global firm should disperse those activities that involve the *least* sacrifice in terms of economies of scale and learning and the least need for close coordination with other activities.

Coordination

The way in which a firm coordinates its activities around the world determines its ability to benefit from a particular configuration. By coordinating methods, technology, and output decisions across dispersed activities, global corporations can achieve a number of potential competitive advantages. These include the ability to respond to shifting comparative advantage (e.g., raw materials prices, exchange rates); to share learning among countries; to reinforce the corporate brand image for mobile buyers who encounter the firm in different places (e.g., for McDonald's or Coca-Cola); to differentiate with multinational buyers who simultaneously deal with several of the firm's units; to gain bargaining advantages with governments through possessing the ability to expand or contract local operations; to respond more effectively to competitors by choosing the location at which to do battle. Conversely, allowing each dispersed site to act autonomously and tailor its activities to local circumstances may be the source of competitive advantage in other situations. Where local needs and conditions vary and where there are few economies of scale and only local customers, a strategy involving high levels of autonomy for dispersed units is favored.

Coordination encompasses the setting of standards, the exchange of information, and the allocation of responsibility among sites. Coordination that involves allocating responsibilities across countries, such as worldwide responsibility for producing particular models, can unleash economies of scale. Coordination involving information exchange is needed to reap the benefits of worldwide learning. Coordination, then, can allow a firm to realize the advantages of dispersing its activities, and a failure to coordinate activities can lessen those advantages.

Coordination across geographically dispersed locations involves daunting organization challenges, among them language, cultural differences, and difficulties in aligning individual managers' and subsidiaries' incentives with those of the global enterprise as a whole. Some forms of coordination, such as allocating responsibilities for component production to different locations, require less ongoing interchange than others. A central issue in coordination is how and where information, technology, and other knowledge from disparate locations is *integrated and reflected* in products, processes, and other activities.

Implications for Global Strategy

This framework allows us to understand and explain the patterns of global competition and to think systematically about crafting a global strategy for competing in a particular industry. Some competitive advantages are location-based; others relate to the overall global network and the way it is managed. There are many patterns of global competition, and they depend on the particular activities that are concentrated and dispersed, their locations, and how activities are coordinated. Competition in an industry globalizes when the competitive advantages of a global configuration and coordination across dispersed activities exceed the costs. The balance of these advantages and costs varies by activity and by industry.

In multidomestic industries, industry structure favors a highly dispersed configuration in which virtually the entire value chain is located in each country. There are strong benefits in such industries to allowing dispersed units nearly full strategic autonomy. In global industries, concentration of some activities to serve world markets and tight coordination among those activities that are dispersed yield significant competitive advantages. As industry economics, buyer needs, and government policies change over time, the pattern of globalization will also change.

Even in global industries, there is no one type of global strategy. Strategies will differ in terms of which activities are concentrated and dispersed, where activities are located, and the nature and extent of coordination achieved. They also differ in the extent to which companies perform activities or rely on partners. Firms have an active role in shifting the benefits and costs of a global strategy: They can redefine competition through strategic innovations that increase the advantages of a global strategy or reduce its costs. Becton Dickinson, for example, created worldwide demand for disposable syringes in favor of reusable glass syringes. By being the first mover, Becton Dickinson was able to emerge as the world leader. Other firms have triggered globalization by pioneering new approaches to competing that increased economies, or by inventing product designs or production processes that reduced the cost of tailoring products to differing country needs. Many global industry leaders emerged because they were the first to perceive and act on these levers. Theodore Levitt's 1983 work on the globalization of markets is typically seen as arguing the merits of world products. Yet his essay is more important than is commonly recognized for its stress on the ability of the firm to *create* world products by pioneering new approaches to segmentation and marketing rather than passively responding to preexisting needs.

A NEW PARADIGM OF INTERNATIONAL COMPETITION

The globalization of competition has allowed firms to gain competitive advantage, independent of location, through the way they configure and coordinate the value chain on a global basis. However, it has not eliminated the importance of location in competition. Global firms seem to have transcended boundaries, but evidence from the performance of economies, the location of international industry leaders, and the location of industries within nations does not support this view, nor does a close look at the global strategies of the three companies selected for case discussion in this chapter (see Box 4–1).

Box 4–1

Case Studies of Three Global Corporations:
(1) Novo-Nordisk Group (Denmark);
(2) Hewlett-Packard (U.S.); (3) Honda (Japan)

To bring life to the discussion of global strategy, we examined the international activities of three prototypical global corporations headquartered in Europe, Japan, and the United States, respectively. For each of these successful international leaders, we profiled their international operations and probed deeply into the international configuration and coordination of their activities.

Novo-Nordisk Group ("Novo"), headquartered in Denmark, is the world's leading exporter of insulin and industrial enzymes. Novo generates 96 percent of its revenues outside its home country and has strong positions in Europe, the United States, and Japan.[*] Twenty-seven percent of its employees are based outside Denmark and 19 percent of its total assets are located outside Europe. Novo has seven R&D locations and nine production sites outside Denmark. The company distributes its products in 100 countries, and has its own marketing subsidiaries in 43 countries. Novo sources animal pancreases, a key raw material for insulin, in more than 20 countries. It also sources its capital from around the world, funding 83 percent of its short-term debt and 54 percent of its long-term debt in currencies other than the Danish kroner. The company is listed on the London and New York stock exchanges.

Honda, headquartered in Japan, is one of the world's leading producers of automobiles and is the world leader in motorcycles.[**] Honda generates 61 percent of its revenues outside Japan and holds particularly strong market positions in Asia and North America.[†] Twenty-two percent of its employees and 39 percent of its total assets are based outside Japan. The company maintains production and assembly facilities in 39 countries and distributes its automobiles and motorcycles in 150 countries. Inputs and capital are sourced worldwide; the company is listed on the Tokyo and New York stock exchanges.

Hewlett-Packard (HP), headquartered in the United States, is the world's largest and most diversified manufacturer of electronic measurement and testing equipment as well as a leader in other products such as printers, medical instruments, and computers. HP generates 54 percent of its revenues outside the United States.[†] Thirty-eight percent of HP's 93,000 employees and 50 percent of its total assets are based outside the United States. HP operates 600 sales and support offices and distributorships in 110 countries. It is listed on the London, Paris, Tokyo, Frankfurt, Stuttgart, Switzerland, and Pacific stock exchanges.

Globalization has led each of these firms to spread their activities around the world. Hewlett-Packard's locational philosophy is instructive. HP locates low-skilled manufacturing activities with high direct labor content in low-cost areas, at an estimated savings of 40 to 75 percent compared to U.S. locations. For example, some component assembly and manufacturing for personal computers (PCs) is

[*] Information on Novo is based on Enright (1989) and field research.
[**] The profiles of Honda and Hewlett-Packard (see below) are based on Porter and Wayland (1994).
[†] Figures are taken from recent annual reports and other corporate filings.

conducted in Singapore, and electronic component manufacturing is conducted in Malaysia. Hewlett-Packard also locates some medium-skilled activities in lower-cost countries. For example, some product and process engineering activities (such as manufacturing cost reduction programs) are conducted at the PC manufacturing facilities in Singapore, process engineering for some new electronic component products has been transferred to the manufacturing plant in Malaysia, and some software coding and maintenance has been subcontracted to countries such as India, China, Eastern Europe, and the former Soviet Union, where college-educated programmers are available at 40 to 60 percent lower cost than in the United States.

The striking differences in economic performance of national, state, and local economies provide the first indication of the importance of location. The national origin of successful international competitors is the second. Patterns of international competitive success have been examined, initially in ten leading trading nations and subsequently in several others.[4] Across the hundreds of industries studied, including services and newly emerging fields such as software, advanced materials, and biotechnology, world leaders were typically headquartered in just a few and often in only one country. The three case studies in Box 4–1 fit this rule. Honda is not the only Japanese success story in the automotive and motorcycle industries—nine of the world's automobile companies and the four dominant global motorcycle companies are all based in Japan. Similarly, Hewlett-Packard is not the only successful U.S. firm in its industries—U.S. firms are preeminent in workstations, PCs, medical instruments, and test and instrumentation equipment. Novo is the world leader in insulin production—the 1989 merger between two Denmark-based companies (Novo and Nordisk Gentofte) only reinforced Novo's position as the dominant insulin exporter. Novo is also a leader in industrial enzymes, a field in which other Danish firms also compete.

Another manifestation of the importance of location is the geographic concentration of leading firms *within* nations. A particularly interesting example is the United States. Despite free trade among the states, a common language and laws, and great similarities along many dimensions, the location of successful competitors in particular businesses is far from evenly distributed. Publishing is heavily concentrated in New York City; movies and television production, in Hollywood; office furniture, in western Michigan; pharmaceuticals, in Philadelphia/New Jersey; hosiery and home furnishings, in North Carolina; artificial hips and joints, in Indiana—and there are countless other examples. Figure 4–2 illustrates some of the many U.S. industry concentrations in particular states, regions, or cities. A pattern of concentration can be found in every advanced nation.[5]

Finally, the importance of location to competitive advantage is manifested in the pattern of international activities of global companies, including those studied in Box 4–1. Accounts citing widespread geographic dispersion of

FIGURE 4-2 Selected regional clusters of competitive industries.

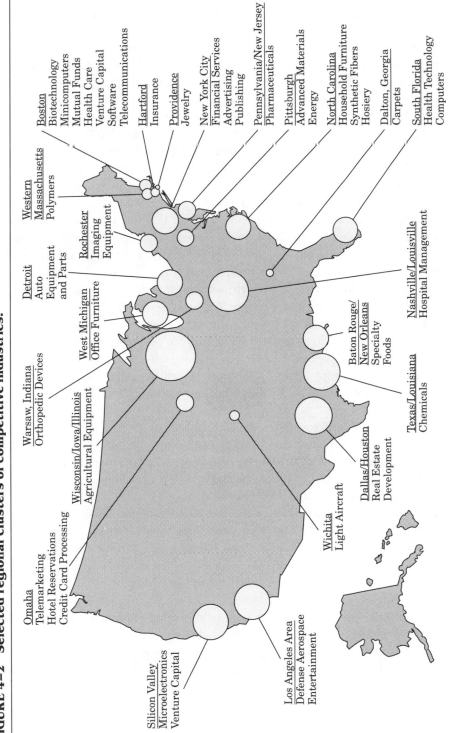

Omaha
Telemarketing
Hotel Reservations
Credit Card Processing

Silicon Valley
Microelectronics
Venture Capital

Los Angeles Area
Defense Aerospace
Entertainment

Wisconsin/Iowa/Illinois
Agricultural Equipment

Warsaw, Indiana
Orthopedic Devices

West Michigan
Office Furniture

Detroit
Auto
Equipment
and Parts

Rochester
Imaging
Equipment

Western
Massachusetts
Polymers

Wichita
Light Aircraft

Dallas/Houston
Real Estate
Development

Texas/Louisiana
Chemicals

Baton Rouge/
New Orleans
Specialty
Foods

Nashville/Louisville
Hospital Management

Boston
Biotechnology
Minicomputers
Mutual Funds
Health Care
Venture Capital
Software
Telecommunications

Hartford
Insurance

Providence
Jewelry

New York City
Financial Services
Advertising
Publishing

Pennsylvania/New Jersey
Pharmaceuticals

Pittsburgh
Advanced Materials
Energy

North Carolina
Household Furniture
Synthetic Fibers
Hosiery

Dalton, Georgia
Carpets

South Florida
Health Technology
Computers

117

activities are misleading, especially regarding company diversification. Foreign activities span many entirely different product areas, but the activities in a given business are far less dispersed. A more important distinction in assessing geographic dispersion is that between the *types* of activities located in different countries. International firms tend to concentrate their most sophisticated activities in their home country—or, if not there, in a single other country. Novo-Nordisk markets its insulin products around the world and sources some inputs globally, but it conducts its most strategically important activities in the value chain—all production and core product and process R&D—in Denmark. Honda has extensive worldwide manufacturing and distribution, but Japan remains the base for production of Honda's most sophisticated components, including all core engine research. Hewlett-Packard's operations encompass over 16,000 product lines sold around the world, yet worldwide responsibility (HP refers to this as "worldwide re") for each product line, including core manufacturing, R&D, and decision making, is concentrated in one particular location.

Additional evidence comes from Asea Brown Boveri (ABB), often cited as the prototype of a company with no national identity (see Cristerna, 1993). ABB has multiple operations located throughout the world, but global responsibility for establishing business strategy, selecting product development priorities, and allocating production for each product line among countries is based in a particular geographic location. Leadership for power transformers is based in Germany, for example; for electric drives, it is in Finland, and for process automation, in the United States. Moreover, multinationals seem to relocate headquarters of particular businesses from one nation to another with increasing frequency.

The apparent paradox between the globalization of competition and a strong national or even local role in competitive advantage can be resolved by taking a fresh look at the nature of international competition and the sources of competitive advantage in international markets. The paradigm that governs international competition has shifted. Formerly, competition was based on static efficiency, and the firm with the lowest factor costs (e.g., labor, raw materials, capital, infrastructure) or the greatest economies of scale won.

The changing nature of competition has overtaken this view. As many observers have noted, globalization allows firms to source inputs such as raw materials, capital, and even generic scientific knowledge in international markets, and to locate selective activities overseas to take advantage of low-cost labor or capital. Similarly, volume gained in the home market is far less important than the ability to penetrate world markets. Equally important in neutralizing the traditional role of location is technological change. Advancing technology has given firms the ability to eliminate, nullify, or circumvent weaknesses in local inputs. Japanese firms, for example, have prospered in many industries, despite the high cost of energy and space in Japan, through pioneering energy-saving technologies and space-saving innovations such as lean production. New technology is also diminishing economies of scale[6] and/or causing large firms to be rapidly neutralized by smaller but more innovative and dynamic rivals (witness the difficulties confronting General Motors, IBM, Philips, and many other large firms).

In a world of rapidly diffusing information and of generic technology that makes basic inputs widely available, globalness alone is not sufficient to sustain competitive advantage. The only way a firm can retain its competitive advantages is to continuously innovate and upgrade its advantages to more sophisticated levels. Innovation refers not only to physical technology but to ways of communicating, marketing, product positioning, providing service, and other forms of competing. The most dynamic and innovative companies can outpace their rivals, even those entrenched competitors enjoying low-cost factors or economies of scale. Competitive advantage results from the rate of dynamic improvement, not from static efficiencies. In the parlance of the earlier literature, the essential source of competitive advantage is not the inputs or scale the firm possesses today; it is the ability to rapidly create and recreate intangible assets that lead industry needs.

In this form of competition, the role of location changes profoundly. Firms operate globally to source inputs and access markets, but competitive advantage comes from a process of innovation that is heavily localized at the firm's "home base"—the location of its strategic management team, of the R&D to create the core product and process, and of a critical mass of the firm's sophisticated production (or service provision) or a particular product line.[7] The home base is where the essential skills and technology reside, where inputs and information sourced from global activities are integrated, and where the most productive jobs are located. The location of ownership, or of the overall corporate headquarters, is far less significant than the location of the home-based activities for each strategically distinct business.

Location-Based Foundations of Upgrading

The capacity to innovate draws fundamentally on the nature of the local environment in which the firm's home base resides. My research (Porter 1990) has highlighted four aspects of the national (or state) environment that take on particular significance: (1) factor conditions, (2) related and supporting industries, (3) demand conditions, and (4) the context for firm strategy, structure, and rivalry. These four attributes, which I collectively term *the diamond,* explain why certain companies based in particular regions are capable of consistent innovation in particular fields, and why they relentlessly upgrade (see Figure 4–3).

Factor Conditions

Factors of production are the basic inputs to competition; they include land, labor, capital, infrastructure, natural resources, and scientific knowledge. Globalization has made basic factors such as roads, bridges, or a college-educated work force easily duplicated and available around the world. General-purpose

FIGURE 4–3 Location-based determinants of competitive advantage: The diamond.

inputs such as an educated work force and a good basic infrastructure are necessary to avoid a disadvantage but no longer sufficient for gaining competitive advantage.

Advantages arise from highly specialized pools of skills, applied technology, infrastructure, and sources of capital that are tailored to the needs of particular industries. In the United States, for example, preeminence in software rests on unique pools of highly trained programmers and other computer science professionals, unparalleled research programs in computer-related disciplines, and well-developed and expert sources of risk capital for software firms (many American venture capital firms specialize in software). Hewlett-Packard benefits from some of these in its computer-related businesses. Nations and regions do not inherit the most important factors of production for sophisticated competition; they must create them. The presence of unique local educational, research, and other institutions that create specialized skills and technology is a potent source of competitive advantage.

More paradoxical is that selective *disadvantages* in basic factors, such as high wages or local raw material shortages, often lead to competitiveness because they trigger innovation. In Holland, for example, a poor climate has led to innovations in such areas as greenhouse cultivation methods, breeding technology, and handling techniques for cut flowers, a product for which the Dutch hold more than 60 percent of world exports. Conversely, the presence of abundant labor, cheap debt capital, and bountiful natural resources leads firms to use these resources less productively and become vulnerable to new global competitors.

Demand Conditions

National and international success grows out of having local customers who are or are among the most sophisticated and demanding buyers in the world for the region's products or services, or who have unusually intense needs for specialized varieties that are in demand elsewhere. Sophisticated, demanding buyers provide a window into advanced customer needs; they pressure companies to meet high standards and prod them to innovate and move into more advanced segments. Sophisticated home customers are particularly valuable if their needs anticipate or shape those of other nations, thereby providing "early-warning indicators" of global market trends. Local customers are far more likely to spur improvement and innovation than are distant customers, because of high visibility, short communication lines, and the opportunity for joint working relationships. Unusual local needs for specialized varieties are important for similar reasons; they cause firms to concentrate on improvement in segments that are ignored elsewhere. All three of the global leaders discussed in Box 4–1 benefited from sophisticated demand at home. Novo, for example, sold to perhaps the most sophisticated group of medical specialists in the treatment of diabetes in the world, and operated in the context of a national health care system that provided generous reimbursement for new treatments.

Related and Supporting Industries

Competitive advantage arises from the presence of a critical mass of competitive, home-based suppliers of the specialized components, machinery, and services that most drive progress in business. Local suppliers are important less for their access to inputs, which has been largely nullified by globalization, than for the advantages they provide in innovation. Suppliers and end-users located close to each other can take advantage of quick and constant flow of information, joint work on improvements, and mutual pressures to advance. Highly applied technology and specialized skills, are hard to codify, accumulate, and replicate. Companies have the opportunity to influence their suppliers' technical efforts and can serve as test sites for new developments, accelerating the pace of innovation. Honda benefited from such a supplier network in both producing its automobiles and motorcycles. General-purpose machinery, standard components, and raw materials are less important to innovation. They can (and must) be obtained globally from the most cost-effective sources.

Home-based competitors in related industries, or in industries that require similar skills, technologies, or customers, provide similar benefits: information flow, technical interchange, and opportunities for sharing that increase the rate of innovation and upgrading. Japanese dominance in electronic musical keyboards, for example, grew out of a success in acoustic instruments combined with a strong position in a wide array of consumer electronics industries.

Firm Strategy, Structure, and Rivalry

The circumstances and context within a nation or region influence how companies are created, how they are managed, and how they compete. Competitiveness grows out of whatever context encourages the types of strategies and organizational structures that foster innovation in a particular industry (e.g., large, disciplined, structured organizations in some industries and smaller, fluid, family-owned companies in others). Also important is a context of social norms, tax incentives, patent laws, and prestige that encourages sustained investment, by both individuals and companies, in the skills, knowledge, and physical assets needed in the particular business.

Among the most significant influences on innovation and dynamism is the presence of local rivalry. Honda, for example, faced competition from eight other Japanese auto companies, all of which compete internationally. Firms rarely succeed abroad unless they compete with some capable rivals at home. Rivalry among a group of locally based competitors heightens pressures to innovate and upgrade. Because local rivals have comparable access to the home market, comparable local inputs, and similar basic circumstances, these are nullified as sources of competitive advantage, and upgrading is encouraged and then reinforced by a rapid flow of information and by *relative* (versus absolute) performance comparisons that stimulate rapid improvement. The presence of local rivals works against comfortable dominance of the home market, and pressures vigorous efforts to compete nationally and internationally.[8] Novo, for example, was pushed to export because it had to compete in Denmark and the rest of the Scandinavian market with Nordisk; most other insulin producers were effectively national monopolies. Although individual companies have difficulty staying ahead for long, the entire local industry progresses more rapidly than competitors based elsewhere.[9]

The Diamond as a System

Together, the diamond's four location-based sources of competitive advantage constitute a dynamic system that is at least as important as any of its parts. How one part of the diamond affects innovation depends on the state of the other parts. For example, having selective disadvantages in factors (e.g., higher energy or raw materials costs) will not lead to innovation unless vigorous local competition pressures investment that will offset them and a technical and supplier foundation exists to overcome them. Conversely, vigorous local competition can degenerate into price cutting and harvesting, if local customers have unsophisticated needs or the local context discourages investment. Serious weakness in any part of the diamond will constrain an industry's potential for advancement.

The four determinants are also self-reinforcing. The role of local rivalry is illustrative. Vigorous domestic rivalry not only pushes companies to improve but also stimulates the development and renewal of unique pools of specialized skills and technology. Local institutions, such as universities and financial institutions, are encouraged by the presence of a number of rivals to adapt and support the industry's distinctive needs. Active local rivalry promotes the formation and upgrading of local supplier industries, as well as new, related industries.

The bonds that hold together the parts of the diamond are the strong relationships, and open information flow, between firms, local suppliers, and customers, between firms and educational and research institutions, between firms and infrastructure providers, between all these entities and government—all relationships weigh heavily in the rate of upgrading and innovation. Vertical collaboration, between customers and suppliers, is a *sine qua non* of competitiveness. Horizontally, between rivals, vigorous competition is a necessity although some forms of collaboration in infrastructure areas (e.g., trade association training programs) can be beneficial.

Competitive advantage, then, grows in a home environment of pressure and challenge. Nationally and internationally, competitive companies are those based in the most dynamic and challenging home environments. Proximity to capable rivals, suppliers, sophisticated customers, and specialized factor providers leads to information flow, faster accumulation of knowledge and skills, more fluid working relationships, and stronger pressures to innovate.

Industry Clusters

Nations, regions, and states are rarely competitive in isolated industries; instead, they host *clusters* of interconnected industries, a prominent feature of every advanced economy.[10] A cluster is a grouping of industries linked together through customer, supplier, or other relationships. Both manufacturing and service industries belong to clusters; often, they are interconnected. The seed of a cluster can come from unusual local needs, natural resource endowments, university areas of excellence, or acts of pure entrepreneurship. As a cluster forms, the industries that comprise it become mutually reinforcing. Aggressive rivalry in one industry spreads vertically and horizontally in the cluster through spin-offs or related diversification. Ready access to local suppliers, skill pools, and a base of sophisticated customers lowers the cost of entry.

Clusters widen as new industries develop upstream, downstream, or in related fields. New industries or segments involving advanced technology emerge, even where the clusters involve mature industries. Less productive and innovative industries in the cluster, conversely, can shrink and decline. Through a cumulative process that often occurs over several decades, the nation, state, or region becomes a unique repository of specialized expertise, technology, and institutions for competing in a given field.

Clusters are often geographically concentrated within a nation, with firms in a field all based in a particular region or city (recall Figure 4–2). This clustering reflects the importance of proximity in motivation (through highlighting relative versus absolute performance), the flow of information, the start-up of new companies, and the responsiveness of local institutions to a cluster's specialized needs.

Location and Competitive Advantage

Competition is increasingly national and global, but the crucial sources of competitive advantage are often local. Generalized factors such as capital, raw materials, and scientific knowledge are highly mobile, and companies can readily tap low-cost labor through global networks. What are not mobile, however, are the critical masses of highly specialized and interconnected skills, applied technologies, firm home bases, supplier home bases, and institutions that reside in particular areas.[11] Firms based in these environments emerge as global leaders. Foreign firms are drawn to invest in these locations; they may establish subsidiaries there and delegate to them worldwide responsibility for the products involved. Finally, individuals with good ideas and specialized skills are drawn to these areas because they offer the greatest excitement and rewards.

Because of the cumulative and self-reinforcing nature of the diamond and the time required to build specialized institutions, knowledge, and a critical mass of firms, there will normally be only a small number of favorable locations for competing in a particular business. The process of cluster formation and upgrading is not inevitable. Healthy diamonds are those characterized by the most vigorous local rivalry, local institutions that are the most responsive to industry needs, the climate for investment and new business formation is the most favorable (this strengthens the feedback loops among the diamond's parts), and strong linkages among firms, suppliers, universities, and other actors. As an established diamond upgrades, it attracts specialized factors, customers, suppliers, and other firms' home bases from around the world; often, these newcomers are relocating from weaker diamonds. In pharmaceuticals, for example, the

Philadelphia/New Jersey diamond has attracted substantial investment by German, Swiss, British, and Japanese pharmaceutical firms because of its superior demand conditions and excellent access to specialized factors. Conversely, activities that become standardized will be dispersed to source cheap inputs or facilitate foreign market access. The most sophisticated parts of an industry (or of particular industry segments) will thus become concentrated in a particular location, making it difficult to develop or attract similar concentrations at other locations. Spillovers among parts of the diamond reinforce the advantages of established concentrations and make it more difficult to replicate them elsewhere. The cycle is interrupted only when major technological changes invalidate past skills, suppliers, and other local advantages, or when upgrading pressure to innovate diminishes because rivalry is eliminated or buyer sophistication lags.

To truly access the advantages of the diamond as a system, a firm must locate its home base for business in a favorable diamond. Co-locating a critical mass of home-based activities at one location fosters rapid progress by promoting communication, cross-functional coordination, and more rapid decision making. Firms benefit not only from spillovers that occur within the local diamond but also from spillovers within the firm. Co-locating the full range of core activities at a single favorable diamond is thus preferred over dispersing these activities, even if each of the dispersed activities was to be located at a sophisticated site for that activity. Activity-specific advantages are outweighed by rapid cross-activity coordination from a single location and by the ability of this configuration to better capture spillovers within a single diamond. Wide dispersion of core activities to areas of functional excellence (as recommended by Reich, 1991b, and Bartlett and Ghoshal, 1989) rarely occurs in practice.

Proximity to a favorable diamond provides best access to the diamond's innovation advantages. Proximity in physical, cultural, and institutional terms speeds the flow of information, facilitates vertical working relationships, and amplifies the pressure from rivalry and the desire to improve relative performance. By having a critical mass of home-based activities at such a location, a firm is better able to assimilate and benefit from local externalities that cut across many activities (functions).

Location within a strong diamond is difficult to offset by firms based elsewhere. Direct contact with knowledgeable customers, educational and research institutions, and suppliers, and proximity to the core activities of capable rivals. These advantages produce information and motivation benefits that cannot be easily duplicated or tapped unless a firm has a home base there. For example, senior management and core R&D personnel of a firm based in the United States will find it difficult, if not impossible, to fully understand their Japanese customers and Japan-based rivals. Mere access to companies, machines, or customers yields no competitive advantage. What is needed, instead, is ready access to specialized knowledge as it develops and evolves over time—an outcome that comes only from proximity. Spillovers are strongest within a local diamond, and they are slow to be transmitted outside.[12]

While competitive advantage is heavily local, however, competition must be global. The firm's home base is the platform for global strategy, not the place where all of a firm's activities should take place. Companies must sell their products nationally and globally. Activities that are not central to the innovation process, such as final assembly, sourcing capital, and after-sale service, must be dispersed to source low-cost inputs and gain access to foreign markets.

A NEW CONCEPTION OF GLOBAL STRATEGY

The new paradigm for international competition carries strong implications for company strategy, especially for the design of approaches to competing globally. Some of the most important implications follow; they are illustrated with examples drawn from the three global companies profiled in Box 4–1.

Setting Corporate Goals

Corporate goals must shift from solely static measures such as return on investment (ROI) or market share to dynamic measures of the ability to improve. Continuous innovation and upgrading must be the central purpose of the enterprise. Companies that emerge as world leaders are those that can sustain innovation over decades, as have the three companies profiled.

Since their founding in the early 1920s, both Novo and Nordisk pioneered the most important innovations in the insulin industry. Nordisk introduced mixing technologies and slow-acting insulin. Novo led in the development of highly purified insulin and was the first truly global competitor.

An orientation toward innovation at Honda goes back to its founder, Soichiro Honda, who had a strong passion for creativity and originality. His philosophy of pioneering led to the development of the first mass-market motorcycle, the CVCC engine, the Accord, and the Acura luxury car concept (the first among the Japanese companies), to cite just a few achievements. An orientation to innovate also prompted Honda's actions after passage of the 1970 Clean Air Act, when it resolved to upgrade the fuel efficiency of its engines rather than join U.S. competitors in battling new regulations.

Among a long list of innovations, Hewlett-Packard developed the first desktop scientific calculator in 1968, pioneered inkjet printing technology in 1984, and led with HP Precision Architecture in 1991. The company was one of the first American corporations to adopt total quality management (TQM) techniques. More than half of HP's orders in 1992 were for products introduced in the previous two years.

Performance must be measured in terms of progress, not today's position. Corporate goals must be expressed as the projected long-term competitive position, not as current profitability. Some of the most sustainable competitive advantages are those created through investment in intangible assets—technology, supplier relationships, employee training, or market access—whose benefits are difficult to quantify and whose effect is to diminish near-term profitability. Goals framed in terms of long-term competitive position are needed to overcome the pressures found in many U.S. corporations for short-term financial returns.[13]

Creating an Innovative Organization

The foundation of competitive advantage is an ability to innovate and upgrade, but neither innovation nor upgrading occurs naturally. There is a tendency in any organization to maintain past ways of doing things and concentrate on improving their execution or just fine-tuning them. Innovation and change are disruptive, difficult, and unsettling. Internal and external feedback is more often negative than encouraging.

The principal role of senior management is to overcome those tendencies and motivate an organization to advance. Companies that are world leaders have a sense of urgency and run a little scared. There is a constant focus on threats and challenges.

Part of the environment for innovation comes from internal management practices. Among the most important practices are those involving performance measurement and capital budgeting. Performance measurement should stress *relative position vis-à-vis competitors* rather than current financial indicators. Capital budgeting should encompass not only physical assets but intangible assets such as R&D, training, relationships with suppliers, and information systems. Investments must be considered not as discrete projects but as a series of complementary resource allocations across a variety of forms.[14]

However, rarely can a leader motivate innovation solely from within. Innovative companies are often those that systematically and culturally draw on pressures and insights from their local environment. To put it bluntly, most companies do not innovate unless they are forced to. Indeed, one can cast the role of a leader as one who is able to harness external pressures and information to motivate change in an organization.

For example, a leader might serve the most demanding local customers, even if they represent only a small part of sales. Another challenge is to tackle the jurisdictions with the most stringent regulations. Avoiding these possibilities, conversely, sends a signal of complacency to the organization and undermines the search for product and process improvements. Capable competitors are another potent motivator of organizational change. The most innovative companies often designate capable rivals for detailed study, and make bettering their results a highly visible goal in the organization.

Selecting Industries and Segments

The diamond provides a way of identifying (1) the industries in which a firm can gain a unique competitive advantage vis-à-vis rivals based elsewhere and (2) those industry segments where home-based circumstances provide the most distinctive benefits. New business development should concentrate in these areas.

The principles of the new paradigm raise cautions about extensive vertical integration. Instead, a company should foster strong relationships with local suppliers of specialized machinery and inputs, while sourcing globally generalized and less technology-controlling inputs. Diversification should be more horizontal and along cluster lines. By diversifying, companies will better leverage not only their own internal assets but also the unique assets of their local environment, such as suppliers, research centers, and skill pools. HP's diversification from measurement and test equipment into information systems and medical instruments has followed these principles, in each case involving a field where the United States has unique strengths. Novo's move from insulin to industrial enzymes followed the same principles, as did Honda's diversification from motorcycles to automobiles. Innovations often originate at the interstices between industries and clusters, when related technologies and skills are combined. For example, to get its start in automobiles, Honda drew on its small-engine technology nurtured in motorcycle manufacture, while drawing strength from the fierce rivalry and supplier base of the Japanese automobile cluster.

Setting Global Strategy

The diamond model casts in a new light the available choices about configuration and coordination. Recent research on global strategy has focused on the benefits of dispersing activities and global coordination, but this is an incomplete view of the problem. A number of key questions that need to be considered in setting global strategy are noted in Table 4–1.

A Clear Home Base for Each Distinct Business

The ultimate source of competitive advantage is not the ability to compete globally, but the unique attributes of a firm's strategy and capabilities, which depend a great deal on conditions in its home base. A firm must have a clear home base for competing in each strategically distinct business, and a critical mass of its home-based activities must be located there. A coordinating center is not enough. The home base should have clear worldwide responsibility in the business and should serve as the integrating point for inputs, information, and technology obtained elsewhere.

The home base should be located in the most favorable diamond for the particular business. This may not necessarily be the country of ownership. The location of overall *corporate headquarters* is less significant. Failure to distinguish between the location of corporate and business-unit home bases is a principal cause of confusion in interpreting multinational corporations' global strategies.

Each of the three companies profiled in Box 4–1 has a clear home base for each major business. Denmark serves as the home base of Novo-Nordisk's insulin

TABLE 4–1   Shaping global strategy: Some key questions.

- Is the industry multidomestic or global?
- Is the company based in a country with a favorable demand for the business? How can the home demand be upgraded?
- What activities in the value chain should be located in other nations to:
  - —Source low-cost inputs?
  - —Access foreign markets?
  - —Tap into specialized technologies?
- What is the best way to establish these activities? In-house? Alliances? Acquisitions?
- How should activities located in different countries be coordinated and integrated?
- How should the company's management systems and processes be changed to facilitate better coordination and transmit the company's distinctive culture to subsidiaries?
- Are there product lines that should be based in another country? Which ones? Where?
- Is the company gaining the maximum competitive advantage from its global presence? Are competitors doing a better job?

business (and of both Novo's and Nordisk's insulin businesses prior to the merger). Even though 95 percent of sales is generated outside Denmark, all insulin purification facilities, which comprise the most critical activities in the production process, are based in Denmark. Denmark's large pig-farming industry has provided the crucial raw material. Insulin purification requires not only large investments but also highly specialized machinery, skilled technicians, and strong quality control systems. Denmark is home to critical suppliers of machinery and other specialized production inputs, in part because of its strong position in the dairy and beer industries, which employ related technologies and skills. All of Novo-Nordisk's core product and process research is also conducted in Denmark, which is home to an array of world-class diabetes research institutes and two leading diabetes hospitals. The demand conditions for insulin in Denmark are also advanced. The country's generous health care system provided early funding for new diabetes testing and treatments. Danish doctors not only examine patients but also conduct and monitor programs that train diabetes patients in their eating and cooking habits. Novo-Nordisk personnel interact directly with hospital doctors to gain quick feedback on the success of new products and on emerging issues facing diabetes patients.

Honda's most sophisticated activities, in both motorcycles and automobiles, are conducted at its Japanese home base. Japan accounts for 76 percent of Honda's production capacity in motorcycles and 68 percent of its automobile production. Foreign production plants are primarily assembly facilities, drawing on sophisticated parts sourced from Japan. Honda's Japanese motorcycle plants have an average capacity of 396,000 units compared to 75,000 for those located elsewhere. Automobile R&D is even more concentrated—95 percent of R&D

employees and *all* core engine research are located in Japan. R&D personnel based outside Japan must undergo two years' training at the Tochigi Research Center in Tokyo before beginning work in their native country.

At Hewlett-Packard, worldwide responsibility for each product line— including core research, the most sophisticated production activities, and decision making—is concentrated in a particular location. Many product-line home bases are located in the United States (the United States hosts 43 percent of HP's physical space dedicated to marketing but 77 percent of the space dedicated to manufacturing, R&D, and administration). Within the United States, product-line home bases are concentrated in particular geographic areas: medical instruments, in Waltham, Massachusetts; printers, in Boise, Idaho; personal computers, in Palo Alto, California; electronic components instrumentation, in San Jose, California.

The Role of Dispersed Activities

The dispersal of activities from the home base should serve one of three purposes:

1. Sourcing basic factors such as cheap labor, raw materials, or capital (adjusted for taxes). A firm shall seek to exploit the comparative advantage of various locations. It must take advantage of global markets to efficiently source inputs that do not affect the innovation process.

2. Securing or improving foreign market access. Locating selected activities near markets signals commitment to foreign customers and allows responding to local needs and tailoring offerings to local preferences. Some R&D activities are often dispersed to support product adaptation and compliance with local regulations. However, modern flexible manufacturing systems and the increased power of information and communications technologies are working to lessen the need for dispersed activities, as customization to serve local needs can be more easily accomplished from a single facility. Greater harmonization of technical standards and diminishing trade barriers have the same effects.

   Activities may also be dispersed in order to respond to actual or threatened government mandates, as has been the case with Japanese auto and consumer electronics assembly in the United States. When a firm must respond to government pressures, dispersing some less scale- or innovation-sensitive activities can allow the firm to continue to concentrate others. The goal should be to deal with government mandates at the least possible sacrifice to efficiency and especially to the rate of innovation.

3. Selectively tapping particular skills or technologies that are not available at the home base. When tapping the capabilities of other diamonds, it is important to supplement the home base, not to replicate it or seek to replace it.

The ultimate aim is to develop capabilities in important skills or technologies at home, in order to facilitate more rapid innovation. Relying too heavily on advantages sourced elsewhere threatens the capacity to innovate. Overall, the principle is to disperse *only* those activities needed to achieve these three classes of benefits.

Alliances with firms based elsewhere can be a means of more effectively or more rapidly gaining these benefits. Market access is often enhanced by a local partner, and the ability to tap advanced skills and technologies in another location may require a partner's well-established presence. Alliances, however, complicate coordination and can slow innovation. The best alliances are (1) highly selective, (2) focused on particular activities and on obtaining a particular benefit, and (3) often temporary. A firm cannot rely on a partner for assets that are crucial to competitive advantage.

Our case studies illustrate all these motivations. Novo-Nordisk ("Novo") has sourced its main raw material, pig pancreases, from 20 countries. Worldwide sourcing not only allows access to larger supplies but also smoothes price fluctuations. Novo funds 83 percent of its long-term debt in currencies other than the Danish kroner, and taps foreign equity markets. To facilitate market access and lower transportation costs, Novo has dispersed four insulin processing plants to France, South Africa, Japan, and the United States. These plants—the only ones that operate outside Denmark—are not full-scale production facilities. Their functions are to add water to concentrated insulin crystals imported from Denmark and then package products for final sale. Dispersing these less scale-sensitive processing plants has allowed Novo to continue to concentrate its more scale- and skill-dependent primary production in Denmark. To improve access to local medical communities and government health care systems, Novo has established marketing joint ventures with local companies in a number of countries. Finally, Novo has established a limited number of highly specialized R&D activities outside Denmark to tap particular skills or technologies not available at home. Zymotech, based in Seattle, Washington, was acquired to access expertise in genetically engineered insulin (a U.S. strength). A Japanese research facility was established as well. After repeated delays in gaining regulatory approval in Denmark, Novo established a genetically engineered insulin production facility in Japan, where approval was more rapid. Novo has not ceded this core technology to foreign operations; its own genetic engineering capabilities have been built up in Denmark. The company is transferring the knowledge acquired in the United States and Japan back to its Danish home base, and has established genetic insulin production there as well.

Honda has also dispersed non-home-base activities for all three reasons given above. Automobiles are assembled in 11 countries and motorcycles in 30 countries, to reduce transportation and tariff costs and to source lower-cost labor. To ensure continued market access in the face of rising concern over Japanese automobile imports, Honda has invested $2 billion in facilities in the United States: two assembly plants, a manufacturing facility for engines, transmissions, and suspension parts, an engineering center, and an R&D facility. Honda's U.S. activities are focused on cost reduction and adaptation of products and processes to the U.S. market. Innovation is centered in Japan. Honda also has a joint venture with Rover in the United Kingdom, oriented toward securing access to the European market. Finally, Honda taps styling expertise available in California, and high-performance design capabilities in Germany, via small, local design centers that transfer knowledge back to the Japanese home base, where it is incorporated into model development.

Coordinating and Integrating Dispersed Activities

Unlocking the full competitive advantage from dispersed activities requires that they be coordinated and that the learning and technology gained from dispersed activities be integrated at the home base. All three of the case studies in Box 4–1 are illustrative, but Novo's case is particularly interesting. Novo's global procurement, production, and marketing activities are tightly coordinated from Denmark. All marketing subsidiaries, agents, and distributors use consistent promotional materials and are trained in consistent selling approaches. Novo works hard to ensure a common image worldwide and reinforces it with periodic sponsorship of physicians' conferences on diabetes sponsored in Denmark.

The dual goal of coordinating subsidiaries and integrating ideas at the home base requires (1) an organizational structure, systems, and norms that all support frequent and open information exchange and (2) decision making that addresses the goals of the global business unit rather than individual subsidiaries. These attributes are difficult to achieve. A full discussion of solutions is beyond the scope of this chapter, but among the key ingredients are information and accounting systems that are consistent worldwide, to facilitate exchange of information and comparisons; active efforts to facilitate mutual learning and personal relationships among subsidiary managers; and an incentive system that weights overall contribution to the company in addition to subsidiary performance.[15]

Upgrading the Home Base

An important part of a firm's competitive advantage resides in its local environment, not within the firm itself. Without a fundamentally healthy home base, the capacity for rapid innovation will diminish. The firm will be unable to assemble the resources and capabilities most essential to competitive advantage. Dispersing sophisticated production or outsourcing critical components and machinery may improve performance in the short run but will threaten the firm's ability to innovate in the long run.

Firms should support specialized training programs and should promote university research in areas that are relevant to their particular business. Local suppliers should be nurtured and upgraded (depending heavily on distant suppliers nullifies a potential competitive advantage). Industry associations can play an important role in sponsoring training programs, funding research on enabling technologies and standards, and collecting market information. Unfortunately, few companies see their local environment as a vital competitive resource. In the United States, for example, many companies take their suppliers for granted and see education and training as the responsibility of government.

Our case studies illustrate how global leaders take an active role in upgrading their home environment. For example, before the merger, Nordisk established the Nordic Insulin Fund in 1926 to support insulin research projects in Scandinavia, and established the Steno Memorial Hospital in 1932 as a center for research and treatment of diabetes. Novo founded the Hvidore Diabetes Hospital and later the Hagedoorn Research Institute in 1957 to conduct basic research on diabetes. The Novo Research Institute was created in 1964 to investigate the causes and origins of diabetes. Today, the Steno Diabetes Center and Hvidore Diabetes Hospital treat 6,000 diabetes patients and conduct 25,000 diabetes consultations each year. Novo-Nordisk also sponsors international conferences on diabetes in Denmark, bringing together local experts and specialists from around the world.[16]

The history of the Danish insulin industry illustrates the power of active local rivalry between two companies to motivate continual innovation. One of the risks of their merger is that, while it will achieve some static efficiencies, it will undermine dynamism. The parent company is aiming to address this and other risks by keeping the two operations separate. A broader principle, however, is that the presence of local rivals creates advantages. Seeking to eliminate local competition is normally misguided.

Product-Line Home Bases at Different Locations

As a firm's product range broadens, the home bases for some product lines may best be located outside the home country. A firm should locate the home base for each product line in the country with the most favorable home diamond in that particular segment of the business. (Figure 4–4 illustrates the resulting configuration schematically.) This approach is far superior to replicating production and R&D activities for the same products in several countries, which is inefficient and dulls innovation. Ohmae's (1985) triad model, in which each regional subsidiary concentrates on serving its home market, gives up important advantages in terms of specialization. Instead, each regional subsidiary should *specialize* in models for which it has the most favorable diamond, and serve those segments worldwide. Instead of dispersing activities individually, as the Bartlett/Ghoshal (1989) and Reich (1991b) models suggest, groups of activities comprising product-line home bases should be located in countries with favorable diamonds.

Hewlett-Packard provides an interesting example of these notions. Its worldwide operations encompass a number of product lines, each with a distinct home base that has worldwide responsibility. Research and development, sophisticated manufacturing, and key decision making are concentrated at this home base. Regional subsidiaries are responsible for some process-oriented

FIGURE 4–4   Model of home-base global strategy.

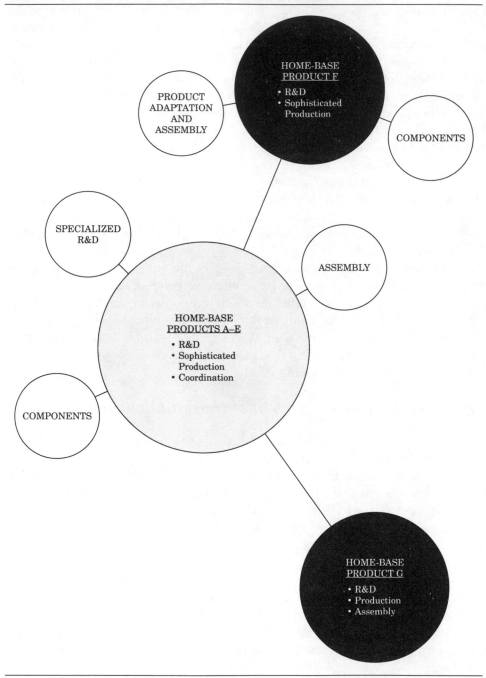

R&D, product localization, and local marketing. At the home base, engineers with specialized expertise are designated worldwide experts; they transfer their knowledge either electronically or through periodic trips to subsidiaries. Responsibility for personal computers and workstations is based in California—home to almost all of the world's leading personal computer and workstation firms. The medical instruments group is based in Massachusetts, the location of several world renowned research hospitals and numerous leading medical instrument companies. Inkjet printer operations are concentrated in Vancouver, British Columbia, with localization for regional markets and assembly in Barcelona (Spain) and Vancouver. Worldwide responsibility for a new line of compact inkjet printers is based in Singapore. This line combines printer technology transferred from Vancouver with Asian expertise in designing space-saving office products.

Honda's home base for automobiles has been entirely in Japan; however, it is beginning the process of creating a product-line home base in the United States. "Project DW," an initiative to develop an Accord station wagon, is based in the United States. Adapted from a sedan designed and engineered in Japan, the station wagon was conceived, designed, and developed in the United States, which is considered to be the leading market for station wagons and has a network of established suppliers of station wagon components. Honda's California R&D design facility created the models and life-size mock-ups of the wagon; the Ohio R&D facility fabricated the metal prototype; and major production tooling, including stamping dies, was made by Honda Engineering in America. Honda has stated that the United States will become its world headquarters for station wagons, and that U.S. designers and engineers will continue to develop and upgrade the product. American Honda also has worldwide responsibility for development of a two-door Civic coupe.[17] By the end of the 1990s, American Honda plans to export 70,000 automobiles from the United States to more than 20 countries.

Preserving National Identity in Business Units

A firm's national identity in a business is not something to shed, as some observers have suggested, but something to preserve. Competitive advantage arises from distinctive attributes of the firm's home environment in a business; they place an imprint on the firm and shape how it competes. Identity and culture, and the company characteristics they connote, are crucial to foreign customers. Most Americans, for example, do not want to buy a German car from a German car company that is acting too American.

When accessing foreign markets, a firm must adapt—in the sense that it tailors its product to local needs and be sensitive to local business practices—yet it should not lose its distinctive identity, which should be preserved and inculcated in foreign subsidiaries. At Honda, for example, managers hired to run international subsidiaries must first undergo two years' training at the Japanese home base.

Relocating the Home Base

If the attractiveness of a firm's home base for a particular business deteriorates because of changes in customer sophistication, the need for new types of suppliers, ineffective local institutions, or other reasons, the first response should be to upgrade at home. If such efforts are exhausted without success, however, a firm may need to relocate its home base to a place that has a more favorable diamond. Shifts of home bases from country to country are occurring with increasing frequency in multinational companies. As global competition exposes firms to the world's best rivals and nullifies advantages in capital, raw materials, and labor, the penalty of an unfavorable home diamond is increasing. Yet, relocating a home base must take place reluctantly, because it involves the need to become accepted as a true insider in a new environment and new culture.

Firms rarely shift the home base of the entire company at once. Instead, they relocate the home base of a particular product line or business segment for which the home diamond is least favorable. One common catalyst (and enabler) of such a shift is the acquisition of a foreign firm already established in a more vibrant diamond. Such an acquisition provides the critical mass for a new home base, which, over time, gains increasing worldwide responsibility and decision making for a business. For example, Nestlé has relocated the world headquarters for its confectionery business to England, centering it around the acquired Rowntree MacIntosh company. England, with its sweet-toothed consumers, sophisticated retailers, advanced advertising agencies, and highly competitive media companies, is a more vibrant environment for competing in mass-market candy than Switzerland. Similarly, Nestlé has moved its headquarters for bottled water to France, the most competitive country in this industry.

Although each of the case study companies in Box 4–1 continues to enjoy a strong home diamond in its principal businesses, not all firms are so fortunate. The Canadian manufacturer Northern Telecom, for example, has shifted its home base for digital central office switching equipment from Canada to the United States.[18] Northern Telecom manufactured and installed the first local digital switch, the DMS-10, in the United States in 1977. The subsequent AT&T divestiture and mandate for equal access reconfigured the U.S. diamond for telecommunications service and equipment, and led Northern Telecom to expand its U.S. operations dramatically. By 1991, the company had relocated its world headquarters for central office switching to the United States. It now conducts all research and development activities for this product line in the United States, with a work force of over 1,000 employees. Virtually all central office switching manufacturing is also conducted in the United States: 7,000 employees occupy 2.2 million square feet at the company's major plant in North Carolina.

The rationale behind Northern Telecom's move to the United States can be seen in the strength of the U.S. telecommunications equipment diamond. Compared to Canada, highly specialized factors are uniquely available in the United States; they include sophisticated software engineering and world-class university research programs in computer science and telecommunications. American buyers and end-users are among the most sophisticated in the world, and the existence of 20 to 25 major independent U.S. switch buyers leads to intense competition that encourages customers to continuously upgrade their central office switching capabilities. American firms in integrated circuit manufacturing and systems-level software design provide strong capabilities in related industries. The local rivalry within the U.S. market is intensified by the high commitment of focused U.S. competitors and the openness of the U.S. market to foreign rivals (in telecommunications equipment, governments have tended to protect local markets and support monopoly suppliers).

In another interesting example, Wesson (1993) describes the shift of Hyundai's home base in personal computers from Korea to Silicon Valley, when Hyundai discovered that it simply could not "keep up" from a Korean base. With all competitors sourcing low-cost parts internationally, the only competitive advantages were in the rapid introduction of new models that met evolving customer needs and the ability to successfully access evolving distribution channels. Here, the United States was far ahead of other locations. Traditionally, foreign direct investment (FDI) has been seen as exploiting home base advantages. Wesson employs statistical evidence to confirm the prevalence of home base *seeking* FDI, or FDI directed at accessing sophisticated advantages of other locations or relocating the firm's home base elsewhere.

CONCLUSION

Since the 1950s, globalization has exerted an ever-increasing influence on competitive strategy. Aggregate statistics confirm the popular view that firms are increasingly global in their sales and operations. The traditional paradigm of comparative advantage has been superseded, and it is tempting to conclude that corporations have come to transcend national boundaries.

Deeper research reveals, however, a striking localization of competitive advantage. This apparent paradox can be explained by adapting a new paradigm of international competition—one based not on static advantages such as input costs or economies of scale but on the ability to innovate and upgrade. This paradigm must guide a new generation of thinking about global strategy in which localization and globalization are integrated in wholly new ways.

Localization was once seen as a necessary evil to be balanced against the compelling benefits of a global strategy. Instead, there are two different roles of localization: (1) innovation and (2) adaptation to local circumstances. The location of the home base is often the root of competitive advantage. Global strategies can extend this advantage through sourcing inputs, accessing markets, or tapping particular information or technologies. To play this role, however, dispersed activities must adapt to local needs and customs. This new synthesis, which recognizes the complex role of location in competitive advantage, will drive competition in the coming decades.

NOTES

1. Among nations, for example, Japan, Italy, and Korea have been prospering during recent decades in terms of world trade and per-capita income, while other nations have been stagnating. Within countries, some states are consistently more prosperous than others. In Germany, for example, Baden Württemberg is the performance leader. In the United States, Massachusetts and New Jersey have ranked in the top ten states in terms of gross domestic product (GDP) per capita for the past ten years, consistently outperforming states such as Arkansas, West Virginia, Utah, and others. States such as Georgia, Virginia, and New Hampshire have gained markedly in the per-capita income ranking; others, such as Michigan, Indiana, and Oregon, have fallen.

2. Porter (1980).

3. Porter (1985).

4. See, for example, Porter (1990); Crocombe, Enright, and Porter (1991); Porter and Monitor Company (1991), and Sölvell, Zander, and Porter (1991).

5. See also Enright (1993 and 1994).

6. See, for example, Jaikumar and Upton (1993).

7. This group of activities, which varies in composition from industry to industry, will be termed *home-based activities* or *core activities*.

8. Thomas (1993) confirms this result in pharmaceuticals, where firms facing local rivals (and strict product approval regulation) are the most innovative.

9. Some observers have cited collaboration rather than competition as an important basis of competitiveness, referring most often to Japan and to the industrial districts of Italy. This view confuses *vertical* collaboration with buyers, suppliers, and local institutions, which the diamond theory stresses, with *horizontal* collaboration among competitors. Horizontal collaboration is rare in successful Japanese and Italian industries (*keiretsu,* for example, do not contain direct competitors) and is limited to general infrastructure.

10. Clusters are also present in developing economies, although they normally lack depth in terms of machinery producers, advanced components, and sophisticated services. See Porter (1990), Chapter 10.

11. See also Kogut (1991). Such location-based advantages are inconsistent with Reich's (1991b) views of mobile resources, information, and technology. His notion of symbolic analyst zones, which is focused only on skilled employees, is an effort to bridge this inconsistency.

12. Given the dynamic nature of competition and the benefits available to early movers, the speed with which knowledge can be transmitted bodes large as a competitive advantage or disadvantage.

13. For a description of these pressures, their causes and effects, see Porter (1992).

14. Porter (1992).

15. For a useful discussion of organizational issues in global companies, see Bartlett and Ghoshal (1989).

16. Enright (1989).

17. Honda's movement toward greater local content is related to establishing new product-line home bases.

18. Wesson (1993) further develops the Northern Telecom case.

REFERENCES

Bartlett, C. A., and S. Ghoshal. *Managing across Borders: The Transnational Solution.* Boston: Harvard Business School Press, 1989.

Buckley, P. J., and M. C. Casson. *The Future of the Multinational Enterprise.* London: Holmes and Meier, 1976.

Calvet, A. L. "A Synthesis of Foreign Direct Investment Theories and Theories of the Multinational Firm," *Journal of International Business Studies* (Spring–Summer 1981), 43–60.

Caves, R. E. "International Corporations: The Industrial Economics of Foreign Direct Investment," *Economica* (1971), 1–27.

Cristerna, H. "The Role of Home-Based Advantages in Global Expansion: Five Case Studies," unpublished MBA research report, Harvard Business School, May 1993.

Crocombe, G. T., M. J. Enright, and M. E. Porter. *Upgrading New Zealand's Competitive Advantage.* Auckland, New Zealand: Oxford University Press, 1991.

Doz, Y., C. A. Bartlett, and C. K. Prahalad. "Global Competitive Pressures and Host Country Demands: Managing Tensions in MNC's," *California Management Review* (Spring 1981), 63–74.

Dunning, J. "The Eclectic Paradigm of International Production: A Restatement and Some Possible Extensions," *Journal of International Business Studies*, 1977, 1–32.

Dunning, J., and A. M. Rugman. "The Influence of Hymer's Dissertation on the Theory of Foreign Direct Investment," *American Economic Review,* May 1985, 228–232.

Enright, M. J. "Novo Industri," Harvard Business School case 9-389-148, 1989.

Enright, M. J. "The Determinants of Geographic Concentration in Industry," Harvard Business School Working Paper 93-052, 1993.

Enright, M. J. "Organization and Coordination in Geographically Concentrated Industries," in *Coordination and Information: Historical Perspectives on the Organization of Enterprise* (Chicago: University of Chicago Press/NBER, 1994).

Ghoshal, S. "Global Strategy: An Organizing Framework," *Strategic Management Journal* (September–October 1987), 425–440.

Graham, E. M. "Oligopolistic Imitation and European Direct Investment in the United States," doctoral dissertation, Harvard Business School, 1974.

Hamel, G., and C. K. Prahalad. "Do You Really Have a Global Strategy?" *Harvard Business Review* (July–August 1985), 139–148.

Hout, T., M. E. Porter, and E. Rudden, "How Global Companies Win Out," *Harvard Business Review* (September–October 1982), 98–108.

Hymer, S. H. "International Operations of National Firms: A Study of Direct Investment." Cambridge, MA: MIT Press, 1976. (From 1960 doctoral dissertation.)

Jaikumar, R. and D. M. Upton. "The Coordination of Global Manufacturing," in S. P. Bradley, J. A. Hausman, and R. L. Nolan (eds.), *Globalization, Technology, and Competition: The Fusion of Computers and Telecommunications in the 1990s.* Boston: Harvard Business School Press, 1993.

Johnson, H. G. "The Efficiency and Welfare Implications of the International Corporation," in C. P. Kindleberger (ed.), *The International Corporation.* Cambridge, MA: MIT Press, 1970.

Kindleberger, C. P. American Business Abroad. New Haven, CT: Yale University Press, 1969.

Knickerbocker, F. T. "Oligopolistic Reaction and Multinational Enterprise," Working Paper Harvard Business School Division of Research, 1974.

Kogut, B. "Normative Observations on the International Value-Added Chain and Strategic Groups," *Journal of International Business Studies* (Fall 1984), 151–167.

Kogut, B. "Designing Global Strategies: Comparative and Competitive Value-Added Chains," *Sloan Management Review* (Summer 1985), 15–28.

Kogut, B. "Designing Global Strategies: Profiting from Operational Flexibility," *Sloan Management Review* (Fall 1985), 27–38.

Kogut, B. "Country Capabilities and the Permeability of Borders," *Strategic Management Journal* (Summer 1991), 33–47. (Special issue.)

Krugman, P. "The New Theories of International Trade and the Multinational Enterprise," in C. P. Kindleberger and D. Audretch (eds.), *The Multinational Corporation in the 1980s* (Cambridge, MA: MIT Press), 57–73.

Levitt, T. "The Globalization of Markets," *Harvard Business Review* (May–June 1983), 92–102.

Magee, S. P. "Technology and the Appropriability Theory of the Multinational Corporation," in J. Bhajwati (ed.), *The New International Economic Order.* Cambridge, MA: MIT Press, 1976.

Mataloni, R. J., Jr. "U.S. Multinational Companies: Operations in 1990," *Survey of Current Business* (August 1992), 60–78.

McManus, J. C. "The Theory of the International Firm," in C. Paquet (ed.), *The Multinational Firm and the Nation State.* Toronto, Canada: Collier-Macmillan, 1972.

Ohmae, K. *Triad Power: The Coming Shape of Global Competition.* New York: The Free Press, 1985.

Ohmae, K. *The Borderless World: Power and Strategy in the Interlinked Economy.* New York: Harper Business, 1990.

Perlmutter, H. V. "The Tortuous Evolution of the Multinational Corporation," *Columbia Journal of World Business* (January–February 1969), 9–18.

Porter, M. E. *Competitive Strategy: Techniques for Analyzing Industries and Competitors.* New York: The Free Press, 1980.

Porter, M. E. *Competitive Advantage: Creating and Sustaining Superior Performance.* New York: The Free Press, 1985.

Porter, M. E. "Competition in Global Industries: A Conceptual Framework," in M. Porter (ed.), *Competition in Global Industries*. Boston: Harvard Business School Press, 1986.

Porter, M. E. *The Competitive Advantage of Nations*. New York: The Free Press, 1990.

Porter, M. E. *Capital Choices: Changing the Way America Invests in Industry*. Washington, DC: Council on Competitiveness, 1992.

Porter, M. E., and Monitor Company. *Canada at the Crossroads: The Reality of a New Competitive Environment*. Ottawa: Business Council on National Issues and Government of Canada, 1991.

Porter, M. E., and R. E. Wayland, "Global Competition and the Localization of Competitive Advantage," in *Integral Strategy*, Greenwich, CT: JA1 Press, forthcoming.

Prahalad, C. K. "The Strategic Process in a Multinational Corporation," unpublished doctoral dissertation, Harvard Business School, 1975.

Reich, R. B. "Who Is Us?" *Harvard Business Review* (January–February 1991a).

Reich, R. B. *The Work of Nations: Preparing Ourselves for 21st-Century Capitalism*. New York: Alfred A. Knopf, 1991b.

Rugman, A. M. "Internalization as a General Theory of Foreign Direct Investment: A Re-Appraisal of the Literature," *Weltwirtschaftliches Archiv.* (1980), 116: 365–379.

Rugman, A. M. "Do Multinationals Have a Future?" *Futures* 243–246.

Rugman, A. M. *Inside the Multinationals*. London: Croom Helm, 1981.

Sölvell, Ö., I. Zander, and M. E. Porter. *Advantage Sweden*. Norstedts, Stockholm, Sweden, 1991.

Thomas, L. G. "Spare the Road and Spoil the Industry: Vigorous Regulation and Vigorous Competition Promote International Competitive Advantage," Emory University Working Paper, 1993.

Tyson, L. D. "They Are Not Us: Why American Ownership Still Matters," *The American Prospect* (Winter 1990).

Vernon, R. "International Investment and International Trade in the Product Cycle," *Quarterly Journal of Economics* (May 1966), 190–207.

Vernon, R. "The Product Hypothesis in a New International Environment," *Oxford Bulletin of Economics and Statistics* (1979), 255–267.

Wesson, T. "The Determinants of Foreign Direct Investment in U.S. Manufacturing Industries," unpublished doctoral dissertation, Harvard Business School, 1993.

POLITICAL STRATEGY: MANAGING THE SOCIAL AND POLITICAL ENVIRONMENT

5

John F. Mahon

Boston University

Barbara Bigelow

Clark University

Liam Fahey

Babson College and
Cranfield School of Management

CORPORATE POLITICAL STRATEGY[1]

Case 1: American Telephone and Telegraph (AT&T) routinely made donations to the Planned Parenthood Foundation of America for over 25 years. AT&T's funding was designated for relatively uncontroversial issues—family planning and sex education. However, in March 1990—in response to concerns that it would become embroiled in a public battle between anti-abortionists and women's rights activists—AT&T announced that it would no longer provide funding. The anti-abortionists had achieved success in their previous campaigns to have other major corporations—among them, JCPenney and Union Pacific—withdraw their financial support of Planned Parenthood. AT&T, in announcing the withdrawal of support, noted that ". . . advocates on either side of the issue began to equate AT&T's support of Planned Parenthood's family planning and sex education as really AT&T's political view of pro-choice. We had to keep explaining ourselves. We feel that [abortion] is not a corporate matter but a private matter." Did this mean that AT&T supports abortion rights? "No, it means that we don't have a stance, nor should we."[2]

Case 2: Anheuser-Busch (AB) found itself the subject of Operation PUSH (People United to Save Humanity) in 1982. Operation PUSH, headed by the Reverend Jesse Jackson, decided to target AB for an "economic reciprocity" agreement. Such an agreement would oblige an organization that makes products that are bought by minorities to select more minority suppliers and support minority-owned banks. Reverend Jackson argued that if African Americans consumed X percent of AB's products, then X percent of AB's suppliers should be African American, and X percent of AB's funds should be deposited in African American-owned banks. Reverend Jackson threatened a national boycott of AB's products if these demands were not met.

Case 3: The coming of a United Europe has been eagerly awaited by some interests and apprehensively anticipated by others. The members of the European Community (EC) have been working for the past ten years to achieve this union, and the recent national votes in support of the Maastricht Treaty are furthering this end. However, there are still many major areas of concern for the conduct of business and international trade. One is: What constitutes a "domestic" corporation within the EC? This definition is crucial for businesses to reap the benefits of reduced trade barriers among EC members. Another area of contention is how to deal with Japanese automobile imports. Northern Europe is willing to let the free market rule, but Southern Europe wants strict quotas on Japanese auto imports. Both of these issues and numerous others will be resolved not just by the economic/business system but by the political system as well.

The essence of strategic management, as argued in Chapter 1, is the design and execution of strategies that anticipate, cope with, and leverage change. However, the conventional views of business strategy, as outlined in Chapters 2 through 4, address change in and around the economic or product marketplace and would not be helpful in dealing with the three cases described above. Political strategy gives managers a methodology for coping with change in the social and political environment. As this chapter will show, political strategy can be critical to the success of organizations' product-market or economic strategies.

The teaching of political strategy is not as well developed as the more conventional "business" strategy; indeed, it is often downplayed or even omitted in strategic management textbooks. A few U.S. companies play the political game superbly. Routinely, they risk their fate on the outcome of decisions in the Pentagon and Congress. Surprisingly, many organizations traditionally pay little attention to political and social change and its implications for economic success. Others have relied on the manipulations and influence of a few individuals to achieve desirable political goals. Few organizations have involved large numbers of their corporate executives in coherent political policy planning or have thoroughly trained their executives to manage political issues. Yet, during the past 20 years, many events that have shaped both individual firms' and industries' direction have occurred in the political and/or social realms. (Many of these changes and their implications for both business and political strategy are discussed in detail in Chapter 7.) Box 5–1 serves as an initial illustration of the linkages between political and social change and change within industries.

It would be wrong to maintain that corporations just react to their environment. The actions of individual firms may also be a source or cause of activity and change in the political and social domains. What firms do in the product marketplace often results in the involvement of political institutions, such as regulatory agencies and the courts, and social entities such as community and public interest groups. Each of the cases outlined briefly in Box 5–2 shows how a firm's business strategy can be the source of both positive and negative change in the political and social environment, and how that in turn affects the outcomes of those strategies.

Three Core Theses

Three related theses undergird this chapter. First, as illustrated in the three cases at the beginning of the chapter and in Box 5–1, subtle changes in the political and social environment can provoke transformative changes in the competitive opportunities of organizations. Thus, organizations need to understand intimately the political and social milieu in which they operate. Second, organizations increasingly recognize the need to develop strategies that explicitly address their involvement in the political and social realm—their political strategy. Third, as illustrated in Box 5–2, organizations not only react to their social and political environment but can be instrumental in shaping it. Thus, well-managed firms' political strategy is part of their overall strategy to shape and influence the external environment (or context) within which they do business.

The scope and sequence of this chapter are as follows:

- We define political strategy, placing particular emphasis on the term *political*.
- We identify and discuss the three principal integrating elements and foci of political strategy: (1) issues, (2) stakeholders, and (3) arenas.
- We detail the types of political strategies and explain how an organization can shape and influence the political and social environment.
- We explore the linkage of political strategy to business or economic strategy.

WHAT IS POLITICAL STRATEGY?

Political strategy is the set of activities undertaken by an organization in the political, regulatory, judicial, or social domain to secure a position of advantage and influence over other actors in the process. The organization's political activities entail identifying which issues it wishes to pursue, who its opponents and proponents are, and in which domain or arena it wishes to act. It is not surprising to discover, as is shown in Box 5–3, that political strategy has a number of

Box 5–1

Political and Social Change and Change within Industries

Political and Social Change	*Industry-Specific Impact*
President Clinton proposes changes in the health care system in the United States, to guarantee access to all citizens. Likely outcomes include a reduction in costs to the patient and the probable rationing or limitation of services.	The entire health care industry (insurers, hospitals, individual providers, health maintenance organizations (HMOs)) will be impacted in as yet unknown and unequal ways. Each group has launched its own lobbying effort to shape the outcome in ways favorable to its own constituency. Reaction of the general public to all these efforts is unknown at this time.
The signing and enactment into law of the North American Free Trade Agreement (NAFTA) among Canada, Mexico, and the United States.	Controversy has arisen regarding NAFTA's impact on jobs and transfer of technology among the three nations. Already, environmental groups have won a court victory requiring the U.S. Government to prepare an environmental impact statement before implementing the agreement.
Growing societal concern over toxic wastes.	The available land space for disposal has declined, raising the cost of disposal to new levels. The impact this will have on different industries and on individual competitors within industries is still uncertain.
Growing German nationalism, violence, and the increased strength of the Deutsche mark raise widespread public concern.	These events will have an impact on the reliability of product delivery and potentially on product quality itself. Which industries will be affected by increased costs of doing business with German suppliers and customers and how the impact will be felt have yet to be determined.

Box 5–2

Business Strategy → Environmental Change → Strategy Change

Business Strategy	Change in the Environment	Change in Strategy
Procter & Gamble (P&G) introduces a new product—Rely —as its first entry into the feminine hygiene products market.	The product is linked with the development of toxic shock syndrome, which can cause death.	For the first time in P&G's history, it withdraws a product from the market. It then announces that it is providing millions of dollars for research into toxic shock.
The hazardous waste industry markets the safe disposal of toxic wastes, but disposal is an expensive process.	Congress passes laws requiring control of toxic substances and hazardous waste sites.	The demand for toxic waste services explodes. Rapid growth occurs in the size and numbers of businesses involved.
Union Carbide seeks out lowest-cost sources for competitive advantage.	An explosion in a Union Carbide plant in Bhopal, India, kills and injures thousands.	Increased attention is given to plant safety. Union Carbide pays OSHA a fine (at the time, the largest fine in OSHA history) for problems at its West Virginia plant.
The insurance industry provides property and casualty insurance to poorer areas of the nation.	Riots in inner cities in the late 1960s cause extensive property damage; continued coverage is in jeopardy.	The insurance industry lobbies the federal government for guarantees against future large losses from such situations.

---

remarkable similarities to the more conventional business strategy. Individual actions by themselves do not constitute a strategy. Rather, an organization has a political strategy when some set of political actions such as those noted in Table 5–1 is organized and integrated by the organization to achieve some specific purpose.

Box 5-3

Parallels between Political and Business Strategies

All strategy is developed and executed within an environmental context. In business strategy, the organization defines the relevant industry setting, its structure and dynamics, and its likely future evolution. In political strategy, the relevant environment includes the industry context noted above as well as the political and social context in which it is embedded.

In business strategy, the firm builds its planning around its products because, ultimately, its products must attract, win, and retain customers. In political strategy, the organization articulates a position (or set of arguments) that serves as the equivalent of a product—the position must attract, win, and retain stakeholders.

Both kinds of strategies involve rivals seeking to outmatch and outmaneuver each other. In business strategy, the rivals offer different mixes of products and services and are commonly referred to as competitors. In political strategy, the rivals may be the organization's product-market competitors, but they can also include other stakeholders, such as public interest groups, governmental agencies, and ad hoc groups, that offer a different mix of ideas, values, and interests.

Each time it is challenged, the organization must carefully deploy its limited resources in order to outmaneuver its rivals. The organization chooses the actions it thinks will best preempt, respond to, and anticipate the actions of rivals. The constant intent is to create and sustain positions of advantage over rivals.

As shown in Table 5-1, and as discussed throughout this chapter, the range of political actions is quite large. They vary from actions that extend over a long period of time and cost a significant amount of money (such as lobbying or mounting a public relations program to improve the organization's image in the community) to those that are ad hoc, short-term, and low-cost (such as limited financial support of a local charity or the assignment of an employee to the charitable organization to assist in management of the effort).

Political strategy is played out or executed within what we shall broadly define as the political system. It includes the *formal* governmental processes—elections, and the legislative, judicial, and regulatory systems—as well as the more *informal* arenas—public opinion, the media, and local community activity. Lobbying a congresswoman and testifying before a legislative committee are examples of activities undertaken in formal arenas. Sponsoring a Little League baseball team and working on the image of the corporation with specific stakeholders are examples of activities in informal arenas.

Gaining positions of permanent or temporary advantage is the purpose of political strategy. Many distinct positions of advantage may be sought. For example, one firm may take another to court to protect its patents. The intended position of advantage may be an injunction from the court stipulating that the other firm cannot use the patent or that it must withdraw one segment of its

TABLE 5–1   Examples of an organization's political actions.

Action Category	Illustrative Action
Narrowly Focused Activities	
Lobbying	A finance officer meets with Senator _____ to discuss tax impacts on the organization as a result of political campaign contributions.
	A check for $1,000 is sent to Representative _____'s election campaign on behalf of the corporate political action committee (PAC).
Letter writing and correspondence	The CEO pens a letter to Representative _____ on a specific issue of interest.
Speakers' bureau	The public relations (PR) department provides a managerial speaker for the local toastmasters club.
Charitable contributions	A donation of $1,000 is made to the United Way Fund.
Arbitration/mediation	Labor and management agree to binding arbitration on some contract issues.
Crisis management	A fire occurs in a local plant; the fire department is immediately contacted; subsequent calls are made to the local media and the plant's next shift of workers.
Broadly Focused Activities	
Advocacy advertising	The organization runs an advertisement expressing an opinion on the federal legislation on weapons control.
Image programs	The organization's slogan is prominently displayed in an intense media campaign.
Public relations/public affairs	The PR department launches a new campaign to deal with recent bad press.
Community relations	The R&D unit sponsors a variety of year-round community liaison activities (softball and bowling teams, fund-raising events).
Testimony before Congressional committees	Legal counsel testifies before the House Labor Committee regarding potential changes in labor laws.
Political risk analysis	The organization is preparing to enter a third-world country and seeks to assess the projected safety of its personnel and the security of its invested capital.

product line from the marketplace. The position of advantage that is obtained may be either temporary or permanent, although the distinctions between temporary and permanent are subtle and easily lost. For example, when a legislative or regulatory action is involved, an organization needs the influence and support at the time of the vote itself, not before or after. That is the "temporary" advantage. But because political and regulatory actions, especially in the formal arena, set the rules of the game, the results of the vote may be long-lived and quite significant for the organization.

Political strategy as described above is inherently adversarial; rival organizations pit their strategies and resources against one another. However, the exercise of corporate political strategy can be, and often is, undertaken in nonadversarial settings and relationships. The establishment of the National Coal Policy Project, which brought together environmentalists and coal-mining firms in a private setting to resolve difficulties and misunderstandings, is a notable example of an attempt to deal with pressing problems in a nonadversarial manner.[3]

Frequent assertions in the popular press notwithstanding, the winners in the political system are not necessarily those with the most money, the largest membership, or the most visibility. Several other mechanisms and forces serve as determinants of success; many of them are detailed in the later discussion of different types of strategy. To win in the political system, the organization must develop a compelling set of arguments framed with very carefully chosen words, get the attention of other stakeholders or actors in the system, and then convince them of the merits of the organization's position over the positions offered by others.[4]

ELEMENTS AND FOCI OF POLITICAL STRATEGY

Issues

Issues serve as the primary focus in political rivalry, yet the concept of an issue is not easily defined. In general terms, issues constitute the points of contention or conflict between an organization and other economic, social, or public policy entities. They involve situations in which the answer to "What should be done?" is seen differently by different groups within society, each of which may have widely differing "stakes" in the outcome. These situations are typically characterized by disagreements over facts (such as the size of the federal deficit or the cost of health care programs), values (Is genetic research morally correct? Should the government fund abortions on demand?), and policies (How should we deal with increasing crime or pollution?).

The nature, scope, and characteristics of *issues* are best illustrated by two well-known, highly visible, public examples: (1) abortion and (2) the use of nuclear power. Few would disagree that abortion constitutes a major public policy issue. The various sides have rallied around very powerful and starkly conflicting organizing themes—the sanctity of life (pro-life) and the sanctity of an individual's freedom of choice (pro-choice). Pro-choice conveys to large segments of this society a message of constitutional guarantees of freedom and of the right of people (in this case, women) to choose. Pro-life argues powerfully on the other side that acceptance of abortion is murder, and murder is forbidden by the laws of any civilized society. Each side of the debate has framed the issue in wording that makes a powerful case to the public but has little to say to opponents. Each argument is almost totally exclusive of the other's position. Pro-choice advocates never have to deal with what their opponents call "murder" because they see the issue in terms of freedom of choice; pro-life advocates are not swayed by the personal tragedy of women—even victims of rape and incest—who would be denied the choice not to give birth, because they see the issue only in terms of life or death.

The second example directly affects many corporations: the history of nuclear power in the United States. The nuclear power industry has been embattled by opponents for the past 20 years. These opponents to nuclear power have adopted the tactic of questioning the safety and security of the power source. In its initial responses, the industry promoted the cost and political advantages: nuclear power was proclaimed to be cheaper than oil in the long run (no longer true) and was said to have the ability to free the United States from dependence on foreign oil (and, by extension, from the influence of foreign governments). The safety issue was definitely not the industry's first choice of topics to debate. As a result, the industry lost valuable time and momentum by not addressing the specific concerns of security and safety earlier. The industry surrendered the "high" ground in the debate to its opponents.

Issues can arise in many ways, but they are always fueled and ignited by change. First, issues often arise for organizations as a consequence of the preferences of other groups in society with regard to change. Second, issues may arise out of broad societal trends and patterns that are outside the control of one organization but are readily identifiable. Consider, for example, a number of demographic trends within the United States today: increases in the total number of ethnic minorities, increases in the average age of the population, reduction in the number of unskilled jobs, and growth in the number of one-parent homes. Some issues that could emerge from these trends are: demands for minority representation within organizations (as in the Operation PUSH example cited at the opening of this chapter), or demands for increased benefits for the elderly, or for corporate support for care of employees' dependents (to include employees' parents as well as their children). Finally, organizations can create issues for themselves as consequences of their own actions, as illustrated in Box 5–2.

There are several ways to characterize issues. One method is based on generic distinctions offered by Bartha.[5] He suggests that there are four types of generic issues: (1) universal, (2) advocacy, (3) selective, and (4) technical. Using these generic issue types, managers can learn to predict where an issue is likely to arise, what stakeholders are first involved, and the likely arena of solution.

Universal issues affect large numbers of people. Exposure to these issues is direct and personal, and personal impact is viewed as serious and imminent. Universal issues arise spontaneously in conversation. The general view is that government is responsible for their resolution. Examples include inflation, unemployment, energy crises, and hazardous wastes. The current debate in the Clinton Administration over the reform of health care in this country has sparked intense and widespread public debate—it is a universal issue.

Advocacy issues affect a smaller number of people than universal issues and stand lower on the list of public concerns. Usually introduced and promoted by spokespersons claiming to represent the public interest, they tend to be potential rather than actual problems. They do not emerge spontaneously in conversation, but, once raised, they cause people to react favorably to the need for action and solutions. The general view is, "Someone ought to do something about this"; the "someone" is unspecified. Consumer issues and improved health care access for the poor are examples of advocacy issues.

Selective issues are the focus of interest groups. They rarely arise spontaneously in conversation; when they are mentioned, usually only those directly affected express an interest or opinion. The problems and solutions are unique and affect only certain identifiable groups. Moreover, the costs of dealing with them are to be passed on to society-at-large; the interest group or those affected by the problems expect to get governmental or corporate support. These issues generate great intensity, commitment, and activism among those most likely to benefit. An example of a selective issue is corporate dependent care. Those favoring it wish to have corporations and nonprofit organizations provide facilities for such care and absorb some of the costs involved.

Whether some issues should be considered universal, advocacy, or selective is a matter of intense politicking. Opponents treat gay rights as a selective issue ("Gay rights should not be forced on the public"); proponents see it as a universal issue ("Gay rights are like any other civil rights").

Technical issues are of absolutely no interest to the general public; people are content to leave them in the hands of the experts until a larger problem arises. Only persons who have technical expertise would ordinarily discuss them. Examples include the application of general legislation or regulation to specific cases, the selection of the appropriate statistical method to analyze data, and the use of morbidity and mortality statistics in health care and insurance.

These categories of issues (universal, advocacy, selective, technical) represent important distinctions for organizations because they suggest the pathways for managing issues, the patterns that issues will follow, the role of the media, and the leaders who will fight for the issues. For example, universal issues have numerous champions, and the arena of action is generally a legislature, the higher courts, or the voting booth. It will be argued that government should do something about the problem or issue, but the costs, in fact, are often passed on to the private sector. The media have intense interest in such issues because they have high public visibility and are newsworthy. Advocacy issues, on the other hand, are articulated by specific groups who face a challenge in persuading the media of the newsworthiness of the issues while simultaneously seeking an appropriate arena for their resolution. Selective issues are championed by the specific groups who are directly affected (working parents, or people with certain disabilities or "orphan diseases"). They face enormous hurdles in obtaining media interest and in gaining access to and support from any specific arena.

Technical issues are ordinarily so complex that both the general public and the media are uninterested in them. Those who articulate these issues must find ways to make their pros and cons clear to the general public and the media.

All of these specific types of issues provide different challenges in terms of arena selection, media interest, and the enlistment of general public support.

The Evolution of Issues

The process by which issues emerge, evolve, and are resolved is difficult to delineate and describe because issues reflect so many different evolutionary paths. Some issues may come and go very quickly; others (such as abortion and health care) may linger on for decades. To aid managers in their understanding of how issues evolve, the "traditional" or public policy-oriented view of issues and their life cycles[6] was developed, as shown in Box 5–4.

A more inclusive view of life cycles, developed by the authors,[7] incorporates the stages included in the traditional model, but focuses attention on earlier stages in an issue's evolution, before it became public. These are the stages in the authors' model:

Stage 1: Stakeholders first become aware of a development or change in the environment. Issues at this emergence stage are ill-defined and poorly understood.

Stage 2: Stakeholders begin to interpret and make sense out of an issue. Because values often provide the basis for these interpretations, and because different stakeholders have different and often conflicting values, an issue may be interpreted in a variety of ways.

The third and fourth stages are similar to those described in the traditional model.

Stage 3: Stakeholders begin to take positions, and the issue becomes increasingly public and visible. During this stage, stakeholders often engage in political tactics such as coalition formation or constituency building.

Stage 4: The issue is resolved in some arena, whether formal or informal. (The traditional model assumes that resolution occurs in governmental arenas.)

Compared to the traditional model, this approach places more emphasis on the early stages of the life cycle. The implication from the point of view of a business is that it can influence the outcome of an issue when it first emerges (for example, by introducing new facts) or as it becomes interpreted (for example, by linking the business's interpretation with widely held societal values), and does not need to wait until the issue has become public and positions of various stakeholders have solidified.

Box 5–4
Conventional/Traditional Public Issues Life Cycle Model

The traditional or public issues life cycle consists of five stages through which an issue develops and evolves. A gestation phase begins when a gap develops between a firm's actual performance and the public's expectation of that performance (stage 1). This gap can be either real or perceived. The alcohol industry continues to deal with the issue of drunk driving and the causality (or lack thereof) of their products in drunk driving and accidents—a difference in the "facts."

As the gap between the alcohol industry's claims and society's perceptions and expectations widens over time, more groups and individuals become involved, and the risk increases that the issue will become politicized (stage 2). (The shift in public sentiment over the effectiveness of the health care system is also illustrative of stages 1 and 2.)

If the issue remains unresolved (that is, the gap is not narrowed by organizational or societal action), a legislative or regulatory phase can occur: The issue enters a specific political or regulatory body for discussion and resolution (stage 3).

After the issue is resolved, a period of litigation often follows. During that time, the interested parties test out the scope of the legislative or regulatory solution (stage 4).

Finally, after public policy has prevailed or the public has exercised its choice through media or community pressure to which the organization acquiesces, there occurs an institutionalization of the matter by the organizations affected (stage 5).

STAKEHOLDERS

Issues are shaped and driven by the actions of stakeholders. The activities listed in Table 5–1 necessarily involve stakeholders. In broad terms, stakeholders may be defined as "any group or individual who can affect or is affected by the achievement of the organization's purpose."[8] Stakeholders include a variety of entities typically seen as outside an industry: public interest groups, environmental and consumer advocacy groups, local community groups, industry and trade associations, and a dizzying array of governmental agencies and organizations. But stakeholders also include the "players" in the conventional meaning of an industry: suppliers, distributors, customers, and competitors. As we shall see, almost any combination of entities external to the industry and industry players may be either the firm's political rivals or its allies with regard to any particular issue or set of related issues. Thus, the relevant set of stakeholders may vary from one issue to another. Typical questions that arise in an analysis of stakeholders that provides input to political strategy development and execution are shown in Table 5–2.

TABLE 5–2 Critical stakeholder analysis questions.

1. What is the issue or set of issues?
2. Who are the relevant stakeholders?
3. What is the "stake" of each stakeholder and with what intensity is that "stake" held?
4. What claims, demands, and counterdemands result from each stake?
5. What differences and similarities exist across these stakes and/or stakeholders?
6. How can these stakeholders affect these issues?
7. How can these stakeholders affect the origanization's interests?
8. What can the organization do to influence these stakeholders?
9. How can these stakes and stakeholders be prioritized?
10. What *should* the organization do?
11. What *can* the organization do?

Stakeholders assume importance in the development and execution of political strategy to the extent that they hold a "stake" in one or more issues. Some stakeholders hold a stake by virtue of their economic role in relation to the organization. For example, customers hold a stake in the delivery of high-quality goods at reasonable prices, institutional investors are concerned with the security of their investment and their rate of return, and local communities are concerned about the security of their jobs. Some stakeholders have a noneconomic stake in the organization. Environmental groups might take upon themselves a stake in many organizations when they consider an organization's actions inimical to a clean and safe environment, and consumer advocacy groups might be concerned with the organization's products.

A stake, whether economic or not, is not an indication of the stakeholder's impact on the organization and its political and economic goals; rather, the impact comes from the stakeholder's willingness to act on that stake. For example, the intensity with which a stakeholder holds a position or point or view can lead to dramatic action. In both the gay rights movement and the pro-life movement, we have examples of intense stakeholders on both sides of the issue. The recent murder of a physician by a pro-life person (and the implication that a pro-life organization allegedly verbally supported the murder) has raised concerns over the reasonableness of the pro-life movement. The radical gay rights group ACT-UP has held numerous protests that have been criticized by other members of the gay community. "Radical" stakeholders can create issues for both their own organizations and the organizations they target.

Irrespective of the source of a stake, it causes stakeholders to place demands or claims on the organization. An industry or trade association, for example, often asks its members to support its efforts to change a specific piece of legislation. Consumer groups demand that businesses provide safer products. Shareholders frequently insist that a firm commit to generating higher financial returns for them. In short, most political strategy is focused on managing stakeholder demands and claims.

Assessing Threats and Opportunities for Cooperation

It is important for organizations to assess both the stakeholders' potential to cooperate and the threat they pose. Among other things, these assessments indicate how each major stakeholder could affect the organization's interests. It is crucial to note that opportunities for cooperation can vary dramatically between the political and product marketplaces and from one issue to another. For example, within the soft drink industry, competitiveness is very high because manufacturers and bottlers are competing for market share. Yet, proposals for recycling or repackaging of soda bottles and cans can lead to cooperation across industry lines to achieve an acceptable "political" solution for all of the players in the industry.

Relationships among Stakeholders

There are two final observations that we would offer concerning stakeholders. First, the relationships between and among stakeholders form a dynamic and complex process that evolves over time and with reference to specific issues and problems. For example, it is not uncommon to find within an industry two competitors who are strong allies with regard to one issue and fierce antagonists with regard to another. Thus, as one issue is resolved and another arises, today's enemies can easily be tomorrow's friends.

Second, stakeholders constitute an intricate interconnected web of relationships that are in a constant state of flux. How the organization chooses to interact with one stakeholder may dramatically affect its relationship with others. A key task in political strategy, therefore, is the assessment of how the organization's actions or position on a given issue can affect relationships with other stakeholders on this issue and *on all other issues currently being dealt with by the organization.* Organizations that do not recognize this simultaneity of issues and stakeholder relationships are likely to commit grave errors. For example, the founder of Domino's Pizza has given his personal funds to pro-life groups as a reflection of his own beliefs. As a result of this action, pro-choice groups have declared a nationwide boycott of Domino's Pizza products, thus attacking Domino's Pizza not in the political realm but in the product marketplace.

Arenas

Arenas are the public and private forums where political strategy is played out. As noted earlier, they may be either formal or informal. The more formal arenas include legislatures and political bodies (international, national, regional, state, or local), judicial arenas (all levels, including formal negotiations, mediations, and arbitrations), and regulatory arenas (again, at all levels). In designing and executing political strategy, organizations need to be aware of the significant differences between formal and informal arenas. The formal arenas are first and foremost public institutions. They are part of the formal governmental process and carry with them many forms of authority. They are capable of making and enforcing laws and regulations. Each type of formal arena has its own particular operating procedures, sets of rules, and norms. For example, in a court at any level, there are clearly defined judicial procedures; precedents have been set that impact on decisions and on the ways that the attorneys can argue specific situations.

By contrast, action and discussion within the informal arenas can occur outside the glare of publicity and public hearings. The participants themselves determine the rules of the engagement and what, if any, enforcement of the outcomes will occur. The ability to influence the "rules of engagement" allows for greater flexibility in solution seeking and finding. In contrast to formal arenas, there are no clearly defined routes of access: it is up to the parties involved, working toward satisfying their mutual interests, to determine how this shall take place. The National Coal Policy Project, for example, had no formal mechanisms or procedures for meeting. The participants made them up as they went along.

The discussion of strategy types later in the chapter will show how difficult it is to separate arenas from issues and stakeholders. Stakeholders typically have some measure of choice in arena selection. Selection of an arena by organizations and their stakeholders is central to the evolution of political rivalry and, in many instances, critically affects the outcome. Many of the examples offered in this chapter demonstrate the skill of stakeholders in selecting arenas that most favor their interests and avoiding arenas in which their interests may be more difficult to advance or defend. For example, U.S. airlines are well aware that no matter where in the world their planes are involved in an injurious or fatal accident, they will face litigation in U.S. courts. Litigants file their claims in U.S. courts because they tend to be far more generous than other legal jurisdictions in the settlements awarded to dependents and survivors.

Many firms have used the courts to their political and economic advantage. Manville, a firm that once made products containing asbestos, by filing for bankruptcy was able to treat victims of asbestosis as creditors in bankruptcy court and not as litigants in civil trials. Public interest groups exercise the same care in arena selection as do organizations. The recent success that environmental groups have had in stalling the implementation of the North American Free Trade Agreement (NAFTA) by petitioning in court for environmental impact statements is yet another example of this tactic.

How does all of this come together in the development and implementation of corporate political strategies? It is to that topic that we now turn our attention.

TYPES OF POLITICAL STRATEGY

The interplay among issues, stakeholders, and arenas is dynamic and ongoing. The nature of this relationship is such that any discussion of one element alone is somewhat artificial. A discussion of issues is incomplete without the recognition of the stakeholders involved. An analysis of stakeholders makes no sense without reference to issues, and a full political strategy analysis demands an intimate understanding of the issue–stakeholder–arena relationship. We will now address the strategy options available to organizations as they seek to manage issues, stakeholders, and arenas (see Table 5–3). In discussing these options, it is important to recall that issues, stakeholders, and arenas interact with one another in every unfolding issue. We must caution the reader that most organizations deal with multiple issues simultaneously. Although this increases the level of complexity, the strategic options for dealing with each issue are the same.

TABLE 5–3   Critical political strategy analysis questions.

Issues

What issues currently confront the organization?

At what stage of the issues' life cycle is each issue?

What issues are likely to emerge in the near future?

What issues should the organization create and/or champion?

What types of issues are they (universal, advocacy, selective, or technical)?

What stake does/will the organization have in each issue?

What stake does/will each stakeholder hold in each issue?

What alternatives are available to the organization to manage the issue?

Stakeholders

What stakeholders are currently involved in each issue?

What stakeholders are likely to emerge regarding each issue?

What are the stakeholders' demands and claims?

What impact are these stakeholders likely to have on the organization?

What is the organization's current and/or future base of power and influence with regard to each issue?

What alternatives are available to the organization in its dealings with stakeholders?

Arenas

In which arena is each current issue?

Can the arena of current issues be changed?

In which arena will each future issue emerge?

What alternatives are available to the organization in selection and operation within arenas?

Managing multiple issues necessitates analysis of a number of core questions (see Table 5–3) that go to the heart of political strategy and execution. As an example of this complexity, consider some of the major issues Ford Motor Company has to manage simultaneously. Ford has to have a coherent policy on: fuel efficiency, automobile air pollution, international manufacture and sales of automobiles, NAFTA, union negotiations and job security issues, the closed nature of the Japanese market, international competition, and automobile safety. Many of the issues overlap and have overlapping stakeholder interests. The unions are concerned about jobs, salaries, and benefits, but Ford has to consider the costs of the car from a customer's view. It might be cheaper to produce cars in Mexico but would their safety suffer and what would be the reaction of unions in Detroit? Cars are a major source of air pollution, but to improve their effect on the environment requires expensive technology that lowers gasoline efficiency and raises the cost of the car to the buyer. All of these issues must be addressed, and many of them will be resolved in the political arena.

The following sections provide examples of organizations engaging in corporate political strategy. The fundamental organizing theme is the issue, although, as should be clear, managing an issue entails developing strategies for stakeholder management and choice of arena. For ease of analysis, the focus is on a specific issue rather than organizations' attempts to manage multiple issues simultaneously.

Managing Early Issue Evolution

It is to an organization's benefit to preempt and contain issues. Although it is difficult to manage emerging issues, organizations always need to consider the option of trying to seize the political initiative by channeling the early stages of issue evolution in a direction that favors their own interests. They can do this in a number of ways including (but not limited to) redefining the issue, appealing to stakeholders, or moving the issue to arenas of the organization's choosing.

A well-known example of managing early issue evolution is the action of Johnson & Johnson (J&J) in a Tylenol tampering incident. The stakes for J&J were very high:

- Loss of consumer faith and trust.
- Significant financial losses from the withdrawal of a market-leading and highly profitable product.
- Potential negative regulatory reaction.

As soon as it became evident that its product had been tampered with and that deaths *might* have been caused by the tampering, J&J immediately pulled all of the product from store shelves. The intent was to send a powerful and unmistakable signal to key stakeholders—consumers—that the firm was committed to preserving and protecting not just its consumer franchise but consumers' safety and health. This decision was not reached easily. The Federal Bureau of

Investigation (FBI), another key stakeholder in this issue, wanted J&J to keep the product on the market. By doing so, the FBI hoped to catch the person or persons responsible for the tampering. When J&J raised the issue of liability for further loss of life, the FBI backed away from its argument. J&J was then able to continue its control of the selection of the arena in which this issue would be resolved. The company specifically rejected the legal arena as the first choice for resolution.

J&J maintained constant contact with the media—another critical stakeholder—with the intent of not just preempting bad press but of signaling to the media that it was committed to solving the crime and ensuring that a similar problem never occurred again. To attain the latter goal, J&J quickly moved the issue to another arena: it began to push a public policy initiative. It suggested that the Food and Drug Administration (FDA) should immediately require that all products such as Tylenol be placed in tamper-proof containers. (One consequence of this initiative was that some of the costs associated with the Tylenol tragedy were shared by all competitors.) In addition, J&J strengthened its position and image with customers as a firm that worries about their safety. As a consequence of its management of the issue, the stakeholders involved, and the arena selection, J&J was able to quickly reintroduce Tylenol and recapture its leading market share.

Issue Redefinition: Redefining Issues Already on the Agenda

In spite of an organization's best efforts, issues will still emerge, evolve, and arrive in arenas that are not of its choosing. The further the issue has evolved, the more likely that many stakeholders are aware of the issue, have developed an understanding or interpretation of it, have assessed their stake in it, and have developed some set of preferences for certain outcomes over other choices.

One of the most powerful strategies available to organizations is to redefine the issue—to recast the issue for existing and potential stakeholders. By redefining the issue, the organization changes stakeholders' perceptions of their stake in the issue itself.

The power of redefining or reshaping issues is evident in most of the examples that have already been noted. J&J reshaped the issue in the Tylenol incident from product tampering to the protection of consumers' health and safety. Activists on both sides of the abortion and gay rights issues are endeavoring to advance their specific issue definitions.

Issue redefinition also serves as a powerful weapon when a number of organizations are engaged in cooperative political strategies. Such strategies are often played out at the industry and trade association level. One continuing example is the efforts of the chemical industry to deal with hazardous waste site cleanup, in particular its responses to major legislative initiatives in the early and mid-1980s—the so-called Superfund legislation. Ironically, the legislative arena for Superfund was selected as a consequence of the oil industry's years-long lobbying for a federal oil spill bill. The oil industry was seeking to obtain relief from varying legislative demands across different states; the aim was to have one set of rules in dealing with spills. When the problem of hazardous wastes became a universal issue (as a result of Love Canal and other highly publicized sites), members of Congress merely appropriated language from the oil spill proposals and introduced bills in both houses. The chemical industry was ushered into an arena that had been already selected by Congressional action.

In the early days of the proposed legislation, the chemical industry attempted to define the issue as a "societal one"; that is, because society benefited from the advances made by chemicals, society should bear the burden of cleaning up waste sites. When that attempt failed, the industry tried to identify the issue as one of "orphan sites": the proposed tax, it said, should be used only to clean up sites where ownership or responsibility could not be determined. The industry reasoned that, because these sites were not numerous, the proposed tax should be very low. The industry's attempts failed, but it is important to note its persistent efforts to redefine the issue as it was up for resolution, and the subtle appeal that each redefinition held for different sets of publics interested in the issue. This example details the events and actions that occurred in a formal arena. Other issues can arise and be resolved in informal arenas, as the following California example indicates.

It is important to define or redefine issues quickly, before antagonists can assume and retain the initiative by successfully defining issues in a way that attracts and energizes a broader base of stakeholders. A classic example is the 1964 California grape pickers' strike, led by the late Cesar Chavez. It was not the first strike to be organized against the land owners (an example of an advocacy issue), and the history of such strikes was one of failure. Chavez succeeded where numerous others had failed because he managed the perception of the issue and made it one of universal appeal. Chavez and his followers portrayed the strike as a battle for the rights of an oppressed minority—migrant workers—not just another union–management conflict that happened to involve grapes. In 1964, civil rights was a sensitive issue, and the rights of the oppressed offered a valuable symbol to gain media attention and other support.

> "I am here," announced an early arrival in clerical garb, "because this is a movement by the poor people to improve their position, and where the poor are, Christ should be and is." Other supporters . . . said much the same thing in their own way: this was part of their battle against society's power structure.[9]

The national boycott of California grapes gave people an opportunity to participate in the struggle of the oppressed. Liberals could support the issue, and Chavez pressed the presidential contenders in 1964 for their position on the strike. The candidates' involvement had the effect of keeping the issue before the general public through national media coverage.

Moving an Issue Off an Agenda

In many instances, the ideal outcome for organizations is not just preemption or redefinition of an issue, but its total elimination. Once an issue is placed on an agenda, its elimination is normally beyond the actions of a single organization. The cooperation of stakeholders who represent diverse interests is most often required to achieve successful removal. Organizations are provoked to try to "kill" an issue when the consequences of how the issue might be resolved are large (or, stated differently, when their stakes in the issue are very high).

Many organizations have successfully gotten issues off either formal or informal agendas by reshaping existing stakeholders' stakes and/or broadening the base of stakeholders. A classic illustration of these tactics occurred in Massachusetts in 1982, when a controversial piece of legislation was introduced calling for dramatic reallocation in health care costs. The reason for the introduction of this legislation arose from federal pressures for changes in Medicare management and payments. The state saw this legislation as a potential opportunity to obtain a waiver from the federal government. Several major stakeholders were involved: the state Business Roundtable, the Massachusetts Hospital Association (MHA), Blue Cross, the High-Technology Council, physicians, the state Commissioner of Insurance, and the Life Insurance Association of Massachusetts (LIAM). A major focus of the legislation was to reduce health care costs and erode the dominant position that Blue Cross held in the state. This would improve the competitive position of the insurance companies in Massachusetts in the health care field. It was clear to all that the issue was "health care cost containment." This had great appeal to business (it would reduce the cost of employee benefits) and to individuals (it would reduce their costs for health care). The MHA, the physicians, and Blue Cross were less than thrilled by this proposal, but it had great public, business, and political backing and appeal.

In assessing the situation, Blue Cross noted that if the legislation passed, it would force the organization to reduce the benefits provided to its 300,000-plus elderly subscribers. That group would either pay more for benefits or receive fewer benefits, or both. Blue Cross called all of these subscribers to let them know of this impact. These subscribers, in turn, caused a massive grass-roots movement—an organized campaign of phone calls to public representatives, letters to newspapers, and representation to the electronic media. The resulting publicity stopped the issue dead. The public debate shifted to "erosion of benefits for the elderly," and no group or organization wanted to support that position publicly.

Another way to move an issue off an agenda, in either a formal or an informal arena, is through quick legislative or judicial action or the threat of such action. The threat of movement to another arena is often sufficient to compel compromises that are favorable to the organization's stakes. The breakup of AT&T illustrates this tendency.

The breakup of AT&T was not a universal issue as defined earlier, but had advocacy, selective, and technical aspects. The advocacy aspect was demonstrated by AT&T's position and posturing on the breakup itself; the issue's selective nature was represented by the actions of MCI, a competitor of AT&T in long-distance service. MCI, headquartered in Washington, DC, saw the opportunity to provide the legislature with a nonpolitical or governmental supporter of the breakup of AT&T. MCI also realized that the breakup of AT&T would yield it competitive opportunities unavailable by any other course of action. The details and other aspects of the breakup (for example, the access charge) were far too technical to elicit public or media interest.

As the breakup proceeded, AT&T became fed up with the slow pace of action and concerned that Judge Greene was going to hurt its interests. AT&T unleashed a flood of lobbyists on Capitol Hill, attempting to transfer control of the breakup from the courts to the legislature or to the Federal Communications Commission (FCC). AT&T was not successful in recapturing the issue from the federal judiciary, but its actions had the intended effect: they raised the specter of a conflict among three powerful stakeholders—(1) the courts, (2) the regulatory agency (the FCC), and (3) Congress—over jurisdiction in this situation, and thus moved the issue away from the regulatory and legislative arenas. Judge Greene got the message, the breakup proceeded at a faster rate of speed, and AT&T achieved many (but not all) of its major goals with the breakup.

LINKING POLITICAL AND CORPORATE STRATEGY

As noted at the beginning of this chapter, an organization's political strategy is not disconnected from its business strategy. Indeed, quite the contrary is true. Political strategy can affect business strategy in a myriad of ways, as is evidenced in the Bell Atlantic–TCI merger (see below). Our intent here is merely to illustrate some of the ways in which political strategy can support and facilitate business strategy.

On October 13, 1993, the largest communications merger in American history was announced. Throughout the summer, top executives of Bell Atlantic and TCI had been meeting, maintaining such a level of secrecy that even among themselves they referred to their companies in code. The final outcome of their meetings was the announcement that Bell Atlantic would buy TCI for stock valued at about $12 billion and would absorb $9.6 billion in debt. The deal included TCI's cable programming arm, Liberty Media Corporation.

Technologically, the merger builds on synergies that can be exploited between, for example, the carrying capacity of cable companies' coaxial lines and the switching capabilities of telephone companies. For consumers, it means vastly extended access to information—whether through video libraries or shopping networks—through new interactive video capabilities. For the industry, it means redefining what business the "Baby Bells" are in. One industry observer has said that businesses that fail to form similar alliances will be out of the picture.

The deal reflects a major strategic move for Bell Atlantic. It will own major equity stakes in, among others, Turner Broadcasting and Home Shopping Network. The merged organization will have access to 22 million customers in 59 of the top 100 U.S. markets. With plans to rebuild TCI's cable systems for phone service, Bell Atlantic, already a leader in innovation among the Baby Bells, will be positioned to challenge other phone companies for local service. Finally, the merger puts Bell Atlantic at the cutting edge of a telecommunications revolution and represents a major step toward laying the groundwork for the future "information highway."

However, the ultimate success of the merger is not affected solely by technological or marketplace advantages. As of this writing (less than two weeks after the announcement), major concerns have already been raised indicating that corporate political strategies will play—and already have played—a major role in the eventual success of the merger and the shaping of the industry that the new organization will compete in.

The issues spawned by the merger, which now must be managed by Bell Atlantic, include:

- The extent to which the proposed merger is perceived by others as a threat to competition;
- The way in which the proposed merger may influence later developments in the telecommunications industry;
- The short-run and long-run implications for customers.

The set of stakeholders likely to be involved in the resolution of these issues is extensive: industry participants such as direct and indirect competitors to the newly combined organization, distributors, customers, suppliers, and vendors; governmental agencies at the federal, state, and local levels; state and federal legislatures; judicial institutions at multiple levels; and public interest and consumerist groups. These stakeholders unquestionably will be confronting each other in multiple arenas: the courts, Congress, regulatory agencies (such as the Federal Trade Commission), the White House, the media, industry and trade associations, and the court of public opinion.

Indeed, it did not take long for the political battles to be initiated. Within days of the announcement, consumer groups were charging that the merger will eliminate competition, and at least one Senator wants to block it legislatively. Both the Justice Department and the Federal Trade Commission must determine whether it does indeed eliminate competition. There is some uncertainty concerning the Administration's position on this issue, although President Clinton has said he would like to help build the information superhighway. Vice President Gore has said the Administration will support any efforts that are procompetition, and Bell Atlantic and TCI officials are already lobbying the White House with assurances that this is such an effort. One of Ray Smith's (the Chairman of Bell Atlantic) missions, according to an editorial in *The Wall Street Journal,* is to gain Vice President Gore's support of the merger. Further, because state governments will be involved in reviewing the merger and municipalities must approve transfers, political efforts will be required at those levels as well as at the federal level.

Contained in this example are the impacts of political and noneconomic actions on the success of the Bell Atlantic–TCI merger. Even after the merger is approved, government actions will play a critical role in Bell Atlantic–TCI's efforts. For example, later in 1993, a task force headed by the Commerce Department was to begin to establish guidelines for the industry. The extent to which the government, rather than industry participants, determines the shape of this burgeoning industry will depend in part on the actions taken by Bell Atlantic–TCI.

At least three key conclusions can be drawn from this example:

1. Political strategy is sometimes necessary for business strategy success. For example, many firms have used political strategy to develop the alliances necessary to put in place the technological standards that were central to the marketplace success of their products. The ability to develop these alliances with key Administration officials is clearly important in the Bell Atlantic–TCI case.

2. Political strategy is sometimes critical to gaining access to marketplaces. For example, Japanese automobile manufacturers essentially negotiate the extent to which they can enter the U.S. marketplace through "voluntary restraints" agreements that govern the number of cars they can export to the United States. The ability of Bell Atlantic to serve its potential customer base may depend on decisions concerning its threat to competition.

3. The corollary of gaining marketplace access is that political strategy can contribute to preservation of marketplace position and protection against new entrants. U.S. automobile and electronics firms have benefited from the voluntary restraints agreements with Japan. Bell Atlantic–TCI's success at getting Administration support will have a similar effect by giving them an advantage in major markets throughout the United States.

CONCLUSION

In developing its political strategy, an organization needs to identify the most salient issues, the stakeholders who are likely to be its allies and antagonists, and how those stakeholders can impact the issues and the arenas in which it has a position of advantage over other current and potential stakeholders. The questions noted in Tables 5–2 and 5–3 provide the necessary framework of analysis. Once the most critical issues have been determined, then the organization has to assess and execute the types of strategy alternatives discussed earlier.

Let us conclude where we began. As illustrated in the Bell Atlantic–TCI case, our thesis in this chapter has been that the need to use political strategy in conjunction with business strategy will increase in the business environment of the 21st century. Business strategy alone will not be sufficient to ensure success in the product marketplace. Managers in the next century will have to demonstrate the same level of skill in dealing with the political environment that they have developed in this century in dealing with the product marketplace. It seems safe to suggest, given the current pace of change in the political and social arenas, that managers will be confronting a greater diversity of issues than ever before. Becoming adept at political strategy is no longer a luxury: It is a survival skill.

NOTES

1. Portions of this chapter draw on the following work of the authors: B. Bigelow, L. Fahey, and J. F. Mahon, "Political Strategy and Issue Evolution: A Framework for Analysis," in K. Paul (ed.), *Contemporary Issues in Business and Society* (Lewiston, NY: Edwin Mellon Press, 1991), 1–26; J. F. Mahon, "Corporate Political Strategy," *Business in the Contemporary World* (November 1989), 50–62; J. F. Mahon, B. Bigelow, and L. Fahey, "Toward a Theory of Corporate Political Strategy," paper presented at the Academy of Management national meetings. Washington, DC August 1989.

2. J. J. Keller, "Abortion Issue Prompts AT&T to End Its Support for Planned Parenthood," *The Wall Street Journal,* March 26, 1990, A3B.

3. T. M. Hay and B. Gray, "The National Coal Policy Project: An Interactive Approach to Corporate Social Responsiveness," in Lee E. Preston (ed.), *Research in Corporate Social Performance and Policy,* Vol. 7 (Greenwich, CT: JAI Press, 1985), 191–212.

4. P. Bachrach and M. S. Baratz, "Two Faces of Power," *American Political Science Review* (1962), 947–952; T. Lowi, "American Business, Public Policy, Case Studies and Political Theory," *World Politics* (1964), 677–715.

5. P. F. Bartha, "Managing Corporate External Issues: An Analytical Framework," *Business Quarterly* (1982), *47,* 78–90.

6. R. Eyestone, *From Social Issues to Public Policy* (New York: John Wiley & Sons, Inc., 1978). Eyestone was one of the first to look at issues and their development.

7. B. Bigelow, L. Fahey, and J. F. Mahon, 1991. "Political Strategy and Issue Evolution," in K. Paul (ed.), *Contemporary Issues in Business and Politics* (Lewiston, NY: Edwin Mellon Press, 1991), 1–26.

8. R. E. Freeman, *Strategic Management: A Stakeholder Approach* (Boston: Pitman Publishing, 1984), 53.

9. R. W. Cobb and C. D. Elder, *Participation in American Politics: The Dynamics of Agenda Building* (Baltimore: Johns Hopkins University Press, 1972), 72.

REFERENCES

Bigelow, B., Fahey, L., and Mahon, J. F. 1991. "Political Strategy and Issues Evolution: A Framework for Analysis," in K. Paul (ed.), *Contemporary Issues in Business and Politics,* 1–26. Lewiston, NY: Edwin Mellon Press.

Bigelow, B., Fahey, L., and Mahon, J. F. 1993. "A Typology of Issues Evolution," *Business and Society.* Spring, pp. 18–29.

Brewer, T. L. 1992. "An Issue-Area Approach to the Analysis of MNE-Government Relations." *Journal of International Business Studies, 23:*295–310.

Cobb, R. W., and Elder, C. D. 1972. *Participation in American Politics: The Dynamics of Agenda Building.* Baltimore, MD: Johns Hopkins University Press.

Dutton, J. E., Fahey, L., and Narayanan, V. K. 1983. "Toward Understanding Strategic Issue Diagnosis." *Strategic Management Journal, 4:*307–324.

Dutton, J. E., and Ottensmeyer, E. 1987. "Strategic Issue Management Systems: Forms, Functions, and Contexts." *Academy of Management Review, 12:*355–365.

Fahey, L., Bigelow, B., Mahon, J. F., and Narayanan, V. K. 1992. "A Political Strategy Perspective on Product-Market Strategy." Paper presented at the annual conference of the International Association for Business and Society, Leuven, Belgium, June.

Freeman, R. E. 1984. *Stakeholder Management: A Stakeholder Approach.* Boston: Pitman Publishing.

Getz, K. 1991. "Selecting Corporate Political Tactics," in J. L. Wall and L. R. Jauch (eds.), *Best Paper Proceedings,* 326–330. Miami, FL: Academy of Management.

Ghemawat, P. 1986. "Sustainable Advantage." *Harvard Business Review, 64:*53–58.

Greening, D. 1991. "Organizing for Public Issues: Environmental and Organizational Predictors of Structure and Process," in J. L. Wall and L. R. Jauch (eds.), *Best Paper Proceedings,* 331–335. Miami, FL: Academy of Management.

Hainsworth, B. E. 1990. "Issues Management: An Overview." *Public Relations Review, 16:*3–5.

Heath, R. L., and Nelson, R. A. 1986. *Issues Management: Corporate Public Policy Making in an Information Society.* London: Sage Publications.

Keim, G., and Zeithaml, C. P. 1986. "Corporate Political Strategy and Legislative Decision-Making: A Review and Contingency Approach." *Academy of Management Review, 11:*828–843.

Kim, W. C. 1988. "The Effects of Competition and Corporate Political Responsiveness on Multinational Bargaining Power." *Strategic Management Journal, 9:*289–295.

Mahon, J. F. 1989. "Corporate Political Strategy." *Business in the Contemporary World, 11:*50–62.

Mahon, J. F. 1993. "Shaping Issues/Manufacturing Agents: Corporate Political Sculpting," in B. M. Mitnick (ed.), *Corporate Construction of Competition in Public Affairs.* Newbury Park, CA: Sage, pp. 187–212.

Mahon, J. F., Bigelow, B., and Fahey, L. 1989. "Toward a Theory of Corporate Political Strategy." Paper presented at the annual meetings of the Academy of Management, Washington, DC, August.

Mahon, J. F., Bigelow, B., and Fahey, L. 1990. "Toward a Theory of Corporate Political Strategy." Paper presented at the meetings of the International Association for Business and Society, San Diego, CA, March.

Mahon, J. F., and Vachani, S. 1992. "Establishing a Beachhead in International Markets: The Direct and Indirect Approach." *Long Range Planning, 25*(3):60–69.

Mahon, J. F., and Waddock, S. A. 1992. "Strategic Issues Management: An Integration of Issue Life Cycle Perspectives." *Business and Society, 31:* 19–32.

Mizruchi, M. S. 1989. "Similarity of Political Behavior among Large American Corporations." *American Journal of Sociology, 95:* 401–424.

Post, J. E., and Waddock, S. A. 1989. "Social Cause Partnerships and the 'Mega-Event': Hunger, Homelessness, and Hands Across America," in J. E. Post (ed.), *Research in Corporate Social Performance and Policy,* 181–206. Greenwich, CT: JAI Press.

Tombari, H. A. 1984. *Business and Society: Strategies for the Environment and Public Policy.* New York: Dryden Press.

Waddock, S., and Mahon, J. F. 1991. "Corporate Social Performance Revisited: Dimensions of Effectiveness, Efficiency, and Efficacy," in J. E. Post (ed.), *Research in Corporate Social Performance and Policy,* 231–262. Greenwich, CT: JAI Press.

Wartick, S. L., and Cochran, P. L. 1985. "The Evolution of the Corporate Social Performance Model." *Academy of Management Review, 10:* 758–769.

Wilson, G. K. 1985. *Business and Politics: A Comparative Study.* Englewood Cliffs, NJ: Prentice-Hall.

Wilson, G. K. 1991. "Corporate Political Strategies." *British Journal of Political Science, 20:* 281–288.

Windsor, D. 1992. "Stakeholder Management in Multinational Enterprises," in S. Waddock (ed.), *International Association for Business and Society Proceedings,* 121–127. Leuven, Belgium: The Association.

Yoffie, D. B. 1987. "Corporate Strategies for Political Action: A Rational Model," in A. M. Marcus (ed.), *Business Strategy and Public Policy.* New York: Quorum.

Yoffie, D. B., and Badaracco, J. L. 1989. "A Rational Model of Corporate Political Strategies." Harvard Business School, Cambridge, MA. Working Paper 9-785-018.

PART THREE

STRATEGY INPUTS: ANALYZING THE EXTERNAL AND INTERNAL ENVIRONMENTS

INDUSTRY ANALYSIS: UNDERSTANDING INDUSTRY STRUCTURE AND DYNAMICS*

6

David Collis
Pankaj Ghemawat

Harvard Business School

Industry analysis is one of the most useful forms of strategic analysis, which is why it is widely practiced as well as preached. Careful industry analysis can help establish whether a particular industry is likely to prove attractive to the "average" competitor and can also shed light on profit differences among the competitors in that industry. More broadly, industry analysis illuminates the competitive landscape in a way that aids the formulation of effective strategies.

The overriding goal of this chapter is to provide two alternative but related frameworks for industry analysis. The major sections deal with these questions:

- What are the objectives of industry analysis?
- How should industries be defined?
- What determines an industry's average profitability? Porter's "five forces" model is discussed here in detail.
- What are the effects of industry-level attributes on intra-industry profit differences? Particular reference is made here to a resource-based model of industry analysis.

* The authors are grateful to Richard Caves, Michael Enright, Liam Fahey, Anita McGahan, Srinivasa Rangan, Joan Ricart i Costa, Richard Rosenbloom, and David Yoffie for their comments on an earlier draft, to Adam Brandenburger for relevant discussions, and to the Division of Research at the Harvard Business School for financial support. The opinions expressed herein are, however, strictly the authors' own.

THE OBJECTIVES OF INDUSTRY ANALYSIS

The first and most popular use of industry analysis is to predict the average level of long-term profitability of the competitors in a particular industry. Research has demonstrated that there are substantial, sustained differences in profitability among industries (Table 6–1). The pharmaceutical industry, for example, has earned far more on average than the steel industry in the United States over the past 20 years. There are technical reasons why one would not expect all industries to show exactly the same profitability. In part, the accounting rates of return shown in Table 6–1 do not correlate perfectly with true economic rates of return; also, cyclical industries should earn higher profits to account for their greater risk. However, the size and durability of these reported differences suggest the value of assessing the extent to which a particular industry will resemble pharmaceuticals or steel in terms of its long-term profit potential.

Assessments of average industry profitability can be useful at several levels of an organization. At the corporate level, they are valuable inputs into decisions to enter or exit particular industries. They also help top management plan the allocation of resources and the evaluation of performance across portfolios of businesses. At the level of the individual business, working through an industry analysis systematizes the identification of *opportunities* and *threats*, the two external components of the venerable SWOT (strengths–weaknesses–

TABLE 6–1   Profitability by manufacturing subsector, 1971–1990.

	Return on Equity	Return on Assets	Return on Sales
Drugs	21.4%	11.8%	13.1%
Printing and publishing	15.5	7.1	5.5
Food and kindred products	15.2	6.6	3.9
Chemicals and allied products	15.1	7.5	7.2
Petroleum and coal products	13.1	6.5	6.5
Instruments and related products	12.9	7.2	6.9
Industrial chemicals and synthetics	12.9	6.2	6.1
Paper and allied products	12.5	6.0	5.1
Aircraft, guided missiles, and parts	12.4	4.1	3.7
Fabricated metal products	12.3	5.7	3.7
Motor vehicles and equipment	11.6	5.6	3.7
Rubber and misc. plastic products	11.6	5.1	3.4
Electric and electronic equipment	11.5	5.4	4.4
Machinery, except electrical	11.1	5.8	3.4
Stone, clay, and glass products	10.4	4.8	4.0
Textile mill products	9.3	4.3	2.5
Nonferrous metals	8.3	3.9	3.6
Iron and steel	3.9	1.5	1.3

Source: Anita McGahan (1992).

opportunities–threats) framework that many firms still use in their formal strategic planning processes.

A second use of industry analysis is to gain some understanding of profit differences among competitors in the same industry. Such profit differences are of interest because they seem to be both large and long-lived. For example, the steel industry features a few competitors that have managed to sustain very attractive rates of return (see Figure 6–1b). Conversely, some competitors in the pharmaceutical industry have not been very profitable (see Figure 6–1a). Industry-level attributes help shape such within-industry differences.

An understanding of intra-industry profit differences has at least two uses:

1. The extent of such differences is a helpful indicator of the scope and type of strategies that might outperform industry averages.

2. Insight into the sources of intra-industry profit differences helps companies develop better matches between their internal resources, competencies, and capabilities (or strengths and weaknesses, to use SWOT terminology) and the industry environments that they face.

INDUSTRY DEFINITION

Before one can begin to analyze an industry, one must define it. This is not a trivial matter. Although the scope of an industry to be considered is often intuitively apparent, drawing industry boundaries very precisely can be difficult. For example, should a definition of the U.S. automobile industry be confined to passenger cars or should it also include light trucks, which are increasingly popular vehicles for personal transportation?

Official statistical definitions such as the Standard Industrial Classification (SIC) codes aren't of much help in addressing such questions. For the U.S. automobile industry, for example, the SIC codes break out passenger cars from trucks, but lump light trucks together with their heavier brethren. This illustrates a general problem with SIC codes: They rarely correspond to competitively relevant industry conditions.

The most helpful principle in defining industries is to account for substitution possibilities, on both the demand and the supply sides. On the demand side, companies need to look beyond their direct competitors: they must also account for indirect competitors that offer products or services that are close substitutes for their own. On the supply side, they must account for technological substitutability as well. Taken together, demand- and supply-side considerations suggest that industries should be defined in terms of companies that share customers or technologies with each other.[1] Thus, a decision about whether cars and light trucks should be treated as part of the same industry depends on both the degree of demand-side substitutability between the two product lines and the extent to which know-how and production equipment can be cross-utilized (supply-side substitutability).

FIGURE 6–1   Average return on assets, 1973–1992 (%).

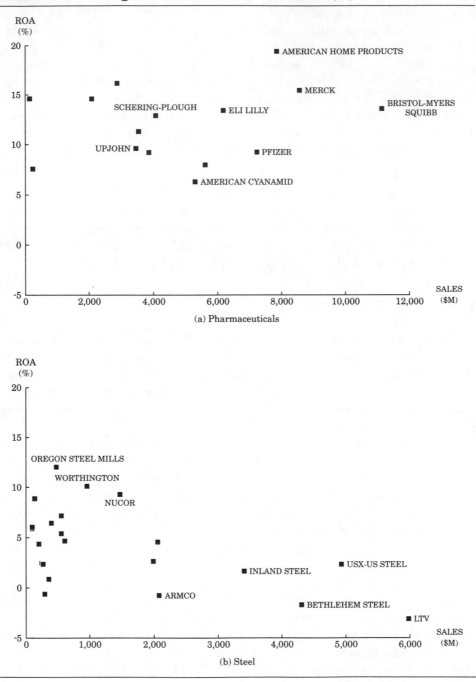

(a) Pharmaceuticals

(b) Steel

Despite the principle of substitutability, the definition of industry boundaries remains as much an art as a science. Most of the ambiguities involve various dimensions of scope:[2]

- Horizontal—across product markets.
- Vertical—along the value chain.
- Geographic—across local, regional, and national boundaries.

Horizontal Scope

The issue of horizontal scope has already been highlighted by the example of passenger cars and light trucks. When it is unclear whether a narrow horizontal definition corresponds to a segment of an industry or a separate industry, it may make sense to analyze the industry based on both narrow and broad definitions. The narrow definition focuses the analysis, and the broad one prevents being blindsided by unexpected new competitors. If it proves very difficult to analyze the broader definition of an industry because of differences among segments, then the industry is properly defined narrowly, not broadly.

Vertical Scope

In regard to vertical scope, the key issue is how many vertically linked stages an industry should be defined to span. For example, can one analyze bauxite mining, alumina refining, aluminum smelting, and fabrication of aluminum products independently of each other? In general, if a competitive market for third party sales exists between vertical stages, the stages should be uncoupled in defining industries; if not, they should remain coupled. In this sense, the tightest coupling in the vertical aluminum chain is between bauxite mining and alumina refining, because most refineries are tied to one source of bauxite. The loosest coupling is between aluminum smelting and fabrication because fabricators can buy aluminum ingot from the London Exchange as well as from different smelters. If competitors specialized to a particular vertical stage thrive, it may make sense to treat that stage as a separate industry.

Geographic Scope

The issue here is whether physically separate markets should be treated as being served by the same industry or by distinct industries. For example, does it make more sense to talk of the U.S. pharmaceutical industry or of the global pharmaceutical industry? Such issues can arise around local and regional boundaries as well as national ones. A key criterion in settling them is whether competitive positions in different geographic markets are interdependent. Because of the importance of amortizing their huge research and development (R&D) expenditures, interdependence across markets is higher for pharmaceutical companies than for steelmakers, suggesting that the pharmaceutical industry should generally be defined to have broader geographic scope.

Additional complexities can arise along each of these dimensions if competitors differ significantly in terms of their chosen scope. In such situations, industry definitions may have to acknowledge the differences among competitors. More generally, it may sometimes be helpful to identify "strategic groups" within an industry—sets of competitors that compete in similar ways for similar customers and interact more directly within each group than with competitors drawn from other strategic groups. In the automobile industry, for instance, luxury car manufacturers constitute a distinct strategic group whose performance is partly independent of competition in the mass market for automobiles.

AVERAGE INDUSTRY PROFITABILITY

Industry analysis is most often used to assess the future prospects for average industry profitability. There is a substantial amount of research indicating that the profit potential of an industry is bounded by basic conditions that are largely exogenous, such as the price elasticity of demand and the production technology. These define the gap between buyers' willingness to pay for products and suppliers' willingness to provide the required resource inputs. The extent to which such profit potential is actually realized by the industry depends on its structural attributes—such as its concentration levels, which tend to be more endogenous—as well as on the strategies adopted by direct and indirect competitors.

By far the most popular application of these structuralist ideas, one that supplements scientific evidence with common sense, is Michael Porter's[3] "five forces" framework for assessing average industry profitability (see Figure 6–2).

The Five Forces Framework

The horizontal dimension of Porter's five forces framework comprises three forces that are uncompromisingly competitive:

1. The degree of rivalry.
2. The threat of entry.
3. The threat of substitutes.

The vertical dimension involves two forces that have cooperative as well as competitive components:

4. Buyer power.
5. Supplier power.

A company usually cannot do without buyers or suppliers, even though it is likely to thrive in the absence of direct or indirect competitors. We will discuss these forces one-by-one, starting with the horizontal or explicitly competitive forces.[4]

FIGURE 6–2   Elements of industry structure.

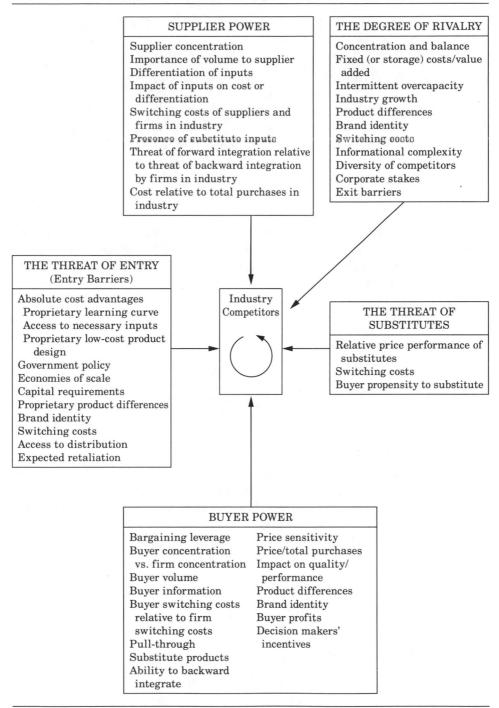

SUPPLIER POWER

Supplier concentration
Importance of volume to supplier
Differentiation of inputs
Impact of inputs on cost or
    differentiation
Switching costs of suppliers and
    firms in industry
Presence of substitute inputs
Threat of forward integration relative
    to threat of backward integration
    by firms in industry
Cost relative to total purchases in
    industry

THE DEGREE OF RIVALRY

Concentration and balance
Fixed (or storage) costs/value
    added
Intermittent overcapacity
Industry growth
Product differences
Brand identity
Switching costs
Informational complexity
Diversity of competitors
Corporate stakes
Exit barriers

THE THREAT OF ENTRY
(Entry Barriers)

Absolute cost advantages
    Proprietary learning curve
    Access to necessary inputs
    Proprietary low-cost product
        design
Government policy
Economies of scale
Capital requirements
Proprietary product differences
Brand identity
Switching costs
Access to distribution
Expected retaliation

Industry
Competitors

THE THREAT OF
SUBSTITUTES

Relative price performance of
    substitutes
Switching costs
Buyer propensity to substitute

BUYER POWER

Bargaining leverage
Buyer concentration
    vs. firm concentration
Buyer volume
Buyer information
Buyer switching costs
    relative to firm
    switching costs
Pull-through
Substitute products
Ability to backward
    integrate

Price sensitivity
Price/total purchases
Impact on quality/
    performance
Product differences
Brand identity
Buyer profits
Decision makers'
    incentives

Source: Michael Porter (1979).

Force 1: The Degree of Rivalry

The intensity of rivalry is the most obvious of the five forces in an industry—and the one that strategists have focused on historically. It helps determine the extent to which the value created by the industry will be dissipated in the competitive struggle. Porter's five forces framework provides a useful reminder that rivalry is only one of several forces that determine industry attractiveness.

The structural determinants of the degree of rivalry in a industry are numerous. One set of conditions concerns the number and relative sizes of competitors. The more concentrated the industry, the more likely it is that competitors will recognize their mutual interdependence and so restrain their rivalry. If, in contrast, there are a lot of small players in the industry, each is apt to think that its effect on others will go unnoticed and so is tempted to gain market share, thereby disrupting the market.

The presence of a dominant competitor rather than a set of equally balanced competitors also tends to lessen rivalry because the dominant player can set industry prices and discipline defectors, while equally sized players often try to outdo each other to gain an advantage. The titanium dioxide industry, for example, is one of the most profitable commodity industries in the world because of its highly concentrated structure and the leadership provided by the dominant competitor, Du Pont.

A second set of structural attributes that influence rivalry is more closely related to the industry's basic conditions. In capital-intensive industries, for example, the level of capacity utilization has a direct impact on the incentive for firms to engage in price competition to fill their plants. More generally, high fixed costs, excess capacity, slow growth, and lack of product differentiation all increase the degree of rivalry. Most of these factors are implicated in the low profitability of the airline industry. In contrast, in consumer goods industries, where each firm positions and advertises its products to appeal to a slightly different set of consumers, firms are less direct competitors and rivalry is reduced.

The degree of rivalry also has behavioral determinants. If competitors have diverse objectives or attach high strategic stakes to their positions in an industry, they are likely to compete aggressively within it. For example, Cummins Engine, a largely family-owned firm that specializes in diesel engines for trucks, unilaterally cut prices almost in half in the early 1980s to stop Japanese competitors from gaining market share, even though this condemned the industry to negative average profitability for nearly a decade.

Force 2: The Threat of Entry

Average industry profitability is influenced by potential as well as existing competitors. The key concept in analyzing the threat of entry is entry barriers, which act to prevent an influx of firms into an industry whenever profits, adjusted for the cost of capital, rise above zero. In the restaurant industry, for example, if a new format (i.e., style of cooking) such as mesquite grilling becomes popular, the limited height of entry barriers allows any interested party with a modicum of resources to open a mesquite grill restaurant, eroding the format's profitability. In contrast, entry barriers exist whenever it is difficult or uneconomic for an outsider to replicate the position of the incumbents. Entry barriers usually rest on irreversible resource commitments (discussed below).

Figure 6–2 illustrates that entry barriers can take many different forms. Some barriers reflect intrinsic physical or legal obstacles to entry. It would probably be hard to discover a diamond mine rich enough to justify entry into the diamond mining industry. Similarly, the existence and efficacy of patents on aspartame (Nutrasweet) and other artificial sweeteners have, until recently, historically impeded entry into new segments of that industry.

The most common forms of entry barriers, however, are usually the scale and the investment required to enter an industry as an efficient competitor. For example, no one is likely to enter the aluminum industry on an integrated basis, because an efficient integrated facility would cost several billion dollars and account for 5 percent or more of worldwide demand, which is already low enough to have led to considerable overcapacity and soft prices. Similarly, when incumbent firms have well-established brand names and clearly differentiated products, it may be prohibitively expensive for a potential entrant to undertake the marketing campaign necessary for effective introduction of a competing product.

Credible threats of retaliation by incumbents can also deter entry. In the diamond industry, the Central Selling Organization (CSO) controlled by DeBeers has a long record of discouraging attempts by diamond producers to market their rough diamonds directly. Zaire, for example, tried to dispense with the CSO in the early 1980s but returned to its fold after a glut developed for the grades of diamonds produced by Zairian mines. The glut was due, in part, to destocking of these grades by the CSO.

Force 3: The Threat of Substitutes

The existence of substitutes that perform the same functions as the products or services being analyzed is a basic condition that caps the amount of value an industry can create. When high-fructose corn syrup (HFCS) was replacing sugar as the sweetener in soft drinks, Pepsi and Coca-Cola were willing to switch only when the cost of the HFCS needed to sweeten a can of cola fell below the cost of sugar. The threat of substitution from sugar therefore capped the price of HFCS. When the cost of HFCS rose above the cost of sugar, HFCS manufacturers were unable to make any profit at all.

The analysis of the threat of (demand-side) substitution must focus on the customer function performed, not just on physically similar products. Overnight delivery services, which provide rapid document delivery, must consider facsimile machines to be an important substitute, even though the two use entirely different means to achieve the same end. Similarly, because potential car buyers can repair their old cars or buy second-hand vehicles, auto manufacturers need to consider the alternative of doing without a new car as a substitution threat that constrains the price they can charge for new cars.

Conceptually, analysis of the substitution possibilities open to buyers should be supplemented with consideration of the possibilities available to suppliers.[5] Supply-side substitutability affects suppliers' willingness to provide required inputs, just as demand-side substitutability affects buyers' willingness to pay for products. Chemical industries that use high-grade wood pulp, for example, are constrained in their ability to push down the prices they pay by the fact that pulp-production equipment can be switched from high-grade pulp to lower grade pulp used by other industries, such as paper products.

Force 4: Buyer Power

Buyer power is one of the two vertical forces that influences who appropriates the value created by an industry. Buyer power allows customers to squeeze industry margins by pressing competitors to reduce prices or to increase the level of service offered without recompense.

Probably the most important determinant of buyer power is the size and concentration of the customers. In its heyday, for example, General Motors (GM) enjoyed enormous bargaining power because it dominated the automobile industry. GM regularly threatened its component suppliers with loss of its business if they failed to offer price or nonprice concessions, and those suppliers, desperate to avoid losing such a large fraction of their business, often agreed. GM's bargaining power was also enhanced by other factors, including the extent to which it was well-informed about supplier costs, the credibility of its threat to integrate backward into suppliers' businesses, and the relatively low costs it would incur if it switched suppliers.

Such buyer bargaining power can, of course, be offset by competitors' concentration (i.e., a small number of competitors) and product differentiation. If only one competitor can provide the precise specifications required by a customer, that customer's buyer power is severely diminished. Thus, suppliers of critical components such as electronic fuel injection (EFI) systems fared somewhat better with GM than the average component supplier because of both their limited number and their attractiveness to the customer's customers (EFI became a key selling point for certain car models).

It is often useful to distinguish potential buyer power from the willingness or incentive to use that power. The U.S. government is one of the most powerful buyers in the market by virtue of its size; yet, unfortunately for U.S. taxpayers, it has not historically been one of the most price-sensitive purchasers. To explain why firms have the incentive to use their inherent purchasing power, it is necessary to look at another, more behavioral set of conditions.

Prime among these conditions is the share of the purchasing industry's cost accounted for by the products in question. Purchasing decisions naturally focus on larger-cost items first. Suppliers of incidental products can, therefore, often escape the keenest attentions of purchasing agents.

Of almost equal importance is the "risk of failure" associated with the use of a product. In the early days of mainframe computers, for example, the head of a management information systems (MIS) department often purchased IBM computers rather than a lower priced, lesser known brand with perhaps equivalent capabilities. Such purchase decisions were based on the risk to the manager's careers of buying from another company a mainframe computer that did not work. If, however, the head of an MIS department bought an IBM computer and it failed, he or she could not be fired for having bought the "best product" on the market. Purchase decisions for items critical to a whole system's operation, such as oil-rig blowout prevention equipment, are usually influenced by such risks of failure, which substantially reduce the buyer's price-sensitivity.

The example of IBM mainframe computers highlights the importance of studying the decision-making process when analyzing buyer power. The interests and incentives of all players involved in the purchase decision must be understood if one is to predict the price-sensitivity of the buyer. MIS department heads often faced incentives that diverged from the interests of their companies, yet they exercised considerable control over the purchase decision because at that time only they—not the line managers or top management—understood computer technology and capabilities. Buyer power can often be reduced if individuals who tend to be more concerned with high performance than low prices—engineers or plant managers instead of purchasing agents—are involved in the buying decision.

Force 5: Supplier Power

Supplier power is the mirror image of buyer power. The analysis of supplier power focuses, first, on the relative size and concentration of suppliers relative to industry participants and, second, on the degree of differentiation in the inputs supplied. The most profitable players involved in the IBM-compatible personal computer (PC) industry, for example, are not IBM, Dell, or other manufacturers, but Intel (microprocessors) and Microsoft (operating systems), which have virtual monopolies on the supply of critical components for IBM-compatible PCs.

The acid test of supplier power is whether suppliers are able to set prices that reflect the value of their inputs to the industry and not just their own production costs. Suppliers of many commodity chemicals and other raw materials, for example, manage to pass along cost increases without necessarily possessing supplier power. Their margins may already be very low, and a price increase simply serves to keep them in business at low rates of return. What must be tested instead is whether suppliers are able to extract most of the value created in the industries that they serve. The ability to charge discriminatory prices between customers is usually indicative of higher supplier power (and low buyer power).

Consideration of buyer and supplier power must always be balanced with the recognition that relationships between buyers and suppliers have important cooperative as well as competitive elements. General Motors and other U.S.

automobile companies lost sight of this fact when they pushed their parts suppliers to the wall by playing them off against each other. Japanese car companies, in contrast, committed themselves to long-run supplier relationships that paid off in terms of quality and the speed of new product development.

Two Examples

The inherent attractiveness of an industry—its expected average profitability—is not determined by just one factor, such as how fast the industry is growing (although this does tend to reduce rivalry and thereby raise industry profitability). Rather, it reflects the interaction of the competitive forces described above. Using the factors in Figure 6–2 as a checklist to determine the strength of each of those competitive forces is, therefore, a critical part of a thorough industry analysis.

To achieve a more holistic perspective on the five competitive forces, we can compare the pharmaceutical and steel industries in the United States, the two industries identified as the most and least profitable in Table 6–1.

Pharmaceuticals

Rivalry in the pharmaceutical industry is limited by patent protection, product differentiation, and the lack of effective substitutes. Barriers to entry are very high: Potential entrants must spend hundreds of millions of dollars to research new drugs and complete an approval process that can take years; they must also make significant investments in marketing and sales. Buyers or suppliers have not historically been in a position to squeeze industry profits. On the demand side, patients lack the information to evaluate competing drugs and must take into account the high personal cost of any substitute's failure. The high personal cost of failure is also a consideration for doctors who may be faced with malpractice suits. In addition, many doctors and patients lack any incentive to hold down the prices paid for drugs because a third party—an insurance company—actually foots the bill. For conventional drugs (as opposed to biotechnological products), inputs are usually available from several commodity chemical companies. Because each of the five competitive forces is favorable to the pharmaceutical industry, its historically high level of average profitability is predictable from the model.

Steel

The U.S. steel industry is characterized by very different attributes. Rivalry in the steel industry is exacerbated by worldwide overcapacity, high exit barriers, and an inflow of cheap imports. The barriers to entry into fully integrated steel-making are very high (for example, the cost of duplicating one of the largest competitors' operations). However, the technology for becoming a small, highly efficient competitor—by using a mini-mill to make steel by melting scrap—has reduced the minimal efficient scale and capital required for steel production by an order of magnitude. Substitutes that are taking markets away from steel include plastics, aluminum, and ceramics. Buyers include such large and powerful companies as automobile manufacturers, who tend to focus considerable attention on steel prices because steel often represents the largest single component of product costs. Historically, the U.S. steel industry has faced a very powerful supplier in the United Steel Workers Union, which was able to bargain steelworkers' wages to well above the levels for other manufacturing industries. These negative competitive forces help explain the steel industry's abysmally low profitability.

Model Assessment

In addition to being widely used, the five forces framework is supported by research findings to a much greater extent than most other strategic planning frameworks. Both considerations suggest that companies can profit from a five forces analysis. Despite this favorable overall assessment, it is nevertheless useful to suggest areas where care needs to be taken in applying the five forces framework

Framework Structure

Why are there five, and only five, forces in the framework? The five forces identified are, at the aggregate level, more or less mutually exclusive, but whether they are also exhaustive is less clear. Some of the relevant issues are:

1. The five forces framework focuses on industry environments rather than macroenvironments: it seeks to understand the impact of macroenvironmental forces—macroeconomic, -social, -political, and -technological—in terms of their implications for the five industry-level forces. This is probably appropriate, although it does imply that macroenvironmental analysis is a necessary input into an effective industry analysis.[6]

2. Buyers and suppliers are treated unevenly in the five forces framework: buyer substitution rates a separate force but supplier substitution possibilities do not. (Painful supplier substitution effects were felt by movie theater owners, for example, when movie studios reduced the theaters' profitability by selling movies to cable TV and releasing them on videotape.) This feature of the model is awkward to justify because suppliers can search out better deals just as buyers can.

3. The framework does not take into account the effects of complements on industry performance. Porter's work on international competitiveness,[7] for example, highlights the critical importance of "related and supporting industries" in making an industry successful.

On the narrower issue of how the intensity of each of the five forces is determined, the framework raises additional issues. Some determinants, such as switching costs, appear to be double-counted. Other determinants can probably be added rather than subtracted. The list of rivalry determinants, for example, could be extended by adding import competition (which tends to increase rivalry) and multimarket contact among competitors (which can reduce rivalry). One might also argue that informational considerations, such as what competitors believe about each other, what they know about buyers' willingness to pay, or suppliers' costs, are even more salient than indicated by the list in Figure 6–2. Once again, Porter's subsequent work suggests new facets to the model:[8] he emphasizes the importance of informational conditions for an industry's international competitiveness.

Finally, although the five forces framework makes it clear that companies should focus analysis on the industries in which they participate rather than just the markets they serve, the framework is still subject to all the problems of industry definition discussed earlier in this chapter. Saying that substitutes from other industries should be taken into account, for example, does not shed much light on whether a particular substitution threat should be taken seriously. For instance, how formidable for the airline industry is the threat from long-distance picture phones?

Long-Run Focus

The five forces framework focuses attention on the average long-term profitability of an industry. The appeal of a long-term horizon should be obvious: it takes years to implement most strategic moves and see their effects. Nevertheless, two qualifications need to be taken into account: (1) an exclusive focus on the long run may not be appropriate and (2) even if it is, the five forces framework may, as usually applied, miss important long-term effects.

Focusing exclusively on the long-term horizon downplays short-run phenomena, such as business cycles, that can be quite important. In the U.S. steel industry, for example, integrated steelmakers' attempts to modernize were regularly and debilitatingly interrupted by cyclical downturns, which increased the profit potential for mini-mills. In the satellite television industry in the United Kingdom, British Satellite Broadcasting and Sky Television lost more than £1 billion in their first four years of operation, before a merger de-escalated the intense rivalry between them. These huge short-run losses reflected the switching costs faced by buyers once they installed a satellite dish that could receive only one of the firms' signals. As a result, the two competitors were trapped into a ferocious battle to build market share in the short run. This example also demonstrates how the short-run effects of structural variables can be different from the long-term ones. As a general rule, buyer switching costs raise average long-term industry profitability, but in this case they actually reduced it in the short run!

In terms of long-term forecasting, the five forces framework needs to be supplemented, except perhaps for mature industries, with some consideration of trends affecting such factors as market growth, buyer needs, the rate of product and process innovation, the scale required to compete, input costs, and exchange rates. Furthermore, analyses based on the five forces often focus on "exogenous" trends, which often are taken as givens, that influence industry structure. There is a danger of ignoring "endogenous changes" to industry structure that are driven by competitors' strategies.[9]

Product Market Focus

The five forces framework tends to focus attention on current product realities: the products that competitors sell, the costs of making them, their value to buyers, and the prices charged for them. It has, for that reason, recently been challenged by strategists who emphasize industry participants' resources—current and potential—instead of their existing products.[10]

   We think that a resource-based perspective is consistent with and augments the product market perspective instead of supplanting it. Because resources are hard to measure directly, in practice it often makes sense to evaluate them in terms of the products they make possible. For example, in order to assess Eastman Kodak and Fuji's technological resources in the photographic film industry, it is likely to be useful to compare, among other things, the film products they offer and the rates at which their product lines improve.

   To say that the five forces framework is consistent with resource-based analysis is not to imply, however, that the latter approach offers nothing new. Resource-based industry analysis promises significant additional benefits to practitioners: It helps explain sustained profit differences within industries—the topic of the next section.

PROFIT DIFFERENCES WITHIN INDUSTRIES

We have seen how industry-level analysis can be employed to explain average industry profitability. It is also a very valuable tool for managers' understanding of profit differences within industries. This opportunity for use is one that many companies ignore. To see why it is worth exploiting, one need only compare Table 6–1 and Figure 6–1. Their juxtaposition suggests that within-industry differences in profitability (Figure 6–1) may be roughly similar in size to the differences in the average profitability of the two most extreme industries in the U.S. manufacturing sector (Table 6–1). Indeed, some researchers[11] think that (relatively) sustained intra-industry profit differences tend, on average, to be several times larger than average differences in industry-level profitability.

   Profit differences within industries are important and therefore worth understanding. They reflect, in part, the fact that competitors pursue different strategies within the same industry, with differing levels of efficiency.[12] Profit differences within industries also depend, however, on industry-level attributes.[13] In fact, resource-related industry attributes determine whether there can be significant profit differences among competitors in the first place. This section focuses on these resource-related attributes and their effects on the size of within-industry profit differences, and then presents a framework for classifying industries in terms of the resources that underpin profit differences within them.

Commitment Opportunities

Different industries afford competitors different opportunities to make commitments to long-lived resources. Such commitments play a critical role in sustaining profit differences among industry incumbents and between incumbents and potential entrants.[14] In the absence of such commitments and the rigidities that they induce, alert competitors would quickly imitate superior strategies and iron out intra-industry profit differences.

The importance of resource commitments is illustrated by the performance of the U.S. airline industry after its deregulation in 1978. The deregulators believed that they were about to equalize all domestic airlines' profits at a level where each would just cover its cost of capital. This belief was based on a deeper one: that resources would be highly mobile within a deregulated domestic airline industry. (In the words of Alfred Kahn, a key deregulator, airplanes were "marginal costs with wings!") The deregulators reasoned that even if a city-pair route within the United States was monopolized, the threat of hit-and-run entry by other carriers redeploying airplanes from other routes would prevent the monopolist from earning above-average profits from its position.

This reasoning has proven to be specious. What has actually happened since deregulation is that profit differences within the airline industry have exceeded those in most other industries. The deregulators overlooked the opportunities for the airlines to make commitments to a range of resources that have turned out to be important in the new competitive environment. Commitments to computerized reservation systems and "hub-and-spoke" route networks— with a central city like Chicago, for example, as the hub—have played a particularly interesting role in this context. To see why, one need only consider in more detail the effects of the hub-and-spoke networks, in which all of an airline's flights within a given area converge on a centrally located hub at roughly the same time and leave a short time later, carrying, for the most part, passengers who have transferred from its other flights.

A hub-and-spoke geometry—when compared with direct flights—can help improve load factors and other elements of efficiency, blunting the threat of hit-and-run entry into particular city-pair routes. In theory, an attacker might still achieve competitive parity by setting up its own hub-and-spoke operation instead of entering piecemeal. In practice, such attacks have been constrained by shortages of gates at many hub cities (in some cities, gates have been contractually tied up for decades by incumbents). There is also the "S-curve" effect, which implies disproportionately high load factors for carriers with more extensive operations out of a particular city (because their flight times are more likely to mesh with passengers' preferences). Finally, there seem to be limits on the number of hub-and-spoke operations that can coexist at the same location (no U.S. airport now supports more than two). Attacks from other hubs have been constrained by the limited number of attractive locations, measured in terms of local plane boardings and geographic centrality.

Deregulation led, for all of these reasons, to a scramble to commit to hub-and-spoke operations at attractive locations. Control of large central hubs accounted for a significant fraction of the total profits earned by the U.S. airline industry in the first ten years after deregulation. A significant fraction of the industry's losses in the subsequent downturn can be ascribed to hubs as well—to locating in marginal cities rather than the most attractive ones. The hub-and-spoke operations that appear to have caused the most problems for the industry leader, American Airlines, for example, are not its large ones at Chicago and Dallas (even though it competes there with United and Delta, respectively) but its smaller outlying ones, such as those in San Jose, California, and Raleigh, North Carolina. By implication, commitments to long-lived resources need to be analyzed with particular care because they can lead to sustained negative as well as positive departures from average profitability.

The fact that long-lived resources and related rigidities are responsible for sustained profit differences within industries suggests a distinction between industries that afford opportunities to commit to long-lived resources and those that do not. The airline deregulators thought that the airline industry would fall into the second category, but it actually fell into the first. The second category of industries, those that offer limited commitment opportunities, is exemplified by the household furniture industry, which exhibits the characteristic symptoms of low investment-intensity, maturity, and fragmentation. Such industries make it very hard for participants to achieve sustained superior profitability, unless they can unlock profitable resource commitment opportunities within the industry or at its boundaries (for example, by opening retail outlets or establishing a brand name in household furniture). By the same token, sustained inferior profitability is also unlikely to be evident in such industries: an absence of commitment leads to zero entry and exit barriers. The absence of commitment therefore shrinks the potential for within-industry profit differences.

A Resource-Based Industry Typology

Within-industry profit differences are nevertheless the rule rather than the exception because opportunities to make resource commitments usually exist in most industries. It is therefore useful to supplement an understanding of the size of such differences with some consideration of their sources. One way to do so is to classify industries in terms of the resources that dominate competition in them and that are likely, therefore, to underpin within-industry profit differences. If particular types of resource commitments are salient in particular industries, investment in and utilization of those resources are likely to play particularly important roles in shaping within-industry profit differences.

Several schemes for classifying industries along these lines have been proposed, especially in recent years (see Table 6–2). Instead of reviewing each of these classification schemes, we will take advantage of the commonalities among them by grouping key resources into three categories:

1. Capacity.
2. Customer base.
3. Knowledge.

Industries dominated by different types of key resources seem to vary systematically in terms of the size, stability, and sources of the profit differences within them.[15] They tend to differ in terms of their structural attributes as well, which suggests that the typology presented below may be a useful supplement to the five forces framework when analyzing average industry profitability.

Capacity-Driven Industries

In capacity-driven industries, physical capital investments tend to be relatively large in relation to cost or value-added. The steel industry is a good example. It still uses physical capital more intensively, on average, than most other U.S. manufacturing industries. Competition takes place mostly on price; expenditures on R&D by the industry are quite limited. It is not surprising, therefore, that Nucor, which has sustained both superior profits and growth in this generally unattractive industry, has done so with a strategy that emphasizes building plants cheaply and running them efficiently.

More generally, capacity-driven industries are relatively likely to be mature, commoditized, and fragmented (except when capacity comes in large lumps). In such industries, rivalry tends to be static, which reduces the instability of market shares, and to be based on price competition, which reduces industry profitability. The pace of productivity improvement is typically modest, forcing most competitors to focus on incremental refinements, production processes, or what one might call static efficiency.

Profit differences within capacity-driven industries usually reflect differences in competitors' costs (or locations) because the prices that competitors charge tend to be uniform. Such profit differences also tend to be relatively limited in size and to change slowly.

Customer-Driven Industries

In customer-driven industries, investments in brands or customer relationships tend to account for a relatively large part of cost or value-added. The U.S. brewing industry is a good example. Brewers compete intensely across a number of functions, including product formulation, manufacturing, logistics, pricing, and the nonprice aspects of marketing. Initiatives in most of these areas appear, however, to provide only temporary advantages—advantages that can readily be imitated by competitors. What competitors cannot easily imitate are the brand

TABLE 6–2 Industry classification schemes.

Key Resource	Capacity	Customer Base	Knowledge
Chandler (1993)	Stable Technology	Low Technology	High Technology
Khandwalla (1981)	Production	Marketing	Research and development
Rumelt (1974)	Production	Market & Distribution	Science-based
Sutton (1991)	Exogenous sunk costs	Endogenous sunk costs	Endogenous sunk costs
Tracy and Wiersema (1993)	Operational excellence	Customer intimacy	Product leadership
William (1992)	Local monopoly	Stable oligopoly	Schurnpeterian

awareness and the positions in consumers' minds that successful beers enjoy. By implication, the key activities in the brewing industry are advertising and new-product introduction. The key resource that they are meant to build up and maintain, a loyal customer base, is the dimension that differentiates a very successful competitor, such as Anheuser-Busch, from less successful ones, such as Stroh or Heileman.

More generally, customer-driven industries tend to be less mature, commoditized, and fragmented than capacity-driven industries, and to exhibit more dynamic rivalry and higher average profitability. The pace of productivity improvement, adjusted for changes in quality, is higher as well, and competitors are more willing to adapt to and even anticipate changes in customers' preferences (at the expense of static efficiency).

Profit differences within customer-driven industries usually reflect absolute or scale-related differences in competitors' access to customers. Profit differences within such industries are often larger than in capacity-driven industries and may also change more quickly.

Knowledge-Driven Industries

In knowledge-driven industries, investments in R&D (or, more generally, innovation) tend to account for a large part of cost or value-added. The pharmaceutical industry is a good example. It is investment-intensive along a number of dimensions, including marketing, but its most striking characteristic is its very high R&D investment rate, one of the highest in all of U.S. manufacturing. As one might expect, pharmaceutical competitors that have outperformed (high) industry averages, such as Merck, appear to have been superior at innovation, particularly in terms of their ability to introduce unique drugs for common diseases.

More generally, knowledge-driven industries tend to be in the earlier stages of their life cycles, and their concentration can vary widely from global oligopolies to almost atomistic structures. Rivalry is particularly dynamic in such industries, and the degree of market share instability is correspondingly high. Productivity improves very rapidly, and competitors tend to pay more attention to their dynamic efficiency at introducing new products and processes than to static efficiency.

Profit differences within knowledge-driven industries usually reflect differences in competitors' abilities to develop significant product or process innovations. Although such profit differences have the potential to be very large, they can also change very quickly.

Classification

To categorize the resource base of a particular industry, it is useful to compare it to the average of all industries in terms of three key ratios:

1. Physical capital stocks to value-added.
2. Advertising expenditures to value-added (or marketing expenditures, if industrial rather than consumer marketing is involved).
3. Research and development expenditures to value-added.

When an industry has a relatively high ratio on one of these dimensions, it can easily be classified in terms of our typology because the three ratios correspond to the three types of industries outlined above. The focus on value-added rather than on sales in the denominators of the ratios reflects the important competitive principle that resources, services, or other inputs that can be purchased in reasonably efficient markets are unlikely sources of competitive advantage (superior profits) within an industry.

Assessment

To assess the typology itself, we begin by recognizing that the three resource-based industry categories are largely but not completely mutually exclusive. For example, the industries that rank in the top one-third in terms of physical capital-intensity, advertising-intensity, and R&D-intensity (the cut-off points, expressed as a percentage of value-added, are 70 percent, 2.8 percent, and 1.7 percent, respectively) show a tendency toward clustering. (See Table 6–3, which lists the two-digit manufacturing subsectors (six apiece) in which the different types of industries, defined at the four-digit SIC code level, tend to be concentrated.) More specifically, Collis[16] shows that five-sixths of U.S. manufacturing industries, defined at the four-digit SIC code level, fall into the top one-third along at least one of the three dimensions and that only one-third of the industries figure in the top tier along more than one dimension. The latter industries (such as semiconductors, in which both capacity and knowledge are important) can be treated as amalgams of the basic industry types described above.

TABLE 6–3 Industry clusters.

A. Capital-Intensive Subsectors		B. Advertising-Intensive Subsectors		C. R&D Intensive Subsectors	
Food processing	15%	Food products	26%	Machinery	26%
Textile fabrics	15	Consumer chemical products	12	Electrical equipment	21
Basic metals	13	Misc. consumer products[a]	9	Chemicals	15
Stone, clay products	13	Household durables	7	Transport equipment	11
Basic chemicals	12	Carpets, etc.[b]	6	Scientific equipment	9
Pulp and paper	8	Glass, ceramic products	5	Food products	5
Subtotal	75%	Subtotal	65%	Subtotal	87%

Source: David Collis (1993).

[a] SIC Code 39.

[b] SIC Code 22.

Note: Percentages indicate the extent to which particular subsectors account for all the manufacturing industries that figure in the top third along a particular dimension. Numbers may not add up exactly due to rounding errors.

Whether the threefold classification of industries is exhaustive is harder to establish. It excludes or de-emphasizes several forms of investment, such as expenditures on information technology, that have soared in recent years. The trouble is that little is known about how such nontraditional investments affect either average industry profitability or profit differences within industries.

From a dynamic perspective, we should add that the ways in which industries are classified can change over time and depend on competitors' strategies. The U.S. brewing industry was capacity-driven for many years after World War II but has since become more customer-driven. In contrast, the moves by Coca-Cola and Pepsi to integrate forward into bottling are making capacity (as well as customer bases) an important factor in the soft-drink industry. One must remember, therefore, that industry classifications are, like industry structure, mutable.

We also recognize that there is usually more than one strategy that can be pursued within each type of industry. The maverick steel maker Chaparral, which emphasizes R&D in its capacity-driven industry, is an example. The scope of Chaparral's contrarian strategy is limited, however, and does not free it from having to pay considerable attention to the pressures for static efficiency that pervade the market for steel products. More generally, such strategic variety is likely to widen within-industry profit differences. Its effects on average industry profitability are more controversial.[17]

Finally, we should acknowledge that our threefold scheme for classifying industries has not been supported by as much research as the five forces framework and is, therefore, more tentative. Previous industry classification schemes have tended to focus on product-market characteristics and have highlighted similarities based on whether products are to be sold to consumers or producers, whether they are durable or not, whether they are differentiated or not, and their life cycle stage. We believe that resource-based industry analysis helps systematize such insights.

SUMMARY

Strategy has always been concerned with achieving superior profitability. The profitability of any firm can be divided into the average industry profitability and the firm's divergence from that average. In this chapter, we have argued that industry analysis sheds light on both components of profitability and is, therefore, immensely important.

Industry analysis can be related to the traditional SWOT (strengths–weaknesses–opportunities–threats) framework for strategic planning. The five forces framework for industry analysis systematizes the analysis of opportunities and threats, and resource-based industry analysis helps elucidate prospective strengths and weaknesses. For these reasons, the popularity of industry-level analysis is likely to continue to increase.

NOTES

1. Derek F. Abell, *Defining the Business* (Englewood Cliffs, NJ: Prentice-Hall, 1980).

2. For related discussions of the concept of scope, see Chapters 1 through 3.

3. Michael Porter, "How Competitive Forces Shape Strategy," *Harvard Business Review* (March–April 1979), 137–145.

4. Readers are referred to Porter's original article (*id.*) for more extensive discussion.

5. Adam Brandenburger and Stuart W. Harborne, Jr., "Value-Based Business Strategy," Harvard University Graduate School of Business Administration, Working Paper, 1993.

6. The linkages between macroenvironmental analysis and industry analysis are detailed in Chapter 7.

7. Michael E. Porter, *The Competitive Advantage of Nations* (New York: The Free Press, 1990).

8. *Id.*

9. Robert M. Grant, *Contemporary Strategy Analysis* (Cambridge, MA: Basil Blackwell, 1991).

10. See, e.g., Margaret A. Peteraf, "The Cornerstones of Competitive Advantage: A Resource-Based View," *Strategic Management Journal* (March 1993), 179–191.

11. See, e.g., Richard P. Rumelt, "How Much Does Industry Matter?", *Strategic Management Journal* (March, 1991), 167–185.

12. See Chapter 2 for a discussion of business-unit strategies and how these strategies relate to competitive advantage.

13. Richard E. Caves and Pankaj Ghemawat, "Identifying Maturity Barriers," *Strategic Management Journal* (January 1992), 1–12.

14. Pankaj Ghemawat, *Commitment: The Dynamic of Strategy* (New York: The Free Press, 1991).

15. See, e.g., Richard E. Caves and Michael E. Porter, "Market Structure, Oligopoly, and Stability of Market Shares," *Journal of Industrial Economics* (June 1979), 289–313.

16. David J. Collis, "The Resource-Based View of the Firm and the Importance of Factor Markets," Harvard University Graduate School of Business Administration, Working Paper, 1993.

17. Miles Grant, Charles C. Snow, and Mark P. Sharfman, "Industry Variety and Performance," *Strategic Management Journal* (March 1993), 163–177.

REFERENCES

Abell, Derek F. 1980. *Defining the Business.* Englewood Cliffs, NJ: Prentice-Hall.

Brandenburger, Adam, and Harborne W. Stuart, Jr. 1993. "Value-Based Business Strategy." Harvard University Graduate School of Business Administration, Cambridge, MA. Working Paper.

Caves, Richard E., and Pankaj Ghemawat. 1992. "Identifying Mobility Barriers." *Strategic Management Journal* (January), *13*:1–12.

Caves, Richard E., and Michael E. Porter. 1979. "Market Structure, Oligopoly, and Stability of Market Shares." *Journal of Industrial Economics* (June), *26*:289–313.

Chandler, Alfred D., Jr. 1993. "Competitive Performance of U.S. Industrial Enterprises since the 1960s," in M. E. Porter (ed.), *Time Horizons of American Management.* Boston: Harvard Business School Press.

Collis, David J. 1993. "The Resource-Based View of the Firm and the Importance of Factor Markets." Harvard University Graduate School of Business Administration, Cambridge, MA. Working Paper.

Ghemawat, Pankaj. 1991. *Commitment: The Dynamic of Strategy.* New York: Free Press.

Grant, Robert M. 1991. *Contemporary Strategy Analysis.* Cambridge, MA: Basil Blackwell.

Khandawalla, Pradip N. 1981. "Properties of Competing Organizations," in P. C. Nystrom and W. H. Starbuck (eds.), *Handbook of Organizational Design, Vol. 1*, 409–432. Oxford, England: Oxford University Press.

Miles, Grant, Charles C. Snow, and Mark P. Sharfman. 1993. "Industry Variety and Performance." *Strategic Management Journal* (March), *14*:163–177.

McGahan, Anita M. 1992. "Selected Profitability Data on U.S. Industries and Companies." Harvard Business School, Cambridge, MA. Case 9-792-066.

Peteraf, Margaret A. 1993. "The Cornerstones of Competitive Advantage: A Resource-Based View." *Strategic Management Journal* (March), *14*:179–191.

Porter, Michael E. 1979. "How Competitive Forces Shape Strategy." *Harvard Business Review* (March–April), *57*: 137–145.

Porter, Michael E. 1985. *Competitive Advantage.* New York: Free Press.

Porter, Michael E. 1990. *The Competitive Advantage of Nations.* New York: Free Press.

Rumelt, Richard P. 1974. *Strategy, Structure and Economic Performance.* Boston: Harvard Business School Press.

Rumelt, Richard P. 1991. "How Much Does Industry Matter?" *Strategic Management Journal* (March), *12*:167–185.

Sutton, John. 1991. *Sunk Costs and Market Structure.* Cambridge, MA: MIT Press.

Tracy, Michael, and Fred Wiersema. 1993. "Customer Intimacy and Other Value Disciplines." *Harvard Business Review* (January–February), *71*:84–93.

Williams, Jeffrey R. 1992. "How Sustainable Is Your Competitive Advantage?" *California Management Review* (Spring), *34*:29–51.

MACROENVIRONMENTAL ANALYSIS: UNDERSTANDING THE ENVIRONMENT OUTSIDE THE INDUSTRY

7

V. K. Narayanan

University of Kansas

Liam Fahey

Babson College and
Cranfield School of Management

A corporation acts minute-by-minute in a microenvironment: its operations, markets, and industry. It is acted on—usually slowly, but sometimes suddenly—by a macroenvironment: the world outside the bounds of the organization's industry. It is not surprising that organizations give their microenvironment most of their attention, but it is alarming that so many organizations pay so little heed to the macroenvironment. There is ample evidence that this inattention can be risky; the favorite stories of daily newspapers and the business press are about political, social, economic, legal, and technological events that suddenly upset carefully planned management decisions, open or close market opportunities, and send stock prices on a roller coaster ride.

The problem for corporations is that monitoring the macroenvironment is a lot like studying geology—the subject is huge, usually ponderous, but sometimes precipitous; and much of what researchers would like to know is buried under something heavy. Momentous change in the macroenvironment can occur so slowly that it's hard to discern until eventually it's uncovered in a focused and systematic search. For example, demographic shifts, movement toward an integrated global economy, changes in governments, and arcane technological developments also have significant implications for the evolution of industries and for organizations' strategies. Surprisingly, strategy analysis as practiced in many organizations barely acknowledges the dire threats of macroenvironmental change. Some organizations that do keep watch for perils are stingy about providing resources for monitoring opportunities in the macroenvironment. In this chapter, we show how analysis of the macroenvironment supports the execution of sound strategy.[1]

Because the macroenvironment tends to be shortchanged in both strategy textbooks and practice, let's review some key reasons why managers should spend time understanding how to monitor it:

1. Many transformations and discontinuities experienced by industries are caused by changes in the macroenvironment. Deregulation has opened the gates for a stampede of opportunities and risks in the airline and telecommunications industries. Changing demographics and life-styles have caused many fast-food chains to focus on families and older age groups as major customer segments. Companies that focus exclusively on industry structure, current products, and current competitors will fail to see threats and opportunities that may be emerging in and around the marketplace.

2. Companies that learn to be among the first to perceive and exploit macroenvironmental changes can gain a valuable competitive advantage, as many of the examples in this chapter will demonstrate.

3. If organizations don't pay attention to environmental changes, they may pay the ultimate price for living in the past—they soon become history.

We need to preface this discussion by clarifying what the objective of macroenvironmental analysis is and what it is not. Like any business assessment of the future, its intent is not to foretell events. That is an impossible task. Macroenvironmental analysis can, however, do the following:

1. Provide an understanding of both *current* and *potential* changes taking place in any industry's external environment.[2] The role of current changes is often emphasized in practice at the expense of potential changes. Understanding current changes is an important guide to anticipating the future. This awareness helps an organization choose appropriate short-term tactical actions. But macroenvironmental analysis should cover a time frame from short run to long run so an organization can also prepare for strategic actions that take years to implement. As many examples in this chapter show, understanding both potential and current change can be vital to organizational survival.

2. Provide critical inputs to strategic management. Although we urge firms to cultivate the ability to recognize and assess change, the truly valuable product of macroenvironmental analysis is its contribution to strategy.[3] Unfortunately, in some companies, analysis merely provides descriptive details of what is taking place in the macroenvironment rather than supplying decision makers with information that is useful in determining and managing the firm's strategies.

3. Facilitate and foster strategic thinking in organizations. An understanding of current and potential social, economic, political, legal, and technological

change can bring fresh viewpoints into the organization. An up-to-date analysis of demographics and life-styles can challenge key market segmentation premises underlying many firms' strategies. An analysis of technology change can challenge an organization's historic practices pertaining to alliances, partnering with other organizations, and outsourcing activities.[4]

These benefits of macroenvironmental analysis, however, are realized only when those doing the analysis are willing to assume the difficult but necessary task of making judgments about the effects of change. As we shall see in the many examples cited in this chapter, it is the role of the analyst to interpret and make sense of change in the macroenvironment. In a turbulent environment, the implications of change for an organization's current and future strategies are never self-evident. Preparing a set of key issues, recognizing pivotal data points, having a sensitive appreciation of the implications of change, and selecting an array of alternatives all contribute to the judgments of those doing the analysis,[5] which is the managerial product of macroenvironmental analysis.

In the sections that follow, we define the macroenvironment and look in detail at its social, political, legal, technological, and economic segments. Next, we address how to capture macroenvironmental change—how to scan, monitor, and forecast it. We then focus on integrating macroenvironmental analysis into strategy development and execution.

DEFINING THE MACROENVIRONMENT

To understand the concept of macroenvironment, it is helpful to visualize a firm's environment as shown in Figure 7–1, where the firm is portrayed as enclosed within several layers or levels of environment.

The *task environment* refers to the customers, suppliers, and competitors that constitute a firm's immediate environment. Much of its day-to-day operations involve activities or decisions related to its task environment. Thus, a firm may negotiate a new source of capital with potential investors, enter into a component codevelopment agreement with a supplier, or attend to upgrading its service to a particular group of customers. The task environment is more or less specific to a firm and is not necessarily shared by its competitors. For instance, its customers may be loyal to its brand, and its suppliers may have granted the firm preferred-customer status.

The *industry* or *competitive environment* surrounds the task environment. The industry environment is the focus of Chapter 6. Environmental factors at the industry level directly affect most competitors, although the effects may be differential. For example, the threat of new entrants may have significant impact on competitors in one product segment of an industry but have little influence on others.

The largest and most complex area affecting an organization is the general environment or macroenvironment—the focus of this chapter. It is important

FIGURE 7–1   Levels of environment.

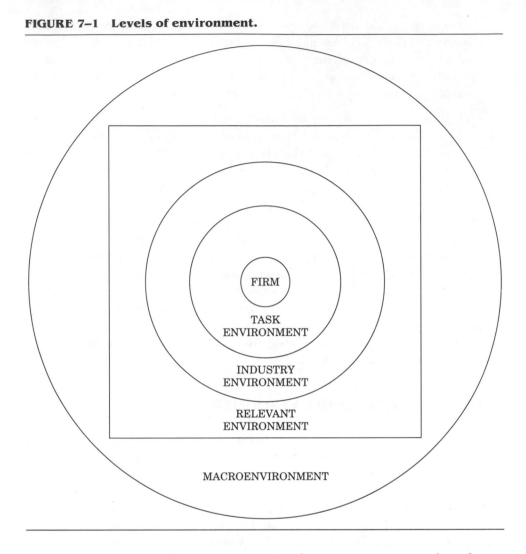

to note in Figure 7–1 that we have narrowed our investigation to the *relevant environment*. To use resources effectively, organizations must learn to manage their analysis of the social, political, technological, legal, and economic environments. Too much focus could lead a corporation to ignore messy, unpleasant, and confusing signals that can be the first warning of profound change. Too little focus makes the analysis prohibitively expensive, time-consuming, and counterproductive.

The relevant environment is defined as the boundaries of the general environment as they are drawn by an organization for analytical purposes. In practice, analysts need to focus on the key aspects of the environment that are most relevant to this particular organization. For example, a consumer goods firm and an industrial products firm may define their relevant environments quite differently. Demographics and life-styles may be of crucial importance to the consumer goods firm but of lesser relevance to the industrial goods firm. All definitions of the relevant environment require judgments, and, as noted at the beginning of this chapter, such judgments are necessary for engaging in worthwhile analysis.

SEGMENTS OF THE MACROENVIRONMENT

To facilitate analysis, we identify four major segments of macroenvironment: (1) social, (2) economic, (3) political, and (4) technological. The principal elements of each segment are summarized in Box 7–1. Each is briefly discussed here.

The social segment consists of the demographics, life-styles, and social values. An analysis of this segment considers shifts in the structure and mobility of the population, how life-styles are changing, and whether social value change is

---

Box 7–1

Key Elements of the Macroenvironmental Segments

The Social Environment

The social environment consists of demographics, lifestyles, and social values.

Demographics may be segmented into the following elements:

Population size. The total number of people in a given geographic area.

Age structure. The number of people within different age bands such as 0–10 years and 11–20 years.

Geographic distribution. Growth rates within and shifts of population across geographic regions.

Ethnic mix:. The mix, size, and growth rates of ethnic groups.

Income levels. The amount and growth rates of income across demographic/lifestyle groups such as family types, age levels, or geographic regions, for example.

Lifestyles may also be segmented into the following elements:

Household formation. The composition, type, rate of change and size of households.

Work. Whether people work; what type of work, where they work; expectations about work, and how long they work.

Education. Type and level of education.

Consumption. What people purchase or consume (or do not purchase and consume).

Leisure. How people spend their spare or non-working time.

Social Values may be broken into a number of types of values:

Political values. Reflected in how people vote and how they feel about major political and social issues (such as, support for the military, abortion, and preservation of the environment).

Societal values. Reflected in attitudes toward work, leisure, participation in organizations, acceptance of other groups, and acceptance of social habits (such as smoking, etc.).

Technological values. Reflected in acceptance of new technologies, choices between costs of technologies, and their benefits.

Economic values. Reflected in pursuit of economic growth, tradeoffs between economic "progress," and its social costs.

The Economic Environment

The economic environment refers to the nature and direction of the economy in which business operates. Two types of change are especially worthy of emphasis:

1. *Structural change* refers to change within and across sectors of the economy such as movements in economic activity from some types of industries to others (such as a decline in steel industry and growth in a number of the electronics industries) and movements in the relationships among key economic variables such as the relative levels of imports and exports as a percentage of GNP.

2. *Cyclical change* refers to upswings and downswings in the general level of economic activity such as movement in GNP, interest rates, inflations, consumer prices, housing starts, and industrial investment.

Political Environment

The political environment may be segmented into formal and informal systems.

The formal system. The formal system consists of the electoral process as well as the institutions of government: the executive branch, the legislatures, the judiciary, and the regulatory agencies.

The informal system. Refers to the arenas outside of government in which political activity occurs. It includes local community settings and the media.

The Technological Environment

The technological environment involves the development of knowledge and its application in "how to do things." It can be broadly segmented into the following domains:

Research. Fundamental or basic research that seeks the principles and relationships underlying knowledge, often termed invention.

Development. Transforms knowledge into some prototype form, often termed innovation.

Operations. Puts the knowledge to use in a form that can be adopted by others, often termed diffusion.

taking place. Changes in the social environment directly affect total market potential for many products, especially consumer products.

The economic environment consists of the general set of economic conditions facing all industries. It includes the stock of physical and natural resources and the aggregation of all the markets where goods and services are exchanged for payment. Economic activity is reflected in levels and patterns of industrial output, consumption, income and savings, investment, and productivity. Changes in the overall level of economic activity directly affect supply and demand in almost all industries.[6]

The political segment incorporates all electoral processes and the administrative, regulatory, and judicial institutions that make and execute society's laws, regulations, and rules. This is perhaps the most turbulent segment of the macroenvironment. Few industries are unaffected by change in the political and legal environment.

The technological segment is concerned with the level and direction of technological progress or advancements taking place in a society, including: new products, processes, or materials, general level of scientific activity, and advances in fundamental science (for example, physics).[7]

A simple way of remembering the four segments is by using the acronym SEPT (social, economic, political, and technological). In the model presented in Figure 7–2, multiple linkages exist among the segments: every segment is related to and affects every other segment, and the macroenvironment ultimately can only be understood as an interrelated system of segments. However, the

FIGURE 7–2   A model of the macroenvironment.

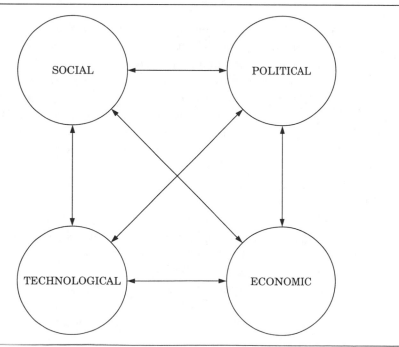

model does not specify the types of linkages; these are deemed to be the output of a process of analysis and the judgments of analysts. In other words, the linkages are to be discerned by analysts during their efforts to scan, monitor, forecast, and assess macroenvironmental change.

SCAN, MONITOR, FORECAST, ASSESS: ANALYZING THE MACROENVIRONMENT

Identifying the key segments of the macroenvironment and their interrelationships is a relatively straightforward first step. But discerning which current and potential changes in the macroenvironment are most relevant to a particular organization means making judgments based on bewildering complexity.[8] This section offers an analytical framework for identifying, tracking, projecting, and assessing significant change in the macroenvironment. It consists of four analytical stages:[9]

1. Scanning the environment to detect ongoing and emerging change.
2. Monitoring specific environmental trends and patterns to determine their evolution.
3. Forecasting the future direction of environmental changes.
4. Assessing current and future environmental changes for their strategy and organizational implications.

Scanning

Organizations frequently scan the environment in order to identify indicators or precursors of current and potential change and issues in the social, political, technological, and economic environments. One intent of scanning is to alert the organization to predictable head-on collisions with its environment so that it will have as much time as possible to consider alternative actions. It is equally important that scanning be sensitive to new opportunities. Indeed, the most successful scanning draws an organization's attention to critical changes and events—both fortuitous and calamitous—well before they have revealed themselves in an obvious way to all other organizations. Many of the critical questions that guide scanning and monitoring are noted in Table 7–1.

Scanning, as detailed in Box 7–2 in the case of a food firm, involves an extensive search of primary (from individuals) and secondary (written) data sources. Many organizations now regularly use computers to tap into an extensive array of electronic databases for items that might be of relevance. Some firms hire vendors to scan for them. For example, a number of consulting firms specialize in providing corporate clients with updates and forecasts on social change. Larger organizations may form one or more panels of both in-house experts and outside consultant so that they can receive regular input about change

TABLE 7–1   Guiding questions in scanning and monitoring.

1. What are the relevant segments of the macroenvironment?
   - Which segments are most important?
   - Which areas within each segment are most important?
2. What are the current and emerging trends?
   - What is each trend?
   - What are the emerging trends?
3. What are the current and emerging patterns?
   - What are the specific patterns?
   - What trends contribute to each pattern?
   - What patterns seem to be on the horizon?
4. What are the indicators of these trends and patterns?
   - What indicator is associated with each trend?
   - Are two or more indicators related to a specific trend?
5. What is the historic evolution of these trends and patterns?
   - How has each indicator changed over time?
   - What is the time period?
6. What is the degree of change within these patterns?
   - Is the degree of change minor or major?
   - How different is the expected change from the present state or a past state?

in one or more of the macroenvironmental segments. Some organizations regularly draw on their own panel of economists for economic analyses and projections; others have panels of technology experts for evaluation and projections of technological change.

Ideally, scanning feeds early signals or indicators of potential macroenvironmental change into monitoring and forecasting. Such scanning is especially useful when macroenvironmental change takes time to unfold. An organization gains valuable lead time to understand the implications and consider its options for action. Most major shifts in the social environment do not occur in days or even in months. They often take years to unfold. For example, many organizations will be affected by a fundamental change occurring in the workplace over the past decade: After a decade-long revolution in communications technology, many types of work are increasingly taking place in the home.

Scanning might unearth such signs of social change as potential shifts toward political conservatism or liberalism, or the emergence of a pro-business judicial or administrative system. Once an organization has become aware of a specific potential change, it can begin to monitor its development, project its evolution, and examine its implications.

On the other hand, scanning may make discoveries that require immediate action. For example, a scan may detect macroenvironmental change that is

Box 7–2

Scanning in a Food Firm

A large food firm that manufactures a variety of canned and other food goods has established "an institutionalized scanning process." At its core are what the managers in the firm refer to as general and focused searches.

Electronic databases serve as a principal means of conducting general searches. The databases cover a massive array of industry and popular magazines and periodicals, trade newsletters, and daily newspapers. Some are directly related to the food industry, some are not.

In scanning the databases, the firm searches for items that might be of interest and relevance to its business. What is deemed relevant is a product of the knowledge and judgment of those doing the scanning. In a general search, the firm is not looking for anything in particular. It is not sure what sources (such as publications) it should cover and often is concerned that it may capture some data but not recognize its value.

Analysts look for indicators that suggest emergent, developing and well-established trends. In seeking emergent and developing trends, analysts look for indicators that suggest change in its early stages. For example, one analyst discovered that a group of local consumers in one small town had objected to how one supermarket had advertised organic products—they claimed that the advertising was false and misleading. Could this episode be an indicator of consumers in other areas objecting to such advertising? If so, what changes in the firm's own advertising might be required?

The firm also conducts general periodic and ad hoc scans through the use of select individuals. It establishes and maintains a series of panels and focus groups. One panel reports regularly on technology developments relevant to the firm's products, manufacturing, distribution, and retail processes. It was through one of these reports that the firm first discovered the vast potential of "scanner data" (the ability of retail outlets to automatically track sales of each specific type of product and communicate that data to manufacturers) as an aid to decision making. In its *ad hoc* scans, analysts simply phone a select set of individuals, such as experts in distribution, retailing, technology, demography, lifestyle change, and politics to ascertain emerging and potential changes that they should be aware of.

General scans often lead to surprises. For example, a general scan led to the discovery that a small group of doctors was making statements that called into question the safety of some food ingredients—they claimed there was some evidence that these ingredients led to an unusual form of reaction in a small percentage of the population. Could this incident be the first step on a path to regulations prohibiting the use of these (and perhaps other) ingredients?

In focused scans, analysts seek whatever data they can obtain pertaining to a particular topic or issue at one point in time. To initiate a focused scan of the electronic databases, an analyst keys in specific terms or words such as laws, regulations, values, eating habits, leisure, household activities, technology, technical developments, and specific food types. These words generate a series of items that are automatically categorized. For example, they might try to generate as much data as possible from the relevant databases on the eating habits of some age group or changes in laws and regulations pertaining to the sale and delivery of food products.

General scans sometimes lead to focused scans. They generate topics or new key words that necessitate an additional, more focused search of the databases. For example, terms or phrases that begin to find wide usage in either the popular press or specialized trade press are added to the predetermined list. When an analyst noticed an increased usage of the phrase "politically correct," he ran a search to gain a better understanding of what it meant and what social and political forces might be propelling its usage. His concern, which proved to be legitimate, was that food labels, brand names, or names of individual product types might be deemed by some group as politically incorrect.

---

already in an advanced state. Such a change may have evolved to the point where it is actual or imminent rather than likely at some unspecifiable date. For example, one firm's scan of life styles discovered a surprisingly high growth rate in single-person households and an increase in the number of people in their twenties who were postponing marriage. A scan of demographic and life-style data might pick up shifts in geographic mobility, household ages, or who is forming households. A scan of the economic environment might reveal shifts in interest rates, productivity, or output in certain sectors of the economy. Scanning is more likely to unearth actual or imminent macroenvironmental change when it explicitly trains an organization's antennas on areas that previously may have been gravely neglected, or when it challenges the organization to rethink areas to which it had paid scant attention.

It cannot be emphasized enough that scanning is not a science; it is an art that relies on the importance of analysts' judgments. Because there are no algorithms or procedures that are applicable to all situations, analysts must be sensitive to the particular nature and intent of each scanning assignment.

Three scanning tasks are so critical they merit special attention:

1. Because scanning is the most ill-structured and ambiguous of the analysis stages, the analyst has to decide on the scope and breadth of the data and data sources. There are essentially no limits on the potentially relevant data. Moreover, a common feature of scanning is that early signals of macroenvironmental change often show up in unexpected places. Consequently, the purview of search should be broad. Sensible schemes for narrowing it make it likely that important early signals will be missed. The result is that scanning must sift through a lot of chaff to find a few grains of valuable information.

2. A related fundamental challenge in scanning is to make sense out of data that are likely to be vague, ambiguous, and unconnected. As the case in Box 7–3 illustrates, the analyst has to infuse meaning into the data and perceive

important connections that signal future events. If the bank manager in the Box 7–3 case had not first recognized that the recent immigrant's complaint was a potentially common customer problem, and then followed up by checking with other primary and secondary sources, he would not have detected the potential market opportunity. In short, scanning involves acts of perception, deduction, and intuition on the part of the analyst.

3. The analyst has to make some critical choices of signals or precursors to consider for further monitoring, forecasting, and assessment. Not all emerging or potential macroenvironmental change is likely to be relevant. As is evident from the questions raised in the food firm case outlined in Box 7–2, the choices of which signals to pursue are influenced by the analyst's judgments about their implications for the organization. These choices therefore depend heavily on the skill and expertise of the analyst and are not easily formalized.

Box 7–3

A Bank Manager's Scanning Incident

A bank manager, who held special responsibility for business development, was travelling from New York to Washington, DC, on a train. He struck up a conversation with a passenger seated beside him, a recent immigrant from Jamaica, who began to talk about plans to expand his business—an innovative software firm. As the head of a sophisticated start-up company, he fervently complained about a pressing problem: his inability to raise money quickly enough.

The bank manager asked why he thought he was encountering this problem. Expecting an answer about the speed of growth of his business, the banker was taken back by the reply, "Bankers are too arrogant and self-important to treat immigrants seriously."

After reflecting on the conversation, the manager began talking to his colleagues and friends who had contact with recent immigrant entrepreneurs to find out if they, too, held this perception of bankers. He began to discover that the opinions expressed by his chance acquaintance on the train were not unique.

He then contacted a market research firm to learn if this attitude was widely held (the bank did not have an extensive market research department). After a number of focus groups, it was discovered that there is a widespread perception among immigrant entrepreneurs that banks are typically unresponsive to their needs and often act cavalierly toward them.

The focus groups also investigated what banks might do that would deal with an array of problems to the satisfaction of the entrepreneurs.

Armed with this data, the bank manager proposed a series of changes to the bank's lending practices and a strategy to reach and satisfy a new group of customers—immigrant entrepreneurs.

Monitoring

Monitoring involves tracking macroenvironmental change over time. Specifically, the focus is on the evolution of trends, such as demographic and economic indicators, sequences of events, such as technological developments or political election results, or streams of activities, such as the actions of regulatory agencies. The trends, events, and activities that the organization tracks may have been identified during scanning, or the organization may accidentally become aware of them, or they may be brought to the organization's attention by outsiders.

The intent of monitoring is very different from that of scanning. Monitoring's purpose is to assemble sufficient data so that the analyst can discern whether certain patterns are emerging. It is important to note that these patterns are likely to be a complex of discrete trends. For example, an emergent life-style pattern may include changes in entertainment, education, consumption, work habits, and domicile-location preferences. The recent emergence of "singles" (that is, households consisting of only one individual) as the most prevalent form of household in the United States reflects a pattern among these trends. A pattern in political opinion shifts might be discerned from a series of election results, referenda, or special ballots or propositions held at various levels of the political process (federal, state, and local) as well as from opinion polls.

Monitoring ensures that the analysts' hunches and intuitive judgments about weak signals observed during scanning are brought to the attention of the organization. The analysts' judgments and those of experts then need to be tracked for confirmation, elaboration, modification, and validation or invalidation. For example, a local city, county, or state election result might indicate a change in the political climate, such as a movement toward more conservatism. To validate that this was a significant trend, the monitoring process would consider election results in other local areas, statements by local and national political leaders and public interest groups, and changes in the policy platforms of political groups and parties.

In monitoring, the data search is more focused and more systematic than in scanning. The analyst is usually guided by prior hunches (seat-of-the-pants hypotheses) based on signals observed during scanning or brought to the organization's attention by consultants or academics. For example, a furniture manufacturer's scan of changing consumer tastes indicated that customers seemed to be moving away from "contemporary" and toward "foreign" and "older" styles. This signal provided a very specific focus for the firm's monitoring efforts. In such cases, the analyst develops a general sense of the pattern to watch for and collects data regarding its evolution. The furniture company's analysts, for instance, collected data on the sales of various furniture styles as well as consumers' perceptions about different styles.

As monitoring continues, trends accumulate into patterns. A picture of change in progress that may have been hazy and uncertain when uncovered by scanning quickly becomes imbued with clarifying details during monitoring. For example, in tracking the emergence of social issues, the first indicators (often picked up through scanning) are feelings of discontent or vague concerns expressed by a few individuals. These sentiments begin to attract the attention of others of like mind, and a social movement may gradually begin to evolve. This was the pattern of evolution of the consumerist and environmentalist movements at the national level and of community-interest movements at the local level.

As with scanning, monitoring requires the analyst to interpret a variety of data. As trends or sequences of events or activities are tracked, the analyst has to make a number of judgments: What data are relevant? What are the valid and reliable data sources? How do the data fit together? How can conflicts in the data be reconciled? When are there sufficient data to declare that a pattern is evident? These are not straightforward judgments. It is often difficult to judge when a pattern is long-lived; many are simply fads. The analyst may be imputing groundless linkages among disparate, unconnected data points. This problem is further confounded when different individuals within the organization make different and conflicting judgments—a not uncommon occurrence.

The outputs of monitoring are threefold:

1. A specific description of environmental patterns to be forecast.
2. The identification of trends and patterns for further monitoring.
3. The identification of patterns requiring future scanning.

In practice, the outputs of monitoring go beyond simply providing inputs to forecasting. Monitoring may identify trends or apparent trends that were not included in the scope of the original monitoring program. Also, it is not unusual for monitoring activities to indicate areas where further scanning may be desirable.

Forecasting

As is evident in every chapter in this book, strategic decision making requires a future orientation: It needs a picture of what is likely to take place in the external environment. The analyst must therefore confront the difficult tasks of laying out possible evolutionary paths of anticipated change in the social, political, economic, and technological environments and then making the connections among them.

The intent of forecasting is to develop plausible projections of the scope, direction, speed, and intensity of macroenvironmental change. Scope refers to the substance of what is being forecast: whether it is a narrowly defined trend such as the number of individuals entering or leaving a particular geographical area or a broadly conceived pattern such as the life-style of some specified group of individuals. Many of the typical foci of forecasting are shown in Table 7–2.

TABLE 7–2 Sample foci of forecasting.

The Social Environment

1. How will the demographic structure (that is, the number of people in different age groups) shift over the next 20 to 40 years.
2. What life-style shifts might occur as those presently in the age group 25–40 move into the age group of 40–55?
   - How will the compositions of their households change?
   - How will their consumption patterns change?
   - How will their work patterns change?
   - What changes will occur in how they use their leisure time?
3. How will social values change?
   - Will there be an increase in political conservatism?
   - Will more people manifest agreement with a reduction in military spending?
   - Will people be more or less willing to bear the costs of curtailing and eliminating pollution?

The Economic Environment

1. What will be the level of inflation over the next three years?
2. Will GNP increase or decrease over the next five years?
3. Which service industries will grow and decline in the next decade?

The Political Environment

1. Which political parties will gain/lose strength in the next two or three elections?
2. What significant shifts will occur in governmental policies, laws, and regulations pertaining to specific industries?
3. What decisions might different levels in the judicial system make that could affect different industries?
4. Will existing social/political movements such as consumerism and environmentalism gain or lose public support?

The Technological Environment

1. When and how might recent breakthroughs in basic research lead to commercial products?
2. What linkages among which technologies would have to occur before a specific technological event or breakthrough occurs (such as high definition TV)?
3. What might be some new applications of currently available technologies?

A few useful terms describe the characteristics of the change pattern:

- *Direction* describes the vector of the specific trend and pattern. For example, interest rates may be moving up or down; more or fewer individuals may be following a particular life-style.
- *Speed* describes how quickly or slowly a trend or pattern is projected to move.
- *Intensity* describes the strength of the forces propelling a trend or pattern.

There are two distinct types of forecasting. The first involves *projections* based on trends that are evident (that is, they are reflective of data over some time period) and can be expected (with some margin of error) to continue unabated over some future period of time. For example, many demographic trends such as the number of children entering high school or the number of people reaching retirement age may be projected with reasonable accuracy. Some lifestyle trends, such as rates of household formation, may also be projected. It is often possible to project some technological trends such as the rates of diffusion of new products.

The second type of forecasting prepares *alternative futures*. They are based on current trends and on judgments regarding events that may take place or that may be made to happen by the firm itself or by other entities such as competitors, customers, suppliers, social and community groups, and governmental agencies. Alternative futures are thus brought about by the interaction of many different social, political, technological, and economic trends and patterns. Alternative futures are obviously more complex and more uncertain than projections. As a consequence, they are considerably more difficult to envision and construct. Scenarios serve as the analytical means by which many organizations conceive and elaborate alternative futures.

A scenario is simply a depiction of how one "future" might unfold.[10] Many firms routinely develop multiple economic scenarios that depict possible future states of the economy. Consumer goods firms frequently develop scenarios that focus on distinct levels of discretionary income across different customer groups and how they might affect spending patterns.

The power of scenarios as a forecasting tool is that simple scenarios based on a limited amount of data can generate significant implications for an organization. Box 7–4 summarizes different scenarios developed by one firm in 1989 with regard to the completion of the European Community's 1992 program (the set of initiatives by the European Community to put in place a single market by the end of 1992). As indicated in Box 7–4, different scenarios may generate quite distinct implications for an organization's strategies.

The significance of the distinctions between projections and alternative futures needs to be emphasized. Projections reflect a largely predetermined future: the trends and patterns will continue for some period of time. Alternative futures, on the other hand, as illustrated in Box 7–4, represent possible futures. They are an acknowledgment that there are many potential pathways to the future, and they enable managers to develop strategies that would be effective in a variety of possible futures.

Without a willingness to consider alternative futures, an organization is likely to find itself constrained and victimized by its implicit presumption that the future is going to largely replicate the past. For example, during the 1970s and 1980s, many firms that did not consider dramatic increases in the price of energy (in large measure, caused by macroenvironmental forces such as governmental policies, OPEC, and changing economic conditions) discovered that their

---

Box 7–4

One Firm's Scenarios about the Future State of the European Community's Single Market*

Scenario 1: The first and most likely scenario was called "EC 1992 Works." The EC would likely meet most but not all of its single market goals by the end of 1992. Progress would be made toward the free movement of goods and services, and the standardization of indirect taxes. But the EC might not achieve banking centralization, with a unified currency and monetary policy. Nevertheless, EC governmental control would grow in strength. East-West relations would become "friendlier." The trade policy of the EC would be no more and no less protectionist than the rest of the world.

   Business Implication: In this scenario, the level of information technology market growth would be medium to high.

Scenario 2: The second scenario was called "EC 1992 Disappoints." The program of policies moving the EC toward the single market would not fail, but they would evolve much slower than in the first scenario.

   Business Implication: Information technology market growth would continue to be moderate, as it had been in the first scenario, despite the slow pace toward single market cohesion.

Scenario 3: The third scenario was called "The EC Fails." This scenario painted a gloomier picture than the second one. Little or no progress would be made toward achieving the single market goals. Disappointment with the EC as a whole would be widespread. Only under these circumstances would EC trade policies be different from the rest of the world, and be less protectionist.

   Business Implication: Information technology market growth would be low.

Scenario 4: This scenario was called the "U.S. of Europe." It expected the single market goals to be reached and perhaps exceeded. A centralized banking system would be in place. Free movement of goods would be achieved. The EC would grow in power to the state of semi-sovereignty—no more or less protectionist than the rest of the world.

   Business Implication: Information technology market growth would be high.

* These scenarios were adapted from Stephen M. Millet, "Battelle's Scenario Analysis of a European High-Tech Market," *Planning Review,* March/April, 1992, pp. 20–23.

---

best laid plans were built on highly erroneous assumptions. Many firms that were unprepared for "unthinkably high" oil prices eventually suffered another shock when oil prices dropped to "unthinkable lows."[11]

   As with scanning and monitoring, a number of key tasks and challenges are central to forecasting. First, analysts have to understand the forces that drive the evolution of trends and patterns. This is a prerequisite to charting the evolutionary path of macroenvironmental change.

The politically charged issue of legislation limiting the freedom to buy and possess firearms, especially hand guns and automatic weapons, offers an example. Many analysts are currently endeavoring to craft scenarios that look at the future in terms of more or less gun control. To develop possible futures involving different degrees of gun control, analysts must make assessments of the forces propelling and resisting gun control. Will the historically powerful lobbying groups that have traditionally resisted almost all forms of gun control, such as the NRA (National Riflemen's Association), continue to lose their power and influence over legislative decisions? Will legislative bodies, prodded by well-organized victims' lobbies, continue to push for more stringent forms of gun control? Will more or fewer average citizens arm themselves as a defense against violent crime? Will social issues, such as the demand for safe neighborhoods, well-publicized deaths and maimings, and the high cost of health care for gunshot injuries, keep gun control an issue in the forefront of public consciousness? The analyst must make three judgments:

- How much power does each participant in this drama hold?
- What are the interests of each of the groups, and what are the areas for compromise?
- How might the groups' choices, and those of the general public, change over time?

Next, the analyst must decide the nature of the issue's evolutionary path—its scope, direction, speed, and intensity. Often, analysts must determine whether a change is a quickly passing fad, or will have some duration, or is cyclical or systematic in character. For example, many firms have failed to appreciate the scope, direction, and intensity of many emerging social movements and social value shifts until they have evolved into widespread, unmistakable patterns.

Finally, the analyst has to delineate the evolutionary path or paths leading to projections and alternative futures. This is the essence of forecasting.

It is both counterproductive and unnecessary for an organization to forecast large numbers of trends and patterns. Instead, the analyst should focus on macroenvironmental changes of importance to the organization—a set of key issues. Forecasting thus requires that the organization identify what it is that it wishes to forecast and why it needs to do so. Before it invests time and effort in forecasting, the organization needs to identify likely organizational implications of the potential macroenvironmental change.

For this reason, forecasting and assessment are intimately linked.

Assessment

Assessment involves the efforts of analysts to identify and evaluate how and why current and anticipated macroenvironmental changes currently affect strategic management of the organization and how their effect will be felt in the future. During assessment, the frame of reference moves from understanding the macroenvironment—the focus of scanning, monitoring, and forecasting—to identifying what that understanding of the macroenvironment means for the organization.

In linking macroenvironmental analysis and strategic management, the critical question is: What are likely to be the positive or negative impacts of macroenvironmental change on the organization's current and future strategies? Many of the specific questions typically asked in the assessment are shown in Table 7–3. These questions compel the linking of macroenvironmental change and the organization's more immediate industry and task environments.

The questions listed in Table 7–3 highlight the intimate linkages between forecasting and assessment. Those macroenvironmental changes or patterns judged to have already had an impact on the organization's strategies, or to possess the potential to do so, are deemed to be *issues* for the organization. The important issues become the center of attention in forecasting.

TABLE 7–3   Assessing macroenvironmental analysis implications.

1. How might each change affect the organizations industry?
   * General expectations about the industry?
   * Emergence of new products?
   * Sales of existing products?
   * Entry and exit of competitors?
   * Emergence of new suppliers?
   * Entry and penetration of substitute products?
2. How might each change affect the organization's more immediate task environment?
   * Demand by existing customers?
   * Changes in existing competitors' strategies?
   * Changes in suppliers' strategies?
3. What might be the implications of each change for the organization's current strategies?
   * Change in existing products?
   * Change in existing target market segments?
   * Change in how the firm competes?
   * Change in the firm's current goals?
4. How might each change affect the organization's future strategy choices and their execution?
   * Potential new products?
   * Potential new customers?
   * Potential new ways of competing?
   * Change in strategy choice criteria?
   * Need for new organization structure?
   * Need for new operating processes?

Typically, macroenvironmental analysis generates a host of issues—far more than any organization can systematically analyze. If an organization attempts to analyze too many issues, it becomes bogged down, and action becomes muddled and less decisive. Moreover, some issues are simply more important than others; that is, they have more serious implications for the organization's current and future strategies.

Identifying issues necessarily entails managers' judgments: they must determine which trends and patterns or alternative futures are affecting or will affect the organization. Judgment involves assessing and prioritizing macroenvironmental change against the specific questions in Table 7–3. Issues can be conveniently arrayed on a *probability-impact matrix* (see Figure 7–3), and a separate matrix can be prepared for each of the three planning periods: short-, medium-, and long-term. Although the scoring system for this assessment of probability and impact can be simple or complex, a general categorizing of high, medium, or low is usually sufficient. Such a matrix display has several merits. It provides a comprehensive, at-a-glance array of issues, orders them in a manner that facilitates discussion and planning, and places them in time frames appropriate to the allocation of resources and management attention. After the issues are arrayed on a matrix display, they can be fed into various strategic analyses.

Linkages among the Analysis Stages

To explain the concepts of scanning, monitoring, forecasting, and assessment, we have introduced them as if they were distinct analysis activities. In practice, however, they are inextricably intertwined. As noted in the discussion of each activity and as illustrated in Figure 7–4, each one can and does influence the others. For example, scanning often generates surprises and signals of change that lead the analyst to implicitly or explicitly assess their impact on the organization's industry and the firm's future strategies. If warranted by the potential

FIGURE 7–3   Cross-impact matrix: An illustrative structure.

Probability and Timing of Events	Event 1	Event 2	Event 3	Event 4
Event 1 (Prob., Timing)				
Event 2 (Prob., Timing)				
Event 3 (Prob., Timing)				
Event 4 (Prob., Timing)				

FIGURE 7-4   Linkages among scanning, monitoring, forecasting, and assessment.

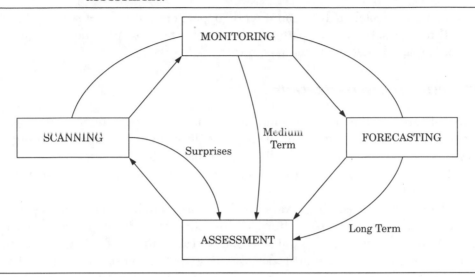

impact, further scanning, monitoring, and forecasting may be deemed necessary. Long-term issues are subjected to ongoing monitoring and forecasting as a source of input to assessment. As noted previously, forecasting requires some initial assessment in order to ensure that the organization expends its efforts on the most critical issues. Assuming that many of those critical issues have been identified, the next critical process involves linking macroenvironmental analysis to strategic management.

LINKING MACROENVIRONMENTAL ANALYSIS TO STRATEGY DEVELOPMENT AND EXECUTION

Before describing the methodology of the assessment phase of macroenvironmental analysis, it is valuable to reiterate three major points about the role of macroenvironmental analysis in strategic management:

1. Macroenvironmental analysis is useful only to the extent that it results in strategy-related actions and decisions.
2. The integration of expectation of change and preparation for it does not just happen; it must be made to happen. Change must be managed: choices and alternatives need to be weighed, the consequences and operating issues involved in actions need to be examined, and resources need to be allocated.
3. Integration needs to take place for short-, medium-, and long-run horizons.

Corporate Strategy

Macroenvironmental analysis can directly impact corporate-level strategy in at least three ways: by altering patterns of diversification, by influencing resource allocation, and by recalculating risk–return trade-offs.

Patterns of Diversification

Diversification is the act of moving an organization into product-market segments unrelated to its existing businesses. As illustrated in Chapter 2, an organization can pursue a number of distinct approaches to diversification, each of which is influenced by both the opportunities confronting it and its own resource profile.

There are at least three ways in which macroenvironmental change can influence an organization's pattern of diversification. First, macroenvironmental change may open up or close out existing patterns of diversification. For example, new political attitudes affecting application of the relevant law on mergers and acquisitions occurred when Ronald Reagan assumed the Presidency and established a "free market" administration policy. As a result, the opportunities for corporate diversification changed overnight. As this example shows, diversification that might be frowned on or even prosecuted by one administration may be allowed by a later one. The Bush Administration's policy on antitrust legislation went a step further: it was pro-merger. "Small" American companies—banks, for example—were seen to be at a competitive disadvantage with foreign giants.

Second, in response to changes in the macroenvironment, corporations can alter the synergies they try to exploit across their business units. For example, Procter & Gamble, Heinz, and a number of other leading consumer product and food firms with nationally recognized brand names are facing increasing competition from "Brand X" products. These leaders are now experiencing difficulties in maintaining and leveraging the marketing synergies based on the brand names that historically have been central to their corporate strategies. Changing demographics, life-styles, and social values and a persistent downturn in the economy have left many consumers increasingly price-conscious, thus making the effort to build and sustain an image of superior "value for money" around their brand names ever more difficult for these firms.

Third, the different patterns of diversification developed in Chapter 2 are susceptible to different vulnerabilities, such as change in technology and the decline of different industry segments. Change in the macroenvironment may amplify these vulnerabilities. For example, a diversification thrust that centers on linkages across certain types of technologies is especially vulnerable to change in technology. Many defense industry firms that diversified around their core technological capabilities now find many of the businesses they developed in the past decade suffering from the same difficulties as their historic core business: a lack of demand because of the end of the Cold War.

Resource Allocation

Macroenvironmental change has important implications for corporate resource allocation—that is, the distribution of investment in business units—for at least two reasons. First, macroenvironmental change can foster opportunities for some business-unit products of a corporation and wreak havoc on the markets of others. Some business units may need an infusion of resources to exploit these opportunities, and others may need substantial resources to overcome market exit barriers. Second, global macroenvironmental change is increasingly affecting where opportunities exist. For example, in the early 1990s, compared to the 1980s, a number of corporations have dramatically added to the resources they have committed to "dipping their toe" in China.

Risk–Return Trade-offs

Political, economic, technological, and social shifts impact the returns and risks of existing and potential portfolios of business units. For example, anticipated changes in key economic indicators such as interest rates, money supply, inflation, unemployment levels, and gross national product often critically affect projected returns in both existing businesses and potential new businesses. To cite merely one example, an industry leader in building materials and supplies whose sales always closely correlate the overall state of the economy, has seen its profits oscillate more or less in line with gross national output over the past 20 years. Many technology-related corporations have had to come to grips with the increasing rate of obsolescence of some of their major product lines. Not surprisingly, these firms search for ways to leverage their existing technology into product enhancements or even new products. Many firms now do extensive political-risk assessments of foreign countries before making commitments to initial or continued investment. For example, some firms such as Digital Equipment Corporation have recently announced they plan to reenter South Africa as a consequence of its efforts to move toward democracy.

Business-Unit Strategy

Macroenvironmental analysis provides critical intelligence in the formulation and execution of business-unit strategy in two distinct but related ways: its effects on industry structure and evolution need to be assessed; its implications for various inputs to strategy development can then be assessed.

Implications for Industry Analysis

At the level of industry or competitive analysis, changes in the macroenvironment may affect:

- The boundaries of the industry.
- The forces shaping industry structure, such as suppliers, customers, rivalry and product substitution, and entry barriers.

- Strategic groups.
- The key success factors.
- The general expectations within the industry.

These elements provide the competitive context within which business-unit strategy is developed.

Macroenvironmental changes can threaten the survival of an industry or specific industry segments. This is perhaps most evident in the way that technological change can render substantial segments of an industry obsolete. As an example, advances in the technology underlying frozen foods have reshaped major sectors of the food industry. In another example, the technology developments facilitating linkages among voice, data, and images are now reconfiguring what used to be distinct industry sectors (telecommunications, television receivers, and optics) into what is now referred to as the multimedia business.

Macroenvironmental change directly influences each of the forces shaping industry structure: suppliers, customers, new entrants, and substitute products (see Chapter 6). It can affect the number, type, and location of *suppliers*, the products they offer customers, supply costs, and the competitive dynamics of supplier industries. Global macroenvironmental change has dramatically shifted the supply sector in many industries. To cite merely one example, the political, economic, and social changes that have occurred in Korea and other Asian countries have spawned many new competitors for American and European firms that previously dominated many raw material and component businesses.

Changes in demographics, life-styles, and social values can affect the size, characteristics, and behavior of the *customer base* in an industry or industry segment. For example, changes in life-styles and related social values, such as greater emphasis on personal health and fitness, generated the necessary consumer base for the array of products now associated with jogging, tennis, and fitness equipment for use in the home.

Product substitution and *new entrants* are most often driven by technological change. Development of "mini-mills" for steel making resulted in products that have displaced much of the product line emanating from old, large steel mills. In the computer industry, voice recognition is likely to make obsolete many types of current software.

Macroenvironmental change differentially impacts various *strategic groups within an industry*. Changes, to the extent that they affect customers' preferences, suppliers' capabilities, substitute products, and so forth, could potentially enlarge or decimate the product-market arenas in which different strategic groups operate. Perhaps more importantly, macroenvironmental changes may afford opportunities for firms in a specific strategic group to overcome mobility barriers, that is, the barriers inhibiting a firm from moving from one strategic group to another.

Macroenvironmental change can potentially affect the *key success factors* in almost any industry or industry segment. At a minimum, such change needs to

FIGURE 7–5   Issue–impact matrix: linking issues to industry analysis.

Impact on Industry

	Industry Boundaries	Forces Shaping Industry	Strategic Groups	Key Success Factors	General Expectations
Issue 1					
Issue 2					
Issue 3					
Issue 4					
Issue 5					
Issue 6					
Issue 7					
Issue 8					
Issue 9					

be assessed in terms of its impact on factors such as desired product quality, product functionality or performance criteria (such as reliability and durability), relative cost positions, image and reputation, and resource commitments for major product-market segments. For example, many industry sectors that depended on door-to-door sales—a critical success factor—have suffered severely because many of the women who were formerly their customers are now working full-time.

The discussion above suggests that macroenvironmental change potentially affects the general expectations about an industry and about the firms within it. One useful means of integrating the above analysis is to develop *issue–impact matrices*. These matrices detail the effect of each of the selected set of macroenvironmental issues on industry-level factors. Matrix displays of the type shown in Figure 7–5 facilitate assessments of these impacts. These assessments should include not only the general direction of change but its timing and intensity. Such assessments form much of the industry backdrop against which business strategies are formulated.

Linkage to Business-Unit Strategy

At the level of business-unit strategy, macroenvironmental analysis, together with industry analysis and competitor analysis, needs to be assessed for its contribution to business-unit strategy in terms of:

- Business definition.
- Assumptions.
- General strategic thrust.

Few concepts are more central to business-unit strategy determination than *business definition*. Professor Derek Abell[12] has noted three critical elements in any firm's business definition: (1) What customers does the business serve? (2) What customer needs are satisfied? and (3) What technologies are employed to satisfy these customer needs? Each of these elements can be affected directly or indirectly by macroenvironmental change. Many businesses have found that demographic and life-style changes have altered not just their served or targeted customer base but also their customers' needs. For instance, the growth in the number of affluent older consumers has caused all kinds of businesses, from insurance and financial services to food and entertainment businesses, to either introduce new product offerings or significantly reshape existing products. In short, as a major segment of the population ages, new opportunities to fill its needs and wants develop and once-promising opportunities wane.

Because strategy is about winning in the future marketplace, assumptions about the current and future environment always underlie any strategy. For example, key macroenvironmental assumptions (as distinct from industry assumptions) might include expectations about shifts in governmental policies, changes in technology developments, and demographic and life-style shifts. These assumptions need to be anchored in a thorough analysis of the macroenvironment surrounding the industry if they are to be realistic and thus, useful for strategy formulation.

Because of the importance of macroenvironmental assumptions,[13] the merits of identifying and challenging them need to be emphasized:

1. By defining assumptions, an analyst is compelled to make a critical assessment of macroenvironmental change. It is not merely enough to identify prevailing change. Assumptions emphasize the importance of projecting and assessing the future direction of change.

2. Consideration of assumptions facilitates and fosters sensitivity analysis. Every strategy alternative is always vulnerable to environmental change. Consideration of assumptions necessarily entails asking what macroenvironmental changes might most negatively affect each strategy alternative.

3. Assumption analysis frequently serves to heighten awareness of macroenvironmental change and its importance to strategic management.

Finally, macroenvironmental analysis must be linked to the business-unit strategic thrusts identified in Chapter 3. This linkage is, of course, related to business definition and assumptions, discussed above. For example, a market-share building thrust presumes some relevant business definition as well as assumptions pertaining to customers, suppliers, new entrants, and substitute products. Thus, macroenvironmental change, through its impact on industry elements, may signal the need for a change in strategy thrust.

THE STRATEGIC ORGANIZATION

As argued in Chapter 1, winning in the marketplace necessitates building and sustaining a strategic organization. Macroenvironmental change must be taken into account in shaping the strategic organization because it affects so many facets of what takes place within organizations. We address here only three broad implications: (1) design of work, (2) design of organizations, and (3) globalization.

Design of Work

Although Chapter 12 addresses changes in work and operating processes, it seems necessary here to emphasize that macroenvironmental change frequently drives changes in how work gets done in organizations. In general, macroenvironmental change affects:

- The nature and conduct of the tasks or routines that constitute work.
- The social setting of work.
- The risks and rewards of employment.

Some examples are in order. Advances in information technology have allowed many people to work at home—a change in the location of work. Demographic change has directly resulted in what is referred to as "diversity in the work force." Employees must now interact in the workplace with individuals of both sexes and of diverse national, ethnic, and religious backgrounds. Change in economic conditions has contributed to organizations' being no longer able to guarantee life-long employment. Indeed, in the past few years, the phenomenon of temporary managers has become common.

Design of Organizations

New forms of organization have been adopted by companies that are winning in marketplaces characterized by increasingly rapid change. The old rigidly hierarchical, procedure-driven, slow-moving, bureaucratic form of organization formerly typical of large corporations simply inhibits the flexibility and speed of action that are now required. At least three organizational design elements are influenced by macroenvironmental change:

1. Degree of hierarchy.
2. Bases of subunit formation.
3. Degree of decentralization.

Middle-management levels and the number of managers at each level have been significantly reduced in many large corporations—in part, because of the increased need for competitiveness and the power of many different types of technology to do the work of middle management. Changes in social values, leading to increased customer demands and expectations with regard to better quality, higher levels of service, and lower cost, have also made it necessary to rethink organizational processes through simplification of reporting relationships, flexibility of organizational structures, and the substitution of technology for labor. All of these factors, in turn, necessitate decentralization of decision making and increasing employee empowerment.

Globalization

As shown in Chapter 4, organizations now have little choice but to extend their global reach. As they do so, change in the global macroenvironment further confounds the choices inherent in building a strategic organization. To cite just a few examples, changes in local or national economies influence factor costs (such as labor, raw materials, and components). As factor costs change across different countries and regions, firms move operations from one country to another and devote considerable attention to developing linkages between operations in different countries. Relationships between countries or regions may also affect organizational choices. Free trade agreements (such as NAFTA—the North American Free Trade Agreement) or trade disagreements (such as the recurring disputes between the European Community and the United States) influence location of facilities, cost structures, and, in some cases, under what conditions products will be allowed into specific marketplaces.

SUMMARY

Macroenvironmental change affects all facets of strategic management. Because it is covered in detail in Chapter 5, we have not addressed the linkages between macroenvironmental change and political strategy. It should be obvious, however, from the discussion in this chapter that macroenvironmental change gives rise to issues, impacts stakeholders and their demands, and affects the arenas in which political strategy is played out.

Macroenvironmental analysis provides critical inputs for all phases of strategic decision making, such as capturing strategic alternatives, developing and evaluating alternatives, and implementing strategy over time. Change is the dominant characteristic of our macroenvironment. Without a clear and purposeful understanding of how possible futures in the social, economic, political, and technological environments may affect evolution of individual industries, an organization is highly likely to adopt strategies that fail to anticipate and leverage beneficial environmental change or protect against harmful change. Continuing macroenvironmental analysis is needed in organizations that hope to adapt and survive in the future.

NOTES

1. Readers interested in a more thorough treatment of analysis of the macroenvironment are referred to Liam Fahey and V. K. Narayanan, *Macroenvironmental Analysis for Strategic Management* (St. Paul, MN: West Publishing Co., 1986).

2. The role and importance of macroenvironmental changes in shaping industry change were noted but not discussed in Chapter 6.

3. For this reason, we devote the final section of this chapter to developing linkages between macroenvironmental analysis and both corporate and business-unit strategy.

4. These issues are examined in detail in Chapter 8.

5. The importance of mindset, discussed in Chapter 1, is evident here. Managers need to be willing to challenge and to have challenged the organization's vision, values, assumptions, and beliefs.

6. Readers interested in a global economic analysis that challenges much economic conventional wisdom are referred to James Dale Davidson and Lord William Rees-Mogg, *The Great Reckoning* (New York: Simon & Schuster, 1993).

7. This chapter pays comparatively less attention to the technological environment because it is a principal focus of the next two chapters.

8. Readers interested in a well-researched and well-argued depiction and assessment of global macroenvironmental changes—demographic, technological, economic, and political—and the linkages among them are referred to Paul Kennedy, *Preparing for the Twenty-First Century* (New York: Random House, 1993).

9. We detail these analytical activities—scanning, monitoring, forecasting, and assessment—in part because of their applicability to other domains such as the analysis of competitors, customers, suppliers, and change in the global arena.

10. For an easy-to-read discussion of philosophy and methodologies involved in scenario development and use, see Peter Schwartz, *The Art of the Long View: Planning for the Future in an Uncertain World* (New York: Doubleday Currency, 1991).

11. Many of the issues involved in identifying and developing "unthinkable" alternatives are considered in Chapter 10.

12. Derek F. Abell, *Defining the Business: The Starting Point of Strategic Planning* (Englewood Cliffs, NJ: Prentice-Hall, 1980).

13. In Chapter 1, assumptions were identified as a core element in an organization's mindset. See also Chapter 14, for a discussion of the difficulties inherent in changing an organization's most fundamental assumptions.

BUILDING THE INTELLIGENT ENTERPRISE: LEVERAGING RESOURCES, SERVICES, AND TECHNOLOGY*

8

James Brian Quinn

Amos Tuck School
Dartmouth College

As noted in Chapter 1, strategy is about creating and leveraging change. Strategy textbooks have typically emphasized environmental change and downplayed or ignored the potential of the organization's own resources as a primary source of marketplace opportunity. In particular, only recently have organizations' own resources, such as knowledge and skills, received systematic attention as building blocks of distinctive competitive advantage.

The scope and intent of this chapter are threefold:

1. To identify the key resources that organizations are now using as the bases of successful marketplace strategies and to discuss how they are doing so. Increasingly, intellectual resources and not physical assets constitute the seeds of marketplace success.

2. To demonstrate how the new intellectual resources are leading to new organizational configurations, some of which involve multiple linkages to other organizational entities such as suppliers, distributors, end-customers, and technology sources. Many of the new organizational networks extend beyond country or even regional borders.

3. To show how the new intellectual resources and organizational configurations are giving rise to distinctive competencies, that is, competencies that generate value and benefits that are important to customers. These competencies increasingly emanate from knowledge-based service activities.

---

* Reproduced by special permission from James Brian Quinn, *Intelligent Enterprise,* The Free Press, New York, 1992.

INTELLECTUAL CAPITAL: THE NEW CRITICAL RESOURCE

At their core, most successful organizations today can be considered *intelligent enterprises;* they convert intellectual resources into a chain of service outputs and integrate these into a form most useful to certain customers. (See Table 8–1 for a brief delineation of the key attributes of an intelligent enterprise.) Enterprises providing law, accounting, financial services, applied research, health care, and most forms of entertainment primarily sell the skills and intellect of key professionals. In manufacturing as well, most of the processes that add value to materials derive from knowledge-based service activities.[1] The most important of these activities are shown in Table 8–2. In the past, investors— particularly venture capitalists—shied away from companies with a strong service orientation because their assets could "walk away any night and leave you with nothing." They wanted "solid assets to offset downside risks." Now that view is changing.

In manufacturing today, most venture capitalists recognize that investments in bricks and mortar provide little security and warrant only the same rates of return as mortgages. They make their money by (1) investing in the special skills and intellect that only highly motivated, knowledgeable people can provide and (2) leveraging this intellect in the marketplace through a few "best-in-world" internal systems and the integrated management of many outsourced activities. Virtually all high-technology start-ups take this approach. Venture capitalists try to keep conventional plant and equipment investments limited—in part because they can be so quickly supplanted by new technologies—and they focus their client companies' management talent and investments on effectively building the intellectual aspects and personal attitudes most important to the needs of a selected customer group. Unless the facilities and manufacturing technologies are themselves part of the core competencies of the company, strategy dictates that they *should* be limited—and outsourced—whenever feasible. This is not an argument against facilities investment per se. It does suggest,

TABLE 8–1 Key attributes of the intelligent enterprise.

- Focus on knowledge-based activities, not products.
- Develop "best-in-world capabilities" in selected activities.
- Continuously upgrade these to stay "best-in-world."
- Benchmark other activities: Consider outsourcing unless "best" or "strategic."
- Focus on the customer, the employee, and the shareholder.
- Adjust measurement and reward systems to reflect this focus.
- Establish a learning culture at the personal, team, and enterprise levels.
- Leverage intellect through training, databases, networks, and motivation.
- Disaggregate organizations, restructure around the task.
- Utilize worldwide "best-in-class" resources.

TABLE 8–2   Critical knowledge-based service activities.

- Basic and applied research.
- Product and process design.
- Software development and management.
- Managing information systems.
- Logistics management.
- Production and quality management.
- Market and competitive intelligence system.
- Managing innovation.
- Marketing, sales, and distribution management.
- Coordinating integrated (materials, process, and human) systems.
- Personnel sourcing, training, and development.
- Professional legal, accounting, public relations, medical, and financial services.

Note: To be effective, each activity usually must cut across several traditional "functional" groupings.

however, that those essential fixed facilities should embody as much of the firm's uniqueness and critical intellect as possible. (A number of the key intellectual resources that firms can leverage are noted in Table 8–3.)

Every few years, *Inc., Venture,* or similar magazines run special articles in which they feature the garages in which today's great companies started—a reminder that ideas and intellect, not physical assets, build great companies. One venture capitalist summarized the issue this way:

> We don't want to invest in hard assets. They are too short-lived and risky. We certainly don't want to invest in bureaucracies. We want to invest in people who have a clear viable concept, who can manage outside contracts with the best sources in the world, and who can concentrate their internal energies on that small core of activities that creates the real uniqueness and value-added for the company. That's where the action is today, but it's a tough sell against traditional thinking.

TABLE 8–3   Key intellectual resources.

- Technological resources.
- Databases about processes and customers.
- Design and innovation systems.
- Management systems and practices.
- Logistics systems and information networks.
- Specialized contact networks and access to new players.
- Fast organizational response systems.
- Motivational systems and corporate culture.

Consider the case of Novellus Systems Inc., the most profitable and fastest-growing company in the semiconductor production equipment field. With only 12 shop-floor personnel, Novellus concentrates on design and engineering of advanced chemical disposition equipment. It disdains internal "metal-bending" activities in favor of long-term strategic relations with a few trusted and specialized parts and subsystems producers. In addition to design, Novellus controls all assembly, test, customer contact, and postsales service work, and uses partners and suppliers to leverage its in-house capital and design resources. In a notoriously cyclical industry, Novellus's profits grew 20 percent during the 1991–1992 recession. Sales averaged $350,000 per employee—almost double the industry's average.[2]

Many large manufacturing companies (Sony, Nike, Honda, Apple, Matsushita, Polaroid, Liz Claiborne, Genentech, or IBM, for example) initially succeeded by following the intellectual holding company model quite closely. At first, they purposely invested limited amounts in plant and standard equipment, produced as few components internally as they reasonably could, and leveraged their limited resources by sourcing externally. Konosuke Matsushita assembled his bicycle lights and portable electric lights using standard parts that were made by others but fitted into his own unique designs. Sony initially rented a bombed-out corner of a department store in Tokyo. Its first permanent quarters were some old warehouses in Shinagawa. The roofs were so leaky that experiments had to be run under umbrellas. Digital Equipment Corporation (DEC) leased some old mills in Marlboro, Massachusetts. Genentech rented warehouse space in South San Francisco and bootlegged other space from its researchers' university-tied laboratories. Genentech primarily performed research and coordinated the complex processes of early-scale production, clinical trials, regulatory clearance, patenting, maintaining a home for advanced researchers, and networking worldwide with university researchers to stay on the frontiers of its remarkable new technology. It licensed the large-scale production, marketing, and distribution of its early "high-volume" products to companies like Eli Lilly and Kabi.

As these and many other successful manufacturers grew to be large companies, they continued to focus on a selected set of service skills and to leverage these against multiple products to develop dominating product-market positions. Others wishing to emulate these firms would do well to address the questions pertaining to intellectual resources that are listed in Table 8–4.[3]

HOW CORE INTELLECTUAL AND SERVICE COMPETENCIES SUPPORT BROAD PRODUCT LINES

The broad lines of all these companies—and some other even more remarkable examples—demonstrate that strategic focus lies not so much in narrowing or limiting one's product lines and product-market scope as in focusing strategy

TABLE 8–4   Thinking about intellectual resources: Some key questions.

- What are the critical intellectual resources of the firm now? How well do they match future needs? How long will it take to build the needed resources?

- How can analysts place a value on a firm's intellectual resources or measure trends in these knowledge-based assets?

- How does the value of a firm's intellectual resources compare to that of the firm's physical resources?

- How can the firm add value to its physical resources or to its intellectual resources?

- Which set of resources is more leverageable? More enduring?

- What are the keys to matching intellectual resources? How do they differ from physical resource management?

around a uniquely developed set of core intellectual and service capabilities that are important to customers. A broad or mixed product or service line may not signify a loss of focus at all. In fact, a broad line may add to strategic focus—when one can coordinate the deployment of an especially potent set of service skills against numerous marketplaces.[4]

In strategic circles, it has recently become popular to seek increased focus by concentrating on fewer and more closely related product lines. After a prolonged period in the 1960s and early 1970s, when ill-conceived financial strategies drove manufacturing companies to over-extend their lines through conglomeration, a reverse fad developed.[5] Those who had made fees from the acquisition programs of the 1960s and 1970s found that they could make further fees by "deconglomerating" and selling off divisions of companies that had followed the preceding fad too far. These narrowing (or divestiture) strategies were often justified as giving the company "greater strategic focus." Unfortunately, as many have sadly learned, such strategies place the company at considerably more risk because it is subject to much sharper drops in sales when the total economy turns down or when its particular segment of the economy goes sour.

By contrast, looking beyond mere product lines to a strategy built around core service competencies provides both a rigorously maintainable strategic focus and long-term flexibility. Once a company develops sufficient depth in a few well-chosen service activities, these can become linchpins for a consistent corporate strategy and a competitive edge that can last for decades. Innumerable new products or services can spring from these core activities over the years, providing the company with constant refreshment for its line and with enough diversity to stabilize earnings and offset downturns—unlike more traditional product-focused strategies. The concept has worked well for companies as diverse as Merck, Sony, Intel, Motorola, Pilkington Brothers, Moulinex, Matsushita, Sharp, Texas Instruments, and Nike. Their widely diversified product lines have been powered by a few core competencies, mostly service activities. 3M Corporation, as detailed in Box 8–1, provides probably the classic U.S. case.

Box 8–1

3M: The Importance of Core Knowledge-Based Competencies

3M's extensive growth has been founded on its R&D skills in three critical, related technologies: abrasives, adhesives, and coating-bonding. In each of these areas, it has developed knowledge bases and skill depths exceeding those of its major competitors. To these core technologies (referred to as historic in Figure 8–1), 3M has attempted to "add" four other compatible sets of core technologies, at least partially from acquisitions. When combined with 3M's remarkable "entrepreneurial-innovation system" and with a strong broad-based distribution system, its "historic technologies" let 3M develop a wide variety of products internally and sustain continuous growth for 6 to 7 decades (through 1980) at a compounded annual growth rate of 10%. From time to time, 3M identified a specific application area, for example, small labels, which offered an opportunity to leverage its core technologies or distribution skills by acquisition. Sometimes it needed the complementary skills of a small manufacturer to realize strategic timing goals or to attain a full product presentation in a key area for its "wave front" of products. But, for decades, 3M's growth basically exploited its core internal service competencies in its 3 or 4 "historical technologies," its unique innovative system, and its broad-based distribution system. However, as 3M began to see its growth rates fall in the early 1980s, it tried to acquire new core technologies well beyond its origins—that is, in imaging and instrumentation. Acquisitions to support these markets were no longer gap filling, but moved the company into new business areas that had less connection to its core service competencies. As 3M moved away from its well-developed competencies, success became harder to achieve. Despite strong efforts to diversify further, businesses built off 3M's adhesives, coatings, abrasives, and nonwoven technologies continued to generate a return on assets, on average, about 50 percent higher than the new areas.

As product cycles become shorter, technological performance or style becomes more important, and product-based experience curves recede in importance, we find that many sophisticated long-term strategists no longer look primarily to market share and its associated cost-reducing potential as the keys to strategic planning.[6] Nor do they build vertically integrated empires to achieve ephemeral scale economies. Instead, they concentrate on identifying those few core service activities where their company has—or can develop—a continuing strategic edge and long-term streams of new products to satisfy future customer demands. They develop these competencies in greater depth than anyone else in the world. Then they seek to eliminate, minimize, or outsource activities where the company cannot be preeminent, unless those activities are essential to support or protect its chosen areas of strategic focus. To develop this kind of service-based strategy, managers concentrate their competitive analyses, not on market share, but on "activity share"—the relative potency of the key service activities

FIGURE 8–1   3M: Technology-driven strategy.

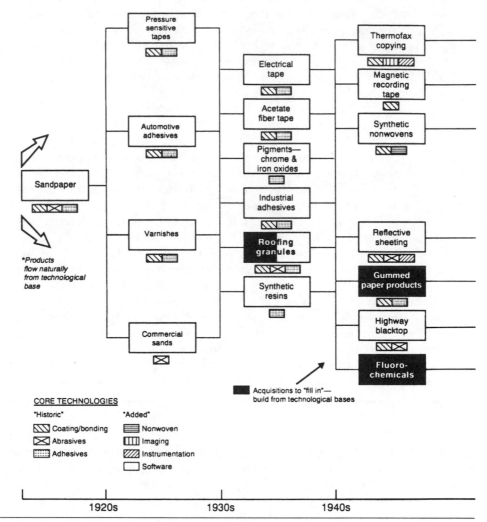

Source: Original chart by Braxton Associates; reproduced with permission.

underpinning their own and all direct and functional competitors' positions.[7] When they fail to do so, the price can be high.

Consider the case of Pilkington Brothers PLC. After thriving as a growing company on its process innovation capabilities (particularly in flat glass and fiberglass), Pilkington eventually stumbled when it forgot that process skills were the wellspring of its growth. As it became the largest flat glass producer in the world, Pilkington relied more on economies of scale and attempted to move into other areas where its skill base was not as applicable. It also maintained an

FIGURE 8–1   (continued)

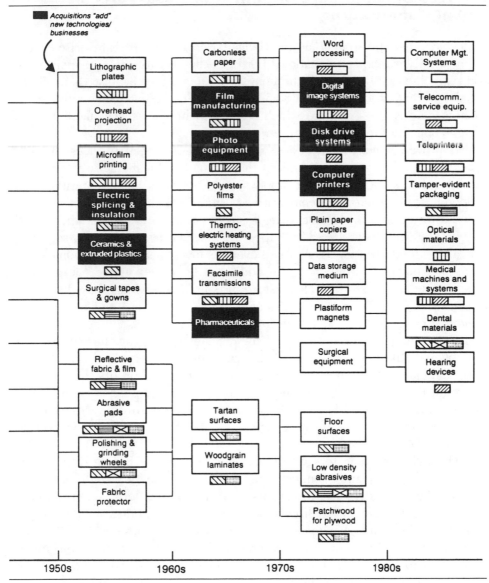

integrated operation when its competitors were outsourcing more. When demand for flat glass fell 4 percent in 1990–1991, Pilkington's profits plummeted 52 percent. Its more disaggregated European rival, St. Gobain, had a loss of 20 percent. Although other glass companies, to be more market-responsive, had flattened their organizations, a combination of Pilkington's conservative personnel policies and the support needed for vertical integration kept its fixed overhead high. Pilkington's 1990 sales per employee were only $83,000, as against $171,000 at Pittsburgh Plate Glass (PPG) and $500,000 at Nippon Sheet.[8]

Services Disaggregate Organizations as a Force in Global Competition

To develop their full potential, knowledge-based intelligent enterprise strategies generally extend across national borders. They try to utilize truly best-in-world suppliers or benchmark the company's capabilities against them. Some global sourcing or joint venturing has always been present in manufacturing. What is new is the extent to which service technologies now facilitate—or force—companies to think globally.

Improved telecommunications, air transport, financial services, storage, and cargo-handling technologies mean that virtually all manufacturers (regardless of size) must either consider supply sources, markets, and competition on a worldwide scale or lose their competitive positions. About one-fifth of the total capital invested in U.S. manufacturing firms has now moved outside the United States.[9] The knowledge-based activities of coordinating production, sourcing, and value-added services among these overseas investments have become critical to multinational profitability. In addition, the places where the greatest value-adding economies of scale exist are usually in knowledge-based services (R&D, marketing, design, informations systems, and so on) and not in plant economies of scale. As a result, many of the profits, royalties, and intracorporate sales these enterprises remit to the United States are among the few strongly favorable net balances of trade that U.S. manufacturing has provided in the late 1980s and early 1990s. In addition to the royalty fees and profits these companies remit to the United States, they account for a major portion of the goods shipped into the United States—that is, their sales from overseas divisions to the United States are significant components of U.S. imports from abroad, as shown in Table 8–5.

Through large importers in certain sectors (like Nike, IBM, or Exxon), U.S. manufacturing companies dominate the design, specification, and location of much of the world's trade. Through its powerful wholesaler–retailer systems, however, the United States directs even more of the world's manufacturing trade. With their purchasing power, these service companies now specify what will be made and often how it will be produced. In addition to the strong influence these capabilities give the United States in world trade, they lower costs for U.S. consumers and increase the purchasing power of those consumers. Through their relative efficiency, these companies increase U.S. workers' purchasing power, giving them higher real wages and higher living standards compared to their foreign competitors. For example, because distribution channels are so much longer and less efficient in Japan, Japanese workers must pay a multiple of the (exchange-weighted) price a U.S. worker pays for the same item. U.S. manufacturers' competitiveness is further supported by America's generally superb and lower-cost communications, finance, and air transportation services.

For *mass-produced consumer goods,* large-scale service enterprises and the power of service technologies to link manufacturing entities are the key factors effecting worldwide coordination of integrated manufacturing, global

TABLE 8-5 U.S. Services Trade Balances, 1982-90 ($ millions)

	1982	1983	1984	1985	1986	1987	1988	1989	1990
Selected Business									
Services, Total	12,873	10,534	10,188	4,077	10,703	11,373	17,369	30,052	35,141
Travel	(1)	(2,202)	(6,255)	(7,492)	(6,473)	(6,656)	(4,163)	625	1,908
Passenger fares	(1,598)	(2,393)	(1,864)	(2,327)	(1,209)	(545)	859	1,987	3,288
Other transp.	607	368	(1,034)	(969)	(1,257)	(805)	(520)	9	(1,056)
Fees & royalties	4,560	4,553	4,674	5,104	6,192	7,644	8,721	9,776	12,647
Other priv. serv.	9,305	10,208	10,188	9,761	13,450	11,735	12,452	17,655	18,354
Selected Income									
Transactions, Total	43,415	37,868	39,322	33,639	28,627	27,609	28,814	32,904	39,870
Direct investment	21,562	21,224	20,755	22,216	25,521	33,390	36,810	42,484	52,662
Other private investment	21,853	20,360	18,567	11,423	3,106	(5,781)	(7,996)	(9,580)	(12,792)
Selected U.S. Gov't									
Transactions	(15,936)	(15,226)	(18,895)	(22,426)	(23,656)	(25,009)	(30,452)	(37,853)	(36,690)
Services, Income, & Government	40,352	36,892	26,136	15,290	15,674	13,691	15,631	25,103	38,321

Source: Bureau of Economic Analysis, "U.S. International Transactions," Table 1, *Survey of Current Business,* June 1991.

product and process development, and functionally segmented manufacturing–distribution joint ventures. Although services drive globalization at many levels, perhaps nowhere else is their effect as great as in the retailer–manufacturer relationships that interconnect world economies so tightly today. These relationships leverage knowledge bases about U.S. customer demand directly into foreign producers' plants on a daily updated basis. As an example, virtually all retail chains—like Kmart or The Limited's group of companies, with their 2,250 and 3,860 retail outlets and sales of $29.5 billion and $4.8 billion, respectively—aggregate the day's sales each night from their Electronic Point of Sales systems. These systems break down sales to the minimum replicable level of detail—type of item, cut, size, material, color, style, number sold, price, margins, and so on. Forecasting programs at corporate headquarters then convert the day's sales into a cutting order for Southeast Asian fabric suppliers for the next day. Within a few days, a wide-bodied aircraft takes off from Southeast Asia for the distribution depots of The Limited or Kmart in the United States. A few days later, the merchandise is on their shelves. Thus, stocks are aligned to current demands, markdowns are limited, and inventories are kept to a minimum. Other programs keep track of sales of new or experimental items being sampled throughout the system. What is stocked is dictated by the customer and the retailer, and manufacturers are linked as directly to their order givers as possible.

For *intermittently produced* or *specialty products,* other manufacturing-service arrangements dominate. For example, VTI Inc. has a flexible worldwide sourcing network to obtain least-cost product design and production of its high value-added, applications-specific integrated circuits (ASICs). Through electronic interfaces, VTI's designers can work with customers anywhere to create new ASIC designs upon request. VTI's software in Silicon Valley converts these designs into photo masks. The photo masks are shipped to Japan, where others etch the chips. The chips are sent to Korea for dicing and mounting, and then to Malaysia for assembly. From Malaysia, they are shipped directly to customers—by overnight parcel delivery, if desired.

For *continuous production operations,* global sourcing networks have long offered advantages. Overhead and direct costs tend to drop markedly with off-shore manufacturing. On the other hand, logistics costs tend to *increase* by a factor of about 20 percent, and tariffs and exchange rates become increasingly significant.[10] In these circumstances, global information concerning local costs, suppliers' capabilities, transportation possibilities, en-route location of materials, and financing potentials becomes a crucial competitive weapon for manufacturers—and a critical component of strategy. So important are logistics costs in worldwide manufacturing networks that before Toyota began its Nummi joint venture with GM in the United States, it set a target of having "the most cost-efficient inbound–outbound logistics system in the world." Because its own costs for production in Japan would be essentially fixed (excluding exchange rates), Toyota's capacity to control the profitability of its Nummi versus Japanese sources depended mainly on logistics. Without very sophisticated capabilities,

Toyota would have been largely competing with itself. Another Japanese group, Mitsubishi, has recognized that its combined financing and logistics functions will be so important to its future profitability that it reportedly is planning to spend up to 20 billion yen on its new MIND logistics system to support world-wide manufacturing and distribution for its broad line of manufactures.

For *economies of scale,* multinational manufacturing operations today usually look more to service capabilities (their technology development, marketing, technology transfer, financial, and logistics functions) than to plant-scale economies, which are dropping in most countries.[11] Many of these services can flow duty-free across borders, offering new strategic flexibilities when a multinational company can handle cross-border data and services flows more effectively than its competitors can. Because a host country can *least* easily reproduce the service and knowledge components of a multinational's capabilities, these become the company's bargaining points in dealing with host nations, with suppliers, and with customers in each country. Unfortunately, host countries increasingly see these data flows as potential tax sources and as threats to their local companies' competitiveness. Maintaining the freedom of these flows has thus become a critical strategy and a delicate political issue affecting the future international competitiveness of both manufacturing and service enterprises.[12]

International simultaneous development of products has become a *sine qua non* for most manufacturers, if they hope to develop the most competitive available products or processes. Potential suppliers and partners must be intimately and continuously coordinated throughout the design process. In fact, many companies find that they can obtain a competitive edge by using the differences in time zones between countries to obtain a 24-hour workday during design cycles. A design team begins working on a product in the eastern United States in the morning, transfers its status to the Japanese team after 11 hours of coordinated work in the United States (an eight-hour day plus three time zones). The Japanese partners pick up the design and work on it through the next eight to 12 hours, before passing it along to European design teams. By the next morning in the eastern United States, when the U.S. designers return to work, two full days of further work have advanced the design. Even without such sequenced design capabilities, many firms are coordinating worldwide development with different supplier groups to obtain "best-in-world" design capability as a matter of competitive necessity.

Restructure of Whole Industries

These types of "intelligent enterprises" are so pervasive that whole industries are restructuring to achieve simultaneous interactions on a variety of projects. These industries are becoming merely loosely structured networks of service enterprises joined together (often temporarily) for one purpose. They remain suppliers, competitors, or customers in other relationships. This phenomenon is common in financial services, where cross-competing consortia constantly form and reform to finance different projects or to spread risks worldwide. But the same is true for enterprises in the mineral resources, construction, publishing, entertainment, or software development fields, among others. Publishers, for example, have become primarily coordinators of intellect, outsourcing virtually the whole process of book creation to independent writers, copyeditors, artwork groups, compositors, printers, binders, advertising agencies, distributors, retailers, and so on, located anywhere in the world. Biotechnology provides another interesting global example (see Box 8–2). Almost all biotech products are developed by intelligent enterprises that coordinate a number of different specialist teams. They join together temporarily for the sole purpose of creating a particular biological entity and introducing it to the marketplace. Different types of highly specialized enterprises have developed at each level of the industry to perform individual functions.

Box 8–2

How Specialized Enterprises Reshape Industries

Many biotechnology research groups—for example, at universities—seek only to identify and patent active biological entities (or proteins) at the laboratory level. Others develop and license the cell lines that are used to reproduce promising entities. (Having identified and cultured cells that contain the genes to "express an entity" is often as important as knowing the active protein and its effects *in vitro.*) Still other companies, like Verax and Damon, have developed pilot-level processes that utilize cell lines owned by others to produce the desired entities in the limited quantity needed for clinical tests and early commercialization. Medical centers handle the highly technical problems of actually administering and running clinical trials. Other enterprises or professional groups may oversee regulatory relationships and FDA clearances. End-product companies—usually major pharmaceutical companies—may take over the large-scale market introduction, detailing, production, and sale of the products, and service companies may handle their wholesale or retail distribution. Once the product is in the marketplace, doctors (another, wider group) prescribe and administer it to patients. In essence, a unique consortium of specialists, intentionally tapping best-in-world capabilities, forms for each stage of research, development, product introduction, and full-scale production.

The semiconductor, Application Specific Integrated Circuits (ASIC), and electronics industries are becoming similarly structured. Independent design, foundry, packaging, assembly, industrial distribution, kitting, configuration, systems analysis, networking, and value-added distributor groups do over $15 billion worth of customized development, generating almost $140,000 of revenue per employee.[13] Even the largest Original Equipment Manufacturers are finding that these groups' specialized knowledge, flexible production facilities, and fast turnarounds decrease investments and increase value at all levels of the value chain.

In advanced technology fields particularly, a single company often cannot effectively span the full chain of activities needed, because of the specialized expertise, high risks, and varying time horizons required at each level of the development process. As a result, many high-tech industries—from biotechnology and ASICs to oil exploration, dam building, nuclear power, or commercial aircraft—are developing as multiple-level consortia, with each consortium and enterprise having its own network of contract and information relationships embracing a variety of research, development, production, finance, and marketing groups around the world. Although biotechnology and ASICs are commonly thought of as manufacturing industries, most of the units that comprise these industry consortia are essentially service centers that perform specialized activities for each other.

New Methods of Financing

These kinds of networks present some financial opportunities that are different from those involved in financing a single company. One can participate at any risk level desired. For example, at the university level, one can sponsor research seeking individual patentable biological entities. The probability that any specific project will succeed is very low, but the investments required are generally low and, if the project is successful, the royalty payoffs are potentially high. Alternately, one can invest larger amounts in companies like Genentech, Biogen, or Amgen (or a new biotech start-up), which are pursuing multiple projects at the research level. At the next stage, financing independent pilot-scale processors (like Verax) allows an investor to average somewhat higher investments—and their associated risks—across a number of projects, yet potentially participate in individually large upside licensing incomes if the investments pay off. Clinical limited partnerships have been developed to spread investments and risks of failure at the clinical trials stage, while sharing partially in larger benefits if successful. Full-scale production and marketing investments—usually undertaken by more integrated companies—are quite large, but their risks are much lower.

Each level has developed some creative new forms of financing. Only in rare instances has a single enterprise financed the complete development of a new biotech entity from research through volume production and marketing. The combination of risks, the huge amount of capital required, and the industry's long time horizons makes such an undertaking unwieldy. Alliances are common in biotech: more than 170 were formed between pharmaceutical manufacturers and other independent biotech groups in 1990. Given the rapid technological advances throughout such industries, companies can lower their risks substantially by specializing, by avoiding investments in vertical integration, and by managing intellectual systems instead of workers and machines worldwide. Because of their high value-added and easy portability, the services that are input to such systems may come from anywhere in the world. The core strategy of participating companies becomes: Do only those things in-house that contribute to competitive advantage, try to joint-venture others, or source the rest from the world's best suppliers.

Interestingly, this opens up opportunities for myriad smaller companies. By concentrating on a few selected intellectual skills and attracting best-in-world talent, they can become the suppliers of larger companies for whom these skills are not specialties. This is the core cause of the growth of the number of smaller companies—and of the changing and increasing outsourcing expenditures of large companies. Price Waterhouse studied 500 software start-ups with an average history of eight years and found that two-thirds got some form of financial help from partners, in the guise of marketing assistance, equipment support, or guarantees from customers or computer builders. Only one-fifth used venture capital. If these companies develop their core competencies in sufficient depth, their small scale, flexibility, and responsiveness make them ideal partners for intellectual holding companies.

GLOBAL FINANCING AND MANUFACTURING STRATEGIES

Another change in the financial realm has been of prime importance in creating more disaggregated intelligent enterprises in manufacturing. The integration of world capital markets (service institutions) through electronic communications (service technologies) has forced almost all manufacturers into some form of globalization, much more disaggregation, and major shifts in their sourcing strategies. The total of all measured goods and services sold in international trade was $4.5 trillion in 1990, but the Clearing House for International Payments (CHIPS) alone handled almost $250 trillion in international financial transactions. Euromarkets and world bond markets added over $1,000 trillion to this sum. Instead of following goods or trade, money now flows toward the highest available real interest rates or returns in safer, more stable economic situations.[14] These factors are generally influenced more by government policies than trade. As money flows have sprung free of trade, exchange rates have fluctuated wildly at times—± 50 percent among major trading partners within a few months in the late 1980s—principally because of fiscal or monetary, not trade or management, decisions.[15] Such fluctuations change enormously, in a short period of time, the relative costs of producing at or importing from particular locations.

Manufacturers cannot cope with changes of this magnitude by merely adjusting their internal productivity rates, no matter how responsive they may be. A manufacturing firm now needs to manage several groups of global portfolios: (1) its financial positions, (2) its market outlets, (3) its assembly sites, (4) its supplier sources, and (5) its subassembly units in different geographical locations, among which it can switch its resources and product developments rapidly and flexibly.[16] Given such high cost variabilities, few firms can afford to own all of their producing entities themselves. Hence the increased need to form the kinds of worldwide coalitions noted above: purchasing arrangements, long-term contracts, alliances, or joint ventures. These are inevitably linked more by information, communication, and mutual interests than by ownership (vertical or horizontal integration) ties. Because of their high value-added potentials and the ease with which their "products" can be transferred across borders, services activities or companies are the central features in many of these coalitions.

Services Create Disaggregation and Global Networks

Why have these disaggregated global ventures suddenly become so much more common?

1. New service technologies in communications, information, storage, transportation, materials handling, and so on, have made it possible for manufacturers to compete directly over wider geographic ranges.

2. The fact that more of the value-added in products comes from services means that one can afford to seek out the best providers (for design, finance, and so on) wherever they exist. Their services can be shipped across borders at very low cost and tariff-free.

3. Most manufactured products now function in conjunction with some other systems from which they obtain specialized inputs, components, software, distribution, or repair services. It is frequently far more effective to obtain such capabilities by forming coalitions with exceptionally strong external units rather than by developing all needed activities internally or acquiring and owning a total vertically integrated operation. (See Box 8–3.)

The purported benefits of vertical integration—greater control, faster response, and profit capture at each level of production—may work well in stable or predictable industries with long time horizons. But there are few such industries today. Technology, worldwide competition, and extreme design and cost variations among different suppliers' capabilities and customers' needs have destroyed the potential benefits of such infrastructures for most companies. Vertical integration forces companies to be expert in more areas than they can possibly sustain as best-in-class. Unless transaction costs[17] are very high, integration is unlikely to offset the costs of having a lesser expertise and a higher investment base in a highly variable marketplace.

Vertical integration exposes a company to all of the risks at each activity level in which it participates, and amplifies the systematic risks of the volatility in its own industry. Whenever there is a downturn, a vertically integrated company must absorb not only the losses in its own final marketplaces, but also those in each of the supplier marketplaces in which it is vertically integrated. Outsourcing lets a company spread these risks upstream to suppliers and downstream to distribution networks. Proper outsourcing and managing of supplier networks allow the company to concentrate on what it does best, surround that activity with enough value-added services to give it uniqueness and depth,

---

Box 8–3

Examples of Services-Driven Global Networks

Liquid crystal displays (LCDs) are crucial to the next generation of computers and perhaps of television. Color-LCD sales (probably made from thin films) are expected to exceed those of memory chips by the year 2000. Exploitation, however, requires multiple skills. One set of skills supports the thin films themselves, another is for the special glass needed for displays, another is for advanced testing equipment to control defects, and another is for the equipment that uses the displays. A number of consortia are forming to link the crucial skills that various specialized companies have, and to reduce investment risks during the expected prolonged development cycle.

   Silicon Graphics, a leading manufacturer of 3D workstations, has been one of the most rapidly growing companies ever located in Silicon Valley. Its high-powered computers sell for around $200,000. Recognizing the need to increase the volume and to lower prices for its complex technologies, it introduced a $10,000 IRIS Indigo workstation. Then it entered licensing agreements with Compaq and Microsoft and opened its software to third-party licensees. To keep it ahead, Silicon Graphics is relying on its accumulated knowledge base about 3D and an enforced fast-response culture. Without such alliances, its CEO, Ed McCracken, felt others could eventually force competing technologies to become the industry's standard.

   By contrast, two electronic home equipment giants, Sony and Matsushita, saw their basic entertainment hardware products moving toward a commodity status in a few years. Instead of entering alliances, they vertically integrated. Each purchased a major software (film and distribution) company to capture the higher margins and more stable revenues available there. It remains to be seen whether their strong consensus-type core design-and-manufacturing cultures will be compatible with the creative, risky, egocentric world of movies, television programming, and rock concerts, or whether alliances would have lowered risks and investments.

---

avoid investments and risks in areas where it is less expert, and tap the innovation and expertise of best-in-world suppliers in the latter areas. As the CEO of a major telecommunications company interviewed with said: "You know how many advanced technology people I have working for me now? About 21,000! Less than 1,000 on my staff and over 20,000 in my suppliers' shops. And they are the best available anywhere in the world."

Disaggregation with a Strategic Focus

Such potential can change the entire concept of strategic focus in manufacturing: a focus on product classes becomes a focus on the activities (usually services) that the company can perform and link uniquely well to customers' needs. In some cases, this may require a single-minded concentration on certain aspects of manufacturing itself. More often, it means surrounding the company's product skills with a complex of service activities that are so integrated as to give the company a unique ability and depth in servicing selected customers' needs.

Despite current admonishments to "stick to one's knitting," for a Xerox to stick to manufacturing and selling reprographic machines or an IBM to only manufacture computers would be a strategic disaster. Xerox became a huge success primarily because it created an invulnerable patent wall around its product, found a unique way to finance purchases by smaller customers so they could pay for their units as they used them, and coped with the product's early erratic performance with the best field service force then available. Finally, at the right time, Xerox expanded into support software and systems to give its customers the flexible image-reproducing qualities and network interconnection capabilities they were then demanding. Both before and after Xerox's products went off patent, the sum of its profit contributions from service activities was at least equal to its profits from the direct sale of equipment.

IBM has long received over one-third of its gross profit from direct sales of software and services, rather than sales of its information-processing equipment. When one takes into account the value of the system software and design services "built into" or associated with the equipment IBM sells, and the value of the equipment sales it would lose without its awesome service support activities, most of IBM's profits are truly due to its service-based focus on its customers' needs. IBM and Xerox have built up a service core that best delivers their carefully defined "document handling" (Xerox) or "information management" (IBM) capabilities as a system to their customers. Yet, as large and as capable as these companies are, neither could have conceivably created and controlled internally the full range of design, hardware, software, communications, and networking capabilities it needed. Hence, both have moved steadily away from earlier attempts to vertically integrate and toward a wide-ranging and constantly changing set of coalitions with outside service and support groups. Their outside sources let them compete globally against similar networks of other companies.

Given the rapid changes in technologies and world marketplaces, IBM in the late 1980s began dismantling the insularity and self-sufficiency that had dominated it in the 1970s and early 1980s. Even its huge multibillion-dollar R&D program—largest in the industry—needed to be leveraged externally. In addition to partnering with Apple on software (RISC, UNIX, and Taligent) and helping the MCT consortium to do basic computer technology research, IBM began teaming with Siemens to launch the next generation of 16-megabit Dynamic Random Access Memory and to design the 64-megabit DRAMS that will replace them. Siemens will sell the chips in Europe. IBM is also trying to forge partnerships with Disney, MCA, Spielberg Productions, and Warner Brothers, to exploit the multimedia worlds of industrial and personal computers. Its traditionally strong skills in industrial marketing, information, and distribution should give it advantages in that market, but it will need coalitions for success in the consumer-entertainment segment of any multimedia ventures.[18]

Networks—like those illustrated in Figure 8–2—have become the basis of competition in many industries.[19] These arrangements look much like the Japanese keiretsu structures (that is, interlocking linkages among manufacturing units, financial institutions, and other entities within a compact family), but with a real difference. For years, combined production–service integration (of banks, producers, and export/distribution companies) has been at the heart of Japan's keiretsu-based trading power. Although some large manufacturing groups may wield enormous economic clout within a keiretsu, the Japanese have been wise enough to practice quasi-integration, not complete vertical integration. Most keiretsu operate largely through multiple, carefully interlocked coordination-and-decision structures based on common interest, rather than on orders from a central authority. Given the Japanese success, it is not surprising that similar coalitions—extended more on a worldwide basis—are providing an essential model for other countries' competitive postures today.

However, the keiretsu's interlocking boards would be illegal in most countries. Besides, companies in those countries can probably gain greater competitive advantage by jumping beyond the mutual partial-ownership ties of the keiretsu and directly into a more flexible, partnership-oriented contract structure. They can avoid much of the bureaucracy and inflexibility that keiretsu relationships cause their Japanese competitors. There are numerous challenges in managing the more disaggregated Western intelligent enterprises, but the form provides very real competitive advantages for those who use it effectively.

MAINTAINING STRATEGIC FOCUS IN THE INTELLIGENT ENTERPRISE

The key to an intelligent enterprise lies in maintaining strategic focus while disaggregating. This does not necessarily mean a tight focus on a limited set of products. Products rarely provide a maintainable competitive edge today; they can be too easily back-engineered or cloned. True strategic focus means developing a selected set of knowledge factors, databases, and service skills (of particular importance to customers) in such depth that the company becomes best-in-world at providing these to customers. It then concentrates its resources on these activities and seeks best-in-world partners (or performance parity) in other areas by careful benchmarking, process updating, and outsourcing to others when it cannot reach best-in-world internally.

To maintain its position from a strategic viewpoint, the company's selected focus *must control some crucial aspect(s)* of the relationship between suppliers and the marketplace. The company must block its suppliers from bypassing it to the marketplace as Giant Manufacturing of Taiwan, originally a bicycle frame subcontractor, did to Schwinn. It must also defend itself from big purchasers

FIGURE 8–2 Competing global networks: IBM and AT&T.

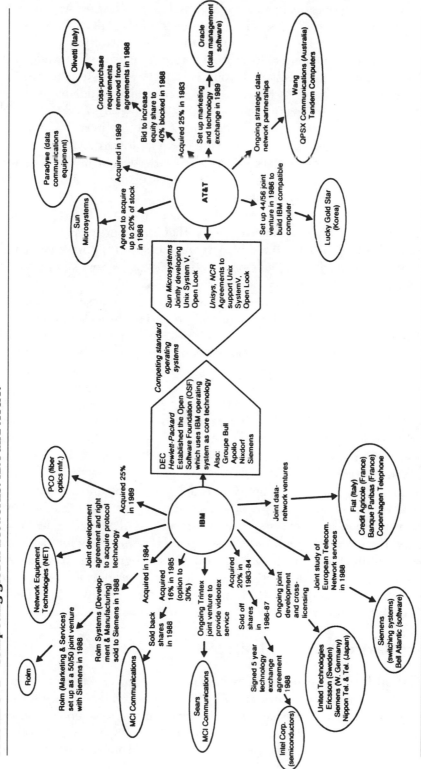

Source: Original chart by Braxton Associates, J. B. Quinn, and P. C. Paquette.

attempting to become vertically integrated into its turf. The best way to do both is to control some key knowledge-based segment(s) of the value chain. As an example, Apple Computer Inc. defended its position by controlling the "look and feel" of the personal computer's operating software and the knowledge about computer demands that it generated from its well-developed user network.

To cite another example, Excel Industries of Elkhart, Indiana, had developed a better method for making auto windows. When Ford tried to bring that production in-house during a recent recession, it could not master Excel's complex process. Ford ended up having to give Excel a multiyear contract as well as investing in the company. Excel's sales grew fourfold, and it reinvested in a faster, more efficient process that cut design cycles by a year. Ultimately, both companies gained by the new relationship.

The company's depth in its selected core activities and the importance of those activities to its customers must be such that customers cannot destroy the company by short-circuiting it directly to its suppliers, and suppliers cannot simply assemble components and sell clones to the market, as Sony's imitators have often attempted to do with its products.

This approach radically shifts the basis of strategic analysis in manufacturing. Strategists must analyze all present and potential (direct and cross-) competitors able to perform the *service activities* on which the strategy focuses. Because there is enormous cross-competition among most service activities, managers cannot simply look at the companies in their own product industry. In practice, they must strategically analyze all those companies that cross-compete in providing the particular function(s) they have chosen as their core competencies and make sure they focus more talent on these areas than any other companies in the world. Simultaneously, they must benchmark other crucial service activities to ensure that they maintain sufficient parity so as not to be overtaken by cross-substitutions.

As companies begin to simplify internal operations and outsource nonstrategic activities—particularly overheads and peripheral activities—they often discover secondary benefits. The overhead cost leverages can be very impressive. For example, Black and Decker found out that as it eliminated steps in its own manufacturing processes, simplified its designs, and consolidated its suppliers, it dramatically decreased the service activities needed to support its product line. It ultimately obtained from overhead cost reduction $3 in benefits for each dollar of direct cost it eliminated from production activities.

A More Market-Driven Strategy

For almost all firms, focusing strategy on a few core service competencies will lead to a more compact organization. The firm usually ends up with fewer hierarchical levels and a much sharper focus on recruiting, developing, and motivating the people who can create most value for the company. Knowing that it can be potentially outsourced, each activity in the company becomes more market-driven to provide better and lower-cost service for its internal users. Some companies establish their overhead service units as small private business units that must sell their services to operating groups on a continuing basis, just as component divisions must sell their products in competition with outsiders. In many cases, the market-driven process can be extended to providing such services directly to outside customers—for example, selling one's accounting or personnel services to outsiders. Some authorities even suggest that if an internal staff group cannot sell at least one-third of its output to outside users, this is a sure sign that the internal activity is not world-competitive and ought to be outsourced.

Some companies, as detailed in Box 8–4, go further by linking services directly to defined customer needs in a strategic mode.

The approaches described above help organizations achieve a greater and more consistent strategic focus. They also shift management's attention away from an internal or functional orientation—and the capacity to manage these functions' associated bureaucracies—and toward those more coordinated, strategic, and conceptual tasks that add greater value for customers. The skills needed at the top level shift strongly toward: (1) coordinative interfunctional skills, (2) logistics and contract management skills, (3) specialist skills at the forefront of their fields, and (4) leadership skills capable of conceiving, implanting, and coordinating a broad vision[20] across the much more geographically diffused activities of a company. With fewer bureaucracies, the company can become much more quality- and customer-focused. (See Figure 8–3.)

Box 8–4
Linking Services to Customers' Needs

Although it is a relatively smaller company (versus its competitors, the "Baby Bells"), United Telephone of Ohio (UTO) is attempting to match up the level of services it offers to customers with the pattern of its customers' true needs. UTO seeks to first understand in depth what services customers most want and need from UTO, and then to allocate its internal resources and scale its organizational units' sizes to better fit the defined service balance. (See Figure 8–3.) UTO tries to benchmark the best available competitive sources for each service and then beat that performance. To make sure that it is best-in-class where it counts with customers, UTO consciously patterns its organizational elements and resource commitments to be overstaffed relative to those needs its customers define as most critical and those in which it is attempting to achieve its own competitive edge. Conversely, services that are less essential or less desired by customers may be consciously understaffed or eliminated to lower overall costs. All systems and organizational elements are aligned to ensure that those activities most valued by customers receive most attention.

FIGURE 8–3 Example: Activity analysis matrix—support activities versus customer needs, large business segment.

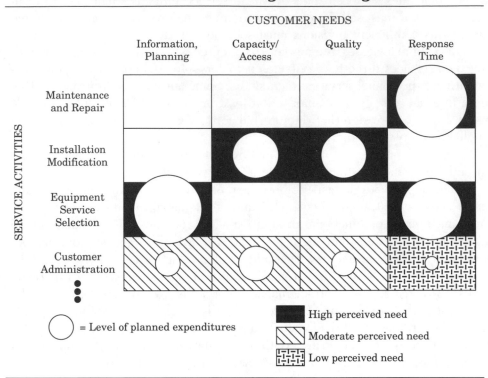

Source: Original chart by Braxton Associates; reproduced with permission.

CONCLUSION

True focus in strategy means the capacity to bring more power to bear on a selected sector than anyone else can. This once meant that one manufacturer owned the largest production facility, research laboratories, or distribution channels supporting a single product line, but such a strategy is no longer desirable or sufficient for most companies. Physical positions (a raw material source, a plant facility, or a product line) rarely constitute a maintainable competitive edge today, especially for manufactured products. They can be too easily bypassed, back-engineered, cloned, or slightly surpassed in performance. A truly maintainable competitive edge usually derives from developing depth in skill sets, experience factors, innovative capacities, know-how, market understanding, databases, or information-distribution systems—all knowledge-based service activities—that others cannot duplicate or exceed.

As a company does this, it needs to concentrate on those particular skills, service activities, or knowledge elements in the value chain where the company is, can be, or must be best-in-world in order to have a competitive advantage its customers deem to be critical. The company must ensure that it is and remains measurably better than competitors in its selected core service activities, developing them in greater depth than anyone else can. Then it must seek to achieve at least parity—either internally or through external arrangements—in most other key elements of its value chain. In pursuing this parity, it must seek out, join with, purchase from, or try to match the best-in-world performance in each activity. Finally, it must surround its selected core competencies with defensive positions, both upstream and downstream, that keep existing or potential competitors from taking over or eroding its selected positions. As it moves toward such a posture, the company tends to become an intelligent enterprise, developing and coordinating intellectual activities worldwide.

Defending and Enhancing the Knowledge Core

Many companies fear that if they follow this approach they may not be able to maintain at the core the knowledge needed to manage specialist suppliers. This can be a real problem if not properly handled. To avoid losing control in the areas they outsource, successful companies maintain at the top a small cadre of sufficiently specialized and talented managers who oversee their outsourced relationships expertly. This often actually means upgrading the top line of people for their new activities. When this is done, despite some initial fears, many companies have found that their new activity coordinators, by riding circuit on all potentially best-in-world outside suppliers, can generate an even greater knowledge of the outsourced activities than the company had when its internal bureaucracies were producing these outputs on a proprietary basis. For example, as a portion of its Taurus/Sable project, Ford installed a "must see before" contracting policy, which forced its teams into the field to investigate alternate suppliers in detail. This led to greater understanding of suppliers and design problems, new ideas for the cars, and a higher level of internal understanding about possibilities than the old process had allowed.

Fortunately, new service technologies—especially on-line systems for remotely monitoring research, design-logistical activities, quality, and cost relationships—can markedly reduce the transaction costs and improve the effectiveness of managing disaggregated systems. Most companies find that their other internal costs and time delays drop as long-standing bureaucracies disappear or are reduced in power, and as their managements concentrate more of their time directly on more coordinative activities and the important core strategic activities of the business. None of this is easy. Implementing this kind of strategy is a formidable undertaking, and it usually must be approached incrementally. However, when successful, the changes in the company's posture can be very impressive.

NOTES

1.   These knowledge-based service activities often underlie many of the operating processes that are discussed in detail in Chapter 12.

2. "Novellus: Thriving—With a Little Help from Its Friends," *Business Week* (January 27, 1992), 60.

3. These questions are integrally related to the discussion of analytics and mind-set in Chapter 1. They are also relevant to the discussion of strategic alternatives in Chapter 10.

4. For a related set of comments, see the discussion of the value chain in the context of business-unit strategy in Chapter 3.

5. Chapter 2 provides a detailed discussion of the logic that led many firms to conglomerate or diversify.

6. D. Abell and J. Hammond, "Cost Dynamics: Scale and Experience Effects," in idem, *Strategic Market Planning: Problems and Analytical Approaches* (Englewood Cliffs, NJ: Prentice-Hall, 1979).

7. This is in line with the argument in Chapter 1 that organizations must develop capabilities and competencies as a source of marketplace advantage.

8. "The Cracks at Pilkington," *The Economist* (October 12, 1991), 78.

9. Peter Drucker, "From World Trade to World Investment," *The Wall Street Journal* (May 26, 1987).

10. "International Logistics Management," *Distribution* (October 1987).

11. R. Shelp, *Beyond Industrialization: Ascendancy of the Global Service Economy* (New York: Praeger, 1981).

12. K. Sauvant, *International Transactions in Services: The Politics of Transborder Data Flows* (Boulder, CO: Westview Press, 1986).

13. "Services Get the Job Done," *Electronic Business* (September 15, 1988).

14. It has been estimated that 95 percent of daily volume in foreign exchange markets is not connected to trade. See S. Bell and B. Kettell, *Foreign Exchange Handbook* (Westport, CT: Quorum Books, 1983).

15. J. Bleeke and L. Bryan, "The Globalization of Financial Markets," *The McKinsey Quarterly* (Winter 1988).

16. The broader context of global strategy within which these decisions are made is detailed in Chapter 5.

17. Transaction costs are the costs associated with making a particular transaction, that is, an exchange in the form of a purchase and sale of some good or service. Transactions may take place in a market—such as purchasing an automobile—or within an organization. Most transactions have lower costs when they occur in a market but in some instances the costs may be lower when they occur within an organization.

18. *Business Week* (April 6, 1992), 64–65.

19. K. Ohmae, "Triad Power: The Coming Shape of Global Competition," *Harvard Business Review* (July–August, 1991).

20. The importance and role of marketplace vision were discussed in Chapter 1.

A STRATEGY FOR GROWTH: THE ROLE OF CORE COMPETENCIES IN THE CORPORATION

9

C. K. Prahalad

University of Michigan

with

Liam Fahey

Babson College and
Cranfield School of Management

Robert M. Randall

Writer and Editor

In the 1970s and 1980s, Japanese and other Asian firms had stunning success in a wide variety of industries that were initially dominated by North American and European firms. Each market triumph fueled the ongoing debate about why the Western firms were not more competitive. By now, we have heard most of the rationalizations: "nonlevel playing fields," the "short termism" of U.S. management, the role of MITI (the Ministry of International Trade and Industry) in Japan, the role of technology, and difficult U.S. trade unions, to name a few.

A central issue that is too often neglected in this debate is the lack of internal capacity for new business development in Western firms. Compared to their Japanese competitors, why have so many large North American and European firms failed to develop new businesses? Why have so few resource-rich Western firms pioneered the newly emerging industries or industry segments? These questions compel us to reconsider the meaning of growth strategy and the role of top management in revitalizing Western firms.

This chapter has three goals:

1. To examine the "scorecard" or performance of top management in Western firms during the past 40 years.
2. To provide a framework for a new perspective on strategy that addresses the underlying rationale and logic for growth in a globally competitive environment.
3. To detail the new perspective on strategy with a particular emphasis on the role and importance of core competencies as the source of new business opportunities.[1]

A SCORECARD FOR GLOBAL COMPETITIVENESS

Let us begin by developing a scorecard for the top management of Western firms during the past 35 to 40 years. From about 1950 to 1980, in a wide variety of industries (including automobiles, semiconductors, tires, medical systems, earth-moving equipment, and reprographics), almost all the world leaders were Western companies. In the automobile industry, General Motors and Ford dominated the world marketplace. In the merchant semiconductor business, Texas Instruments (TI) and Motorola were the undisputed leaders.

During the 1980s, however, industry leadership proved to be even more difficult to retain than it was to acquire. A "who's who" of companies providing the "intellectual leadership" in major industries would be a very different list of firms than one for the prior 30 years. The changing pattern of leadership in many different industries is illustrated in Table 9–1. For example, intellectual leadership in the automobile industry is now increasingly being provided by companies such as Honda and Toyota, whether the criterion is use of new technology, new features, new standards of quality, customer orientation and service, or price–performance relationships.

Loss of leadership occurred in many different industries (Table 9–1). If it had happened in just one industry, we might be tempted to attribute the decline to industry-specific external factors such as the role of MITI in Japan, the cost of capital, or the attitude of trade unions.

However, the fact that Western management stumbled in so many industries suggests that something more systemic was at work. This becomes more evident when we consider the other categories of Western managements' scorecard—for example, *internally generated growth* at the top 25 electronics companies during the 1980s. The giants at the beginning of the decade were IBM, GE, ITT, Philips, and Siemens. Most Japanese firms were small. Hitachi, with around $12 billion in sales, was about half the size of IBM. Sony at $3 billion, was about one-fifth the size of Philips. Keep in mind that high-volume electronics was a "fortunate" industry during this decade: It experienced an average growth rate of 14 percent through the 1980s. However,

TABLE 9–1 The changing pattern of industrial leadership.

Industry	Leaders 1950–1980	Major Challengers 1980–1990
Automotive	GM Ford	Toyota Nissan Honda
Semiconductors	TI Motorola	NEC Toshiba Fujitsu Hitachi
Tires	Goodyear Firestone*	Michelin Bridgestone
Medical systems	GE Philips Siemens	Hitachi Toshiba
Consumer electronics	GE* RCA* Philips	Matsushita Sony
Photography	Kodak	Fuji
Xerography	Xerox	Canon

*Has been acquired.

there were wide variations in the rate of growth of various companies within the industry. The Western firms were all on the low end of the curve: 12 percent for IBM, 11 percent for GE, 5 percent for Philips, 8 percent for Siemens. Four Japanese firms were far more successful: Hitachi grew at 17 percent, Matsushita at 16 percent, Toshiba at 15 percent, and NEC at 23 percent.[2]

The disparity in growth rates among these firms in essentially the same industry category, combined with the evidence of shifts in leadership noted in Table 9–1, raise a number of unavoidable and critical questions:

- Why do some firms in the same industry grow at 5 percent and others at 20 percent for 10 years?
- How did the market leadership in so many industries shift in such a short period of time?
- What were the marketplace strategies of the rivals noted in Table 9–1 and how did they contribute to the shift in leadership?
- In view of the many advantages U.S. firms enjoyed during the period from 1950 to 1980—such as superior technology, larger size, global distribution, reputation, and management know-how—how did the intellectual leadership slip away?[3]

The conclusion is that most large Western firms have not learned how to succeed in opportunity (growth) management. Let us use a simple equation to evaluate the scorecard of a company's capacity to grow, say, during the period from 1985 to 1991. If total sales for a corporation was 100 for the year 1985, the capacity-to-grow index during the period from 1985 to 1991 can be computed as follows:

Capacity-to-grow index = (sales revenue for 1991 − acquisitions during the period
from 1985 to 1991 − inflation + divestments during
the period from 1985 to 1991).

By eliminating growth through acquisitions and inflation, this index measures *internal capacity to grow.*

Unfortunately, for most large Western firms, this index for the period from 1985 to 1991 is not very flattering. It indicates that these firms had relatively little internally generated sales growth. Top managers in these firms must ask themselves:

- What opportunities have we lost?
- Why? What internal factors have caused us to lose these opportunities?
- Who is responsible for these missed opportunities?
- Should the compensation of top management be adjusted to reflect lost opportunities?[4]

Let us take this analysis one step further by comparing the growth of three companies: Westinghouse, General Electric (GE), and Hitachi. Westinghouse grew from $8.5 billion to $12 billion during the 1980s. Westinghouse primarily divested itself of major businesses and acquired a few. GE also aggressively pursued a strategy of portfolio shuffling through acquisitions and divestments.[5] However, Hitachi grew from $12 billion to $50 billion through internal development. This pattern is no different if we consider RCA and Philips versus Sony and Matsushita, or GTE versus NEC.

Why have these results occurred? Why did Hitachi and Westinghouse experience such radically different revenue performance? The market opportunities for both firms were similar around the globe. Their initial technological capabilities were comparable. In fact, throughout the 1970s and 1980s, U.S. firms like Westinghouse led in technology in almost every field.

Reflection on this scorecard suggests that explanations must focus not on the differences in starting resource positions but on the differences in the ability of managers of successful firms to leverage corporate resources. Thus, we need answers to these questions:

- Is our orientation to management and exploitation of technology and market opportunities appropriate?
- Is there a distinctly different underlying logic (as compared to the financial portfolio logic) to profitable growth? What is that logic?

- What should top managers do in order to change their orientation from cost cutting to opportunity management?

These questions are the focus of the rest of this chapter.

THE MOTIVATION FOR RETHINKING THE SCORECARD

The fundamental business issue for the 1990s is *growth* in revenues. Creating the potential for revenue growth must become the all consuming focus or agenda for top management. Without revenue growth, organizations cannot invest in their future; they cannot create their future.

Downsizing, restructuring, and streamlining organizations cannot substitute for vigorous, internally generated growth. Downsizing in the form of "reducing headcount" rarely enhances sales revenues. Restructuring by acquiring and/or divesting business units or recombining existing business units without rethinking the focus and agenda of management inevitably leads to further restructuring. Many large U.S. firms have restructured themselves more than once (and some, many times) in the past ten years. Despite this management effort, the business difficulties that prevent these firms from growing never seem to get resolved.

If growth and new business development are the real issues, *value creation* will be the scorecard for managers during this decade. This scorecard will consist of three parts (see Figure 9–1):

1. *Managing the performance gap.* Organizations must be assessed on how well they improve performance across a wide variety of dimensions, such as quality, cost, cycle time, productivity, and profitability.
2. *Managing the adaptability gap.* Organizations must be assessed on how well they anticipate industry change and initiate and manage industry transformations. This is dramatically different from managing to enhance

FIGURE 9–1   Scorecard for top management: Value creation.

Performance Gap	+	Adaptability Gap	+	Opportunity Gap
Restructuring		*Reshaping*		*Revitalization*
Quality		Portfolio choices		Growth
Costs		Product mix		New business development
Cycle time		Channels		New market development
Logistics		Price–performance		Strategic direction
Head count		New business model		Resource leverage
Productivity				
Administrative systems				

Value Creation

performance in an existing industry or being the "best of breed" in a given industry segment.

3. *Managing the opportunity gap.* Organizations must be assessed on how well they create new businesses, pioneer new markets, and discern and communicate strategic direction. The defining challenge for organizations aspiring to global leadership is their capacity to identify, create, and exploit fundamentally new business opportunities—opportunities that do not exist in today's industry.

The Need to Address Opportunities

This three-part scorecard is necessary because so many industries are undergoing major structural change. Industry change adds urgency to the need to manage the adaptability and opportunity gaps. Merely outperforming existing competitors in terms of product quality, cost, and features is increasingly unlikely to provide the basis for breakthrough business opportunities.

Consider how structural change has affected the computer industry. For decades, IBM was the increasingly powerful leader of the computer industry, the epitome of a highly vertically integrated firm: from components, to mainframes, to operating systems, applications engineering, and software. IBM also owned its own distribution channels. Today, the computer industry is "deverticalized." IBM was slow to change as this new industry structure evolved. The companies that pioneered new growth segments of the industry are strong, and IBM is downsizing. The component part of the industry (for example, microprocessors) is dominated by Intel and Motorola. The operating system that drives most computers is provided by Microsoft. The applications software is dominated by specialists such as Lotus. There is considerably more variation in distribution channels: from value-added resellers to owned distribution to mail order houses and large retail operators such as Computerland and Sears. In short, the entire industry landscape has changed.

Such structural change is evident in most industries. Indeed, in many cases, the degree of change is so extensive that it is often difficult to delineate the boundaries or borders of an "industry." Consider the so-called "multimedia" business. It seems safe to suggest that the dividing lines that distinguish consumer products, professional and office products, computing, telecommunications, software (especially publishing and entertainment), and content providers are significantly blurred. Moreover, scenarios of what the "structure" of the multimedia industry will look like a mere five years from now vary widely.

Industries are undergoing various degrees of structural change for many reasons: deregulation, excess capacity, mergers and acquisitions, changing customer expectations, and technological discontinuities, to name a few.[6]

The persistent change in and around industries poses one overriding issue for every manager: What is the capacity of my organization to anticipate and manage the transformation of the industry? Unless managers seriously challenge their capacity to understand the project industry change, they are destined to be followers rather than leaders.

The ability to generate industry foresight and change proactively can be scored by measuring the *adaptability gap*. Given the evidence that an adaptability gap exists in most large Western corporations, managers must rethink their business model. The model has two parts:

1. Understanding the environment.
2. Competing to win in the marketplace.

Using this model requires corporations to rethink the logic underlying their business portfolios as well as their price–performance assumptions in each business.

While firms are coping with the performance and adaptability gaps, they have to address simultaneously the *opportunity gap*. How are they going to initiate new business opportunities that lie outside the purview of their current product portfolio? They must profitably deploy resources to create new markets and new businesses and establish a broad strategic direction.

During the past decade, management attention has been focused primarily on the performance gap, sometimes on the adaptability gap, and rarely on the opportunity gap. Managing the performance gap—fixing the problems of profitability, cost, quality, cycle time, logistics, and productivity—is the legitimate task of management. Managing the performance gap, if done well, ought to create a *large investment pool*. The question for managers, then, is how to utilize the investment pool, in the pursuit of new opportunities for growth. To create value, management must address operational improvement (performance gap) and strategic direction (opportunity gap) simultaneously. Value creation is not just a matter of catching up with the competition and eliminating the performance gap. It also must include the active management of the opportunity gap—the development of opportunities not available in current industry configurations. The remainder of this chapter addresses the underlying logic of opportunity management.

A NEW FRAMEWORK FOR VALUE CREATION

The logic of opportunity gap management consists of at least four interlinked parts (see Figure 9–2):

1. Managing the aspiration level.
2. Leveraging resources.
3. Creating new competitive space.
4. Energizing the whole organization.

Each will be briefly described and then addressed in more detail.

FIGURE 9–2   The new concepts in strategic management.

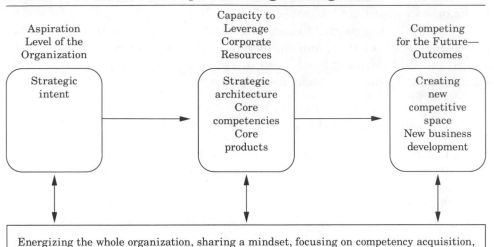

Organizational Capabilities

Managing the Aspiration Level

Organizations can accomplish unprecedented achievements when they are motivated to do so. Therefore, a fundamental challenge for top managers is: How can they foster a high aspiration level in terms of a strategic intent, so that their organization will push or entice its members to strive for goals that are beyond all prior achievements?

Motivation for change results from an aspiration or broadly defined goal that all employees can identify with and feel committed to. Aspirations must represent a stretch; they must exceed the current resources of the company. Therefore, by design, strategic intent must cause a "misfit" between aspirations and current resources/current approaches to using resources. The aspiration must focus the energies of the organization toward building its position in the marketplace through internal business development and marketplace innovation. This can occur when the business team finds a way to change the rules of the competitive game in a particular industry setting.

Leveraging Resources

A high aspiration level (compared to the resources available) leads to the need for resource leverage. Thus, another fundamental challenge faces managers: How do they acquire and use resources most effectively to generate new marketplace opportunities?[7]

The process of resource leverage is best accomplished through defining and developing a *strategic architecture.* As indicated in Figure 9–2, a strategic architecture necessitates identifying and fostering *core competencies* and *core products.*

Creating New Competitive Space

An internal capacity to leverage resources is a prerequisite for inventing new businesses. This may be called *creating new competitive space.* The required management skills are different from those needed to compete more effectively in existing businesses. The strategic intent is to shape a new business context, to provide unique offerings or solutions for customers. Creating new competitive space and managing growth efficiently are the essence of "competing for the future."

The commitment to create new businesses requires:

- A framework for identifying new opportunities.
- A break with the organization's old ways of looking at the world.
- A focus on functionalities rather than on current products and services.
- A dramatic altering of the price–performance relationships in an industry.

Energizing the Whole Organization

This new approach to managing strategically is not just a technical task or a senior management task; it is a task for the *whole organization.* The role of top management, therefore, is essentially one of energizing the entire organization—all members, at all levels, in all functions, and in all countries. One key step is to develop a shared mindset and shared goals. Another is to develop strategies for competency acquisition and development.

Senior managers must therefore focus on these questions:

- How do we stretch the imagination of all employees?
- How do we challenge the organization?
- How do we enhance the motivation of individuals and teams and link them to the corporation's aspirations?

Using this framework, the remaining sections examine, one at a time, the building blocks of value creation.

STRATEGIC INTENT

Strategic intent is the articulation of the organization's aspirations.[8] It provides a means for stretching the imagination of the total organization. It creates a focus for developing "barrier-breaking" initiatives such as identifying radical new directions for investigation of business opportunities. It provides a way of creating an obsession with winning in the marketplace that encompasses all participants at all levels and functions of the organization.

This obsession must translate into a shared competitive agenda that is sustained over a long period of time. Frequently, it is an agenda for global leadership. Specific corporate examples are NEC's goal of C&C (computers and communications) and Kodak's strategic intent to remain a *world leader in imaging.* Kodak chose not merely to be a leader in chemical imaging or electronic imaging, but to attempt the creative combination of both electronic and chemical imaging. Once leadership in *imaging* was accepted as Kodak's strategic intent, debates inside the company on whether chemical imaging was superior to electronic imaging, or vice versa, subsided. The focus shifted to creating new hybrids—products and services that creatively combined both chemical and electronic capabilities.

Extraordinary accomplishment often is based on a clearly articulated strategic intent. We in the United States have experienced the power of a clear national strategic intent. In the 1960s, the Apollo program's goal, to "Put a man on the moon by the end of the decade," was a "stretch" target. If successful, the result would be global leadership and the domination of space. The goal was competitively focused; the Soviet Union was the archrival. The goal was very clear and easy to understand. Although the goal was specific, managers of the project had to discover the means—new technologies had to be rapidly developed. How do we account for the inventiveness that was characteristic of the effective NASA efforts during the 1960s? Why is the "spirit" of the Apollo program seldom rallied to transform Western firms?

As the Kodak and NEC examples show, strategic intent may be stated in different ways in different firms. But, in all cases, it must represent a competitive agenda for the whole company. Such an agenda requires an architecture.

STRATEGIC ARCHITECTURE

Aspirations at the heart of strategic intent should suggest direction; but they do not indicate how to get there. Once an organization has developed a shared aspiration, it needs a framework for leveraging corporate resources that is consistent with the strategic intent.

Strategic architecture provides the necessary corporationwide framework. It serves as the bridge between strategic intent and resource leveraging/competency building. As discussed in the next section, a strategic architecture should, ideally, serve as a road map of the future that identifies which core competencies to build and cultivate—the essence of enhancing the corporation's long-run competitiveness.

A number of firms in transition, including Vickers (a division of TRI-NOVA), Sharp, Colgate-Palmolive, Kodak, and NEC, have developed strategic architectures to guide their managerial actions.

An example of strategic architecture is NEC's concept of C&C, the convergence of *computing and communications* (see Figure 9–3). NEC believes that the evolution of computing is being driven by two market forces: (1) the need for decentralized processing and (2) rapid changes in communication and component technologies. C&C is NEC's road map for developing products and services to compete in a marketplace created by the convergence of these two evolutionary forces.[9]

It is not the purpose of a strategic architecture to generate specific product plans. Rather, its purpose is to indicate basic stepping stones in the evolution of

FIGURE 9–3   NEC's concept of computers and communications (C&C).

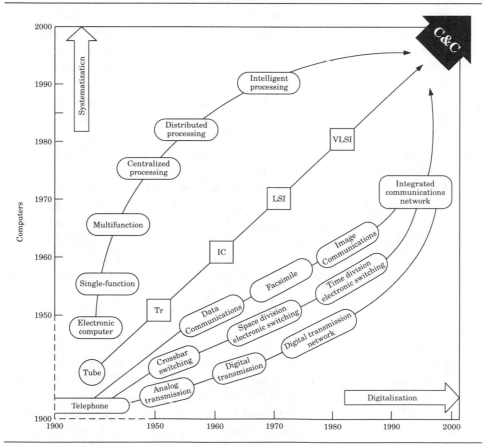

Source: From Koji Kobayashi, *Computers and Communications: A Vision of C&C* (Cambridge, MA: The MIT Press, 1986).

an industry or in the evolution of a series of technologies. As such, it suggests preliminary answers to many questions, including:

- What are the new technological possibilities?
- How might these technologies or different combinations of them change the interface with customers?
- How are our current and future competitors positioning themselves to approach this industry?

Because it integrates answers to these types of questions, strategic architecture offers an organizing system for distilling a great deal of conflicting information. It is a way of capturing both major discontinuities and current trends in and around the industry.

Yet, we must ask more specifically: What are the benefits of a strategic architecture? In the case of NEC's C&C, the framework of C&C has been used as a central organizing idea behind the firm's strategy, at the broadest level of strategic management, for the past 15 years. The NEC portfolio of businesses includes enormous product variety, technology diversity, and distinct bases of knowledge. Strategic architecture provides an understanding of the logic behind this diverse portfolio. All business units and product areas are derivatives of C&C. The framework has provided consistency and direction to complex decisions involving individual markets, customers, and technologies across multiple business units.

More specifically, strategic architecture should guide resource allocation. Consider NEC's R&D expenditures. The firm's R&D budget, during the period from 1980 to 1990, was considerably smaller than either IBM's or AT&T's. But NEC generated a growth record of 23 percent per year for over a decade, with significantly smaller investments in R&D.

How did NEC achieve this growth and how did strategic architecture help? NEC supplemented its investments in R&D by a series of carefully targeted alliances: from 1965 to 1987, NEC participated in over 130 alliances. The logic for this network of alliances was derived from the strategic architecture. Each alliance was intended to augment the firm's technology resource base. In fact, one can track all the alliances for this period and position them in the overall strategic architecture of the company.

However, selecting and investing in alliances is not enough. The strategic architecture also provided the framework to learn from these alliances. The intent of each alliance was to fill in some of the missing pieces in the overall architecture. This required the organization to commit itself to learning about the technology and knowledge of its alliance partners. It is important to understand how NEC used its alliance partners as a means of leveraging its internal resources. NEC also used its strategic architecture as a means of communicating to the rest of the world what the corporation was all about: Its C&C theme appeared in its advertisements.

What have been the results for NEC? We have already noted the superior returns (compared to IBM) on its R&D investments. More generally, in the early 1990s, NEC occupied one of the top five positions in telecommunications, computing, and semiconductors worldwide. Yet, it was only a $3 billion company in 1980!

A primary lesson of the NEC case is that establishing strategic architecture is a key function of top management because it is a useful framework for effectively managing innovations. *Innovation is the fundamental job of a general manager.* Strategic architecture provides a framework for everyone involved in the innovation process. Top management can use it to identify targeted acquisitions, alliance partners, and investments in technology and knowledge. When viewed from the perspective of long-run corporate competitiveness, the underlying assumption must be that innovation is a line, rather than a staff, job. Senior managers must set the architecture. Viewed in this light, innovations cannot be left to skunk works or "off-line activities" such as internal entrepreneurship or internal venture teams.

It is not enough for a small group of technical people to have a vision or an integrating view of the future of their industry. What is needed is widespread management agreement and understanding of the concept of strategic architecture, a process that requires extensive and dedicated salesmanship efforts by top management. An architecture, such as NEC's C&C, can be easily developed by the technical community, but getting universal agreement among several levels of managers inside a company is a much harder task. It is an effort that takes skill, time, and patience.

CORE COMPETENCIES

A strategic architecture allows managers to identify *which core competencies they have and which ones they need to develop.* Core competencies reside at the heart of the process of leverage and the creation of new business opportunities.[10]

How does an organization identify its core competencies? Three simple tests or sets of questions can reveal the key characteristics of core competencies:

1. Is the competence a significant source of competitive differentiation? Does the competence generate distinct value and benefits for customers? Core competencies manifest themselves to customers in the form of the firm's products and their attributes.
2. Does the competence transcend a single business? Does it cover a range of businesses, both current and new? A core competency should provide access to a variety of product marketplaces.
3. Is the competence hard for competitors to imitate? Is it difficult for others to learn how the firm does what it does?

Examples or core competencies that meet these tests include: miniaturization at Sony, network management at AT&T, billing at the Regional Bell Operating Companies, user-friendliness at Apple, and high-volume manufacturing at Matsushita. Sony's miniaturization and Apple's user-friendliness are unique signatures of these companies. These competencies underlie the competitive differentiation they have attained across a variety of end products. However, it is difficult for someone to visit Matsushita or Sony and define precisely why one is so good at manufacturing and the other excels at miniaturization.

Few companies are likely to build and sustain world leadership in more than five or six core competencies. The knowledge required to achieve world-class status and the speed of technological change render it difficult for any organization to possess more than a few core competencies. It is little wonder, then, that organizations invest so heavily in alliances and other forms of relationships in order to acquire the resources necessary to build desired competencies.[11]

Because core competence is a term that is often misunderstood, it is important to define precisely what it means. Many managers regard the concept of core competencies as synonymous with core technologies and/or capabilities. Core technologies are a component of core competencies. But core competence only results when firms learn to *harmonize multiple technologies.* For example, miniaturization, which has been the unique "trademark" of Sony, requires expertise in several core technologies, such as microprocessors, miniature power sources, power management, packaging, and manufacturing. It also requires an understanding of user-friendly design, a knowledge of ergonomics, and an awareness of emerging life-styles. For example, Sony product designers need to know how and why customers will want to use miniaturized products such as a radio that is no bigger than a business card.

The example of miniaturization highlights a key characteristic of core competencies: they are more than a collection of technical capabilities. Core competencies involve the *creative bundling* of multiple technologies along with customer knowledge, marketing intuition, and the skill to manage them all synergistically.

A second source of misunderstanding occurs when core competencies are confused with capabilities. Capabilities are, in some cases, prerequisites to be in a business. For example, just-in-time (JIT) delivery is now a prerequisite to be a "tier 1" supplier to the auto industry. It is the price one has to pay to get into the game. In the terminology of gamblers, capabilities are the equivalent of "table stakes." A capability is crucial for survival but, unlike a core competence, it does not confer any specific differential advantage over other competitors in that industry. Also, capabilities are often unique to a particular function or group within a business unit and therefore do not carry advantages over to other businesses.

Because competencies require (1) the management of complex, iterative processes, (2) the bundling of technologies, and (3) the integration of learning in many parts of the organization, they are difficult to imitate. Managers need to understand that any competence permeates the whole organization. In comparison, technology can be stand-alone (for example, the design of VLSI—very large system integrated circuits); competence, on the other hand, means getting consistently high yields in VLSI production. Competence transcends a specific technology or design capability. The process of converting good designs into high yields requires that multiple organizational levels (for example, workers on the shop floor and product development engineers) and multiple functions (for example, applications engineers and manufacturing groups) work together.

Much of the understanding and learning by individuals at different organizational levels and in the different functions that make up a competency is tacit. Leveraging tacit learning requires constant communication across hierarchical and functional boundaries.

The key to understanding competence is that, although it incorporates a technological component, it also involves the *governance process* inside the organization (the quality of relationships across functions within a business unit or across business units within a multibusiness firm), and *collective learning* across levels, functions, and business units. We may conceptualize competence as follows:

Competence = (Technology × Governance process × Collective learning)

Let us examine the implications of this view of competence, using, as a hypothetical example, a typical U.S. firm. The usual assumption is that, if its managers pour a lot of money into technology, the firm will become competitive. Using the equation above, let us consider this hypothetical firm to be rich in technology—commanding, say, 1,000 units of technology. However, let us assume that the various businesses within this corporation do not work together. They earn just 20 units for the governance process—the capability to work across business and functional unit boundaries. Let us also assume that, in this firm, the capacity for collective learning is low: 5 units for this dimension. Using the formula above, the firm's overall competence score is 100,000 (1,000 × 20 × 5) units.

For comparison, let us look at a company that is not blessed with as much technology. It rates only 200 units of technology, using the same scale that was used for the previous firm. However, this firm has fostered the capacity to work across organizational boundaries and is fully focused on organizational learning. It earns 100 units for governance and 500 for collective learning, which leads to a competence of 10,000,000 (200 × 100 × 500) units. The assertion is simple: Investments in technology, unless accompanied by investments in *governance* and the creation of a *learning environment* at all levels in the organization, will remain underleveraged.

This relationship among technology, governance, and learning environment suggests that the logical approach to improving the management of the core competencies for Western firms (and the means to correct their competitiveness deficiency, noted earlier) is to focus on improving the *quality of their organization.*

For evidence of the logic underlying this assertion, consider the case of Honda (see Figure 9–4). Honda's multiple businesses depend on a competence

FIGURE 9–4   Honda: Leveraging core competencies example.

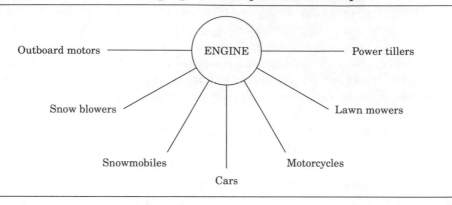

in engines. However, if each of its business units behaved as if it were discrete and only focused on (and was willing to pay for) the functionalities (i.e., specific engine design attributes) it needed, Honda's engine competence could be compromised. For example, in power tillers, managers may demand and be willing to pay for a light and powerful engine. However, noise reduction is not a major priority for power tiller managers because they target their products for use in villages in the developing world. On the other hand, the business-unit manager developing lawn mowers for sale in the United States may need a light and powerful engine that is as quiet as possible. Suppose that business-unit managers could uniquely define the functionalities that they need. If each Honda business unit merely optimized its own needs without maintaining a perspective on the implications of its parochial approach for the protection and development of an overall competence, the skill base would be eroded. Often, a single-minded focus on the strategic business unit (SBU) structure, without checks and balances, can destroy the very basis of nurturing and exploiting core competencies.

Competency development is also inhibited by prevailing organizational models. Historically, the dominant corporate model has been that of a portfolio of businesses. If the portfolio model is the only one used, then cost reduction within those businesses will appear to be the primary task, sometimes accompanied by the goal of product-line extensions. However, if we model the corporation as a portfolio of core competencies (as we shall demonstrate in the final section of this chapter), the result will be greater attention to new application opportunities. This will help make new business development top management's priority.

At Sharp, Sony, and Canon, the businesses in the portfolio share core competencies. For example, Canon sells a wide variety of end products—copiers, laser printers, fax machines, cameras, and camcorders. All of these businesses share access to core products (or components), such as Canon lens systems and Canon laser engines. To be world-class, these core products depend on Canon's core competencies—miniaturization, mechatronics, and so on.

Each end-product business has an independent identity and a specific set of customers and markets. But underlying that market focus is a structure of core products and core competencies that are shared. As a result, within Canon, there is an opportunity for gaining economies of scale in core products and an ability to anticipate new functionalities and leverage technical resources.

Core products are often the physical embodiment of one or more core competencies. Compressors at Matsushita and laser printer engines at Canon are examples of core products. Canon not only uses its laser printer engine in several businesses, it also markets it to external customers. Firms such as Canon distinguish among their market share of end products (such as copiers), their manufacturing share (such as share of market gained by providing manufactured products under private label to others), and their share of core products (such as laser printer engines sold to others). Canon has gained a predominant market share of over 85 percent worldwide in laser printer engines. However, the firm remains a small worldwide player in laser printers—the end product.

Consideration of core competency adds to the need to recognize that competition for core products is distinctly different from competition for end products and services. Consider, for example, the color television business. In order to succeed, firms must have access to core products such as picture tubes, signal-processing integrated circuits (ICs), tuners, and line output transformers. If we disaggregate businesses to the core product level—say, VCRs, camcorders, or laptop computers—we find that very few Western firms have sought leadership.

Understanding the importance of core products compels us to evaluate competitive rivalry differently. For example, in the VCR business, we can explain an important reason why Matsushita and JVC won the battle for their VHS format over Sony's Beta Max. Their combined market share for the end product—VHS VCRs—was only 24 percent. However, their manufacturing share (that is, the share of market gained by providing manufactured products under private label to others) was 41 percent, their VHS format share through licensing was 80 percent, and their core product share for decks was 85 percent. Eighty-five percent of the world's demand for VCR decks was met by one company!

Managers tend to underestimate the power of core product dominance. Such dominance gives rise to a critical issue: Who controls critical technologies? Given the dependence on a foreign supply base for critical core products, what are the chances that U.S. firms can create an indigenous high definition television (HDTV) business, even if resources are not constrained? The supplier base (and access to and control over core products) is a fundamental part of competitiveness. The key point here for both firms and countries is this: Technological superiority (including a world-class supplier system) without a corporate competence will likely be a short-term victory.

In summary, the emerging global competitive picture should force senior managers to ask themselves these questions:

- How long can this erosion of core product capability in the West be sustained?

- Who are the custodians of the technical virtuosity of individual companies? Managers of business units, as discussed above, have no natural inclination to concern themselves with core product share or competencies.

- How can group and sector executives transcend the concerns of the business units and play a role in protecting the basis for long-term competitiveness of their firms?

- Who should protect the disciplines that require multiple business units to work together?

It is important to recognize that competition today takes place on multiple planes (see Figure 9–5). To build and sustain market and intellectual leadership on a global scale in the long run, an organization will probably have to win on all planes. First, there is competition for end-product markets and services, that is, price–performance competition represented by market share battles for today's market. Managers have to fight in that arena. There is also a less visible battle for dominance in core products. These are the building blocks that create the capacity to lead in the development of products with new functionalities. Finally, there is competition for competence—the capacity to create new businesses or new competitive space.

CREATING THE NEW COMPETITIVE SPACE

How can firms create totally new products and services? Consider new businesses such as personal fax machines, a Global Positioning System (GPS) for

FIGURE 9–5 Competition at three levels.

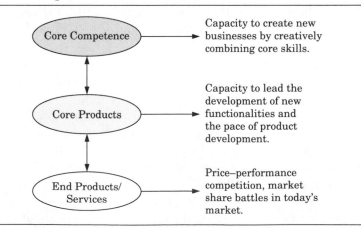

hikers, photo CDs, and camcorders. The *opportunity list* for the next decade, in high-volume electronics alone, could fill several pages. The key question for consideration by senior managers is: What do we have to do to capture our share of new business development?

New business development requires a new mindset on the part of most enterprises. Such a mindset has the following characteristics:[12]

1. *A persistent challenging of existing price–performance assumptions.* Why can't we create a color fax machine that sells for $200? Why should it cost $5,000? Canon, in copiers, and Lexus or Honda, in the luxury car segment, are good examples of firms that dramatically challenge the prevailing price–performance assumptions in the industry.

2. *Understanding the meaning of "customer-led."* Most firms have only recently learned to listen to customers and to give them what they ask for. That's important and beneficial but it's not sufficient. It is also necessary to lead customers. As customers, many of us may not have anticipated, ten years ago, our emerging dependence on fax machines in our homes. Being a customer-led company is important, but leading customers is what competing for the future is about. Managers must understand product functionalities and customer needs, and then create products with a price–performance ratio that makes them attractive for people to buy.

3. *Avoiding the tyranny of the "served market."* Most managers are so focused on their current market that they cannot see opportunities emerging elsewhere. A served-market orientation puts too much emphasis on current businesses and reduces the capacity to foresee new opportunities that arise outside the current market scope, especially those that fall in between two or more current business units. If we wish to re-ignite corporate imagination, we have little choice but to de-emphasize the served-market orientation and emphasize exploiting the opportunity horizon. Managers must not just defend markets, but create markets. Managers must not be comfortable with incrementalism in price–performance enhancement but commit to stretching price–performance goals. It is not enough just to benchmark the competition; managers must plan to outinnovate it. Firms must move:

   - From satisfying needs to anticipating needs.
   - From being close to customers to leading customers.
   - From thinking in terms of products to focusing on functionality and rapid market incursions.
   - From a focus on core business to diversifying around core competencies.

   These shifts would constitute radically new aspirations for most firms. Managers have traditionally sought to satisfy current customers, analyze current product-markets, and grow existing business units. But in order to achieve exponential growth based on core competencies, managers need both a new mindset and new managerial capabilities. The competency-based view of the corporation allows it to share knowledge and components across business-unit and functional boundaries.

The arguments advocated in this chapter suggest that serving only current business units, customers, and markets does not lead to long-run competitive success. This corporate focus does not result in significant new business development. Strategy analysis therefore needs a new perspective that *starts with a strategic intent, creates a strategic architecture, and understands core competencies and core products.* Only with this perspective will a logic of opportunity development emerge for business units, both current and new, and will leverage based on continuous reconfiguration of these competencies be continually addressed.

The new managerial mindset must address not just the intent or vision embodied in the commitment to develop and exploit new opportunities. For an organization to realize both the *stretch* (the difference between aspirations and available resources) and the *leverage* that strategic intent implies, it must develop a set of values and beliefs that is consistent with the goal of profitable growth. Values and beliefs will strongly influence how an organization answers the following questions:

- What is the unit of analysis for resource allocation?
- How do we manage interbusiness unit linkages? Interfunctional linkages?
- How do we create organizational capabilities, such as global–local capability, or cycle time?
- How do we think about administrative processes such as budgeting or planning?

If the dominant values and beliefs are competency-oriented rather than business-unit- or business-portfolio-oriented, then these questions will be answered differently than is the case in most Western corporations today.

CONCLUSION

Corporate strategy needs new guiding principles. Nothing short of a radical rethinking of current strategy analysis methodologies is required. The intent of this chapter has been to provide the requisite framework of concepts: strategic intent, strategic architecture, and core competency. Strategy must be aimed at growth; growth must be the new agenda for corporate management. Restructuring and other ways of delayering organizations cannot be the focus. Dramatic growth will not take place if the focus is on technology alone; it will take place only if the focus is on competencies, with technology as a component.

NOTES

1.   The ideas developed in this chapter will be illustrated with examples drawn primarily from high-volume electronics. I believe these concepts are equally applicable to industries as diverse as agricultural processing, chemicals, and, at least in some cases, defense electronics. I do not claim that the concepts presented here have universal applicability to all industries. However, I have found them useful in a wide variety of industries.

2.   These figures represent the annual compounded growth rate during the decade.

3.   These questions reinforce (a) the importance attributed in Chapter 1 to marketplace leadership as a central goal of organizations and (b) the need for senior managers to continually challenge how such leadership can be sustained.

4.   The importance of generating opportunities was emphasized in Chapter 1. Chapter 10 addresses many of the analytical and organizational issues involved in identifying opportunities.

5.   Some of GE's activity in realigning its scope was identified in Chapter 1. GE is further discussed in Chapter 14.

6.   Two related frameworks for industry analysis that are intended to identify and analyze the forces shaping industry change and evolution are examined in Chapter 6.

7.   See Gary Hamel and C. K. Prahalad, "Strategy as Stretch and Leverage," *Harvard Business Review* (March–April 1993), 75–84.

8.   The notion of strategic intent was briefly introduced in Chapter 1. For a full treatment, see Gary Hamel and C. K. Prahalad, "Strategic Intent," *Harvard Business Review* (May–June 1989), 63–76.

9.   See Koji Kobayashi, *Computers and Communications: A Vision of C&C* (Cambridge, MA: The MIT Press, 1986).

10.   A detailed exposition of the concept of core competence can be found in C. K. Prahalad and Gary Hamel, "The Core Competence of the Corporation," *Harvard Business Review* (May–June 1990), 79–91.

11.   These relationships are extensively discussed in Chapter 8.

12.   For a fuller discussion of the mindset required in exploiting opportunities, see Gary Hamel and C. K. Prahalad, "Corporate Imagination and Expeditionary Marketing," *Harvard Business Review* (July–August 1991), 81–92.

PART FOUR

STRATEGY MAKING: IDENTIFYING AND EVALUATING STRATEGIC ALTERNATIVES

10 IDENTIFYING AND DEVELOPING STRATEGIC ALTERNATIVES

Marjorie A. Lyles

Indiana University

AT&T (American Telephone and Telegraph) was facing its toughest competition in many years. Its aggressive challenger, MCI, had just announced an alliance with British Telecommunications, a signal that rivalry within the industry would intensify. AT&T could lobby for changing the regulations that prevented it from competing internationally. But AT&T needed to become more price-competitive in its home markets, and that meant analyzing various alternatives for cutting costs. A management committee generated a list of conventional alternatives: early retirement for large numbers of managers and employees, downsizing, and increased production efficiency. Senior management replied with a request for more creative and unique alternatives—alternatives that went beyond the ones that came readily to mind. The next set of alternatives picked a different target: offices and work space. Tossing out previous assumptions, the recommendations included a "reengineered" concept of office space. The concept took the perspective that most offices are largely wasted space used to store personal items like old files, sweaters, and umbrellas. At $40 per square foot in New York City, this was decidedly expensive storage space for items of little value to the corporate rent payer. Implementing a startling alternative, AT&T Sacramento decided to test eliminating the offices of its salespeople and, instead, giving them laptop computers, cellular telephones, and portable printers. As an added benefit, this alternative would allow its salespeople to work out in the marketplace, talking with and listening to customers. After observing the Sacramento unit's success, AT&T corporate headquarters decided to adopt the approach. It told its salespeople to create their own "virtual offices." For many managers, this was an "unthinkable" alternative.[1]

Most managers readily admit that generating alternatives as part of problem solving or leveraging opportunities is not something they do well. Indeed, when pressed, they'll admit it is not something that they routinely do.

Yet, because organizational and environmental change is so prevalent and so risky to ignore, as is shown in many chapters of this book, generating alternatives is both a necessary and a critical component of strategic management. When crafting an organization's future strategic direction, managers typically begin by identifying and considering a list of the organization's principal strategic alternatives. By practicing the process of generating alternatives that can be developed into viable and challenging strategic options, managers increase their organizations' chances of winning in the marketplace.

This chapter describes how organizations cultivate strategic alternatives and how organizational processes can enhance the quality of their choices. The next section defines what a strategic alternative is, and subsequent sections lay out the analytical and organizational steps involved in generating alternatives. A concluding section reviews factors that can influence the process of alternative generation.

UNDERSTANDING STRATEGIC ALTERNATIVES

What Is an Alternative?

An alternative is one of various means by which a goal can be attained, a problem solved, or an opportunity achieved. For example, there are frequently various alternative ways to enter a new geographic market, introduce a new product to the marketplace, or preempt a competitor's anticipated moves to lure away customers. To quickly illustrate the nature of alternatives, Table 10–1 shows

TABLE 10–1   Strategic alternatives: Gaining share in a particular market.

1. Add new items to the product line.
2. Add new features that would add to the product's appeal for some customer segments.
3. Provide off-site service that would allow the firm to meet many customers simultaneously.
4. Seek new distribution channels.
5. Endeavor to move more product through existing channels by altering the current incentive structure for each channel.
6. Develop a new advertising program in order to change the image of the firm and its products.
7. Restructure the sales force by realigning sales territories and modestly changing its incentive system.

different alternatives that an organization might consider as a means to gaining a major increment of share in a particular geographic market.

Alternatives are important because they define the choices available to a manager who must make a strategic decision. As illustrated in Table 10–1, managers gain a set of options that they can consider and evaluate; they can then choose a specific option.

Alternatives typically involve opportunities for shaping an organization's future strategic direction. This chapter emphasizes strategic alternatives, which have the following characteristics:

- They provide choices about marketplace strategy or about configuring the organization.[2]
- They address issues of central importance to the organization.
- They have uncertain outcomes.
- They require resources to develop before action can be taken.

Types of Alternatives

Alternatives can differ greatly along a number of key dimensions: the extent to which they are logical extensions of existing strategies, the extent to which they are creative or inventive, and the extent to which they break away from previously acceptable options and are "unthinkable" in the context of current operations. It is useful to categorize alternatives into three distinct types:

1. *Obvious alternatives* arise from an organization's current strategies, typically as extensions or corrections to the thrust of current strategies. Many of the alternatives noted in Table 10–1 fall into the category of obvious alternatives.

2. *Creative alternatives* embrace a new approach to the issue or decision. They take different conceptual approaches than existing strategies do. They require fresh thinking to break away, to some degree, from the assumptions and beliefs underlying current strategies.

3. *Unthinkable alternatives* reflect a radical departure from the organization's historic mindset. Frequently, such alternatives are "unthinkable" not because no one in the organization thought of them (or could think of them) but because they break the rules of what is appropriate in the organization. In most instances, such alternatives have a very low probability of being accepted by management. Yet, it is often crucial that they be included in an initial set of alternatives, if for no other reason than they can jump-start new lines of thinking throughout the organization. Unthinkable alternatives can illuminate the status quo in a radically different light and provoke managers to propose creative solutions.[3] For example, for many AT&T managers, eliminating offices for salespeople was an unthinkable alternative solution to the problem of cost-cutting.

Identifying and Developing Alternatives

It's important to distinguish between identifying an alternative and developing it into information that is useful for managerial decision making. Managers often identify an alternative as a "possibility," and most such possibilities are actually highly unlikely. For example, the alternatives noted in Table 10–1 might be considered possible alternatives. However, until an alternative that is possible has been considered in a variety of contexts, it is not ready to be assessed and evaluated.[4] For example, Table 10–2 illustrates how strategic alternative 3 in Table 10–1 might be probed for its actual potential to the company. Only after alternatives receive the due process of "pretrial discovery" and a creative "hearing" can they be reasonably evaluated. For brevity, we shall refer to alternative identification and development as alternative generation.

Different individuals may be involved in alternative generation. A task force may be formed or a group of middle managers may be asked by a senior executive to develop one or more alternatives around potential acquisition candidates or ways to divest a specific business. Sometimes, outside consultants are hired to add substance and context to alternatives that have been initially identified by individuals within the organization.

When Are Alternatives Generated?

The thesis of this chapter is that alternatives should be continually generated, even when managers may believe there is not a need to do so. This is recommended for two reasons:

1. Organizations should always be looking for ways to enhance the returns from their existing strategies. Among the outcomes of environmental change, discussed in Chapters 6 through 9, are new opportunities that can be exploited by adjusting and adapting the firm's current strategies. However, unless the organization is committed to seeking such opportunities, they are not likely to be captured.[5]

2. The fundamental strategic challenge noted in Chapter 1—the need to build for tomorrow while exploiting today—necessitates the development of alternatives that will allow the organization to position itself for the future marketplace. In short, whether the organization is preoccupied with optimizing its existing strategies or preparing for tomorrow, the extent and rate of change are such that opportunities and threats are continually unfolding. As discussed in Chapter 1, strategic management is essentially about capturing and leveraging such change. Alternative generation is the critical first step in doing so.

    Alternatives are more necessary at some times than at others. For example, when there is a clear need for a strategic change, such as when a continued deterioration in performance occurs, a list of alternative courses of action must be generated.

TABLE 10–2   Exploring a potential strategy alternative.

"3. Provide off-site service that would allow the firm to meet many customers simultaneously." [Strategic alternative, Table 10–1]

Steps Needed for Assessment and Evaluation

Identify the service(s) to be offered.

Identify to which customers the service(s) would be offered.

Determine what groups of customers should receive the service(s) simultaneously.

Determine the best type of off-site location.

Determine how many sites should be covered and in what order.

Determine how many individuals from the firm would be involved and whether the same individuals should cover every site.

Estimate the costs involved in providing the service(s).

Identify the benefits and values associated with delivering service in this way.

Identify a method for monitoring the impact of the service(s) on customers' loyalty and purchasing behavior.

Estimate the overall value or returns associated with this level of service.

How Are Alternatives Generated?

In spite of the fact that seasoned managers usually have considerable experience generating alternatives, most companies don't have sophisticated analytical and organizational processes for alternative generation. Even organizations with a systematic approach may not get high paybacks from mere diligence. Here's how the typical system works in practice: a number of individuals are assigned the task, they dutifully identify a set of alternatives, prune the initial set down to a few that are "doable," and perhaps arrive at a small set described in terms of actions, consequences, and resources. Yet, in the same organizations, alternative generation is a significant and spontaneous part of decision making. Alternatives are crafted rather quickly, without any intent to identify whether they are "good" or "bad" and without seeking the advice of others, outside or inside the organization, regarding which alternatives might be worth considering.

Because there are no simple algorithms for alternative generation, the next major section details how alternatives typically evolve. First, however, it is important to consider what is meant by a superior alternative.

What Are the Qualities of a Superior Alternative?

We noted above that organizations seldom attempt to determine whether alternatives are good or bad. The purpose of evaluating strategies, as discussed in the next chapter, is to determine which alternatives are best for the organization. It is also important for anyone involved in alternative generation to understand what constitutes a truly useful alternative. This understanding leads to more efficient alternative development processes and to alternatives that are more likely to enhance organizational performance.

Although there is no definitive set of criteria by which to judge the quality of any individual alternative or set of alternatives, organizations have found the following guidelines helpful:

- The variety of the alternatives. Having wide-ranging alternatives is important because the merits or demerits of one alternative or a set of related alternatives often only become apparent when they are judged against others. Unfortunately, too often the alternatives considered are merely variations on a theme. For example, a group of product managers was asked to prepare alternatives that would enhance their firm's competitive posture. Each alternative involved a price reduction. The managers made no real progress until they considered an alternative that required enhancing the product's functionality and associated service. Exploring this avenue, they stumbled on an alternative that could lead to a viable action plan for a price increase rather than a price decrease.

- Differences among the alternatives compared to the present situation. Among other benefits, such differences compel decision makers to reappraise the quality of the present strategy.

- The costs and difficulties of implementation. If the alternatives are too easy to implement, it is most unlikely that any unthinkable alternative has been identified.

- Do they challenge existing goals? Superior alternatives cause managers to demand more from existing expectations, aspirations, and objectives. As a consequence, long-held assumptions and beliefs may be challenged.

In summary, a set of superior alternatives presents different viewpoints and assumptions. A good list therefore creates real choice: Decision makers can select from among distinctly different alternatives. To the extent that alternatives are mutually exclusive, they should help decision makers avoid locking into a particular alternative too quickly.

A word of caution is in order. As the next section shows, generating (and evaluating) alternatives is not a simple linear process. Raising and considering distinctly different alternatives may lead to change in the criteria for making a strategic decision. Restructuring the issue or changing the criteria may mean that a new list of alternatives will have to be generated.

A MODEL OF THE ALTERNATIVE GENERATION PROCESS

The alternative generation process is complex and multidimensional, as illustrated in Figure 10–1. It is also recursive: It involves various points of starting, stopping, and returning to earlier points. The flow of the process, as depicted in Figure 10–1, suggests that alternatives may evolve in a linear fashion or, as

FIGURE 10–1   Model of alternative generation process.

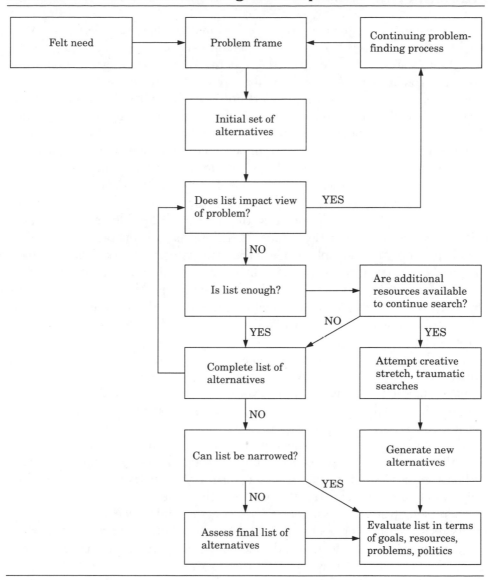

is most typically the case, they may involve cycling back and forth among the steps.

The model in Figure 10–1 helps managers think through the various steps or stages in the evolution of alternatives. By understanding this evolutionary process, managers can develop better organizational approaches to generating superior alternatives, and can anticipate and manage organizational and analytical difficulties that may arise. Before we detail some of the analytical and organizational approaches to developing alternatives, it is useful to examine Figure 10–1 for some of the key steps involved in alternative development.

Problem Frame

In most instances, strategic alternatives are created when managers perceive a need for them. But what provokes the perception process?

As indicated in Figure 10–1, the impetus for alternative generation often emanates from a "felt need"—a general awareness that the organization is facing or will face a potential problem, opportunity, or issue. Often, managers do not fully understand what the issue is. For example, a manager may have a sense that the rate of growth in sales of a particular product line is likely to slow down. This anticipation may be attributed to intuition, to conversations with a small set of customers, or to a potential entry of a substitute competitor. To deal with different alternative futures, the manager may feel compelled to identify and investigate alternative actions in the event of a sales downturn in the product line.

For strategic issues, formulating the nature of the felt or, vaguely perceived, need becomes a critical aspect of the alternative generation process. In the chapter-opening example, when AT&T cut its costs, it could have framed the problem as a production problem, in which alternatives would be generated to minimize costs in production; as a human resource problem, with the obvious alternatives of freezing new hires and encouraging early retirement; as a real estate problem, where the alternatives addressed would reduce the amount and cost of plant facilities.

As these examples illustrate, managers often must develop a frame that clarifies what the problem or issue is and what might be causing it. Developing an understanding of an issue often involves the scanning and monitoring that were detailed in Chapter 7. For example, a manager who anticipates a sales slowdown might scan various publications to pick up indicators of sales difficulties among competitors or of customers' purchasing substitute products.

Whatever data sources or indicators are tapped, managers must piece together a sense of exactly what issue is calling for alternatives to be developed. This "problem frame" clarifies the nature of the issue.

Problem frames are important because they influence managers' judgments regarding how critical the situation is and whether alternatives need to be generated. If a sales decline is deemed to be temporary, a manager may see no need to change and may conclude that, if the firm continues operating as usual, the pressures for change will eventually disappear. IBM's support of its mainframe business in the face of gloomy market forecasts is a good example. Its initial set of developed alternatives might have contained only one option: Maintain the status quo. Firms committed to "business as usual" will tend to make positive statements about their current strategy and hopeful assertions about the future.

In summary, an unavoidable role of management is to assign meaning or a problem frame to the pressures that are creating a felt need. As illustrated in the AT&T and sales downturn examples, the way that the problem frame is defined will limit the set of alternatives that are considered relevant.

Generating a List of Alternatives

In most organizations, strong pressures exist to quickly define and solve problems or resolve issues: managers see themselves as problem solvers, and they want to be seen as ready to take action. Prolonged consideration of alternatives is viewed as "paralysis by analysis." Under such behavioral pressures and mores, managers who commit time and resources to producing superior alternatives may be seen as going against the tide. In practice, by unquestioningly accepting just one problem context for study, managers often foreclose any possibility of generating alternatives that would lead to original courses of action. Managers therefore need to encourage the generation of creative and unthinkable as well as obvious alternatives (extensions of the current strategy). The length and variety of the list will depend on the issue and its complexity. The specificity of the alternatives will depend on the amount of information available and the predictability of an alternative.

The process of generating an initial list of alternatives often gives rise to new information that sheds further light on the strategic issue at hand or causes the problem frame to be altered. Indeed, new information may lead to the generation of new alternatives. For example, one firm that was seeking alternative ways of entering a foreign market discovered that some of its competitors might be interested in selling their businesses "if the price was right." This information led to the generation of a new alternative: the acquisition of one or more competitors that already had a presence in the relevant foreign markets. The problem frame was switched from one of "going it alone" to procuring a business that was already in the market. The intensity of the search for new information depends on the importance of the issue to the future of the firm.

As suggested above and as indicated in Figure 10–1, as the initial list of alternatives evolves, it is quite likely that the problem frame itself will be reevaluated. Indeed, managers must ensure that this takes place. They must continually ask:

- Has the issue or problem been formulated in more than one way?
- What alternatives are generated from each problem frame?
- What insights can be gained by redefining the issue?

Limiting the Number of Alternatives

The initial list of alternatives helps managers to see the many options that are potentially available; it is obviously not possible or desirable to fully explore each one. Thus, managers always face the dilemma of limiting the number of alternatives that are seriously developed, without being sure of which ones most merit investigation.

Implicitly or explicitly, managers use many criteria for deciding which alternatives they will examine and which ones they will bypass. For example, when it sought to reduce costs through divesting real estate, AT&T first identified only alternatives that were viable and satisfactory in the existing environment: selling properties, closing some offices, renting out office space, and reducing the amount of space that it needed for its employees. The number of alternatives on any list will depend on the goals and the resources available for generating and assessing them. List makers need to address the political realities involved in implementing alternatives. Merely announcing that an alternative is being considered can affect the likelihood that it will become a viable option. Announcing prematurely that a corporation is considering eliminating the offices of its salespeople would ignite a personnel relations firestorm in almost any business.

ANALYTICAL APPROACHES TO ALTERNATIVE GENERATION

Analytical approaches to alternative generation can be categorized in multiple ways. Each approach helps to frame the types of alternatives being considered. To simplify the analytical challenges inherent in alternative generation, we group the approaches according to the organization's strategy context: current strategy, business-unit strategy, or corporate-level strategy.

One approach that is applicable to all organizations is to build on the existing strategy and the need to create change by developing both obvious and creative alternatives. Another approach is to presume that the organization needs to invent a new strategy. The analytical merit of this presumption is that it often forces unthinkable alternatives: the organization has to invent alternatives that simply would not be considered in the identification of extensions to the present strategy. Many organizations attempt to use both approaches.

Before we detail the various analytical approaches, a few critical considerations need to be emphasized:

1. As discussed above, the alternatives that emerge are shaped by the operative problem frame. Thus, they can only be as good as the problem frame.
2. Organizational context and goals influence the process. If managers are trying to dramatically increase financial performance, they are very likely to search for and approve development of alternatives that satisfy the enhancement of financial returns.
3. It is well to remember that current and future strategy choices involve complex issues: changes in technology, competitive environments, global competition, and host governments.

Thus, the technical aspects of alternative detection and development can be quite challenging. In other words, beware the rush to adopt simple alternatives for complex issues.

Extensions of Current Strategy

The current strategy provides a logical basis for generating alternatives such as those identified in Table 10–3. These alternatives are aimed at extending the firm's market share within both end-customer and distribution channel segments by extending its current product lines and/or penetrating existing and new customer segments. These alternatives are obvious in the sense that they represent the types of alternatives that most firms should (and usually do) consider on an ongoing basis.

Obvious alternatives can be transformed into creative ones. For example, an organization can develop innovative ways of reaching its customers with its existing or new products. Often, such alternatives represent a major departure from the normal modes of operating or the conventional wisdom within an industry.

General Motors (GM) provides a case in point. In the face of deteriorating marketplace performance over a number of years, GM sought to regain market share and compete more effectively. The auto giant had little choice but to generate a set of alternatives that would win back many of its old customers and attract new ones. Thus, it attempted to identify alternatives that would (1) add to and extend its product lines within each major product sector, (2) improve product quality and functionality, (3) enhance its image and reputation in the eyes of existing and potential customers, and (4) offer superior value for price. The overall intent was to find ways to improve market share and increase profits, using its existing strategy as a point of departure.

Alternative generation almost always requires consideration of the implications for the organization's core operating processes.[6] One consequence of the alternatives chosen by GM was that some of its core operating processes had to be changed. For example, in the development of GM components, its internal suppliers had to compete directly with outside vendors. GM decided to choose among its internal and external suppliers in order to increase the quality and decrease the price of its parts.[7]

TABLE 10–3 Alternatives stemming from current strategy.

1. Extend the variety of models, styles, or types of each product within each of the firm's product lines.
2. Add new products to one or more of the existing product lines.
3. Reach customers in new geographic areas with the firm's current products.
4. Reach customers in new geographic areas with additions to the current product lines or new products.
5. Penetrate new distribution channels with the existing products.
6. Reach new customers within existing geographic markets.

Generic Business-Unit Strategy

Every business can consider alternatives that address revenue enhancement, cost minimization, or differentiation creation. These alternatives are not mutually exclusive: alternatives that enhance revenues often lead directly to unit-cost reduction.[8]

Revenue enhancement alternatives, a constant goal of managers, aim to increase revenues within the current business. The alternatives noted in Table 10–3 can be viewed as means of revenue enhancement.

Adapting to change in a declining industry provides a challenging opportunity for the generation of alternatives aimed at revenue enhancement. Yet, unless a firm commits itself to seeking strategic alternatives that enhance revenues, it will almost certainly incur declining sales. Harris Corporation, faced with a declining defense market, saw as an alternative the acquisition of other firms' defense units. Harris purchased General Electric's semiconductor business for $206 million in 1989. Many Wall Street analysts thought the most viable alternative for Harris was to exit from the semiconductor industry. Instead, Harris installed new management and shifted the product strategy from low-margin items such as logic and memory chips to higher-margin specialty chips.[9] Strategy shifted from a low-cost emphasis to a focus on differentiation. Another alternative that Harris identified and implemented was a shift of its customer base from defense contractors to civilian, government and commercial businesses. These alternatives were successful at increasing Harris's revenue base.

Cost minimization builds on a philosophy of being a low-cost producer and generating alternatives that keep the cost structure low. More intense rivalry in many industries, coupled with the general slowdown in economic conditions, has compelled many organizations to seriously search for cost reduction alternatives. Some questions that typify the search for cost minimization are noted in Table 10–4.

Many industries could be cited as examples in which cost minimization strategies have emerged as critical to the survival of individual firms. For example, many U.S. airlines have had to consider reducing capacity, decreasing the number of personnel, and canceling orders on new aircraft. Several airlines began to keep costs to a minimum by reducing the number of hubs that they supported.[10]

Differentiation creation defines alternatives that enhance the organization's competitive posture, that is, how the firm distinguishes itself from its competitors in the eyes of customers.[11] The emphasis is on identifying potential ways in which the firm can differentiate itself in each of its product-customer segments. The sources of differentiation may vary considerably, from unique skills and capabilities to market position (market share and reputation), but the intent in identifying differentiation alternatives is to develop specific means to get and keep customers.

TABLE 10–4 Identifying cost minimization alternatives.

1. How can the organization reduce manufacturing or operations costs? Is it possible to extend capacity utilization? Is it possible to reduce or eliminate waste?

2. How might the organization reduce or control raw materials and input costs?

3. What might be some lower cost sources of components, raw materials, and other supplies?

4. What possibilities might exist now or at some point in the future to use substitute components, raw materials, or supplies?

5. What might the firm outsource as a means of reducing costs?

6. What purchasing policies might be changed?

7. What distribution efficiencies might the firm be able to effect?

8. Where might further economies of scale exist?

9. How might the firm partner or align with others (such as vendors and distributors) as a means of lowering costs?

Generating differentiation alternatives requires the organization to ask the types of questions listed in Table 10–5. These questions are likely to spawn alternatives that combine the dimensions shown in Table 10–5.[12] Such alternatives may range from customization (adapting the firm's offering for each customer) to mass marketing the firm's product line at the lowest possible price or to mass customization (mass-producing customized goods or services).

Generic Corporate Strategy[13]

The identification of strategic alternatives is just as important for multi-business corporations as it is for business units. As discussed in Chapter 2, many corporations are now dramatically shifting their strategies. Thus, at some earlier stage, corporate managers must have identified and assessed their options and chosen a change of course. We will consider here only some of the major alternatives.

Diversification provides an analytical framework for corporate expansion in both related and unrelated business areas. Some firms find their major business area maturing and unable to provide the sustained level of performance that management wants. Consideration of diversification inevitably follows. Conglomerate or unrelated diversification offers a wide spectrum of alternatives. Firms can identify and explore almost every imaginable option pertaining to entry into businesses that are new to the corporation. For example, one large U.S. conglomerate has claimed that, at one time or another, it has investigated the possibility of diversifying into almost every industry that exists.[14]

The importance of continually generating and considering corporate strategic alternatives is well-illustrated in the fact that many firms that adopted conglomerate diversification in the 1960s and 1970s found themselves desperately trying in the 1980s to identify the alternative that would best refocus them

TABLE 10–5 Generating differentiation alternatives: Sample questions.

1. What are our current customers' needs and wants?
   How do they appear to be changing?
   What might they be in two, three, or five years?

2. What are the needs and wants of our competitors' customers?
   How are they changing?
   How different are they from those of our current customers?

3. What are the needs and wants of our substitute competitors' customers?
   How different are they from our customers'?

4. To what extent are customers falling into clearly identifiable segments based on buying behaviors, volume of purchases, demographic considerations, or other criteria?

5. What are some of the key trends in customers' buying behaviors?

6. What opportunities might be suggested by these needs and wants?

7. Given answers (however tentative) to the above questions, how might the firm differentiate itself in terms of:
   • Product line width?
   • Product features?
   • Functionality?
   • Service?
   • Availability?
   • Image and reputation?
   • Selling and relationships?
   • Price?

on their core businesses. On the other hand, firms such as Dow Chemical have been successful at conglomerate diversification. Dow needed to identify alternatives that would overcome the cyclicality of its commodity chemical business. It did so with the acquisition of drug and specialty chemical operations.

Acquisition or merger is a generic corporate strategy that opens the door to many alternatives.[15] It is obviously an alternative that has found favor in many corporations: during the 1980s, $1.3 trillion was spent in the United States on acquisitions, mergers, and takeovers.

The strikingly high failure rate in acquisitions and mergers suggests the importance of analysis in *identifying* potential acquisition and merger candidates. It has frequently been noted that many of these failures occurred because the acquisition or merger decisions relied too heavily on the input of financial analysts for both generating and evaluating the alternatives.[16] The better deals were based on strategic analysis and addressed alternatives that fit alongside the current corporate strategy. Examples of successful acquirers (and their acquisitions) include General Electric (RCA), May Department Stores (Associated Dry Goods), and Quaker Oats (Stokely-Van Camp). Before making an acquisition, a firm usually does a detailed analysis of potential targets. AT&T, for example, studied Digital Equipment Corporation (DEC), Hewlett-Packard, and Apple Computer Inc. as potential alternatives before launching a hostile takeover bid for NCR Corporation.

Divestment is often initially an unthinkable alternative because it is hard for management to even contemplate divesting a business after perhaps spending many years cultivating it. The reality, as evidenced in the large number of corporations shedding one or more substantial business units, is that divestment is a very viable and highly appropriate corporate-level decision.

Frequently, divestment is identified as an option when it has not been fully studied. This seems to be especially true when the business unit is profitable or in a growing market. When the divestment alternative is thoroughly scrutinized, management may realize that a particular business unit does not fit with the corporate intent or vision.[17] Funds from sale of the business unit may be urgently needed to promote other, more viable business areas.

Global Strategies

As discussed in Chapter 4, organizations must develop, increasingly, alternatives that address the global business arena. Typically, consideration of global strategy involves the generation of myriad alternatives: selection of different countries and regions; the products suitable for the selected areas; how best to enter these areas; what strategies to pursue in penetrating these markets.

Sara Lee provides an example of a firm that has greatly globalized its strategy in its apparel, personal-care items, and baked goods markets in the past decade. What alternatives might it have considered? That is, what alternatives might have been responsible for its quick penetration of major national markets overseas? Acquisition was one alternative that it identified and fully developed: recent acquisitions have added to its businesses in seven countries.

Another alternative might have been the extension of its products across national borders. This potential alternative flies in the face of considerable conventional wisdom. The food industry traditionally has been dominated by adherence to unique national tastes, customs, and eating habits. Thus, products had to be designed specifically for individual markets. Sara Lee and other food companies, however, are beginning to find that certain products can be offered successfully "as is" in many national markets.

Unthinkable Alternatives

Unthinkable alternatives, as noted earlier, require decision makers to break out of their mental models, assumption sets, and ways of thinking about businesses. Unless they do so, there is little chance they can reinvent their business—that is, create ways of doing business that are new to the marketplace. As argued in Chapter 1, strategic renovation and, in particular, strategic reinvention require the development of strategic alternatives that are premised on an understanding of possible futures and not on how and why the organization's strategies were successful in the past.

Managers must systematically generate unthinkable alternatives, for at least two reasons:

1. If they don't do so on their own initiative, they may be forced into doing so. The actions of competitors have compelled many organizations to seriously consider what previously might have been seen as unthinkable. Some firms simply would not consider divestment or merger until their circumstances became so dire (through the loss of market share to rivals) that the only choices were one of these alternatives or going out of business.

2. Once unthinkable alternatives are identified, they may prove, upon reflection, to be quality alternatives. For example, both Apple and IBM found it very difficult to seriously consider any form of cooperation or alignment because of the intensity of the long rivalry between the organizations. Yet, once an alternative in the area of technology development was explored, it became apparent to both organizations that the alternative had strong potential to be a "win–win" relationship.

Cooperative Strategies

Cooperating with current or potential competitors is an increasingly employed alternative. Many different types of alliances, relationships, and networks are reported in the business press every day of the week. Indeed, many of these cooperative relationships represent options that firms with established franchises (like Apple and IBM) would never have considered a few years ago.

One of the challenges in generating cooperative alternatives is that so many distinct possibilities potentially exist: joint ventures, cooperative R&D, integrated marketing and distribution, cross-licensing of technology, and outsourcing of manufacturing, to name but a few. One of the dangers of this alternative is that in gaining an ally, an organization may be creating a future competitor. Thus, it is important to consider in advance the consequences of cooperating with current or potential competitors. Many American firms have discovered, much to their surprise, that cooperative agreements with their Japanese counterparts have greatly enabled the Japanese firms to learn about their business, their technology, and their customers—precisely the knowledge needed to displace the American partners from the market.

ORGANIZATIONAL PROCESSES TO AID IN ALTERNATIVE GENERATION

Alternative generation can be greatly aided and abetted by the design and development of appropriate organizational processes and procedures. Among the many processes that could be discussed, we will concentrate our attention here on five distinct processes that have proven their usefulness in aiding alternative generation: (1) scenarios, (2) conflict generation, (3) brainstorming, (4) chaos theory, and (5) group work support systems. These may be used at any of the various levels (corporate, business unit) within the firm. They are useful to any manager who wants to stretch the thinking of the individuals involved in the alternative generation process.

Scenario Generation

Scenarios are alternative depictions of the future. Some organizations refer to them as integrated stories about the future. They address what might be, what could be. They are explicitly intended to allow any group of individuals to envision the future; they provide a means for decision makers to think about the future without the constraints of the past. The power of scenarios is that they allow several alternative pictures of the future to be developed simultaneously, as described in Box 10–1. Managers can experience and prepare for different possible industry futures before they take place.

Each of the different possible futures thus may give rise to distinct strategic alternatives. For example, a firm may develop scenarios ranging from massive upheaval in its industry (such as the replacement, by substitute products, of a large percentage of current competitors' product lines) to a baseline scenario that is a continuation of the industry's key current trends. The organization then

---

Box 10–1

Different Industry Scenarios as Input to
Generating Strategic Alternatives

Scenario 1: The industry will maintain its current rate of overall growth. No new competitors will enter. No major technological shifts will occur. Existing competitors will generally maintain their current strategies.

Scenario 2: The industry will maintain its current rate of overall growth, but competitors will introduce new products and modify existing products. Customers will more clearly segment into groups seeking different types of "solutions."

Scenario 3: Industry growth will slow down as a result of penetration of existing customer segments. Rivalry among competitors will intensify. Competitors will thus be forced to seek ways to differentiate their offering.

Scenario 4: The industry, as currently configured, will slowly but surely succumb to the onslaught of substitute products. Technology will continue to drive and refine the substitute products.

has to develop specific alternatives that would allow it to operate and prosper in the competitive environment spelled out in each scenario. Not surprisingly, many of the alternatives are likely to be not only creative but unthinkable.

Scenarios also stimulate managers' thinking by letting them experience time running backward. That is, scenarios first develop pictures of some future and then let managers trace back how that future happened and plan what they must do to operate in that new environment.

Conflict Generation: The Use of Assumption Analysis

The problem frames discussed earlier are really distinct sets of assumptions for looking at the world in terms of, for example, future growth of specific product-markets, competitors' strategies, the evolution of technology, governmental policies, and the organization's own cash flows. Unfortunately, if these different assumptions are not identified, explicated, and critiqued, they unwittingly influence the generation of alternatives.

There are two philosophies regarding the management of assumption conflicts:

1. They need to be acknowledged, channeled, and managed.
2. They need to be generated in order to enhance the probability that quality alternatives will be generated.

Indeed, one role of scenarios is to sensitize managers to the role and importance of assumptions.

It is widely accepted that conflict generation can enhance the alternative generation process. Mason and Mitroff[18] suggested that managers are frequently unaware of the assumptions they hold and that examining them through a process of debate or conflict generation can lead to a rich understanding of the prevailing problem frames within an organization. Research suggests that structured conflict helps to confront basic assumptions and to improve the decision-making process in generating and evaluating alternatives.

Two specific processes are useful:

1. "Devil's advocacy," a process in which an alternative is examined with the perspectives of heaven and hell reversed. In addition to searching the proposal for inconsistencies, inaccuracies, irrelevancies, the advocate must critique the proposal from a contrarian perspective, at least in part.[19]
2. "Dialectic inquiry," a utilization of groups to present the most divergent alternative views of the issue. Individuals are often grouped in order to build heterogeneous viewpoints across groups. The groups develop alternatives and then debate them. An important aspect of this process is the identification of underlying assumptions.

Conflict generation must be managed because it may have undesired consequences. Intense debate may be detrimental to the quality of the alternatives developed and how they are later presented and evaluated. Debate is an uncomfortable activity for many individuals, and it may leave unresolved feelings of conflict because individuals get too tied to their positions in the debate and analysis.

Brainstorming

Sometimes, managers need organizational processes that are less formal than scenario development and conflict generation and are designed specifically to help generate creative and perhaps unthinkable alternatives. An environment conducive to such creative processes is one characterized by openness, trust, freedom from criticism for failure or nonconformity, and playfulness.

Brainstorming is one such creative process. According to its rules, participants can come up with any alternative, no matter how obtuse, without fear of criticism. Four rules are usually suggested: (1) no criticism, (2) no bounds on the nature of the ideas, (3) no limit on the number of ideas that can be generated, and (4) no restraints on using ideas to create new ideas.

Brainstorming is especially useful when individuals have found it difficult, over some period of time, to get beyond obvious alternatives. For example, a group of managers should try to brainstorm if the alternatives generated appear to be merely extensions of the present strategy.

Chaos Theory

A number of authors have advocated a theory of managing organizations under conditions of chaos.[20] A principal underpinning of this approach is that it is impossible to predict a planned or envisioned future because the linkages between cause and effect disappear and are impossible to trace. Successful organizations seek bounded instability and move away from the norms of equilibrium. They encourage multiple cultures, conflict around issues, lack of cohesion, and lack of consensus.

Alternatives are created in a spontaneous manner. They address the unwritten issues, aspirations, and challenges to which key groups of managers are attending. By addressing these strategic issues, managers create instability in the existing system. Through an informal process of discussion and debate, they choose an alternative that shatters the existing order. Thus, alternative generation becomes a spontaneous process for challenging and changing relationships in the firm, and success depends on destabilizing the current organization.

Group Work Support Systems

Several different types of organizations are utilizing computer tools to facilitate interaction among groups of individuals in alternative generation. Indicative of this thrust is work developed by The University of Arizona, which uses a room that has 24 workstations and a variety of media equipment. It allows a group of managers to generate ideas and surface assumptions utilizing computers and other media. A facilitator, providing expertise in decision making and group dynamics, helps to lead the group through the stages of alternative generation.

Electronic brainstorming (EBS) is a technique in which ideas are generated anonymously and entered into a computer. By having the ideas submitted anonymously, any reliance on the perception of the individual submitting the idea is eliminated. Power and status of individuals become less important, because no one knows who created which idea. The files are shared from workstation to workstation to allow others to build on the ideas. Ideas are simultaneously submitted. Ideas can change, grow, or inspire other ideas. The resulting ideas are then categorized and grouped according to issues. Out of this mode of interaction come potential alternatives that probably would not be crafted by any individual working alone.

FACTORS INFLUENCING THE GENERATION OF ALTERNATIVES

The identification, development, and evaluation of strategy alternatives are conducted by humans in an organizational context and setting and are influenced by both human and organizational factors. An understanding of how these factors affect alternative generation can aid decision makers in shaping quality alternatives.

Human Factors

Among the human constraints that influence the generation of alternatives are: short-term memories, difficulties in considering a large number of alternatives, limited ability to process a large amount of information, individual framing based on past experiences and values, and cognitive biases (such as varying propensities to use quantitative data).

These constraints influence alternative development and evaluation in many ways. For example, individual managers may interpret the same alternative or set of alternatives differently. Bounded rationality (the inability of managers to consider many alternatives simultaneously) suggests that in generating (and evaluating) alternatives managers cannot deal with all the possible alternatives. Their cognitive abilities are bounded by their values, skills, and abilities. Managers are also limited by the amount of information that they can process. In the AT&T example used at the beginning of the chapter, it was probably not the human resource manager who suggested that the cost-cutting objective could be defined as a real estate problem. The source of the idea was more likely a manager who had been dealing with real estate costs. As a rule of thumb, managers will generate and develop alternatives only to the point of finding the one alternative that satisfies their minimum criteria. Thus, managers will not look for alternatives that extend and stretch the organization's objectives but will stop searching when they find an acceptable alternative. This saves time in the alternative generation process, but it limits the number of alternatives considered.

Escalation of commitment (individuals become more committed to an alternative over time) also biases how managers develop alternatives. For example, managers sometimes identify an alternative that they think is appropriate and stick with that alternative even when new evidence emerges that suggests they should seriously consider alternative courses of action.

Organizational Factors

A number of organizational factors influence alternative generation: pressures for conformity, group think, shared problem frames, political alliances, and the extent of organizational learning.[21]

Pressure for conformity (such as the desire to be seen as a member of the team) gives rise to tendencies to avoid developing alternatives that significantly change the firm's strategy or a group's position pertaining to specific alternatives. Group think and shared problem frames (individuals manifesting shared frames of reference and recall of past events, the creation of stories and myths that reinforce assumptions and beliefs, vicarious learning, and shared and tested memories) can quickly lead to downplaying or even rejecting development of specific alternatives.

Individuals may also form temporary political alliances to support or oppose alternatives, depending on self-interest. To influence strategy, each coalition may advocate its own position through such mechanisms as task forces, special reports, advocacy of preferred goals, reframing of data, and redefinition of issues.[22] These different coalitions may attempt to influence others and to gain the agreement of others about their interpretation of the issues and of viable alternatives. For example, in one firm, a group of individuals lobbied key senior managers to reject development of an alternative to divest its original product line because it would signal to others within the organization that the firm was not committed to this product sector. Their unstated concern was that divestment would affect overhead allocations (and potentially cause a decline in profitability of their product lines) and could lead to organizational restructuring (thus potentially threatening job security).

The presence or absence of organizational learning may also influence the generation of alternatives. "Smart" organizations have the potential to learn, unlearn, or relearn to adjust to a changing environment. They have the capacity to develop insights and knowledge and to transmit them throughout the organization. In short, organizations that cease to challenge the merits of their current strategies, the veracity of their underlying assumptions and beliefs, and the efficacy of their operating processes have stopped learning. Such organizations are hardly likely to identify and develop creative or unthinkable alternatives.

ROLE OF TOP MANAGEMENT IN ALTERNATIVE GENERATION

How and when is top management involved in the alternative generation process? With particular reference to alternative generation, the top management team often exerts considerable influence over the problem frame, as well as the organizational culture[23] within which ideas are created, nurtured, and challenged. Input from top management is especially crucial in certain sectors of the model of alternative generation depicted in Figure 10–1. Top managers are particularly important at the beginning and the end of the process. They can frame the issue at hand as a problem, an opportunity, or a crisis and thereby influence the alternatives generated. The attitudes and subjective criteria of top managers become an important indication of their predispositions toward the process of alternative generation and of their willingness to accept the alternatives. They communicate their view through speeches, statements, and actions, and these will influence how others in the firm interpret the importance of events in the environment.

Unfortunately, alternative generation is frequently poorly executed because it is not considered important by top management, for several reasons:

- It is not seen, within the organization, as the job of top management; instead, it is viewed as falling within the domain of middle management. Top management's role is seen as choosing among alternatives, not developing them.
- It is too time-consuming. Top management simply does not have the time to become involved with alternative development.
- Top management does not have the knowledge to develop alternatives in sufficient detail.

At a minimum, top management's role in alternative generation must be to remove obstacles to effective creativity, to provide resources for the generation process, and to encourage multiple alternative assessments. By words and deeds, top management should emphasize the need for alternatives that stretch and create learning rather than those that extrapolate the present into the future. The role of vision is of critical importance because it provides a guide for building on the present but still allowing the development of creative alternatives. A vision should provide a challenge for the future that opens to members of the firm an opportunity to generate new possibilities that stretch the current organizational analytics and mindset.

CONCLUSION

Effective strategic management is much more than just recognizing that there is a decision to be made. The successful manager relies on an alternative generation process that addresses obvious, creative, and unthinkable alternatives. Sensitivity to the various assumptions and factors that influence the alternative generation process is required. Intuition plays an important part by signaling when something additional needs to be done, like brainstorming, or when the process needs to reach a conclusion and it is time to make a decision. The top management team has an important role in the generation of strategic alternatives. It sets the tone, champions specific alternatives, and is responsible for making the choice among the alternatives.

NOTES

1.   M. Pacelle, "Vanishing Offices: To Trim Their Costs, Some Companies Cut Space for Their Employees," *The Wall Street Journal* (June 4, 1993), A1, A6.

2.   These are the principal foci of Chapter 1.

3.   The analytical and organizational processes discussed in Chapter 16 in the context of reinventing a firm's strategy often result in the generation of unthinkable alternatives.

4.   The evaluation of alternatives is the focus of the next chapter; therefore, this chapter addresses only the identification and development of alternatives.

5.   This is a good example of the role and importance of mindset, discussed in Chapter 1. If an organization's values are such that identifying opportunities is accorded importance and prominence within the organization, then individuals will seek ways to identify and leverage change without continuous admonitions from senior executives to do so.

6.   The importance of core operating processes was discussed in Chapter 1. It is also the focus of Chapter 12.

7.   See, for example, *Business Week* (June 22, 1992), 30–31.

8.   For a detailed discussion of business-unit strategies, readers are referred to Chapter 3.

9.   M. Brannigan, "Harris Finally Digests Big Semiconductor Acquisition," *The Wall Street Journal* (October 13, 1992), B4.

10.   See "Ready to Soar Again? The Big Flyboys May Be Bouncing Back at Last," *Business Week* (April 26, 1993), 26–28.

11.   For a detailed discussion of competitive posture or differentiation, see Chapters 1 and 3.

12.   This is in keeping with the observation in Chapter 1 that a posture that results in some degree of sustainable differentiation almost certainly results from the integration of the dimensions shown in Table 10–5.

13.   See Chapter 2 for a detailed discussion of corporate strategy.

14.   This is largely a true statement if one accepts that the provision of suppliers or raw materials constitutes involvement or participation in an industry.

15. Acquisition or merger is the means by which firms often execute a diversification strategy.

16. The difficulties in integrating financial and other considerations into evaluation of strategic alternatives are explicitly considered in the next chapter.

17. The notions of corporate intent and vision are discussed in Chapters 1 and 9.

18. R. O. Mason and Ian I. Mitroff, *Challenging Strategic Planning Assumptions* (New York: John Wiley & Sons, Inc., 1981).

19. See C. Schwenk, *Essence of Strategic Decision Making* (Lexington, MA: Lexington Books, 1988).

20. See, for example, R. D. Stacey, *Managing the Unknowable: Strategic Boundaries between Order and Chaos in Organizations* (San Francisco: Jossey-Bass Publishers, 1992).

21. Again, one of the purposes in discussing these organizational factors is the pervasiveness of their influence on many facets of strategic management beyond alternative generation.

22. Many of these mechanisms are akin to the political strategies discussed in Chapter 5 in the context of organizations' effort to influence their external stakeholders. For example, issue redefinition received particular attention in Chapter 5.

23. The role and importance of organizational culture in shaping and executing strategies are fully developed in Chapter 15.

11 EVALUATING STRATEGIC ALTERNATIVES

George S. Day

The Wharton School, University of Pennsylvania

Unless we change our direction, we are likely to wind up where we are headed.
—Ancient Chinese proverb

Poor choices of strategic direction are costly. Beyond the obvious out-of-pocket drains are the hidden costs of foreclosed opportunities and the neglect of the rest of the business while the management team struggles to contain the damage.

How can the likelihood of bad decisions be reduced, and good decisions be encouraged? The strategy development process, the continuing theme of this book, suggests three answers:

1. Understand the situation fully.
2. Surface a rich set of alternatives.
3. Subject these alternatives to a rigorous strategy review.

This chapter proposes a series of challenging test questions that are critical to any strategy review.

Had the management of Convergent Technologies squarely confronted these test questions before rushing the Workslate notebook computer to the market, a costly debacle that forced the firm's withdrawal from the burgeoning personal computer market might have been avoided. The events leading to the withdrawal are described in Box 11–1. We will refer to the Workslate experience as we develop the logic of a strategy evaluation framework.

Despite the excellence of the Workslate product, prospects for successful implementation of the entry strategy were never good. What questions should

Box 11–1

Convergent Technologies Learns an Expensive Lesson

In 1983, Convergent Technologies was a well-regarded designer and manufacturer of powerful workstations, which were sold through other brand names. Management was anxious to diversify into other computer markets to reduce the firm's exposure to a single volatile market, to establish its own brand name, and to capitalize on the promise of rapid growth and high volumes in the emerging personal computer market. The Workslate computer was the firm's first foray into a mass market under its own name.

The initial reception left no doubt that the Workslate was an outstanding product that had a substantial lead over the Japanese competition. The designers had managed to package a powerful small computer into the shape and size of letter paper, with a thickness of one inch. They accomplished this feat in less than a year by skipping field testing and going straight from design to manufacturing.

Soon after its introduction, the Workslate appeared on the covers of three major computer magazines, was featured in the American Express Christmas catalog, and was touted in various mailings. One computer retailing chain forecast that it could sell every Workslate that could be made. When the company saw this reception, it made ambitious plans to sell 100,000 units in the first year, at a retail value of $90 million. So confident was management because of these signals of acceptance that it was decided that research into the market was not necessary and would only delay proceedings. For the same reason, the president rejected the marketing manager's request for a $7 million launch budget, and only reluctantly agreed to spend $700,000.

The first cracks in the plan emerged when the project ran into production difficulties. The company was a manufacturer of workstations for large computer suppliers, and was unused to large-volume production of standard units. The factory soon fell a month behind schedule and missed most of the Christmas season. Lack of production wasn't the real problem, however; customers weren't buying the Workslates that were available. In fact, it wasn't clear that this was a consumer product that could be sold as an ordinary personal computer. Unfortunately, the company used a totally new sales force to reach mass market consumers, and ignored the existing sales network of business sales teams and distribution that might have delivered steady sales. Confusion was also created in the market by frequent price changes; after starting at $900, the retail price soared to $1,300, but soon dropped to $1,100 because of buyer resistance. The accountants were apparently responsible for the price hikes after they discovered that, even at the most optimistic production levels, Workslate was not profitable at a unit price of $900. Costs were high because of very high expenses, including carrying 50 engineers in the R&D budget.

Only 1,000 units were sold in the first quarter of 1984. The losses were mounting so rapidly that the company was forced to cease production by July and take a $30 million write-off. As serious as the cash loss was to the company, this sum did not begin to reveal the true extent of the damage. Senior management and the R&D group had been so distracted by this problem that they neglected their core workstation business and lost ground in a fast-moving sector that they have never recovered. Worse, the company lost a chance to become a significant player in the booming PC market, because "once bitten (they were) twice shy" as the old saying reminds us. Although these "opportunity costs" did not appear in any financial statement, the management was appropriately held accountable for the bad judgment that was the cause.

have been asked by management to help reveal these problems? Each of the test questions formulated in this chapter is posed as a measure of the credibility of a proposed strategy; the answers determine whether senior management has confidence that the promised returns on the investment will be realized.

The test questions work best when there is a rich array of strategic alternatives from which to choose.[1] There is mounting evidence that superior strategic choices are made when the decision makers explicitly search for and debate several alternatives at a time. The variety gives managers a basis for comparison and enhances creativity by suggesting combinations of different strategies. However, the debate over which alternatives should be chosen will only be productive when the alternatives are compared in terms of the strategic fundamentals that underlie the creation of shareholder value.

This process involves much more than a comparison of the promised financial results, using common criteria such as market share gains, payback of investment, or return on investment. Most evaluations of strategy are flawed because of the misguided presumption that they are primarily financial analyses. Financial results are the outcomes of decisions; they will be valued and meaningful only if they credibly address the three fundamental issues that determine the payoff from a strategic choice:

1. The prospects for superior profitability.
2. The chances that superior profitability will be realized.
3. The acceptability of the risk–reward ratio.

The prospects for superior profitability depend on the attractiveness of the market opportunity[2] and the ability of the business to gain and sustain a competitive advantage: These two sources of profits are represented schematically in Figure 11–1, which displays the distribution of profits of all the rivals in a market at a given time. The bell curve indicates that a few are doing well, some are doing poorly, and the majority are bunched in a range of average success. Confidence that a strategy is worth supporting will go up if there is persuasive evidence that the average rate of profit of all rivals is high and/or that a competitive advantage will be gained and held.

The second fundamental issue is whether the intended strategy, which promises superior—or at least acceptable—profitability has a reasonable chance of being realized.[3] Can this strategy be implemented with the skills and

FIGURE 11–1   Distribution of profits across rivals.

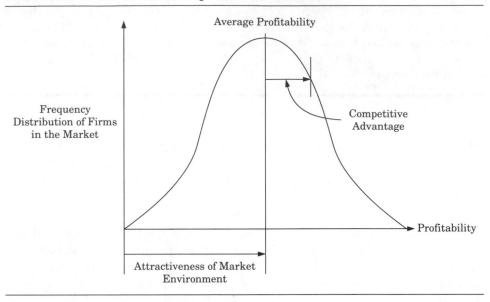

resources at hand? If not, can the deficiencies be overcome without too much extra cost or time delay?

The third issue asks whether the risk–reward ratio is acceptable. Specifically, what things might go wrong? Can the damage that might be wrought be contained? Will credible forecasts of revenues, costs, and investments yield profit returns that warrant taking these risks?

VALUE-ADDING STRATEGY REVIEWS

The Workslate entry (Box 11–1) was not subjected to a rigorous review before major financial commitments were made. The go-ahead decision was made by advocates who were simply validating their conviction they had picked a winner. The result was collective self-delusion, a condition that permitted management to ignore some awkward realities. An effective, tough-minded review by an informed and objective top management group would have led to a search for an entry strategy that better suited the capabilities and assets of the firm.

The root of the Workslate disaster was the unwarranted belief by the development team that the excellence of the product would sell itself to all comers. Such a belief is seldom warranted, no matter how good the new product, but it is especially dangerous when it obscures the need to introduce the product to the right market through the right channels. Because neither the Workslate team nor the parent management had any experience with retail chains, they did not consider the lack of a match between what their product could do and the needs of the market they were trying to reach. Had this mismatch been confronted earlier, other strategies—using available channels to reach business markets, or partnerships to gain market access—might have been seriously considered.

A strategy review should be much more than a detailed scrutiny of financial projections as the basis for a go or no-go decision. To add value to the strategy development process, the review should be designed to serve four functions:

1. Provide top management with a sound basis for resource allocation decisions and for negotiation of performance objectives. There will be modifications of the proposed strategy alternatives as insights into strengths and vulnerabilities are revealed. By the end of the review process, the relative merits and drawbacks of each alternative should be clearly evident, to allow a fully informed choice.

2. Focus the business team on the drivers of profitability and shareholder value. If, instead, the focus is on the financial forecasts, it is very hard to know whether the numbers have been arrived at by the simple expedient of working backward from the profitability requirements that have to be satisfied before funding can be approved. If the company requires a two-year payback and an 18 percent internal rate of return, the forecasts of prices, costs, growth, and share may have been subtly massaged to predict that these targets will be exceeded.

3. Create a forum for surfacing and testing critical assumptions. Choices among alternative strategies are arguably the least structured decisions that managers make. To cope with the inherent ambiguity, all participants in the decision make assumptions about how customers, competitors, channels, and costs will respond, and about how well the organization will implement the programs. Good decisions are based on valid assumptions grounded in defensible evidence, not on faulty, uninformed guesses. Only through relentless questioning can the valid assumptions be distinguished from those that are unexamined, possibly wrong, and potentially misleading.

4. Help to isolate risks, contingencies, and control factors. The actual results from a chosen strategy will almost always differ from the forecasts. To minimize the damage from these "surprises," the management team needs to think through all the things that could go wrong, prepare contingency plans that acknowledge the likelihood of these surprises, and supply remedies in advance of their occurrence. This line of thinking will help to identify control factors that can be monitored as early indicators of trouble and can trigger remedial action. Flexibility and responsiveness can be built into the organization and the strategy when these protective measures are present.

A key presumption of a value-adding strategy review is that the top management reviewers and decision makers, as well as the business team developing and proposing the strategic alternatives, fully understand these four fundamental functions. When the underlying criteria are communicated in advance, there is no uncertainty about what is expected, and the management team can do its strategic thinking in anticipation of the questions they know they will have to answer. The quality of the strategies being proposed is then much improved, and the resulting choices are more resistant to political pressure and short-run expediency.

Strategic fundamentals can then be addressed with the following test questions, which can be applied to business strategies in any competitive market:

Test One: How attractive is the market opportunity?

Test Two: How sustainable is the competitive advantage?

Test Three: What are the prospects for successful implementation?

Test Four: Are the risks acceptable?

Test Five: Will the forecast financial results be achieved and increase shareholder value?

TEST ONE: HOW ATTRACTIVE IS THE MARKET OPPORTUNITY?

Market attractiveness analysis should present a balanced view—the threats versus the opportunities uncovered during the situation assessment. Included here is the anticipated impact of events and trends in the aptly named PEST environment (the political, economic, social, and technological forces covered in Chapter 7). Supplementing these factors are the specific attributes of the competitive market to be served:

- Market size and growth.
- Cyclicality of market demand: Will forecast demand be steady with small fluctuations or be vulnerable to economic swings or the fortunes of related industries?
- Present and prospective intensity of competition, as revealed in the industry analysis. Here we employ the methods of Chapter 6 to assess the forces of competition: direct rivalry, bargaining power of suppliers and customer, substitutes, and threats of entry.
- Degree of market fragmentation, which determines the presence of protected market segments.
- Ease of channel access: Is this going to be a high- or low-cost market to serve?
- Break-even share: Is this a high or low fixed-cost business? This is a useful measure of the vulnerability of profits to volatility in market demand.

The better the market opportunity measures up on these criteria, the higher the long-run average profitability of all the players in the market. The potential of high average profit provides a degree of encouragement for the new entrant. The reasoning is, in the event the strategy falls short of its market penetration objectives, there might still be some profit possibilities. However, each competitor will have a different perspective on the optimum levels of each attribute. Small companies will value smaller markets (which have numerous protected niches they can safely occupy) quite differently than will large companies. Incumbents will celebrate high barriers to entry, which are very costly for new entrants to surmount. These same barriers may make entry completely unattractive to outsiders. Even a high forecast growth rate is not always a good thing, if it draws in an overabundance of competitors and erodes overall profitability.

The management of Convergent Technologies spent relatively little time on this test; after all, industry pundits were unanimous that prospects were favorable. The current high rate of growth seemed to support the belief that there would be plenty of room for new entrants. Management might have reflected instead on the relentless pace of technological change and the implications of unforeseen entrants and continuous downward pressure on prices. Further inquiry into the volatile nature of customer behavior might have sent up a warning flag. Taking this volatility into account, management would have recognized the pivotal importance of access to distribution channels if the company was going to be able to reach and assure prospective customers about product performance, reliability, and service support.

Full-fledged assessments of market attractiveness must consider events and trends in the macroeconomic and industry environment as well as conditions within the segments of the market the strategy proposes to target. After all, the competitive war will be waged within the market segments. Table 11–1 shows how one manufacturer viewed prospects in two segments and then justified a growing emphasis on segment B—large, global customers. This decision was a major departure from the previous strategy of emphasis on midsize, nationally focused customers.

TABLE 11–1   Comparison of customer segments by a manufacturing firm.

Criteria	Segment B (Large, Global Customers)	Segment D (Midsize Nationally Focused Customers)
Size ($, units)	Large	Medium
Growth (average for next three years)	+ 5%	± 1%
Cyclicality	Moderate	Moderate
Intensity of competition	Moderate	High
Access of channels	Easy	Easy
Break-even share	Moderate	High
Costs to serve	Low	High
Overall attractiveness	+ + +	−

TEST TWO: HOW SUSTAINABLE IS THE COMPETITIVE ADVANTAGE?

Economists, who take a long-term view of markets, have a bleak answer to all questions about sustainability of competitive advantage. Called the Law of Nemesis, this tenet holds that nothing good lasts indefinitely; that is, other competitors will invariably find ways to share the wealth of the market leader. Attractive opportunities always motivate competitors to try to match, leap-frog, or offset the advantage the leader has achieved. Thus, the anticipated extra profitability that a competitive advantage promises may not materialize or may quickly dry up.

This law is vividly illustrated by the Japanese consumer electronics market, where new products—usually variants in a theme—are matched in months or less. Sony has had to introduce 160 models of the Walkman to withstand the onslaught of clones. Innovations are copied within six to 12 months. The frenetic pace of "innovative imitation" ensures that closely matched competitors who understand each other well, and closely watch each other's moves, can anticipate and respond rapidly. The only basis of sustainable advantage appears to be an ability to continuously innovate. This raises daunting questions when customers, no longer valuing the blizzard of features and minor variations, start to buy for other reasons.

At the other extreme are those firms with highly durable advantages based on gaining a resource or capability that is unique and tightly secured within the organization. A classic example is the patent-protected pharmaceutical industry, which, in the five-year period that ended in 1990, yielded the best return on capital (20 percent) of all U.S. industry groups. Other revealing examples are the Microsoft MS-DOS operating system and the Lotus 1-2-3 spreadsheet; each still holds 60 percent of its market in the face of aggressive price cutting. These firms' unassailable positions are based on (1) the "first-mover" advantages of being able to set standards and create high customer switching costs and (2) high visibility as leaders in the market. Some of the most durable competitive advantages are derived from close personal relationships, such as those investment bankers often achieve with their clients. The actual investment products—investment advice, merger screening, balance sheet management—are sophisticated but readily available elsewhere. However, in a pressured, high-stakes deal environment, the clients are willing to work only with advisers whom they know and trust. Such confidence is earned over a very long period of time.

Because competitive advantages are becoming increasingly difficult to sustain, emphasis is shifting from seeking an unassailable static advantage to building organizations that continually seek new sources of advantage. This is how DELL Computer became a *Fortune* 500 company only eight years after its founding. The genesis of the firm was the recognition that sophisticated personal computer buyers were getting little from traditional store-front retailers. Initially, DELL reached this high-end market segment directly through ads in trade magazines; low prices were the offered incentive. It soon became apparent that this strategy was readily imitable: price was not a sustainable edge. The next stage was to augment the core product with guarantees, unlimited toll-free technical support, and one year of free on-site service. To keep ahead of the clone makers who simply assembled standard components, DELL raised the stakes by manufacturing PCs to order. This kept inventories and financing costs low, and investments in flexible robots enabled DELL to become a low-cost manufacturer.[4]

The most durable source of DELL's advantage remains its mastery of direct-relationship marketing. DELL has a capability to monitor and analyze each of the 25,000 calls received each day, and to extract from them some valuable, fine-grained insights into problems, needs, and emerging segments. Dealers and competing manufacturers have yet to get this kind of direct feedback from their market. This advantage is presently being married to heavy investments in R&D, to make DELL a technology leader. The company can listen closely to how the market responds to its innovations, and act quickly on what is learned. Will this keep DELL ahead of its competition, especially when the recipe is already being emulated by others? The two big draws of direct sales—price and convenience—are being matched by low-price electronics superstores, and competitors like Compaq have entered direct marketing with promises of faster delivery, longer warranties, and new installation services. Will the pressure of continuous innovation and rapid growth cause DELL to compromise its quality and slow its responsiveness in an era of heightened expectations? DELL's position is not invulnerable, and leadership will be difficult to maintain in the volatile PC business at a time when prices are continuing to plummet. Michael Dell's response is appropriate: "We're constantly reinventing ourselves."

Evidence of Sustainability

The pessimism of economists (the Law of Nemesis) notwithstanding, sustainability is a matter of degree. Most advantages are contestable because they can be eventually duplicated. The most contestable are price advantages, which can be rapidly countered by competitors, and most product innovation. It is estimated that competitors are able to secure detailed information on 70 percent of all new products within a year of their introduction. Even improvements in internal processes are hard to protect—60 to 90 percent of all learning eventually diffuses to competitors.

How does a business assess how long its advantages will last and will continue to yield superior profitability? A response requires answers to three related questions:

1. Of the advantages the business now possesses, which ones yield a price premium because customers get either superior value or lower costs?

2. How will the proposed strategy enhance these differentiation or cost advantages, or create new advantages?

3. How difficult will it be for competitors to imitate those advantages, and how long will it take them? A thorough understanding of the intentions and capabilities of competitors and of the barriers to imitation is required here. These barriers can be roughly divided into two categories: (1) supply-side barriers and (2) demand-side barriers.

Supply-Side Barriers

Based on internal strengths that permit the business to outperform the competition, supply-side barriers are:

1. *Distinctive capabilities.* These are complex bundles of skills and knowledge—exercised through an organization's processes—that ensure superior coordination of activities and superior utilization of assets. Because such capabilities are deeply embedded in the organization and contain a large measure of tacit knowledge, they are very hard for competitors to understand, much less copy. They cannot be as readily acquired as a new numerical machine tool or a software program. Distinctive capabilities have multiple uses; they can be implemented to speed the firm's adaptation to environmental change.

2. *Proprietary technology.* Product, process, and managerial innovations can be protected with patents, copyrights, or confidentiality. Whether patents offer significant protection depends on how difficult it will be for the competition to invent around them. Merrill Lynch was able to obtain a patent for its Cash Management Account, which integrated four investor services into one account, but competitors were able to match the technology readily because what they needed could be easily obtained. What competitors lacked was the organizational infrastructure for successfully bringing the innovation to market.

3. *Economies of scale and/or scope.* Substantial cost advantages can be realized and protected through investments that cannot be readily copied by other firms—either because they lack sufficient capital, or because the market is not big enough to warrant the investment. Scale economies can be achieved with almost any value-adding business activity.

Demand-Side Barriers

These barriers stem from the links the firm has to the market. Two classes of links are especially valuable:

1. *Customer and channel relationships.* At one time, buyer–seller relationships emphasized arm's-length, adversarial bargaining. Now, customers, as well as major channel members such as IKEA and Wal-Mart, are seeking

much closer, collaborative relationships based on a high level of coordination, shared assets, participation in joint programs, and close communication linkages. The ability to engage in joint problem solving and to coordinate numerous activities is a difficult set of skills to master. Competitors can't easily match them and, once the joint investment has been made, the customers face high costs if they decide to switch suppliers.

2. *Brand equity.* A strong brand name serves as a proxy for quality and creates positive images in consumers' minds. It is a significant and durable advantage because it represents a long history of superior value that cannot easily be matched by imitators. A strong brand name also helps firms to deal with changing markets because it eases their extension into new markets or product categories.

There are few, if any, market opportunities where the Law of Nemesis doesn't apply. Whether it can be postponed depends on the ability of the strategist to envision how to protect or continuously enhance the advantages. Strategic alternatives that can persuasively demonstrate that the advantages that ensue can be protected are much preferred.

TEST THREE: WHAT ARE THE PROSPECTS FOR SUCCESSFUL IMPLEMENTATION?

The first two tests asked about the attractiveness of the market opportunity and the likely payoff from the intended strategy. This test asks whether the intentions can be realized. Three conditions must be fulfilled before we can be satisfied that a strategy can deliver the promised results: (1) feasibility, (2) supportability, and (3) consistency.

Feasibility: Does the Business Possess the Necessary Skills and Resources?

If the business does not possess the skills and resources it needs, is there time to acquire or develop them before the window of opportunity closes? Financial resources (capital funds or cash flow requirements) and physical resources are the first constraints against which a strategic alternative is tested. If these limitations are so restrictive that undertaking a strategy would actually jeopardize the competitive position, then the strategy has to be modified to overcome or live within the constraint—or perhaps be rejected. Imaginative solutions—innovative financing methods using sale and leaseback arrangements, or the tying of plant mortgages to long-term contracts—may be necessary.

The next constraints to be tested are access to markets, technology, and servicing capabilities. Is there adequate sales force coverage? Is the sales force capable of the selling job demanded by the strategic alternative? Is the advertising effort likely to be sufficient? What about the cost efficiency and coverage of the present distribution system—including order handling, warehousing, and delivery? Are relationships with jobbers, distributors, and/or retailers strong enough to support the proposed new strategy? Negative or uncertain answers should trigger a search for modifications to overcome problems, and may lead to eventual rejection of the strategy. (The Workslate project in Box 11–1 failed these tests.)

The most rigid constraints stem from the less quantifiable limitations of individuals and organizations. The basic question is: Has the organization ever shown that it could muster the degree of coordinative and integrative skills necessary to carry out the change in strategy? Any strategy that depends on accomplishing tasks outside the realm of reasonably attainable skills is arguably unacceptable.

Supportability: Do the Key Implementers Understand the Strategy and Are They Committed to It?

A broad-based commitment to successful implementation requires two conditions:

1. The premises and elements of the strategy must be readily communicable. If they are not understood, then not only is the strategy likely to be flawed, but its capacity to motivate support will be seriously compromised. A good strategy is one that can be easily understood by all functions; they must not be working at cross-purposes. For this reason, a good strategy is one that can be adequately explained in two or three pages.
2. The strategy should challenge and motivate key personnel. Not only must the strategy have a champion who gives it enthusiastic and credible support, but it must also gain acceptance by all key operating personnel.

If managers have serious reservations about a strategy, are not excited by its objectives and methods, or strongly support another alternative, the strategy must be judged infeasible. This test must be applied with care, however. The Convergent Technologies case warns us that excessive enthusiasm by a highly placed champion can be counterproductive. Apparently the president in particular overrode criticism and suppressed any doubts about the soundness of the strategy.

Consistency: Does the Strategy Hold Together?

To achieve consistency, there should be minimal conflict within each level of strategy and between the levels. The elements of strategic thrust must fit with the supporting functional strategies. Table 11–2, which shows how the functional elements might mesh with the alternative investment strategies, was

TABLE 11–2 Alternative functional strategies.

	Strategic Thrust				
Functional Elements	Invest/Build	Selectivity Growth	Maintain/ Protect	Selectivity/ Manage for Earnings	Harvest/ Divest
Product design	Lead, differentiated ◄──────────────►				Cost reduction
Product line	Proliferate ◄──────────────────►				Prune
Pricing	Value oriented, build experience ◄────►				Generate margin
Distribution	Exclusive, selective ◄────────►				Margin oriented
Promotion/sale	Create demand, capture share ◄──────►				Least cost
Service	Quick fix, applications ◄──────►				Only for profit
Technology	Innovate ◄────────────────►				Minimum necessary
Costs	Pursue scale benefits ◄────────►				Ruthless cutting
Capacity	Lead demand ◄──────────────►				Divest for utilization
Inventory	Anticipatory ◄─────────────►				Minimum response
Risk	Accept, contain ◄──────────────────►				Avoid

developed by a manufacturer of process equipment to aid in testing the suitability of individual functional programs.

The second concern about fit involves the couplings among the functional strategies. Without an acceptable degree of fit in either instance, effective coordination cannot be achieved. The obvious price is management energy needlessly devoted to organizational conflict, and functional "finger pointing" intended to shift blame. A less obvious price is the diffused and uncertain impression of the business in the market. The customer has the best view of the inherent contradictions in the strategy—a quality claim contradicted by shoddy packaging, or a service-intensive selling program without the essential back-office support to expedite deliveries and troubleshoot problems.

The "consistency test" is seldom pivotal; few strategies are conclusively rejected for inconsistency. However, this test can be useful in improving and refining the strategy to ensure that all elements are pointing in the same direction. It may also indicate that the degree of change necessary to bring the elements into line is simply not feasible with the available resources. Functional managers can only cope with a few changes simultaneously while they try to maintain continuing operations. It may not be possible to upgrade old product lines, enter new markets, modernize the costing system, and build a new manufacturing plant all at once.

TEST FOUR: ARE THE RISKS ACCEPTABLE?

The overall level of risk reflects the vulnerability of key results if pivotal assumptions are wrong or critical tasks are not accomplished. For example, an aggressive strategy that increases investment intensity also elevates the break-even point. The strategy alternative is then more sensitive to revenue short-falls than is a "manage for current earnings" strategy.

Overall risk reflects the combined threats from both *environmental* uncertainties (Can competitors easily match, offset, or leap-frog the prospective advantage? Will the target customers respond as anticipated? Will the government regulations be more restrictive than expected?) and *internal* uncertainties about the ability of the business to implement the strategy. Both sources of risk proved too much for the Workslate computer. Either would have crippled the undertaking; in combination, they were lethal.

Assessing Risk

The usual procedure begins by identifying the major environmental and internal uncertainties. These could result from events ("We can't launch the new product in time for the annual trade show") or trends ("The growth of the target market segment isn't materializing"). Essentially, the risk is a joint function of (1) the probability that the adverse event or trend will happen and (2) the consequent effect on long-run performance. The outcome of this analysis is an identification of the key leverage points, as shown in Figure 11–2.

A risk assessment should not stop with an enumeration of all the things that might go wrong. The benefit of this evaluation comes from helping the management team to take preemptive steps to reduce the probability of bad things happening. If there is a significant risk that a major customer will branch out into a supplier's business (leaving the supplier with unused capacity and adding to the available capacity serving the market), what can the supplier do to lessen the probability of this happening? Sometimes, it is not possible to take effective protective action, especially with events and trends that are beyond managers' control. In such circumstances, the best response is to activate the contingency plans—the plans that are only triggered when some kind of threshold is reached. A contingency plan might be stated:

> If demand falls 20 percent below forecast levels, we will do the following: cut prices selectively, reduce the work force, and accelerate the new product activity.

Robust versus Fragile Strategies

Some of the riskiest strategies will achieve desired results in only one industry situation or one environmental scenario. Success is then highly dependent on certain conditions—high growth being realized, currency levels remaining stable, or competitors behaving as they have in the past. If the needed scenario doesn't materialize, performance results are likely to be poor. This is the hall-mark of a fragile strategy: It withers under adversity. To test for how fragile a

FIGURE 11–2   Key leverage points.

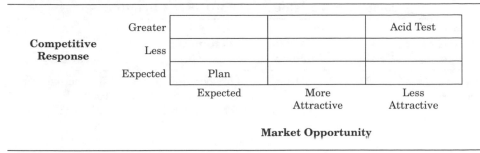

Competitive Response		Expected	More Attractive	Less Attractive
	Greater			Acid Test
	Less			
	Expected	Plan		

Market Opportunity

strategy is ask this question: What if the fundamental assumptions about the attractiveness of the market opportunity are excessively optimistic, and the major competitors' reaction is far more significant than expected? Conversely, a robust strategy may not be the most optimistic; in fact, it may underperform other alternatives if the expected scenario unfolds. However, a robust strategy will succeed in a variety of scenarios because it won't be nearly so damaged by undesirable events.

Assumptions: The Achilles Heel of Strategy Formulation

A hard-nosed risk assessment can help isolate critical assumptions but cannot evaluate their underlying soundness. For this, a validity test is needed. Such a test is especially important whenever a major departure from past performance is anticipated. The key question is: Is there evidence to support the forecast? Table 11–3 shows how the supporting evidence for a proposed strategy was compiled for an industrial components business. Forecasts were: an increase of $51 million in sales and $7 million in net income between 1983 and 1987.

The first step in a validity test is to isolate each of the assumptions about the reasons for the forecast changes. For example, sales and profits were expected to benefit from: a combination of price increases close to the rate of inflation, real market growth of 7 percent per year in the forecast period, and substantial share gains in both market segments. The next step is to evaluate the evidence used to support each assumption. In Table 11–3, the basis for the assumptions about share gains and real market growth appears especially tenuous. How can any share gains be realistically justified when the new products in the commercial segment do not appear to offer a competitive advantage, and the business is trying to hold prices in the industrial segment close to inflation while countering potential Japanese competition? On this evidence, one has little confidence that the proposed strategy will deliver the promised results. New evidence has to be provided and the forecasts have to be adjusted to fit market realities and reflect trade-offs between conflicting performance objectives.

TABLE 11-3   Testing key strategic assumptions of an industrial components business, 1983–1987 ($ in millions).

Sources of Change	Sales	Net Income	Key Assumptions/ Actions	Validity
Price increase	$23	$12	5.5% per year (inflation rate forecast = 6%)	7.6% increase in 1981 5.3% increase in 1982 80% industry capacity and Japanese threat
Share improvement	$17	$ 4	31% to 34% in industrial segment 20% to 27% in commercial segment	0.6% per year increase in 1979–1982 but with minimal price increase Industrial segment is a highly price-sensitive market New products in the commercial segment are catchups
Real market growth	$10	$ 2	7% per year	2% per year, 1980–1982 20% from unproven new market X
Cost productivity	$ 1	$ 1	3% per year	70% of annual productivity increase (3% per year, 1978–1982) was a single technical process breakthrough
Compensation		($12)	24% increase in head count	1983 head count same as 1980 with 10% less volume
Total change	$51	$ 7		

Anyone who does a strategy evaluation must be constantly on the alert for the deep-seated optimistic bias that managers bring to their forecasts. Such a bias is usually the outcome of the following habits managers have developed for coping with ambiguity:

- *Anchoring.* Decision makers tend to "anchor" on a particular outcome they believe will occur. This expected outcome dominates their thinking and suppresses consideration of uncertainties. As a result, downside risks are understated.

- *Selective perception.* Several biasing elements work together to foster selective perception. For example, people tend to structure problems in light of their past experience and training (marketing people, for example, will tend to interpret a general management problem as a marketing problem). Another cause of this bias is that people's anticipation of what they expect to see will influence what they actually see. As a consequence, conflicting evidence will be disregarded.

- *Illusion of control.* Planning activities may give decision makers an illusion that they can master and control their environment. At the same time, decision makers have a tendency to attribute success to their own efforts and blame failures on external events and "bad luck."

- *Availability.* Emphasis is usually given to facts and opinions that are easy to retrieve. Often, these are hard data about past successes, which are given greater weight than soft assessments of future adversity. As a result, the ability of new competitors to gain market acceptance and penetrate previously secure markets is often underestimated.

A rigorous strategy review (1) recognizes that the quality of strategic thinking is dependent on the quality of the underlying assumptions and (2) uses the tough questions to identify the critical assumptions and challenge their validity.

TEST FIVE: WILL THE FORECAST FINANCIAL RESULTS BE ACHIEVED AND INCREASE SHAREHOLDER VALUE?

All strategy alternatives must eventually be tested for their financial attractiveness. The raw materials for this test are valid assumptions about the future revenues, costs, and investment requirements to be achieved by each alternative. These in turn are based on persuasive evidence of sustainable competitive advantage. Which yardstick should be used for judging the financial merits of these strategies? There is growing evidence that conventional yardsticks such as return on sales, revenue growth, and earnings offer inferior guidance because they ignore risk and timing considerations.

A more defensible yardstick judges a strategic alternative by its ability to enhance shareholder value. The basic premise of this approach is that the market value of stock depends on investors' expectations of the cash-generating abilities of each business in the firm. This means that investors willingly invest in a firm only when they expect management can get a better return on their funds than they could get on their own—without exposing themselves to any greater risks. Their minimum expected return is the firm's cost of capital.

These ideas apply neatly to strategy evaluation because any strategy needing new investment will be justified only if the promised returns are greater than the cost of capital. To account for differences in the timing and riskiness of financial benefits and up-front costs, the overall value of the strategy is estimated

---

Box 11–2
The Valuation of Strategies

There is a close affinity between shareholder value-based methods of strategy evaluation and the familiar discounted cash flow (DCF) methods widely used to evaluate capital investment projects such as the addition of plant capacity. The extension of the DCF method to the comparison of business strategies had to wait until business units had their own profit and loss statements and balance sheets. These are the necessary conditions for the estimation of annual operating cash flows, which are the raw material of this method. These cash flows reflect the sales, profit, working capital, and fixed capital investment consequences of a strategic alternative within a particular environmental scenario.

The total shareholder value a business expects to realize from a strategy has three components:

1. The present value (PV) of cash flows during the planning period. This period may be three to five years, depending on the industry. The discount rate used to bring future cash flows to the present depends on the parent's cost of capital and the riskiness of the strategy being proposed. A radical departure from the present direction will have a sizable risk premium, whereas a continuation of the current strategy in a low-volatility environment will have a low risk premium.

2. To this present value is added a "residual" value, which is the present value of the cash flows to be received after the end of the planning period. In effect, this is what the business is worth at the end of the planning period. For many strategies—especially those that require heavy up-front investments—this may be the largest source of total value.

3. From these two present values is subtracted the market value of debt assigned to the business.

This calculation results in an estimate of total shareholder value. This is equivalent to the initial shareholder value plus the value created by the proposed strategy. The initial value is essentially what the business is worth today without taking any account of the value created by prospective investments.

by discounting all relevant cash flows. The discount rate is the cost of capital adjusted to take into account the riskiness of the strategic alternative compared to other investments the firm could make. The best strategy for a business—if there are several choices—will create the most value. Interested readers will find more details of this evaluation method in Box 11–2.

Cash flows have the advantage that they are not distorted by the accounting conventions that afflict forecasts of net earnings. Suppose a business maintains market position by allowing customers increasingly long periods to pay for products or services. Even though profits are realized, the business may not have enough cash inflow to pay for the increase in working capital as well as other investments. Rapid sales growth may turn a business into a heavy cash consumer. A distributor of medical lasers recently filed for bankruptcy, after a year in which sales trebled. Although reported earnings were high, the accounts receivable grew even faster. The company found itself so short of cash, because of this surge in working capital needs, that it had to write down its receivables, which eliminated most of the next year's earnings. This was a dramatic evaporation of shareholder value, but any business that persistently needs more cash than it generates is eating into shareholder value.

Because the estimates of value are so dependent on the quality of assumptions about market-share revenues, costs, and timing, a business would be unwise to use the results as the ultimate arbiter of strategic decisions. These methods are better used as a defensible framework for a sensitivity analysis of key assumptions. How much would prices, market share, timing of entry, costs, and so forth have to change before a strategy became unattractive? Whether this scenario can be reasonably anticipated depends on an understanding of the competitive situation, the prospects for sustainable advantage, and the ability of the business to implement the strategy. This approach shifts the emphasis back to where it belongs—to an understanding of the fundamentals that create shareholder value. The questions that will reveal these fundamentals are summarized in Table 11–4.

SUMMARY: IMPLEMENTING A VALUE-ADDING STRATEGY REVIEW

Recently, a major telecommunications firm conducted a postmortem of its failed diversification activities so that it could avoid repeating the same mistakes. These were expensive lessons; the cumulative loss on six ventures exceeded $56 million. The firm concluded:

> The plan review process led to unrealistic profit projections. Year one was an operating plan, with the numbers in years 2 to 5 simply adjusted to meet known criteria. Everyone knew they had to break even in three years; therefore they backed into their projections. . . .

TABLE 11–4   Questioning the strategic fundamentals.

Test One: How attractive is the market opportunity?

How big is the market?
How fast will it grow?
How intense will competition become?

Test Two: How sustainable is the competitive advantage?

What target market segments will be served?
What advantages will be achieved in these segments?
What are the outcomes of these advantages?
How long can they be sustained?

Test Three: What are the prospects for successful implementation?

Feasibility: Do we have the necessary skills and resources? If not, can they be
    obtained in time?
Consistency: Does the strategy hang together?
Supportability: Do the key implementers understand the premises and the strategy?
    Are they committed to it?
Does the plan address the major issues?

Test Four: Are the risks acceptable?

How vulnerable are the forecast results if pivotal assumptions are wrong or critical
    tasks are not accomplished? What actions can be taken to minimize the exposure
    to the risks?
How robust is the strategy?

*Test Five: Will the forecast financial results be achieved and increase shareholder
    value?*

How sensitive are the results to changes in the forecasts?

> There was a built-in lack of accountability that encouraged people to put to-
> gether and approve unrealistic long-term plans. . . .

> We didn't know what we didn't know. The reviewers didn't have the expertise or
> market experience to add value in the review process. As a result, the reviews
> were based more on format than on content.

This is certainly a damning indictment of a misguided effort to diversify
into markets where the firm had few competencies. It is also symptomatic of
strategy evaluations that don't add value because they suffer from several deficiencies. Senior managers are disconnected from the early development of the
strategy, so they don't appreciate the range of possible alternatives or the trade-
offs to be made. Instead, the business team makes a choice among the alternatives already selected for consideration. By the time the team proposes its
preferred strategy, team members are completely committed to that direction
and have foreclosed other possibilities. During the strategy review, the emphasis tends to be on the financial forecasts—which deflects attention from the
strategic fundamentals we have emphasized in this chapter. When approval is

given, the team often accepts the performance objectives but provides less funds than requested—partly because there are not enough funds available, but also because team members suspect that the resource requirements have been inflated. This leads to an unhealthy amount of game playing as the business teams anticipate that they will cut back and adjust their estimates accordingly.

A healthy strategy evaluation process should be an integral part of the planning process—not a single event at the end of the strategy development process. A well-informed senior management team will provide guidance, using tough questions to probe the strategy at several points during the planning process. During the early stages, the emphasis is almost exclusively on the qualitative factors covered by the first four test questions and on the validity of the underlying assumptions. As the feasible alternatives are refined, the attention turns to quantifying the performance results, capital investments, and risks. In this approach to strategy evaluation, management is more deeply involved and can exercise a leadership role throughout the process, while still coaching the business team on the important factors to consider and clearly communicating well-grounded expectations. For this entire process to be productive, both the reviewers and those reviewed must be working with the same mental model of the attributes of a sound strategy. Hence, it is essential that all parties fully understand the five test questions given in this chapter and their underlying premises. This uniformity ensures the complete transparency of the strategy evaluation process. The payoff is realized in informed and committed managers who will implement sound strategies with above-average prospects for success.

NOTES

1. The importance of developing diverse alternatives and how to go about doing so have been discussed in the previous chapter.

2. Chapter 6, which addresses industry analysis, discusses in detail how industry structure and evolution affect the attractiveness of opportunities—and thus, profitability.

3. For further discussion of the distinctions between intended and realized strategy, see Chapter 15.

4. Dell has also been discussed in some detail in Chapter 1.

REFERENCES

Day, George S. *Market-Driven Strategy: Process for Creating Value.* New York: Free Press, 1990.

Porter, Michael E. *Competitive Advantage.* New York: Free Press, 1985.

Rappaport, Alfred. *Creating Shareholder Value: The New Standard for Business Performance.* New York: Free Press, 1986.

PART FIVE

MANAGING STRATEGIC CHANGE: LINKING STRATEGY AND ACTION

12 STRATEGIC CHANGE: REALIGNING THE ORGANIZATION TO IMPLEMENT STRATEGY

Russell A. Eisenstat

Management Consultant

Michael Beer

Harvard Business School

The technology for developing business strategy is formidable. The past 20 years have seen a burgeoning of sophisticated techniques for competitor analysis, market segmentation, and product positioning. Chief executives have had considerable assistance in the use of these powerful tools. Most large firms have created strategic planning departments; in addition, U.S. businesses spend billions of dollars every year on strategy consulting.

Too often, strategies devised by consultants or strategic planning departments fail to be implemented effectively. Millions of dollars spent in analysis and strategy formulation yield little more than fancy presentations and reports. The behavior of functional departments, staff groups, or unions, which must adapt to new competitive realities, remains largely unchanged. Why?

The behavior of individuals and groups—organizational behavior—is shaped by multiple facets of the organization: structure, the leadership behavior of key managers, the people who have been recruited and promoted, and the information, measurement, and reward systems that create incentives and control. These are designed over time by management to stimulate and reinforce attitudes, skills, and behavior needed by the firm to succeed in its marketplace. As the firm succeeds in its endeavors, its organization and human resource policies and practices become entrenched. Alignment fosters the consistent skill, attitudes, and behavior—the organization's capability—needed to implement strategy.

As the competitive environment changes, new attitudes, skills, and behavior are required. Past structure, systems, policies, and practices foster behavior that is no longer functional. The organization is out of alignment with new competitive realities. As the organization reformulates its strategy, it must also realign itself so that new attitudes and behaviors required to implement strategy are encouraged and reinforced.[1]

The case of Honeywell's Commercial Aviation Division (CAvD), headed by John Dewane, its newly appointed general manager, is detailed in Box 12–1. How could Honeywell, so successful in developing and selling a new technology in the military avionics business, be so unsuccessful in commercializing it? The Commercial Aviation Division is a classic case of an organization out of alignment. Concerned about air superiority, the military customer cared about innovative technology more than about speed in developing the product or its price. Quality was important, but it was ensured by military inspectors stationed in Honeywell's plants. Consequently, managers and workers never saw quality as something for which they had to take full responsibility.

The division's hierarchical and functional approach to management fostered little of the teamwork required by the new business environment. Although the CAvD had many individuals who were talented technically, the organization as a whole lacked the capability to respond to new competitive demands. Dewane quickly realized that he had to develop organizational capability in response to new market demands and that this would require organizational as well as individual change. How he should go about realigning the organization with strategy was less clear. The gap between them presented a challenge with which Dewane struggled for several years.

A SYSTEMIC APPROACH TO REALIGNING THE ORGANIZATION WITH STRATEGY

Successfully implementing business strategy involves a complex matching game. It requires a general manager and his or her team to identify opportunities for competitive advantage in the marketplace, and to develop an organization with a capability for realizing those opportunities.[2]

By "capability," we mean much more than the competence of the many employees who make up the business unit. The organization as a whole must be able to coordinate the efforts of individuals and groups in a way that allows it to sense what the market demands and then to respond as a unified whole. It was one thing for John Dewane to realize that the future viability of the Commercial Aviation Division depended on speeding the process of product development; it was quite another for him to mobilize the multiple employees and functions of his organization to accomplish this task.

Realigning an organization with strategy appears deceptively easy: Analyze what is needed, and then simply redesign the organization and its management

---

Box 12–1

Honeywell CAvD Case

The Commercial Aviation Division (CAvD) had been floundering for two years in its efforts to commercialize a new technology for aircraft navigation developed for its defense business. Convinced that the new technology had commercial applications that could propel Honeywell into a major new business, top management created this new division. But, it was making little progress. New commercial products were long overdue. Customers were so angry they vowed to cancel their orders. Losses threatened Honeywell's return on investment. The future of the business was in doubt. What was the problem?

When John Dewane was appointed to replace the first division manager, he found a top team that did not work well together. Consistent with past practice, business strategy had been developed by the general manager and the director of marketing without involvement of the full staff. Little consensus existed about the strategy or commitment to it. The results were: conflicting directions from functional managers and unclear priorities.

Communication was extremely poor. Dewane found that directions discussed at the top did not reach lower levels, possibly because of an excessive number of levels in the organization. Consistent with practices that worked in the defense business, engineering had designed the product with little influence from manufacturing. Then, according to managers in manufacturing, engineering "threw an incomplete product over the wall to manufacturing." Many costly engineering changes were required to make the product manufacturable at the specified cost. All these changes created cost overruns in manufacturing for which its managers were held accountable. Consequently, manufacturing distrusted engineering and viewed its personnel as arrogant and imperious.

The commercial business required not only rapid product development but a responsiveness to customer needs and lower costs than in the military business. Locked in a competitive battle brought about by deregulation, airlines put pressure on aircraft manufacturers to reduce the cost of an airplane. The manufacturers, in turn, pressured subcontractors like Honeywell's CAvD to lower costs. Simultaneous demand for rapid product development and lower cost could only be met by close interfunctional coordination, particularly among marketing, engineering, and manufacturing.

The demand for a lower-cost product required a production work force committed to lowering costs while maintaining quality. A history of distrust between management and the union still blocked cooperative efforts.

---

policies and practices. Because analysis of the organization's alignment requires a systemic, objective, and rigorous approach, consultants are often brought in to do the analysis and make recommendations. Alternatively, staff groups, in conjunction with key executives, perform the analysis and plan the changes needed. Because they are developed by outsiders or at the top, however, desired changes are frequently not implemented effectively.

The Three Tasks of Strategy Implementation

Over the past five years, we have studied strategy implementation in a range of business units across a number of different corporations. None of these corporations was on the verge of immediate failure, but all were under considerable competitive pressure. The most successful implementation did not occur when staff groups and/or consultants developed a sophisticated new organizational design. It occurred when sophistication in analysis and design was combined with appropriate involvement of employees in organizational analysis and change. As a result of our work, we have identified three tasks whose successful completion is vital to the effective implementation of strategy. General managers must:

1. Develop a partnership with organization members to implement strategy.
2. Assess the organization's capability to implement its business strategy.
3. Orchestrate change initiatives that will realign the organization with its business strategy in such a way that commitment builds and learning occurs.

We will use the Honeywell Commercial Aviation Division (CAvD) case to illustrate how a manager might go about accomplishing each of these tasks. We begin with an overview of Dewane's response to the crisis he faced. Throughout the chapter, we will return to the CAvD case to highlight how Dewane's actions illustrate the role of the three tasks in developing an organization capable of implementing its strategy.

Dewane began his change effort by working with his top team. His staff, which had never been part of the strategy formulation process, spent many meetings reviewing data about the competitive environment—market trends, customer reactions to CAvD's product, and financial goals—and ended with consensus on the strategy. It defined its strategy as a three-part sequence:

1. Develop the new commercial product.
2. Develop good customer service.
3. Reduce cost, once volume has been established.

In the first few years, product development was the key.

During the same period, Dewane held several off-site meetings, facilitated by a consultant, to discuss relationships among the staff. At the meetings, the directors discussed their views of themselves and their jobs, and their approach to managing. Dissatisfaction with the current organization and its management practices grew as a result of these discussions. Dewane recalled that the group evolved toward agreement with his own view: "This is garbage; why the hell are we living in a mess like this? There should be some pleasure in this work. Let's look at some more modern organizations; let's try to find a better way to do things."

Looking for a Model

Once Dewane and his staff had decided to seek some type of change, they formed a team of volunteers to visit other companies' and Honeywell's plants, with the goal of identifying an organizational model that could be used at CAvD. The team, which included a cross-section of employees ranging from a union steward to a director reporting to Dewane, was impressed by a visit to Honeywell's Chandler plant. Employees were working in teams, with cooperation between management and the union. A production employee remarked: "After seeing and feeling that atmosphere at Chandler, I realized what an improvement it would be in Commercial Aviation to have parts come in correct, to be able to ask for engineering support and get it, and to find everyone genuinely concerned about solving problems, to have everyone proud of their work area, with everyone having a chance to contribute to the whole."

A second team, including John Dewane, was sent to the Chandler plant. Back home, a discussion developed about the barriers CAvD's functional organization posed to the development of new products and how Chandler's team approach might be used to overcome these problems. Dewane recalled that the team concept had been met with resistance and skepticism by some members of his staff.

In response, Dewane appointed a design team composed of management and production employees. Their task was to identify organizational barriers to product development and recommend a new model for organizing and managing to overcome barriers.

The design team quickly concluded that all work in CAvD, especially product development work, cut across functional lines. They proceeded to recommend a team structure, at the divisional and plant levels, that brought people together around tasks. Product development teams, which brought together engineering, marketing, manufacturing, and other functions, were the most important part of the proposal.

The design team formed a larger "core group" composed of 90 employees. Their assignment was to review the organizational model developed by the design team, suggest modifications, and craft a statement of values for the division. At the end of a week, the core group agreed on a new organizational model and the values that would drive it. After reviewing these, Dewane and his staff assembled all employees in an auditorium where the design team and core group presented their recommendations. What came to be known as the Total Involvement Program (TIP) was born.

The Record of TIP

In the second year of change, it became apparent that some employees at several levels did not fit the new model of management. The operations manager agreed to transfer out to another part of the company. He was not replaced, and the number of reporting levels in the division was thereby reduced. Several supervisors who found it difficult to work within the new framework were given different jobs or transferred. The union president objected to the new approach to management, but the local union steward convinced him that the approach was one to which production employees were committed.

Efforts to change began to penetrate each of the functions in the second and third years of change. Engineering undertook an analysis of its organization in the context of the new cross-functional team organization that was in place. So did the marketing function. Manufacturing organized itself to participate in product development decisions and work on continuous process improvement. In each function, the structure and/or management process was altered after an analysis showed how its approach to managing was not aligned with the new team organization.

Clarence Asche, director of engineering, commented on the improvement in cross-functional coordination, the central objective of the organizational realignment: "I certainly have seen relationships improving. We have people from other departments on our teams. They are recognizing that they have an obligation to make a contribution to the development process as opposed to evaluations downstream, when it's too late to do anything. I also see a stronger orientation in design work toward making product cost a driving force in design."

Dramatic Results

The realignment of the organization with strategy produced dramatic results. By 1986, CAvD was a market leader in inertial reference and inertial navigation (IRS/INS) products. The division estimated that 80 percent of the IRS/INS systems installed on air transport airplanes and 95 percent of the IRS/INS systems installed on business aviation jets were made by Honeywell. Studies showed that customers thought Honeywell's systems were three times as reliable as competitors' products; the actual figures were higher: competitors' products averaged some 2,000 hours between failures, compared to 7,000 hours mean time between failures for Honeywell's products. The division's reputation for customer service was excellent. Honeywell's costs of producing products was estimated to be quite a bit lower than competitors'. In 1985, the division became profitable for the first time—a dramatic turnaround from the substantial losses of previous years. This improvement reflected dramatic reductions in scrap, rework, and inventory costs since the implementation of TIP, as well as a significant improvement in value-added sales per employee.

John Dewane's efforts to realign the organization illustrate a significant departure from conventional approaches. He involved members of the organization in analysis and change. The result was not only an organization that was aligned with strategy but employees who were committed to learning how to work within the new alignment.

DEVELOPING A PARTNERSHIP TO IMPLEMENT STRATEGY

The case of the Commercial Aviation Division suggests that the foundation for effective strategy implementation is a partnership. A way must be found to rally employees in different levels and parts of the organization around the task of implementing strategy.

Competition is forcing most companies to find ways to improve coordination among various parts of the organization. Few sources of sustainable competitive advantage can be realized through the efforts of any one function. As the CAvD case illustrates, product quality and cost are affected not just by manufacturing but also by R&D, where the product is designed for manufacturability. An important role is played by the purchasing and logistics functions, which ensure that raw materials consistently meet specifications. In fact, partnership must go beyond the boundaries of the firm to include its suppliers and customers.[3]

Partnership is necessary not just in the newly aligned organization but also in the change process itself. Why? Employees in various parts of the organization who must coordinate their efforts know better than those at the top what type of coordination is needed and where the barriers to coordination are.

Barriers to Cross-Functional Coordination

The problem is that much of what employees know is typically undiscussable. Barriers to cross-functional coordination at CAvD were rooted in the arrogance within the engineering function. In the military avionics business, superior technical solutions were valued by the military customer so highly that it made sense for engineers to be in complete control of design decisions. Engineering's role was to design a sophisticated product; manufacturing's responsibility was to make it. Because cost was not very important, product designs were not examined from manufacturing's point of view. Over the years, engineers learned that their unit was "king." Engineering managers further reinforced this learning by hiring engineers for their technical expertise, not for their interpersonal sensitivity. This translated into a dictatorial style at every level and into hostility and distrust between the heads of manufacturing and engineering.

Deep-seated issues of this type are very difficult to surface and discuss publicly. Without the capacity to surface them, however, the organization is unable to redesign its structure and management practices to correct them. If general managers have grown up in the organization, as had John Dewane's predecessor, they may be blind to these problems—indeed, they may be contributing to them. Even if they are vaguely aware of problems, they may have a difficult time assessing their significance. If they assess their significance correctly, they may lack the capacity to confront them or to mobilize groups to deal with them. These are "iceberg issues"—the issues below the surface of the organization's public conversations that are most likely to sink new strategic initiatives. This is clearly a case where what you don't know *can* hurt you.

Just as often, the barriers to partnership are in vertical relationships. Employees and/or the union may distrust management, preventing engagement in the kind of open dialogue and cooperation that identifies problems and develops commitment to solutions. The use of top-down programs to change the organization also reduces commitment. This was the response of the union president at CAvD to John Dewane's preliminary ideas about change, well before Dewane decided to involve lower levels: "You do it that way, you can count me out. We have really had enough of all these damned programs that come and go, and they have no support from the people. When you've got people's support, and you can prove it to me, I'll back you on a program like that."

When the barriers to strategy implementation are the attitudes and behavior of top management, these issues are even more difficult to discuss. If ways are not found to make a dialogue possible, the organization cannot realign itself with strategy.

For these reasons, creating a partnership for implementation across organizational levels and between different parts of the organization is essential. Senior management, because of its knowledge of both the external environment and the overall business, can define a broad strategic direction; however, the top management group cannot do it alone. Those at lower organizational levels, who are deeply involved in the daily details of actually implementing a business strategy, tend to have a better sense for where the hidden organizational icebergs lurk.

John Dewane developed a partnership among different functions and levels (including production workers and union leaders) by involving them in managing change. Representatives of these diverse stakeholders were on the teams that visited the innovative Chandler plant, on the design team, and in the core group. Employees knew from years of experience where the barriers to cross-functional teamwork and labor–management cooperation lay. They translated this knowledge into a completely new team model of management, something that would have been difficult for Dewane and his top team to do alone. The senior managers knew less about the details of the problems, and the new team-based organization was a potential threat to their traditional roles and responsibilities.

Two Models of Partnership

Becton Dickinson

The Becton Dickinson Corporation has formalized and institutionalized the idea of partnership for strategy implementation. After completing its strategic plan, each business unit at Becton Dickinson enlists the help of an employee task force to assess the organization's capabilities to implement its strategic tasks. The task force feeds back to the top team the results of interviews they have conducted with employees about organizational barriers to accomplishing these tasks. Problems in interfunctional cooperation, top team effectiveness, changing priorities, and uncoordinated resource allocation, as well as deficiencies in technical and managerial competence, are typically surfaced.

The task force is able to present these potentially embarrassing and threatening problems by means of a carefully crafted process intended to promote a nondefensive discussion. Members of the task force, seated in an area called "the fishbowl," in the middle of the room, discuss their findings with each other while top management sits in an outer circle listening. They engage the task force in a discussion about findings under commonly agreed-on ground rules for nondefensive dialogue. A trained internal facilitator from the strategic planning or human resource department helps both groups follow the ground rules.

The top team then develops a diagnosis of why and how the organization is not aligned. Next, they work up a model of how the business unit should be organized and managed to support the strategy more fully. Often, employee teams are enlisted to help develop particular parts of the change plan. At Becton Dickinson, managers are expected to go through this process periodically, but particularly if a major change occurs in the business's strategic direction. Strategic human resource management (SHRM) profiling, as it is called within the company, enables business-unit managers to examine typically hidden and undiscussable deficiencies in the organization's capabilities to implement strategy.[4]

The GE Workout

General Electric's "workout" process provides a somewhat different model for developing a partnership for realigning the organization. Each workout session is based on a critical business issue or a key business process. All the individuals, across organizational levels or functions, who are necessary to address this issue are brought together in an off-site meeting. In some cases, suppliers and customers are also included. These individuals are assigned to small groups in which they brainstorm ideas for improvement. The suggestions from these sessions are then presented in a "town meeting" to the leaders of the business, who must decide on-the-spot whether to accept each suggestion, reject it, or ask for further study. Finally, a process is put into place to follow up and ensure that the accepted recommendations are actually put into effect.[5]

How to Develop a Partnership for Strategy Implementation

To develop a partnership for strategy implementation, an organization begins by building a consensus around the business's strategic tasks. Strategic tasks are whatever has to be done to create or sustain a competitive advantage in the marketplace. This consensus must be created both within the senior management team and in the larger organization. To develop this consensus, key individuals must be convinced that certain actions are good for both the overall business and for them. Honeywell's John Dewane helped his top team understand the business problems facing them, and the importance of developing new products more quickly and at lower cost, through a series of off-site meetings in which the business was reviewed. Information about customer dissatisfaction (and the disastrous consequences if it continued) helped develop commitment to change. So did the realization, triggered by the visits to the Chandler plant, that there was a better way to manage.

The competitive crisis that Dewane faced made it relatively easy to align individual and organizational interests. The problem is more difficult when the external crisis is less severe—individual interests are less likely to align with those of the overall organization. In these instances, it is extremely important that the top team engage in a joint process of data collection and analysis. The process allows them to come to a common understanding of both the risks and the opportunities inherent in the new strategic direction. The general manager must also send the message that members of the team will be evaluated on their willingness to act for the good of the overall organization, not just on their functional performance.

If the top team is committed to accomplishing a common set of strategic tasks, those lower in the organization are less likely to receive conflicting direction. However, this does not necessarily ensure widespread organizational commitment. Developing this commitment usually requires sharing with those at all levels of the organization the information that led the top team to decide on a common strategic direction. Often, it involves sharing far more information about competitors and customers than has been customary in many companies. It also requires some imagination and creativity. For example, some companies have arranged visits to customers' facilities for production workers as well as salaried workers. In other companies, customers have been invited to demonstrate how a product is used, or competitive products have been displayed on the shop floor for all employees to inspect.

The Barrier of Fear

One of the barriers to developing a partnership is that those who have the most to contribute also have the most to lose. This is most apparent when the strategic objective is cost reduction. It is difficult to ask managers to recommend reductions in their budgets, and virtually impossible to ask them to eliminate their jobs. Yet, these managers may know more than anyone else about the impact of alternative cost-reduction strategies on effectiveness.

Mandating a fixed percentage of across-the-board reductions in costs for all functions is a common approach to addressing this problem. Managers in each department are asked to determine the best way to make cuts. This approach has great limitations. Not all departments or areas are equally important strategically: some areas should be cut more deeply, others less so. Moreover, strategic effectiveness is typically not dependent on the cost-effectiveness of single functional departments. It depends on how all of the functional departments work together. Without considering the organization as a whole—a perspective that requires a partnership among different levels and parts—it is difficult to come up with the best way to reduce costs.

A more sophisticated approach has been developed by the process reengineering movement. A team of high-potential managers from all relevant functions is taken out of their current jobs for an extended period of time and given the responsibility for developing a radically more effective organization. Because they are the company's "best and brightest," they are explicitly told their jobs are secure. Because they are a team representing different functions and are assigned to analyze a cross-functional work process, the solution developed is more likely to align with the needs of the organization as a whole.

The Barrier of Old Assumptions

It is often difficult for the managers who know the organization best to go beyond their deep-seated assumptions, especially if the organization has been successful in the past. It is hard to accept that what worked before may not work in the future. Executives fear that those who know the most will have the greatest difficulty breaking the frame of "how we have always done things around here." This concern leads executives, intent on implementing a radically different strategic approach, to go it alone.

There are two obvious dangers with this approach. First, the concerns of those who have been with the organization longest may have merit. They can be ignored only at the peril of the implementing manager. For instance, David Halberstam's book *The Best and the Brightest*[6] suggests that one reason for our difficulties in Vietnam was that the Kennedy Administration ignored the advice of regional specialists in the State Department who knew the area best. Second, individuals with long tenure usually have competence that is critically important to implementing the new strategy. It is difficult to gain their commitment without their involvement.

A better alternative is to help experienced managers break out of their old paradigm, or mental model of the situation.[7] This is one reason why external consultants are brought in. When they facilitate a process of diagnosis and change rather than give their own recommendations, they can help managers break into a new frame of thinking without incurring resistance to change. Benchmarking, a method of comparing one's own performance and practices to those of companies that have adapted radically different approaches to implementing similar strategies, is also useful in pushing people to go beyond previous assumptions about what is possible. Visits to Honeywell's Chandler plant by employees of the Commercial Aviation Division stimulated them to conceive the radically different team-based organization.

In summary, developing a partnership among management and organizational members is essential in the development of an organization capable of implementing strategy. Involvement in defining the demands of the competitive environment and the organizational barriers to an effective response is the first step. It engages people's hearts but, by itself, is insufficient. Developing organizational capability also requires rigorous analysis.

DIAGNOSING ORGANIZATIONAL CAPABILITY TO IMPLEMENT STRATEGY

Just as successful strategy *formulation* requires a comprehensive scanning and assessment of the external competitive environment, effective strategy *implementation* demands an equally rigorous assessment of the organization's internal environment. The analysis should answer whether the organization possesses the capabilities it needs to achieve the chosen strategy, and, if not, what barriers are preventing the development of these capabilities. The most effective managers continuously conduct this assessment intuitively, tracing back organizational problems to their root causes. The resulting causal map is valuable in determining what must change to implement business strategy.

Unfortunately, many managers do not apply rigorous analysis to the questions of how and why their organization is not implementing strategy effectively. One reason is that they do not possess an analytic framework for asking the right questions. Figure 12–1 is a systemic framework for making an organizational diagnosis. In the following sections, we discuss each element in the framework, using a series of questions managers must answer to make an assessment of organizational capability. Given the requirement for partnership outlined above, the answers to these questions ideally should be developed by the top team with the involvement of the larger organization. This can be done in a variety of ways ranging from CAvD's core group of 90 employees to Becton Dickinson's SHRM process or GE's workout.

FIGURE 12–1   Assessing the readiness to implement strategy.

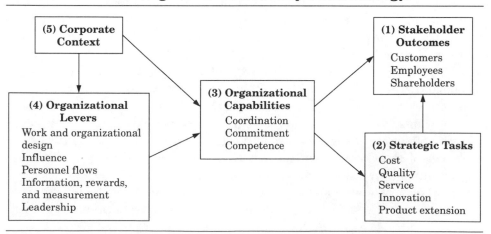

The model, summarized in Figure 12–1, is based on a few simple premises:

1. Organizations can continue to exist only if they anticipate and meet the needs of their stakeholders—customers, employees, and shareholders.
2. Business strategies must be articulated in actionable terms. What are the key tasks the organization must accomplish to satisfy stakeholder needs?
3. The ability of the business to accomplish its strategic tasks is dependent on three organizational capabilities:
   (a) coordination among parts of the organization that must work together to accomplish the strategic task;
   (b) commitment of individuals and groups to accomplishing the strategic task; and
   (c) technical and managerial competence to solve problems and coordinate solutions.
4. The organizational capabilities are related to how the organization is designed and managed—its structure and systems; who has a say over key decisions; the types of individuals who are hired and promoted; its information, rewards, and measurement systems; the character and behavior of its leaders.
5. How the organization is designed and managed, as well as its capabilities are in part determined by the nature of the larger corporation of which the business unit may be a part.

Table 12–1 outlines diagnostic questions for each element of the model. These will enable managers to assess systematically all aspects of an organization's readiness to implement a proposed business strategy.

STAKEHOLDER OUTCOMES

How Adequately Is the Organization Meeting the Needs of All of Its Stakeholders—Customers, Employees, and Shareholders?

For a business organization to remain viable, employees must be willing to provide their labor, customers must be willing to buy its products, and shareholders must be willing to provide the necessary financial capital. The interests of shareholders are generally defined by financial measurements such as sales growth, profitability, return on sales, return on investment, and stock price appreciation. In the 1970s and 1980s, shareholder interests may not have been adequately represented in the financial measurements utilized or the goals set. In the 1990s, boards of directors, pressured by shareholders, have exerted heavy influence on management to redefine measures and goals.

The ability of the firm to attract and keep employees is a proxy measurement for employee satisfaction. Labor markets are not efficient, however. For a

TABLE 12–1 Assessing organizational readiness for strategy implementation.

Stakeholder Outcomes

How adequately is the organization meeting the needs of all of its stakeholders—customers, employees, and shareholders?

Strategic Tasks

What are the strategic tasks for the organization?

Is the top team clear and in agreement with the key strategic tasks?

Is the rest of the organization clear and in agreement with the strategic tasks?

Organizational Capabilities

Does the business have the appropriate level of coordination or teamwork to accomplish the task?

Do the members of the organization have the necessary technical and managerial competencies to accomplish the task?

Does the necessary level of commitment exist among the key functions, suppliers, and customers identified above?

Organizational Levers

• The organization of work.

How does each of the following either support or hinder accomplishing the strategic task?

The formal organizational structure.

The presence or absence of cross-functional mechanisms such as meetings or formal teams.

The specification of individual roles, responsibilities, and relationships.

• Influence.

Are decisions made with appropriate influence from relevant functions in the organization?

Are decisions made with appropriate influence from all organizational levels?

• Personnel flows.

Do individuals in key organizational positions have the appropriate skills and abilities?

What types of attitudes and behaviors does the promotion process reward?

• Information, rewards, and measurement systems.

Do the information and measurement systems provide the data needed to accomplish the strategic task?

Do the measurement and reward systems motivate behavior that supports the strategic task?

• Leadership.

Do the actions of the general manager and his or her top team encourage and reinforce lower levels to behave in a way that supports the business's strategic task?

Corporate Context

To what extent do the policies, procedures, or culture of the larger corporation make it difficult for the business unit to implement its strategy?

variety of reasons, employees do not always leave when they are unhappy, and their lowered commitment can hurt the firm's capacity to implement its strategy. Other measures of satisfaction—surveys of employee attitudes, grievances filed, legal suits regarding fair treatment, a desire to unionize, and/or the relationship of the firm with the union—must, therefore, be used as indicators of employee satisfaction. It is important to recognize that a firm's policies can satisfy top management and discourage lower-level managers or workers. For this reason, data about employee satisfaction must be collected from all levels.[8]

Market share is a proxy measurement for customer satisfaction. More sensitive and direct measures include surveys of customer reaction, warranty returns, and customer loyalty. In response to the competitive environment, many firms are developing multiple methods for measuring customer satisfaction. They are learning that a downward trend in these measures indicates that the firm will have difficulty meeting its financial targets in the future. Consider the shock of a new general manager who, based on financial measures, thought he was inheriting a healthy business, only to find that customer satisfaction was low and declining.

A firm can satisfy one set of stakeholders in the short run, without satisfying others. Paying a dividend while laying off employees and decreasing investments in new products puts shareholders ahead of employees and customers. Retaining employees on the payroll when profits are inadequate puts employees ahead of shareholders. A major task facing general managers is balancing these interests in such a way that the business will remain viable over time.

STRATEGIC TASKS

What Are the Strategic Tasks for the Organization?

The foundation for strategy implementation is a clear and shared understanding of a business's strategic tasks. We have seen how a general manager can use the process of defining the strategic task and communicating it widely to develop a partnership with employees in realigning the organization. Strategic tasks are simple statements of what has to get done in a business to create or sustain a competitive advantage in the marketplace. In Honeywell's CAvD, the strategic task had changed from developing a high-technology product without much regard to time or cost to developing products rapidly with considerable regard to cost.

The accomplishment of a given strategic task depends on the organization's ability to accomplish certain key work processes.[9] For example, developing high-quality and lower-cost products rapidly at Honeywell's CAvD was strongly dependent on a process that translated a technical innovation in engineering into a manufacturable and commercially viable product. This process involves many trade-offs among marketing, engineering, and manufacturing.

Strategic tasks can be defined at any organizational level. Within a manufacturing plant, accomplishing the strategic task of improving product quality requires coordinated effort across the various parts of the plant. Within a business unit such as Honeywell's CAvD, the strategic task of product development required work processes that spanned a number of functions. Corporate strategic tasks are accomplished through work processes that span multiple businesses. These tasks define ways in which the corporation as a whole contributes to the competitive advantage of its various businesses through such work processes as multidivisional sales to large customers, or through the transfer of technologies from domestic to overseas businesses.

Is the Top Team Clear and in Agreement on the Key Strategic Tasks?

In many organizations, despite an enormous amount of time spent developing strategic plans, there is no consensus within the senior team about the business's strategic tasks. Strategic planning documents contain discussions of long-term trends in technology and customer buying behavior and incisive analyses of competitors' strengths and weaknesses. Yet those formal plans say little that would help an employee decide on a day-to-day basis what activities would be most helpful in making the business successful.

One division we studied developed the following strategy statement: "Fortify our quality, product cost, and market share strengths, while also transforming the industry through expanded customer knowledge and product/service innovation." Undoubtedly, the business must do all of the things in the statement, but not all of them are equally important for competitive advantage. The strategy statement provides little organizational guidance as to which of the factors—quality, cost, or product and service innovation—is more or less important, and why.

Just as often, what substitutes for clarity on strategic tasks is a list of quantitative business objectives such as profitability, sales growth, return on assets, and market share, and a list of programs and projects for achieving them. This is very different from providing a sense of the overall task the organization needs to complete if it is going to be successful in the marketplace.

Why are strategic tasks not better defined? A common reason is that senior teams are uncomfortable about making tough choices. Each of the functional heads who make up the top management group of a business unit stands to gain or lose because of the strategic choices made. An emphasis on decreasing product cost will tend to tip the balance of power toward manufacturing; an emphasis on innovation will move power toward R&D. Vice presidents responsible for quality will push for increases in product reliability; those responsible for sales will be especially interested in increasing market share.

Many top teams tend to paper-over their differences, rather than directly confront hard trade-offs. The results are vague statements that incorporate too many strategic tasks or rely on numbers, but provide little direction to the larger organization. They allow each functional head to pursue his or her own objectives. Not surprisingly, the response of employees is strategic confusion.

Is the Rest of the Organization Clear and in Agreement on the Strategic Tasks?

Communicating a business's strategic tasks allows those responsible for implementation to work from a common strategic story. This story explains to individuals and groups how their job activities are contributing to critical work processes, and how the quality of these processes in turn relates to long-term success in the marketplace. These tasks help guide action when unforeseen problems arise.

Defined strategic tasks do not and should not eliminate conflict. Discussions can be quite contentious when different parties debate how the strategy applies in particular circumstances. Strategic focus on product development at Honeywell increased the debate among engineering, marketing, and production at the top and within product development teams.

Short-term financial pressures, a reality in most organizations, can cause senior managers to act in ways perceived as inconsistent with accomplishing strategic tasks. Well-articulated strategic tasks can, however, force a debate about inconsistencies. Lower levels have a basis for challenging managerial action. Senior managers are given an opportunity to explain why they are deviating from strategy. Because they know that large inconsistencies will cause them to lose credibility, managers are pushed to consider closely the logic behind a chosen course of action. If convinced that their course is still correct, senior managers are in a better position to explain to employees the complex set of business pressures that has made a "temporary detour" necessary.

As this discussion suggests, the articulation and communication of strategic tasks have the potential to change the fundamental relationship among various parts of an organization. Without a shared understanding of strategy, those at lower levels have little choice but to do as they are told. Conversely, when a shared understanding exists, individuals at lower levels have a basis for challenging the actions of their managers: Are they consistent with the stated organizational strategy?

The importance of developing a common understanding of strategic tasks depends on the strategy to be implemented. Strategies that can be implemented by only a few people at the top of the firm—asset rationalization, and portfolio management, for example—do not require the knowledge and commitment of others and therefore do not have to be widely understood. Improving quality or customer service, on the other hand, depends on the competence, commitment, and coordination of many individuals and groups. Consequently, a much wider circle of individuals and groups must have a shared understanding of the strategic tasks and how they fit into competitive realities.

We caution, however, that even in cases of corporate restructuring, the larger organization's understanding of the reasons for top management's actions is helpful. After the restructuring is completed, management will still have to run a business. If employees understand the rationale for difficult decisions made by senior management, they are more likely to emerge from the restructuring with their morale and effectiveness intact.

ORGANIZATIONAL CAPABILITIES

The key questions that must be answered here are:

- Does the business unit have the appropriate levels of coordination or teamwork among functions, suppliers, and customers that are needed to accomplish the strategic task?
- Do the members of the organization have the necessary technical and managerial competence to accomplish the task?
- Do the key functions and levels have the level of commitment that is necessary to accomplish the strategic task?

Making the strategy clear and developing commitment to it are necessary first steps. They are not enough, however. Successful strategy implementation requires organizational capabilities. Managers in Honeywell's CAvD knew that product development was the key to their success, but this knowledge did not enable them to develop products at the cost and speed required. Knowing the strategy merely identifies the competitive game. It does not determine whether it is a game that the organization knows how to win. Winning depends on three critical organizational capabilities:

1. *Coordination.* Few sources of sustainable competitive advantage can be realized through the efforts of any one function. Knowledge and expertise can be bought, but the capability of the organization to implement strategy through teamwork among different parts of the organization cannot be purchased at any price. At Honeywell's CAvD, product development was impeded by a lack of teamwork among engineering, production, and marketing, and this discord was a reflection of a lack of teamwork at the top of the division.

2. *Competence.* Successful strategy implementation requires two types of competence: (a) technical/functional and (b) managerial. Honeywell's CAvD required and had engineering talent to solve technical problems. Highly competent engineers were not enough, however; for the functions to coordinate their efforts effectively, managerial and interpersonal competencies were needed at the top and lower levels. John Dewane's top team in CAvD had to develop new competence in resolving conflict constructively. They set out to do this through a number of off-site team-building

meetings with an outside facilitator. They also had to develop skills and methods for prioritizing programs and allocating resources across programs. Lower-level employees needed to develop skills in project management and group decision making in order to implement programs.

3. *Commitment*. Effective teamwork at lower levels cannot be ordered from the top. It can only come about when employees are willing to work cooperatively with each other to do "the right thing." In CAvD, engineers had to become interested in meeting customer needs as opposed to making technological enhancements to the product. Production workers had to learn to take initiative in identifying quality and cost improvement opportunities, and to communicate these to engineering and other relevant departments whose cooperative effort was needed to realize them.

Coordination, competence, and commitment are all needed to implement strategy. A deficit in any of them will lead to failure. The problem is not unlike the challenge facing basketball coaches. Players with the right skills are needed (competence), but they must also understand how to play as a team (coordination), and they must possess the dedication to win (commitment).

When failures of strategy implementation occur, one or more of the three strategic capabilities is inevitably lacking. Like Honeywell's CAvD, companies seeking to decrease time to market for new products often create cross-functional product development teams. After teams are created, however, they are apt to discover that team effectiveness is undermined by low commitment to the new organization from strong functional heads whose authority is threatened. They also may find out that effective teamwork requires competence typically not developed in a strongly functional organization. Skills in project management, conflict resolution, and leadership are missing.

The simultaneous need for coordination, competence, and commitment was dramatically illustrated by events at Kodak in 1993. To improve lagging performance, Chris Steffan was brought in as the company's Chief Financial Officer (CFO). The news of Steffan's joining Kodak led to an increase in the market value of the company's stock of over $2 billion. According to the financial press, shareholders felt that Steffan brought the necessary competence to improve the company's bottom-line results. They also interpreted his hiring as a signal that the senior management of Kodak had the necessary commitment to engage in the painful work of restructuring. Three months later, Steffan resigned from Kodak and the company's stock fell dramatically. What the financial analysts hadn't seen was that, as an outsider, Steffan was unable to develop the level of coordination or teamwork with Kodak's executives that was necessary to implement the changes he proposed.

What is a manager to do when confronted with a deficit in coordination, competence, or commitment? To determine the most appropriate course of action, deficits in organizational capabilities must be traced back to their root causes.

ORGANIZATIONAL LEVERS

Figure 12–1 shows five organizational design levers that strongly influence the development of the capabilities needed to implement strategy:

1. The organization of work.
2. The amount of influence that different levels, parts, and functions of the organization have on decisions.
3. The flow of people into, upward within, and out of the organization.
4. The information, rewards, and measurement systems.
5. The leadership of the general manager and her or his top team.

The role of these levers in causing lower-than-desired levels of coordination, competence, and commitment is analyzed in the following subsections.

The Organization of Work

- How does each of the following either support or hinder accomplishing the strategic tasks?
  —The formal organizational structure.
  —The existence and quality of cross-boundary teams to integrate parts of the organization.
  —The specification of individual roles, responsibilities, and relationships.

The Formal Organizational Structure

The formal organizational structure has a major impact on organizational levels of coordination, competence, and commitment. Because functional organizations encourage specialization, people in such organizations develop high levels of skills in their particular function or technical specialty, but a narrow perspective in their approach to business problems. In these organizations, individuals often progress from job to job within one function. This career progression does little to provide managers with the general management orientation or interpersonal and conflict management skills needed to manage outside of the formal chain of command.

Narrow job descriptions also can lead to problems of commitment. They can rob employees of the sense of meaning and accomplishment that comes from completing a whole task. This is particularly true at lower levels of the organization—on the manufacturing floor or in the back office of a bank. Problems in motivation and cooperation experienced in these organizations often arise from exceedingly narrow work. The results can be low productivity and poor customer service. This syndrome of problems has given rise to methods for reexamining the design of jobs. Professors Hackman and Oldham[10] provide a framework that managers can use to systematically analyze how to increase the motivating potential of a job.

The narrow perspective encouraged in functional organizations makes it difficult to create the cross-functional coordination required to accomplish many strategic tasks. When problems emerge between R&D and manufacturing, or marketing and sales, the general manager emerges as the only individual with the formal authority to resolve them. This is the problem John Dewane faced at Honeywell. Recurring conflicts between manufacturing and R&D could only be solved by him. He had limited time and expertise, however, to make decisions for all new product developments in two different businesses—business aviation and commercial aviation.

John Dewane might have solved his problem by decentralizing his division into separate business units for business aviation and commercial aviation. Decentralized organizational structures make it easier to coordinate around key tasks; a corporation divided into a set of focused business units is more apt to be responsive to the needs of distinct market segments than one that is functionally organized. That is why the CAvD was set up by Honeywell in the first place.

However, decentralized organizations also have their costs—in potential duplication of resources, as well as in the breakdown of coordination among decentralized units. Instead of one marketing, R&D, and manufacturing director, Honeywell's CAvD would have had several. It is unlikely that each of the functions would have been able to develop or afford the depth of expertise that was available in the previous organization.

Expense is not the only cost of decentralization. Decentralization facilitates coordination within each of the new business units, but coordination between units is made more difficult. For example, some airplane manufacturers make both business and commercial airplanes. Had two divisions been formed by John Dewane at Honeywell, they would have had to coordinate their selling and customer service efforts. Because the navigation devices for commercial and business airplanes are very similar, it would have made no sense to create two factories. A common plant—a shared resource—for two divisions would have caused serious coordination problems.

The Existence and Quality of Cross-Boundary Teams to Integrate Parts of the Organization

As the above examples demonstrate, the functional organization is good at developing specialization but incurs problems of focus and coordination as the organization develops new products and enters new markets. The decentralized organization solves problems of focus and coordination, but incurs problems of cost and creates potentially new problems of coordination across business units—particularly when resources must be shared. Neither organizational structure is perfect.

When growth requires the organization to focus on multiple products and markets, but it cannot afford decentralization, another solution must be found. Increasing competition is forcing more companies into this position.

To deal with this complexity, formal functional and decentralized organizational structures are often supplemented by *ad hoc* mechanisms such as cross-functional teams. The new product development teams created by John Dewane were an overlay on the functional structure. Team members retained their functional affiliation and reporting relationship but took on a new affiliation and accountability as business or product team members. Teams can span larger and more complex organizations. For example, the Becton Dickinson Corporation is organized into two worldwide sectors, one for medical diagnostic devices and the other for medical devices such as insulin syringes, hypodermic needles, and blood collection tubes. Because of the importance of differences in national markets, each sector is divided into a set of geographically based product divisions. An important strategic opportunity for Becton Dickinson lies, however, in transferring product technology developed in the United States to overseas divisions. To facilitate this overseas transfer, the corporation has created worldwide teams for each major product family. The teams consist of the regional division presidents in each geographic area. Their job is to develop a worldwide strategy to coordinate R&D and manufacturing.

In the 1970s, many companies formalized the notion of teams through the matrix structure. Members of teams reported to both functional bosses and the product or business team leaders. Without the right attitudes and skills and reinforcement by the organization's culture, many found the structure difficult to implement and abandoned it. As companies are forced by competition to develop the attitudes and skills needed to make ad hoc teams work, the matrix structure may reappear as an option.

The Specification of Individual Roles, Responsibilities, and Relationships

Even if the appropriate formal organizational structure or cross-functional teams are in place, the intended levels of teamwork, commitment, and coordination may not necessarily result. Formal organizational charts and cross-functional team rosters are too crude to capture the complex patterns of coordinated behavior required in any successful business. A parallel problem exists in professional basketball. A team's roster tells the players who is playing at center, at forward, and at guard, but this barely begins to specify each player's role, or how they need to work with one another to have a winning team.

Coordination breakdowns commonly occur when individuals are not clear about their roles, responsibilities, and relationships, and/or have not accepted them. For example, in the Communications Products Division of a real company we will refer to as Alpha Corporation, product development teams were initiated to decrease time to market for the business's high-speed modems. However, a year after the teams began work, managers were frustrated that the organization seemed to be no more productive than it had been in the past. The problem was that the teams existed only on paper; the roles and responsibilities of the key players who had to make the system work—the team leaders, team members, and functional heads—had not been clearly defined and accepted. For example, members of the organization were still struggling with these questions:

1. Who should have the responsibility for committing functional resources— the team representatives for a functional area or the functional head?
2. Who should be responsible for evaluating the performance of a functional representative on a team—the team leader or the functional head?
3. What should be the role of team leaders? Should they be facilitators of the team's efforts or the individuals who have primary responsibility and accountability for driving for results?

Unless these difficult questions of roles, relationships, and responsibilities are clarified, even the most elegant organizational design is unlikely to achieve its intended effects. The answer is not job descriptions. Instead, organizational members must meet to discuss their perceptions of roles and negotiate them. A typical tool used to facilitate this process is the responsibility matrix. For each anticipated decision, functional heads, team leaders, and team members must agree on who will have the authority to make the decision, who must be consulted, and who must approve.

Influence

Are Decisions Made with Appropriate Influence from All Relevant Functions in the Organization?

One of the most subtle, yet powerful factors affecting the success of strategy implementation efforts is the pattern of organizational influence—what individuals or groups have a say in decisions. To the extent that those who know the most have the most to say in decisions, the organization is able to make the best possible use of the competence it possesses to get the job done. Consider the case of Apple Computer Inc. The influence of technical people in R&D was so high in 1988 that their desire for technical superiority resulted in a 22-pound laptop computer that few customers wanted. Apple's marketing unit, which knew that light weight was favored by customers, did not have sufficient influence. Moreover, had the marketing people had more influence on the decision, they would have been more committed to it. The result would have been better implementation of marketing plans.

Changes in strategic task usually require changes in patterns of influence across functions as well as across levels. The new emphasis on rapid development of new products that can be manufactured at competitive costs required Honeywell's CAvD to boost the amount of influence production and marketing had on decisions. As many companies struggle to become less inwardly focused and more oriented toward customer needs, they find that there is a need to shift relative influence from the previously dominant manufacturing and

R&D functions toward marketing and sales. That is what happened at Apple after 1988. The shift in influence helped the company develop a stream of new, attractive, lower-cost products in 1990.

Are Decisions Made with Appropriate Influence from All Organizational Levels?

When the implementation of the strategic task requires delegation of authority to lower organizational levels, upper levels must relinquish power. For example, at Honeywell's CAvD, the introduction of cross-functional product development teams, composed of engineers, middle managers, and, in some cases, production workers, required functional heads to remove themselves from day-to-day decision making. This transformation occurred at CAvD, but other organizations have not had the same success. The problem is that functional managers have difficulty giving up influence they have had in the past.

These problems were well-illustrated in the new product development teams established at Alpha's Communications Products Division. Although the teams existed on paper, they were not able to accomplish very much. Team meetings were frustrating and inconclusive because of functional heads who prevented their representatives from making commitments for their function. Very quickly, the team leaders discovered that if something had to get accomplished in manufacturing or R&D, the person to speak to was not the functional representative but the functional head. Because the functional heads refused to allow team leaders a role in the performance appraisal of team members, team leaders had little recourse when functional representatives did not complete team responsibilities on time or failed to attend meetings.

When external consultants informed the senior team of these problems, team members acknowledged their unwillingness to cede authority. Although they had been frustrated by their work overload before the teams were formed, they found it difficult to relinquish authority for decisions. If they delegated decision-making responsibility to the teams, what would be left for them to do? What would this mean for their careers? Their perception that corporate management was evaluating them on their knowledge of business details did not help them overcome these fears.

Assessing mismatches between levels of influence and the demands of the strategic task is not easy. Assumptions about the level of influence certain functions and levels of the organization should have tend to be deeply ingrained. It is also natural to assume that the most influential functions and people have the greatest level of competence. This assumption is reinforced by a natural tendency for the most competent individuals in an organization to gravitate to functions that have traditionally been the most influential.

Close examination of the management approaches taken by those in other companies can be valuable in coping with the issues of power. John Dewane, his managers, and union leaders were impressed by what they saw at the Chandler plant—a high-performing, team-based plant within Honeywell. Many companies have been helped to improve union–management relationships by sending joint union and management groups to visit Japanese companies, where they have developed insights into a different model of influence.

Personnel Flows

Do Individuals in Key Organizational Positions Have the Appropriate Skills and Abilities?

Personnel flows—the systems for hiring, promoting, and developing employees —have a vital impact on an organization's ability to implement its business strategy. If these systems have been effectively managed, they provide the organization with a core resource—a supply of talented and motivated employees—that will facilitate the implementation of virtually any business strategy. Corporations such as General Electric have prospered in a range of different industries on the strength of their recruitment and management development practices.

However, most managers have relatively little control over these broad corporate systems. They face a more immediate problem. Implementing a new strategic direction requires key organizational players to act in very different ways on the job. A definition of a new organizational design may specify the behaviors required, but employees often do not have the competence to enact these behaviors. When confronted with these gaps in skills and motivation, executives must make a difficult assessment: Can key managers be developed or do they need to be replaced? Managers have available to them a number of techniques for assessing managerial skills and competence, ranging from observation of on-the-job behavior to off-site assessment centers or paper-and-pencil tests. Placing people in new roles is often the best place to start: It offers the most credible test of their capacity to learn, and it makes visible to them and to management the skills and attitudes they must develop. New, additional assessment and training can be more helpful. If they do not show the capacity to learn, they can be removed without doubts about the justice of the decision.

What Types of Attitudes and Behaviors Does the Management Succession Process Reward?

Promotion decisions made over time send strong signals to employees about what is valued. It will be very difficult to gain wide-scale commitment to the new behavior required to implement a new strategy, if the old criteria for promotion remain in place. This is an area where it is critical to look not at what an organization says, but what its practices are. The CEO of a consumer products company was frustrated that business-unit managers were not moving faster into new products and markets. At the annual retreat for the company's top 100 managers, the CEO declared that more entrepreneurial and risk-taking managers were needed. Over drinks that night, the business-unit managers talked about how unlikely it was that they would heed the CEO's words. So long as those promoted continued to be only from mature businesses where it was easy to deliver high margins, there would be no incentive to take risks.

More generally, realigning an organization in a way that reduces career development and promotion opportunities makes it more difficult to develop commitment to change. Concerns about the consequences for their careers were an important reason for the unwillingness of the senior management team of the Communications Division of Alpha Company to share power with the new product development teams. Organizational changes prompted by a new strategy must therefore be examined from the point of view of the professionals and managers affected. In those cases where organizational realignment reduces layers of management, personnel systems may need to be modified to recognize and properly reward broadened job responsibilities and increased authority, in addition to hierarchical promotions. If internal opportunities do not exist, managers must be helped to find career opportunities elsewhere.

Many strategic changes require that the organization restructure and employees be laid off. Such reductions change the psychological contract between employees and the organization—they reduce loyalty and increase employee self-interest. How much help those laid off receive and how they are treated are key to the attitudes of survivors. The company's ability to redefine its psychological contract, from security in return for loyalty to personal and career development in return for high performance, will determine the commitment and the competence the company will be able to obtain in the future.

Information, Rewards, and Measurement Systems

Do the Information and Measurement Systems Provide the Data Needed to Monitor and Manage the Strategy Implementation Process?

Information and measurement systems are intended to provide the data that allow managers and other employees to assess how well they are doing in accomplishing the strategic task. Shifting strategic direction, without an appropriate information and measurement system, is about as easy as driving a car down a dark country road without headlights.

Westinghouse's Nuclear Fuels Division was a recent winner of the Malcolm Baldrige National Quality Award. Faced with reduced demand for nuclear fuel, the division managers had to sustain sales levels by increasing market share. They had no way to measure customer satisfaction, however, nor did they have operating measures that informed them early of quality problems.

Within a year of their quality improvement initiative, the division's top management team commissioned a quality task force to develop what came to be called "pulse points" for managing the health of the business—something financial measures provide only after it is too late. One pulse point was a quantitative measure of customer satisfaction obtained through structured interviews. Others were operating measures that informed management about the effectiveness and productivity of the manufacturing process. With participation of employees at all levels, improvement goals were set each year and reviewed monthly. Individuals on the general manager's staff were assigned responsibility for leading projects that would improve these measures.

When new strategy requires a major shift in patterns of coordination, it is safe to assume that changes in the organization's information system will be needed. The introduction of new product development teams may be a first step in creating the coordination needed to reduce time to market. But teams will be limited in their effectiveness unless the accounting system is modified to allow each team to track the costs of the functional resources it is utilizing, as well as the sales and the profitability of the products or services it produces. Measuring speed to market will also be necessary. The information and accounting systems of functional organizations do not typically consolidate data by product, customers, or market—only by function.

Initially, new information requirements can be met by informal efforts to consolidate existing information in a different way. Thus, changes may not require a major reworking of the formal MIS system. Eventually, however, formal systems have to be developed to provide the needed data and measures in a timely fashion.

Do the Measurement and Reward Systems Motivate Behavior That Supports the Strategic Tasks?

Information and measurement systems have a powerful effect on the levels of organizational commitment. Providing individuals with information on the consequences of their actions is a strong internal motivator for improving performance. Measurement systems also establish an organization's scorecard. They help managers figure out which actions on their part will be valued by the organization.

There is little doubt that actions that are measured and rewarded will occur more frequently than those that are not. Salespeople who receive higher commissions for selling certain items will be more apt to pitch these items to their customers. When these systems are out of alignment with the strategic direction of the organization, they can create substantial difficulties. For example, in a plant manufacturing drinking glasses, a barrier to improving quality was a bonus system that paid operators based on the quantity rather than the quality of the glasses produced. Many companies have found that financial incentive systems that emphasize individual divisional performance are a significant impediment to creating the cooperation needed to implement corporate strategies that span business units.

Do financial rewards have to be tied to performance measures and goals in order to motivate behavior? It is well-established that promising to pay for achieving certain goals will cause people to make an effort to achieve them.

Unfortunately, it will also cause them to focus so hard on achieving these goals that they may not always do what is required by unanticipated circumstances. There is also evidence that motivating through commissions and bonuses makes people compliant and reduces internal motivation and creativity.[11]

Given these problems, we believe it is generally better to use information, involvement, and measurement to motivate while making an effort to pay equitably. When management reviews performance against agreed-to measures and goals, people make a good-faith effort to achieve them. Accomplishment is rewarded through satisfaction from a job well done, recognition, and the prospect of career advancement. These inducements produce motivation without dysfunctional consequences. People must be paid fairly, consistent with their market value and performance, but this can be accomplished through long-term adjustments in their pay, through promotions, and by avoiding the risks associated with financial awards that are tightly coupled to results.

Leadership

Do the Actions of the General Manager and His or Her Top Team Reinforce Effective Performance of the Business's Strategic Tasks?

The organizational levers described above have a powerful impact on whether the coordination, competence, and commitment needed to implement strategy exist. Organizational design alone does not ensure that desired organizational capabilities will be developed, however. Bringing managers together on a committee does not necessarily mean they will be able to work together successfully. We have observed many instances in which organizations with similar strategic tasks used similar organizational designs to facilitate implementation of their strategy and achieved very different levels of success.

The difference is leadership—the behavior of the general manager and the top team. It is difficult for managers at middle levels of the organization to work together effectively when the heads of their functions are unable to reach a meaningful consensus, set priorities, or agree on the behavior they want to reinforce. Commitment at lower levels is also directly affected, as we illustrated earlier, by the amount of authority the senior group is willing to delegate.

Conversely, an effective general manager and top team can make up for flaws in organizational design by the actions they take. Consider the new plant manager of the glass plant discussed above. He inherited an organization in which the hot end and the cold end of the plant were at war with each other. He developed a cohesive top team first; then they, as a group, broke down some of the barriers to cooperation by serving as facilitators for regular shift meetings. The plant manager also spent a great deal of his time coaching managers on his staff. They in turn coached those at lower organizational levels on how to develop the competence demanded by the new organization. Shared commitment to improving quality was developed, despite the fact that the formal reward system, which rewarded productivity rather than defect reduction, was not changed. Managers in the plant reported that they were both working harder and having more fun since the new plant manager had taken over.

Top teams that do not share commitment to a common strategy and values cannot develop a shared diagnosis of the barriers to strategy implementation or a vision of how to organize and manage differently. Thus, the leader and the top team's cohesion and effectiveness are crucial in both organizational design and implementation of the design.

CORPORATE CONTEXT

To What Extent Do the Policies, Procedures, or Culture of the Larger Corporation Affect the Strategy Implementation Process?

A business unit cannot realign its organization with strategy without considering the corporate context in which it operates. It would have been far easier for John Dewane at Honeywell to realign his organization with strategy if he had not faced the constraints imposed by the Aerospace and Defense Group of which his division was a part. Procedures and systems developed for the defense business did not apply to the commercial business. Consider a general manager of an electronics business, where rapid product development must be led by the marketing function. The larger corporation imposed a control system that measured manufacturing plants on gross margin. Not surprisingly, plant managers were reluctant to introduce trial runs of new products in their plants. To do so would have interrupted their long manufacturing runs and reduced gross margin. Our research shows that often, the businesses that are most creative in redesigning their organization for effective strategy implementation are farthest from corporate headquarters. Awareness of the constraints imposed by the corporate context should not be used as an excuse for inaction. Short of freedom to do what is right for one's business, general managers must devise strategies for convincing corporate management to allow deviations. If this is not possible, they must exert the leadership needed to produce change despite corporate constraints.

We have described a systematic framework for diagnosing organizations. But how does a manager actually go about redesigning the organization and making changes? We began this chapter with the proposition that a partnership between management and members of the organization is crucial for the development of organizational capabilities, particularly commitment. Making partnership a reality, however, is very heavily dependent on the sequence of interventions—actions to change the organization—managers choose as they move change along. Should changes in formal organizational design be made first? Must people be replaced before any meaningful change can occur? How should these and other interventions be sequenced? The sequence chosen enables or limits the possibilities for partnership. We now turn to these crucial questions. How they are answered is every bit as important as the accuracy of the diagnosis and the elegance of the organizational design.

MANAGING CHANGE TOWARD THE NEW STRATEGICALLY ALIGNED ORGANIZATIONAL MODEL: THE PROBLEM OF SEQUENCING INTERVENTIONS

The analytic framework in the previous section provides a rigorous means for diagnosing how an organization is out of alignment with strategy. If the diagnosis is done in partnership with members of the organization, energy for change can be mobilized.

The manager is then faced with the question of what actions to take and how to sequence the actions chosen. Figure 12–2 presents a list of interventions or actions managers can take; they range from changing structure to replacing people and training new people. We have classified these interventions into those that require little or no change in formal organization and those that impact the formal structure, systems, and policies (top and bottom quadrants respectively). We have also classified the interventions into those that impact the organization as a whole and those that impact the individual or group (left and right quadrants respectively). The resulting two-by-two matrix provides the manager with clusters of intervention points. If partnership is to be the guiding principle for change, we argue for a sequence of interventions that approximates the sequence shown by the numbers in each quadrant of the matrix.

FIGURE 12–2   Sequencing interventions for learning.

		Level of Focus	
		Unit Level	Individual or Group Level
Intervention Seeks to Modify:	Informal Behavior	(1) Redefinition of roles, responsibilities, and relationships	(2) Coaching Counseling Training Process consultation Team building
	Formal Design	(4) Compensation system Information system Organizational structure Measurement system	(3) Replacement Recruitment Career pathing Succession planning Performance appraisal

The Design-Driven Approach to Change

The most common approach to realigning the organizational design with strategy is the design-driven approach depicted in Figure 12–3. Having had the benefit of their own or consultants' analysis and recommendations, most managers proceed to drive change by changing the formal organizational design. They begin with the hard organizational levers, such as the formal organizational structure, the financial incentive system, the individuals who are selected for certain key jobs, or the MIS system—the interventions in the bottom quadrants of Figure 12–2. It is assumed that these changes will lead in turn to needed modifications in organizational behavior.

The evolution of the Advanced Data Systems computer business, described in Box 12–2, illustrates the design-driven approach. In this instance, changes in the formal organization were used as the lever driving strategy implementation.

The Advanced Data case shows both the strengths and the weaknesses of the design-driven approach. In the original splitting of the mainframe and the services businesses, the structural change worked as expected—managers did focus their efforts more fully on growing the two separate businesses. However, it proved much harder to put "humpty dumpty"—mainframes and services—back together again.

Why? The reorganization enabled the two new business units to develop the appropriate levels of specialization each needed to prosper. Advanced Data's senior management realized that the strategies for success in the services business differed from those in the mainframe business and that each demanded different managerial skills. Further, the original structural change enabled the services managers in the field to focus on growing the services business, something to which they were already committed. It was experienced by them as removing an obstacle to their effectiveness, rather than as driving strategic change. It gave them freedom to act independently and develop their own identity, something human beings find far more rewarding than losing their identity and independence. Consequently, the design-driven approach to change—where formal structure and systems are changed first and, if needed,

FIGURE 12–3 The design-driven approach.

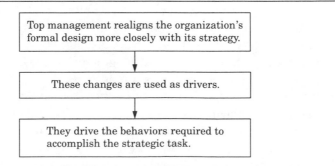

Top management realigns the organization's formal design more closely with its strategy.

These changes are used as drivers.

They drive the behaviors required to accomplish the strategic task.

Box 12–2

Advanced Data Systems

Advanced Data, our fictitious name for a real company, was a significant player in the mainframe computer business. Its computers were sold and installed by one of a number of geographically decentralized branch offices. In the 1980s, in addition to installing large computers, Advanced Data branches began to develop a services business, which provided customers with computer peripherals, contract maintenance, and support for either the company's own or other vendors' machines. Managers responsible for the services business were frustrated that they were being constrained by the dominant culture, which valued "pushing mainframes out the door" above all else. To encourage the growth of the services business, a separate computer services division was created in 1985. This organizational change proved successful, and the services business grew rapidly. The problem was that coordination between the services and mainframe divisions suffered. Common customers found themselves dealing with two competitive sales forces. Administrative and technical resources were unnecessarily duplicated.

To address these issues, the sales forces for the mainframe and the services businesses were reintegrated in 1989. In most cities, the branch manager for either services or mainframes was chosen to head the new integrated branch office. Advanced Data's senior management found, however, that if the mainframe manager got the top job, the services business tended to suffer, and if the services manager got the top job, the mainframe business usually took a back seat. The problem was that substantial differences in culture and perspective had developed between the two divisions. These differences were not easily overcome by a simple structural change.

---

people are replaced immediately—is an option when the redesign calls for specialization and focus.

However, many of the knotty strategic alignment problems facing organizations in the competitive environment of the 1990s require improvements in coordination between interdependent functions and units. The recombination of the services and mainframe businesses attempted to use a structural change to encourage closer coordination between two previously independent businesses, and had far less success than the first change. By selecting a mainframe or a services manager to head the new integrated business, the commitment of managers from the other business was diminished.

Like those at Advanced Data Systems, most formal design changes that attempt to improve coordination lead to losses in power, independence, and identity, and, consequently, to a loss of commitment. When those affected by the changes lose commitment, they are less likely to coordinate their actions and make their competence available to the organization. In the case of the changes at Advanced Data, the manager who was not chosen to head the newly combined business and his or her subordinates were underutilized by the manager who was chosen to run the combined organization. Moreover, lower-level managers on the losing side tended to be less committed and consequently were not actively working to make the integration a success.

Unfortunately, too many efforts to realign organizations make the mistake made by Advanced Data. Immediate changes in structure, rewards/information/measurement systems, or key executives result in losses that tear the fabric of the organization. The sense of partnership that may have existed is lost. That loss causes significant numbers of people to reduce their engagement in making change happen and in learning from it.

The Task-Driven Approach to Change

When coordination, as opposed to lack of specialization or focus, is the barrier to strategy implementation, getting the right people to work together on the right things in the right way is the key. This is difficult to do without developing a partnership that includes all key actors. In those instances where the design-driven approach to change destroys partnership and commitment, an alternative sequence of interventions must be employed. We call that approach the task-driven approach (see Figure 12–4).

The task-driven approach uses shared desire to implement strategy as the source of energy for change. It begins by developing a consensus among all relevant parties on the importance of accomplishing the strategic task. The top management team, often with the help of design teams composed of key employees or union leaders, then develops a new, strategically aligned model of the

FIGURE 12–4   The task-driven approach.

organization. That model does not specify changes in formal structure or systems. Instead, it defines an *ad hoc* organization—task forces, committees, and changes in management process at the top and lower levels, which bring the right people together to work on the right things at the right time, regardless of formal affiliation (quadrant 1 in Figure 12–2). Its aim is to improve coordination around the strategic task. Honeywell's Commercial Aviation Division started with this approach. Its general manager and his top management team committed themselves to a team-based organization recommended by a design team and elaborated by the core group.

If the right people have indeed been assigned to do the right thing, strategic tasks will begin to be implemented more effectively. Team members will begin to feel that they are making a difference where the former organization failed—a feeling that raises their commitment and enhances teamwork. As the new pattern of working together takes hold, new required competencies—skills in teamwork and problem solving, and a less parochial attitude—are developed on-line. If aided by coaching and training (quadrant 2 in Figure 12–2), learning is further enhanced. Training at an earlier point—before the new ad hoc organization is put in place—is hard for people to apply.

Honeywell's CAvD unit followed the sequence we have recommended here. Engineers, production managers and workers, and marketing representatives began to learn new attitudes and skills from their experience on teams. This learning was supported by six human resource specialists who sat in on early meetings and coached the teams, as well as by a training program in interpersonal communication. The general manager's top team utilized an outside consultant at several off-site meetings to facilitate the development of an effective team.

The organizational learning process that begins to unfold in this sequence is one to which people become increasingly committed, but it also exposes the capability of people to fit into the new pattern of management. It is inevitable that some people will be unable to learn rapidly enough—or at all. These are the people who will have to be replaced after a certain period of time. Their departure will be seen far differently than if they had been fired at the very beginning.

High-level replacement decisions, when they are made, do not just affect the competence level for an individual position; they also have symbolic value[12] for the larger organization. A decision to replace a senior manager can either energize an organization or demoralize it. Employees can either view the manager who makes the replacement decision as finally having the courage to confront a personnel problem that has been acting as a roadblock for the whole organization, or as "killing off" a valuable co-worker. If the sequence in Figure 12–2 is followed, the former perception is more likely to be true. By the time managers are moved, employees are committed to the new organization, and removal of employees who have not adapted is perceived as necessary and fair. Because personnel changes are occurring in a context of a now well-accepted organization, those who survive will not be left to argue over what the replacement decision implies about desired managerial behavior. The interventions in quadrant 3 of Figure 12–2 are therefore recommended after the organization and its people have had time to learn and adapt to the new pattern of management.

At Honeywell's CAvD, several staffing changes occurred between the first and second year of change. The operations manager, a member of the team, was helped by Dewane to see that he would not fit into the new pattern of management and was transferred. Several leaders of teams were ineffective and had to be replaced. Slowly, a new standard for hiring and promotion took hold in the division.

As the pattern of management proves itself effective (as it should, if it aligns with strategy), changes in the formal organizational levers can be made as needed (quadrant 4 of Figure 12–2). Now these changes simply ratify and reinforce behavior already learned. At CAvD, formal structure was modified organically as people left. The operations manager was not replaced and the structure flattened. The need for better information and a measurement system for new product development teams was becoming evident after two years, and plans were being made for these changes.

The task-driven sequence of activities maximizes readiness for change. There is more agreement in most organizations on the necessity for confronting core business problems than on the need for a structural reorganization or for personnel replacements. When changes in the formal organization are made, they come only after they have been identified as barriers to the new pattern of management. Similarly, personnel changes are made only after it is obvious to all that certain individuals will not or cannot change.

Despite the power of the task-driven approach, there are a number of reasons why it is not used more frequently. The first is that it takes a little longer than design-driven changes. Therefore, we do not recommend it for businesses on the verge of bankruptcy. We do, however, urge more managers to rethink the prevailing assumption that design-driven changes from the top are the only way to turn around a business. Honeywell's CAvD managed a dramatic improvement in profits in three years while also developing a more effective organization for the future.

Some managers do not use the task-driven approach for another reason. Often, the organization does not possess the competence needed to use such a process. The task-driven approach is quite dependent on the talents of the manager leading the process. Dewane's skill enabled a fractious group of managers on his staff to come together as a team.

Because the task-driven approach tends to depend on those currently in the organization (managers are not removed as a first step), managers typically fear that the resulting changes are likely to be only incremental. The changes at Honeywell, and at other organizations like it, disconfirm this assumption. When the leader is effective and the organization uses outside resources—visits to innovative organizations, advice from managers outside the company, and consultants with knowledge of innovation in other companies—frame-breaking change is possible using the task-driven approach.

CONCLUSION

The successful implementation of a business strategy requires both an accurate assessment of internal capabilities and the mobilization of a broad partnership to make needed changes in organizational structure and systems. This requires accurate and fact-based information that can flow freely up and down the organization.

This approach to strategy implementation is much easier to describe than to enact. It is easy to intellectually acknowledge the importance of getting at the fundamental and deep-seated barriers to strategy implementation, but actually surfacing and dealing with these issues are usually painful and uncomfortable. Similarly, many managers are not used to engaging in a rigorous causal analysis of the human barriers to strategy implementation. We have found that many of the managers who are most skillful in using the analytic tools of strategy formulation face the highest learning curve in taking a similarly dispassionate and logical approach to the emotionally messy issues that can arise during a discussion of how the organization needs to be realigned to implement strategy.

Even the most skilled managers cannot fully anticipate the consequences of the actions they set in motion during the change process. This makes strategy implementation less a linear sequence and more an iterative one, where certain organizational actions are taken, the consequences are assessed, and appropriate modifications are initiated. The iteration and interaction between diagnosis and action are the organizational learning process needed for continuous improvement. Only in this way can the organization augment its capabilities of coordination, competence, and commitment—the essential ingredients for strategy implementation—while also developing the capacity to make further adaptations when the competitive environment again demands them.

NOTES

1. See Michael Beer, Russell A. Eisenstat, and Ralph Biggadike, "Developing an Organization Capable of Implementing and Reformulating Strategy," Harvard Business School, Cambridge, MA, Working Paper, 1993.

2. The importance of partnership across functions in developing and honing capabilities is also clearly evident in the discussion of operating processes in Chapter 13.

3. Again, Chapter 13's discussion of operating processes is relevant here.

4. See Beer, Eisenstat, and Biggadike, cited in note 1.

5. See R. N. Ashkenas and T. Jick, "From Dialogue to Action in GE Work-Out: Developmental Learning in a Change Process," in *Organizational Change and Development,* JAI Press, Vol. 6, 276-287, 1992, for further information on GE's workout program.

6. David Halberstam, *The Best and the Brightest* (New York: Penguin, 1983).

7. Chapter 15 explores in great depth the difficulties involved in breaking out of a long-held paradigm and how a paradigm pervades an organization's way of doing things.

8. Dan Dennison, *Corporate Culture and Organizational Effectiveness* (New York: John Wiley & Sons, Inc., 1990) demonstrates that employee survey data correlate with financial performance in future years.

9. These work or operating processes are the central focus of Chapter 13.

10. Richard Hackman and Greg Oldham, *Work Redesign* (Reading, MA: Addison-Wesley, 1980).

11. See Alfie Cohen, "Why Incentive Systems Cannot Work," *Harvard Business Review* (September–October 1993), 54–63.

12. The power of symbols as signals of change is discussed and illustrated in Chapter 15.

REFERENCES

Argyris, Chris, *Overcoming Organizational Defenses: Facilitating Organizational Learning* (Needham, MA: Allyn and Bacon, 1990).

Beer, Michael, Bert Spector, Paul R. Lawrence, D. Quinn Mills, and Richard E. Walton, *Managing Human Assets* (New York, NY: The Free Press, 1981).

Beer, Michael, Russell A. Eisenstat, and Bert Spector, *The Critical Path to Corporate Renewal* (Cambridge, MA: Harvard Business School Press, 1990).

Beckhard, Richard and Rubin T. Harris, *Organizational Transitions: Managing Complex Change* (Reading, MA: Addison-Wesley, 1987, 2nd Ed.).

Galbraith, Jay, *Organization Design* (Reading, MA: Addison-Wesley, 1977).

Hackman, J. Richard, Ed., *Groups that Work (and Those that Don't): Creating Conditions for Effective Teamwork* (San Francisco, CA: Jossey-Bass, 1990).

Hackman, J. Richard and Greg Oldham, *Work Redesign* (Reading, MA: Addison-Wesley, 1980).

Lawrence, Paul R. and Jay W. Lorsch, *Developing Organizations: Diagnosis and Action* (Reading, MA: Addison-Wesley, 1969).

Nadler, David A., Marc S. Gerstein, Robert S. Shaw and Associates, *Organizational Architecture: Designs for Changing Organizations* (San Francisco, CA: Jossey-Bass, 1992).

Schaffer, Robert H., *The Breakthrough Strategy: Using Short Term Successes to Build the High Performance Organization* (Cambridge, MA: Ballinger, 1988).

STRATEGIC CHANGE: RECONFIGURING OPERATIONAL PROCESSES TO IMPLEMENT STRATEGY

13

Ellen R. Hart

Gemini Consulting

Had the CEO of Woodbridge Papers[1] applied conventional wisdom when he was called in to resolve an ongoing dispute between his manufacturing and marketing people, he probably would have put his company right out of business. Here's the situation he was supposed to resolve: the marketing people couldn't say "No" when customers asked for custom, rush, and special orders. Every time one of those orders was accepted, it threw off the entire production scheduling system and cost thousands of dollars in machine setups.

As a result, the orders sabotaged the manufacturing division's operational goals. Worse, they boomeranged for marketing because customers placing regular orders often experienced delays when the production system tried to digest the special orders. Frequently, the special orders also were delivered late, and they were unprofitable to boot. Customers were griping and managers were frustrated.

Manufacturing offered a solution. It noted that Woodbridge's largest competitor had a much smaller product line—just 140 items—and, as a result, delivered orders much faster. "If we were to streamline our unwieldy product line from 440 to fewer than 200, and install a new production scheduling system," the manufacturing people argued, "we could match that delivery time and recapture customers."

Marketing couldn't come up with a forceful counterproposal. On the surface, manufacturing appeared to have defined the problem and offered the right solution.

This conflict between manufacturing and marketing had its roots in legitimate issues. But all the finger pointing over who was to blame was striking evidence of the poor relationship that exists in many companies between managers who are close to the customer and managers who drive operations. In some firms, the two groups barely communicate. In the past few years, more and more companies have recognized that such disconnects are destructive. Recently, a few organizations have learned how to unite into powerful market-focused systems. The first step is to abandon a purely functional view of operations. The next step is to imbue the organization with an integrated view of business processes—processes driven by the market.

In the case of Woodbridge, for example, a seemingly reasonable strategy might have been to streamline its product line, quit accepting those irksome special orders, and match the competitor's delivery time. What Woodbridge did instead was to define a strategy based on the needs of customers for special services. It developed business processes that delivered both standard and custom orders reliably and profitably. This entailed first understanding the precise requirements of specific customers, and then mastering processes for meeting these needs. With this approach, customers' special orders were no longer considered disruptions to Woodbridge's operations; instead, they were recognized as a source of its strategic advantage.

Remember that company with the quick delivery but standard product line that was seemingly such a fearsome competitor? Once Woodbridge got its act together, the competitor's market share eroded so badly that it elected to exit the business.

The goals of this chapter are to:

- Explain the concepts and practices involved in forging powerful linkages between strategy and core business processes.

- Discuss the evolution in operations management from approaches grounded in functional perspectives to approaches grounded in business processes.

- Distinguish between core business processes and supporting processes.

- Provide a framework for the analysis, planning, and implementation necessary to reconfigure operations and align them with the needs of the customer.

- Learn how traditional organizations change to prepare themselves to design and implement processes capable of generating significant competitive advantages.

PROCESS REDESIGN USED TO ADDRESS ONLY PRODUCTION

From the industrial revolution to as recently as ten years ago, most companies viewed and managed corporate strategy, operations, information technology, and human resources separately. This was a legacy of the Frederick Taylor theory that specialization by each functional group—and the responsibility of each function for only its part of the business process—created efficiency. To the extent that major process redesign initiatives took place, they typically involved fixing only production processes. Production costs, however, typically represent less than 10 percent of total costs. Information technology was viewed merely as a way to mechanize or automate existing ways of working, particularly production processes, not as a way to promote communication among the functions.

In the past few years, many companies have mounted initiatives to streamline other functional processes. Unfortunately, many effective tools and programs for improving processes—benchmarking, best practices, business process redesign (BPR), total quality management (TQM), continuous improvement,[2] and the Baldrige Award[3]—often inadvertently reinforce an incremental approach. In many organizations, the theory seems to be: Fix the parts and somehow the whole will improve. Every company should strive to continuously improve its operations, but such an approach seldom results in sharp jumps in performance or creates competitive advantage. Such incremental fixes may simply keep a company focused on its neck-and-neck competition in a narrow area.

Recently, there has been a growing awareness of the limitations of such functionally driven and vertically organized companies. Although they can optimize the performance of individual functional activities, they tend to focus on the missing piece rather than on the whole puzzle. Moreover, they lack the kind of strategic cohesion that provides a meaningful framework for management.[4] Understandably, it's hard for specialists in finance, procurement, human resources, or transportation to be perfectly sure what it means for them personally when the strategy is: "To be the premier provider of _____ and do it profitably." As a result, individual or departmental decisions can easily be at odds with others made within the organization. The compelling evidence of such a lack of common purpose at Woodbridge was the direct conflict between marketing and manufacturing tactics.

What Changed?

There has recently been a revolution in expectations of both strategy and business operations, and in understanding of the power of the linkages between them. The heightened emphasis on forging powerful links between strategy and processes is driven by a number of factors:

- *The nature of competition has changed drastically.* There are simply more and smarter competitors who can replicate virtually any one-dimensional competitive advantage a company develops—turnaround time, quality, product line, cost. Increasingly, a company has to compete along multiple dimensions.[5]

- *The window of time available to a company to execute its strategy is shorter.* The reaction to intelligence or signals from the marketplace must be virtually instantaneous and pervasive. Whole organizations have to be aligned in ways consistent with the shifting requirements of the market-place. The management of individual functions provides too narrow a horizon for this objective.

- *Smarter workers are available, and they have smarter tools to assist them.* Every ounce of talent in an organization must be harnessed productively and synergistically. Usually, the value-added output of an organization is complex and emanates from a group or a process; it seldom resides solely in an individual. Moreover, organizations may achieve high performance in specialized functional subparts, such as engineering, marketing, or production, but they typically perform much less well—from the customer's point of view—in the hand-offs between functions. Process-oriented management allows the organization to maximize functional interdependencies and outputs.

- *Many processes were designed before there were advanced computer and communications capabilities.* Today, however, information technology (IT) can be the vehicle through which intra- and interorganizational and customer linkages are achieved. Rather than simply automating or facilitating business processes, IT can fundamentally alter how and where business is conducted.

- *Financial results are the byproduct of market performance.* Customer-focused performance provides unity to the organization, creates a framework for operational decisions, and is the driver of financial performance.

We expect any organization's strategy to be tied to real marketplace opportunities and to be articulated so that it provides meaningful guidance to the organization. "Earning a 15 percent return on assets for our shareholders" is a financial objective, not a meaningful statement of strategy. In comparison, "Putting a Coke within arm's reach of everyone" is a powerful statement of strategy. Strategy should determine how a business actually works to deliver value, and the value an organization delivers is the output of its business processes.

A Focus on Processes, Not Functions

Departments or functions used to be defined in terms of the functionality or utility they provided to the organization. For example, marketing was defined by its ability to generate customers; production, by its ability to create products; and sales, by its ability to generate orders. But organizations suffer when each function blindly pursues its own goals. For example, sales might take unprofitable orders to hit sales targets; marketing may accept variations from the standard product, which production can accommodate only with great effort; production may miss delivery commitments in the interest of reducing costs. Often, one function in the company is powerful enough to demand the lion's share of the resources. When this happens, eventually the other functions become starved for investment and perform poorly; as a result, the organization's competitiveness is impaired.

THE ALTERNATIVE: A PROCESS-BASED APPROACH

The standard definition of a business process is: an ordering of activities or tasks, over time, which takes an input, adds value to it, and provides a specific output. The new process-based approach to business reorders activities into a horizontal flow of suppliers, processes, and customers, where each department or area aligns its objectives with those of its neighbors to deliver maximum customer satisfaction.

In the past, many firms organized themselves into systems that were finely tuned to increase the ease and convenience of the internal organization, not the customer. This reflects functional thinking. The new emphasis is on customer-oriented processes, not functions. The changing names that organizations are giving to their core processes reflect this customer-focused shift. For example, the process of "product realization" could include not only the way a product is developed, but the way it is marketed and serviced. The process of "order to delivery" helps focus on the customer order, not the multiple departments or entities it must pass through to be fulfilled. Some other examples of core business processes include: concept to market, customer acquisition, loan processing, postsales service, claim adjudication, and reservation handling.

In Figure 13–1, core business processes are the organizing principle for delivering value to strategically selected customers. This principle is often easier to describe than to implement because we are in the midst of changing our conception of how organizations and businesses work. The bricks-and-mortar control/command models are becoming obsolete more rapidly than replacement models are being introduced. Nonetheless, to increase the likelihood that their strategy will be effectively implemented, leaders need to focus more on the processes that control the value companies deliver to their customers.

FIGURE 13–1   Core business processes—the engine.

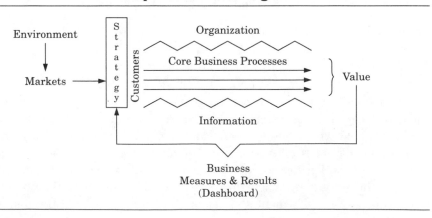

Intracompany Processes

Fedex Innovates Twice

Federal Express is an example of a company that defines its strategy in terms of a customer value and builds business processes that are derived from and linked to the customer. Federal Express's strategy is to provide speedy and reliable delivery of packages. Every process within the organization has been designed to achieve this objective. This is why Federal Express decided to locate one hub in Memphis and to centralize all shipments there. This is also why the company decided that owning its own planes was the only way to achieve the desired level of service, in spite of the huge investment that this fleet represents. In mapping out the company, Federal Express rewrote the rules of its industry. Rather than look for ways to mechanize and improve on traditional methods of sorting and delivering mail, it combined changes in infrastructure, information technology, and traditional processes (that is, distribution and logistics) in new ways to create a market.

By 1990, however, a one-size-fits-all approach to the express courier business was no longer sufficient. As customers became more sophisticated and their expectations increased, a second market segment started materializing. It cared less about speed and was willing to trade off the "before 10:30 the next day" delivery promise for a "within the next day" delivery and a lower price. Federal Express had to reevaluate its strategy and realign its business processes to capture this market segment. Had Federal Express only improved on its traditional delivery process to handle increased volume along the dimensions of speed and reliability (that is, simply undertaken a total quality or continuous improvement program), it could have missed an entire customer segment.

GE Medical Systems

In the case of GE Medical Systems (GEMS), which is detailed in Table 13–1, the third, fourth, and fifth processes are most connected to today's customers, the first and second are focused on tomorrow's customers, and the sixth is focused on the company's internal organization. Mapping the business in this way makes it easier to allocate resources strategically.[6]

Industry Processes

The Fedex and GE examples illustrate intracompany processes. Let's look now at core business processes for whole industries. For example, within retailing, at least four major processes touch the entire value chain from supplier to distributor to store outlet to consumer, and most directly impact consumer needs for products, convenience, and price (see Table 13–2).

Although each of the core processes identified in Table 13–2 could be improved in isolation by each player in the chain, the potential for productivity

TABLE 13–1   Architecture at GEMS (GE Medical Systems) built on six basic processes.

1. *Advanced Technology:* The process of developing the basic technologies on which future products will rely.

2. *Offerings Development:* The design of products and services based on those technologies.

3. *Go-to-Market:* The identification of market needs—including individual national markets—and the fine-tuning of product designs to meet them.

4. *Order-to-Remittance:* Encompasses everything that gets done from the placing of the order to the delivery of the equipment, including sales, purchasing supplies, manufacturing, distribution, on-site installation, testing, billing, and collection.

5. *Service Delivery:* Providing repairs and upgrades to the installed base of GEMS machines.

6. *Support:* All the staff functions from finance to human resources to government relations.

and revenue improvement through cooperation across the chain is much greater. Just as intracompany advances require cooperation among company units—departments, functions, plants, regions—likewise, intercompany advances require the cooperation of industry players, for the good of the customers.[7] For example, in the introduction of new products, detailed point-of-sale information on consumer buying habits and tastes, collected by retailers, can allow the suppliers to identify the need for niche products or make valuable product refinements. In the replenishment dimension, the more synchronized the retail store, the distributor, and the supplier are in terms of real consumer demand, the more they can reduce inventory and capital costs across all three. This is a key intended benefit of the recent strategic alliance of Wal-Mart and Procter & Gamble (P&G).

The P&G/Wal-Mart Alliance

Wal-Mart, the retailer, is close to the customer; P&G operates in that same value chain, further upstream, as a manufacturer and supplier. Their core business processes, however, are driven by a similar mission—to get the right products to the customer. A critical business process to Wal-Mart is inventory management; a critical business process to P&G is order processing. Their performances are dependent on the same information: How quickly are Wal-Mart's

TABLE 13–2   Retail industry core processes.

1. Ensuring ease of shopping and optimum variety at retail level.

2. Replenishment (ensuring product is there when needed).

3. Communicating the value (creating demand and pull-through for the product).

4. Introducing new products.

consumers buying P&G products? As a result of their alliance, information connects the business processes of the two companies to track sales and ensure that the Wal-Mart customer doesn't have to go to Kmart to buy Tide.

This linkage of core business processes does not mean that the two companies have to operate in the same way, only that they share a resource—information—to support each other's business processes and anchor them to the customer. There is still room for cultural differences, language differences, and organizational differences between the corporations. Wal-Mart likes team management; P&G marches to the drums of hierarchical management. The salient commonality is that each knows what to do, and when, if a Wal-Mart store is running low on Tide.

In the preceding sections, we have described the customer orientation of a core business process perspective (see Table 13–3). In the next section, we will discuss the value-chain view and the holistic perspective this approach requires.

THE VALUE CHAIN AS A FRAMEWORK

Successful companies need a thorough understanding of their industries, not just their businesses. Maps of industry interrelationships reduce the complexity of, and provide a framework for, understanding the components of the business and making better decisions. The value chain charts the connection between the upstream and downstream components of the business and their relationships to one another.[8] Business processes organize the flow of an interrelated set of activities, information, and resources along the value chain and, in so doing, help achieve the strategy of individual organizations.

A company can choose to operate anywhere along an industry's value chain. The value chain in the oil and gas business, shown in Figure 13–2, starts with something as fundamental as Exploration (find oil), progresses to Exploitation (lift the oil out of the ground and transport and distribute it), and then to Acquisition/Disposition (manage the land, refine the oil, trade it, distribute it, and sell it to customers). A giant oil company such as Royal Dutch Shell or Exxon can choose to be in all of these businesses. The strategy of some smaller oil companies is to operate in only one or two parts of the value chain. Oryx Energy, for example, operates upstream and concentrates on exploration and production. Ashland Oil focuses on the refining stage. Southland operates downstream and concentrates on marketing and sales.

TABLE 13–3   Characteristics of a core business process perspective.

- Market-focused and linked.
- Value-chain view—how upstream activities drive downstream performance; inherently boundary-crossing.
- Holistic, interdependent perspective, optimizing the whole, not the part.
- Measurable; results not activity-oriented.

FIGURE 13–2   Simplified value chain of an integrated oil company.

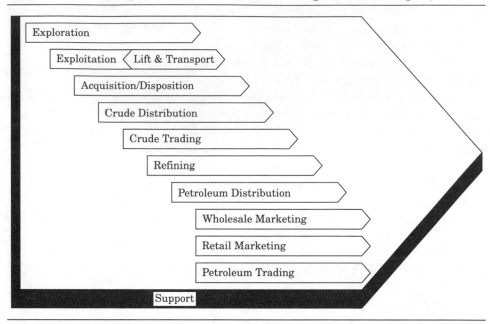

A tenet of strategic management is that a company should focus on the part of the value chain in which it can excel. Based on this criterion, the core or "mission critical" business processes of a company (for example, order fulfillment, new product development, sourcing, or customer service) should be readily apparent. Whether it operates in the services or manufacturing arena, a company usually has only a few truly critical business processes. Internal, support, or managerial processes are those primarily focused on internal customers (human resources, inventory control, records management, facilities management, budgeting). They do not typically provide the same level of leverage as core processes. In a case in point, a chemical company that mapped its improvement efforts, particularly information technology "fixes," against all its business processes was surprised to find that more than half its improvement efforts were focused on support or noncore processes. A wiser use of management resources would be to focus on re-engineering core processes instead.

A Systems or Holistic View

Strategically leveraging business processes has enormous implications for the business system as a whole. It requires a recognition that any meaningful change within the organization affects the entire organization. Without a systems view of core process redesign and aggressive targets, both the identification of the problem and the proposed solutions will often fix only symptoms. For example, an insurance company consistently exceeded the State Insurance Department's legal limit for processing claims. Its average processing time often exceeded 45 days; many claims took 70 to 80 days. The Insurance Department required the payment of interest if processing a claim exceeded 30 days. As a result, this insurance company faced fines and, more importantly, so much customer dissatisfaction that it was losing business to other insurance providers.

The company's initial assessment of the problem suggested several solutions: adding more people, computerizing the current people-intensive process, and creating special teams to deal with the difficult cases that slowed down overall processing. These corrective steps probably could have achieved the 30-day turnaround time.

The company looked beyond the immediate crisis and realized that a 30-day turnaround was not a good enough objective in its increasingly competitive marketplace. Instead of electing incremental improvement, it crafted a customer service and retention-focused strategy based on a better understanding of its customers, the value they were seeking, the causes of attrition, and the costs of acquiring new business. It articulated key performance objectives around the value it planned to provide, and created the processes that would achieve its goals. Although the effort involved many changes, the integrating concept was to organize customer account teams to handle every need of their assigned customers. Previously, the company had been organized functionally—enrollment, claims, billing—and customers' paperwork and phone calls were getting lost in the movement from one department to another.

A new one-stop approach to customer service was established. The company instituted organizational and process changes that enabled it to increase its customer retention rate dramatically and to handle greater volume without having to expand its resource base. New processes were linked to:

- An expert system to assist processing the majority of claims.
- A communications system that allowed direct customer input and response.
- Training in business issues, customer focus, and technical and group skills.
- A participative redesign and people-selection process.

Improved management priorities and reporting systems provided customer teams with reinforcement and feedback on their results, especially at the customer level. As a result, claims adjudication currently averages seven days and many claims are processed in 24 hours. Even more importantly, the process enhancements directly improved customer retention levels.

Business Process Improvement versus Core Business Process Reconfiguration

Nowadays, virtually all companies are involved in some kind of process change. Too often, the targets they set are far short of what they need to achieve a competitive advantage. At the same time, the world is not standing still while a company tinkers with improvements. How does a company know if it needs to undertake the giant step of reconfiguring core processes? There are at least three conditions that indicate the time is right to initiate a major reconfiguration:

1. There has been a pronounced shift in the market the process was designed to serve.
2. The company has found it is markedly below industry benchmarks on its core processes.
3. To regain competitive advantage, the company must leapfrog competition on key dimensions.

Figure 13–3 shows the potential range of impact from a process improvement approach to a core business process reconfiguration approach.

The effort to reconfigure business processes as a strategic activity requires a different mindset than that which is required in continuous improvement programs. Because companies have tended to overlook the powerful contribution that processes can make to strategy, they often undertake process improvement efforts using their current processes as the starting point. Without a fresh examination of customer needs, the analysis of processes and the selection of options will be based on time-honored ways of doing work. The next section describes a framework and the steps required if a company has determined that it must go beyond incremental improvement.

RECONFIGURING CORE PROCESSES: A FRAMEWORK

Seven broad steps are involved in reconfiguring business processes in alignment with strategy (see Figure 13–4). Both analytical and managerial components are necessary to align core processes to strategic objectives. The analytical steps build on each other; the managerial challenges—guiding the organization through change—overlay the entire process. The change model and approach

FIGURE 13–3   Business process redesign continuum.

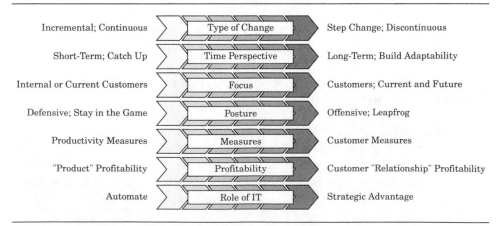

Incremental; Continuous	Type of Change	Step Change; Discontinuous
Short-Term; Catch Up	Time Perspective	Long-Term; Build Adaptability
Internal or Current Customers	Focus	Customers; Current and Future
Defensive; Stay in the Game	Posture	Offensive; Leapfrog
Productivity Measures	Measures	Customer Measures
"Product" Profitability	Profitability	Customer "Relationship" Profitability
Automate	Role of IT	Strategic Advantage

FIGURE 13-4   Reconfiguring core business processes.

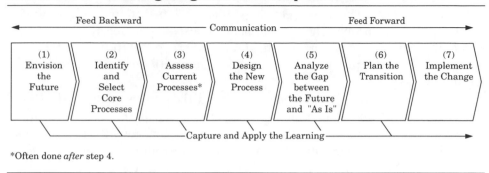

*Often done *after* step 4.

should be identified at the outset. Its essential components are: communication and learning.

The following sections describe the steps necessary to align strategy and core processes, the information each step should provide, and guidelines for accomplishing them.

Step 1: Envision the Future

To align strategy and processes, a company must create scenarios for the future that are unconstrained by current ways of thinking about the business. (See Figure 13–5.) The temptation, when looking toward the future, is to assume that the environment will develop along a linear trajectory; managers are most comfortable when markets progress in some predictable way from the present. Certain elements of the environment may, in fact, evolve in a predictable way; for example, it is indisputable that the Baby Boomers are aging. The real purpose in envisioning the future, however, is to speculate about revolutions in technology, customer preferences, and how a product could be created, delivered, or used.

When companies do not analyze the marketplace of the future, they risk losing major opportunities. A major telephone company invested considerable

FIGURE 13-5   Step 1: Envision the future.

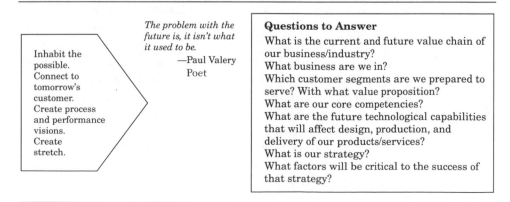

time and effort in redesigning one of its core business processes, order activation, without considering new technology. It revised its system for physically installing phones in people's homes—a labor-intensive approach that focuses on improving logistics and managing a field services group. All the while, the technology to activate the phones remotely—a cost-effective alternative—was within its grasp.

When IBM and Apple Computer studied the future in the early 1980s, they both saw skyrocketing potential for personal computers. Early PC users were sophisticated and extremely enamored of the inner workings of the machine. IBM assumed that future users would also be willing to master the electronic logic of the computer before using it. In contrast, Apple expected future customers to be indifferent to the intricacies of the computer's operating systems, but infatuated with using applications—the more the better, and often simultaneously. Both companies designed their strategies, products, and processes accordingly. Apple's view—ease of user interface, icon-driven "personal" computers—became the standard for subsequent hardware and software design. Later, when the Apple-like Windows© software environment became available, its eager adoption by IBM PC owners was another validation of Apple's earlier vision.

In designing processes for the future marketplace, it is crucial not to be hampered by existing ways of thinking[9] or be unable to differentiate between minor industry adaptations and major industry shifts. It is also necessary to take both an outside-in view (consider the "as yet to be realized" customers and the product/service value they will seek) and an inside-out view (what core competencies must be built to serve those future customers?)[10]

It is typically very difficult for an organization to adopt the outsider's view—either to evaluate itself fairly or to imagine the future unconstrained by current practices and norms. A range of perspectives should be sought as the vision of the future unfolds—including cross-functional perspectives from within the business as well as the perspectives of suppliers, distributors, franchisees, customers, and the ultimate end-user—customers' customers. It is also beneficial to seek out the view of a vertical cross-section of the organization—senior managers as well as the people closest to the work.

Breakthrough results[11] in processes are possible when designing a new product or service. The Saturn division of General Motors, for example, conceived of a future in which making the purchase of a car a pleasurable experience could be a critical success factor for the auto industry. Had Saturn not attempted to tinker with tradition, franchise arrangements, existing infrastructure, or tried-and-true marketing strategies, its revolutionary approach to selling cars would have been stillborn. Existing organizations have to approximate this kind of freedom and keep this dictum in mind: "Don't play for safety. It is the most dangerous game in the world."[12]

Following mergers or acquisitions, many companies try to mix or pick the best from each organization when redesigning their processes. However, because of heightened politics, what often occurs is a dilution that serves no one well. A major retail company, for example, decided to rely on certain common systems after a merger rather than retain what had historically been completely autonomous subsidiaries. The initial plan was to identify best practices throughout the enterprise, then select the information software that would best meet everyone's needs. After two years of work, managers were frustrated by their lack of progress and convened a senior group to figure out what was going on. The trouble they identified was that the original group had envisioned, as their charter, meeting every subsidiary's information needs. The retailer wound up with a system that was "plain vanilla with functionality that everyone wanted," but with no improvement over the past.

The group of senior managers learned that they had made at least three tactical errors:

1. Building from "as is" and from the inside out, they were guided by the current ideas about the business, not by the customer or by a vision of the future.

2. They tried to have lower-level people (who did not feel empowered to raise the broader questions) patch together a "consensus quilt" of a system, one in which conflicts were not resolved and breakthroughs were not the primary focus.

3. The strategic question of how the subsidiaries should intersect for their mutual advantage was not dealt with, primarily because it required a loss of perceived power by the subsidiary presidents. Since none of the essential issues or perspectives was challenged, the solutions, even if they had been implemented within the two-year frame, would have fallen far short of the synergy and productivity that could have been created.

Step 2: Identify and Select Core Processes

The identification and selection of core business processes must be preceded by an articulation of future strategy, the factors that are critical to the success of that strategy, and the sources of competitive advantage. (See Figure 13–6.) In other words:

- Here's the business we are in.
- This is the value we need to deliver to the customer.
- These are the business processes that must perform exceptionally well to deliver that "value proposition."
- These are the processes that, although valuable to our customers, can be offered more effectively by other partners.

An organization chart is a poor starting point for this kind of analysis because it is typically a graphic representation of the historic build-up of relationships between people and power. Organization charts do not reveal much about how a business should actually be run, only how relationships and resources have been demarcated in the past.

FIGURE 13–6   Step 2: Identify and select core processes.

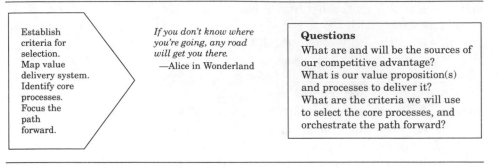

Establish criteria for selection. Map value delivery system. Identify core processes. Focus the path forward.

If you don't know where you're going, any road will get you there.
—Alice in Wonderland

Questions
What are and will be the sources of our competitive advantage?
What is our value proposition(s) and processes to deliver it?
What are the criteria we will use to select the core processes, and orchestrate the path forward?

. . . that not-yet-existing business is the best source of information for what the future organization should look like. *The best place to look for the basis of organization change is in the future business, and the worst place to look is in the current organization.* The present organization, however, may be a good predictor of what will *prevent* you from developing the kind of organization you will need. Like all creatures, it has a vested interest in continuing to exist.[13]

A company's strategic vision should provide guidance on which business processes are core. In advance, the company should spell out the criteria that will be used to select which processes are most significant—in other words, pick out processes that are most directly linked to the customer, that make a business unique, and that provide a meaningful competitive advantage, such as a potential for breakthrough performance.

Maps can help. Core business processes can be identified by drawing the value chain of the business, listing the expectations of customers who are served by each element of the value chain, and charting where the processes touch the customers and affect their perceptions of value.[14] This type of map conceptualizes the business as a value delivery system.

A value-chain map of the industry allows businesses to describe the larger business network, where boundaries of businesses are not fixed. Its ability to extend a critical business process view beyond intercompany boundaries allowed National Semiconductor to make important competitive headway—a strategic decision to establish assembly plants in Southeast Asia. The logistics and distribution aspects of its facilities would obviously be critical to the success of the entire venture. Rather than build its own capabilities to ensure reliable delivery of semiconductors, National Semiconductor contracted with Federal Express Business Logistics Services to store, inventory, and ship its goods. Immediately apparent were the direct net savings: National Semiconductor was able to close nine warehouses. More importantly, however, the contract provided the company with access to a level of excellence in logistics and distribution far beyond what it could have achieved on its own. It thus could leverage its excellent manufacturing process *and* Federal Express's excellent distribution processes.

Selectivity is important in pursuing an advantage through core business process redesign. Improvements can be eked out on multiple fronts, but time and focus are critical to achieving significant results and managing change. Some experts in process management think there can be as many as 20 mission-critical business processes, but most agree that the number is more likely four to eight. "Without focused attention on a few key operating goals at any one time, improvement efforts are likely to be so diluted that the company ends up as a perpetual laggard in every critical performance area."[15]

Step 3: Assess Current Processes

"Things are the way they are because they got that way"[16] is one explanation of how many business processes evolved. Activities and functions that have not been managed as part of an overall process tend to reflect the individual personalities of those who manage and do the work. Despite our earlier emphasis on planning and selection unconstrained by current ways of doing business, it is eventually critical to understand those current ways. (See Figure 13–7.) Detailing the "as is" situation (that is, the current way that work is actually accomplished, not procedural or ideal descriptions of how work is supposed to be done) creates a baseline for measuring operations in relation to time, cost, resources consumed, and volume. An analysis of the "as is" in comparison to the "future ideal" demonstrates the magnitude of the gap that needs to be closed and forms the foundation for the implementation plan.

The majority of approaches to process improvement focus on the modeling component of the analysis. There are formal and rigorous approaches to developing the model; others are less rigorous in terms of the documentation of process flows. The basic elements of a work process flow include a pictorial representation of how the work actually proceeds, showing process inputs, activities, and outputs. The outcome is a detailed map of the work and the information required to accomplish the work, and should include, at a minimum, the elements noted in Table 13–4.

The level of detail required in the model will often be driven by the nature of the work, as well as by the cultural practices of the business. Engineering environments often prefer analytically detailed and rigorous approaches; sales-driven organizations are often satisfied with directionally correct, descriptive displays. A warning: If the methodology develops any of the following

FIGURE 13–7   Step 3: Assess current processes.

| "As is"—how work is actually accomplished and measured. Baseline. Uncover and categorize opportunities. | *Face reality as it is, not as it was, or as you wish it were.*
—Jack Welch, CEO of General Electric | **Questions**
How is work actually accomplished:
• At what level of investment?
• For what kind of output?
What are our strengths?
Do we understand our weaknesses and vulnerabilities?
Have we unseated our complacency?
What's the potential cost of not making a change? |

TABLE 13–4   Elements of a process model.

1. The steps or activities performed.
2. The roles and responsibilities for each step.
3. The infrastructure (e.g., equipment, physical plant) for each step.
4. The activity-based cost for each step.
5. The performance measurement system for each step.
6. The information technology for each step (i.e., the software and hardware).
7. The skills required to perform each step.
8. Overall key performance indicators (e.g., volume, frequency, cost, cycle time, service levels) for the process.

symptoms—the search for infinite detail, analysis paralysis, or iterations to infinity—it is time to alter the approach. Many companies effectively use facilitators at this stage, but, in developing the model, it is important to involve those who actually do the work and to solicit the input of customers and suppliers in diagramming how work actually happens.

There are a number of ways to analyze how work gets done and to measure its efficiency and effectiveness. Flow charts, run charts, Pareto diagrams, histograms, scatter charts, root cause analysis, fishbone diagrams, and problem-solving techniques are just some of the tools to identify strengths and weaknesses. Although this stage requires adopting an industrial engineering (IE) mindset, the analytical steps are only as important as the change management approach that accompanies them. The most effective approaches are inclusive (rather than exclusive), multiperspective, iterative, and validated by both the "doers" of the work and the "customers" of the output. From a broader change perspective, a primary motive for this stage is to make people uncomfortable with the present. This is the "push" aspect of change; the earlier visioning, hopefully, provided the "pull."

Both short- and long-term opportunities for improvement will suggest themselves from the evolving map of current work flows. If the effort were focused solely on a single business process, many of its suggestions could be adopted easily. But what makes one process effective is often what makes another process ineffective. Therefore, the redesign of any process within an integrated system requires appreciating the impact of the redesign on other processes. For example, the transportation department often wants to wait until the truck is full before shipping any product to its destination, because the department is measured on cost-per-mile-transported. Conversely, the customer service department, which is judged by its ability to make the order-to-delivery cycle time as short as possible, would like the truck to leave as soon as the product is available, whether the truck is full or not.

By thinking of opportunities for improvement in the following four dimensions, it may be easier to gauge the breadth of change required:

1. Technical (for example, improve the quality of the equipment or the availability of information).

2. Behavioral/cultural (risk aversion results in slow or overworked decisions).
3. Organizational (multidepartments or layers slow the rate of work).
4. Political (sales and marketing communicate poorly because their respective directors are in competition).

It might be wiser to conduct the analysis of current processes *after* the design of the next evolution, especially if there is a need to alter deeply entrenched ways of doing business.

Step 4: Design the New Process

By now, the organization should have a vision of the competitive performance levels it must achieve, an understanding of customers' expectations around performance and the value it can deliver, and a vision of the processes that would enable it to gain a competitive advantage. It also should have a realistic picture of its relevant business processes. These ingredients are necessary to design and evaluate alternative business processes. The broad objectives for new processes are that they be:

- Effective—they deliver the intended result.
- Efficient—they consume the least amount of resources for the intended value.
- Adaptable, flexible—they can change as customers, market forces, and technology shift.

The input for the redesign can come from many sources, not simply from the internal or market analyses that have preceded it. Wal-Mart, Disney University (the training unit of Disney Corp.), and many other companies host a steady stream of benchmarkers on pilgrimages to learn about inventory management or customer service. These observers don't have to operate in the retailing or entertainment business to gain useful ideas from the innovative approaches of pacesetters.

Before GM's Saturn division designed its business processes, GM dispatched management and union people to other companies to observe how they designed, manufactured, and sold products, and how they interacted with customers. The trips provided a healthy dose of culture shock for managers steeped in the GM tradition. Separated from the normal ways of conducting business in Detroit, they were exposed to alternatives and had the mandate to create "visions of the future."

To provide its managers with a fresh perspective, General Electric established a global executive development process. It required leaders to spend six months visiting other companies to see how they approached their businesses. These visits helped to broaden the participants' thinking and their perceptions of the possible. Such altering experiences could have occurred before Step 1 (Envision the Future) or at this step. When they occur before Step 1, it is important at Step 4 to recreate the learning for the next layer of the design group.

Defining the next evolution of business processes involves benchmarking relevant best practices, identifying breakthrough performance levels, developing alternative models of delivering those performance levels, and then prototyping a new process. (See Figure 13–8.)

Establish Benchmarks

Benchmarks can be established by looking within an organization, at its competitors, and at other industries. David Kearns, CEO of Xerox Corporation, defines benchmarking as "the continuous process of measuring products, services, and practices against the toughest competition or those companies recognized as industrial leaders."[17] Benchmarks need to be realistic and, even if they require a stretch, attainable within the company's environment.

In observing how people operate and how processes have been reconfigured in other organizations, it is important not only to see what people do, but also to seek out the transition stories—how they got there. It helps to adopt an anthropologist's perspective: honor the native culture; understand that the process of observation alters the observed; see the behavior within their world, not yours; and consider what in their environment makes that kind of behavior possible and supportable. Without such a view, companies often adopt ideas/approaches as silver bullets with magical properties. Not surprisingly, the miracle seldom occurs.

Identify the Unique Value Proposition

A value proposition is a statement of the benefits a company chooses to provide to its customers and the price it charges to provide these benefits. It implicitly makes a choice between customer segments the company will and will not pursue. In contrast to traditional demographic segmentation (for example, serve the middle-age upscale male market), a value proposition describes customers in

FIGURE 13–8   Step 4: Design the new process.

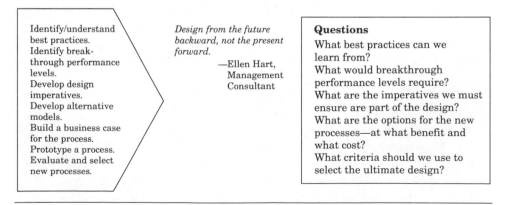

Identify/understand best practices.
Identify breakthrough performance levels.
Develop design imperatives.
Develop alternative models.
Build a business case for the process.
Prototype a process.
Evaluate and select new processes.

Design from the future backward, not the present forward.

—Ellen Hart, Management Consultant

Questions

What best practices can we learn from?
What would breakthrough performance levels require?
What are the imperatives we must ensure are part of the design?
What are the options for the new processes—at what benefit and what cost?
What criteria should we use to select the ultimate design?

terms of the benefits the customer values, for example: "Serve customers who value ease of shopping." The value delivery system—also known as core processes—is how the benefits are delivered.[18]

Design a New Model of Work Activities and Processes

This phase requires a creative approach. The emerging model should be zero-based and designed without regard to current organizational lines, boxes, or form; political or emotional constraints; players or personalities. People in the early stages of design efforts should challenge themselves to transcend boundaries and embody a broad business view. Customers, distributors, suppliers, and consultants can be brought in to provide the "outsiders'" perspective. This is also the stage at which design imperatives must be explicit. For example, when Ford was retrenching in the 1980s, its vision included a major emphasis on being number one for quality. As a design imperative, this might include customers' perception of quality being used as the final determinant in a conflict situation.

It is important that someone (or some team) knows he or she will "own" and be accountable for the entire process that is being created. Those accountable for the process should have an important role in designing it. In the past, people had ownership of parts—the functions or groupings of activities—but there was no core leadership for the whole, and little accountability for the process measures or the process outcomes.

Some organizations design only one model; others design a couple of alternatives. The design selection process should be used as a vehicle for achieving buy-in. In designing the next evolution, the criteria shown in Table 13–5 might be applied in selecting among options.

Prototype the New Model

By creating a prototype, a company can walk through the new process, determine how it actually would alter the business, and test it to ensure that it meets the necessary criteria. Information technology (IT) can provide a useful platform to create a virtual reality or working prototype.

TABLE 13–5 Selection criteria for alternative designs.

- Provides competitive advantage.
- Maximizes use of assets.
- Is customer-anchored and customer-friendly.
- Maximizes the company's distinctive value-added (e.g., time, space, reliability, low cost).
- Is measurable in ways that promote continuous improvement.
- Is adaptive and flexible.

Design Measures of the Process and Its Outcomes

In the example of Woodbridge Papers, at the start of this chapter, the manufacturing function had been measured in terms of traditional performance standards—unit cost and turnaround—but that measurement penalized the group every time it filled a small custom order. Once the strategy of the company was redefined, two distinct manufacturing processes were aligned with plant and distribution capabilities. One process provided quick turnaround at low cost to fulfill price-competitive standard orders. The other provided quick turnaround on customized orders at a price that yielded good margins. The manufacturing function was thus measured primarily in terms of how it contributed to fulfilling the objectives of the two processes.

An aligned measurement system keeps strategy and operations in sync over time by having clear and widely understood measures of both the process and its outcomes. Everyone knows the measures, receives frequent and consistent information, knows how pieces contribute to the whole, and feels able to impact the results.

Breakthrough performance levels should have been identified via benchmarking and knowledge of the benefits sought by customers. The current performance level and the breakthrough performance target are like two fingers with a rubber band stretched between them. If the fingers are too far apart, the rubber band will snap. If they are too close, the rubber band will go slack and create no tension. Reach must exceed grasp when setting performance levels.[19]

Step 5: Analyze the Gap between the Future and "As Is"

The process vision says the organization should be way over there; the managers' perception of "as is" says it is way back here. How big a leap is necessary to get from here to there? Some of the dimensions to examine in order to assess the magnitude of the gap are noted in Table 13–6.

The purpose of analyzing the gap is to determine the capabilities, technologies, information, measurement systems, and organizational dynamics that separate breakthrough performance levels from today's reality. (See Figure 13–9.) Is incremented change required, or is a quantum leap necessary? Which elements causing the gap provide the greatest challenge to remedy? By which measurements is the organization closest to the desired performance levels? Which changes are within grasp from an operational perspective, but daunting from a cultural or political perspective? Identifying the characteristics of the gap allows an organization to establish targets and objectives, determine the specific changes that are necessary, and begin thinking about timing and sequencing.

When it becomes apparent that the makeover will cause disruption and great pain, commitment to the magnitude and speed of the change can become seriously challenged. During this stage, an organization's ambition and fortitude are laid bare, exposed for all to see. The enormity of the required change can cause an organization to lose its willpower and make compromises that

TABLE 13–6   Dimensions for assessing the gap.

- Skills/capability.
- Information technology.
- Reward system.
- Measurement system.
- Infrastructure.
- Roles and responsibilities/organizational structure.
- Work flow and decisions.
- Culture.

shortchange its future potential. When this happens, visions become platitudes and entropy reclaims the organization. To be successful, a change effort should anticipate and manage the need for periodic recommitment.

Step 6: Plan the Transition

Successful execution is the most critical factor in reconfiguring business processes. Transition planning is not an isolated "sixth step." It is an ongoing effort complete with formal plans to gain buy-in to the activities, behaviors, timing, and measures necessary to implement the new business processes. The plans anticipate and address both the hurdles and enablers that are crucial to effecting change. (See Figure 13–10.) Those who craft the plan should have a realistic understanding of how successful change has occurred in the organization in the past, and whether that approach will be sufficient this time. It is also helpful to do postmortems on some "failed" change efforts to understand the factors that contributed to them.

Postmortems usually indicate that human, cultural, and managerial factors were to blame. Either the organization simply automated current processes (which were inherently broken) or too much emphasis was placed on the technical and systems components, with little regard for the behavioral or cultural dimensions that supported the way work was currently being done.

FIGURE 13–9   Step 5: Analyze the gap between the future and "as is."

Identify resource requirements. Understand and analyze gaps. Revisit the design.

It doesn't work to leap a twenty-foot chasm in two ten-foot jumps.
—American proverb[19]

Questions
How broad a change will be required to achieve the desired competitive position?
What strengths can we rely on to accomplish the change?
Have we understood the gap on multiple levels, including the rational, the emotional, and the political?
How does the gap alter our design?

FIGURE 13–10   Step 6: Plan the transition.

Create a
pathway.
Ensure buy-in
to path, timing,
goals, priority.
Devise milestones
and progress
measures.
Clarify
accountabilities.
Link to rewards.
Stack the deck
for success.

*If you want to truly
understand something,
try to change it.*
—Kurt Lewin,
Psychologist

Questions
What is our blueprint to make this
change happen? At what level of
investment?
How will we know when to declare
victory?
Who must be involved and
committed to ensure the success of
this effort?
How will we keep a spotlight on this
effort?
Have we prepared the key players to
capably handle their role during the
transition and have we linked
consequences to implementation
success?

A good transition plan takes into account that a change in one part of the system will likely alter other parts of the system. There are multiple models for looking at the organizational implications of making a change, but the model illustrated in Figure 13–11 charts the key aspects that require management.

Barriers to performance breakthroughs are typically rooted in the skills, leadership, culture, systems, or structure.[20] If, for example, the gap analysis shows the problem is lack of clear leadership, and misaligned performance measures have derailed changes in the past, then judgments can be made about how these elements can be altered to support the necessary future changes. Alteration may involve raising leader skills, encouraging a performance-driven culture, and redesigning the measurement systems.

There are some emerging organizational trends which, experience has shown, can derail the change effort or conversely ensure its sustained impact. Whether these issues help or harm the process depends on whether a company

FIGURE 13–11   The key aspects of change.

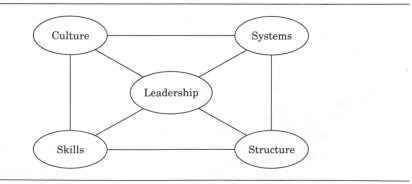

treats them as incidental or integral to the design, transition, and implementation process. Some of these are listed in Table 13–7.

Step 7: Implement the Change

In some change efforts, this phase marks the first time those actually doing the work and managing the work are required to alter their behavior, not just their attitudes or ideas. It is realistic to anticipate new waves of resistance. The degree of resistance to change is often in direct proportion to:

- The degree of mobilization and buy-in generated throughout the prior phases, in people now most affected by the change.
- The magnitude of the change required.

Throughout the prior phases, wholehearted commitment to change can be fostered two ways: (1) by demonstrating that current ways of doing business produce competitive disadvantages and risk the organization's survival (the push) and (2) by creating a vision of the future worth achieving (the pull). This push–pull tension can help managers to mobilize the organization.

If possible, the implementation should begin with a pilot project. (See Figure 13–12.) (This may require more time than some organizations dare take.) The selection of the optimum pilot area should ideally be based on the probability of a visible and transferable success. The deck can be stacked in favor of a successful pilot by peopling it with a critical mass of committed leaders and influencers, by providing the necessary training and coaching for people to feel emerging competence as early as possible, by creating communication and feedback loops that identify issues and reinforce progress, and by rewarding new behaviors as quickly as possible.

TABLE 13–7   Organization trends.

- Customers, and the intended value the company is prepared to deliver, will be the driving force for organizational behavior.
- Self-organizing principles and team dynamics will drive more behavior than procedures and job descriptions.
- Teams, not just individuals, will be primary units of focus.
- Decision making will be knowledge-driven, not hierarchically driven; information will flow to where it is needed.
- There will be wide spans of control and few layers of management.
- Work will be approached as a process with intended outcomes, not a collection of tasks; there will be a result (not activity) focus.
- Labor/management will blur (or disappear) as an organizational distinction; the managerial role will shift to more coaching and supporting of those doing the work, as well as to "anticipator" of changes in the environment.
- There will primarily be generalists, supported by a smaller number of specialists.

FIGURE 13-12   Step 7: Implement the change.

Pilot.
Modify and
stabilize.
Migrate.
Measure.
Continuously
improve.

One doesn't discover new lands without consenting to lose sight of the shore for a very long time.
—André Gide,
Philosopher

Questions
Which potential pilot area has the greatest probability of success or the highest impact?
Have we planned for refinements while encouraging stabilization?
Have we cross-fertilized migration targets?
Have we measures in place to monitor the success of implementation?
Have we built in the capability and means for continuous improvement?

THE TRANSITION MANAGEMENT CHALLENGE

Beginnings are always messy.—John Galsworthy

Many organizations have the technical skills and even the project management skills to effect core process redesign, but many others lack change management skills. Figure 13–13 describes the five key elements that are necessary for successfully reconfiguring core business processes:

1. Vision and guiding principles.
2. Leadership.
3. Sense of urgency.
4. Game plan and structure.
5. Capacity to change.

Each is discussed in the following subsections.

Vision

A vision is an articulation of the aspirations a company has for its future. To be successful, it must be grounded in the future, provide guidance and congruence for ensuing efforts, and have some constancy over time. For people to be motivated by a vision, they must perceive it as representing a future in which they want to participate.

Guiding principles often describe how we will operate and behave in that future place. For example, when Ford began changing in the early 1980s, "Quality Is Job 1," and "employee involvement" were more than buzzwords; they became a way of doing business.

FIGURE 13–13   The key elements of successful redesign.

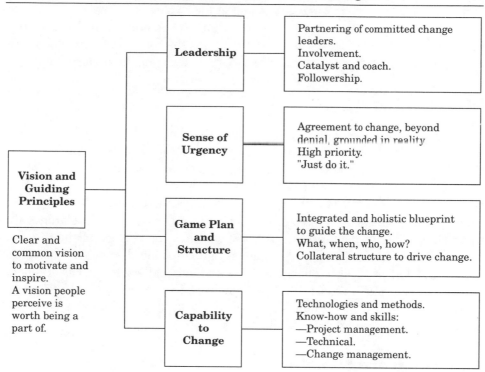

Leadership

Senior management must be the catalyst for broad-based change efforts, for a number of reasons:

- They have the big-picture view and are accountable for the strategic direction of the firm.
- They have access to the resources to make change happen.
- Their stewardship can be focused on the optimization of the whole over the part.
- Without their commitment and participation, the change will be stone-walled or eviscerated.

The leadership factor, more than any other, correlates with success or failure in change efforts. Experience shows that organizations seldom succeed at getting out ahead of their leadership for extended periods of time. More typically, organizations wait to see if something is "real" by observing the behavior, not just the rhetoric, of their leadership. Leadership's role relative to change involves serving as *catalyst* to set things in motion, as *champion* by continuously communicating the message, and as *coach* in shaping new behaviors. Leaders, particularly those who have the influence to marshal internal resources while maintaining an outsider's view, are essential for change.[21]

A critical mass of senior management must be committed if the change is to be successful, but the level of commitment and the role of catalyst, champion, and coach must be replicated within successive layers of the organization.

Sense of Urgency

There are countless examples of companies that have gone through extraordinary change as a result of a crisis. The greater challenge may await the company that wants to change while it is successful. Jack Welch faced that challenge when he began his changes at GE.[22] Increasingly, companies are realizing that the time to change is when things are good. Creating urgency is about focus, time, and willingness; as momentum builds, it includes a certain intolerance for distractions. The Nike phrase "Just do it!" captures the essence of the urgency required. The shoe company's ads create a context for the slogan. Their message is—mental and physical barriers can be overcome, and exciting goals attained, by people who take responsibility for their lives. [Managers, note: The context of your message is all-important. Try saying the Nike slogan while imagining you are a "boss" commanding a subordinate.]

Game Plan and Structure

Because change is necessarily destabilizing, a well-articulated game plan and change structure can provide purposeful direction in a time of ambiguity. The initial game plan should contain all the elements that would typically be contained in a good project plan. However, a parallel game plan should be created and used to help build buy-in and commitment to the effort. It should serve as a road map to the future and articulate the elements of *how to get there* (a high-level synthesis of the project management elements), as well as the vision of *where you are going* (either the end state or the descriptors of the value you intend to deliver to customers when you get there).

To retain focus and to accomplish the change within a certain time frame, most large efforts should set up a shadow or collateral structure,[23] that is, a temporary group of teams that are free to focus on the change effort, while tapping the rest of the organization's resources as needed. The advantages of this arrangement are listed in Table 13–8.

The collateral organization should include:

- A *steering group* (or committee) comprised of the executive leadership who allocate the resources, monitor and remove the barriers to progress, and champion the effort.
- A series of *teams* empowered to do the work of each of the phases. These include design teams, which are primarily accountable for doing the analytical and design work (and which draw additional resources from the

TABLE 13–8 A shadow or collateral organization.

- Can be singularly focused on change.
- Develops future leader skills.
- Breaks with old and allows experimentation with new behaviors, norms, practices.
- Focuses accountability.
- Can potentially increase objectivity.
- Can operate in alternative time dimensions, particularly the future.
- Can make the past uncomfortable to return to.

organization as needed) and implementation teams, which are primarily composed of those who will be most accountable for performing the work in the future. These teams should be peopled with those who can bring knowledge and insight to the process (regardless of prior or current roles), as well as those who can provide leadership going forward.

- Consultative or *facilitative* help, which serves to further the efficiency and effectiveness of the group process and insights.
- A *project management* approach, and leadership that provides the means to motivate, measure, cross-fertilize, and integrate.

Capability to Change

Much of our emphasis has been on the commitment aspect of change. Competence is equally important. Often, people's resistance to change is based on a fear of the unknown driven by concerns about personal fitness or capability to accomplish the work at hand. People ask themselves: Can I envision the future? Do I have the skills to succeed in that future? Do I have the technical skills to help design or implement future processes? How do I manage people in a collateral structure? Can I succeed in a team environment? How can I help people accept and thrive in the change? Acknowledging these concerns—and providing training, coaching, and an environment that makes it acceptable to ask for help—can foster risk taking and real change.

Along with ensuring that the five elements described above are put in place, there are some guiding principles to bear in mind. These are listed in Table 13–9.

SUMMARY

In recent years, organizations have begun to understand how strategic leverage can be created by re-engineering core business processes. Pioneering companies expected to gain much of the strategic advantage from employing the latest information technology. But it turns out that a more important source of advantage is re-imagining business processes in ways that can make them among the

TABLE 13-9   Transition management principles.

- Incremental adaptations can occur without senior-level focus; major change cannot. Do not delegate accountability for major changes.

- Let customers, especially future customers, be the drivers of change.

- Help people understand the emerging model of business (i.e., a network of business processes and competencies organized to provide superior value to customers).

- Simulate multiple frame-breaking events; cultivate the outsider's objectivity.

- Create a shift in strategic focus and an ambition that requires stretch to achieve. Strive for breakthrough performance levels, but build in interim successes.

- Articulate and apply a change model so people can understand and anticipate the process. Be systematic in understanding whether barriers are rational, political, or emotional.

- Make progress visible and publicly reward changed behavior and improved results. Create multiple feedback processes; orchestrate an early alert system.

- Plan investments in education, training, and alterations in people-support processes (e.g., career pathing, compensation).

most critical success factors of an organization. These reconfigured processes often have attributes that competitors would find most difficult to imitate.

Reconfiguring core business processes is a big job—one that affects virtually every component of an organization. The dimensions of the initiative are bounded only by the needs of future customers and their concepts of value. The intent of forging powerful linkages between strategy and operations is to make a strategic leap and leverage every ounce of talent and energy of the organization in the process. Managing change is as important as planning the direction of change the organization will take.

NOTES

1.   In some instances, we will use actual company names, in others we will not. Woodbridge Papers is a fictional name for a real company. See Francis J. Gouillart and Frederick D. Sturdivant, "Spend a Day in the Life of Your Customers," *Harvard Business Review* (January–February 1994), 116–127, for a full description of the Woodbridge case.

2.   Continuous improvement—or a comparable concept, *Kaizen*, in Japan—is based on the notion that people should continuously seek better ways to do their work rather than wait for improvement to be triggered by breakdowns, crises, and so on.

3.   The Malcolm Baldrige National Quality Award's purposes are to promote U.S. awareness about the importance of improving quality in products and services, to recognize quality achievements (of U.S. companies), and to communicate successful quality strategies. Up to two awards in each category are given each year to manufacturing, services, and small businesses.

4. This point is also argued forcefully in Chapter 8's discussion of the need to develop knowledge-based processes.

5. This argument reinforces the discussion in Chapters 1 and 3: Organizations need to provide multiple types of values to customers; they cannot compete on one dimension (such as services or price) alone.

6. As quoted in Noel Tichy and Stratford Sherman, *Control Your Own Destiny or Someone Else Will* (New York: Doubleday, 1993), 225.

7. Based on ideas contained in *Efficient Consumer Response*, Kurt Salmon Associates, Atlanta, GA, 1992.

8. The value chain was discussed in some detail in Chapter 3 as a critical piece of analysis in shaping business-unit strategy.

9. Chapter 15 illustrates how "the existing ways of thinking" are embedded in the organization's culture and how difficult it frequently is to change how organizations think. Chapter 16 details the trauma that often accompanies the radical shift in an organization's thinking that is necessary in reinventing or transforming strategy.

10. Gary Hamel and C. K. Prahalad, "Corporate Imagination and Expeditionary Marketing," *Harvard Business Review* (July–August 1991), 81–92.

11. How breakthrough insights can lead to reinventing strategy is the focus of Chapter 16.

12. Attributed to Sir Hugh Walpole in *Fortune* (May 3, 1993), 41.

13. Stan Davis and William Davidson, *2020 Vision* (New York: Simon & Schuster, 1991), 113. See Chapter 16 on the role and importance of an understanding of the future as an input to strategy reinvention or transformation.

14. Michael Lanning and Lynn Phillips, *Building Market-Focused Organizations*, a Gemini Consulting monograph, Morristown, NJ, 1991. The use of the term *value* may be confusing here. In the Lanning and Phillips model of building a market-focused organization, value is used to express the net effect a customer gets due to obtaining an end-result benefit minus the price. Customers select among competing options by choosing the most positive values. In the recent concept of the value chain, value has come to mean the portion of a business chain of activities that adds value to customers in general; for example, refining adds value by turning crude oil into usable form, whereas recruitment of new employees (while important to a company's success) is not typically in the value chain. For further discussion of the value chain, see Chapter 3.

15. Gary Hamel and C. K. Prahalad, "Strategy as Stretch and Leverage," *Harvard Business Review* (March–April 1993), 79.

16. Attributed to Kenneth Boulding.

17. In the late 1970s, Xerox compared U.S.-made products to those of its Japanese affiliate and was shocked to discover they were selling at prices equivalent to U.S. manufacturing cost. By 1983, Xerox had incorporated benchmarking as a key element in its corporate-wide improvement effort. See James H. Harrington, *Business Process Improvement* (New York: McGraw-Hill, 1991), 222.

18. Lanning and Phillips, cited in note 14.

19. As quoted in William Bridges, *Managing Transitions* (Reading, MA: Addison-Wesley, 1991), 32.

20. Chapter 12 addresses how structure and systems can be used as means to fashion tighter integration between strategy development and strategy execution.

21. See John P. Kotter and James L. Heskett, *Corporate Culture and Performance* (New York: The Free Press, 1992), for multiple examples of the role of the leader in shaping change, particularly the cultural dimension.

22. Noel Tichy and Stratford Sherman, cited in note 6.

23. The definition of collateral is "side by side, lateral, descended from the same ancestors but in a different line, for example, Theodore Roosevelt to Franklin D. Roosevelt." Shadow can be defined as "to represent faintly, mystically or prophetically; to prefigure." *Webster's New Universal Unabridged Dictionary,* 2nd ed. (New York: Simon & Schuster, 1993). See also Ellen Hart, "From Current to Future State" in *Executive Excellence* (September 1993), 10, for a broader description.

REFERENCES

Davenport, Thomas. *Process Innovation—Reengineering Work through Information Technology.* Boston: Harvard Business School Press, 1993.

Gouillart, Francis, and Sturdivant, Fred. "Spend a Day in the Life of Your Customers." *Harvard Business Review* (January–February 1994), 116–125.

Hamel, Gary, and Prahalad, C. K. "Corporate Imagination and Expeditionary Marketing." *Harvard Business Review* (July–August, 1991), 79–91.

Hamel, Gary, and Prahalad, C. K. "Strategy as Stretch and Leverage." *Harvard Business Review* (March–April 1993), 75–84.

Hammer, Michael. "Reengineering Work: Don't Automate, Obliterate." *Harvard Business Review* (July–August 1990), 104–112.

Harrington, James H. *Business Process Improvement.* New York: McGraw-Hill, 1991.

Kotter, John P., and Heskett, James K. *Corporate Culture and Performance.* New York: The Free Press, 1992.

Pine, Joseph B., II. *Mass Customization; The New Frontier in Business Competition.* Boston: Harvard Business School Press, 1993.

Rummler, Geary A., and Brache, Alan P. *Improving Performance—How to Manage the White Space on the Organization Chart.* San Francisco: Jossey-Bass Publishers, 1990.

Short, James, and Venkatraman, N. "Beyond Business Process Redesign: Redefining Baxter's Business Network." *Sloan Management Review* (Fall 1992), 7–21.

STRATEGIC CHANGE: MANAGING STRATEGY MAKING THROUGH PLANNING AND ADMINISTRATIVE SYSTEMS

14

John H. Grant

Katz Graduate School of Business,
University of Pittsburgh

Careful attention to systematic procedures for managing strategy making can reduce the chances of serious omissions or misguided actions involving the many important activities that provide critical information and understanding. Planning and administrative systems (PAS) offer mechanisms for coordinating strategy development and execution on either a regular or ad hoc basis for the purpose of achieving intended organizational objectives.

The goals for this chapter are:

- Introduce the purposes, characteristics, and scope of PAS, to make readers familiar with such systems and their potential contributions to improved organizational performance.
- Illustrate the applications, design trade-offs, and effects of PAS in selected organizational settings.
- Outline procedures for critiquing or designing such systems in an organizational context.

PAS: SOME PRELIMINARY COMMENTS

When we discuss planning and administrative systems (PAS) in this chapter, we are describing more than just sets of formal documents, rigid meeting schedules, and computer support. Our working definition of a PAS is much broader. It includes the diverse conditions, activities, and facilities that can be managed to effect desired future behavior and organizational performance. Data availability, physical visibility, perceived risk taking, employee educational levels, and many other elements contribute to and interact to comprise the total PAS.

The design goal is not to make PAS more comprehensive and detailed, but rather to make them more effective and efficient in economic, organizational, and human terms. In practice, it is possible to paralyze and eventually bankrupt firms with overly detailed and excessively formalized PAS. Managers must strive to make the systems agile, flexible, and resilient enough to meet changing organizational needs.

PAS contribute substantially to the quality, timeliness, and structure of information that general managers have readily available for important decisions. Without such systems, executives may fail to recognize shifting consumer tastes, changing output quality, rising investor expectations, or other trends in critical success factors (CSF) for the organization. Or, they may learn the proper lessons but not in time to be first to market or to take corrective strategic action. In many markets where quality and timeliness of information are increasingly important to profitability or other performance measures, the proper design of the PAS can be crucial to both the recognition of opportunities and the capacity to act effectively.

One of the purposes of this chapter is to provide guidelines regarding the design and uses of PAS and how to adapt them over time to the changing requirements of particular organizations and their leaders. Design trade-offs are difficult because they involve the balancing of components along at least four crucial dimensions:

1. Technological feasibility.
2. Behavioral effects.
3. Scheduling sequence.
4. Economic costs and benefits.

Technology brings both speed and efficiency to many PAS components, but there are currently limits to the analytical technologies of forecasting, data gathering, and the monitoring abilities of computer-based scanners. In short, technology can aid managerial judgment but it cannot substitute for it.

The behavioral effects of different PAS configurations are often difficult to predict. For example, managers at the same organizational level may react very differently to the same incentive system. Decision makers provided with the same data from a strategic issue analysis may draw distinctively different action implications.

Given the interdependence of PAS components, the scheduling sequence demands attention. For example, if computers are installed before operators are trained, old subsystems may be discontinued before new ones have been tested.

Managers with responsibility for economic evaluations of a PAS must include the balancing employees' needs for stability in their work environments against the task needs for frequent changes. Constant minor adjustments can be costly to communicate and confusing to those affected. On the other hand, lack of periodic refinement allows operations to become unresponsive or insensitive to new management perspectives, particularly in dynamic marketplaces.

Linkage to Other Chapters

This chapter can be studied and used as a separate document, but important materials in other chapters relate to the content given here. For example, planning and control subsystems relate to both the industry analysis in Chapter 6 and the macroenvironmental analysis in Chapter 7. The organizational analyses in Chapter 9 are important components of each PAS cycle described here. The generation of strategic alternatives, detailed in Chapter 10, comprises important input to the PAS processes. The design of PAS is expected to be valuable to the implementation and reconfiguration processes described in Chapter 13, and to be an important component of the transformation and reconfiguration options presented in Chapter 16.

Linkage to Specific Organizational Contexts

PAS exist in every organization, whether by deliberate design or by a process of evolution—paper flows, human interaction over time, and customer and supplier transactions require them. Our discussion will focus on ways to improve PAS. To provide varied organizational contexts for applying these concepts, Box 14–1 presents data on three major organizations with various PAS needs: General Electric Company (GE), Ciba-Geigy (C-G), and the Sands Hotel and Casino (SHC). GE is a very large, highly visible, diversified U.S. firm with global operations and a reputation for giving active attention to seeking improvements in its management systems.[1] C-G is a major Swiss firm that sells the vast majority of its numerous chemical-based products outside its relatively conservative and somewhat secretive home country. SHC is predominantly a service business operating in a heavily regulated industry. Concerns about the social consequences of the industry are often sharply debated in political settings.

Individuals and Organizational Performance

Before discussing the ways to coordinate human actions for organizational purposes through PAS, we should acknowledge the important insights being offered in related literature about the valuable contributions that come from "empowered individuals," "teams," and "learning organizations."[2] Nothing we have to say about "systems" should be construed to imply that organizational participants must be "harnessed and controlled" in order to be productive organizational contributors. On the other hand, whole books have been written about the difficulties that arise when the PAS do not help automotive

Box 14–1

General Electric (GE), Ciba-Geigy (C-G), and Sands Hotel and Casino (SHC)

General Electric (GE) is a diversified manufacturing and service firm with more than $60 billion in sales from such sectors as power systems, financial services, aircraft engines, and industrial systems. In more than a decade of CEO Jack Welch's leadership, the company has acquired, divested, and restructured billions of dollars in assets and tens of thousands of jobs.°

The process of designing planning and administration systems (PAS) that provide motivation and delegation without significant loss of control in resource allocation and risk taking is a continuing challenge. Extremely effective PAS design is crucial in a publicly traded firm operating within an aggressive capital market like that of the United States. Many firms that once operated in GE's markets became the subjects of hostile takeovers and break-ups when the corporate headquarters were viewed as detracting from, rather than adding to overall corporate value.

As noted in Chapter 1, the scope of products and services offered by GE has been changing in recent years, but the characteristics of the PAS have perhaps been altered even more. For example, extensive documentation of strategic business units' (SBUs) plans has been greatly reduced, the number of employees in staff roles has been substantially reduced, the responsibilities of general managers have been increased, the decision-making cycles have been shortened, and the rewards or incentives for innovation have increased.

The changes in the characteristics of GE's PAS have been influenced by:

- Customer reactions to the technological changes surrounding many of GE's SBUs.
- Heightened competitive pressure—often from international sources.
- Demands from capital markets.
- Expectations of employees.

The driving objective has been to improve the strength of selected market positions in order to attract the capital, customers, and employees necessary to perform effectively over extended periods of time. There is every indication that, as competitive arenas evolve, Jack Welch will continue to rearrange the elements of GE's PAS so the company can either perform well or divest itself of those operating units that cannot.

Ciba-Geigy (C-G), a pharmaceutical company based in Basel, Switzerland, is a publicly held firm that produces and sells hundreds of products of varying complexity in dozens of countries around the world.°° Because of the difficulty

---

° Based on material from "General Electric (1984)" #9-385-315 and "GE—Preparing for the 1990s" #9-390-091 (Boston: HBS Pub.); M. Dickson, "All for One & One for All," *Financial Times,* September 3, 1992; N. Tichy and R. Charan, "Speed, Simplicity and Self-Confidence," *Harvard Business Review* (September–October 1989), 112–121.

°° Based on material from "Ciba Geigy (A)," #184-185 (HBS Pub. Div.); C. Kennedy, "Changing the Company Culture at Ciba-Geigy," *Long Range Planning* (1993) 26: 18–27.

of predicting changes in the technical and political environments for all its ethical drugs, chemicals, and agricultural products, C-G needs to retain timely, centralized awareness about certain aspects of the business. At the same time, the corporation must delegate a substantial degree of local autonomy to managers operating in many different cultures.

Among the challenges in PAS design at the firm are those associated with technical and regulatory risk sharing, measurement across fluctuating currencies, and communication through many different languages and cultures.

The stimulus for a recent major change in the PAS at C-G was an environmental disaster at a competitor's plant in Europe during the autumn of 1986. When large quantities of toxic compounds spilled from a chemical plant into the Rhine River during a fire, there was public resentment toward the entire chemical industry. This inspired the management of C-G to make a fundamental reassessment of the assumptions underlying its operations. The detailed control system of the past was replaced by an information system that provided more division-level flexibility. New procedures shortened the decision cycles, and central service units (CSUs) had to become fully competitive against outside suppliers. To provide greater opportunities for younger employees, a policy of mandatory retirement for all employees at age 60 was implemented. In an effort to adapt to the changes in the European Community (EC), C-G restructured its operations around specific geographic regions where it expected competitive characteristics to be similar.

Sands Hotel and Casino (SHC) is currently a wholly owned subsidiary of Pratt Hotel Corporation. SHC operates a major hospitality and entertainment complex in Atlantic City, New Jersey.[†] This company experiences rather extensive government regulation because of America's societal ambivalence toward the gambling industry. The potential tax revenues are tempting for taxpayers and politicians, but the concerns about illicit activities associated with the industry remain troublesome.

Efforts by corporate marketers to create a recreational "happy-go-lucky" ambiance must be balanced with tight controls over cash, chips, and gambling behavior. This duality of purpose in the industry creates PAS design problems. Some firms are experimenting with PAS based on cheap, computer-based technologies; others are relying on expensive, experienced personnel.

The planning process for casinos in the United States requires close coordination with regulatory bodies (in this case, the New Jersey Casino Control Commission), which have the authority to regulate matters ranging from aspects of building design to the mix of gaming activities and the processes of counting and depositing cash. The PAS at SHC encompasses extensive, highly structured screening procedures for new employees, optical scanning systems for monitoring customers and employees, and other control features intended to provide an effective balance between society's desire to closely monitor casino environments and operators' quest for operations that will attract profitable customers.

[†] Based on material from "Controls at the Sands Hotel and Casino," #9-184-048 (HBS Publishing); N. Barsky, (1991) "New Jersey Relaxes Its Grip on Casinos," *The Wall Street Journal,* (March 19, 1991), B1, B6.

manufacturers isolate and highlight production cost or quality problems, nor help mainframe computer manufacturers understand the consequences of smaller, networked computers for many of their customers' uses.

The extent of personal knowledge and commitment that individuals can add to the work of an organization represents a vital component of the overall PAS. To the extent that a firm has the capacity to combine and share the insights of many creative people through systems for organizational learning, that firm is well on its way toward the much sought objective of continuous quality improvement (CQI). In other words, the balance between internal or intrinsic components and the external or extrinsic ones used by a company or any other type of organization depends on the types of people attracted to it. This in turn determines the way in which the capabilities of a firm are to be stored and transferred, whether through individual development and training or through more mechanical means like reports, computer programs, and instruction manuals. Let us now consider some of the system components that can comprise PAS for managers.

SYSTEMS FOR INTEGRATING STRATEGIC PROCESSES

Typical PAS consist of a number of subsystems for environmental scanning, corporate resource assessment or "audit," strategic issues analysis, capital budgeting, human resource development, operations, and various levels of control. An overview of the various PAS components can be seen in Figure 14–1. For a description of the components in Figure 14–1, see Box 14–2.

Across the top of Figure 14–1 is represented a sequence of analyses, choices, and evaluations being performed in conjunction with the functioning of the PAS. A key component of the overall PAS is the set of critical success factors (CSF) by which an organization chooses to measure its performance over time.

To implement the overall PAS framework within a given organization, it is necessary to assign activities to specific individuals or groups and to allocate their performance over time. The A-I-T-L (activity–involvement–timing–linkage) chart in Figure 14–2 is a useful way of presenting such relationships.[3] The interrelated subsystems are constructed of many components; a brief description of the A-I-T-L elements will aid the subsequent discussion.

Activities are the various tasks and procedures performed during the analysis, coordination, and implementation of the PAS. They can be undertaken by various individuals or groups inside the organization or by consultants hired for specific purposes. Illustrative activities might include environmental scanning, budget simulation, reward distribution, decision making or numerous other managerial tasks.

Involvement refers to the participation of various people and organizational units in the development of assumptions and issues, the execution of activities, and the assessment of results. Degrees of involvement will vary from

FIGURE 14–1   Planning and administrative system: Overview.

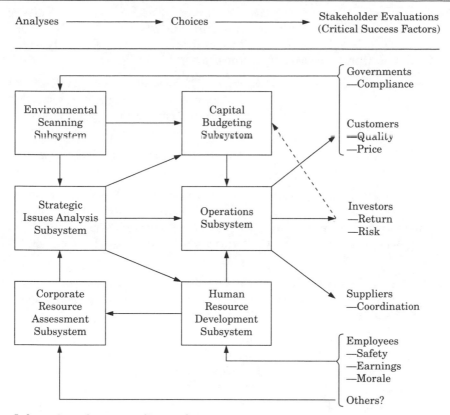

Analyses ─────────────▶ Choices ─────────────▶ Stakeholder Evaluations
(Critical Success Factors)

Information subsystems = lines and arrows.

continuous full-time commitment to ad hoc part-time responsibility for gathering data, organizing analyses, participating in decisions, or other activities.

Timing refers to the calendar sequence for the performance of particular activities by those involved. Some activities should occur sequentially; others may be performed simultaneously during the PAS cycle. Although the timing of most PAS activities should be determined by the nature of the businesses involved, some activities are efficiently linked to external reporting requirements and others are dependent on the competitive actions of rival firms or important customers. A cycle is a sequence of various processes involving linked subsystems that address similar activities over time. Although some subsystems are activated on a regular daily, monthly, or annual basis, others, like personnel selection, are cycled only when there is a specific stimulus for action.

Linkage mechanisms are devices that tie together the activities and subsystems. They may be as structured and rapid as computer software that combines databases and analytical models, or as unstructured and time-consuming as a series of negotiation sessions aimed at reconciling investment requests with available financing. Other examples include individuals who convert reports into

Box 14–2

PAS Component Descriptions (Figure 14–1)

Environmental Scanning Subsystem: The process of identifying those parts of the world outside the firm that are particularly important to its well-being, and then analyzing the related trends and issues for the purpose of identifying opportunities or threats to future performance.°

Corporate Resource Assessment Subsystem: The process of comparing a firm's physical, human, and technological resources with those of competitors and with the "best" known to exist. The process of locating and measuring against the "best available for application" is often referred to as benchmarking.

Strategic Issues Analysis Subsystem: The process of comparing internal and external trends to identify major concerns or opportunities developing over time.

Capital Budgeting Subsystem: A subsystem of activities that identify and evaluate financial investment opportunities, whether directed toward plant expansion and equipment, major marketing programs, acquisition opportunities, or other such commitments where the returns are expected to extend a few years into the future.

Operations Subsystem: Used to plan and control the flow of materials, scheduling of employees, delivery of completed products and services, and collection of invoices from the daily operations of the organization.°°

Human Resource Development Subsystem: Should be given special attention because of the mobility of most personnel and the substantial knowledge and investment many of them represent. Includes enhancing the reputation of the firm as an employer, the recruiting procedures, training and internal placement, incentive programs, succession planning, and outplacement services.

Information Subsystem: Various devices for gathering, sorting, storing, and transmitting data between external parties and parts of the company play essential roles in the effective function of PAS. While some of the devices consist of computers and telecommunications devices, others are written reports and even more informal verbal exchanges.

Stakeholder Evaluations: The system of measures used by an organization to judge its performance from the perspectives of various important constituencies or stakeholders; often called the critical success factors (CSF) or key performance indicators. Figure 14–5, later in the chapter, shows that it is useful to develop a pattern of relationships among these indicators so that complementary and competing measures can be readily recognized.†

° More is described in Chapter 7, and further insights are noted in J. E. Prescott and P. Gibbons (eds.), *Global Perspectives on Competitive Intelligence* (Alexandria, VA: Society of Competitive Intelligence Professionals 1993).
°° These subsystems represent many of the operating processes that are described in detail in Chapter 13.
† R. G. Eccles, (1991) "The Performance Manifesto," *Harvard Business Review* (January–February 1991), 131–137; T. Hiromoto, "Another Hidden Edge—Japanese Management Accounting," *Harvard Business Review* (July–August 1988), 22–27.

FIGURE 14–2 A-I-T-L (activity-involvement-timing-linkages) chart.

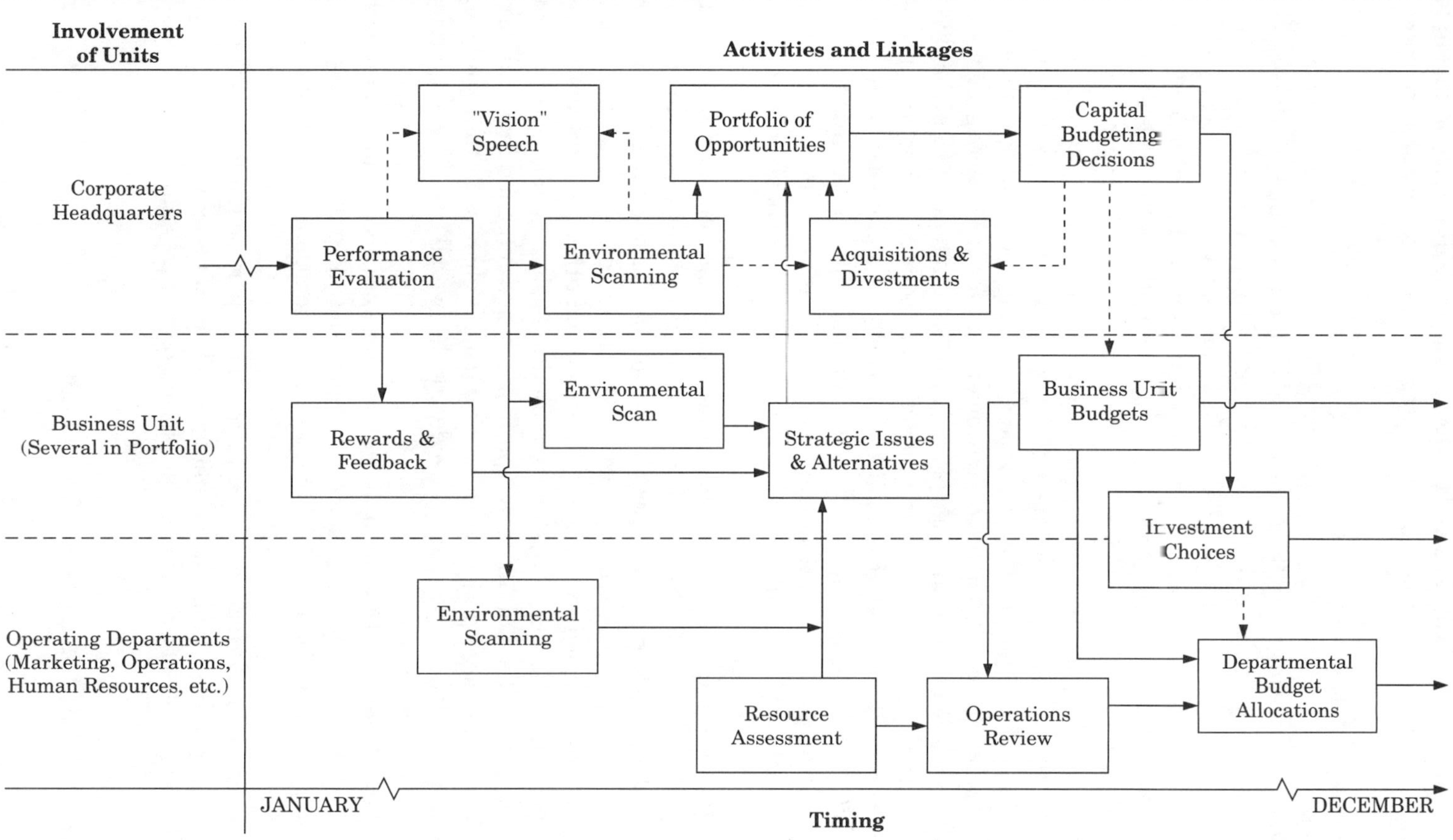

Source: Based on J. Dermer, *Management Planning and Control Systems* (Homewood, IL: Richard D. Irwin, 1977).

397

instructions for personnel, calendars that require the allocation of time to tasks, and speeches that seek to orient employees' energies to a common purpose.

Illustrating a PAS

Various components of a PAS, as they could be used in a company during a given period of time, are illustrated in multidivisional firms such as GE or C-G. Such a firm might begin an annual PAS cycle in February with a statement by the CEO or other officer at the corporate headquarters (CHQ) level. The statement might emphasize or revise the vision or mission of the entire company, based at least in part on the performance evaluation of the preceding year or another recent period. Employees at the corporate level might then gather environmental and competitive trend data for various sectors from capital markets, government agencies, and other sources, and division-level employees might scan and interpret technological developments, customers' preferences among competitors' products and services, and other factors of specific interest to a given division.

At the same time the environmental scanning is occurring, other analysts might summarize the relative quality of the tangible and intangible resources of the firm. When the resource analysis is combined with the environmental scan, the strategic issues and options can be described as bases for future choices by the company. (The strategic issues subsystem deserves special attention and is covered in the next section.)

In a diversified firm, the sets of strategic options from the various business units can be combined to provide the portfolio of investment and divestiture opportunities available at the corporate level. It is at this point that important changes in a company's strategy can be effected and communicated clearly to competitors, customers, employees, investors, and other stakeholders.

Capital budgeting subsystems are used to evaluate alternative investment patterns as a method of improving profitability and retaining financial flexibility. When very large projects are being pursued, changes in the firm's capital structure may have to be synchronized with the overall cash flow requirements of the firm.

Simultaneous with capital budgeting decisions, the business unit and departmental operating budgets are developed and integrated in order that the firm may forecast the expected financial performance a year or more into the future.

Ongoing performance analyses from the departmental levels are periodically aggregated at the business-unit level. Changes in marketing programs and production levels can then be accomplished on a timely basis.

STRATEGIC ISSUES SUBSYSTEM

As analysts and managers examine external trends and the evolving resource base inside the firm, there is a need to interrelate critical factors in meaningful ways. One way to organize data effectively is to identify key internal developments and a similar list of external trends and arrange them in matrix form, as shown in Figure 14–3. The third axis should be a measure of time: Appropriate technical, legal, and other expert personnel can be asked to monitor trends and interrelationships over periods of years or months, depending on the rates of change.

For example, when toxic waste spilled into the Rhine from a C-G competitor's plant fire, it triggered a strategic issues analysis at C-G. Managers recognized that their macroenvironment had changed because of the public's new environmental sensitivity. A macroenvironmental analysis also had a profound impact when GE was assessing the future role of consumer electronics following its acquisition of RCA. Management realized that prospective customers' expectations for design, performance, and price made it seem unlikely that GE's R&D, manufacturing, and distribution systems could compete effectively over

FIGURE 14–3   Strategic issues subsystem.

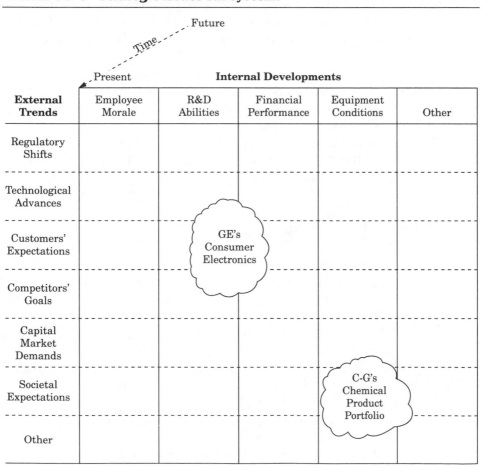

the long term. As a result, management decided to divest the consumer electronics operating unit.

Strategic issues subsystems may function on a routine annual cycle as long as the organization's industries and the broader macroenvironment are relatively stable. However, as discussed in Chapters 6 through 9, change is the dominant feature of most organizations' environment.[4] Moreover, analysis should not focus on isolated events or environmental segments: The connections and linkages among the segments of the environment give rise to opportunities and problems. For example, a change in the political environment, such as the election of a new administration or a change in regulations, may give rise to a change in customers' expectations. Because of a goal of the Clinton Administration, the pharmaceutical operations at C-G should closely scan for indicators of potential change and should monitor emerging attitudes in the healthcare industry in the United States, as government officials and representatives of many healthcare industry stakeholders[5] debate alternative cost, quality of care, and availability considerations. Strategic issues subsystems must have the flexibility to respond to both anticipated and unanticipated events that might have strategic importance.[6]

Crisis management systems exist in many organizations to deal with a subset of strategic issues that executives feel are so critical and urgent that most normal operating procedures cannot cope with them.[7] Under such circumstances, the PAS design typically allows for the delegation of much greater authority to individuals with particular skills. For example, a faulty GE jet engine that caused a fatal crash would be expected to trigger the crisis management system in GE's jet engine unit, and a major drug-tampering incident or toxic waste spill at C-G would initiate the same reaction.

The capacity of the organization to identify strategic issues on a timely basis and to act on them efficiently and effectively is highly dependent on the availability and use of a reliable information system.

INFORMATION SYSTEMS

An organization's information system includes a broad array of data types (financial, technological, marketplace) gathered from many different sources and stored or retained by many different means. For example, in many firms much of the information needed for strategy development and execution resides in the memories of individual employees. Increasingly, large quantity of data is stored in computer-based systems.

For purposes of PAS design and evaluation, it is often helpful to visualize a three-dimensional "data cube" (see Figure 14–4). The axes in Figure 14–4— focus (internal versus external), types (qualitative versus quantitative), and frequency (routine versus nonroutine) provide managers and others with a useful means to identify distinct data categories.[8]

One overriding benefit of the data cube shown in Figure 14–4 is that it helps to avoid data use that is driven by availability alone—a situation found in

FIGURE 14-4   Data varieties for PAS.

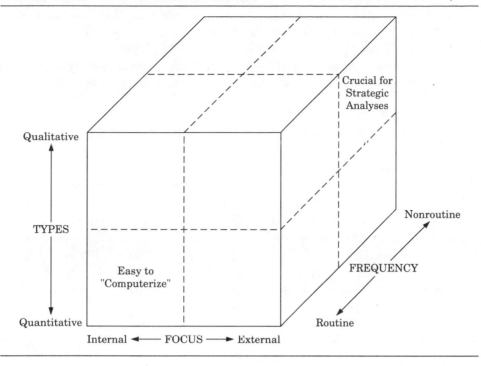

many organizations today. Unfortunately for many managers and analysts, PAS often become dominated by data that are in the quantitative-internal-routine cell because such data are typically easy and inexpensive to mechanize or computerize. However, the data in the qualitative-external-nonroutine cell are often most critical to strategic issues identification and thus to major shifts in resource allocations. For example, the early indicators of political, regulatory, social, economic, and technological change—a statement by a government official, an announcement of breakthrough findings by scientists, or a major change in consumers' behavior—almost always fall into the qualitative-external-nonroutine cell.[9]

When refining an information system designed to support other PAS components, two other dimensions are often important:

1. Distribution (personal versus shared).
2. Availability (archival versus on-line).

Because information tends to convey power or strategic position and direction in many organizational situations, the need for secrecy or personal control over the distribution of certain types of data can be crucial. Hence, information subsystems designers need to determine the breadth of access of data at various points in time. The mode of availability is equally important because it will determine the speed, geographic distribution, and multiplicity of uses of particular data. For example, customer account data on a time-sharing computer system can be used by marketing researchers, financial planners, and accounts receivable personnel for very different purposes and from dispersed locations simultaneously. On the other hand, an uncopied paper file describing an acquisition candidate is available to only one person in a single location at a particular time.

The next section examines the ways in which these various types of data can be used for linking PAS activities and performance measurements.

LINKAGE MECHANISMS AND PERFORMANCE CRITERIA

As noted earlier, linkage mechanisms are those structured and unstructured devices that tie together the activities and subsystems. It is particularly important that they be related to measurement criteria and performance levels because of the wide differences in the goals and associated performance measures across functions and between levels within the organization.[10] For example, at the corporate level in a publicly traded company, the CEO and board of directors might aspire to a particular earnings level or stock price. On the other hand, a team in a production department might seek to make a product that meets certain quality and cost standards.

A framework for associating different linkage mechanisms and performance criteria to various organizational levels, from the individual employee through the corporate and nation-state levels, is shown in Figure 14–5. On the horizontal axis are criteria ranging from individual attributes to government regulations. For example, if a manager at GE or C-G is interested in improving the company's stock price, a logical question is: What actions will improve investors' perceptions of the future potential of our company? Two quite different actions might be implied in the framework: (1) seek to improve the return on assets (ROA) or the economic value added (EVA) of divisions within the company or (2) redeploy the portfolio toward industry sectors where the company might find opportunities for successful innovations.

In another example, managers might consider whether investment programs designed to enhance market share might improve the ROA and whether standard costs might be reduced without sacrificing quality. Those analyses would inevitably lead to the most micro level in Figure 14–5: the assessment of individual personnel to see whether they have the skills and technology needed to perform as effective competitors in the external marketplaces.

On the diagonal of performance criteria, upward from the corporate level are the (CSF) that society uses to evaluate individual firms. Pharmaceutical firms like C-G will be asked whether their ethical drug products are as innovative and cost-effective as alternative treatments, and SHC will be asked whether the casino is cost-effective for the taxpayers of Atlantic City.

At the level of a nation's entire economy, the criteria become tax rates, emission levels, employee safety, and other pervasive concerns of citizens. In other words, the organization must ask whether it is meeting the expectations and demands of the myriad stakeholders who constitute the macroenvironment.

FIGURE 14–5 Linkage mechanisms and performance criteria.

Levels	Internal Technical Emphases		Capital Markets	External & Societal Criteria	
	Performance Criteria				
	Individual Attributes	Product Markets & Costs	Financial Markets	Industry Structure	Government Regulations
Nation-State					Taxes Emission Control Employee Safety
Industry				Concentration Ratios Innovation	
Corporate			Stock Prices		
SBU or Division			ROA or EVA		
Product Line		Market Share			
Department		Standard Costs			
Individual	Skills Values				

The PAS within and surrounding a firm will determine how directly linked these various measures are. However, the trade-offs for both managers and government officials are between the rigidities resulting from tight linkages versus the apparent injustices arising from overly loose connections. In general, the PAS should seek tighter linkages over internal relationships because most are more directly controllable. On the other hand, most government policies and regulations are adjusted slowly in democratic societies, so managers will have both opportunities and constraints that may be out of phase with the technical possibilities in their markets.

PAS designers should be careful to incorporate valid measures of performance, rather than simply convenient ones. C-G made substantial changes in its financial measurement system to avoid using historical book values for assets; it estimated current replacement or market values in order to calculate performance ratios. Newer EVA and value-based planning procedures seek to incorporate the real economic costs of assets into their calculations rather than permitting valuable but depreciated assets to imply higher-than-actual ROAs.[11]

As managers develop ideas for taking action based on the performance criteria which have been analyzed, a next logical step is to become concerned about establishing priorities and assigning responsibilities. If this step is not handled properly, some future options may be precluded or the time of expensive, senior people may be wasted. Hence, a mechanism for deciding which activities are most critical or important to the future well-being of the organization and which must be accomplished first can be a valuable decision aid. If more detailed analyses are warranted at a subsequent stage, the PERT (Program Evaluation and Review Technique) charts or CPM (Critical Path Method) diagrams can be developed and urgency dimensions sorted properly.

The importance–urgency activity framework shown in Figure 14–6 can be used to sort and integrate activities on a timely basis and with reference to the person or organizational unit responsible under radically different circumstances.[12] This framework should help PAS designers and managers think effectively about the ways their associates are asked to use their time and energy. For example, the CEO or managing director of a major firm or business unit must expect that a portion of his or her schedule will be disrupted by critical events that arise without forewarning—a hostile takeover threat, a major toxic waste spill, or a promising change in regulations that demands testimony at a Congressional hearing. Other line managers should be assigned responsibility for urgent matters that have low importance individually but are collectively crucial to organizational performance.

Such a framework can help in the design of information systems that must be prompt, even though approximate; an example is C-G's "hot line" to corporate headquarters for technical or political crises. Alternately, product-testing procedures in laboratories at GE must provide precise and reliable data if new components are being considered for mass-produced home appliances or medical equipment.

FIGURE 14–6   Importance–urgency activity framework.

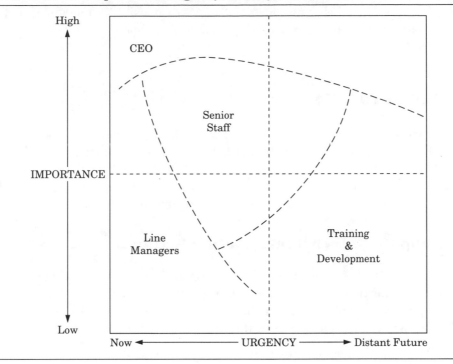

MEASUREMENT AND EVALUATION PROCESSES

Measurement and evaluation processes are crucial because of their impacts on the rewards for information sharing, the motivation for risk taking, the resulting organizational learning, and other factors. Educating diverse employees as to why the performance criteria vary across job descriptions is important for maintaining morale and cooperation, particularly in loosely linked professional organizations like research laboratories, orchestras, hospitals, and similar institutions.

Incentives and penalties must be related to desired behaviors, and this relationship must be clearly conveyed to all members of the organization. Thus, it is becoming increasingly common for high-performance executives to use stock options, quality awards, innovation bonuses, and other mechanisms to communicate the important contributions that other managers and employees in many arenas can make to enhance the strategic performance of the company.

In diversified, related-product organizations, the transfer pricing process often creates particular evaluation problems.[13] Firms such as C-G and GE, which hope to benefit from the sharing of knowledge or other assets across sub-unit boundaries, frequently encounter difficulties distributing the related costs or investments in ways that are viewed as equitable. The specific techniques for balancing market prices and administered costs are too complex to address here, but it is crucial that managers with PAS responsibility recognize that if special attention is not given to these matters, major dysfunctional consequences can result.

BUILDING THE PAS

The process of developing a PAS for a particular organization depends on the size of the firm, the nature of the markets in which it competes, the types of people involved, and the resources available. All such systems require continual modification, but the initial steps in designing and developing a PAS remain fairly uniform. They are described in the following subsections.

Develop the Internal Information Requirements

The purpose here is to maintain the core operations. Core operations extend from the acquisition of materials, employees, and financing through the value-adding processes involving manufacturing or operations, and on to the sales and collection stages. Typical questions that should be considered include:

- What are the key operating processes in the organization?[14]
- For each key operating process, does the organization have thorough and timely data? For example, what is the quality of the organization's data pertaining to production planning, procurement efficiency, and inventory management?
- Can the economic costs associated with each operating process or activity be calculated in order to perform effective benchmarking?

Identify the Key External Information Requirements

This is often a difficult task, although some critical information needs—customer locations, purchasing patterns and preferences, components and raw materials suppliers' prices changes, entry and exit of competitors, and competitors' behaviors—are available through straightforward research methods. Key questions include:

- What are the most relevant changes taking place in the organization's environment (its industry and macroenvironment)?
- Does the organization have procedures for tracking/monitoring and projecting competitors' product/service developments, customers' behaviors, and distribution channel changes?
- Can the organization effectively scan and monitor important technological developments, regulatory changes, and other macroenvironmental trends in ways that permit timely identification of strategic issues?

Identify the Critical Success Factors (CSF)

CSF are particularly required for measuring the short-term performance of the business unit. Typical factors include sales patterns, production volumes and quality, order backlogs, margins on sales, and employee turnover. After the essential data requirements are developed, the manager must select those people who will need to be involved either because they will possess key data or because their participation will aid implementation steps. Typical questions include:

- What are the critical success factors? Do they vary from one business unit to another? Do they vary from one geographic market to another?
- Given the objectives of the organization, which key stakeholders must be satisfied with what measures of performance? Do owners want profit measures? Do contributors to a charity want evidence of services provided?
- How do the CSF relate to one another over time? For example, does reduced employee turnover lead to better customer service and does this in turn lead to more profitable sales?
- What persons within the organization possess critical data with regard to each CSF? How can they be motivated to contribute to developing and sustaining each CSF?

Identify the Key Reports or Other Outputs

PAS are designed for the purpose of providing outputs that are useful to decision makers. Thus, it is imperative to determine what types of outputs are required by which decision makers, and what will be needed in terms of information characteristics, schedule of preparation, and sequence of distribution. Key questions include:

- Among the decision makers, who will require written reports, who will need verbal communication, and who can be contacted via computer systems?
- What schedule of information distribution is needed to help each decision maker perform his or her task both effectively and efficiently?
- Ideally, what information should departments, levels of management, and key individuals receive?

Assess Technology Requirements

As noted frequently in this chapter, technology can play a major role in shaping desired PAS outputs. Thus, technology must be assessed in terms of its cost-effectiveness for the various subsystems, given the expected volume of data and the resources available for handling it. Key questions include:

- How computer-literate are various employees, suppliers, and customers? What is their current state of computer technology?

- Does the business require the speed and precision of integrated computer systems, or should most systems be less structured and seemingly more personal?

Develop Initial Systems

At some stage, systems need to be operationalized or put in motion. Thus, the elements of the strategic issues, information, measurement and evaluation, and other systems must be put in place. In the early stages, these systems can be regarded as tentative: the intent is to learn from their execution. As learning accrues, each system can be refined and enhanced. Key questions include:

- What minimum systems will be required to satisfy various regulatory agencies, including tax authorities, employment monitors, pollution control agencies, and so on?
- What documentation will be helpful for new employees if the business expands and more complex PAS components need to be added?

CONCLUSION

This chapter has underscored the importance of PAS design and characteristics to the effective strategic management of organizations. Many factors appropriately deserve attention, but neither managers nor analysts must be attracted to systems only because they are quick-and-easy to implement.

PAS are *not* an end in themselves. Their purpose is to facilitate attainment of the organization's goals; indeed, they can contribute to identifying what the goals of the organization should be. Strategic issues, planning and control, and information systems should generate the data necessary to challenge whether the organization is pursuing only easy-to-reach goals or stretching its resources to seek higher-yield opportunities.

As noted throughout this chapter, PAS must never be allowed to stand still. Change in the environment always tests the validity and relevance of existing systems; for example, changes in technologies that cause a shift in the types of products offered in the marketplace often provide a test case as to whether and when they were identified by the strategic issues subsystem. In short, PAS must be continually assessed and refined.

NOTES

1. General Electric was discussed at some length in Chapter 1.

2. J. C. Camillus, "Crafting the Competitive Corporation," in P. Lorange, et al. (eds.), *Implementing Strategic Processes* (Oxford, U.K.: Basil Blackwell, 1993).

3. See J. Dermer, *Management Planning and Control Systems* (Homewood, IL: Richard D. Irwin, 1977); A. P. de Geus, "Planning as Learning," *Harvard Business Review* (March–April 1988), 70–74.

4. Worth repeating here is the argument in Chapter 1 that change is the central concept in strategic management.

5. For a discussion of the role and importance of stakeholders in understanding environmental change, see Chapter 5.

6. For more discussion, see J. E. Dutton and S. E. Jackson, "Categorizing Strategic Issues: Links to Organizational Action," *Academy of Management Review* (January 1987), 76–90; J. E. Dutton, L. Fahey, and V. K. Narayanan, "Toward Understanding Strategic Issue Diagnosis," *Strategic Management Journal* (Vol. 4, 1983), 307–323; J. Camillus and D. Datta, "Managing Strategic Issues in a Turbulent Environment" *Long Range Planning* (April 24, 1991), 67–74.

7. P. Shrivastava and I. Mitroff, "Strategic Management of Corporate Crises," *Columbia Journal of World Business* (Spring 1987), 5–12; G. Siomkos and P. Shrivastava, "Responding to Product Liability Crises," *Long Range Planning* (October 1993), 72–79.

8. Adapted from J. C. Camillus, *Strategic Planning and Management Control* (Lexington Books, 1986); J. H. Grant, "Indicators of Strategic Performance," Working Paper, University of Pittsburgh, 1975; R. Saberwahl and J. Grant, "Integrating External and Internal Perspectives of Strategic Information Technology Decisions," in J. Henderson and N. Venkatraman (eds.), *Strategic Management* and *Information Technology* (JAI Press, in press).

9. Readers are referred to Chapter 7 for a detailed discussion of the scanning and monitoring that are necessary to detect and develop the early indicators of macroenvironmental change.

10. Distinct levels of goals were noted and discussed in Chapter 1. Different types of goals in the case of business units were noted in Chapter 3.

11. See S. Tully, "The Real Key to Creating Wealth," *Fortune* (September 20, 1993), 38–40, 44–45, 48, 50.

12. See J. H. Grant and W. R. King, *The Logic of Strategic Planning* (Boston: Little, Brown & Co., 1982).

13. R. G. Eccles, "Control with Fairness in Transfer Pricing," *Harvard Business Review* (November–December 1983), 149–161; E. J. Kovac and H. P. Troy, "Getting Transfer Prices Right: What Bellcore Did," *Harvard Business Review* (September–October 1989), 148–154.

14. Operating processes are the primary focus of Chapter 13.

15 STRATEGIC CHANGE: MANAGING CULTURAL PROCESSES

Gerry Johnson

Cranfield School of Management

In 1989, David Dworkin was trying to launch a management buyout for Bonwit Teller, the department stores group, when he was approached by a management recruitment firm to take over BhS, an ailing U.K. clothing stores chain. BhS, with 130 stores and a turnover exceeding $1 billion, was part of the troubled Storehouse Group whose share price was dropping. BhS, as the main business in the group, was a major cause of this decline. It faced stiff competition from the powerful Marks & Spencer chain and showed little prospect of improving its low sales and profit. Taking the job of CEO, Dworkin's first impressions of BhS were not favorable. In his assessment, the stores were shabby, the managers were conservative and unimaginative, and the organization was top-heavy and unwieldy. However, by the time he left BhS in 1993, both a Harvard case study and the U.K. financial press were heralding the business as a major turnaround success.

Some of the actions Dworkin took followed the prescriptions in most management textbooks. He modernized the merchandise; cut costs dramatically; delayered the organization; removed many of the conservative, long-serving managers and brought in new blood. However, some of his other actions were less conventional: "BhS staff still recall the shock of attending meetings when Dworkin strolled in wearing a tee-shirt, cycling shorts and bare feet, eating a pot of yogurt."[1] In the face of the staid male-dominated culture, he recruited three women onto the board. The new open style of communication was initially shocking for some. At his first meeting with corporate staff, he promised them that things would change and that the company would be successful. Then he added, "The bad news is that, unfortunately, many of you won't be here a year

410

from now." They were not. Three hundred office staff personnel were removed. However, few on the sales side of the business departed. Under Dworkin's leadership, the proportion of employees engaged in sales activities rose from 60 percent to 80 percent. In addition, the de-layering and the openness meant that real responsibility was passed down the chain of command, dramatically changing the day-to-day jobs of store managers and shop staff.

David Dworkin understood that his changes in strategy for BhS had to be accompanied by appropriate metamorphosis in the company's culture. Such a transformation is a vital process in the management of strategy. However, if the connections between strategy and organization culture are to be managed, there must be a clear understanding of how strategy and culture are related and how they affect behavior in the organization.

Cultural influences on strategy are the formidable hidden hands that cause consternation not only for many managers just starting their careers, but also for some seasoned managers who take an overly mechanistic approach to the development and execution of strategy.

Figure 15–1 summarizes the flow of this chapter. An overview of how strategy is developed in organizations begins the discussion. The crucial difference between strategy as planned or intended and strategy as actually realized by an organization is then shown. This is an important distinction because it

FIGURE 15–1   A framework for managing strategic change.

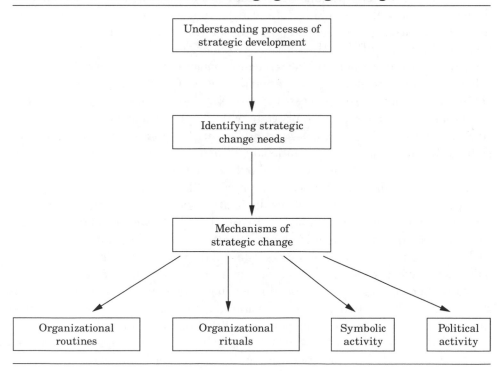

helps to explain how organizational culture either inhibits or fosters strategy development and implementation, and it drives home the point that the management of strategic change requires the redirection of strategy as it is actually evolving. In seeking to implement strategic change, therefore, managers need to "lay their hands on" the processes that give rise to the realized strategy.

The chapter then addresses how strategic change can be managed through the cultural processes of the organization and the closely related political processes. It does this, first, by providing a framework—the cultural web—that explains the linkages between organizational culture and strategy. Next, it explains (1) the reasons for resistance to strategic change and (2) why organizations are likely to drift away from their strategic focus. The ever-present danger is that organizational culture can nurture resistance to strategic change. However, by gaining an understanding of corporate culture, a manager can facilitate strategic change. The rest of the chapter explains how to accomplish strategic change by identifying barriers to change, and how to operate the mechanisms of strategic change.

STRATEGY DEVELOPMENT IN ORGANIZATIONS

The changes Dworkin sponsored at BhS were transformational; such dramatic shifts of direction are milestones in a company's history.[2] Normally, most organizations go through long periods when strategies develop incrementally; that is, decisions build one upon another. In effect, an accumulation of past decisions molds future strategy. Incremental change can be a good practice: no organization could function efficiently if it were to undergo frequent major transformations of its strategy. Incremental strategic change can therefore be seen as a valuable adaptive response to a continually changing environment. However, a closer examination of the processes of strategy development suggests that this observable incremental pattern of strategy development may not always be the consequence of intentional management planning. It can also be seen as an outcome of the influence of organizational culture.

Typically, strategy is written about as though it were the result of a straightforward, mechanistic planning process. Most textbooks describe a systematic formulation process that results in strategic direction, an implementation plan, and a timetable (route 1 in Figure 15–2).[3] However, much evidence suggests that, in many organizations that attempt to formulate strategies in such systematic ways, the intended strategies do not become implemented or only part of what is intended comes about (route 2 in Figure 15–2).

Just because an organization doesn't implement its planned or intended strategy doesn't mean that the organization has no strategy. If strategy is defined as the choices that set the long-term direction of the organization, then a firm can have an emergent process of strategy development (route 3 in Figure 15–2). How this works in practice will be discussed later in the chapter and will

FIGURE 15–2   Different explanations of strategy development.

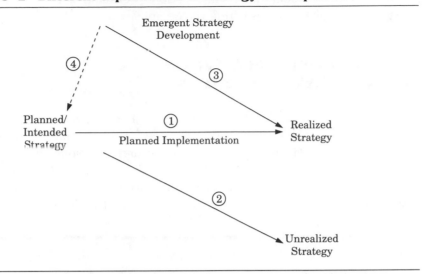

help to explain how cultural influences are likely to play an important role in shaping strategy.

Even in companies with a stated, intended strategy that appears to have come about through some sort of formal planning process, the real strategy development may occur behind the scenes. For example, the planning process may perform the role of monitoring the progress or efficiency of an emergent strategy, or it may perform the role of pulling together the views and the collective "wisdom" management has built up over time. Indeed, a common complaint of chief executives is that their planning systems seem to have degenerated into little more than routine exercises in post-facto rationalizations of how the organization's strategy was conceived, developed, and executed. Such retrospectives become the basis for projecting future strategy direction (route 4 in Figure 15–2). This illusion of rationality can be dangerous. While the organization appears to be taking a proactive, systematic approach to strategy development, the planning activities may actually mask a complacent, unrealistic view of the situation the organization is in.

There are other explanations of how strategies originate. Strategies may be the product of opportunism or the vision of executives;[4] strategies may be imposed on an organization by an outside agency (such as government) or by the environment in which the organization exists.[5] However, historical studies of organizations suggest that, typically, strategies change in incremental ways,[6] and that the impact of organizational culture on the processes that give rise to such patterns is important.

In summary, managing strategic change entails changing the realized strategy of an organization. This means that managers must recognize and deal with the processes that account for emergent strategy development. To do so requires managing cultural processes within the organization.

A CULTURAL PERSPECTIVE ON STRATEGY DEVELOPMENT

We think of strategy as the choices that define an organization's longer-term direction. There must be some set of influences or forces guiding those choices. However, such guidance may not be explicit and conscious, as is assumed in much of the strategic management literature. To see how strategy may evolve in a manner unintended by top management, consider the case of EngCo, a composite of the history of several real firms, which is discussed in Box 15–1.

Box 15–1

The EngCo Case: The Influences on Strategy Evolution

EngCo, which could be one of many engineering-based businesses in any number of Western economies, manufactured electrical distribution equipment and had done so for 40 years. It had always manufactured components and undertaken metal fabrication work to mount these components into units built for specific purposes. Over time, the firm gained a reputation for technical reliability and experience in meeting specific needs of industrial buyers. In the 1980s, fundamental market changes took place: lighter-weight imported Japanese components became available, low-cost fabricators took advantage of the product change to enter the market, and industrial buyers cut back on their in-house engineering specialists and came to rely more on contractors who, in turn, started to squeeze prices. Although new entrants saw themselves as fabricators using bought-in components for buyers mainly interested in price, EngCo managers still saw the company as a manufacturer of high-quality electrical components for a technically sophisticated market. The emphasis on in-house component manufacture thus continued. In the face of falling prices, they put more and more pressure on lowering manufacturing costs. This realized strategy of specially designed high-specification products, combined with cost reduction, inevitably squeezed margins, reduced retained earnings, and left the company with insufficient funds for reinvestment. The dispassionate observer might have counseled the firm to consider alternative strategies: use bought-in components and concentrate on enhanced service delivery, develop a product range that made the company less vulnerable to imported components, focus on a market segment valuing traditional quality, and so on. When a new chief executive finally did address these options, the established strategy of the business had persisted for many years. Not surprisingly, he found that, despite his decisions to shift substantially to bought-in components, lower-level management still continued to design own-made components into the products.

The EngCo story is an example of what research confirms: strategic decisions are strongly influenced by corporate history and managerial experience, which filter external information and make sense of internal capabilities. This tacit "guidance" that gives rise to strategy is, then, a product of the web of assumptions, beliefs, and values that organizations take for granted. These are the invisible constraints of organizational culture.

There are many definitions of culture. A working definition is: culture is the "basic assumptions and beliefs that are shared by members of an organization, but operate unconsciously and tacitly define an organization's view of itself and its environment."[7] These assumptions relate to the day-to-day behavior in an organization, and this behavior, in turn, reinforces the assumptions. Over time, as an organization develops (and especially if it develops successfully), the culture becomes more and more installed. So it was in EngCo. Assumptions about the needs of buyers and the quality of products determined day-to-day work patterns in the design office and on the factory floor. Unfortunately, this culture either failed to detect or downplayed the significance of signals from the marketplace.

Individual managers may hold quite varying beliefs about many different aspects of their organizational world, but a core set of assumptions has to be held in common. Without a commonality of core assumptions, an organization cannot function. This core set of assumptions has variously been called a mental model, a mindset, a dominant logic, or the term used here: a paradigm.[8] The difficulties in adapting the paradigm to facilitate strategic change are highlighted in the examples depicted in Box 15–2.

At their most beneficial, the core assumptions encapsulate the unique or special competences and skills of an organization and can promote competitive advantage. Marks & Spencer, the famous British store chain mentioned earlier, is a good example. One of the most consistently successful retail businesses in the world, its reputation is built on quality products and services; indeed, quality is at the very heart of its culture. Managers and staff alike are imbued with the notion of quality—in products, merchandising, training, staff, facilities, and design of buildings. Assumptions about the significance of quality are reflected in everyday behavior. In turn, this has created for Marks & Spencer a distinctive image that competitors find extremely difficult to imitate. This quality culture enhances the firm's ability to launch new products or to develop new stores. Retail property developers are keen to attract Marks & Spencer stores to new sites in order to enhance the sites' reputation. However, these assumptions can also be problematic. Marks & Spencer often lags behind in the introduction of fashion goods. In its geographical expansions into France and Canada, it ran into major problems because it assumed that the Marks & Spencer way would be invariably appropriate there too.

Environmental forces, such as those discussed in Chapters 6 and 7, and an organization's resources and capabilities (see Chapters 8 and 9) undoubtedly affect the performance of an organization. Yet, they do not, in and of themselves,

---

Box 15–2

Some Examples of Paradigms at Work

The managers of a local newspaper for a major U.K. city had always assumed that they were in the business of providing local news to a local community and that people would pay for that news. The reality: 70 percent of the revenues came from advertising, there had been substantial inflow and outflow of population in the community, the distribution of free newspapers had grown, and market research showed that local readers valued advertising and television listings more than local news.

———

The paradigm for a major defense contractor was closely linked to its long-established reputation in the design and building of military aircraft. Throughout the organization, the core role of military aircraft was assumed; linked to this assumption was a focus on the necessity of technical perfection. Not surprisingly, this firm was having difficulty in diversifying into worldwide project management of defense installations.

———

Police forces throughout the world have an assumed role of law enforcement, catching criminals, and achieving prosecutions within a strict hierarchical system. This role can conflict with community expectations of trust and public service.

———

U.K. banks, faced with banking deregulation in the 1980s, found it difficult to adjust their strategies, given their long-held assumptions of employment for life, the indestructibility of their organizations, and concentration on professional integrity rather than market focus.

create organizational strategy. People create strategy. And people are influenced—perhaps even indoctrinated—by the paradigm that the company culture uses to make sense of and filter external and internal stimuli. Figure 15–3 is a representation of this process. Change strategies that managers advocate are typically limited to actions that fit the logic of the paradigm.

What happens when changes in the environment threaten organizational performance? In many organizations, even if mangers perceive such changes, they may not acknowledge those that are in conflict with the paradigm their company culture accepts. Devising a strategy to adapt to the new environment—one that changes the rules of the game—can cause culture shock.

There are many examples of managers' striking aptitude for ignoring or downplaying environmental change:

- Executives who discount competitor activity or changes in buyer behavior as aberrations.

FIGURE 15-3   The role of the paradigm in strategy formulation.

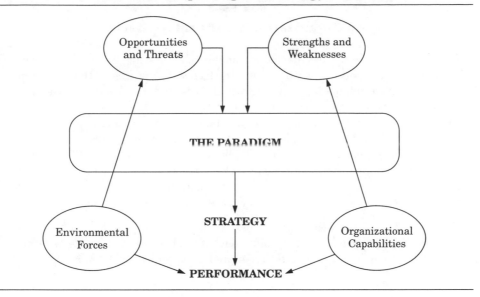

- Managers who persist with outmoded practices.
- Managers who remain committed to dying products, even in the face of declining markets or competitor substitution.
- Management teams that ignore or minimize the evidence of market research, the implications of which question tried and tested ways of doing things.

There is usually a tragic/comic quality to these situations. They are comic because outsiders who are not initiates into the culture can usually see quite easily that the old strategy doesn't fit the new environment. The tragic aspect occurs when people's lives and careers are sacrificed to wage futile battles with outmoded, inappropriate tactics. Any manager who has encountered the frustration of trying to use apparently objective evidence to persuade a management team of the need to change its core beliefs will be familiar with the problem.

How likely it is that a paradigm can dominate the development of strategy and cause resistance to significant change? Consider the wider cultural context in which it exists. The paradigm, as a set of assumptions and beliefs more or less collectively owned, is likely to be inseparable from the web of cultural artifacts specific to the organization. These cultural artifacts are briefly delineated in Box 15-3.

It is a grave mistake to underestimate the power of a company's paradigm or to write it off as merely a set of abstract beliefs and assumptions that have little measurable effect on organizational action. The paradigm is inextricably bound within a cultural web (see Figure 15-4) that bonds it to the day-to-day action of organizational life. In turn, this web of cultural artifacts serves to

---

Box 15–3
An Organization's Cultural Artifacts

Routines: The routine ways in which members of an organization behave toward each other, carry out their work, and interface with entities in their environment, including suppliers, customers, distributors, and social and political organizations. This is "the way we do things around here," which is intimately linked to the core assumptions of the paradigm and, in effect, provides a repertoire of actions that form the day-to-day reality of those in the organization. At their most beneficial, such routines lubricate the working of the organization, providing a distinctive and beneficial organizational competency. However, such routines can also take the form of a repertoire of activity that is extremely difficult to change and highly protective of core assumptions in the paradigm.

Rituals: The rituals of organizational life—such as training programs, promotions, and assessment procedures that point to what is important in the organization. They reinforce "the way we do things around here" and signal what is especially important.

Systems: The control, measurement, and reward systems that focus attention and activity on what is seen to be important in the organization. They do so in more formal, often measurable ways.

Stories: The stories told by members of the organization to each other, to outsiders, to new recruits, and so on. They embed the present in the successes and disasters of organizational history, flag important events and personalities, often as "heroes" or "villains," and identify mavericks who "deviate from the norm."

Symbols: The more symbolic aspects of organizations—logos, offices, cars and titles, and the type of language and terminology used. Such symbols become a shorthand representation of the unique nature of the organization.

Power: The weighted effect is likely to be associated with the key constructs of the paradigm. The most powerful managerial groupings in the organization are likely to be the ones most associated with core assumptions and beliefs about what is important, not least because they may represent that which has given rise to past success.°

Organizational Structure: The formal organizational structure, or the more informal ways in which the organization works, are likely to reflect or even preserve power structures and, in this respect, delineate important relationships and emphasize what is important in the organization.

° D. J. Hickson, G. R. Hinings, C. A. Lee, R. E. Schneck, and J. M. Dennings, "A Strategic Contingencies Theory of Intraorganizational Power," *Administrative Science Quarterly* (1971), *16*(2): 216–229.

FIGURE 15–4   The cultural web of an organization.

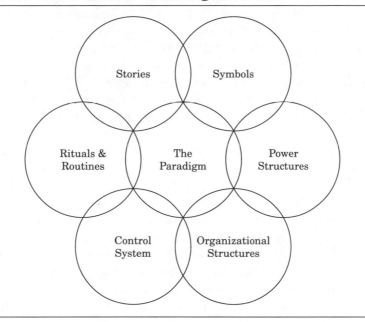

institutionalize the paradigm. (Box 15–4 (page 426) provides an example of a cultural web for a major professional services firm.)

STRATEGIC DRIFT[9]

A manager's working definition of organizational culture is: the inherent beliefs and assumptions that are widely shared in the organization, and the routine behavior and organizational artifacts that reinforce those beliefs and assumptions. Over time, the beliefs and assumptions will change gradually, but they are likely to have a powerful conservative or constraining influence on the organization and its strategy.

The Risk of Strategic Drift

The textbook definition of strategic management is: A planned, intentional activity in which there is a logical search for a match between external forces and internal capabilities. It is axiomatic that when external forces or internal capabilities change, strategies need to change. However, as our cases have shown, when faced with crucial signals of changes in the external environment, managers are likely to interpret them in ways consistent with the organization's existing paradigm. Even if the situation calls for radical alteration of behavior, managers are nonetheless likely to deal with the situation in ways that align with the paradigm and the cultural, social, and political norms of organizational life.

Rather than being a logical process of planning, analysis, and evaluation, strategic management can be understood in terms of an organizational response over time to an environment that is logical in terms of the paradigm.[10]

This model of strategic change indicates how difficult it will be to take action that is outside the scope of the paradigm and the constraints of the cultural web. To undertake such change would require substantial change to core assumptions and routines. Desirable as this may be, it does not occur easily. Most agents of change assume, wrongly, that managers can perceive the need for such change. Even if they do, they are likely to attempt to deal with the situation by searching for definitions of problems and solutions in terms of the existing paradigm and in ways that can be accommodated within the existing culture. This seems to be especially so in organizations in which there is a high degree of homogeneity in the beliefs and assumptions that comprise the paradigm. Managers will typically attempt to minimize the extent to which they are faced with ambiguity and uncertainty by relating to that which is familiar.

Figure 15–5 illustrates the problems that strategic change encounters. Faced with a stimulus for action (in this case, declining performance), managers first seek ways to improve the implementation of existing strategy—for example, a reduction of costs or tightening of controls. In effect, they seek to enforce their accepted way of operating. If this is not effective, then a change of strategy may

FIGURE 15–5   Strategic change and the paradigm.

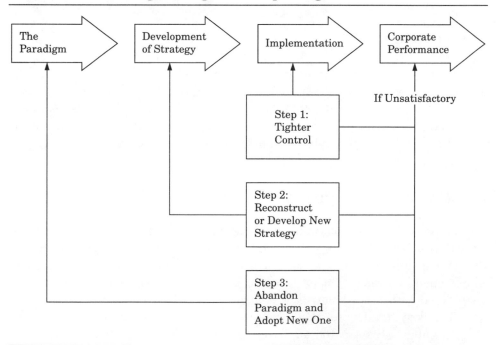

Source: Adapted from P. Greinyer and J. C. Spender, *Turnaround: Managerial Recipes for Strategic Success* (Associated Business Press, 1979), 203.

occur, but it is likely to be a change that is congruent with the existing paradigm. For example, managers may seek to extend the market for their business but will assume that it will be similar to their existing market. They then make plans to manage the new venture according to past practices and beliefs.

Changing the strategy within the paradigm may make a good deal of sense. After all, the paradigm encapsulates the experience of those in the organization and permits change to take place within what is familiar and understood. However, the outcome of this process may not be an adaptive strategy sufficient to address environmental change. Too often, firms create new strategies to fit old paradigms. If this happens, eventually the forces in the environment will adversely affect performance (see phase 1 of Figure 15–6). In cases of strategic drift, the organization's strategy gradually, usually imperceptibly, loses its focus on the demands of its environment. Indeed, Miller[11] points out that many firms become victims of the very success of their past. For example, Digital Equipment Corporation's success was based on the excellent design of its flexible, cheaper minicomputers. As a result, the company fostered an engineering monoculture in which technological fine-tuning became such an obsession that customers' needs for smaller, more economical, more user-friendly machines were ignored. In another example, Chrysler's success in doubling its U.S. market share and tripling its international share was substantially due to its aggressive marketing and its sporty styling of cars. However, preoccupation with style and image led to a proliferation of product lines and a triumph of packaging over content. Critics say the results were a lack of focus, rising costs, and reduced quality in Chrysler vehicles.

By the time strategic drift becomes apparent, performance usually has been seriously affected (see phase 2 in Figure 15–6). Strategy development is

FIGURE 15–6   Strategic drift.

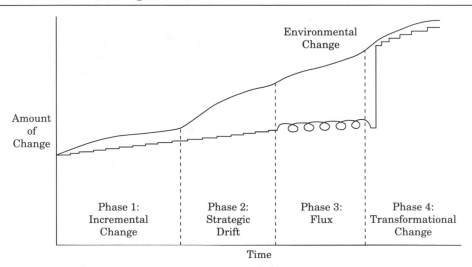

Phase 1:
Incremental
Change

Phase 2:
Strategic
Drift

Phase 3:
Flux

Phase 4:
Transformational
Change

then likely to go into a state of flux, with no clear direction (phase 3). If this situation is not confronted quickly, performance is likely to get worse. Eventually, a transformational change is the appropriate response, or the organization is doomed (phase 4).

This seems like an overly gloomy prognosis of organizational development. However, the facts do bear it out. Several studies show that many of the most successful firms of 50 or 60 years ago are no longer successful, have been taken over, or have gone out of business. It is a fallacy to assume the inevitable longevity of apparently powerful, dynamic business organizations.

Managers should draw three lessons from this:

1. Learn the skills of strategic management, many of which are articulated and discussed in this book.
2. Develop sensitivity to the signals and symptoms of strategic drift.
3. Learn to effectively manage the strategic change of an organization—the subject of this chapter.

Detecting Strategic Drift

How can a manager gauge when strategic drift has occurred and transformational change may be required? Unfortunately, there is no absolute set of conditions that forecasts or describes a state of strategic drift. However, some of the symptoms internal to an organization can be identified:

- A highly homogeneous organizational culture and internalized paradigm. In this sort of organization, there are few differences of beliefs and assumptions about the institution and its place in the external world. Established routines are not deviated from and are little related to the needs of customers and the market. Newcomers are taught powerful symbols and stories of "the good old days."

- Little toleration of questions about or challenges to the prevailing assumptions and beliefs. There is a readiness to dismiss new ideas with "We've tried this before and it didn't work." Old hands indoctrinate new recruits to conform, to "see the world the way we do."

- Major power blockages to change, either because of resistant dominant leaders or because a group or layer of management is resistant to change. One executive in a manufacturing company complained: "Our problem is our senior operations managers: they've been here years and most of them are going nowhere and know it; but they can block anything if they choose. They are our 'concrete ceiling.'"

- An organization with little focus on its external environment. Firms that don't have a market focus are at great risk of drift. Symptoms include: a lack of market information, a bias toward "selling what we make" rather than responding to market and customer requirements, and competition on the basis of price, rather than the delivery of added value to customers. Such organizations are likely to be building their strategy on internalized views of their competencies and the dynamics of their markets.

• Deteriorating performance. The appropriate measurement is performance relative to competition—the potential of future competitors as well as the abilities and results of historical competitors.

None of these symptoms is truly difficult to detect. However, in most organizations, the formal means of reporting such problems are limited to either the measurement of decline in performance or formal feedback from the market place. A surprising number of firms don't do the kind of market research that would uncover the symptoms of strategic drift.

Another problem is that a decline in performance can manifest itself many months, or even years, after the organization has begun to drift. Some successful organizations exert such powerful control over their markets that they can disregard customer criticism and dealer complaints—for a time. Early warning signals of strategic drift are insular departmental structures, a reluctance of senior management to listen to the junior personnel who are in contact with customers, a rigidity in routine behavior, and indoctrinated conformity. Quite likely then, behavioral symptoms, not formal organizational measures, are the early signs of drift. The irony is that those outside the firm—consultants, visitors, suppliers, and customers—often see the early stages of drift more readily than the managers do.

Problems of Strategic Planning in a Cultural Context

A major limitation of most strategic planning is that the thinking and the recognition of opportunity take place within the confines of a mental box—the limits of the paradigm. Often, signals of change or threat are simply not recognized by the most powerful people involved in the planning. Middle managers frequently contribute to the problem by focusing on, or even magnifying the signals in the environment that fit the paradigm. Front-line managers may be subtly discouraged from challenging the status quo. In short, the paradigm exerts a limiting role on the environmental analysis and evaluation of the plan.

How can managers critically examine the cultural aspects of their organization that can lead to this drift? Using the structural or control mechanisms of the organization may be one method (see Chapters 12 and 14). Critical outsiders such as consultants or nonexecutive directors can play a positive role in identifying strategic drift. Some companies have become antihierarchical and are promoting the involvement of (and critique by) people at different levels in the organization, especially those who are close to customers. The planning system may need to be adapted to pay greater attention to the symptoms of strategic drift.[12] Some firms have set about identifying their cultures and its links to strategy development through workshop activities involving managers, staff, and informed outsiders. The strategic manager must be as sensitive to managing the culture of the organization, as to managing marketing, financial analysis, and planning.

STRATEGIC MANAGEMENT IN A CULTURAL CONTEXT

At the beginning of this chapter, we briefly reviewed different ways of looking at the strategy development process. We urged questioning of the idea that strategic plans necessarily lead to intended strategy. We proposed instead that strategy development be seen as an emergent process. The cases and commentary have shown how an understanding of organizational culture also helps to explain how such a process may take place.

Our model of strategy development raises questions about the role of strategic management in the context of organizations' culture. The aim of strategic management is to decide on, formulate, and plan the implementation of strategies. The presumption is that the strategies will give rise to significant strategic change. The frustration felt by many executives when strategic planning systems do not promote such changes can be explained in terms of the powerful influence of organizational culture and the hidden assumptions of the organization's operative paradigm. Our proposition is: Strategic management is unlikely to cope with the inertial forces of organizational culture unless such forces are specifically considered and addressed.

The Politics of Strategy

A very different type of problem—resistance to strategic change—often pops up when a new plan is proposed. For example, a recently hired marketing director of a clothing company complained that the stated strategy of the firm—to market popular but fashionable clothing—was not being advanced. Instead, the firm was making a pattern of decisions that reinforced its image as a low-priced mass marketer. The research the marketing director commissioned supported his complaints. Customers saw the clothing as having reasonably good value but as being dowdy, out-of-date, and of a lesser quality than competitors' garments. The products were selling on price alone. The marketing director, armed with his powerful analysis, decided that he would present the evidence to the board, the members of which had been associated with the company for many years. The presentation of the research was followed by a relatively brief discussion in which powerful individuals on the board found reason to dispute the analysis, criticize the presentation, and dismiss the findings. The market research and its implications were ignored. The marketing director commented afterward: "I realize that what I had thought was a statement of analysis was in fact a statement of considerable political threat." The most powerful members of the board owed their reputation and their standing to the firm's historically successful capability to sell large volumes of standard, low-priced merchandise. The new market research raised questions about the validity of such an approach, implied that a fundamental strategy shift was needed, and threatened old assumptions and the enshrined ways of doing business. In sum, the research threatened the power bases of the established management.

As this case illustrates, the idea that analysis and planning are politically neutral is naive.

Although the exercise of analysis, evaluation, and planned implementation, which comprise strategic planning, is valuable, one should not assume that such intellectual endeavor will necessarily change organizational behavior or culture. A manager in a major chemicals firm observed, after considering the culture of his own company: "This is one hell of a tight molecule. I don't think we are likely to change it by having an intellectual argument about its nucleus" (by which he meant the powerful inner core of managers). To transform the strategy of an organization requires recognizing hidden assumptions and the implicit rules that govern the current ways of doing things. The first step toward fostering and managing significant change may be this realization: "It's where you are that makes it hard to get where you could be."

From Strategic Direction to Critical Success Factors

A useful first step in the process of identifying the means of achieving strategic change is to write a statement of strategic direction in terms of critical success factors (CSF).

This step translates the overall strategy into a relatively few but critical dimensions requiring change. The senior executives of most firms could rapidly prepare such a list, but a better practice is to create project teams made up of different levels of managers and let them do the analysis. For the professional services firm described in Box 15–4, such a list of CSF might include:

- Greater understanding of the strategic needs of clients.
- Tailoring of services to those needs.
- A more integrated delivery mechanism for services.
- A focus on those clients whom the firm can serve superbly and, by implication, the referral of work for clients whom it cannot serve equally well.
- The delivery of effective and practical solutions.
- A greater percentage of staff with wider strategic skills.
- Less division between partners and others.

Such CSF are likely to be somewhat general. The benefit of the activity is not in the achievement of precision, but in isolating the relatively few critical aspects of the organization's activities and behavior that need to change. It is essential that the managers involved recognize that, unless they are translated into more specific action, they are not of much practical value. To do this, they need to clearly understand the barriers to strategic change.

Box 15–4

The Cultural Web of a Professional Services Firm

A major region of an international professional services firm embarked on a strategic change program. Partners from the firm's audit, consultancy, taxation, and corporate recovery services undertook a culture audit using the cultural web as a framework for their deliberations on the need for and means of achieving strategic change. A cultural web based on their work is shown in Figure 15–7.

What does the web signify? The assumptions within the paradigm are about the standing and reputation of the firm, particularly the professionalism of its individuals. The firm's perceived superiority is closely linked to individual, and especially partner, capabilities and to closeness to clients. A "generalist" view is often expressed in the belief that these individuals could do anything for clients. Professionalism is associated with the conservative, uncontroversial, low-risk approach reflected in much of the routine behavior and control systems concerned with quality control.

Given this paradigm, it is not surprising that individual partner power was seen to be significant. This might be represented in named individuals, but, as in most partnerships, the hierarchy of power was not clear. In many respects, indeed, power has to be seen within the context of a partnership as a complex network that can be represented as a complex matrix. However, the extent to which the organization actually operates on the basis of its formal structure was being questioned: The networking between partners built up over many years and largely based on trust and proven expertise was especially important. As with many professional service and consultancy firms in which manpower is a key cost, controls over bookable time spent with clients and fee-earning were of central importance, as were the quality control procedures, particularly those concerned with, for example, the reports issued to clients. These controls were also somewhat cumbersome, time-consuming, and historically based.

The routines and rituals reflected much of this complexity. Because partners are central in the firm, looking after partners was as important as looking after clients. Professionalism and quality were reflected in the practice of partners' "signing off" anything that was going to a client, for example, reports and written correspondence. Individual responsibility of partners was reflected internally in the proliferation of committees and meetings. Partners might take personal responsibility with regard to clients, but they also wanted to have their say internally. Collective decision making (or, cynics might say, lack of decision making) was therefore the norm. Perhaps the most important ritual was the progress toward partnership, which began with induction into the culture of the firm and was periodically formalized in the appraisal systems.

Many of the stories were about individuals—heroes, villains, and mavericks. Other stories reflected the network structure or the almost tribal nature of the firm, with one "tribe" telling denigrating stories about another. It was recognized by the partners themselves that many stories were told by the managers about the differences between partners ("them") and everyone else ("us"). A good deal of the symbolism was related to partnership, especially in terms of the difference between partners and everyone else, which was underlined in partners' access to dining rooms and their other privileges.

FIGURE 15-7   The cultural web of an organization.

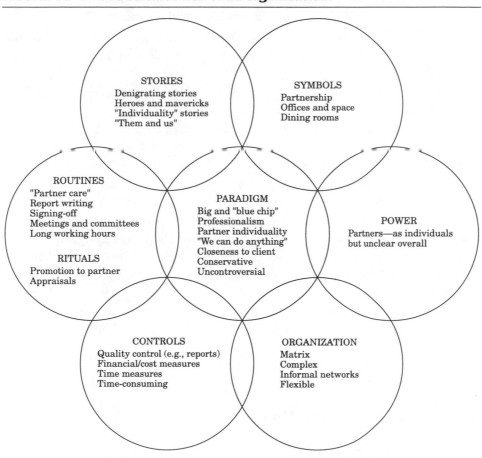

Identifying Barriers to Strategic Change

The process of identifying the organizational culture in its various components—or mapping the cultural web—can be useful in a number of respects. First, a culture audit sensitizes managers to an aspect of their organization that they know is important, in general terms, but of which they have no precise understanding. There is considerable value in identifying some specifics of a culture. Second, managers can often see how different aspects of the culture support each other. For example, in the professional services firm in Box 15–4, the core assumptions about professionalism and the ability to be a generalist are embodied in the institution of partnership, fostered by many of the stories, ritualized in the training programs for new recruits, and symbolized in the distinctions that exist between those who are partners and those who are not.

Most important of all, the mapping of organizational culture can help identify blockages that are likely to be faced in effecting strategic change. We can use the map of the professional services firm (Box 15–4) to indicate where some of the blockages to the delivery of the strategy might occur:

- If clients are looking for services tailored to their needs, is this compatible with a "we can do anything" approach centered around individual partner skills?
- Given the degree of complacency around an assumption of quality service, will the energy for change be achieved?
- What does "closeness to the client" mean? The risk is that it involves closeness to particular individuals—almost social relationships—rather than closeness to the problems that the client perceives as important.
- The loose, individually based power structure of the firm could be a problem if change is required. "Resistance movements" might well occur and be difficult to overcome where power is fragmented.
- Many of the routines and control systems are about "quality," but there is some evidence that quality is seen in relatively formal terms—for example, the production of reports. Does this relate to clients' needs if the clients are looking for the solution to problems?
- The routines of individuality in service delivery but collectivity in internal decision making might make refocusing on integration and coordination problematic.
- To what extent will the dominant role of partners linked to a "them and us" system militate against ownership of the new strategy throughout the firm?

Trading-In the Old Symbols

It is important to understand that an organization's cultural artifacts—its routines, stories, rituals, jokes, and symbols—can be used to challenge and amend status quo thinking. Organizational routines are, in effect, the everyday way in which core assumptions are translated into action. Stories are myths and legends that identify and dramatize what is meant by success or failure. Rituals embody and magnify the aspects of the organization that are especially significant. Renewing such aspects of organizational life can have powerful effects.

Mechanisms for Managing Strategic Change

To produce strategic change, strategic direction must be translated into strategic action. Too many senior executives equate the management of strategic change with changing the organizational structures and control processes and perhaps also with changing the power configurations of the organization. In effect, they are attempting to manage strategic change by starting within two, or perhaps three, elements of the cultural web—organizational structures and controls, and power bases in the organization. Too often, they fail to realize that for many—arguably, most—of those who execute the strategy in the organization, the more routinized and symbolic aspects of organizations are the day-to-day realities. Retail strategies are delivered by sales clerks as well as by the merchandise in the store. Strategy is communicated by the people who answer an organization's 800 number, as well as by its project engineers and truck drivers. The attitudes, ambitions, and work practices of factory employees as well as those of mechanical engineers drive the strategic action of manufacturing businesses.

Statements of strategy, organization charts, and formalized control procedures may be important, but their effect doesn't really begin until they impinge on the more mundane aspects of organizational life. How is a new strategy reflected in organizational routines, signaled in symbols, and talked about in stories? Until a strategic innovation touches the day-to-day experience of most individuals in the organization, it's likely to be discounted as merely a whim of senior executives. The wise manager takes the trouble to make changes in strategies that are relevant at the level of mundane reality. Lasting change must challenge and alter the core assumptions of the organizational paradigm. Figure 15–4 has made this point: it acknowledges the importance of changes in structures and control systems but identifies the changes in routines, rituals, and symbols that are required to change the paradigm.

The extent of the cultural change will, of course, depend on the extent of the change of strategy direction. In every organization, there is always likely to be a need to manage changes in culture. The rest of this chapter considers how this might be done and reviews the role of political processes in this context.

Changes in Organizational Routines

Routines are the institutionalized "ways we do things around here"; they tend to persist over time and guide how people do their jobs. Routines are also likely to be closely associated with the assumptions of the paradigm. For example, in the case of the professional services firm (see Box 15–4), the routine of getting all reports and correspondence to clients "signed off" by a partner and the day-to-day deference by managers to partners are obviously linked to the core assumptions about partnership centrality, low risk, and professionalism. Changing such routines may well question and challenge deep-rooted beliefs and assumptions in the organization. The changes may appear to be mundane but they can have significant consequences. Here are some examples:

- The management of a transport and distribution firm, seeking to emphasize rapid response to customer needs, established a routine for answering telephones in the head office. The routine had two rules: (1) no phone was allowed to ring more than twice before being picked up by someone and (2) no one was allowed to ignore a ringing phone ("It might be a customer").

- The main activity of branch personnel in many U.K. retail banks was the tedious process of filling in forms. In effect, this paperwork routine became more significant than dealing with customers. In the 1980s, when the banks introduced computerized systems, staff costs and paperwork were greatly reduced. As one manager put it: "If you haven't got a form to fill in, you have to attend to customers, and that is at the heart of our strategy."

- Buyers in a major retailer had always "bought long" (that is, committed themselves to large quantities of stock) to obtain the greatest discounts. A new managing director wanted a more responsive, fashion-oriented operation and insisted on cutting buying lead-times by half.

- An engineering company that was suffering from high costs and from low morale among its work force reduced its factory space by half. This required repositioning equipment, redesigning work areas, reducing space available for each operation, and, consequently, changing work routines. This was initially a cost-saving initiative, and it did reduce the work-in-progress on the factory floor, but there were other benefits. Factory employees began to take better care of their work areas, even down to repainting the walls and personally labeling cleaning materials.

As these instances show, strategies are abstractions until they are delivered at this mundane level. It's worth stressing the observation that senior executives often fail to identify the sort of changes in routine that drive core assumptions and deliver a strategy. Perhaps this is evidence that they aren't keeping a watchful eye for these day-to-day routines.

The translation of strategy into organizational action at the routine level is better undertaken by those in the organization who are intimately involved in those routines. Moreover, involving different levels of management in the strategy development process enhances the likelihood of more widespread ownership of and commitment to the strategy throughout the organization.

Rituals and Strategic Change

Anthropologists have long known the importance of rituals as ways in which communities preserve their cultures by acting them out. Organizations also have rituals that serve to reinforce their culture. We will discuss here some ways in which rituals can be employed to signal and effect change.[13]

Rituals of passage, which can include induction training courses or the training programs that fast-track executives attend, can be used to introduce new goals and promote new norms of behavior. The case of the professional service firm (see Box 15–4) provides a good example. Prior to the strategic change workshop, most of the partners had simply attended external training programs that had nothing to do with the internal development of the firm. Indeed, the workshops were not initially recognized, by the partners attending them, as having direct practical relevance to their firm. However, once the potential impact of the workshops was recognized, it galvanized real energy and commitment to effect strategic change. This had an even greater effect at the levels below partner. Middle managers had never before been involved in processes central to strategy development and change. Their participation signaled changes in manager–partner relationships, and therefore in the central assumptions about the role of partners.

Rituals of enhancement, such as awards ceremonies at company conferences, can be used to signal approval of individuals for their accomplishments and to motivate others toward similar efforts that are in line with the desired strategy. This device is frequently used by firms to magnify the importance to the firm of, for example, personnel who have shown attention to meeting customer needs, or have contributed to improved efficiency, or have contributed substantially to a new strategic direction. The new president of a financial services business introduced "birthday parties." As one manager described the ritual, "If it was your birthday, you could come and have coffee and ask any questions you wanted. People asked the stupidest questions sometimes, but there was always an answer immediately or in 24 hours. This signaled to me that [the new CEO] really cared about making this company better."[14]

Rituals of renewal, such as the appointment of consultants or task forces, can be used to signal that problems are being tackled and are being taken seriously. Banks throughout the world have faced the problem of developing more customer sensitivity. In the ANZ Bank in Australia, a customer care program was developed to enhance customer sensitivity. Informal networks of "diagnostic groups" were set up across levels of management to search for service quality changes. These groups were legitimized and provided with internal coherence by a variety of symbolic and ritualistic processes, including "well presented program guides, network directories . . . and certificates of merit [and] . . . formal presentation ceremonies to Regional Managers for discussing results achieved in service quality improvement. . . . There are also other rituals which provide a sense of identity and continuity . . . like the "groupie handshake," a special way of sitting on chairs, and "magical mystery tours."[15]

It has long been recognized that corporate social events can incorporate powerful *rituals of integration.* Surprisingly, rituals such as planning and budgeting can have similar influences. Seasoned executives know that one of planning's main purposes is to get the "blessings" of top management on the integration of the activities of different parts of the organization. Changing planning and budgeting systems can signal significant changes in strategy. For example, the consolidation of business plans according to strategic business units in General Electric (GE) a decade or so ago signaled a significant shift from a heavily diversified business toward a more focused strategy.

Rituals of degradation, such as firing top executives or moving them sideways publicly signal that the old order changeth. It is quite typical for a new CEO or an acquiring business to substantially disband an existing board. On the surface, this is the equivalent of firing the coach when it's really the players who are dropping the ball. But the new management is signaling the organization that it should not associate future strategy with the past regime. The strategy has changed.

Senior executives who have made their way up through the ranks in hierarchical firms are likely to have a highly developed sensitivity to corporate ritual. They can more readily identify and change training programs, company conferences, planning systems, the appointment of consultants, and many other rituals. They need, however, to reconsider what current rituals signal and what changing such rituals would signify.

Symbolic Activity in Managing Strategic Change[16]

An organizational symbol can be thought of as "any object, act, event, quality or relation that serves as a vehicle for conveying meaning usually by representing another thing."[17] These symbols "are signs which express much more that their intrinsic content."[18] They therefore link everyday aspects of the organization to more fundamental organizational meaning. For this reason, symbolic aspects of the organization act to preserve the paradigm. Consequently, symbols are especially important when it comes to managing strategic change. Management Consultant, Tom Peters has argued that "mundane tools that involve the creation and manipulation of symbols over time have impact to the extent that they reshape beliefs and expectations."[19] This is one reason why changes in routines and rituals (discussed above) are important; other such "mundane" aspects include the stories that people tell, buildings, clothing, particular people, status symbols such as cars or sizes of office, the type of language and terminology used, and even the technology of the organization and its history. The reward systems, the information and control systems, and the very organizational structures that represent reporting relationships and, often, status are also symbolic in nature. Even budgeting and planning systems come to take on symbolic significance insofar as they can represent the everyday reality of day-to-day organizational life peculiar to those in an organization.

Consciously or unconsciously, managers—indeed, all of us—manage symbolic aspects of everyday life. We arrange our office in a particular way; we dress in a particular style; we drive particular models of cars. The manager of change, however, needs to understand that, if symbolic aspects of organizations act to preserve the paradigm and exert forces for conformity, then they can also be used to influence change. There are many examples of such symbolic actions effecting changes:

- In the days when he established his reputation as a change agent at General Motors, John de Lorean deliberately promulgated stories to ridicule the dominant culture. He also introduced routines that were in direct contradiction of established values, and underlined his refusal to accept current norms through his personal dress and office decor.[20]
- A new chief executive of a transportation company ordered that the logos on vehicles were to be removed and all the vehicles were to be painted white. When managers complained, he requested that they come up with proposals for a new livery. In effect, he was (1) challenging them to

rethink what should visibly symbolize the future strategy of the business and (2) demanding that they do it without preconceptions rooted in company history.[21]

- Managers at a long-established industrial products company were reacting far too slowly in the face of declining markets. They realized that their new CEO "really meant business" when he closed the executive dining facilities. Managers were then required to eat in the same facilities as the work force, many of whom the managers knew they would have to fire.

- In a textile firm, equipment associated with "the old ways of doing things" was taken into the yard at the rear of the factory and dismantled in front of the work force.

- Salespeople in a clothing retailer, where the strategy was to move from a down-market, staid-product range to more fashionable merchandise, were asked to wear only the new clothing when they came to work. This move was doubly potent: (1) they complained to the buyers if the merchandise was not of good quality—a change in behavior that had political significance in itself—and (2) as one executive observed: "They had to wear the new strategy."

The action taken may be both substantial in terms of changes in strategy and symbolic in its significance. For example:

- When the new president of Asaki Breweries in Japan introduced Koku-Kire beer, he signaled a fundamental shift in product policy and required commitment to the new product, not only with a highly visible publicity launch and a change in company logo, but by recalling the old product from 130,000 stores and dumping it.[22]

- The way selection interviews are conducted is likely to signal, to those being interviewed, the nature of the organization and what is expected of them. A highly formal interview procedure may signal a mechanistic, hierarchical organization. More informal dialogue will signal a more open, organic organization.

One of the major signals of both substantive and symbolic change is the physical relocation of an organization's head office. Relocation often accompanies change in work processes, staffing, senior executives, logistics, and so on (substantive change), and, quite often, the head office is associated with the history and traditions of the organization (symbolic change).

The language used by change agents is also important. Change agents must learn to use metaphor and symbolism appropriately. Language is not simply about communicating facts and information; because of its symbolic nature, it is simultaneously able to carry several meanings at once. For example, it may link the past to the future—perhaps by attacking or undermining an image of the past—and therefore carry a very serious message. Yet it may do so in a playful way that evokes emotional feelings as strongly as does rational understanding. For example:

- One chief executive of a company facing severe strategic threats chose to indicate the urgency and need for radical rethinking through the language he used to his board and senior executives: "We need to think of ourselves as bulls; and we have a difficult choice. We face the abattoir or the bull ring. I am clear about my preference; let's talk about yours."

- In the professional services firm discussed in Box 15–4, the senior partner/sponsor made a presentation outlining the proposed changes. It included pop art visuals with words like "wham" and bubble-speak such as "Wow, I'm being asked to participate." As the senior partner said: "Now you may think that this is pretty ordinary; but my audience was accustomed to nothing more exciting than slides with a neat printing and our logo. So, if nothing else, my pop art images made an impact and contributed to a real atmosphere of change."

- As British Telecom, the previously nationalized telecommunications company in the U.K., started to adjust to its new commercial role, difficulty was found in getting managers to commit themselves to action and take responsibility. The company issued directions to project managers to use certain words in their reports rather than others—specifically, to use words like "reduce, eliminate, improve, remove, and meet target" and not to use words like "discover, explore, revise, devise, and review."

- The language used by Sir Ralph Halpern in his description of the head office long associated with Burton's, a family-run business in the U.K., showed dramatically both his commitment to running a commercial enterprise, rather than a family-controlled interest, and the primacy of the retail side of the business. The head office was located on the same site as the company's huge clothing factory: ". . . it was a feudal castle. They had their lunch in the feudal canteen, the feudal barons called Burton turning up and administering the rites and allowing employment to be granted; and there would be a medical man on the premises and a bit of billiards and a bowling green. So the whole of the village set up was really to show that we could protect you there. . . ."[23] Halpern closed the factory, signaling that the company was irreversibly a retailer rather than a vertically integrated menswear clothing company and that the family dominance had ceased.

Perhaps the most powerful symbol of all, in relation to change, is the behavior of top executives. The behavior, language, and stories associated with them can signal powerfully the need for change and appropriate behavior relating to the management of change. Their behavior can also substantially undermine change processes. Too few senior executives understand that, when they have made pronouncements about the need for strategic change, it is vital that their behavior be aligned with such change. It is one thing to analyze a strategic position carefully or to conceive of a future strategy; but, for most people in an organization, their day-to-day reality is one of deeds and actions rather than of abstractions. The visible actions of the change agents, therefore, need to be in line with the strategic thrust being advanced. In one major retail business, for example, where there was an espoused strategy of customer care, the CEO, on visits to stores, typically ignored staff and customers alike: he seemed to be interested only in the financial performance of the store. It was not something he was aware of until it was pointed out. Afterward, his insistence on talking to staff and customers during his store visits became a story that spread round the company and helped reinforce the strategic direction of the firm.

Whether consciously or unconsciously, change agents employ symbols, language, and metaphor to galvanize change. However, there is a danger that change agents do not realize the power of the language they employ and, while espousing change, use language that signals the importance of the status quo or their personal reluctance to change. In short, those involved in change need to think carefully about the language they use and the symbolic significance of their actions.

Political Processes for Change: The Links to Organizational Symbols

In managing strategic change, it is likely that there will be a need for the reconfiguration of power structures in the organization. This may well be part of the process of legitimizing dissent and empowering those in the organization who are questioning the existing ways of operating. Managers need to be sensitive to the political dimensions of their activities and to understand the links between organizational power and organizational symbols. As was pointed out earlier, there is likely to be a link between the paradigm, (a historically rooted set of assumptions and beliefs that may be linked to past success), and the power elites in the organization. Particularly in long-established organizations that have undergone little transformational change, the most powerful people or groups are likely to be those associated with the core assumptions of the organization. Again, not only is strategic change likely to require political change; but political change itself is therefore both substantially and symbolically important if changes are required in core assumptions.

In the context of the management of strategic change, political activity may be used to:

- Build a power base.
- Encourage support or overcome resistance.
- Achieve commitment to change.

The control and manipulation of organizational resources create a source of power. For example, acquiring or allocating resources, or being identified with significant resource areas or areas of expertise, can be an important means of overcoming resistance or persuading others to accept change. Association with powerful elites in the organization is of importance in building a power base. Building alliances can also be important in overcoming the resistance from more powerful groups because some parts of the organization (or individuals) are likely to be more sympathetic to that change than others are. The likelihood of political change within an organization can even be mapped by rating factions in terms of their relative power and the stake they have in a change in strategy.

To build power, the manager may initially seek to identify with the very symbols that preserve and reinforce the paradigm—working within the committee structures, becoming identified with the organizational rituals or stories that exist, and so on. On the other hand, in breaking resistance to change, removing, challenging, or changing rituals and symbols may be powerful means of achieving the questioning of what has been taken for granted. Symbolic activity can also be used for consolidating change: by concentrating attention or "applause" and rewards on those who most accept change, wider adoption of the change is more likely. There may also be means of confirming, through symbolic devices such as new structures, titles, office allocation, and so on, that the change is to be regarded as important and irreversible. In that way, symbolic activity is linked to political activity and, as was seen earlier, political action may itself take on symbolic significance.

CONCLUSIONS

This chapter has provided (1) a framework for the consideration of strategic change in terms of the cultural processes in organizations and (2) explanations for the strategic inertia that so often exists in organizations and the consequent strategic drift that can occur. The chapter has also proposed ways to consider managerial change processes in cultural terms that can help achieve strategic change in organizations.

In their study comparing successful versus less successful cases of strategic change in the 1980s, Pettigrew and Whipp[24] concluded that no one characteristic was more important than another for successful firms. Managers who concentrated on a number of key activities effected change in their organizations most successfully. These characteristics included organizationwide sensitivity to the environment; coherence in strategic planning, to match organizational capabilities to changing environmental pressure; and the effective development of the human resource base of the organization. However, they also stressed the importance of linking strategic and operational change, not only in the sense of linking strategic direction with detailed resource planning and control procedures, but also by ensuring that the need for change and the direction of change were communicated through the everyday aspects of the organization that make up its culture (and have been the subject of this chapter). Moreover, they found that the successful leader of change was one who could sensitively construct change programs in the context of an understanding of the culture of that organization.

As Peters and Waterman[25] argued, the successful manager of change:

> . . . must be the master of two ends of the spectrum: ideas at the highest level of abstraction and actions at the most mundane level of detail. . . . With soaring lofty visions that would generate excitement and enthusiasm for tens of hundreds of thousands of people. . . . On the other hand, it seems the only way to instill enthusiasm is through scores of daily events.

This master of two ends of the spectrum will simultaneously understand the need for careful analysis and evaluation, to invite confidence in the strategies to be followed, and the need to relate to the routines, rituals, symbols, and stories that are the reality of organizational life. Managers recognize the powerful influence of cultural and political systems in organizations: they use them every day. What they lack is an explicit framework that makes sense of the links among strategy, culture, and managerial processes of strategic change. This chapter has set out to provide such a framework as a means of better considering problems and means of strategic change.

NOTES

1. *The Financial Times* (November 4, 1992), 20.

2. Strategic transformations are the focus of Chapter 16.

3. The framework presented here builds on the discussion in H. Mintzberg and J. A. Waters, "Of Strategies Deliberate and Emergent," *Strategic Management Journal* (1985), *6*(3): 257–272.

4. See D. K. Hurst, J. C. Rush, and R. E. White, "Top Management Teams and Organizational Renewal," *Strategic Management Journal* (1989), *10:* 87–105.

5. See H. E. Aldrich, *Organizations and Environments* (Englewood Cliffs, NJ: Prentice-Hall, 1979).

6. D. Miller and P. Friesen, "Momentum and Revolution in Organizational Adaptation," *Academy of Management Journal* (1980), *23*(4): 591–614.

7. E. H. Schein, *Strategic Change and the Management Process* (Oxford, U.K.: Basil Blackwell, 1987).

8. G. Johnson, *Strategic Change and the Management Process* (Oxford, U.K.: Basil Blackwell, 1987).

9. This section is adapted from G. Johnson, "Re-Thinking Incrementalism," *Strategic Management Journal* (1988), *9:* 75–91.

10. K. E. Weick, *The Social Psychology of Organizing* (Reading, MA: Addison-Wesley, 1979).

11. D. Miller, *The Icarus Paradox* (New York: HarperCollins, 1990).

12. For a discussion of the role of planning and other administrative systems in anticipating and dealing with strategic drift and environmental change, see Chapter 14.

13.   H. M. Trice and J. M. Beyer, "Using Six Organizational Rites to Change Culture," in R. H. Kilmann et al. (eds.), *Gaining Control of the Corporate Culture* (San Francisco: Jossey-Bass Publishers, 1985).

14.   L. A. Isabella, "Evolving Interpretations as a Change Unfolds: How Managers Construe Key Organizational Events," *Academy of Management Journal* (1990), *33*(1): 24.

15.   D. Ballantyne, *Management of the Diagnostic Review Process in Service Quality Management*, Cranfield School of Management, Working Paper Cranfield SWP 3/90, 1989.

16.   G. Johnson, "Managing Strategic Change: The Role of Symbolic Action," *British Journal of Management* (1990) *1*(4): 183–200.

17.   Same reference as endnote 13, 394.

18.   L. R. Pondy, R. J. Frost, G. Morgan, and T. C. Dandridge (eds.), *Organizational Symbolism*, (Greenwich, CT: JAI Press, 1983), 5.

19.   T. Peters, "Symbols, Patterns, and Settings: An Optimistic Case for Getting Things Done," *Organizational Dynamics* (Autumn 1978), *7*(2): 2–24.

20.   J. Martin and C. Siehl, "Organizational Culture and Counterculture: An Uneasy Symbiosis," *Organizational Dynamics* (Autumn 1983), *12*(2): 52–64.

21.   Adapted from E. H. Schein, *Organizational Culture and Leadership* (San Francisco: Jossey-Bass Publishers, 1985).

22.   T. Nakajo and T. Kono, "Success through Culture Change in a Japanese Brewery," *Long Range Planning* (1989), *22*(6), 29–37.

23.   G. Johnson, "The Burton Group," in G. Johnson and K. Scholes (eds.), *Exploring Corporate Strategy, Text and Cases* (Englewood Cliffs, NJ: Prentice-Hall, 1993), 699.

24.   A. M. Pettigrew and R. Whipp, *Managing Change for Competitive Success* (Oxford, U.K.: Basil Blackwell, 1991).

25.   T. J. Peters and R. H. Waterman, *In Search of Excellence* (New York: Harper & Row, 1982), 287.

RE-INVENTING STRATEGY AND THE ORGANIZATION: MANAGING THE PRESENT FROM THE FUTURE*

16

Tracy Goss
Author, Lecturer, Consultant

Richard Pascale
Author, Lecturer, Consultant

Anthony Athos
Author, Lecturer, Consultant

In the past few years, Kodak, IBM, American Express (Amex), and General Motors (GM)—all corporations that had for decades prided themselves on their venerable management traditions—suddenly sacked their CEOs. The end began for each CEO when the board, no longer content to provide genteel oversight, began to press for results. When these were not forthcoming, the board was willing to take tough remedial action.

That these firms had intractable problems was not a secret. Each of the ousted CEOs had promised a "turnaround" that never came. All were able managers with records of sustained success. Beyond these common traits, there were few similarities save one: in the aftermath, all four CEOs seemed bewildered by the unraveling state of affairs that had led to their downfall. Why had the measures they employed to correct the situation fallen so far short of what was needed?

---

* This chapter is drawn from the same research as Goss, Pascale, and Athos, *Harvard Business Review*, Nov.–Dec. 1993, pp. 97–108.

439

Each leader had spearheaded vigorous programs of downsizing, delayering, and reengineering of core business processes. Most of these endeavors showed promise: lowering costs, accelerating productivity, and improving profitability . . . for a while. But beneath the sound and fury of restructuring, the competitive vitality of their enterprises continued to ebb away. Ultimately, they were faulted personally for "inadequate leadership" and "lack of a strategic vision."

These corporate leaders had many resources available to revitalize their companies. That they failed may point to a larger issue—we often attack symptoms, not root causes, as we go about the task of authentic corporate renewal. Current difficulties finding appropriate remedies for such management problems are reminiscent of the search for reliable medicine to cure the wide variety of illnesses that plagued Europe during the Middle Ages. Owing to the ignorance about the underlying sources of disease, changing doctors (or shifting from leach treatments of the arm to leach treatments of the groin) didn't do a lot of good.

The authentic revitalization of companies requires rebuilders to dig deeper. There are four essential steps:

1. Step outside the current management context (or paradigm) to take a fresh and creative look at the source of the difficulties and how to address these root causes.

2. Establish whether the organization needs to change incrementally or reinvent itself fundamentally. Most companies talk transformation while setting a course that can, at best, improve performance only incrementally. Most companies find true metamorphosis unimaginable. Unless this choice of incremental change or real transformation is conscious and well-considered, the ensuing muddle will almost certainly diffuse the power of whatever remedial action is taken.

3. Galvanize the organization around a powerful future that people would currently predict is not possible. Then "manage the present from that future." This step sounds strange, but it turns out that the attention and energy of the organization and its key executives need to be refocused on executing a definitive break with the past. To do this, top management must design a set of difficult challenges (we call them "breakdowns-on-purpose," or "re-invention projects") that dramatically interrupt the organization's historical way of doing things and require inventing ways of operating that are consistent with the new context.

4. Initiate certain processes and steps in the re-invention of an organization that are essential to success.

Even when executives become convinced that re-inventing their organizations is the only hope for the future, they are likely to have serious reservations. In the history of management, few executives have been able to turn a corporate behemoth (or even a small organization with fewer resources) on a behavioral dime. Companies *know* a lot about improving things incrementally, and most firms do a respectable job of downsizing and drastically reducing costs when those steps are required. But when it comes to dramatic shifts in an organization's capabilities in such areas as cycle time, quality, service, or rate of innovation, the remedies offered almost always fall short of expectations.[1]

WHY RE-INVENTION?

For an organization to re-invent itself fundamentally, it must shift the *context* of work, as distinguished from the *content,* such as CAD/CAM or expert systems, or the *processes* through which work is accomplished such as total quality management (TQM) or business process reengineering. Altering an organization's context is always the decisive factor in paving the way for transformation.[2] The deposed leaders of Kodak, IBM, Amex, and GM either failed to realize this or "couldn't find the handle" to set the process in motion.

Re-invention entails a bona fide metamorphosis, the organizational equivalent of changing from a caterpillar to a butterfly. In contrast to change, re-invention is not about improving on what is, but about creating what isn't.[3] The butterfly is not "more caterpillar," or a "better or improved caterpillar," or even a "changed caterpillar." It is a new and entirely distinct being that flourishes in a different environment, seeks different sources of nourishment, and has a different source of power.

To re-invent itself, an organization creates a new realm of possibility that did not previously exist. The outcome is seen in unprecedented results that previously were considered impossible in three key areas:

1. Financial performance (such as profitability and return on investment (ROI)).
2. Industry benchmarks (such as quality, service ratings, cycle time, and market share).
3. Organization and culture (as measured by surveys of key employees, usually the hardest to fool, who say: This is a different company than it was three to five years ago.).

At Ford in the 1980s, for example, the financial pendulum swung from a $3 billion loss at the start of the decade to the industry leadership in earnings. Quality improved from worst among the Big Three automobile manufacturers to best, and cycle time to build a car halved from eight years to four. Climate surveys and focus groups of both union and salaried employees reported dramatic shifts in perceptions of management, and improved morale and company loyalty.[4]

These are impressive achievements, but there is a hitch—sustainability. Of the handful of companies that have produced these outcomes, fewer still have been able to sustain the new momentum as an ongoing way of doing business. The ability to continuously renew one's organization is a much-sought-after but highly elusive goal. To re-invent an organization for the long term, its leaders must continuously put at risk the success they have become for the possibility they could be.[5]

ALTERING THE CONTEXT

The term *context* encompasses the underlying assumptions or invisible premises on which an organization and its strategy are based.[6] Unless the context is articulated, acknowledged, and grappled with, shifts of fundamental importance cannot occur. That is why the recent appeals to executives to "stretch" their "strategic horizons" or to declare their "strategic intentions" have produced grandiose ambitions, a lot of "trying harder," and underwhelming results.[7] In effect, there has been a lot of grunting and groaning without ever getting the lid off the jar. Unless the context is shifted, it is virtually impossible to create an entirely new realm of possibilities.

An organization's context is the sum of all the views and perceptions of its members, and the product of its experience (which, by definition, is always derived from the past) and interpretations about the past. These often unspoken and even unacknowledged conclusions determine what is possible for the future. Context determines the outcome, no matter how clever the new processes and improvement in work content may be. For this reason, many prescriptions for fixing processes (TQM, just-in-time, workout, continuous improvement) have had only modest results. The context is also determined by the key individuals in the organization, especially top management. They must re-invent themselves if unprecedented outcomes are to be created and persist. When senior executives seek to alter everything but themselves, re-invention cannot occur and outcomes are disappointing.

An analogy will help to explain the nature of the context. Suppose you inherit your grandmother's house. Unknown to you, it has one peculiarity: All the light fixtures have bulbs that cast a slightly blue light. While renovating, you find that the color of the new furnishings you like in the sales rooms takes on an unpleasant hue once installed. You continue to spend a lot of time and money repainting walls, reupholstering furniture, and replacing carpets. Then one day you notice the blue lights and change the bulbs. Seen in this new light, everything you've "fixed" is "broken."[8]

Context is about the color of the light, not the objects in the room. Context colors everything that it illuminates, without our being aware of it.

Much maligned IBM is a good example of a firm that tried to fix many processes to solve a contextual problem. It was among the vanguard in pioneering many contemporary business techniques, such as "six-sigma quality," "empowerment," delayering, and downsizing. Yet IBM has steadfastly been unable to achieve lift-off because it has failed to alter the fundamental context in which all these techniques were embedded. The IBM way is to control and predict— to demonstrate, in an upbeat and positive way, that the organization knows exactly how a course of action will play out five steps in the future before it embarks on step one.[9] This establishes a context that has circumscribed the potency of the business techniques employed. On the other end of the spectrum, Motorola, with an awareness of how its context was holding it back, has repeatedly chosen to break out of its traditional context and re-invent a new one. Of all companies we have researched, only Motorola qualifies as having mastered the art and science of re-invention.[10] (See Box 16–1.)

A NEW TERRITORY—"THE DOMAIN OF BEING"

The "Doingness" Trap

The problem today is that we doggedly talk about "re-invention" while proceeding along a path that is predestined to stay within the old change boundaries. With no awareness of the power of context, we continue to beat our heads against a wall that we can't see.

What are we missing? This parallel from the history of physics may help. All scientists at the turn of the century treated time as a universal constant. Time just "was." However, physicists studying properties of light (photons) had increasing amounts of experimental evidence that indicated the universe wasn't performing as everyone believed it should. Yet they held fast to the then-extant "ether wave theory" of light and its central premise that time was a constant (and the speed of light was a variable).

When Einstein speculated that the speed of light might be a constant, he was drawn to look elsewhere for a variable that could account for the elasticity of the cosmos. There was only one candidate—time. Einstein created an intellectual puzzle that forced him to look "outside the box" for a solution. His speculation about totally new possibilities launched him on the intellectual odyssey that produced the General and Special theories of Relativity and revolutionized the world of physics. Stated differently, he created a new context for how we look at the world around us.[11]

There is a modest parallel in the field of management. The constant accepted as valid without question in all management theories is that effective prescriptions and methodologies prescribe *doing* this or *not doing* that. *Doing* is the apparent constant; to manage is to *do*. Managers are selected and promoted based on their ability to *get things done*. But what if something else is the constant and *doing* is actually the variable?

Einstein engaged in the mental experiment of riding on a photon of light to see what the world looked like from that perspective. So too, the executive who would master re-invention must journey into a largely unfamiliar and, perhaps at first, uncomfortable territory. In this territory, a crucial dimension is hidden until we learn to distinguish it. This is the territory or domain of *being*.[12]

Box 16–1

Motorola

For those who wish to master the art of re-invention, Nordstrom and Motorola represent two of the most instructive success stories available. While in very different businesses, they have many qualities in common—qualities that highlight the concepts advanced here. Both have enjoyed the benefit of several generations of family leadership that was willing to "do whatever it takes to succeed." Both have strong operating systems and disciplined financial controls, but neither is obsessively bottom-line-oriented. Both companies make extensive use of contention and orchestrate conflict to keep everyone on his/her toes. Both advocate an upside-down organization with the customer at the top, and both go overboard in taking outrageous customer requests as a provocation to continuously reexamine how they do things. Both firms have a team management approach on top and intentionally choose individuals of differing styles and talents to provide complementary vision and debate. Both companies are unusually focused on the future, and these deep convictions about how the future will turn out lead to day-to-day decisions that might truly be characterized as "managing the present from the future." Both firms orchestrate "breakdowns-on-purpose" to push the envelope and challenge conventional ways of doing things.

With $14 billion in sales and 100,000 employees worldwide, Motorola shows few signs of the machine like bureaucracy one would expect of a company of its size. In the past five years, sales have risen from $3.5 billion while total employment has remained essentially unchanged. In the same time frame, it has become the market share leader and low-cost provider in pagers, cellular phones, and two-way radios. It is a strong and profitable producer of microelectronics (i.e., computers on a chip), ranking second behind Intel, and has outperformed Japanese heavyweights like NEC and Matsushita in all of the above markets. The firm estimates it has saved a total of $3.1 billion since 1988 by reducing its defect ratio in manufacturing by 99.5%.[a]

The following managerial practices contribute to this high level of performance:

Managing the present from the future. Throughout its history, Motorola has done something few companies do: It has moved *proactively,* long before its business was at risk, to position itself in whole new industries that it bet on for the future. In 1949, founder Paul Galvin and his son Robert bet the company on the then nascent semiconductor business, diverting resources from its bread-and-butter consumer electronics lines. In 1974, sensing the coming Japanese dominance in consumer electronics, Robert Galvin, now chairman, bet the company again—this time on microchips, wireless phones, two-way radios, and pagers—and sold off consumer electronics while its businesses were still seen as healthy.

Described as one of the most far-thinking business executives of this century, Robert Galvin has a clear grasp on the benefits of leading from the

[a] For an excellent description of Motorola today, see G. Christian Hill and Ken Yamada, "Motorola Illustrates How an Aged Giant Can Remain Vibrant," *The Wall Street Journal* (December 9, 1992), A1, A18.

future. "At times," he states, "we must engage in an act of faith that key things are doable that are not provable." "Too often," he adds, "our expectation level is too little compared to what is possible."[b] In 1982, as Galvin stepped down, he charged Motorola with being "the world's premier company." His head of strategic planning, Richard Heimlich, remembers, "People snickered. He [Galvin] countered with, 'Why not? Someone is going to do it. Why not us?' This goal has since become the 'future' of Motorola. One of its highly important SEPs [senior executive projects] is to create a road map to achieve this goal."[c]

Re-invention projects and "breakdowns-on-purpose." In the 1967–1977 time frame, Motorola observed the sobering debacle of the Japanese destroying two businesses in the United States: (1) color television and (2) CB radios. In both cases, Japanese dumping was extensive (and subsequently proven in court). Motorola noted the Japanese willingness to kill a U.S. market while excluding U.S. firms from retaliation in Japan.

At the first of what became Motorola's Biannual Officers' Meetings in 1979, Galvin assembled his top 140 managers to gauge their awareness of the impending threat. He found them overconfident. Then one officer stood up and said, "While we're patting ourselves on the back, let me tell you something. Our quality stinks."[d] (Such a comment is permissible at Motorola, where self-criticism is cultivated.) Galvin seized on this opening to drive his concern home. He announced that the company should commit itself to a 10X improvement in quality. At the next meeting in 1981, Galvin again sought the pulse of urgency. This time he broke the attendees into groups of 25 and asked for recommendations for areas needing change. He listened in silence to the read-out, then stood up. "I am very disappointed," he stated. "Ten percent incremental improvement won't do it, guys. If we don't change discontinuously, we'll be out of business in two years."[e] Heimlich recalls, "People were stunned. Was he serious? Feelers went forth to the executive office on Monday. Was this for real? The answer: Damn right, he's serious!"[f]

Soon thereafter, Galvin ratcheted his quality expectations upward to "six sigma" (which translates to 3.4 defects per million), a standard comparable to the best of the Japanese. By 1987, he had added more pressure by announcing two further productivity goals that his subordinates considered impossible. He wanted Motorola to reduce manufacturing defects by 70 percent every two years, and cycle time by 90 percent every five years. To ensure these reinvention projects were taken in earnest, he tied quality and cycle time gains to compensation and began each of his monthly executive committee meetings with a review of current status against these goals. He also embarked on a program, called the Bandit Project, to invade the Japanese pager market. Motorola was the world's low-cost producer and believed that if it could succeed with any product, this was it. Prospective Japanese customers stalled, then refused to provide specs, and then begrudgingly placed their orders

[b] Robert W. Galvin, *The Idea of Ideas* (Schaumburg, IL: Motorola University Press, 1991), 8, 24.
[c] Interviews with Richard Heimlich, Motorola, Schaumburg, IL, October 28, 1992.
[d] Hill and Yamada, *op. cit.*, A18. Also see John J. Coleman, "Motorola's Japan Strategy," Harvard Business School, Cambridge, MA, Case Study 387-093 (1986), 8–18.
[e] *Id.*, A18.
[f] Heimlich, *op. cit.*

under diplomatic pressure from the U.S. Special Trade Representative. Angry, the Japanese pager manufacturers retaliated by dumping in the U.S. market. While Motorola pursued and won the subsequent antidumping litigation, they hung tough during the price war and surprised themselves by lowering the prices of pagers and cellular phones by 80 percent. When the dust cleared, the Japanese were vanquished and Motorola dominated the Japanese and U.S. markets.[g]

Shift in being. In 1983, Galvin wrote a 13-page memo that launched the Organizational Effectiveness effort. It challenged Motorola's strong not-invented-here culture, its arrogance, and its complacency. Galvin advocated ongoing change as a way of life. This initiative soon led to massive retraining and education programs aimed at all levels of Motorola's hierarchy.

A highly effective video chronicling the Japanese invasion and subsequent elimination of once proud names like RCA, Philco, and Magnavox had the effect of evoking terror in the ranks. "It truly created a sense of urgency," recalls strategic planner Heimlich.[h] It became a seminal event. Motorola went on to establish Motorola University and invested over $100 million in the education and re-invention of its employees over the next five years.

Purposive differences. Any organization that re-invents itself does not do so without costs. Firms like Honda, Nordstrom, and Motorola are all pressure-cooker environments that relentlessly ask: "What have you done to add value *today?*" Galvin coined the term "purposive differences," a virtue he extolled.[i] His own three-person executive team (and the three individuals he chose as its successor) draws on strong-willed individuals with divergent but complementary views and capabilities. Motorola, according to one source, "makes a cult of dissent and open verbal combat." Each employee is entitled to a minority report if he feels his ideas aren't supported. The reports are read by the bosses of the worker's bosses. Unlike other firms that have (but subvert) such devices, retribution at Motorola is considered "un-macho." Engineers are encouraged to dispute their supervisors and one another vigorously at open meetings. The ferocity of conflict can be shocking, especially to newcomers. "It gets wild," says new president George Fisher. "I was amazed when I came here from Bell Labs in 1986. The discussions get violent—verbally, fortunately."[j]

"Motorola's cult of conflict quickly identifies and fixes mistakes," states industry expert Ken Yamada.[k] "It unmasks and kills ill-conceived projects, tends to ensure top managers are informed, and occasionally unearths enormous opportunities that have been passed by." Like Honda, Motorola points to some of its biggest breakthroughs (and subsequent financial successes) and assigns their survival against all odds to the company's willingness to tolerate conflict. The high-speed workstation microprocessor 880000 and the Iridium low-flying satellite-based world cellular phone are examples. Both were rescued by conflict-surfacing devices known as "minority reports," "technology road maps," and the routine top management practice of coming into town and meeting with bench-level engineers. In a culture that conditions people to speak up, buried proposals get a hearing.

[g] Hill and Yamada, *op. cit.*, A18.
[h] Heimlich, *op. cit.*
[i] Galvin, *op. cit.*, 83–91.
[j] Hill and Yamada, *op. cit.*, A18.
[k] *Id.*

Being: **The Hidden Dimension**

Organizations and the people in them are *being* something all the time. On occasion, we describe them as being "conservative" or "hard-charging" or "resistant to change." However, aside from such casual generalizations, we concentrate mostly on what we are *doing* and let *being* fend for itself.

We have few mental hooks—or even words—for excursions into the *being* terrain. It smacks of something philosophical—or even worse, theological—and therefore is presumably of little relevance to management. But what if the difficulty we are experiencing in getting our minds around the terrain of *being* is a real-time example of the blind spots we have been talking about. Who we are *being* is a critical (and almost always ignored) factor in re-inventing organizations.[13]

Remarkable shifts in action and results can occur only when there is a shift in *being*. Executives who decide to undertake re-invention must take two steps into this domain:

1. Become aware of and come to terms with the way the organization is *being*.
2. Shift the way they are *being,* to be consistent with the new context.

If accomplished effectively and publicized properly, these two unconventional management decisions can alter the organization's perceptions of what is possible (creating opportunities that managers weren't able to see before). This enables them to take action in entirely new ways and to achieve unheard-of outcomes that were previously inconceivable and are required for performance in the new competitive situation. To tie all this together, re-invention entails the creation of a new context: The art and craft of continuously engineering shifts in being, which in turn produce sustainable unprecedented results. An example of how this can happen is given in Box 16–2.

The acid test of a shift in *being* is whether it is intellectually and/or emotionally jolting. Shifts in *being* are not merely upbeat intellectual "ah-ha's." When a shift in being is experienced, "Eureka!" isn't as likely to be exclaimed as "Oh, my God!" is to be whispered. Mort Meyerson, the former president of Electronic Data Systems (EDS), is largely credited for building the firm into the information technology giant it is today. Currently, as the chairman of Perot Systems (an information systems company that is assisting many corporate re-inventions), he is thoroughly familiar with the jolting shifts in being that re-invention entails. He warns:

> The journey to re-invent yourself is not as scary as they say it is . . . it's worse! You step into the abyss out of the conviction that the only way to compete in the long haul is to be a totally different company. By definition, because the undertaking is not an incremental one, it's a sink-or-swim proposition. As the senior executive, you feel a huge responsibility for crossing this river of no return. It causes upsets and conflicts. Many times you ask yourself, "Am I making the right decision?"

Box 16–2

Europcar[a]

Executives at Europcar (the second largest rental car company in Europe, behind Avis) understand the *being* dilemma. For years, they tried to *do* what Avis and Hertz did until they took on the challenge of shifting who they were being (i.e., from a follower to a leader; from a controlled, risk-averse company to one that takes on big challenges and banks on the exceptional performance of its personnel).

Europcar has been built through acquisition. Its strength lies in its comprehensive presence in the primary and secondary cities of Europe. It dominates the self-move truck-rental market and caters to local in-country businesspeople and vacationers. It has less of a presence at Europe's major international airports. Worse, its operating systems were built and maintained by the separate country fiefdoms—and these were plainly inadequate when dealing with the increasing numbers of international and local cross-border travelers—the big growth sector in the swelling Pan-European market.

In January 1992, CEO Fred Dellis surveyed the competitive situation and did not like what he saw. Revenues were rising slowly; profits were plummeting. Dellis, a 12-year Hertz veteran and a Belgian by birth, approached the problems in a careful and deliberate fashion. He estimated that it cost Europcar $13 to process each rental agreement (much of it by hand) compared to $1 at Hertz and Avis. Past attempts at incremental improvement had failed to close the gap.

Characteristically, Dellis did not embark on his efforts to transform Europcar with a big meeting and high drama. Instead, he commissioned one of his most energetic and hard-charging executives to revamp Europcar's entire operating system—how reservations were made, how rental operations flowed from check-out to check-in, and the financially critical activities of fleet purchasing and fleet utilization. The project was called Greenway—tying to Europcar's green logo and evoking images of a fresh approach to the future.

Over 100 high-potential Europcar middle managers were conscripted from their in-country jobs and housed in London to re-engineer the information flows of the enterprise. Their challenge, together with their partner in the process, Perot Systems, was to implement the new approach in 18 months. The experts insisted it could not be done in less than two years—more likely, three. Europcar stuck to its "impossible" deadline.

As the design process moved forward, all of the many ways in which the beliefs from the past subvert the hopes for the future began to be encountered by the design team. The separate countries claimed they did not have enough information on what was being built and could never implement the new approach in time. Many countries insisted on such high degrees of tailoring to their own market as to compromise efficiencies of scale.

But in Nice, France, on February 24–27, 1993, a small miracle happened on the road to transformation. The 35 top managers from Europcar headquarters

[a] This description of Europcar is based entirely on Richard Pascale, "Transformation at Europcar" (Spring 1993), unpublished.

and member countries assembled to take a hard look at competitive realities and their current cost position. Slowly, painfully, a consensus arose: Nothing short of transformation would suffice. The Greenway Project, precisely because it was so difficult and all-encompassing, was just the right medicine to shake the company awake before its survival was at stake. It was also recognized that, through Greenway, Europcar could leapfrog competition and become the most user-friendly and efficient rental car company in Europe.

Picture now the Greenway Fair held in a very large hotel ballroom, separated by partitions into booths (or meeting areas). Because senior management had belatedly recognized the importance of Greenway to Europcar's competitive future, the middle management designing team that had been invited to demonstrate the system now arrived with low expectations of their seniors. The designers had made enormous headway with very little support, input, or encouragement from these senior sponsors who had complained that "Greenway was too slow, too expensive, too complex" and so forth. Underneath the push back, they could discern that the underlying agenda of the management of the country units was to maintain their local prerogatives by preventing the companywide system from taking hold.

As the Greenway Fair commenced, the senior 35 managers (now sensitized to the crucial importance of Greenway and the necessity of thinking and behaving as a non-European company) were assigned the task of bridging the gulf of distrust and misunderstanding between themselves and the design team. The seniors were divided into subgroups, each scheduled to rotate through each of the six booths for extensive one-and-a-half-hour briefings on each of the components of the new operating system—rental operations, fleet utilization, finance, sales and marketing, and so on.

Zoom in on the rental operations booth. Its partitions are decorated with diagrams of essential work flows, photographs of rental counter layouts, and blowups of the simplified rental contract. A slide projector hums at the back of the booth. The senior executives gather around an articulate midlevel manager who describes her Scottish design team's work efforts. A console is on the table. There are many questions, a lot of give and take. Slowly, disbelief and alienation on behalf of both designers and senior managers fade away. A subtle sense of excitement of what might be possible for Europcar starts to take form. This is the ineffable, hard to describe stuff of *being*. From this sense of unity and possibility, a new future for Europcar was born—the future of a company that could coalesce across borders and levels of hierarchy, work as a team, and lead as an innovator in its field.

An awareness of differences in being (although we never think of it in these terms) occurs to many of us when we first travel abroad. We come home saying, "I learned more about my own country than the country I visited." What we are describing is the discovery that the community in which we were raised imported certain unspoken rules. These social conventions are implicit—like the appropriate speaking distance between people in conversation or polite levels of voice or gestures. These are rarely, if ever, articulated as explicit rules of conduct. Those of us who have lived abroad for an extended period of time experience "culture shock." As the novelty wears off, we must come to terms with a whole new way of being. We must truly alter our nature to blend in and effectively cope with the new society.[14]

It is difficult for us to focus on *being*. Everyday language contributes to its invisibility. We do not generally say, "How are you *being* with regard to total quality management?" Instead, we say, "What are you doing in the quality arena?" Our difficulty in discerning what a business is being (which then shapes action, which in turn shapes outcomes) is at the heart of why so many efforts at corporate re-invention have failed. We see dramatic examples of this when many companies strive to copy competitors. In the mass retailing arena, a relative newcomer, Nordstrom, has dominated other established department store chains like Saks or Macy's. The embattled rivals talk about "transforming themselves" and have attempted to copy everything Nordstrom does. And they continue to lose ground. Lacking insight into what Nordstrom is *being*, all they can *do* is reverse-engineer Nordstrom practices and remain behind the power curve. (See Box 16–3.)

INVENTING A POWERFUL FUTURE

When a company is struggling to re-invent itself, the process can be painfully embarrassing. Usually, the CEO leads off with a videotape that capsulizes the new vision. This act of executive imagination is intended to excite the work force, but more often it bewilders and even amuses employees. They wonder how the CEO could so earnestly make such an awkward pronouncement about a future that their experience says will never be.[15] The action plans that result are inevitably built on past experience (that is, "How things really work around here," and "What happened to the last change attempt of this kind").

What is the alternative? As we have said, a pivotal factor in re-invention entails creating a new possibility for the future—one that past history and current predictions would indicate is not possible. Sir Colin Marshall did this by declaring British Airways "the world's favorite airline" when it ranked among the worst. Until it was privatized in 1980, British Airways had come to be known as "Bloody Awful" to the flying public who endured its frequent maintenance-related delays, poor food, and disdainful service. Marshall's declaration was the start of re-inventing the way British Airways was being.[16]

At Häagen-Dazs, the ice-cream maker and retailer, a future of creating a special experience of fun and excitement associated with the brand held the keys to overcoming snack food giants like Mars and Nestlé. Like British Airways' initiative, this can an extraordinarily ambitious goal. What differentiated these big ambitions from empty words was that these leaders had listened very closely to what really mattered to customers and employees. (See Box 16–4.)

A declaration by the leaders is essential for re-invention.[17] It creates a new possibility that evokes widespread interest and commitment. Why is this so important? Because a powerful future is required to create a new context. Standing

---

Box 16–3

Nordstrom[a]

Like all retailers, Nordstrom has struggled during the recessionary 1990s but it has fared far better than most. It survived a bitter strike by a disgruntled group of Seattle employees when the overwhelming majority of employees voted to decertify the union. Tension and lack of accountability led to the elimination of one of Nordstrom's three co-presidents. Meanwhile, the company has expanded into electronic catalog sales and continues to demolish competitors as Nordstrom opens more stores in shopping malls across the United States.

What has driven competition crazy is that they can copy a specific Nordstrom practice—like the "personal shopper" or more user-friendly policies toward refunds—but somehow they don't close the gap in the customers' eyes. Why? Because Nordstrom's secret lies in what it is *being*, not just what it is doing. How does this come about?

Nordstrom employees, carefully screened and always promoted up through the ranks, internalize as a condition of employment that the tie-breaking value of the company is *customer service*. This ties to a *future* that galvanizes Nordstrom's work force from top to bottom—a deep-seated belief that they *are* the future of mass retailing. One means through which Nordstrom has pioneered this future is via the concept of the "personal shopper."

Nordstrom maintains its vitality through an ongoing "re-invention project" without ever calling it that. It is embedded in one omnipresent motto: "Respond to Unreasonable Customer Requests!" This leads to daily "heroics" (as "Nordies" call it). The majority of Nordstrom's responses to "unreasonable customer requests" entail no more than going a little out of the salesperson's way to provide extra service. But occasionally it extends to hand-delivering to the airport items purchased by phone by a customer leaving on a last-minute business trip, or changing a customer's flat tire, or paying a customer's parking ticket when gift wrapping in the store has delayed the customer's departure until the parking meter ran out. "Respond to Unreasonable Customer Requests" is an ongoing source of breakdowns (which, remember, are not "bad"; they are learning opportunities because they continually place stress on the Nordstrom system and cause it to question its policies and processes).

With a reputation for extraordinary service and a sales force motivated to *look for* opportunities to go the extra mile, there is a built-in tension at Nordstrom between service excellence and taking the idea to such extremes that the business loses economic viability. As management sees it, that is just the tension they want. Nordstrom sustains a relentless high-performance environment. Management feels that the sales force commitment to move mountains to give customers what they want is the surest way to stay in touch with the mood of the consumer and a foolproof way to expose any organizational orthodoxies and bureaucracy that stand in the way of doing that. In other words, providing extraordinary service

[a] Much of this narrative on Nordstrom is drawn from Richard Pascale, "Continuous Self Renewal at Nordstrom" (November 1991), unpublished.

generates breakdowns. Management doesn't always approve of every act of "heroics." But they regard the opportunity to decide whether a good thing is being taken too far as the most provocative stimulus to remain outward looking.

It is important to note that when "Respond to Unreasonable Customer Requests" effectively serves as an ongoing re-invention project, it is life-giving. This is not just a "strategic intent"—it is much more concrete, operational, and self-renewing. Nordstrom employees appear to have a relationship with this motto that makes it "a place to play from," not a threatening "ought" that is tied to punishment or survival. As one interacts with most Nordstrom employees, one gets the impression that they are having as much fun pleasing the customer as the customer is having with being pleased.

Nordstrom sales personnel are entirely on commission and typically earn about twice the wages of their counterparts at competing stores. Within each store, the separate departments (e.g., women's shoes, menswear) work on an incentive scheme tied to revenue and growth in sales.[b] The company steadfastly encourages the individuals who head these departments to see themselves as "running their own business"—with Nordstrom underwriting the floor space and inventory. This feature likewise generates ongoing tensions and breakdowns. It positions the department head on parity with the Buying and Merchandising Department. Buyers are typically the prima donnas of retailing. At Nordstrom, they work in close partnership with the department heads. The ambiguity of authority and responsibility among store managers, department managers, buyers, merchandisers, and sales personnel is so complex that the company refuses to publish job descriptions or organization charts. There *are* many ambiguities at Nordstrom and these stimulate dialogue, communication, and competition—all held from splintering apart by Nordstrom's (1) growing presence as a national retailer, (2) "magnetic north" of putting the customer first, and (3) shared sense of pioneering the future of the industry. This is the source from which "What Nordstrom is Being" arises.

It is almost impossible for competition to emulate properties of this nature precisely because they are so multifaceted and subtle.

[b] For an excellent discussion of Nordstrom's economic engine, see Margaret Gillian, "First Boston Equity Research Report" (October 28, 1991), 5.

in the new future, British Airways CEO, Marshall took actions that were consistent with being "the world's favorite airline" now. From the platform of the re-invented future, the leader reaches back to grab the present, yanks it into that future, and leaves the past behind. Re-invention requires leaders to stand in the desired future as if it were a place, and lead from there.[18]

Before we go on to detail what we know now about how to do what we are advocating, let us make one distinction clear. Please notice that we are not against doing, in favor of being; that would not be sensible. Rather, we want to point out that what we do and how we do it is shaped by the way we are being. In sum, an altered way of being will lead to new processes and desired outcomes.

Box 16–4
Häagen-Dazs[a]

In Häagen-Dazs's view, it does not just sell ice cream, it sells "pleasure," a great concept in the hedonistic 1970s and 1980s. Then along came Ben and Jerry's, which sells "social responsibility," "small is beautiful," and exemplary corporate citizenship—along with all those delectable calorie-crammed combinations.

Our research has taken us to Häagen-Dazs Europe where Ben and Jerry's is still an insignificant speck on the horizon. A team of young hard-charging recruits from the world's leading food products companies joined Häagen-Dazs to launch the brand in Europe in June 1989. Could Häagen-Dazs's high-margin "pleasure" concept succeed in a skeptical European market where tastes for ice cream were varied and competitors ranged from giants like Mars and Nestlé to thousands of "home recipe" boutiques? Against all odds, this tight-knit team was committed to giving it a try.

What has this got to do with a "powerful future"? A great deal. European president John Riccitiello makes the story come alive. "I think that anyone who starts a new business has to believe in it very deeply to overcome all the 'good reasons' for not taking the risk. I just *knew* that Europe was ready for a product like Häagen-Dazs. I could feel it in the focus groups and when I met with the trade. I searched until I found a half-dozen people who shared my near-religious zeal. When you get a critical mass who believe something is possible, it's contagious."

Their kick-off maneuver was a daring ad campaign featuring amorous couples (in scant clothing) indulging in the pleasures of ice cream. Extensive press coverage carrying reprints of these stunning photographs catapulted Häagen-Dazs into the public eye. Within 18 months, Häagen-Dazs was the leading dairy ice cream throughout Western Europe and has been singled out for one of the most successful new product launches in the packaged food industry.

Then an interesting thing began to happen. Once victory was realized, all that seemed to be needed was a mopping-up operation. Häagen-Dazs began to behave more like a comparable division at Nestlé or Mars. Paris headquarters began to quarrel over turf with country management teams. Marketing began to flex its muscles at the expense of sales and shops' operations.

As president, John Riccitiello observed these early signs of bureaucratic mischief. He concluded that the big problem was that Häagen-Dazs Europe had already used up its "future." Riccitiello, an incisive, 34-year-old executive from Pepsi, took comfort from the fact that his company was far from moribund. But, having savored the earlier dynamism, he was convinced that incremental improvement could never restore the previous momentum. Häagen-Dazs needed a new and powerful purpose. Listening closely to employees and customers, Riccitiello became convinced that what attracted people to Häagen-Dazs was something intangible—its excitement and pizzazz. Employees, in fact, commonly referred to it as "Häagen-Dazs magic." Riccitiello declared that Häagen-Dazs would commit

[a] This description of Häagen-Dazs is based on Richard Pascale, "Transformation at Häagen-Dazs" (Spring 1993), unpublished.

itself to two new and much more ambitious aims: (1) to become the leading premium *food* brand in Europe and (2) to generate "ten million special relationships" (shorthand for keeping the magic alive with its employees and customers).

> We shifted our recruitment policy to select people who were committed to sustaining this excitement. For example, in the shops, we aren't just looking for people to clear tables and dispense ice cream. We wanted our shops to be an *event*—where the customer and the staff celebrate the experience of something that tastes great and gives you, even if just for a moment, a sense that it's worth being alive. It became our mission to provide that feeling. We've created a senior position which we humorously refer to as "Director of Magic." The woman who fills this slot works tirelessly with shop managers and scoopers: "How can we make it fun to work at Häagen-Dazs?" Yes, it's a minimum-wage, routine job. But if this is what you signed up for to help you through school or over a summer, what ideas do you have that would make you *look forward* to coming to work? Of course, what makes a job like this worthwhile always boils down to the chemistry among people. You'd be amazed at the ideas our people have generated. One of the most important has altered our whole approach to hiring. We want people with a theatrical sense who enjoy being playful. We've adopted the suggestion to conduct our "employment interviews" like a theatrical audition. A group of prospects come in. We give them impromptu situations and see what they do. Do they ad lib, laugh at themselves, or freeze and look for the "right" answer? We ask them to juggle ice cream cones. When you get a whole organization being that kind of company, it is very hard for competition to match.

> Häagen-Dazs Europe's success was not lost on the struggling U.S. operations. Europe's number-two executive, Tony McGrath, will soon become president of North America, to chart the course for the U.S. parent company. There, Ben & Jerry's has displaced Häagen-Dazs as the leader in most major markets. Ben & Jerry's is propelled by a genuine sense of purpose (which, to repeat, is what a powerful future always provides) and this contributes to its innovations and momentum in the marketplace. Can Häagen-Dazs U.S. (whose "purpose" today is to "hunker down and protect market share") re-invent a bold new future? Can it come up with something that is fresh, motivationally compelling to its employees, and sufficiently in tune with customers to meet the Ben & Jerry's challenge? This quest is at the heart of re-invention.

Who were the employees at British Airways or Cable News Network (CNN) or Honda *being* when they accomplished extraordinary things? As we've proposed, a lot turns on how they related to the future. Fritz Roethlisberger, a pioneer in the field of organizational behavior, once observed: "Most people think of the future as the ends and the present as the means, whereas, in fact, the present is the ends and the future the means."[19]

Roethlisberger's ideas fueled the thinking of two other individuals, Ronald Lippitt, a founder of NTL (National Training Labs) and futurist Edward Lindaman (who planned the Apollo moon shot). The two joined forces to help organizations break free of their past. They had observed that executive teams that compiled long problem lists became increasingly depressed. The obstacles identified were often regarded as beyond the participants' control.

Lippitt and Lindaman tried an experiment. They began to ask participants to generate an action plan working backward from a desired future state. To their surprise, groups developed energy, enthusiasm, and commitment to what was earlier regarded as unattainable.[20]

Every now and then, companies come along that defy the odds and prevail. Some examples are: fledgling CNN (outflanking entrenched CBS), infamous British Airways (outmaneuvering venerable Pan Am), innovative Sony (vs. RCA, the industry pioneer of long ago), late starter (in automobiles) Honda (vs. virtually everybody), and clever Canon (vs. powerhouse Xerox).

As one way of explaining such successes, each of these companies had a deep-seated belief in the way the future was going to turn out. No basis in verifiable fact would have led Sony or Honda or CNN or Canon to aspire to the dominant positions they enjoy today. The leaders of these companies simply believed in the possibility to which they dedicated themselves, and this became a compelling view of the future to the employees who joined in. These convictions determine how resources are allocated.

One doesn't "creep up" on a big future incrementally. Rather, it is boldly declared and serves as the catalyst for all the action that follows. When President Kennedy declared in 1961 that the United States would put a man on the moon by the end of the decade, there were no solutions to the problems at hand. All the many seemingly insurmountable things that needed to happen—Congressional approval, appropriation of funds, technological breakthroughs, the creation of NASA (to supplant the rival Army, Navy, and Air Force rocketry programs)—all came into being after the declaration. The same could be said of the management teams of Häagen-Dazs Europe or EuropCar, who undertook to achieve a level of performance well beyond what was prudent or foreseeable. "Not so," skeptics may protest; "those things were destined to happen." When we look *backward* at any success story, we can almost always construct a rationale for "why success was inevitable." But 20-20 hindsight is mostly illusory. In real time, leaders who accomplished extraordinary things—politicians like Gandhi or entrepreneurs like Honda's Sochiro Honda or CNN's Ted Turner—aspired to a future that seemed well beyond the reach of their resources and capabilities.

Perhaps readers have experienced being in a group that accomplished something unexpected and truly extraordinary. Typically, someone gives out an assignment that seems to be a "mission impossible" and says, "I don't know if or how you can pull this off, but give it a try." Alternatively, something needed to happen and even though there were many reasons why it should never happen, someone felt so deeply committed to the cause that he or she took it on, no matter what the odds. What happened next, typically, was immersion in the challenge and completion of whatever was necessary to bring it off.

Such occasions of extraordinary accomplishment are unfortunately infrequent in most lives. Because of our preoccupation with *doing* (and our tendency to overlook or ignore how we are *being*), we usually examine these breakthrough experiences after the fact, with an eye toward capturing the formula of What We Did. "We started with A, jumped to C, went back to B . . . ." That may be an accurate historical account of what was done in the particular instance, but it misses something. Who we were *being* was so committed to a future we believed in that we just "made it happen."

Standing in that commitment, in that future, and continuing to take action regardless of the circumstances, we cause results to occur—one way or another. Any subsequent account of the "steps taken" only captures what we did to achieve the end result—not who we were *being*, which in turn produced the behavior and the result. *Being* the right way makes *doing* the right thing a lot more likely. More important, doing the right thing, in and of itself (that is, following the formula), does not produce the same result time after time. *Being* the future shapes actions so that big breakthroughs are produced and are consistent with the future. When these are intertwined with a big or difficult future that people become committed to, the keys to producing continuous re-invention are in hand.

EXECUTIVE RE-INVENTION

Many executives have impenetrable defenses against uncomfortable change. Over the past 35 years, particularly among the most senior echelons of corporations, we often have found a resistance to personal introspection at a level of intensity that necessarily produces discomfort. Not infrequently, we find senior executives or a corporate hierarchy perched like a threatened aristocracy, entitled, aloof, and sensing doom. Flurries of restructuring, delayering, and "right-sizing" (a disingenuous term for headcount cuts) are akin to the desperate attempts of uncomprehending heirs who try to slow the decline of the family estate. Each successive reaction is misconstrued as bold action to "set things right." Predictably, the action does not have the desired effect, and no deep examination of "why not" is undertaken.

In fairness, few of us have had any preparation for what is required by re-invention—gut-wrenching, messy, chaotic, wild, and, at times, frightening experiences that are not possible to control well. It is not surprising that so many senior executives decline invitations to re-invent themselves and their companies. As many executives come face-to-face with their organization's needs to re-invent itself, they often opt for the less painful path of incremental change.

Executives, when leading an organization into the future, sooner or later come to a fork in the road. Even when "re-invention" is the chosen path, feet get cold when the going gets tough. Thrown into the unfamiliar, unpredictable territory of re-invention, where action developments are at times unpredictable, many executives decide that the "responsible thing" to do is to "get things back on track"—that is, abandon re-invention.

We assert that there is another choice; we call it "executive re-invention."[21] This serious inquiry into oneself as a leader is not a psychological process to fix something that's wrong. It's an inquiry that can reveal what we call the "executive's personal paradigm"—the source from which choices are generated.

People have contexts just as organizations do. On the surface, our context is our formula for winning, a "success strategy" that is the source of our success. On closer examination, this context is our hidden strategy for surviving. It is the box within which a person operates and it determines the limits of what is possible and impossible for him or her as a leader and, by extension, for the organization. This context is unapparent, yet it focuses one's attention, defines a way of *being* and a way of thinking, and establishes a world view that has given executives the great competence and strength that have brought them where they are. At the same time, this context has imposed limits on the actions they can take and the ideas they can have that are "outside the box"—outside the organizational paradigm.[22]

Some radically different futures are painfully difficult to imagine, much less attain. A good example is a CEO who wanted to expand his successful $80 million family-run manufacturing business to $200 million as quickly as possible. He had been working very hard toward this goal for a number of years and was dissatisfied with the slow, incremental improvements.

But when someone brought him a plan for expanding the organization—by adding a new product line or entering a new market—all he could see were the incredible problems that would arise with the new outside executive leadership that would have to be brought on board and the new expertise that existing executives and managers would have to acquire (many of them senior family members who were comfortable working the way they were). He would refuse to endorse the plan, or, if he did let a plan go forward, he would call it to a halt whenever contention arose. Unknown to him, he was focusing on a future of avoiding conflict, not of growth. If anyone asked him how he had spent his day, he would say, "I spent it working on the growth of the company." But when he finally stopped to examine the way he was *being*, he discovered that, even though he was spending all his time, energy, and resources *doing* things to expand the business, he was operating from a context of avoiding conflict—a context that was inconsistent with a commitment to ambitious growth, and permitted only the incremental growth that would successfully avoid the conflicts that achieving ambitious expansion would entail. Once he saw this, he was able to put a clear choice in front of the board (all family members): Either pursue becoming a $200 million company with their eyes open—knowing there would be chaos, conflicts, and upheavals—or allow an incremental growth to $100 million. The board decided on the latter and charged the next generation to achieve the larger horizon.

The outcome of the executive re-invention process is: The CEO and the senior management team have the ability to generate a new context for themselves and a new context for the organization that will allow them to lead the organization into an unprecedented future.

MANAGING THE PRESENT FROM THE FUTURE

The concrete activities involved in re-inventing an organization require persistence and flexibility. Some extend over the entire effort and others are steps along the way. The order of these steps can vary, depending on the situation, but all need to be undertaken sooner or later.

Assembling a Critical Mass of Key Stakeholders

The odyssey organizations must undertake to re-invent themselves should never be limited only to the top eight or ten executives. It is deceptively easy to generate consensus among this group; they are usually a tight-knit fraternity, and it is difficult to spark deep self-examination among them. (Even if an epiphany occurs, its new truths influence only a small circle.) The design, therefore, must encompass a "critical mass" of key stakeholders. Most top-management teams can readily identify the 50 to 100 or so employees "who really make things happen" (or not happen!). Some of these individuals hold sway over key resources; others are informal leaders or are central to networks of opinion. The group may often include critical but seldom seen people like a key technologist or a leading process engineer. There is no absolute number, and the exact makeup depends to some degree on the size and nature of the business. What is sought is a "flywheel effect"—enough key players get involved and enrolled to create the momentum needed to carry the process forward.

At EuropCar, an organization of 11,000 employees, the top 50 have spent three days together each quarter since they began to re-invent themselves. They have surfaced conflicts, assessed the predictable results of continuing to perform as they have in the past, and concluded that more of the same was not nearly enough. Before much can occur, a group of such key opinion leaders needs to be convinced that re-invention is necessary.

Why is a tactical matter such as group size so important? Because shifts in being require a permanent shift in how people relate to and interact with one another. Organizations must involve a fairly large number of influential people to achieve this.

These key stakeholders must first determine whether their company has what it takes to remain competitive, and, if not, what to do about it. In the course of doing so in the first of several workshops, the group often surfaces contention, puts unspoken grievances and suspicions on the table, learns to work together, and respects nonconforming opinions. All of this constitutes an evolution in the relationship of the participants, and changes how people work together. In this environment, the management team typically becomes less resigned, more open, and more trusting. The team begins to create a powerful new partnership in which real disagreements are expressed, mutual respect increases, and shared beliefs and values start to crystallize into a social contract among participants. All this constitutes a shift in the way the participants are *being;* they are moving from a relationship of distrust and resignation toward an authentic, powerful partnership. This is not easy, nor is it enough; but it is a beginning.

It is noteworthy that significant shifts in how these managers are being (that is, working with one another) frequently reveal themselves "when no one is watching." Once a shift in being has taken place, a new realm of possibility is available, and actions and reactions that could not have occurred previously happen quite naturally with surprising results. Often they come about when a group is engaged in very intense doing. (This occurs, for example, in Marine boot camp: a very intense set of strenuous and menial activities unfreezes young recruits and alters who they are *being* in relation to authority, trust, teamwork, and courage.)

Such a watershed event occurred at Ford in the 1980s. The dozen upper-level managers in charge of the Engineering and the Powertrain divisions were assembled. Lou Ross, then senior vice president in charge of factories, got right to the point. "Here's the problem," he said. "For 25 years, Engineering and Powertrain have been fighting with each other. Enough is enough. We don't care how long it takes, but we want you to answer one single question: Will Engineering report to Powertrain, or Powertrain to Engineering?" Then he left the room. There was hell to pay.[23]

Now picture a meeting room eight months later. Many of the same people from the Powertrain and Engineering divisions were on their hands and knees discussing the merits of the various organizational charts that covered the floor. There was a lot of give and take. Someone asked, with an edge of frustration, "Which of these organizational charts is best?" Then someone answered, "Maybe *this* is [meaning the hands-and-knees process they were now engaged in]." A hush fell on the room. It gradually dawned on them that "the medium was the message." This way of working together was more important than finding the "perfect" organizational structure. It took another month to put together an "organization" that didn't reorganize at all, but simply realigned the flows of communication across the traditional Engineering and Powertrain "chimneys." In part because of shifts of this kind, Ford's cycle time decreased from eight years (to develop a new model from scratch) to five. Quality improved dramatically.[24]

To repeat, once a shift in *being* occurs it can frequently be seen by peripheral vision, usually when a difficult task has the rapt attention of key players. Only later does it become clear that what seemed at the time to be peripheral to the task at hand is, in fact, central. Such revelations can have a big payoff by radically altering an organization's ability to function cooperatively.

Harnessing Contention

An obscure law of cybernetics, the Law of Requisite Variety, postulates a universal truth of nature: any system must encourage and incorporate variety internally if it is to cope with variety externally.[25] This law seems pretty innocuous until one inquires into how "variety" shows up in organizations. Usually, it takes a distasteful form—deviant behavior, siphoning off scarce resources from main stress activities to back-channel experiments, disagreements at meetings, and so forth. Strange as it seems, in any social system (which is one way of describing an organization), almost all significant norm-breaking opinions or behavior (that is, "variety") are synonymous with conflict.[26]

Conflict can be substantive or interpersonal, muted or passionate. It might be called tension or dynamic contention (we will use the terms interchangeably). But the Law of Requisite Variety tells us that any living system needs a certain amount of contention to sustain vitality. Paradoxically, most organizations suppress it because top managers, among others, cannot stand to be confronted as much as is necessary; they assume they should be "in charge." But, control kills invention, learning, and commitments.[27]

Conflict jump-starts the creative process, which is why the design of the large group process described earlier encompassed such a large number of stakeholders. When participation is extended to those who are really accountable for critical resources, or who hold entrenched positions, or who have been burned by past change attempts, conflict is guaranteed. A major reason behind all the competitive analysis and identification of core problems is the intent to surface these withheld and suppressed disagreements. Breakdowns inevitably occur, but as these issues are faced and handled, there is a shift in how the group is *being* in relation to contention. Participants learn to disagree without being disagreeable. There is a big difference between creative tension and dysfunctional tensions like rage or excessive anxiety. True, strong emotions often accompany "creative tension," and these emotions are not altogether pleasant. But as the group learns to work together, it learns that healthy levels of tension are associated with cutting-edge performance. Participants learn not to shun conflict but to generate it and ultimately employ it.[28] (See Box 16–5.)

The common denominator of companies that have produced unprecedented results (for example, British Airways and Ford) or that appear to undergo continuous re-invention (for instance, Honda and Motorola) is that they consciously cultivate and utilize high levels of contention. At Honda, for example, conflict is legitimized through a process called *waigaya*. Any employee, however junior, can call for a *waigaya* session. The rules of engagement are that people lay their cards on the table and speak directly about problems. Nothing is out of bounds, from supervisory deficiencies on the factory floor to perceived lack of support for a design team. *Waigaya* legitimizes the disconnects and breakdowns so that learning can take place.[29]

At Intel, conflict is so blunt at times that it can seem brutal to the uninitiated. On a field trip to Tokyo to assess Intel's competitiveness against Japanese quality and service standards, the entire top-management team became involved in a fierce debate. Underlying the finger pointing were long smoldering resentments by those representing internal Intel customers who could not get the quality and service they desired from Manufacturing. Craig Barrett, then the head of Manufacturing (and today the president of Intel), was a combative partisan in the melée. An observer states, "Four-letter epithets flew back and forth like ping pong balls in a Beijing masters' tournament. The outside facilitator was in tears. He had never experienced such heat and intensity."

Two days later, the same teams sat down together, sorted out their differences, and put into motion actions that enabled Intel to match or surpass its

Box 16–5

The Honey Pot—A Lesson in Constructive Contention

Elaine Camper provides this possibly apocryphal account of constructive contention in action. It concerns one of the small electric utility companies for the Cascade Mountain region of the Pacific Northwest. The Operations Division was faced with an ongoing problem that resulted in an unsafe job situation for the linemen.

The Pacific Northwest experiences ice storms in the fall and spring. These result in the accumulation of a significant ice load on power transmission lines. If not removed, the ice accumulates until it overstresses and breaks the lines. The method used to remove the ice was to send linemen out into the field to climb the icy towers and shake the lines with long hooked poles. Linemen hated the job. It entailed long treks in the woods, climbing to precarious heights, and shaking the lines under extremely unpleasant conditions. A number were hurt in falls from the utility structures.

The Operations Division, after conducting a number of brainstorming sessions with no positive results, turned to an outside resource to organize another try. The consultant suggested that a group be assembled that had diverse experiences and unrelated jobs, in order to generate conflicting viewpoints and jostle the thought process. The brainstorming session included linemen, supervisors, accountants, secretaries, and mailroom clerks.

Several hours into the session, it appeared that this effort would be as unproductive as previous ones. Then, during one of the coffee breaks, the facilitator overhead two of the linemen talking. "There has got to be a better way to skin this cat," said one. "I really hate this job. Last week, I was chased by a bear. I could have been badly hurt."

Trying to stimulate the group, the facilitator retold this tale when the session reconvened. The anecdote of the bear was about to be disregarded as an insignificant aside, when a participant asked, "Why don't we train the bears to climb the poles? Their weight would oscillate the poles enough to shake the wires and knock the ice off."

After the laughter subsided, an informal leader in the group refuted the idea on a number of obvious grounds and pressed his colleagues to get back to business.

Then another lineman suggested that, although the bears could not be trained to comb each pole sequentially, perhaps the placement of honey pots on pole tops would solve that problem.

More objections followed, centering on the fact that the bears might choose to empty the honey pots in fair, not foul weather, or that they would lose their interest in honey, or that other scavengers (raccoons) would raid the pots, and so on. Tension began to rise in the room as a few persisted with the idea and the majority were itching to explore more practical alternatives and call it a day. One of the more senior (and sarcastic) linemen said, "How about expropriating the executive helicopters that the fat cats use to fly around? We could place the honey pots on top just after an ice storm."

> Then one of the secretaries spoke for the first time. "I was a nurse's aide in Vietnam. Injured soldiers were flown into the field hospitals by helicopter. The down wash from the helicopter blades was amazing. What if we just flew the helicopter over the power lines at a low altitude? Would the down wash be sufficient to knock the ice off?"
>
> This time there was no laughter—just silence. Valuing diversity and tolerating conflicting viewpoints had produced a breakthrough. Today, the utility uses helicopters to fly over the power lines after ice storms. But if the brainstorms hadn't tolerated sufficient conflict to buck the norms, detour from the agenda, and debate the honey pot suggestion, they may never have found the helicopter solution.

Japanese rivals. Craig Barrett states, "I've got pretty thick skin. It takes a lot to penetrate my strongly held convictions sometimes. This kind of hard-hitting session is precisely what we all needed to strip us of our illusions. It brought us all to face one another, the games we were playing, and how this prevented us from facing Japanese competitive realities." Says one observer: "If you're used to tennis, Intel plays rugby and you walk away with a lot of bruises. They've created a company that takes this direct, hard-hitting disagreement as a sign of fitness. You put it all behind you in the locker room and it's forgotten by the scrimmage the next day."[30]

It may seem odd to cite Honda, a Japanese company, as an example of constructive conflict. We do not think of the Japanese as conflictual. With their concern for face saving and their emphasis on consensus, a naive observer may think that conflict is prohibited. But this is an erroneous first impression. The Japanese have learned to "disagree without being disagreeable" and to harness conflict in a wide variety of ingenious ways. One of their fundamental principles of organizational design is redundancy. This takes the form of overlapping charters, business activities, and managerial assignments, and duplicative data bases and lines of inquiry. Westerners are quick to judge such arrangements as "counterproductive" or "wasteful," quick candidates for elimination in a business process re-engineering purge. With our deeply ingrained mindset of organizations as machines, all this overlap seems both inelegant and costly. But in the Japanese view, redundancy and ambiguity spur tension and encourage frequent dialogue and communication. They also generate internal competition—particularly when parallel paths are pursued in new product development.[31]

Such techniques are often employed at Honda and Sony, where competing teams are given the same assignment. Periodic project reviews determine which team gets funded to build the final prototype. Sony's compact disk player was developed in precisely this fashion. The manager in charge handed two teams a block of wood (the size of a small paperback book) and said, "Build it to fit in this space." He recruited designers from Seiko and Citizen—watch companies familiar with miniaturization and ignorant of the traditional "givens" of audio design—and paired them with Sony designers. Then he stood back and let them figure it out.

There is, of course, a human and organizational cost incurred from conflict. But conflict is also an essential fuel to self-questioning and revitalization. Some Western companies have incorporated constructive conflict into their designs with this trade-off in mind. Intel is one example; Nordstrom is another. Not surprisingly, Nordstrom employees report high tension levels at work. States one executive, "It's wrong to think of Nordstrom as a happy place. But the tensions tend to be productive and yield higher performance."

Creating Urgency: Discussing the Undiscussables

An unspoken "code of silence" that is honored in most corporations has the effect of concealing the full extent of a corporation's competitive weaknesses. However, those excluded from the "family secrets" usually have a sixth sense that something worrisome is in the wind. There may be many good reasons to withhold bad news ("It will leak to the press" or "It will demoralize the troops"); but a threat that everyone perceives but no one talks about is far more debilitating to a company than a threat that has been clearly revealed. Companies, like people, tend to be as unhealthy as their secrets.

The Book of Five Rings, a guide to Japanese Samurai written four centuries ago, advocates the practice of visualizing death in battle as vividly as possible before taking the field.[32] Having "experienced" death beforehand, there is not a lot left to be afraid of, and the warrior fights with abandon. In confronting the inevitable, it almost magically becomes less inevitable.

It is noteworthy that the companies that formed the cornerstone of our research confronted the inevitable head-on. Ford was poised on the brink of bankruptcy. Rather than play its cards close to the vest, management fully revealed the company's predicament (and the financial facts) to employees. The starkness of this reality mobilized the collective action that altered Ford's destiny. At Motorola, near-term insolvency was not an issue, but management artfully communicated the full portent of the Japanese threat and built a powerful case that Motorola's eventual demise, like RCA's (an imminent victim of inaction) and Philco's (already defunct), was almost a certainty unless transformative action was taken. Likewise, at British Airways, Häagen-Dazs, and EuropCar, management generated a sense of urgency that galvanized the organization into action.

Whether the urgency is the result of a desire to break new ground, a loss in momentum, or a serious threat to the existence of a company, a strategic business unit, or a functional group, it is necessary for people to behave outside their prior social norms.

The Ford and British Airways examples are illustrative in another respect. Both companies "transformed" themselves in one episodic orgy of commitment. Today, both struggle to re-invent themselves as an ongoing way of doing business.

Doing an Organizational Audit

The process usually begins, as we have noted, by assembling a large (often, surprisingly large) group of key stakeholders. In these sessions, this group first uncovers and then examines the real competitive situation and articulates a desired response. As it does so, the barriers to significantly and fundamentally shifting the organization come to light. In effect, this process begins to reveal the strategic and organizational way of *being*. It is important to do this thoroughly, yet avoid "pointing the finger" (that is, "convicting" particular individuals or departments for how things have been in the past).

The best approach is through a diagnosis test that generates a *complete* picture of "how things really work around here." It starts with a discussion of the currently enacted strategy (as compared and contrasted to what is espoused). Will it lead to a viable future? What assumptions are we making about business practices and customer needs that may no longer be valid? What changes are needed? Next, how is the organization structured? Which functional units are most influential? Will these high-status units remain as important in the future as in the past? Next, what are the key systems that drive the business? What are the primary stylistic characteristics and shared values? Demographically, what are the major groupings of personnel in the company, in terms of profession or education or interests? What are the core competencies or skills of the current enterprise or business unit? These types of questions, if explored in sufficient depth, provoke responses that form a mosaic of "how things *really are* around here."[33]

At the heart of this endeavor is a heard-learned lesson—sooner or later, an organization must learn to face any discrepancy between what it likes to believe about itself and the truth. It must squarely confront the implications of its current performance, given competitive realities, and determine whether its current trajectory (or incremental improvement on that trajectory) is adequate to deliver the future. If not, re-invention is necessary. Premature discussion of re-invention is unauthentic until the needs of the current situation have been fully revealed. No company can get from "here" to "there" without first knowing where "here" is. Nor can it intelligently elect to choose re-invention without knowing where "there" is.

Re-Invention Projects and the Art of Generating Breakdowns

The earlier discussed notion of a "compelling" future is rather ephemeral unless it is based on concrete realities. The sources of these realities are re-invention projects.[34] The latter are tangible milestones along the way to sustained corporate re-invention, or substantive tasks with deadlines. The real purpose of re-invention projects is to cause the organization to experience what we call "breakdowns."[35] Advocating a breakdown may seem hard to swallow, especially when most organizations in need of this kind of shock are probably already experiencing considerable pain. We're not proposing that random provocation of breakdowns, conflict, and chaos is a good thing. Nothing could be further from the truth. Instead, after careful consideration, the executive team needs to identify the core competencies it wishes to build, the soft spots in existing capabilities, and the re-invention projects that, if undertaken, will surface the breakdowns needed to build new capabilities. Europ-Car fostered precisely these kinds of breakdowns in overhauling its *entire*

Box 16–6

Honda City: An Example of a Re-Invention Project

In 1978, Honda sought to achieve a design breakthrough to stem the erosion of its midsize automotive market in Japan.[a] A new product development team of young engineers and designers was assembled (the average age was 27). Top management gave the team two and only two design parameters: (1) come up with a product concept fundamentally different from anything Honda had ever built before and (2) make a car that is inexpensive but not cheap. So far, a pretty typical project charter—concrete and challenging. Project team leader Hiro Watanabe introduced the context shift that successful re-invention projects require. He asked his team: "If an automobile was an organism, how would it evolve?" At first it seemed an engineer's version of a Zen Koan—like contemplating the sound of one hand clapping. But as team members debated and reflected on what Watanabe's question might mean, they generated the concept: *man-maximum; machine-minimum.* This captured the team's conclusion that, over time, automobiles would evolve from their current state (where passengers conform to machine constraints) to the automobile's being a near-organic extension of the passenger—providing both comfort and mobility. The subsequent Honda Civic's revolutionary styling and engineering were a tremendous success. The car inaugurated an entirely new approach to design and led to the new generation of "tall and short" cars now quite prevalent in Japan. Over the history of Honda, there has been a whole series of such re-invention projects that continually cause the company to transform itself along with its products.

Watanabe's cryptic question, which seems silly to most Western readers, was, in fact, highly effective in drawing the design team into the future. Managers everywhere recognize the serendipitous quality of innovation. But how do we "manage serendipity"? (An oxymoron, right? "Serendipity," by definition, means *chance* occurrence.) Standing in a "future," where automobiles were an evolving organism, enabled the design team to see the inevitable evolution. This emboldened them to discard beliefs that constraints of the past/present, the "sacred truths" about design. Through such devices, and with a deep understanding that the design team needed to *be* highly committed and creative (not just *do* what was expected of them), Watanabe was able to influence "serendipity."

[a] Ikujiro Nonaka, "The Knowledge Creating Company," *Harvard Business Review* (November–December 1991), 96–103.

operating system in an impossibly short time frame. In so doing, management knew it would surface the deep-seated behavioral patterns that had to be faced and surmounted if re-invention was to take place.

The whole point behind the re-invention project is not just to produce unpredictable results—such as overhauling an organization's entire operations, as EuropCar is doing today. Rather, the true purpose is to produce the breakdowns that will provide the opportunities needed to cause a shift for both the organization and the executives managing the projects. In this "learning through adversity" model, difficulty fosters insight. Paradoxically, a company can fail at the project (as has often occurred in the path to scientific discoveries and in the careers of entrepreneurs) and succeed in achieving a shift in *being*.

THE RE-INVENTION ROLLER COASTER

Re-invention is not a smooth process. As shown in Figure 16–1, those who pursue it sign up for a challenging experience. The organization encounters peaks and troughs in morale, as initial euphoria is dampened by conflict and dogged task-force work. Morale rises again as alignment among stakeholders occurs—then recedes in the long and demanding task of enrolling the cynical ranks below. It is a demanding up-and-down journey—an adventure, to be sure. And it is destined to be that way.

FIGURE 16–1   The re-invention roller coaster.

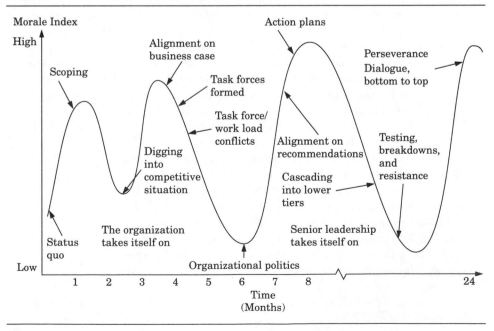

NOTES

1.   See, for example, discussion in Richard T. Pascale, *Managing on the Edge* (New York: Simon & Schuster, 1991), 18–22.

2.   Tracy Goss, "Organizational Re-Invention," unpublished lectures and workshop notes, Paramount Pictures (September 1988). The assertion "an organization's context is always the decisive factor in transformation" is fully developed.

3.   Tracy Goss, "Executive Re-Invention Program," unpublished transcripts (December 1989–December 1993), the distinction between change and transformation is a central theme and extensively treated.

4.   *Richard T. Pascale, Managing on the Edge* (New York: Simon & Schuster, 1991), see Pascale, Managing on the Edge, op. cit., Chapters 5 and 6.

5.   This definition of Re-Invention is drawn from Goss, "Executive Re-Invention Program," unpublished transcripts, op. cit.

6.   Tracy Goss, Richard Pascale, Anthony Athos, "The Re-Invention Roller Coaster," *Harvard Business Review* (November–December 1993).

7.   This theme is well-developed in Gary Hamel and C. K. Prahalad, "Strategic Intent," *Harvard Business Review* (May–June 1989), 74–75; and "Corporate Imagination and Expeditionary Marketing," *Harvard Business Review* (July–August 1991), 10.

8.   This metaphor was inspired by Werner Erhard, conversation in London, October 19, 1992; unpublished.

9.   Richard T. Pascale, "Stagnation of IBM" (September 1992), unpublished working paper.

10.   Richard T. Pascale, "Continuous Renewal at Motorola" (March 1993), unpublished working paper.

11.   Richard Rhodes, *The Making of the Atomic Bomb* (New York: Simon & Schuster, 1986), 169–170.

12.   We are indebted to numerous philosophers, scholars, and thinkers who have inquired into the nature of doing and being especially Werner Erhard "Transformation and Its Implications for System-Oriented Research," unpublished lecture (Massachusetts Institute of Technology, Cambridge, Massachusetts, April 1977) and "The Nature of Transformation," unpublished lecture (Oxford University Union Society, Oxford, England, September 1981); Martin Heidegger, *What Is Called Thinking?* (New York: Harper & Row, 1968), *On the Way to Language* (New York: Harper & Row, 1971), *On Time and Being* (New York: Harper & Row, 1972); and Ludwig Wittgenstein, *Culture and Value* (Oxford: Basil Blackwell, 1980). Concern with *being* can be traced to Lao Tzu in the sixth century B.C. in China, and is the central focus of Middle Eastern philosopher Ibn 'Arabi in the 12th century B.C. This is discussed in Mark P. Kriger, "Being and the Perfect Man According to Ibn 'Arabi and Lao Tzu" (September 1975), unpublished Master's thesis, MIT. Source references to these works are A. E. Offifi, *The Mystical Philosophy of Muhyid Din-Ibn'l 'Arabi* (Cambridge, England: Macmillan, 1939); Toshihiko Izutsu, *A Competitive Study of the Key Philosophical Concepts of Sufism and Taoism* (Tokyo: The Kiro Institute of Cultural and Linguistic Studies—Volume I, 1966 and Volume II, 1967); Max Kaltenmark, *Lao Tzu and Taoism* (Palo Alto: Stanford University Press, 1969). The paradox of doing

versus being is also reflected in the work of such Western poets as John Keats (in his discussions of "Negative Capability") and T. S. Eliot, *Complete Poems and Plays* (New York: Harcourt, Brace & World, 1971).

13. This theme—a shift in *being* is critical to re-invention—is the central premise and is discussed at length in Goss, "Executive Re-Invention Program" unpublished transcripts, op. cit.

14. Conversations with Richard Pascale, 1993; unpublished notes.

15. This observation was provided by Anthony Athos, "The Re-Invention Roller Coaster" (co-authors: Tracy Goss and Richard Pascale), *Harvard Business Review* (November–December 1993).

16. Richard T. Pascale, "Transformation at British Airways" (October 1992), unpublished.

17. The work on acts of speech that evoke action and generate possibility was pioneered by J. L. Austin, *How to Do Things With Words* (Cambridge, MA: Harvard University Press, 1962). This work has been made considerably more accessible through the work of Werner Erhart and Fernando Flores. See for example, Terry Winograd and Fernando Flores, *Understanding Computers and Cognition* (Reading, MA: Addison-Wesley, 1986).

18. A considerable amount of authors have grappled with the relationship of past, present, and future. See especially Werner Erhard, "Organizational Vision and Vitality: Forward from the Future," unpublished lecture (Academy of Management, San Francisco, California, August 1990); Edward Lindaman and Robert Lippitt, *Choosing the Future You Prefer* (Washington D.C.: Development Publications, 1979); Fritz Roethlisberger, *Training for Human Relations* (Boston: Harvard University, Graduate School of Business Administration, Division of Research, 1954); Marvin R. Weisbord, *Productive Workplaces: Organizing and Managing for Dignity, Meaning, and Community* (San Francisco: Jossey-Bass, 1991), 282–85. Among the earliest authors was St. Augustine, who observed "The past doesn't exist." See F. J. Sheed (trans.), *Confessions of St. Augustine* (New York: Sheed & Ward, 1943), 276. This view is shared by Karl E. Weick in *The Social Psychology of Organizing* (New York: Random House, 1979), 177, 189, 198–202. Kierkegaard, *op. cit.*, noted that although life can only be understood backward, it must be lived forward. In relating these concepts to an organizational context, see the pioneering work of E. Lindaman, *Thinking in the Future Tense* (Nashville, TN: Broadman Press, 1978), and E. Lindaman and R. Lippitt, *Chasing the Future You Prefer* (Washington, DC: Development Publications, 1979). These techniques have been incorporated in Marvin R. Weisbord's "Future Search" process as reported in Weisbord, *Productive Workplaces* (San Francisco: Jossey-Bass Publishers, 1991), 283–285. Also see Fritz Roethlisberger, *Training for Human Relations* (Boston: Harvard University, Division of Research, Graduate School of Business Administration, 1954); Weick, *op. cit.*, 200–202; and Stanley Davis, *Future Perfect* (Reading, MA: Addison-Wesley, 1986), 36–41.

19. Roethlisberger, *op. cit.*

20. Lindaman and Lippitt, *op. cit.*

21. This discussion about executive re-invention is drawn from Goss, "Executive Re-Invention Program," unpublished transcripts, op.cit.

22. The scope, role, and importance of an organization's paradigm are extensively treated in Chapter 15.

23. See Pascale, *Managing on the Edge, op. cit.,* 152–153.

24. *Id.*

25. W. R. Ashby, *An Introduction to Cybernetics* (New York: John Wiley & Sons, Inc., 1956); also see Ludwig von Bertalanffy, *General Systems Theory* (New York: Braziller, 1968). This notion is discussed in Weick, *op. cit.,* 188–189, citing R. C. Conant and R. W. Ashby, "Every Good Regulation of a System," *International Journal of Systems Science, 2,* 89–97.

26. The value of contention in organizations is developed at length in Pascale, *Managing on the Edge, op. cit.*

27. *Id.*

28. *Id.*

29. *Id.,* Chapter 7.

30. Richard T. Pascale, "Constructive Contention at Intel" (July 1990), unpublished.

31. Ikujiro Nonaka, "The Knowledge Creating Company," *Harvard Business Review* (November–December 1991), 100.

32. Miyomoto Musashi, *A Book of Five Rings* (English translation) (Woodstock, NY: The Overlook Press, 1974), 38–39.

33. This discussion is based on the "Seven S Framework" as discussed at length in Richard T. Pascale and Anthony G. Athos, *The Art of Japanese Management* (New York: Simon & Schuster, 1981), and Tracy Goss, "Transforming the Organization's Past, A Group Process," unpublished work papers (Monsanto, February 1988).

34. Based on research at Paramount Pictures where Re-Invention Projects were first developed and described fully in Tracy Goss, "Designing a Re-Invention Project," unpublished work paper (Paramount Pictures, Fall 1988).

35. Breakdowns are discussed at length in Winograd and Flores, *op cit.,* 36–37, 66–69, 77–79, 150, 157, 165–173. An in depth treatment of breakdowns is developed in Werner Erhard, "A Methodology for Breakdown," unpublished lectures (Center For Management Design, Sausalito, Calif., February 1987); and in Scherr, Allan L., "Managing For Breakthroughs in Productivity," *Human Resource Management* (Fall 1989, Vol. 28, Number 3), 403–424.

ABOUT THE AUTHORS

Anthony George Athos, Ph.D., held the Jesse Isidor Straus Chair of Business Administration at the Harvard Business School until June 1982, where he focused upon the field of organizational behavior. He has taught in one of Harvard's 13 week executive programs, and has served as chairperson of the school's Strategy Committee.

Anthony Athos co-authored, with Richard T. Pascale, *The Art of Japanese Management*.

Michael Beer, Ph.D., teaches in the Advanced Management Program at the Harvard Business School, and is chair of strategic human resource management, an educational program for senior human resource executives. Prior to joining the Faculty at Harvard, Michael Beer was director of Organizational Development at Corning Glass Works.

Professor Beer has written numerous articles, and authored or co-authored seven books including *The Critical Path to Corporate Renewal*. He is also senior author of *Managing Human Assets*.

Barbara Bigelow, Ph.D., is an assistant professor of management at Clark University Graduate School of Management. She conducts research and teaches in the area of strategic management with particular emphasis on strategy in the health care industry and nonprofits and on corporate political strategy. She has published widely in a range of scholarly journals and books in the fields of corporate political strategy and health care, including *Business & Society* and *Medical Care Review*. Professor Bigelow has also been an active participant in a number of professional associations such as the International Association of Business and Society and the Academy of Management.

H. Kurt Christensen, Ph.D., is professor of management and strategy and associate director of executive education at the J.L. Kellogg Graduate School of Management, Northwestern University. His research focus is on the strategic determinants of corporate performance and on the cognitive and organizational processes facilitating successful performance. He is currently completing projects on how organizations can develop the capabilities needed to build and maintain externally perceived competitive advantages and on how companies can analyze synergistic potential and develop and maintain positive synergies. He has also consulted and taught in management development programs in the United States, Europe, Latin America, and Asia.

George S. Day, Ph.D., is the Geoffrey T. Boisi professor of marketing, and director of the Huntsman Center for Global Competition and Innovation at the Wharton School of the University of Pennsylvania. He previously taught at the University of Western Ontario, Stanford University, IMD (International Management Development Institute) in Lausanne, Switzerland, and the University of Toronto, and has held visiting appointments at the Harvard Graduate School of Business Administration and the Sloan School of Management at M.I.T.

Dr. Day is editor of the West Publishing series on Strategic Market Management, and serves on seven editorial boards. He has written over 80 articles for leading marketing and management journals and has authored 10 books in the areas of marketing and strategic business planning. His most recent book is *Market Driven Strategy: Processes for Creating Value.*

Russell A. Eisenstat, Ph.D., is an independent consultant specializing in the management of corporate change and innovation, strategy implementation, and improving work team effectiveness. His prior work experience includes six years on the faculty of the Harvard Business School. His most recent book, *The Critical Path to Corporate Renewal,* written with Michael Beer and Bert Spector, received the Johnson, Smith & Knisely Award for New Perspectives on Executive Leadership.

Liam Fahey, an Adjunct Professor of Strategic Management at Babson College and Visiting Professor of Strategic Management at the Cranfield School of management (UK), has received awards for his teaching, research, and professional activity. This is the sixth book he has authored or edited. The editor of *Planning Review,* a bi-monthly magazine on strategic management and planning, he also serves as co-chairperson of an annual strategic management conference sponsored by The Planning Forum. He consults for a number of leading North American and European firms in the areas of competitive strategy and competitor analysis and is a frequent speaker in executive education programs and business management conferences.

Pankaj Ghemawat, Ph.D., is professor of business administration of Harvard Business School. During 1982 and 1983, Dr. Ghemawat was a consultant with McKinsey & Company, London. Since then he has been teaching at the Harvard Business School teaching industry and competitive analysis, an advanced course on strategy formulation that he now heads.

Professor Ghemawat's current research centers on decisions that involve significant amounts of commitment or irreversibility, such as entry into new markets, exit from old ones, capacity expansion and product and process innovation. He has written more than 30 articles and cases on this broad topic and also serves on the editorial boards of the *Journal of Economics and Management Strategy* and the *Strategic Management Journal.* His recent book on irreversible decisions is *Commitment.*

Tracy Goss is an expert in the area of Transformation. She is the originator of a body of work called Re-Invention—a unique methodology designed to produce a fundamental paradigm shift in both an organization and its top management resulting in the organization transforming itself to sustain excellence and competitive leadership. A consultant, lecturer, and author, she works with CEOs and top management of major companies.

Ms. Goss has lectured on the Re-Invention Methodology at Stanford University Graduate School of Business and as a member of the AVIRA faculty at INSEAD in France. She has co-authored with Richard Pascale and Tony Athos "The Re-Invention Roller Coaster: Risking the Present for a Powerful Future" and is the author of forthcoming book, *Re-Invention for People Who Want to Change the World*.

John Grant, D.B.A., is The Robert Kirby professor of strategic management in the Katz Graduate School of Business at the University of Pittsburgh. He pursues research and consulting involving planning and control systems for diversified firms.

He is a member of the Planning Forum; Strategic Management Society; the Academy of International Businesses; and the Academy of Management, where he has served as chairperson of the Business Policy and Strategy Division. His articles have appeared in the *Strategic Management Journal, Academy of Management Review, Long Range Planning, Journal of Management* and other publications.

Anil K. Gupta, Ph.D., is professor of strategy and international business at the College of Business and Management, The University of Maryland at College Park. Dr. Gupta has also served as a visiting professor at the Tuck School at Dartmouth College, Bocconi Business School (Milan, Italy), Helsinki School of Economics and Business Administration (Finland), and IPMI (Jakarta, Indonesia). His core research interests lie in strategy implementation, organizing for international competitiveness, coordination and control within diversified corporations, the management of synergy, and executive leadership.

Ellen R. Hart, Ph.D., is vice president of Gemini Consulting and head of their Organization and Management Development Practice in North America. She specializes in organizational development and design, executive team development, change management, and organizational learning.

Gerry Johnson, Ph.D., is professor of strategic management, and director of the Centre for Strategic Management and Organizational Change at Cranfield School of Management in the United Kingdom. He has taught at Aston University Management Centre and at Manchester Business School. He took up his appointment at Cranfield University in 1988.

Professor Johnson is author of *Strategic Change and the Management Process*, co-author of *Exploring Corporate Strategy*, editor of *Business Strategy and Retailing*, the *Challenge of Strategic Management*, and *Strategic Thinking*.

Marjorie A. Lyles, Ph.D., is associate professor of strategic management at Indiana University. She previously taught in the Schools of Business at the University of Illinois and Ball State University. She is a member of the American Management Association's International Council. She has been an Invited Scholar and consultant for the U.S. Department of Commerce in the Peoples' Republic of China. In 1984, she was a visiting Professor of Business Policy at the European Institute of Business Administration (INSEAD) in Fontainebleau, France.

She has presented and authored over 50 articles on strategic management. Her research has appeared in such journals as *Academy of Management Review, Strategic Management Journal, Long Range Planning,* and the *Journal of Business Strategy.*

John F. Mahon, Ph.D., is a professor of management policy at Boston University. He has authored or co-authored over fifty papers published in the *Academy of Management Review, Business in the Contemporary World, Business and Society Review, Industrial Crisis Quarterly, Journal of Contemporary Business, Long Range Planning, Medical Care Review, Strategic Management Journal* and other journals. He is also the author of numerous book chapters and the co-author of an introductory text on management, and the author or co-author of over forty cases in strategy and public policy/public affairs.

V. K. Narayanan, Ph.D., is currently professor of strategic management and associate dean of academic affairs in the School of Business at the University of Kansas. He is also the director of the Center of Technology in the School of Business. He has taught at the University of Pittsburgh, the Graduate School of Management at Rutgers University, New Jersey, and the University of Kansas, where he was a Phillips Petroleum Fellow during 1984 to 1986.

Professor Narayanan has published over 30 articles and book chapters. With Liam Fahey, he has authored *Macroenvironmental Analysis for Strategic Management.* Recently he completed a monograph for NASA entitled "The Management History of the Space Station" (co-authored with Tom Lewin). He serves on the editorial board of *Organization Science.*

Richard Tanner Pascale, Ph.D., was a member of the faculty at Stanford's Graduate School of Business for 20 years and taught an MBA course on organizational survival. Dr. Pascale, with Anthony Athos, wrote the best-selling *The Art of Japanese Management.* In addition, he has published numerous articles and received the McKinsey Award for 1978's best article in the Harvard Business Review. In 1990, he published *Managing on the Edge: How the Smartest Companies Use Conflict to Stay Ahead.*

Michael E. Porter, Ph.D., is the C. Roland Christensen Professor of Business Administration at the Harvard Business School and a leading authority on competitive strategy.

Professor Porter is the author of 14 books and over 45 articles. His book, *Competitive Strategy: Techniques for Analyzing Industries and Competitors,* published in 1980, is widely recognized as the leading work in its field. In its 45th printing, it has been translated into 15 languages. His 1990 book, *The Competitive Advantage of Nations,* develops a theory of how nations compete and their sources of economic prosperity.

C. K. Prahalad, Ph.D., is Harvey C. Fruehauf Professor of Business Administration at the University of Michigan's Graduate School of Business Administration. He has been a visiting research fellow at Harvard, a professor at the Indian Institute of Management, and a visiting professor at the European Institute of Business Administration (INSEAD).

Professor Prahalad, with Yves Doz, wrote *The Multinational Mission: Balancing Local Demands and Global Vision.* He is currently working with Gary Hamel on a new book, *Competing for the Future.*

Professor Prahalad's contributions to strategic thinking are widely acknowledged. *Business Week* (8/31/92) described him as "A brilliant teacher at the University of Michigan, Prahalad may well be the most influential thinker on corporate strategy today." Professor Prahalad has consulted with the top management of such firms as Ahlstrom, AT&T, Bowater, Cargill, Colgate Palmolive, Eastman Kodak, Honeywell, ICL, Philips, Rockwell, Steelcase, and TRW.

James Brian Quinn, Ph.D., is an emeritus professor of management at Amos Tuck School at Dartmouth and a recognized authority in the fields of strategic planning, the management of technological change, entrepreneurial innovation, and the impact of technology in the service sector.

He has also had extensive international teaching assignments at the Centre d'Etudes Industrielles (Switzerland), Monash and University of Western Australia (Australia), and the International University of Japan, where he served as Academic Dean for the University's newly established International Management MBA program.

Professor Quinn has published extensively on both corporate and national policy issues involving strategic planning, research and development management, the management of entrepreneurial organizations, and the impact of technology in services. He has thrice received the McKinsey Prize given annually for the most outstanding management articles to appear in *Harvard Business Review.* His book, *Intelligent Enterprise,* was named the outstanding book in the Business and Management category for Excellence in Professional and Scholarly Publishing in 1992 by the Association of American Publishers.

Robert M. Randall is the managing editor of *Planning Review,* an award winning strategic management publication. He was a member of its founding team in 1972, and his interviews of CEOs, management theorists, and innovative corporate managers appear regularly in the journal. His publishing company specializes in management magazines, business books, and annual reports. A former Time Inc. writer/editor, he was on the original staff of its magazine *Money.* He has held management positions in several "*Fortune* 500" companies, including the first editorship of Babcock & Wilcox's *Interface,* a magazine about the corporation's strategic issues for its decision makers. He and Liam Fahey are working on another book, *Strategic Scenarios: Teaching Your Organization to Learn from Its Future,* to be published by John Wiley & Sons, Inc.

Index